HIGHER EDUCATION: HANDBOOK OF THEORY AND RESEARCH
Volume II

HIGHER EDUCATION:
HANDBOOK OF THEORY AND RESEARCH

Volume II

Edited by

John C. Smart
Virginia Polytechnic Institute and State University

AGATHON PRESS, INC.
New York

Le

© 1986 Agathon Press, Inc.
111 Eighth Avenue
New York, NY 10011

ISBN: 0-87586-078-8
ISSN: 0882-4126

Printed in the United States

CONTENTS

Contributors

JOHN M. BRAXTON is Visiting Assistant Professor of Higher Education at Loyola University of Chicago. He serves as a consulting editor for *Research in Higher Education* and on the Editorial Board of the *Review of Higher Education*. His publications have focused upon the measurement of faculty scholarly performance, the relationship between teaching and research, and the effects of departmental colleagues upon publication productivity.

PAUL T. BRINKMAN is a Senior Associate at the National Center for Higher Education Management Systems (NCHEMS). He has written on the economics of higher education, cost analysis, interinstitutional comparisons, financial indicators, and decision support systems.

KIM S. CAMERON is Associate Professor of Organizational Behavior and Industrial Relations in the Graduate School of Business Administration and Associate Professor of Higher Education in the College of Education at the University of Michigan. His research investigates organizational decline, organizational effectiveness, organizational life cycles, and organizational design and has published in a variety of management and higher education journals. He is the author or coauthor of five books on organizational effectiveness, management skills, and strategic adaptation, and he is currently working on books focusing on effectiveness in colleges, decline, and the management of paradox.

MONIQUE WESTON CLAGUE is Associate Professor in the Department of Education Policy, Planning and Administration at the University of Maryland. She has written on legal theory, French history, and a variety of issues at the intersection of law and education, including competency testing, corporal punishment, retrenchment, and voluntary affirmative action. Her current research focus is on programs designed to increase the supply of minority doctorates.

CLIFTON F. CONRAD is Professor of Higher Education in the Center for the Study of Higher Education at the University of Arizona. He has written on liberal and general education, academic change, and college and university curriculum. He is editor of the *ASHE Reader on Academic Programs in Colleges and Universities*.

MARY BETH CROWE is Staff Associate in the Office of the President, The Pennsylvania State University. She was affiliated with the Continuing Professional Education Development Project at Penn State for four years. Her interests include program evaluation, performance assessment, and continuing professional education.

GORDON K. DAVIES is director of the State Council of Higher Education for Virginia. He has been president of the State Higher Education Officer's association, and is a frequent speaker, writer, and consultant on higher education in the states. For more than a decade, he has observed something like the principle of entropy at work in American higher education.

CAMERON FINCHER is Regents Professor of Higher Education and Psychology, and Director of the Institute of Higher Education, at the University of Georgia. He has written on policy, administration, evaluation, and assessment in higher education and has been designated a Distinguished Member of the Association for Institutional Research. In

1982 he was the first recipient of the Ben W. Gibson Award given by the Southern Regional Council of the College Board for outstanding contributions to education.

LARRY L. LESLIE is Professor and Director, Center for the Study of Higher Education, University of Arizona. He has written on many aspects of higher education finance including tax policies, the steady state, student aid, collective bargaining, community colleges, tuition policies, facilities financing, costing, and voluntary support. Currently, he and Paul T. Brinkman are collaborating on a book about the economic value of higher education.

CARL A. LINDSAY is a staff member with the Division of Planning Studies and Associate Professor of Education at The Pennsylvania State University. He directed the Continuing Professional Education Development Project, a five-year effort funded by the W. K. Kellogg Foundation and Penn State, which developed new types of continuing learning programs for professionals and examined a number of issues related to continuing professional education.

ANNE M. PRATT is Assistant to the Vice President for University Advancement at The College of William and Mary. Her writing and research address ideas about the curriculum of higher education, liberal education and the arts, individual and organizational learning or change, and the fit of development (or fund raising) in the university.

JONATHAN Z. SHAPIRO is Associate Professor of Education in the Department of Administrative and Foundational Services of the College of Education at Louisiana State University. His research interests include program evaluation and policy analysis.

WAYNE D. SMUTZ is Head, Office of Continuing Professional Education and Assistant Director, Division of Planning Studies within The Pennsylvania State University's Commonwealth Educational System. His interests and publications focus upon continuing professional education, collaborative relationships between universities and other organizations, and institutionalization of continuing professional education within the higher education context.

JOHN R. THELIN is Associate Professor and Director of the Higher Education Doctoral Program at The College of William and Mary; he also is a member of the American Studies Program Faculty. His research interests include public policy, social history, and institutional imagery. He is the author of *The Cultivation of Ivy* (1976) and *Higher Education and Its Useful Past*. His works in progress include studies of intercollegiate athletics, campus architecture, and analysis of historical statistics.

VINCENT TINTO is Professor of Sociology and Education at Syracuse University. He has written and consulted extensively on issues of higher education, particularly on student retention and the impact of higher education on student growth and social attainment. He is the author of a forthcoming book, *Leaving College: Rethinking the Causes and Cures of Student Attrition*, to be published by The University of Chicago Press.

DAVID O. ULRICH is Assistant Professor of Organizational Behavior and Industrial Relations in the Graduate School of Business Administration and Faculty Associate in the Institute for Social Research at the University of Michigan. He is currently engaged in two major research projects on strategic human resource management, strategy implementation, and transformational leadership. His publications have appeared in several management and human resource journals.

RAYMOND F. ZAMMUTO is Assistant Professor of Management and Organization, Graduate School of Business Administration, University of Colorado at Denver. His current research focuses on how organizations adapt to changing environments and, more specifically, on the management of declining enrollments and revenues in colleges and universities.

TRANSFORMATIONAL LEADERSHIP IN COLLEGES AND UNIVERSITIES

Kim S. Cameron and David O. Ulrich
University of Michigan

It is not news that American higher education currently faces an environment unlike any in its history. Reductions in government support, a decline in the number of 18-year-olds, and questioned credibility have been discussed at length in the higher education literature. What is less often recognized, however, is the fundamental transformation occurring in the broader context in which colleges and universities exist that threatens to change the very nature of higher education in America—from particularism to universalism, from monadism to pluralism, from a domestic to a global outlook, and from a monopolistic orientation to a competitive one. This fundamental shift in context will have a profound impact on colleges and universities in the future. The basic premise of this chapter is that a new kind of leadership—transformational leadership—will be required in higher education to adapt to these new conditions. Both the quality of higher education and the survival of the industry in its present form are at stake.

In the first section of this chapter, we discuss the meaning of transformation and outline some of the reasons for the current transformation in the context of higher education. The second section outlines a model of transformational leadership and provides illustrations from organizations that have undergone transformation. The final section provides suggestions for how this model of leadership has been applied in colleges and universities.

TRANSFORMATIONS

Transformations differ in nature from other types of changes, such as transitions, renewals, alterations, or adjustments. *Transformation* implies a metamorphosis or a substitution of one state or system for another, so that a qualitatively different condition is present. *Transformation* implies a change *of systems, not just a change in* systems. The transformation of a caterpillar to a butterfly and the transformation of an agrarian economy to an industrial economy are examples. Other types of changes may suggest merely a variation on a

1

theme or an evolution from one condition to another. For example, the transition from one life-cycle stage in an organization to another (e.g., from an early state of exploration and creativity to a later stage of formalization and efficiency) implies an alteration of conditions; previous characteristics are not replaced. Elements in the original condition are still recognizable after the change occurs. Whereas the environment of higher education is clearly characterized by numerous transitions, the possibility, even the likelihood, of a complete transformation requires rethinking leadership roles in higher education.

The likelihood of a transformation in higher education is greater today than ever before. Pressures for change have been mounting for years because, as service organizations, colleges and universities are in business to meet the needs of various strategic constituencies. It is from these constituencies that they acquire needed resources and obtain the acceptance of outputs and the services required for survival. As higher education's key constituencies go through transformations, like an incoming fog these transformations are likely to engulf higher education as well. Rather than be caught blind by the changes that permeate the context in which higher education exists, we can use transformations within other types of organizations as previews and models for leaders of colleges and universities. A few examples of change in American demographics, financial services, health care, manufacturing, and public education illustrate why the future of higher education may be about to encounter the beginnings of a radical transformation.

Demographics

It is estimated that by the year 1990, one third of the average salary in this country will be spent on social security. The reason is that in the next decade, the fastest growing population cohort will be those over age 65. Each day 5,500 Americans turn 65 in the U.S., and there are more than 26 million in that age category already. If we compare that number with fewer than 12 million students currently enrolled in institutions of higher education, the relative importance of this potential constituency becomes evident. By the year 2000, 32 million Americans will be over age 65, and 13.6 million will be over 85.

In addition, households headed by persons over age 55 control 28% of all discretionary income, double that of the under-35 group. Households in this category currently have 68% of the savings and 75% of the certificate balances, but only 5% of the debt. Of retirees, 78% own their own homes, and only 14% have mortgages.

These demographics lay the groundwork for four potentially dramatic transformations in higher education. First, there will be 850,000 fewer students in the traditional college-age group by 1995. If that decrease were distributed equally over all institutions of higher education in America, the average would be 450 fewer students per institution. With more than 700 schools having fewer than 450 students enrolled, large increases in closings are probable unless other age groups become targets of higher education. Even under present conditions, colleges have a death rate substantially higher than that of business and government organizations. The mortality rate for business organizations is approximately 57 per 10,000, for government organizations it is 28 per 10,000, and for higher education it is 117.6 per 10,000.

Second, with more adults becoming targets of higher education, what is taught and how it is taught may have to be altered significantly. In lieu of meeting students needs for initial career selection, higher education institutions will be attracting students who are near the end of their careers or who have already retired. These students will attend college less to gain job entry than for personal development. The traditionally desired outcomes that students attach to courses—such as good test scores and high grades—are likely to become increasingly irrelevant. One-way instruction from professors to eager young students will very likely become a less acceptable pedagogy, as dialogue, debate, and discussion of a lifetime of learning enter the classroom with older students.

Third, traditional linkages between financial aid and higher education may become fundamentally different with demographic changes. Government funding may become more difficult to obtain for education given the increasing demands of the aging population for social services and medical care. In addition, aid for these older returnees may come from nontraditional sources. Corporate sponsorship of education and payment for individual courses, rather than for degrees, may become more commonplace. Part-time versus full-time enrollment percentages may thus change dramatically as well.

Finally, the demand for quality in education by more mature students is likely to take a form different from the demands of traditional college-age population. The demands of mature, dedicated students are certain to be high, and rather than merely complaining about their dissatisfactions as younger students often do, older students may simply cease to purchase the service from the provider and may look elsewehere for education opportunities.

In sum, the social, economic, and cultural implications of these demographic changes are dramatic. Leaders in colleges and universities may need to take a hard look at recruitment practices, types of curricula offered, desired outcomes of college courses, location of teaching stations, admissions standards, sources of funding, and so on, in order to address the needs of this dramatically different student constituency.

Financial Services

Many in this industry now estimate that banking as it existed at the beginning of this decade will not survive to the year 1990. A fundamental transformation is occurring. In 1983, 48 banks failed, setting a record for the most failures since the Great Depression. In 1984, 79 banks failed. And in 1985, 113 more had failed, resulting in the projection that 130 would close in 1986. Nationwide, 865 branch banks were closed in 1984, the most ever. One reason for this failure rate is the change in the very foundations of American banking. In the past, for example, banks had an exclusive product franchise: only they could handle checking accounts, and virtually every household and corporation was forced to do business with a bank. Most checking-account money was "free" since no interest was paid on it, and service charges on accounts produced even more revenue. Now, deregulation has made checking accounts available to savings and loan associations, credit unions, stock brokerage firms, and almost any other financial services organization. Nationwide credit and debit card systems, along with automatic tellers, threaten to entirely eliminate paper checking.

A second reason for bank failures is the geographic protection from competition that came with laws against interstate and international banking. Deregulation, and a loophole called *bank holding companies,* has now made interstate banking almost universal. For example, Bank of America may now compete with small banks in states such as Mississippi and South Dakota, whereas it used to be restricted to its home state of California. Even more dramatic is the recent purchase by Sears of banks in several states, the opening of branch banks in shopping malls by Montgomery Ward, and the announcement by J. C. Penney Company that it will do the same. Even Southland Corporation, owner of the Seven-11 convenience stores, has announced plans to enter the financial services industry, not to mention General Motors, IBM, and AT&T. In addition, foreign banks have made large inroads into the American financial services market. Japanese banks, for example, have increased from $-\$6$ billion to $+\$18$ billion in long-term capital flows worldwide in the last three years, and five of the ten largest banks in the world are now Japanese (three are American, one is British, and one is French). Profits per employee at these Japanese banks are nearly double those of the best U.S. banks.

The relevance of these changes to American higher education is that the same type of environment is beginning to emerge for colleges and universities as is now typical in U.S. banking. Deregulation has transformed the environment from service-oriented to businesslike, from stable and protected to turbulent and competitive, from a function and process orientation to a product and market orientation, from secure employment to lack of employee security, from a local and specialized focus to a global and generalized focus, from unquestioned credibility to challenged credibility, from traditional technologies and delivery systems to high technology and innovative delivery systems, from slow change and conservative cultures to rapid change and risky cultures, from few mergers to many mergers, and so forth. Like bankers, leaders in colleges and universities may face a need to rethink their institution's relationship to products, markets, competition, globalization, innovative technology and delivery systems, rapid change, risk and innovation, mergers, and other such issues. The exclusive franchise that was once enjoyed by colleges and universities is no longer present. Consider a statement made recently by one college president on this topic:

> We talk about Orwell in 1984, but who in this room ever would have thought, even a year ago, that in 1984 our institution and J. C. Penney would be competitors in the same market? We are now. Last summer J. C. Penney made a corporate decision to get out of the auto service business. . . . What J. C. Penney got into was the business of education and training. And believe me, I don't think a corporation like J. C. Penney would make a decision to do that if there wasn't some evidence that there is a market out there that isn't being adequately served by current competitors. [A. L. Lorenzo, 1984]

Corporate expenditures for education and training now exceed expenditures by colleges and universities, and at least sixteen corporations are accredited to offer college-equivalent degrees. Because the value and relevance of college degrees is more and more in question, competition for non-traditional students has become intense. Furthermore, the likelihood of even more vigorous competition is substantial when one considers data from a summary of studies correlating success in college (as measured by grades) with adult achievement (as measured by a variety of factors including salary, promotion, life satisfaction, and notoriety). The mean correlation coefficient was only .16 (Samson, et al., 1984), not a particularly encouraging statistic for the competitive advantage of colleges and universities.

Health Care

U.S. businesses currently pay more in health care costs than they do in dividends to stockholders (approximately $80 billion per year). Health care costs have risen by a staggering 700% since 1970, and there has been an increase of 80% in just the last five years. Spending on health care now amounts to 11% of America's GNP. The Aluminum Company of America, for example, could have doubled its profits last year if it had been able to reduce medical costs by just 10%. Net profit was $10 million, but health care costs were more than $100 million. Approximately $600 of the price of a new automobile is directly attributable to medical care costs (that's almost 10% of the cost of a small car such as a Plymouth Horizon, a Ford Escort, or a Chevy Chevette). Dramatic transformations are now under way in health care in the form of health maintenance organizations, fee-for-service schedules, shoppingmall clinics, mass media advertising by hospitals, increases in numbers of home nurse practitioners and midwives, retirement communities, health spas in hospitals, and so on. All these measures are designed to decrease, limit, or make up for high and spiraling costs. Third parties (such as insurers) have acquired substantial power in the industry, and they have begun to have a major impact on cost containment in the health care profession, mainly by taking the initiative that once resided solely in hospital administrators and doctors.

The parallel between higher education and the health care industry is not perfect, but similar environmental conditions are emerging. Rising costs (including health care costs for college employees), along with competition from other kinds of service providers, may create a future that differs markedly from the traditional college or university environment. Third-party intervention in education by those with a stake in its outcomes (e.g., employers, students, and professional associations), as well as other cost containment and quality-enhancement measures, could have an important impact on transformations in the higher education industry similar to those in the health care industry.

As one example, current interactive videodisc technology makes possible far less expensive and more effective teaching than is traditionally done in colleges. Students in several experiments using this new technology have learned quicker and more effectively than with traditional approaches, and this kind of teaching/training can be done without an instructor present. In one study at the University of West Florida, for example, students using interactive videodisc finished the course an average of 25% faster than a control group that completed the course using traditional instruction. When given a final exam, 66% of the videodisc students passed, compared to 50% of the traditional students. In a National Science Foundation study, not only did videodisc students learn faster than traditional students, they required 40% less study time. At AT&T, a 30% savings in training time was achieved through the use of videodisc technology, (DeBloois, 1984). Because of the prohibitive expense associated with this technology, virtually all interactive videodisc education is being conducted in private corporations or the military. No college or university to date has made use of the technology on a broad scale. And without alternative sources of funding, it is unlikely that these institutions will be able to afford the high initial costs. The competitive advantage is simply being seized by organizations other than colleges and universities.

Manufacturing

Almost every major American manufacturing firm has begun to seek offshore facilities, joint ventures, or a foreign labor force, with the goal of reducing costs of production. The reasons are clear. In the automobile industry, for example, U.S. costs for blue-collar labor are 40% higher than in Japan, and for white-collar labor, they are 150% higher. The gap is even wider in comparisons to Korea, Singapore, Taiwan, and South American countries.

Even more profound, however, is the difference between quality and productivity in America and in other countries. A recent study by Gavin (1982), for example, compared the room-air-conditioner industries in Japan and the U.S.—industries that are identical in technology, equipment, and standardized product. Nine U.S. firms manufacture air conditioners; seven firms manufacture room air conditioners in Japan. When comparing the highest quality producers to the lowest quality producers, Gavin discovered that failure rates were from 500 to 1,000 times lower. More shocking was the difference between U.S. quality and Japanese quality. For example, the U.S. industry averaged 63.5 defects per 100 units on the assembly line. Japan averaged .95. The U.S. firms averaged 10.5 service calls the first year (under warrantee) per 100 units; Japanese firms averaged .60. The cost of failure for the U.S. industry was 4.0% of sales; for Japan, it was 1.3%. But the differences were not due to slower, more careful production in Japanese plants. Productivity in U.S. firms averaged 1.3 units per labor hour. In Japanese firms, the average was higher: 1.8 units per labor hour.

In the mid-1970s, a TV manufacturing plant near Chicago, owned by Motorola, was sold to the Japanese firm, Matsushita. The work force remained the same (100% American labor), but the number of white-collar workers was reduced by 50%. A comparison between the results produced by Matsushita's management and Motorola's management is dramatic. Under U.S. management, the defects produced per 100 TV sets averaged 150. Under Japanese management, the average was 4. Outright products rejects under Motorola management were 60%; under Matsushita management, rejects averaged 3.8%. Warrantee costs were $17 million per year under U.S. management, $3 million under Japanese management. And again, these results were not produced by slowing down production. In fact, productivity doubled, from 1,000 sets per day under American management to 2,000 sets per day under Japanese management.

A comparison of the printed-circuit-board industries in the United States and Japan in 1980 showed similar results. The error rate in American firms averaged 5%; in Japanese firms, it averaged .05%. The yield in the United States was 70%; in Japan, it was 92%. The complexity of the board being manufactured could account for the error rates, but in this case, much more complexity was produced by the Japanese manufacturers. The U.S. firms produced approximately 1200 styles, whereas the Japanese firms produced approximately 17,000 styles. The refinement of the printed circuits at that time in the United States was 15-millimeter spacing, but in Japan, it was 4-millimeter spacing.

A Public Agenda survey recently uncovered data that help explain some of these results. Only 23% of American workers indicated that they work at full potential. Half indicated that they don't put more effort into the job than is required. Three quarters said that they could be more effective in their job than they are.

This condition in U.S. manufacturing has not been without consequences for the American economy. In 1960, the average annual rate of growth in GNP in the United States was 4.1%; in 1970, it averaged 2.9%; in 1984, it was essentially zero. In 1950, the United States accounted for 40% of the world's GNP; in 1980, it accounted for 21%. In 1960, the United States accounted for 25% of the world's trade; in 1980, it accounted for 11%. In 1972, the standard of living in the U.S. was ranked highest in the world; in 1985 it ranked fifth.

According to most economists, service industries such as higher education are dependent on a strong manufacturing base in America. The reason is that the service sector can grow only to the extent that manufacturing and production expand. Yet the relevance of these statistics to American higher education does not lie merely in this dependency. A more important implication is illustrated by data that the Strategic Planning Institute has gathered annually over several years on American business units (known as the *PIMS database*). One of the most consistent conclusions from those data is reported in Figure 1. Regardless of the type of external environment an organization faces, profitability is significantly related to quality. In fact, quality is more powerful than any other variable in accounting for organizational effectiveness.

The quality of America's colleges and universities, likewise, is of critical concern. In a survey of administrators in 400 selected colleges and universities, Cameron and O'Reilly (1985) found that research on organizational effectiveness was the top-ranked topic for which research was needed. However, a survey of the literature in three major higher-education journals (*The Journal of Higher Education, Research in Higher Education,* and *The Review of Higher Education*) from 1980 through 1984 found that not a single research study had been published on that topic. Because investigations of quality and effectiveness are so difficult to conduct in a valid and reliable way (see Cameron, 1978, 1985, for discussions of the obstacles to studies of effectiveness in higher education, and Webster, 1985, for a discussion of problems in quality studies), researchers have paid relatively little attention to this topic. Yet it is precisely this topic that may predict the future of higher education as an industry. Because quality is so closely linked to organizational success, and because the statistics above suggest that American workers and organizations have become somewhat complacent and a little sloppy since the mid-1970s, special attention to the quality of colleges and universities (especially the nonelites that do not appear in national prestige polls) may be a key to their long-term survival in the environment of the future. No evidence exists that the quality of American higher education is lower than that of other countries' higher education systems, but the fact is that very few reliable data on quality exist at all. The danger is that attitudes displayed in the manufacturing sector may begin to characterize higher education as well.

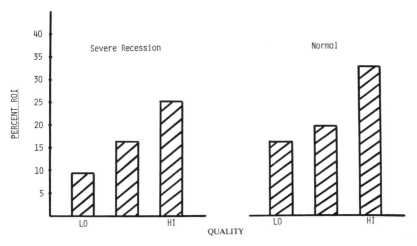

Fig. 1. Quality and Profitability. *Source:* PIMS.

Public Education

Many statistics related to public education have appeared recently in the popular press, but a brief summary here from two National Institute of Education Commission reports (1983, 1984) is a reminder of the need for, and the likelihood of, transformation in higher education. For example, in international comparisons of student achievement in industrialized countries on 19 academic tests, American students were never first or second, but they were last seven times. Nationwide, 13% of all high-school graduates are functionally illiterate, and among selected minorities, the percentage is as high as 40%. The U.S. Navy reported that one quarter of its recruits could not read at the ninth-grade level, the minimum needed to understand safety instructions, and one large U.S. city found that almost 60% of its students could not read at the 9th-grade level. Average scores on the Scholastic Aptitude Test (SAT) declined every year in America from a 1963 high of 502 on the math portion and 478 on the verbal portion to a 1981 low of 466 (math) and 424 (verbal), a decline of 36 points and 54 points, respectively. Recovery by 1985 was only 5 points in math and 2 points in verbal. Moreover, both the number and the proportion of those demonstrating superior performance on the SAT has declined dramatically, without recovery. Science achievement-test scores have similarly declined since 1969, and other tests indicate that 40% of high-school graduates cannot draw inferences from written material, that 80% cannot write a persuasive essay, and that 66% cannot solve a mathematical problem requiring several steps.

There may be several reasons for these rather dismal statistics. In 1965, 12% of high-school students selected the less rigorous "general track" instead of an "academic" or "vocational track" in high school. In 1980, the percentage was 42%. Of the credits earned by general track students, 25% are in physical education, health education, remedial courses in math or English, and personal service and development courses such as marriage preparation. Only 31% of high-school graduates in 1980 completed intermediate algebra, only 13% completed introductory French, only 16% completed geography, and only 6% completed calculus. The amount of homework done by high-school seniors has decreased substantially since the mid-1960s, while average grades have risen. Many industrialized countries now spend more than three times the amount of classroom time on mathematics and the sciences than even the most rigorous American high schools. Expenditures for textbooks and learning materials for classrooms has decreased consistently in this country, and instead of the recommended 5% to 10% of the school budget, these expenditures average 0.7%. Furthermore, it is estimated that half the newly employed mathematics, science, and English teachers are not qualified by training to teach these subjects, and that more than two thirds of physics teachers are unqualified.

The results of these educational deficiencies have been significant for higher education. Over 25% of all mathematics courses taught in colleges are remedial, an increase of 72% since 1975. Remedial English courses constitute almost one third of the offerings. The average tested achievement of students graduating from college is also lower than in years past. Society has been affected as well. In the last ten years, America has endured a 25% decrease in the number of patent applications. In 1984, 30% of all patent applications in the United States were initiated by the Japanese. Whereas in 1960 the U.S. marketed 82% of the world's inventions, now it ranks fifth. On April 1, 1985, Japan completed a coast-to-coast fiber-optics system that makes possible the linking together of all telephones, televisions, and computers in that country. The significance of such a development lies in the ability to transcend the electronic era and to move directly into the optics era in communication. The U.S., with only the New York City to Washington, DC, corridor at the same stage of development, is more than a decade behind. Fujitsu, a firm that has promised to be world's largest computer company by 1990, recently developed a supercomputer than can simulate 100,000 sets of variables in a matter of minutes in order to test an airplane's design. The fastest computer produced by America's IBM would take forty-four years to do the same task.

In brief, public education in America has failed to compete successfully with public education in other countries, and the effects on American society have been dramatic. Trends must be reversed if institutions of higher education are to prevent similar mediocrity. Either way, the pressures created by these stark realities create a climate for higher education ripe for transformation.

Summary: Information, Turbulence, and Complexity

Many other examples of change in the context of higher education have been chronicled in the popular press. Various authors have even coined labels to describe the environment that most predict will be characteristic of America in the 1990s. Terms such as "postindustrial environment" (Huber, 1984; Simon, 1973), "technetronic era" (Brzezinski, 1970), "the information society" (Masuda, 1980), the "telematic society" (Martin, 1981), and "the third wave" (Toffler, 1980) communicate a transformed environment where three main characteristics will permeate institutions: more and increasing information, more and increasing turbulence, and more and increasing complexity.

For example, academic journals are currently increasing at the rate of 11% per year from a base of approximately 100,000. Laser disc technology makes possible the storage of the equivalent of a law library on 10.5-inch disc, and visual scanners make possible the transfer of the contents of printed material to the disc in short amounts of time. Access to more information, in increasing amounts and almost instantaneously, therefore, will lead to more and increasing turbulence. That is, decisions will need to be made ever faster as both the amount and the rapidity of the data being encountered are increased. However, because all individuals are limited in the amount of information they can process at one time (Simon, 1973), leaders in colleges and universities (and other organizations) will find that short time frames and timeliness of decisions will begin to permeate management activities as turbulence increases. In turn, this increasing turbulence will create a condition of more and increasing complexity as well.

Complexity consists of three factors: numerosity (i.e., the number of relevant elements increases), specialization (i.e., the elements become more and more distinct from each other), and interdependence (i.e., changes in one element create changes in other elements). For leaders in higher education, this complexity means both more specialization, in order to avoid information overload, and more generality, in order to retain the ability to attend to a multiplicity of environmental elements. That is, a paradox exists in the requirements for leading an institution of higher education in this new environment. On the one hand, leaders will require the ability to maintain efficiency, stability, and smooth functioning. On the other hand, they will be required to be visionary, discordant, and innovative. Many observers of higher education have argued that the former characteristics are typical of many (if not most) administrators in higher education, and it is the latter characteristics that must be developed and demonstrated. For example:

Unquestionably, universities are among the worst managed institutions in the country. Hospitals and some state and city administrations may be as bad, but no business or industry except Penn Central can possibly be. [Bennis, 1973, p. 26]

The university, like the family and the church, is one of the most poorly integrated of institutions, and again and again it has been completely resistant to changes that were clearly demanded by changing conditions around it. [Stone, 1975, p. 35]

The crisis of leadership today is the mediocrity or irresponsibility of so many of the men and women in power, but leadership rarely rises to the full need for it. The fundamental crisis underlying mediocrity is intellectual. If we know all too much about our leaders, we know far too little about leadership. [Burns, 1978, p. 2]

As implied by Burns, the challenge in leading institutions of higher education in a transformed environment lies in developing and displaying, simultaneously, characteristics of administration (i.e., administering existing policy and procedures), management (i.e., managing multiple constituency demands both reactively and proactively), and leadership (i.e., creating new visions of the future and a readiness for change). Of course, leaders in higher education cannot ignore traditional internal administrative and management responsibilities, such as organizing, controlling, planning, and budgeting. However, if leaders persist in myopically excelling in such management tasks and ignoring the dramatic transformations occurring around them, the demise of many institutions may be assured. The kind of leadership that is requisite, but rare, is concerned more with "doing the right things" than with "doing things right," and with leadership of the intellect as much as with leadership of action. It is a proactive and anticipatory action as well as visionary perspectives. Instead of resembling the leader of the crew that rearranges the deck chairs on the *Titanic*, leadership in higher education must be much more concerned with new directions if the ship is to be preserved. This type of leadership we refer to as *transformational leadership*, and we describe and illustrate its characteristics in the following section.

TRANSFORMATIONAL LEADERSHIP

As the name implies, transformational leadership involves a process of fundamental change. This change results in a new way of interpreting reality, in a different set of motives, in a higher vision of possibilities, not merely the implementation of alternative actions or plans. It is as much concerned with helping people to think differently about the problems they face as it is with creating solutions for those problems. It is as much the management of meaning as it is the management of substance. Authors such as Burns (1978), Bennis (1984), Tichy (1985), and Tichy and Ulrich (1984) have analyzed and chronicled the activities of well-known transformational leaders, including such figures as Martin Luther King, Jr., Abraham Lincoln, John F. Kennedy, Winston Churchill, Mao Tse-tung, and Mahatma Gandhi in politics, and Thomas Watson, Lee Iacocca, Alfred Sloan, Henry Ford, and Frederick Taylor in organizations. From the writing of these and other authors, we suggest a five-step agenda for transformational leadership that has been typical of almost all these well-known figures. We describe these five steps below and then discuss how they apply to leadership in colleges and universities. The five steps are:

1. Creating readiness.
2. Overcoming resistance.
3. Articulating a vision.
4. Generating commitment.
5. Institutionalizing implementation.

Creating Readiness

Without an acknowledged need to change, organizations tend to remain largely the same because change almost never occurs without discomfort. For example, a summary of the organization and group-stage-development literature by Cameron and Whetten (1981, 1983) was applied to the life cycle typical of institutions of higher education. In brief, the progression in organizations tends to move, after the birth of the enterprise, from an early stage of loose, informal structure, entrepreneurialism, and dependence on external resources, through a collectivity stage in which organizational identity and mission become clarified, through a third stage called *formalization and control*, in which rigidity, hierarchy, and rules and policies become predominant, to a fourth stage characterized by an elaboration of structure, differentiation, and diversification. Certain pressures that are inherent in organizations make this progression common, but it is also not unusual for resistance forces and recalcitrance to inhibit these changes. On the one hand, inertia is created in organizations over time that helps to perpetuate stability and predictability. On the other hand, the seeds of destruction are present in any organization when it ceases to be adaptable and flexible in a changing environment; hence, no set of characteristics will be effective continuously, and pressures for change therefore exist. Organizations that are unable to progress and to maintain adaptability find themselves locked into a pattern that eventually becomes non-adaptable, and organizational demise is a frequent result of the resistance forces that derail change (see Quinn and Cameron, 1982). That is, colleges and universities, like all organizations, tend to resist change even when inertia exists for creating it.

One important role of the transformational leader is to create a readiness for change in the organization and its members so that a transformation can truly occur. The leader must unfreeze the organization and create enough dissatisfaction with the *status quo* so that individuals are motivated to change. Unless present circumstances are viewed as unsatisfactory, there is no reason to expect a needed transformation to occur. The question is, How does one go about creating productive dissatisfaction, or the kind of dissatisfaction that leads to desired change rather than discouragement and criticism? Among the many ways of creating this need for change are the following:

1. *Comparisons with referents.* One way to create dissatisfaction is to generate information about current performance or the organization's current condition, and then to compare it to a referent or standard. For example, performance figures, questionnaire responses, or the results of a stakeholder analysis (e.g., customer or user preferences) can produce data that can then be compared with one of the following:

A. Comparative referents—comparisons with other, similar organizations (e.g., "We are doing worse than our competition!").
B. Ideal referents—comparisons with an idealized standard or the best condition that could possibly exist (e.g., "We are not maximizing performance!").
C. Goal referents—comparisons with the stated goals of the organization (e.g., "We have not achieved the goals we set for ourselves!").
D. Improvement referents—comparisons with the past performance of the organization (e.g., "We are not doing as well as we have in the past!").
E. Trait referents—comparisons with characteristics valued by the organization (e.g., "We do not have the characteristics in our organization that we want!").
F. Stakeholder demand referents—comparisons with the demands or expectations held for the organization by certain interest groups (e.g., "We are not meeting customer demands!").

Which referents are most useful depends, of course, on what discrepancies exist in the comparisons, which referent has the most legitimacy with the organization members, and which referent is perceived to be reachable. The purpose, simply, is to make clear the inadequacy of present conditions and the need to make a change. Creating the expectation that a transformation will narrow or eliminate the gap is a role of the transformational leader.

2. *Personnel changes.* Readiness for change can result from introducing new people into the organization who bring fresh perspectives or varied experiences. Because norms and expectations governing interactions and relationships become rigid over time, it is difficult to create a desire for change when no changes occur in the players. Shared interpretations of reality are created and reinforced to help protect the organization from threat and uncertainty, and those interpretations often inhibit the emergence of any dissatisfaction. The introduction of fresh ideas by new people, however, can help create an awareness of alternatives that unfreezes individuals from the standardized interpretations and behavioral rituals.

The paradox of this strategy is that new people must be integrated into the organization's culture and must become socialized in order to have credibility and to adequately perform their roles. Yet it is precisely the absence of such socialization that makes new people valuable as change agents. Creative and useful ideas may emerge from people who haven't yet been confronted with the large number of new-idea-killers that exist in most organizations, such as "We tried it before," "It's against our policy," or "The president (or dean or department head) won't go for it." A balance must be maintained, therefore, between the elimination of new perspectives by means of socialization and the absence of socialization that eliminates legitimacy and credibility.

3. *Creation of a new language.* Another way to create a readiness for change is to help organization members to use a different language to describe old realities. When new language is used, interpretations change. For example, new employees at Disneyworld are taught the first day on the job that they were hired by central casting, not the personnel department; they are cast members, not employees; they wear costumes, not uniforms; they serve visitors and guests, not tourists; they work in attractions, not rides or arcades; they play characters (even as grounds keepers), not merely hold a job; during working hours, they are onstage and must go offstage to eat, socialize or relax. The intent of this alternative language is simply to create a perspective in individuals that leads them to change how they think about work. This language helps to unfreeze old interpretations and to create new ones. A similar phenomenon is evident in many social movements, where an alternative language is almost always present (e.g., beatniks, hippies, black power groups, Valley girls, and yuppies).

Bennis (1984) observed that the most successful leaders in education, government, business, the arts, and the military have been those who have special language characteristics. Most notable is the absence in their vocabularies of the word *failure*. These individuals simply haven't allowed themselves, or others around them, to think about failure. Alternative descriptors have always been substituted such as *nonsuccess, temporary slowdown, false start, mistake, error, blooper, miss, loss, stumble, blotch, bungle, foul-up, constraint, obstacle,* and *disappointment*. These leaders have used language as one mechanism for interpreting reality for others around them and for creating a willingness to try again, not to become discouraged. *Failure* implies finality; *blooper* or *false start* implies the first steps toward eventual success. In a similar way, transformational leaders are sensitive to the power of new language to create a readiness in organizations to change.

4. *Development and training of organization members.* On any given day, approximately 25% of IBM's work force is engaged in formal training activities. The corporate training budget approaches $400 million. One payoff for such heavy investments in reeducation and training of employees is an increased capacity for change and adaptation. Despite a highly turbulent and complex industry, IBM continues to be a runaway number one in its industry and to increase its market share. It is widely recognized as being among the

most successful corporations in the world. While employment in the computer and semiconductor industries has declined 27% since the beginning of 1985 (a decrease of more than 272,000 jobs), IBM has maintained its no-layoff policy. Over 5,000 workers were retrained for new jobs within the corporation in 1985.

This IBM example illustrates the principle that creating readiness for change is dependent on the continuing development of an organization's employees. When new knowledge and skills become available to individuals, the likelihood that employees will look for new opportunities to apply them is strong. Consequently, to enhance the probability of change, transformational leaders invest in the development of employees so that the needed competence base is present to make the change successful. The most recalcitrant individuals in organizations are those who have no option but to continue present behavior patterns because of a lack of training. The most ready to change are those who have a repertoire of competencies that can be applied in the new condition. A role of the transformational leader, then, is to help prepare the competency base that improves the capacity for change.

5. Identification of external threats. Another technique for inducing readiness to change is to identify an external threat to the organization's well-being. When survival is at stake, readiness for change is almost always high. For example, Franklin D. Roosevelt has been accused of allowing the bombing of Pearl Harbor in 1941 to mobilize the American people to enter the war. The launching of *Sputnik* created a threat that led to an increase in support for education that was unprecedented in U.S. history. The loss of U.S. markets to foreign companies has begun to mobilize corporate research-and-development efforts and to increase attention to quality and productivity as never before. The National Institute of Education's National Commission on Excellence in Education (1983) chose to report its findings of declining educational excellence as an open letter to the public in order to emphasize the threat to American society and to mobilize public support for change. The report began with the statement

> If an unfriendly foreign power had attempted to impose on America the mediocre educational performance that exists today, we might well have viewed it as an act of war. As it stands, we have allowed this to happen to ourselves. [p. 5]

Transformational leaders can create a readiness to change by identifying factors in the outside environment that threaten the well-being of the organization or its members. If the threat being identified exists inside the organization, conflict and rigidity among organization members, rather than readiness for change, are frequent consequences. People tend to place blame on one another for their uncomfortable condition, and needed change is difficult to implement. On the other hand, when the threat being identified exists externally, forces within the organization tend to mobilize against it so that conflict and resistance are overcome. Creating readiness simply involves raising the consciousness of people inside the organization to these external threats.

In summary, a variety of approaches exist for creating a readiness for change in an organization. The five discussed here are among the most effective. Each depends on the ability of the transformational leader to manage the interpretations of those in the organization who must change. These approaches involve as much a symbolic or perceptual process as a substantive process. The objective is simply to create enough productive dissatisfaction with the *status quo* so that needed change can occur.

On the other hand, despite the presence of productive dissatisfaction, resistance to change is still a universal phenomenon in organizations. Even though a need is recognized, resistance often scuttles the best laid plans. Identifying and overcoming those resistance forces is, therefore, the second agenda item for the transformational leader.

Resistance to Change

Even though transformational leaders have created a readiness to change, changes of the magnitude of transformations are resisted in organizations because they destroy things. Normal levels of performance, communication channels, organizational values, power relationships, and even careers are destroyed when this kind of change occurs. Whereas individuals would probably not resist a positive change, such as a 10% pay increase, or a small change, such as the addition of another course to the curriculum, transformational change has much broader implications for individual behaviors, expectations, and relationships. The mere magnitude of this kind of change requires giving up certainty for ambiguity, security for risk, stability for instability, and predictability for opportunity. Resistance of many types tends to emerge.

One well-known model for identifying the types of resistance that are most likely was proposed for Kurt Lewin and is called *force-field analysis*. Figure 2 illustrates this model. Current levels of performance are a product of multiple forces working in opposite directions. One one side of the model are restraining forces, or constraints, that inhibit any improvement in performance. They are matched exactly by driving forces, or motivators, that encourage improvement in performance. The reason that performance exists at its current level is the balance of forces. Positive, desired change results from the creation of an imbalance in forces—either a decrease or an elimination of resistance forces, or an increase or multiplication of driving forces. Because the addition of driving forces almost always produces a matching self-generated resistance force (i.e., if the pressure to perform at a higher level is increased, an equal amount of resistance will naturally occur), the most effective way to change a system is to eliminate or decrease resistance forces, that is, to overcome the obstacles and constraints inhibiting change. Transformational leadership, then, is as much like playing guard on a football team as it is like playing quarterback.

DRIVING FORCES   CURRENT LEVEL   RESTRAINING FORCES
                        OF FUNCTIONING

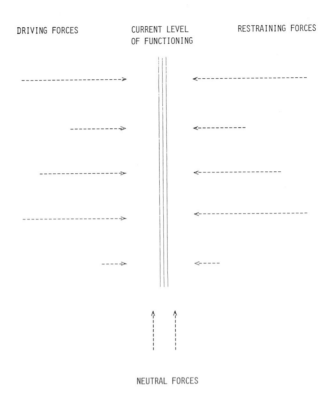

NEUTRAL FORCES

Fig. 2. Force-Field Analysis.

Eliminating potential obstacles to desired change is at least as important to effective transformation as is calling the plays. Clearing the way can be accomplished, however, only when the resistance forces have been identified.

Following Tichy (1983), we can categorize resistance forces into three different types: technical, political, and cultural. A brief discussion of each of these types of resistance follows: then we discuss ways to overcome resistance in order to clear the way for transformational change.

Technical resistance forces. Technical resistance emerges from the technology, the structure, and the interaction patterns that exist in organizations. Change is often resisted, for example, because it threatens habitual social interaction patterns and interpersonal relationships. In a classic study of change in a coal mine in Great Britain, for example, Trist and Bamforth (1951) studied the effects of a mechanized approach to mining coal that made possible mining on a long portion of a wall instead of on short faces. It was predicted that this new method would increase productivity exponentially, but instead productivity decreased. It was discovered that the social groups and interaction patterns that had formed as the miners worked together in groups were disrupted when they were spread out along a long wall and made to work individually. The new technology failed because of social resistance forces.

Other types of technical resistance forces also exist, such as (1) sunk costs in current technology that make additional investments seem too costly; (2) "local pride" or the desire to remain unique, so that change is resisted because it might dissipate that uniqueness; (3) structural reporting relationships that inhibit information flows and efficient action; (4) a low tolerance of ambiguity, a fear of the unknown, or an aversion to risk, which produces conservatism and rigidity; and (5) the absence of adequate know-how or training to cope with the change. In general, technical resistance forces are the most obvious and the easiest to overcome, as we discuss below.

Political Resistance Forces. Political resistance emerges from a disruption in critical organizational resources, such as power, money, career opportunities, and recognition. When a loss of rewards is threatened, for example, resistance forces will be strong. These threatened rewards may be either intrinsic or extrinsic.

An example from the University of Michigan's Graduate School of Business Administration is illustrative. The Burroughs Corporation provided a large grant to the Graduate School of Business Administration that resulted in all secretaries' and faculty members' receiving a new personal computer. Many young secretaries who had become familiar with this new technology in their recent schooling were initially much more comfortable and adept with the computers than were the older secretaries who had relied mainly on typewriters. These young secretaries became the sources of information and expertise, and they were able to perform their new tasks more effectively. The traditional power relationships based on tenure and experience began to be replaced by a new form of power based on technical ability. To prevent disruptive political resistance, steps had to be taken within the school to reestablish and reconfirm the old power relationships and to overcome the natural resistance to change. Involvement and training were high priorities in allocating budgets to overcome this potentially disruptive resistance.

Other forms of political resistance may result from (1) threats to coalitions and interest groups, whose centrality or criticality may be eroded; (2) the loss of discretion or control over resources; (3) threats to feelings of self-worth, which are produced by scapegoating and indictment by those who resist the change; and (4) perceptions that hierarchical superiors are not supportive.

Cultural Resistance Forces. Cultural resistance emerges from the values, norms, biases, and underlying assumptions that develop in organizations. These underlying dynamics in organizations create a special identity and sense of uniqueness for the organization. Psychologists have long claimed that preservation of "face"—a sense of personal worth and individual identity—is the primary motivator of human beings (see Goffman, 1955). Organizations develop similar identity-preservation instincts, which become institutionalized as culture. For example, just after the Arab oil embargo in the mid-1970s, the chief executives of two major American oil companies announced well-developed strategic plans to diversify out of the oil business. Their carefully formulated projections suggested that long-term growth in oil could not be supported by the business environment, and their firms faced serious political threats from outside forces. After several years of floundering in attempts to acquire and build new businesses, however, both firms are now solidly in the oil business and both chief executives have been replaced. The cultural resistance forces in each firm that became mobilized when company identity was threatened sabotaged all attempts to change.

Similar cultural resistance in higher education was evident when schools of business and finance were first introduced into the university curriculum. One well-known critic suggested that a college of commerce was "incompatible with the collective cultural purpose of the university. It belongs in the corporation of learning no more than a department of athletics" (Veblen, 1918, p. 154). Another, in referring to the first established business school at any university, stated: "The first and most important destructive influence at Pennsylvania of the atmosphere important for the nourishment of the humane arts is the Wharton School of Finance and Commerce" (Whyte, 1957, p. 93). These statements were not an indication of an inability to incorporate a business curriculum into the university, or of a threat to the political power of special-interest groups; rather they were a product of underlying values and biases about the nature and identity of the university.

Cultural resistance may be manifested as ethnocentrism, where the impression exists that because something is characteristic of our organization, it must be the best; selective perception, where contradictory or nonsupportive information is filtered out in order to preserve a sense of worth; shared stereotyping, where all threats to the organization, whether they be individuals or events, are given negative labels in order to render them impotent; creating stories and folklore, the purpose of which is to reinforce and buffer core organizational values by identifying and separating outsiders; and so on. Cultural resistance is especially difficult to overcome because it is often unarticulated and unrecognized even by those who are resisting. It is the taken-for-granted nature of culture that makes it both powerful and difficult to change.

The categorization of restraining forces by Eicholtz and Rogers (1964) is different from Tichy's, because of their investigations in educational organizations. Table 1 enumerates their five types of resistance, all framed on the personal rather than the organizational level of analysis. These "forms of rejection" supplement Tichy's technical, political, and cultural resistance forces, and they help to identify a variety of ways of overcoming resistance to change. We now turn to that discussion.

TABLE 1. A Framework for the Identification of Forms of Rejection

Form of rejection	Cause of rejection	State of subject	Anticipated response
Ignorance	Lack of dis-semination	Uninformed	"The information is not easily available."
Suspended judgment	Data not *logically* compelling	Doubtful	"I want to wait and see how good it is before I try."
Situational	Data not *materially* compelling	1. Comparing	"Other things are equally good."
		2. Defensive	"The school regulations will not permit it."
		3. Deprived	"It costs too much to use in time and/or money."
Personal	Data not *psychologically* compelling	1. Anxious	"I don't know if I can operate the equipment."
		2. Guilty	"I know I should use them, but I don't have time."
		3. Alienated	"These gadgets will never re-place a teacher."
Experimental	Present or past trials	Convinced	"I tried them once and they aren't any good."

Source: Eicholtz and Rogers (1964).

Overcoming Resistance to Change
Transformational leadership involves not only identifying the potential roadblocks to change but also overcoming or reducing them. We identify seven principles for accomplishing that aim based on a rather extensive literature in organization development and on our own investigations of change and transformation in colleges and universities (see, for example, Bennis et al., 1969; Cameron, 1984b).

1. *Participation and information dissemination.* A core principle for reducing resistance is to involve those to be affected by the change in gathering data and diagnosing a need for change, in formulating implementation plans, in helping to project outcomes and consequences, and in communicating that information to others. Representatives of strategic constituencies can be important advocates and allies if they are involved in planning and implementing changes. Resistance is lessened when individuals feel that all relevant information is available to them; hence, feedback must be frequent and must be

directed to those affected by the change after the transformation begins to take shape.

2. *Autonomy and discretion.* Resistance is lessened when individuals feel that they have some control over the changes being made. This control can be merely decisions about when or how to implement changes (as opposed to what changes will occur), but some participant autonomy is a prerequisite to implementing successful change. Without it, change is viewed as an externally imposed requirement that is almost always defined as a threat, not an opportunity.

3. *Hierarchical support.* The more the power and prestige held by the initiator of change, the less will be the resistance to it. Therefore, the support of both formal hierarchical leaders and informal opinion leaders in organizations must be fostered by transformational leaders. Change need not be from top down, but top-level support must be obtained in order for change to be institutionalized. As one example, after studying innovation and change in large numbers of organizations, Kanter (1982) identified coalition building among important power groups both inside and outside the organization as the key to successful change.

4. *Supportive group influences.* The consensus of a group can work either for or against transformational change. Extreme consensus can take the form of "group think" and drive out any consideration of change (Janis, 1976). Fault finding and criticism are much more likely to occur in organizations than praise and support (see Argyris, 1970; Cameron, 1984c); hence, negative energy can be reinforced by group consensus. On the other hand, groups can be powerful influences in overcoming resistance to change when they are given a chance to buy in early in the process. When a sense of belonging exists, when the group is attractive, and when it has continuing membership importance (as opposed to a temporary group), group acceptance is powerful in overcoming resistance. Establishing relationships of high trust and social support with key groups is one of the most important roles of the transformational leader.

5. *Advocates versus opponents.* Similarly, when advocates display empathy with and understanding of the resistors' viewpoint, zero-sum definitions are likely to be avoided. That is, instead of defining change as a win-lose proposition, transformational leaders can smooth the way for change by carrying on open, honest dialogues with opponents instead of trying to railroad the change through, regardless of resistance. Identifying the advantages that will accrue to all interested parties as a result of the change is another important mechanism for reducing resistance. Displaying an understanding of the resistors' views and being open to the modification of plans are important characteristics of transformational leaders.

6. *Interesting and nonthreatening approaches.* Change is least likely to be resisted when it reduces rather than increases burdens on organization

members, or when it presents interesting new opportunities. Helping organization members to see the change as increasing rather than decreasing their opportunity to obtain rewards is a key way to lessen resistance. Change that is requested almost always encounters less resistance than change that is imposed, and change initiated from inside the organization generally encounters less resistance than change initiated from the outside. The reason is that more information, more control, and more certainty can be obtained about internal, requested change than about external, imposed change. Organization members are more likely to find ways to turn this kind of change to their advantage. On the other hand, when change threatens the security, power, position, or reward structure of individuals, resistance will be strong. Therefore, transformational leaders must help the organization to interpret needed change as an opportunity rather than a threat in order for it to be supported.

7. *Desirable values.* Bennis (1984) cited a study showing that individuals would rather follow leaders they can count on, who display a consistency of values, even when the disagree with them, than leaders whose positions shift frequently. Kohlberg (1976) found that the most influential leaders are those who display a consistent, comprehensive, universalistic set of values that define clearly what they stand for. Burns (1978) equated transformational leadership with "moral leadership," which "returns to the fundamental wants and needs, aspirations, and values of the followers" (p. 4). These findings illustrate the principle that overcoming resistance to change is enhanced by articulating and exemplifying a core set of values. The relevance of cultural change is not ignored. Transformation is fostered when leaders tie the practicalities of change to the fundamental values that reside within the culture of the organization. Whereas cultural resistance forces are difficult to counter, successful transformational leaders often counter them by facing head-on the relevance of human values.

Numerous other mechanisms for overcoming resistance also exist, but those discussed here are among the most powerful in helping transformation to come about. Clearing away obstacles from the path of change is an important agenda item for the transformational leader. Without a clear idea of where one is going, however, a clear path does little good. Therefore, the third agenda item for the transformational leader, to which we now turn, is the articulation of a vision.

Articulating a Vision
In addition to overcoming resistances, transformational leaders articulate a vision of the future. Visions establish universalistic and consistent principles that give individuals and organizations a sense of direction—a moral viewpoint about what the future holds. Visions evoke deeper meanings than goals. Goals

that call for "increased enrollment," "increased graduation percentages," or "lower costs" may be valuable goals, but they are not visions.

The transformational leader's vision deals with fundamental principles, moving beyond specific targets or goals. Burns (1978) suggested that transformational leaders set visions founded on moral principles. Using Kohlberg's research (1976) on stages of moral development, he suggested that transformational leaders work with Stages 5 and 6. In these stages, choices for action are driven by universalistic principles that govern all behavior. Individual behavior stems from an acceptance of these principles and a personal commitment to them.

As applied to organizations, transformational leaders articulate visions that establish, communicate, and perpetuate principles in which the organization can believe. Thomas Watson at International Business Machines established the principle of service first. The slogan "IBM means service" became more than a short-term program; instead, it became an enduring principle that permeated IBM's culture. Martin Luther King, Jr., based his dream of a "brotherhood of man" on principles of equality. His dream, based on a fundamental principle, guided both his own behavior and the behavior of those who followed him.

Transformational leaders determine, teach, and reinforce principles that come from their own internal values, not from those that seem to be popular or widely accepted. For example, Bennis (1984) found that individuals preferred to follow leaders who demonstrated a consistent set of moral principles, even if they disagreed with the principles or the behavior, much more than leaders who were inconsistent in their behavior. Thomas Watson personally believed in service and demonstrated it; Martin Luther King, Jr., personally believed in equality and acted accordingly. These principles were not worn while at work and then discarded in personal affairs. The principles were encompassing and deeply felt. Teaching principles to organization members requires constant attention to these principles. In speeches, visits, interviews, meetings, and discussions, transformational leaders teach them. Above all, living the principles, and making sure that they represent a personal value statement, teaches them to others.

Reinforcing the principles also comes from hiring employees who support the values, rewarding and promoting employees in a manner consistent with the principles, and allocating resources to ensure that the principles will be maintained. The "IBM look" reinforces the principles that Thomas Watson inculcated. Employees, to succeed, fit the image. They accept the values; they live them; they believe in them. Employees who find the principles at IBM inconsistent with their personal beliefs leave the corporation.

Visions based on principles allow employees to govern themselves. When employees share a common set of beliefs, they are more likely to strive toward a common vision. When employees understand and believe in the ends, or goals, they are more likely to accept the means, or organization processes, for accomplishing the ends. Outsiders make more fun of the "white shirt" image at IBM than do internal employees. Internal employees accept this image as a means of accomplishing a common end.

In the development of a set of principles that establish a vision of the future, two ways of thinking need to be managed: left-brain and right-brain thinking.

Left-Brain Thinking. Transformational leaders develop the left-brain part of a vision. Left-brain thinking emphasizes logical, rational approaches to problem solving and creating a vision. Visions formed from left-brain thinking emphasize the deductive, specific, and concrete processes for organizational success.

Transformational leaders who create visions with left-brain thinking emphasize traditional strategic-planning activities. They worry about such issues as setting goals for the future that are specific and concrete; defining the organization's distinctive competence through careful analysis of the strengths, weaknesses, opportunities, and threats facing the organization; and carefully assessing environmental niches that may lead to future growth. The visions from the left brain often focus on numbers, such as growth rates, productivity rates, graduation rates, retention rates, or revenue goals. These left-brain numerical goals are complemented with clear plans of action that lay out responsibility matrices and PERT charts. The process of setting out left-brain visions also follows a logical format. Discussions are held with key decision-makers, and information is codified into prescribed forms to ensure consistency and accuracy.

Transformational leaders using the left brain respond to some specific questions in forming a vision:

1. *What business are we in?* This question emphasizes the fundamental purpose of the organization. Is the university in the business of producing knowledge (research) or delivering knowledge (teaching)?

2. *What major problems and obstacles do we face?* Being successful in the defined business means that obstacles must be overcome. Recognizing what those obstacles are precludes overcoming them. Succeeding as a research institution means overcoming obstacles of financial support, hiring quality personnel, and maintaining a culture of research.

3. *What information do we require?* To meet the needs for the future, organizations require information. Transformational leaders who create the left-brain vision identify needed information and establish procedures for obtaining, codifying, and processing it.

4. *What are our resources?* Meeting the organization's objectives requires an assessment of current resources. Resources may include personnel, facilities, supplies, and finances. This resource base may be very different for a research university and for a community college, in terms of both its source and its nature.

5. How do we communicate our vision? In letting employees know of the future state, transformational leaders pay attention to the manner in which the vision is perpetuated. Speeches, video, newspaper articles, and one-on-one discussions may each be helpful in different ways in communicating the vision.

Left-brain thinking rewards specifics and detail. Transformational leaders need to appreciate and use the left brain in creating visions so that others can understand and accept the logic of the vision. The visions that come from left-brain thinking engender continuity and stability. However, overdependence on the left brain results in elegant written visions that fail to capture attention or imagination.

Right-Brain Thinking. Complementing left-brain thinking in creating a vision is right-brain thinking. Whereas the left brain focuses on detail, the right brain highlights gestalt; the left brain identifies concrete facts, and the right brain, wholistic images; the left brain delivers, the right brain conceives; the left brain emphasizes intellectual activity, and the right brain, emotional activity. Transformational leaders formulate visions using the right brain as well as the left.

The right brain emphasizes the intuitive, imaginative, insightful, and creative aspects of a vision. It focuses less on the "how-to's" and more on the "what's." The visions articulated with the right brain capture the imagination of the followers and generate emotional commitment to the vision. Martin Luther King's "I Have a Dream" speech painted a picture of equality and freedom. The speech captured imagination and helped both believers and nonbelievers to understand the purposes of Dr. King's work. The speech did not lay out a neatly organized plan for gaining equality. Likewise, President Kennedy's vision in the early 1960s to "land a man on the moon in this decade" captured the imagination of the American people. He did not have the plans formulated that led to Neil Armstrong and Buzz Aldrin's walk on the moon in 1969, but he formulated and articulated an engaging mental image of what he wanted the space program to accomplish.

To articulate the vision, transformational leaders use symbols and language that evoke meaning and commitment. In lieu of speaking about numerical goals, right-brain visions often speak to future hopes. They emphasize the opportunities for a better future that come from a dedication to the present. They are generally punctuated with personal meaning since they reflect the personal values of the leader.

In preparing a vision of the future, transformational leaders invoke both left- and right-brain thinking to enhance the commitment of organization membrs. Often, leaders fall into the trap of responding to daily barrages of meetings, memos, and management. Once into the quicksand of responding, it is difficult to emphasize the importance of perceiving and preparing visions that speak to the future. Given the choice of spending time on today's problems versus visions of the future, it is obviously easier and less stressful in the short-run to work with today's problems. However, emphasis on the short-run creates efficiency at the expense of effectiveness: doing things right versus doing the right things. In 1890, the Pennsylvania Railroad was the largest employer in the United States, with over 110,000 employees. Penn Railroad's vision focused on efficiency in managing the railroad business. It prospered in its vision. It succeeded. Unfortunately, being efficient in the railroad business deflected attention from a changing world in which the transportation business prospered while the railroad business faltered.

Generating Commitment
Once a vision of the future is developed and articulated transformational leaders generate commitment to the vision. A great deal of the commitment to a vision comes from the elegance with which the vision is developed and articulated. The charisma of Dr. King and President Kennedy helped to commit others to the visions that they represented. While the vision itself can evoke commitment, transformational leaders also expend personal effort to generate commitment among followers. Some of the effective ways this is done are as follows:

1. *Ensuring public commitments.* One principle of commitment is that people are committed to act out their public declarations (Salancik, 1977). The need for personal congruence ensures that public statements will be followed by behavior consistent with the statements. A surefire way to commit oneself to behavioral change (e.g., losing weight, or stopping smoking) is to tell one's friends that the change is under way. After making public pronouncements, individuals become committed to what they have espoused.

In order to increase the commitment of newly hired engineers, Hewlett-Packard requires that they spend time recruiting on college campuses. While having engineers do the recruiting helps to attract good engineers, it also commits these newly hired recruiters. To recruit college students, the engineers must publicly praise Hewlett-Packard. The process of making such public statements commit the engineers to the company.

When the Tennessee Valley Authority (TVA) was attempting to build a dam in the late 1940s, it found the local farmers resisting the efforts. To overcome this resistance and to elicit the farmers' commitment to the project, the TVA made local farmers members of the board that would supervise the construction project. These local farmers began to make public statements on behalf of the TVA project and, over time, became committed to it (Selznick, 1949).

Transformational leaders look for opportunities to have key employees make public statements in favor of the vision. Assigning key officers to represent the vision to employees or outside groups, forming discussion groups about how to implement the vision and designating a spokesperson for the group, and asking key officers to join the leader in a program where the vision is discussed may be means of publicly committing others to the vision.

2. *Encouraging participation and involvement.* A second psychological process that evokes commitment is creating ownership of and personal identification with the vision. When individuals feel that the vision is not imposed but shared, they are more likely to be committed to carrying it out. Generating ownership comes, to a great extent, from participation and involvement.

At Texas Instruments, one week a year is spent reviewing the corporate vision and strategic plans. This one-week series of meetings includes the top 150 managers of the corporation. In this week, a number of debates and discussions are held so that each executive feels that his or her points of view have been incorporated into the strategic plan. At International Business Machines, key staff officers have the responsibility to "nonconcur" with the strategic plan if they cannot personally support it. By eventually reaching an agreement with the plan and making a public statement of concurrence, these staff officers assume ownership of the plan and its contents. When the Federal Aviation Administration decided to generate a new culture that supported increased employee participation, the top officers organized an administrator's management team to discuss and debate what the new culture needed to be. After much discussion, these top twenty-five executives each felt ownership of the cultural statement that emerged.

In each of these cases, commitment followed involvement and participation. Transformational leaders involve others in key decisions and thereby gain commitment to the vision.

3. *Setting effective goals.* Many organizations go through round after round of goal setting. Often these rounds become battles that no one seems to win. If goals are set effectively, commitment follows. Setting effective goals requires the inclusion of at least four processes (Latham and Yukl, 1975). First, goals need to be specific. Who needs to accomplish what, when, where, and why should be answered in the goal-setting process. Nonspecific goals do not give the required psychological direction for ensuring commitment. Second, goals need to be set by participation. As discussed above, when individuals participate in setting goals, they feel ownership of the goals. Such ownership leads to commitment. Third, goals must be challenging. Goals that are unrealistically challenging fail to generate commitment because individuals realize that they can never accomplish the goals. Goals that are too easy also fail to generate commitment because they do not stretch individual performance. Moderately challenging goals force individuals to work hard to meet the goals that are attainable. Fourth, goals must be set so that feedback follows the efforts to attain the goal. When individuals receive direct feedback on their efforts to

reach the goal, they are more committed to working toward the goal. Finally, goals are more likely to be accomplished if there is a specific and valued reward for attaining the goal. When individuals see value in successful attainment, they become more committed to reaching the goal.

In World War II, the military learned that feedback and rewards had a very positive impact on commitment to accomplishing goals. Draftees were given a choice. They were told that they had six months to learn Japanese. At the end of six months, they would receive feedback through passing or failing a test. Those who failed would be given a rifle and sent to the front lines. Of those enrolled in the program, 99% passed the exam. Commitment ran high. The soldiers received feedback, they had explicit goals, and most important, they received a reward (and avoided punishment) by accomplishing the goal.

4. *Selecting and socializing key people.* Commitment is also enhanced when transformational leaders perform a political analysis on the organization and identify the key political actors. The key political actors are likely to be the informal leaders to whom others turn for direction and insight. Once these informal leaders are identified, transformational leaders ensure that they will personally and publicly support the vision. This effort builds the coalition necessary for supporting the vision. Selecting key people to help implement the vision ensures that others will also become committed.

Often, when a new chief executive officer (CEO) assumes office, he or she begins by organizing a new staff. This process of selecting a staff is a critical time for communicating a new vision. Selecting those individuals who are known to support the vision of the new CEO alerts others in the organization to the vision and builds organizational commitment to it. When Michael Blumenthal became the CEO at Burroughs Corporation, he changed 22 of the top 23 executives within the first 18 months. By making a careful selection of new executives, he ensured that there would be a commitment to his vision throughout the organization. Others in the organization became aware of his priorities through his choices of new executives, and they learned quickly that it was politically expedient to support the new vision.

After selecting new individuals, transformational leaders orient them. They work to socialize these new organization members so that they feel a part of an exclusive club. By feeling unique, they become even more committed. Selecting and socializing individuals serves the psychological process of creating loyalty and justifying decisions, thus increasing commitment. Once individuals are allowed to join an exclusive club because of the transformational leader, they are more likely to be loyal to that leader and to be committed to accomplishing his or her vision. The new executives at Burroughs developed a commitment to the vision espoused by Blumenthal in part because of their loyalty to the person who hired them. Once individuals have overcome barriers to entry into an organization, they psychologically need to justify their membership. Members of fraternities who endure the initiation rites become increasingly committed to the fraternity because they have overcome the obstacles needed to obtain membership. Transformational leaders build commitment to a vision through the selection and socialization of key people.

5. *Starting with simple successes.* To build commitment to a future vision requires incremental successes. While individuals may not accept or understand the overall vision, they may be willing to take initial steps are taken, the individuals become increasingly committed to the overall vision.

For example, to become committed to overcoming alcoholism, individuals must take some initial steps. Recognizing the problem, joining Alcoholics Anonymous, making a public statement about the alcohol dependency, and finding a buddy who can work with the reforming alcoholic are simple steps that lead to a long-term commitment to overcoming alcohol dependence. Each initial step toward accomplishing a vision reinforces the previous step.

Institutionalizing Implementation

After generating commitment to the vision, the transformational leader works to institutionalize it, to make it an ongoing part of daily life in the organization. In the short run, it is difficult to determine whether a vision has been institutionalized. However, over time, the vision becomes ingrained as a natural part of the organizational process. To facilitate this institutionalization, a number of tools have been used by transformational leaders.

1. *Human resource systems.* Organization memories exist through generations of people in the organization. Transformational leaders institutionalize the vision through paying attention to and managing carefully the human resource systems of selection, appraisal, rewards, and development (Fombrun et al., 1984).

Selection refers to both who is hired and who is promoted. Hiring key individuals who support the vision enhances institutionalization. In the hiring process, transformational leaders pay careful attention to the criteria used to hire new employees, making sure that the new employees adhere to the vision. In the promotion of key individuals, similar concepts apply. Transformational leaders can monitor the succession systems to ensure that those who move up the organization will concur with the underlying vision.

In the appraisal process, criteria are established for evaluating performance. Ensuring that these criteria are consistent with the vision provides another way of making it a part of the fabric of the organization. Similarly, the reward system that supports these appraisal criteria provides incentives for behavior that are consistent with the vision. As reward systems are designed and managed correctly, institutionalization of the vision becomes a natural part of ongoing human-resource-management activities.

Development programs can be used to institutionalize the vision by ensuring that the management skills and the philosophy incorporated in training and development experiences will be consistent with the vision. The impact of development programs may be more evident over time, but as employees participate in training and personal development experiences, attitudes and behaviors can be focused so that they are consistent with the vision.

The human-resource-management tools of selection, appraisal, rewards, and development are often undermanaged. Leaders may assume that these systems will naturally fall into place. When the human resource systems are managed and used by leaders, they can be valuable levers for the institutionalization process. When unmanaged, they can impair any long-term changes.

2. *Organizational frameworks.* In addition to the human resource system, transformational leaders recognize other organizational factors that influence how visions are implemented. Many organizational frameworks serve as checklists to identify the organization factors that influence performance. The seven-S framework (Waterman et al., 1980) describes seven critical aspects of an organization that influence organization change. This framework is shown in Figure 3.

Using the framework, leaders identify the organizational factors that must be managed in institutionalizing change. Some of the specific issues needing to be considered include:

Strategy. *Strategy* refers to the actions that an organization plans in response to or anticipation of changes in its external environment. Strategy communicates how the organization will create unique value for those requiring products or services. Visions are institutionalized by strategies that are consistent over time, that reflect the principles of the vision, and that are translated into action through the other organization issues.

Structure. Organization structures provide a basis for specialization and coordination. They allow different units in the organization to function independently, yet to remain unified. Reporting relationships defined by the organization structure help to institutionalize visions. For example, departments may function independently or they may be tightly coordinated and connected. The ways in which departments are organized influences how the vision is institutionalized.

Systems. *Systems* refers to formal and informal procedures used to carry out basic organizational activities. For example, capital-budgeting and cost-accounting systems can be used to institutionalize a vision by ensuring that these systems will reflect the underlying principles of the vision.

Style. Leadership style often reflects the attitudes and beliefs of the top administrative team. *Style* refers to how administrators spend their time, what they talk about, and what they emphasize in their communications to employees. Administrators translate a vision into style by making sure that their actions coincide with their words.

Staff. *Staffing* refers to the human-resource-management practices discussed above. As discussed, transformational leaders pay close attention to human resource systems.

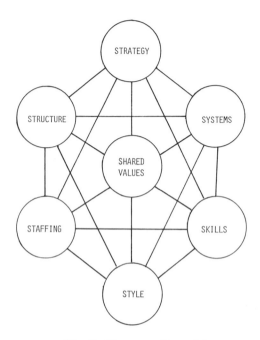

Fig. 3. The seven-S model.

Skills. Visions become institutionalized when organizations develop skills to fulfill the vision. Skills are the distinctive competencies that characterize the organization. For example, Harvard Business School professors count as a major strategic competency skills in teaching by the case method. These skills reflect the vision of graduate business training at Harvard. To fit into the culture at the Harvard Business School, the faculty must work very hard to develop case material and to practice teaching by this particular method.

Shared Values. Shared values are guiding concepts that underlie the business success. They are similar to the fundamental principles discussed earlier that drive the creation of a vision.

When transformational leaders are attempting to institutionalize a vision, frameworks such as this one are useful in two ways. First, they serve as a checklist to ensure that several organizational factors will be considered when change is being created in a system. No one "S" will ensure that the vision will be institutionalized. All seven need to be considered and managed for institutionalized visions to occur.

Second, the seven S's are interdependent. When any one system changes, it affects other systems. When an organization changes its strategy from teaching undergraduate students to teaching adult education, the other six systems must also change. New skills are required to that faculty can relate to the adults. New systems are needed in marketing the curriculum and defining financial controls. New structures may be needed to schedule flexible evening or weekend courses. The process of institutionalizing a vision requires that the systems be managed independently and interdependently.

Institutionalizing a vision requires constant attention. Recidivism is high and is likely to occur. Institutionalizing change requires that such recidivism be counteracted by administrative attention to stability-producing mechanisms such as human resource systems and the seven-S framework. The goal, simply, is to generate an institution that will develop the capacity to pursue the vision long after the transformational leader has gone.

In summary, the five steps that we have reviewed for transformation leaders are not easy to follow. They require that the transformational leader believe in the need for change. They require dedication and effort. They require patience. They require sacrifice. They require endurance. However, these five steps provide an agenda for successful fundamental transformations in institutions of higher education.

TRANSFORMATIONAL LEADERSHIP IN HIGHER EDUCATION

Thus far, we have relied mainly on examples of transformational leadership in organizations other than institutions of higher education, mainly because such examples are more visible and frequent than in colleges and universities. These institutions have felt less need for transformation than business organizations, which are being barraged by heightened competition and turbulent environments. Despite widespread enrollment and revenue declines in the last decade, higher education has been slow to recognize the need to institute significant changes. Belt tightening, curriculum revision, and increased marketing efforts have occurred, but a fundamental transformation has been rare.

A few notable exceptions have been noted, however, and we describe two of them below. Neither case has received widespread publicity, but each exemplifies transformational leadership in individual institutions. In the first case, the change was begun only two years ago, so few results are available. In the second, the transformation was initiated several years ago, so the results of the change are now evident. Both cases illustrate, however, the implementation of the five-step agenda for transformational leadership discussed in this chapter.

Northern University
The president of Northern University took office in 1983 in the midst of severe financial difficulties and sharp enrollment declines. Several additional conditions compounded this already dismal situation. The institution, located in a rural area, was heavily dependent on public funds for support, but because of a hard-hit economy in this industrialized state, normal budget allocations

had been markedly cut back. No large industry existed in the region of the state in which the university was located, and many small businesses had failed or moved. Institutional revenues had declined approximately 20% between 1980 and 1982, and as a result of that decline, 126 positions were eliminated, 44 of them faculty positions. This cutback was especially difficult because the faculty were unionized, and over 80% were tenured—100% in some departments. Some areas within the university were understaffed, such as the counseling and health center, the placement office, and the business school, and could not handle the current student demand. No funds were available to hire anyone, however, and no integrated planning or budgeting system existed for addressing these conditions in the long run.

Enrollment had been declining since 1977, and the total decline had reached over 15%. Even more severe, partly because it was unexpected, was a 25% decline in enrollments in the vocational skills center. Unfortunately, no enrollment or recruitment strategy was in place to respond to these trends. Key professional programs were not accredited, so the normal attractiveness of job-related and professional programs to students was diminished. Of the approximately 8,000 students, 95% came from in-state; only 5% represented minority groups. Although admissions standards existed formally, over 95% of all applicants were admitted, and the typical class had high-school grade-point averages and ACT scores below the national average.

Probably the most important condition faced by the new president was a formally declared state of financial exigency in 1982. Formal plans had been drawn to lay off large numbers of personnel, including those with tenure. A salary freeze was in effect, and tense relationships existed among administrators, the union, and the nonacademic staff. Clearly, the institution was in need of a transformational leader.

Although changes are still in the formative stage, the new president of Northern has exemplified the model of transformational leadership as effectively as any president we know of. Because no transformation can take place quickly, we expect that the results of this leadership will not be obvious for several more years. On the other hand, signs of important change are already in evidence.

Creating a Need. Creating a need for change was not difficult, given the state of financial exigency and the threatened loss of a large number of positions. Such a condition, however, often leads to conflict, turmoil, defensiveness, and further degeneration of morale. The president was careful to define his arrival as the end of the degeneration phase of school's history and the beginning of the regeneration phase. Open discussions were initiated with the union, which eventually led to no further layoffs, despite financial exigency. Much time was spent in reestablishing a sense of security among personnel and in communicating a need to work as a team in making the needed changes. Interpretive leadership more than substantive leadership played a key role in this phase of the transformation.

Overcoming Resistance. Among the most important actions implemented by the new president was the formation of task forces and internal review committees composed of both institution members and representatives from external constituencies. These task forces were charged with the responsibility to study the strengths as well as the problems of the university in selected areas and to make recommendations for change. A high degree of involvement and interaction was fostered, focusing on important institutional issues. The prioritizing of issues and emphases for the future were accomplished with the broad involvement of members of several constituency groups. In addition, several new people were hired for or transferred into the president's cabinet, so that a new administrative team could start the transformation process without encumberances from past policies. The administrative duties of some existing cabinet members were also shifted as part of the reorganization. The result was a growing sense on the campus of movement and progress, and traditional resistance forces became less powerful.

Articulating a Vision. After the initial reorganization, the president spent a large amount of his time on the road. He defined his primary responsibility as projecting a new vision of Northern. External constituencies both in the region served by the university and state- and nation-wide heard the president discuss plans for a transformed institution. The message was essentially a "pockets-of-excellence" message in which the institution was positioned as being, first and foremost, a service organization for the region and, secondarily, an institution that had among the best selected programs in the country.

That vision was operationalized by obtaining the nation's only Olympic training center directly associated with a university. The plan was to have potential Olympic athletes be able, for the first time, to attend school at the same time that they trained for competition. A mathematics and science center, endowed and named after a local Nobel laureate, was also established to conduct scientific research particular to the institution's geographical region. A unique consulting and development unit was formed that provides help for new and small businesses in the region and for other types of economic development activity. The intent was to use the university's resources to encourage and enhance the economic rejuvenation of the region. The vocational training center was integrated more closely into the regular curriculum in order to upgrade its quality and to provide interested students with a unique mix of vocational and liberal arts preparation. In brief, an effort was made to change the image of the university in the eyes of strategic constituents from a lackluster performer to an institution that neither the region nor the state could live without, because of its pockets of excellence.

Generating Commitment. Commitment to the vision had to start at the top of the institution, so the president scheduled an off-site workshop with his cabinet members. One intent was to articulate the vision and to make plans for its accomplishment, but more important, the goal was to create commitment among that administrative group to operationalize the vision in their own areas. Two days were spent with an outside facilitator getting members of the cabinet to clarify for themselves what the vision of the institution was to be and how it could be implemented.

A second way the president began to generate commitment was to appoint a Commission on the Future of Northern University. Well-known leaders from outside the university were asked to serve on an ongoing basis as a sounding board, to advise the president and the regents, to help to define the university's future, and to assist in identifying needs. The public visibility of these individuals provided one enhancement of commitment since they tended to be opinion leaders among their constituencies, and they were carefully oriented by the president regarding his vision at the outset of their service. In addition, the coalitions that were formed both politically and socially as a result of the commission's work provided a strong incentive for unity and commitment among this important group.

The twelve task forces established by the president also provided another mechanism for generating commitment inside the institution. At least one faculty member or administrator worked directly with the outside chair of each task force as the liaison and informant. It is difficult to remain uncommitted when serving as the representative of the institution on an important issue to an outside group, and it is expected that commitment to the transformation will be enhanced by such an arrangement.

Institutionalizing Implementation. Integrating the president's vision into the fabric of the institution will be successful only if it has the support and commitment of top administrators and representatives of strategic constituencies. Most of the president's energy up to now has been spent on getting others to share and articulate the vision as their own. Little attention will be given to operational-level issues until the vision has been accepted by top administrators and opinion leaders. Recently, however, more energy has begun to be spent on encouraging cabinet members, commission members, and task force members to serve as missionaries for the university's message. In addition, the staffing and organization are beginning to be put in place for the new Olympic, research, and service centers so that the vision can become a part of the fabric of the institution.

In sum, what makes this president a good example of a transformational leader is not just his success in averting layoffs and halting decline. It is not just the formation of task forces or advisory groups. Rather, it is his beginning to create a different image, to change the interpretations people have of Northern University, that makes his leadership exemplary. The transformation of the university certainly is substantive, but equally important, it is also symbolic. Individuals both inside and outside the institution are beginning to think differently about the school and their role in it.

Eastern College
Eastern College is a small, private liberal arts college for women. Traditionally, it has enjoyed a good reputation in its geographic region, particularly for those in the middle- and upper-income groups. Almost all students come from relatively well-to-do families, and only 40% receive any kind of financial aid. A new president was hired in 1977 in a period of widespread rumors that the institution would soon close because of financial difficulties and declining enrollments. In fact, the college was beset with problems. (We have relied on Chaffee et al., 1983, for many of the following statistics.)

Whereas the college had grown from a student population of 376 in 1959 to 711 a decade later, by 1976 yearly declines had caused the enrollment to slip back to 542. Only 2% of the students were minority students, and 40% came from in-state. Most of the rest came from the surrounding geographic region. A marked decline of 120 points in entering students' SAT scores had occurred since 1969. A major reduction in faculty size had occurred in 1974 in the face of declining enrollments, and a permanent freeze had been imposed on the number of faculty positions available. Personnel were still receiving a 5% increase in salary per year, but the operating deficit had reached $390,000 on an annual budget of $3.2 million. At least a half million dollars had been transferred from the endowment fund and another half million from the capital fund to meet short-term operating costs. The size of the endowment was at the same level as it had been in the late 1960s (approximately $2 million), but the market value trend was downward.

Of special concern to the new president upon her arrival in 1977 were two challenges, one publicly known and one secret. The secret was that the college was unofficially bankrupt. The new president discovered that there was not enough money to meet salary obligations for the next month. The public challenge was that an academy adjacent to Eastern's campus had failed in 1977 and had recently put its campus up for sale. The acreage was approximately three quarters the size of Eastern's campus with several large buildings including physical education facilities (which Eastern lacked). The sale of the property for an incompatible purpose would seriously diminish the attractiveness of Eastern, yet there was neither the money nor the mood to expand Eastern's campus and facilities by 75%. The challenge faced by the new president was to transform the institution from a declining school on the brink of failure to the high-quality, elite institution that it had been a decade before. Unfortunately, her impression on taking over the new job was "We need to get substantially better even to have another school interested in merging with us."

At the end of seven years in the presidency, the following are indicators of
the success of the transformation that this leader was able to accomplish.
Enrollments had increased 50% to over 820 students; retention rates were up
from 53% graduating in four years to 61%; revenues had more than doubled,
and surpluses had accumulated at the end of each year; the endowment size had
quadrupled and gift revenue had doubled; the campus had increased by 75%
with the purchase of the new campus; and an adult education program had
been formed with a 1982 enrollment of 140 students and 79 degrees granted.
These indicators are merely reflections of the real change, however. A
transformation in the vision and interpretation of what the college was all
about had occurred. The president's vision had been institutionalized to the
extent that the operation of the college was completely different. Here is a brief
description of some of her actions.

Creating Readiness. The first year of the president's tenure was spent
communicating the message frequently and boldly that the institution was in
severe financial straits but had no intention of closing its doors. Faculty and
students were called on to conserve resources and find ways to cut costs. All
alumni, not just wealthy donors, were asked, for the first time in history, to
contribute regularly to the institution. Readiness was created by
communicating not so much a gloom-and-doom message as a message that the
involvement of everyone was needed in order to preserve the institution. In
addition, an entirely new administrative team was put in place and was charged
with the responsibility of carrying out the president's vision.

Overcoming Resistance. In addition to the involvement of faculty, students,
and alumni in suggesting ways to cut costs, a remarkable recommendation was
made to the board of trustees at the first meeting after the new president took
office. The previously formulated budget was to be approved, calling for
another large deficit for the year. The new president recommended that board
not approve the budget. She astounded but delighted board members by
promising to operate in the black for the year. Potential resistance from that
group was quickly put to rest by her show of determination and fiscal
responsibility. In addition, whereas during the first year of her presidency
salary increases remained at the same low rate, beginning with the second year
averages increases of 10% with merit pools were instituted, with the predictable
result of strong support from the faculty and staff.

Articulating a Vision. Much time has been dedicated by the president to
communicating both personally and officially with constituencies inside and
outside the institution. The vision of an elite liberal arts institution with high
personal and academic standards was reinforced in a variety of ways. The newly instituted business major, for example, was given a heavy liberal-arts core
requirement, as was the adult degree program. Corporate executives were
courted for the first time and were asked to support the institution's basic

mission of providing excellent, well-rounded liberal-arts training, and remarkable success was achieved. Most significant, however, was the handling of the new campus acquisition. After learning that the adjacent campus was for sale, the president took to the road day and night for a month in order to raise capital and negotiate a favorable agreement with the sellers. Instead of interpreting this as a desperate or even financially irresponsible move, however, the new president communicated the message that this was a sign of the end to the degeneration phase and the beginning of the regeneration phase of the school's history. Things were not so bad as people thought, because the new campus provided so many new opportunities for increasing excellence. It was interpreted as a God-send, not an albatross. The vision of a college on the move replaced the vision of a college in trouble.

Generating Commitment. The president generated commitment both by publicizing the successes that were being achieved (e.g., increased revenues, higher enrollments, and new programs), and by reinforcing the role of the faculty in the changes. When concern was expressed with the academic quality of the new adult-education program, the faculty was given responsibility for quality assurance. Board members were asked to take a much more active role that ever before in being advocates and fund raisers for the institution, not just watchdogs. Several board members were replaced with people who were committed to that role. Workshops were held, facilitated by outside consultants, between the president and the top administrative staff to iron out problems and to improve working relationships. No assumption was made that this was a one-woman show, and all administrators were encouraged to voice concerns so that these could be openly worked on.

Institutionalizing the Vision. A reorganization of the academic structure in the school, coupled with the reorganization of the administrative structure, helped to disseminate the vision throughout the entire institution. Simply put, a structure was put in place to reinforce the strategy. In addition, relationships with board members and with corporate executives were established and nurtured so that the vision could continue to be financially supported. Physical manifestations of success, such a remodeled buildings, a new art gallery, and new academic programs, also helped to demonstrate the permanence of the vision and to communicate it to more peripheral constituencies, such as community members, potential students, and potential donors. In sum, while the transformation took the better part of seven years to complete, Eastern College now exemplifies the vision of its transformational leader.

SUMMARY

Our intent in this chapter has been threefold. First, we have tried to demonstrate the impending transformation that is likely to affect institutions of higher education in America. As has happened in many industries in this country, not being aware of the threats and opportunities provided by these changes creates quick demise. By the time certain American businesses awoke to the condition of their industries in the early 1980s (e.g., video cassette recorders and 256-K drams), it was simply too late to respond. We have tried to highlight similar potential conditions that colleges and universities will face in the near future. In a small way, we have tried to trigger a rethinking of the strategies being pursued by top administrators in American higher education.

Second, we have presented a five-step agenda for responding to this potential transformation. Research by Cameron (1983, 1985) on college and university effectiveness has clearly demonstrated the power and importance of top administrator strategy in institutional performance. The model of transformational leadership presented here is merely an operationalization of effective leadership for a time of change. Its principles were derived from studies of leaders in many types of organizations throughout history who have been responsible for significant changes. In brief, transformational leaders create a readiness for change among their followers, manage the natural resistance to new conditions and new requirements, and articulate a vision of the future that mobilizes commitment and creates successful institutionalization throughout the system. This model of leadership emphasizes symbolic and interpretive transformation at least as much as substantive transformation.

Third, we have presented two examples of transformational leadership, one in a medium-sized public university and the other in a small private college, in order to illustrate its successful use in higher education. Both leaders faced conditions that threatened the survival of their institutions, and those conditions created an obvious need for transformation. Both presidents accepted jobs at their institutions under unfavorable conditions, and in addition to successful turnaround management, they were able to markedly change how others thought about the institution. Although success can seldom be achieved in the short-run, these two leaders are excellent examples of the transformational agenda even though, in the first case, the changes are just beginning to occur. We expect that a successful transformation will be apparent at Northern University in the future.

As was articulated by Abigail Adams in a letter to Thomas Jefferson in 1790, "These are the hard times in which a genius would wish to live." Similarly, we are convinced that these also are the times that can foster successful transformational leaders as higher education begins to cope with its future. Not only will improvement in the quality of America's higher education institutions depend on such leadership, but the very survival of the system may be at stake.

REFERENCES

Argyris, C. (1970). *Intervention theory and method.* Reading, MA: Addison-Wesley.

Bennis, W. G. (1984). The four competencies of leadership. *Training and Development Journal* August: 20–24.

Bennis, W. G. (1973). *The Leaning Ivory Tower.* San Francisco: Jossey-Bass.

Bennis, W. G., Benne, K., and Chin, R. (1969). *The Planning of Change.* New York: Holt, Rinehart and Winston.

Brzezinski, Z. (1970). *Between Two Ages: America's Role in the Technetronic Era.* New York: Viking Press.

Burns, J. M. (1978). *Leadership.* New York: Harper & Row.

Cameron, K. S. (1978). Measuring organizational effectiveness in institutions of higher education. *Administrative Science Quarterly* 23: 604–632.

Cameron, K. S. (1984). Organization adaptation and higher education. *Journal of Higher Education* 55: 122–144.

Cameron, K. S. (1984b). The effectiveness of ineffectiveness. In B. M. Staw and L. L. Cummings (eds.), *Research in Organizational Behavior, Vol. 6.* Greenwich, CT: JAI Press.

Cameron, K. S., and O'Reilly, B. (1985). The problems of higher education in America: another look. Working paper, Center for the Study of Higher Education, University of Michigan.

Cameron, K. S., and Whetten, D. A. (1981). Perceptions of organizational effectiveness across organizational life cycles. *Administrative Science Quarterly* 27: 524–544.

Cameron, K. S., and Whetten, D. A. (1983). Models of the organizational life cycle: applications to higher education. *Review of Higher Education* 6: 269–299.

Chaffee, E. E., Whetten, D. A., and Cameron, K. S. (1983) *Case Studies in College Strategy.* Boulder, CO: National Center for Higher Education Management Systems.

DeBloois, M. (1984). *Effectiveness of Videodisc Training: A Comprehensive Review.* Falls Church, Va: Future Systems Inc.

Fombrun, C., Tichy, N. M., and Devanna, M. A. (1984). *Strategic Human Resource Management.* New York: Wiley.

Eicholtz, G., and Rogers, E. M. (1964). Resistance to the adoption of audiovisual aids by elementary school teachers. In M. Miles (ed.), *Innovation in education.* New York: Teachers College Press.

Gavin, D. A. (1983). Quality on the line. *Harvard Business Review* (September–October): 65–75.

Goffman, E. (1955). On face-work: an analysis of ritual elements in social interaction. *Psychiatry* 18: 213–231.

Huber, G. P. (1984). The nature and design of post-industrial ernvironments. *Management Science* 30: 928–951.

Janis, I. L. (1972). *Victims of Groupthink: A Psychological Study of Foreign Policy Decisions and Fiascos.* Boston: Houghton-Mifflin.

Kanter, R. M. (1982). The middle manager as innovator. *Harvard Business Review* (July–August): 95–105.

Kohlberg, L. (1976). Moral stages and moralization: the cognitive developmental approach. In T. Lickona (ed.), *Moral Development and Behavior.* New York: Holt, Rinehart and Winston.

Latham, G., and Yukl, G. (1975). A review of research on the application of goal setting in organizations. *Academy of Management Journal* 18: 824–45.

Lorenzo, A. L. (1984). Speech to the Faculty of Macomb Community College. Detroit, MI, December.

Martin, J. (1981). *Telematic Society: the Challenge for Tomorrow.* Englewood Cliffs, NJ: Prentice-Hall.

Masuda, Y. (1980). *The Information Society.* Bethesda, MD: World Future Society.

National Commission on Excellence in Education. (1983). *A Nation at Risk*. Washington, D.C.: National Institute of Education.

Quinn, R. E., and Cameron, K. S. (1983). Organizational life cycles and shifting criteria of effectiveness: some preliminary evidence. *Management Science* 29: 33–51.

Salancik, G. R. (1977). Commitment and the control of organizational behavior and belief. In B. M. Staw and G. R. Salancik (eds.), *New Directions in Organizational Behavior*. Chicago: St. Clair Press.

Samson, G. E., Gaude, M. E., Weinstein, T., and Walberg, H. J. (1984) Academic and occupational performance: a quantitative analysis. *American Educational Research Journal* 21: 311–321.

Selznick, P. (1949). *TVA and the Grass Roots*. Berkeley: University of California Press.

Simon, H. A. (1973). Applying information technology to organization design. *Public Administration Review* 34: 268–278.

Stone, L. (ed.). (1975) *The University in Society*. Princeton: Princeton University Press.

Study Group on the Conditions of Excellence in American Higher Education (1984). *Involvement in Learning*. Washington, D.C.: National Institute of Education.

Tichy, N. M. (1983). *Managing Strategic Change*. New York: Wiley.

Tichy, N. M. (1985). *Transformational Leaders*. New York: Wiley.

Tichy, N. M., and Ulrich, D. O. (1984). The leadership challenge: a call for the transformational leader. *Sloan Management Review* Fall: 59–68.

Toffler, A. (1980). *The Third Wave*. New York: Morrow.

Trist, E., and Bamforth, K. (1951). Some social and psychological consequences of the long-wall method of coal getting. *Human Relations* 4: 3–38.

Veblen, T. (1918). *The Higher Learning in America*. New York: Hill and Wang.

Waterman, R. H., Peters, T. J., and Phillips, J. R. (1980). Structure is not organization. *Business Horizons* June: 50–63.

Webster, D. S. (1985). Institutional effectiveness using scholarly peer assessments as major criteria. *Review of Higher Education* 8: in press.

Whyte, W. F. (1957). *The Organization Man*. Garden City, NY: Doubleday Anchor.

MANAGING DECLINE IN AMERICAN HIGHER EDUCATION

Raymond F. Zammuto
University of Colorado at Denver

It's difficult to attend a professional meeting of higher education managers or researchers and not hear people talk about declining enrollments and revenues. Decline has become one of the most common topics discussed when either group gets together. It's also difficult to read an issue of *The Chronicle of Higher Education* without seeing at least one article about the enrollment or revenue problems of some college, university, or state system. Perhaps the most amazing thing is that although decline is much talked about, there do not appear to be ready answers about how to manage it.

This chapter examines how colleges and universities do and should manage declining enrollments and revenues, based on the literature that has developed since the mid-1970s. The chapter is divided into a number of sections. First, the enrollment projections and predictions that initially gave rise to this concern are reviewed. Much of the confusion surrounding the management of decline is related to the variety of projections that have been made, which range from the pessimistic to the mildly optimistic. Thus arises the question of whom one believes, since that has much to do with how managers plan for their institutions' futures. Part of the answer to this question lies in a careful examination of the *past* rather than the *future*. This statement may sound contrary to prevailing wisdom, but it will be shown that most projections and predictions tend to miss a number of essential points about managing decline.

Once this initial argument has been made, the management of colleges and universities with declining enrollments and revenues is examined. The discussion draws heavily on the published literature, and it focuses on creating an overview of the principles of managing under conditions of scarcity. Theory and research from a variety of areas, including business, public administration, and higher education, are examined, as is appropriate. The review is divided into three major sections. First, what an institution should do before it encounters declining revenues and enrollments is discussed. Then, the organizational dynamics associated with decline and their dysfunctions are reviewed. The final section focuses on the formulation and implementation of institutional retrenchment strategies once a period of decline has begun, and on the role that cutback management plays in the successful implementation of a retrenchment strategy. This final section also provides a number of guidelines for the cutback process that can help prevent the dysfunctional dynamics associated with decline.

As will be seen in the following section, higher education managers may or may not be faced with a tumultuous decade. Institutional enrollments and revenues at any particular institution may or may not decline. Regardless of whether they do, it is essential that higher education managers have the ideas and tools necessary for coping with the types of problems that they may encounter during the next ten years.

ENROLLMENT PROJECTIONS

Twenty years ago, Allan Cartter (1965) published an article discussing the potential effects of then newly declining birthrate on the future supply and demand for teachers. Cartter's projections did not gain much attention at that time. But by the early 1970s, many students of higher education began to take notice of the declining birthrate and its potential effect on future college and university enrollments. In part, this attention may have been focused by the impact of the declining birthrate on other organizations, such as elementary-school systems and baby food manufacturers, which had already experienced the effects of the downturn on their operation.

During the early 1970s, a number of projections of future college and university enrollments began to appear. Generally, projections for the 1970s were for a significant increase in aggregate enrollments nationally. But most projections for the 1980s suggested that moderate to significant declines in enrollments would occur. For example, Dresch (1975) foresaw a 45% decrease in degree-credit enrollments during the 1980s. Other forecasts projected significant declines, but of a lesser magnitude. Crossland (1980) predicted a 15% decrease in aggregate enrollments during the 1980s. Similarly, the Carnegie Council (1980, Chapter 3) projected about a 15% decrease in full-time equivalent enrollments between 1981 and 1996.[1]

In contrast, a number of other authors forecast that enrollments would not decline significantly. For example, Leslie and Miller (1974) envisioned a "steady state" for higher education, where slowing enrollment growth rates rather than decreasing enrollments would create conditions of decline for many institutions. Frances (1980) suggested that total enrollments were likely to increase slightly during the 1980s, once factors offsetting the effects of demographic trends were taken into account. And in a similar vein, Bowen (1984) indicated that many factors could lead to increasing rather than decreasing enrollments during the next decade.[2]

The question that comes immediately to mind for most institutional managers is, Who do you believe? Does higher education have a bright or a dismal future? This is the wrong question to ask, for two reasons. First, to borrow a term from Kenneth Boulding (1982), the future is "irreducibly uncertain." And as Bowen and Glenny (1981) have noted,

> the major causes of this uncertainty are only too well known by all: declining enrollment pools and shifts in the ethnic composition of those pools, inflation, increasing and sometimes conflicting governmental demands for accountability, collective bargaining or its prospect, the apparent tax revolt by the public, and changing student curricular interests.
>
> These and other factors, the national and local economic picture for example, are threads in a seamless web of pervasive uncertainty that confounds institutional planning, even planning in the narrowest sense of scheduling next year's classes. [pp. 142–143]

As a result of this uncertainty, we can not accurately project what institutional enrollments or revenues will be over the next few years because there are too many factors to take into account. Moreover, we do not have a good understanding of the relationships between those factors and enrollments and revenues, nor do we understand how those factors interact. In effect, we will know with some precision what happened to enrollments in the 1980s sometime in 1990, when the decade's enrollment statistics have been compiled, which is much too late for institutional managers.

It's interesting that even in the face of these uncertainties, Baldridge et al. (1982) found that college presidents were generally optimistic about their institutions' enrollment and revenue prospects. In the 1981 National Enrollment Survey, only 16% of the presidents queried expected enrollments at their institution to decline by more than 5% between 1981 and 1986; 26% saw their institutions' revenue prospects as being either fair or poor. Baldridge et al. (1982) interpreted these results as being indicative of a "last survivor mentality," which caused presidents to believe that their institutions were immune to problems caused by the demographic trends of the 1980s. An alternative explanation is that projections have been so inconsistent that presidents have ceased to pay serious attention to the prognosticators.

Even if we were able to project aggregate enrollments with accuracy, they would tell us little about the enrollment or revenue prospects of individual institutions. For example, Krakower and Zammuto (in press) showed that enrollment levels at different types of institutions during the 1970s were not affected to the same extent by changing economic conditions or federal aid policies. The enrollments in some sectors of the higher education community were more affected than others. Similarly, Zemsky and Oedel (1983) argued that the various sectors of the college and university population recruit from different enrollment pools, some of which are affected more than others by changing population demographics. In short, even an accurate prediction of aggregate enrollments would do little to assist the managers of individual institutions in planning for the future.

What may be of more use is examining the past to create a context in which to understand the future. Examining changes in institutional enrollments and revenues during the 1970s can provide some insight into the extent to which higher education managers should be concerned about the next decade. The following section presents an analysis of changes in college and university enrollments and revenues between 1972–1973 and 1981–1982.

ENROLLMENTS AND REVENUES: 1972–1973 TO 1981–1982

The 1970s are generally thought of as the tail end of a period of rapid growth for higher education. Aggregate institutional enrollments continued through the decade while the size of the traditional college-aged cohort leveled off. Even though aggregate enrollments increased, many institutions experienced enrollment and revenue problems. This section examines the enrollment and revenue experiences of colleges and universities during that period. The analysis shows how overall population dynamics changed over time.

Institutional enrollments were defined as full-time equivalent enrollments, and institutional revenues were defined as inflation-adjusted total revenues (Halstead, 1980, and updates). The Higher Education General Information Survey (HEGIS) opening fall enrollment and institutional-finance databases were used for the analysis. All institutions having complete information for the time periods described below were included in the analysis.

The ten-year period was divided into three segments: 1972–1973 to 1975–1976, 1975–1976 to 1978–1979, and 1978–1979 to 1981–1982. These discrete time segments were attended by different conditions that affected institutional enrollments and revenues. For example, during the 1972–1973 to 1975–1976 period, the size of the 18-to-21-year-old population continued to grow while the economy slid into a recession following the energy crisis. During the 1975–1976 to 1978–1979 period, an economic recovery occurred with a high rate of inflation. The size of the traditional college-aged cohort stabilized during this period, while the level of federal student aid increased. The 1978–1979 to 1981–1982 period was marked by another recession, lower rates of inflation, the beginning of the long-expected decline in the size of the traditional college-aged cohort, and a stabilization in the amount of federal student aid available. These different conditions variably affected the institutional sectors of higher education.

Figure 1 presents an analysis of changes in institutional enrollments for each of the three time periods.[3] Growing enrollments were defined as an increase of

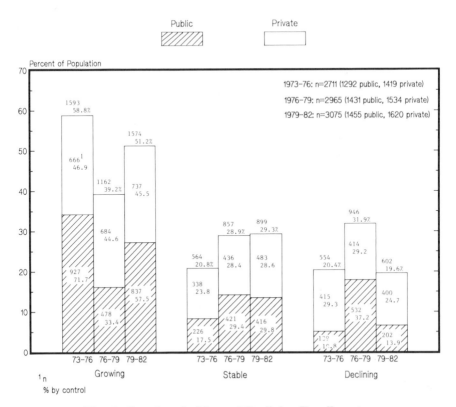

**Fig. 1. Growing, Stable, and Declining Enrollments
by Institutional Control: 1973–1976, 1976–1979, and 1979–1982.**

more than 5% from the base year to the end year of a time period. Declining enrollments were defined as a decrease of more than 5% in enrollments of the period. Stable enrollments were defined as those that varied between plus and minus 5% from the first to the last year of a period. Figure 1 can be interpreted as follows: Each bar represents the prorportion of the total population of colleges and universities experiencing growing, stable, or declining enrollments for a given time period. The numbers at the top of the bar indicate the number and percentage of all institutions experiencing a given enrollment condition. The numbers in the clear section of the bar present the number and percentage of private institutions experiencing a given enrollment condition. The numbers in the hatched areas provide the same information for public institutions.

As can be seen in Figure 1, the proportion of institutions experiencing growing enrollments over the three time periods varied considerably. Over half of the institutions in the college and university population had growing enrollments during the 1973-1976 and the 1979-1982 periods. Only about 40% of the institutions experienced growing enrollments during 1976-1979. The proportion of private institutions experiencing growing enrollments remained about the same across all three periods, but there was substantial variation in the public sector.

The proportion of institutions with stable enrollments increased in both the public and the private sectors, from about 21% in 1973-1976 to 29% during 1976-1979. A slightly higher proportion of private as compared to public institutions experienced stable enrollments during 1973-1976, but the proportions became nearly equal during the two later periods. The incidence of declining enrollments varied substantially over the three time periods. About 20% of all institutions experienced declining enrollments during the 1973-1976 and 1979-1982 periods, while 32% had declining enrollments between 1976-1979. The proportion of private institutions with declining enrollments varied slightly between 24% and 29% across the three time periods. In contrast, the incidence of declining enrollments at public institutions ranged between 10% and 37%.

Overall, the data indicate that declining enrollments have been a problem for a significant proportion of the college and university population, even when the size of the traditional college-aged cohort was increasing. Moreover, the data indicate that the enrollment experiences of public institutions were more volatile than those of private institutions. The major period of declining enrollments corresponded with an economic recovery, a fact suggesting an inverse relationship between economic conditions and enrollments. Such a relationship has been discussed in other research (Dresch, 1977; Rusk et al., 1982; Krakower and Zammuto, 1983).

Figure 2 presents similar information for institutional revenues, with the same percentages used to define the growing, stable, and declining revenue categories. The data show a decreasing proportion of the population having growing revenues across the three time periods, from 63% during 1973-1976 to 42% in 1979-1982. The proportion of private institutions with growing revenues varied slightly, between 49% in 1979-1982 and 57% in 1976-1979. There was much more variation in the public sector, reflecting an overall downward trend in institutional revenues; during 1973-1976, 77% of public institutions had growing revenues, while during 1979-1982 only 35% did.

The proportion of institutions experiencing stable and declining revenues increased across the three time periods. The proportion of private institutions with stable revenues remained fairly constant across the three time periods, going from 24% in 1976-1979 to 32% in 1979-1982. In contrast, the proportion of public institutions with stable revenues nearly tripled, from 14% in 1973-1976 to 39% in 1979-1982. The data also show that that proportion of private institutions experiencing declining revenues decreased, from 24% in 1973-1976 to 19% in 1979-1982, while the proportion of public institutions

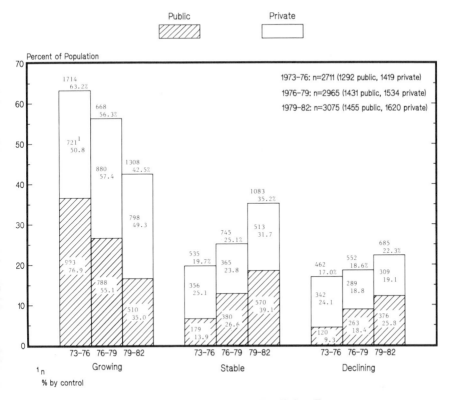

**Fig. 2. Growing, Stable, and Declining Revenues
by Institutional Control: 1973–1976, 1976–1979, and 1979–1982.**

with declining revenues nearly tripled over the same period, from 9% in
1973–1976 to 26% in 1979–1982. Overall, the revenue data indicate a clear
slowing in the growth of institutional revenues between 1973 and 1982,
particularly in the public sector. Initially, the private sector experienced slowing
revenues more than the public sector, but the situation reversed itself by the end
of the time period, when proportionately more public institutions were affected
by decreasing revenues.

Table 1 presents the distribution of institutions by changes in enrollments
and revenues for the three time periods. The upper left cell of the table indicates
that there was a steady decrease in the proportion of colleges and universities
that had both growing enrollments and revenues, from 47% of the population
in 1973–1976 to 27% in 1979–1982. Careful examination of the remaining
cells of the table shows that the types of enrollment and revenue conditions
faced by colleges and universities varied considerably through this ten-year period. For example, the proportion of institutions experiencing stable revenues

TABLE 1. Growth, Stability and Decline in Revenues and Enrollments: 1973–1976, 1976–1979, and 1979–1982

	FTE			
Revenue	Growing	Stable	Declining	Totals
Growing				
1973–76	1,288	277	149	1,714
,,	47.5	10.2	5.5	63.2
1976–79	892	458	318	1,668
,,	30.1	15.4	10.7	56.3
1979–82	833	330	145	1,300
,,	27.1	10.7	4.7	42.5
Stable				
1973–76	190	201	144	535
,,	7.0	7.4	5.3	19.7
1976–79	185	296	264	745
,,	6.2	10.0	8.9	25.1
1979–82	519	367	196	1,082
,,	16.9	11.9	6.4	35.2
Declining				
1973–76	115	86	261	462
,,	4.2	3.2	9.6	17.0
1976–79	85	103	364	552
,,	2.9	3.5	12.3	18.6
1979–82	222	202	261	685
,,	7.2	6.6	8.5	22.3
	1,593	564	554	
	58.8	20.8	20.4	
Totals	1,162	857	964	
	39.2	28.9	31.9	
	1,574	899	602	
	51.2	29.2	19.6	

and growing enrollments more than doubled, from 17% between 1973–1976 and 1979–1982. Other institutions experienced declining revenues with growing enrollments, declining enrollments with stable revenues, and so on.

Surprisingly, there has not been any substantial increase in the proportion of colleges and universities experiencing both declining enrollments and declining revenues. In fact, the joint distribution of institutions by declining enrollments and revenues shows that around a third of all institutions experienced declining revenues or enrollments (1973–1976, 28%; 1976–1979, 39%; 1979–1982, 33%). Of these institutions, only about one third experienced both declining enrollments and declining revenues simultaneously, and the proportion of institutions decreased steadily over the period of the analysis (1973-1976, 35%; 1976-1979, 32%; 1979-1982, 25%). This finding is contrary to the common wisdom that declining enrollments and declining revenues go hand in hand.

A number of tentative conclusions can be drawn from this analysis. First, it is clear from the findings that a decreasing proportion of colleges and universities are experiencing both growing enrollments and growing revenues, and that human and financial resources have become increasingly scarce over the past decade. One interpretation is that the higher education system as a whole is becoming more susceptible to major shocks caused by changing environmental conditions because the amount of slack in the system has decreased since the mid-1970s. As a result, it may take a less potent event or trend in the future to cause significant enrollment and revenue problems for a large number of colleges and universities than has been the case in the past.

Second, variations in the incidence of declining enrollments and revenues[4] in the higher education system suggest that factors other than the size of the traditional college-aged cohort have a significant effect on institutional enrollments and revenues. While the size of the traditional college-aged cohort is known and fixed over the next few years, other factors affecting institutional enrollments and revenues are not. The result is a great deal of uncertainty about the future.

Finally, given the variety of enrollment and revenue experiences of colleges and universities (growing enrollments and declining revenues, declining enrollments and stable revenues and so on), it becomes clear that it is impossible to specify "cookbook" management techniques that are applicable to the majority of institutions. Indeed, Krakower and Zammuto (1983) showed that there is no ordered pattern in the types of sequences of actions selected by colleges and universities in response to declining enrollments and revenues. The conditions faced by individual institutions are unique, as is the capacity of each institution to cope with them. Therefore, it would be difficult if not impossible to discuss specific actions for coping with declining enrollments or revenues.

On the other hand, it is possible to talk about the process of how institutions should position themselves to enhance their potential for success during the uncertainties of the next decade. It also is possible to talk about the processes and pitfalls of managing institutions with declining enrollments and revenues. If institutional managers prepare now for the coming decade, and if they understand how management in declining institutions differs from that in growing institutions, they are more likely to be successful in guiding their institutions through an uncertain future.

The remainder of this chapter is directed toward that end. The next section describes the steps that institutional managers should take *now* in preparing for the future. Included is a discussion of the role that mission review plays in setting priorities, an examination of an institution's priorities for fit with that mission, and suggestions for understanding the educational marketplace of which the institution is a part. The following section focuses on the dynamics commonly exhibited in institutions that are experiencing decline. As will be shown, institutional dynamics take on a different cast under conditions of decline, and the processes for managing a declining institution are different from those for managing a growing institution. The final sections discuss guidelines for developing and implementing retrenchment strategies once declining enrollments and revenues have occurred.

POSITIONING INSTITUTIONS FOR AN UNCERTAIN FUTURE

Given the uncertainty described in the preceding section, what should an institutional manager do? The cry of wolf has been heard so often that it's relatively easy to discount the likelihood of future enrollment and revenue problems. Perhaps the best advice for institutional managers is provided by Mingle and Norris (1981). They concluded their study of retrenchment in colleges and universities by noting that

> precious time can be lost debating the likelihood of decline. The best advice may be to plan for the worst and hope for the best. Early action is needed to mobilize support. Institutions which waste away the last gasp of growth will be worse off than those which use that time of growth to prepare for decline. [p. 67]

There are a number of good reasons for this advice. First, the slack resources necessary for assessment and planning activities usually disappear with the onset of declining enrollments and revenues because the first priority is to fund operations. Second, the organizational dynamics associated with decline (described in detail later) reduce an institution's ability to formulate effective courses of action for recovery. For example, the centralization of decision making that usually accompanies the onset of decline makes it difficult to foster widespread participation, which is necessary to enhance commitment to an institution's retrenchment strategy.

Moreover, decreasing resources bring the latent conflicts within an institution into the open. While slack resources could be used in times of growth to satisfy conflicting demands, a period of decline can make resource allocation a zero-sum situation in which one party gains only at the expense of another. As a result, eliciting the participation and cooperation of institutional members in formulating an institutional retrenchment strategy is much easier before a period of decline has begun. And many of the steps suggested in this section are simply *good management practices* that institutional managers should undertake regardless of whether they believe declining enrollments or revenues are imminent.

Five different aspects of positioning institutions for an uncertain future are discussed in this section: (1) the role of a review of an institution's *mission*; (2)

the notion of *enrollment management* and how it can be used to identify problems and opportunities; (3) the use of *environmental assessment* to increase awareness of, and to sensitize institutional managers to, uncontrollable trends or events that may affect enrollments and revenues; (4) the purpose of *program review* in setting institutional priorities for a period of retrenchment; and (5) the role that *contingency planning* can play in helping to make the transition from a period of growth to one of decline.

Institutional Mission

As Peck (1984) noted, an institution's mission is its driving force, its reason for being. The higher education literature on retrenchment shows that a clear understanding of and consensus about mission is essential for an institution to successfully cope with a period of decline (e.g., Brantley et al., 1979; Mortimer and Tierney, 1979; Bowen and Glenny, 1980; Mingle and Norris, 1981; Chaffee, 1984). For example, Peck (1984) found that a primary characteristic of successful small colleges was that they were dominated by a strong commitment to their missions. In contrast, Jonsen (1984) reported that closed institutions had been plagued by serious conflict and confusion about their missions.

All colleges and universities have a statement of mission as part of their charters. However, these mission statements are usually little more than shorthand phrases summarizing an institution's philosophical reason for being. Unfortunately, broad statements of mission do little to guide an institution during a period of decline (Bowen and Glenny, 1980). Thus, the first step in positioning an institution for the future is a review of its mission that focuses on stating it in operational terms (Mingle and Norris, 1981; Dube and Brown, 1983).

For example, consider the following mission statement of a public urban university: "X University is committed to meeting the needs of the metropolitan community. Academic, public service, and research activities are geared to the demands of the urban population and environment." This mission statement is very broad, providing only a general statement of educational intent. In order for this mission statement to provide guidance in setting priorities, it needs to be phrased in operational terms. The following mission statement does this: "X University is committed to meeting the needs of the metropolitan community by providing comprehensive educational opportunities for working adults. Academic, public service, and research activities are geared to meeting the demands and needs of an urban population and environment." This seemingly minor change focuses the mission statement by identifying both the primary population served (working adults/nontraditional students) and the range of programs that the institution will offer (academic and professional). Moreover, by identifying the population, the institution takes a step in specifying the type of educational delivery system that is appropriate. In this case, it means a delivery system that meets the needs of nontraditional students, which would probably include evening and weekend classes and student service functions that are tailored and scheduled to meet the needs of the older student.

Once the mission statement has been reformulated in operational terms, assess the extent to which faculty, trustees, administrators, and other important constituencies agree that it reflects their understanding of the institution's purpose. Consensus is important because the mission statement is one of the yardsticks against which the centrality of individual programs to an institution is measured during the program review process. If there is a low degree of consensus about the appropriateness of the reformulated mission statement, institutional leaders need to reframe it so that it is consistent with constituent perceptions or to change these perceptions so that the mission statement is accepted. When the mission statement is clarified and agreed on, a number of steps can be taken sequentially or in concert: an assessment of an institution's enrollment flows, an assessment of the institutional environment, program review, and contingency planning.

Assessment of Enrollment Flows[5]

In order to make educated guesses about what may happen to future enrollments, institutional managers must have a good understanding of what has happened to actual enrollments over the past few years. Most institutions collect a wealth of data about enrollments through day-to-day operations such as admissions. Unfortunately, this information is not often used for enrollment management purposes. Enrollment management can be conceived of as a process by which an institution monitors information about the inflow, progression, and outflow of students, with the intent of determining how and where it can positively influence recruitment and retention. As Hossler (1984) pointed out, some of the levers available to institutions are student recruitment and marketing efforts, pricing and financial aid policies, academic and career advising, academic assistance programs, orientation, retention programs, and a variety of student services. But before an institution decides which levers to pull, it needs to know what types of actions have the highest potential payoffs.

A beginning step toward such knowledge is to visualize enrollments as a flow over time, as depicted in Figure 3. For any given period of time, there is an inflow of students through the admissions process and an outflow through attrition and graduations. By studying changes in the flow of students through the institution over time, it is possible to identify potential enrollment problems and opportunities. The types of information that can be developed and used by institutional managers are illustrated by the following sets of questions.

With regard to the inflow of students to your institution, consider the following types of questions: Has the number of applications received by your institution increased, decreased, or remained the same over the past five years? Have the ratios of applications to admissions and of admissions to registrations changed? Where do these applications come from—new students, transfers, or

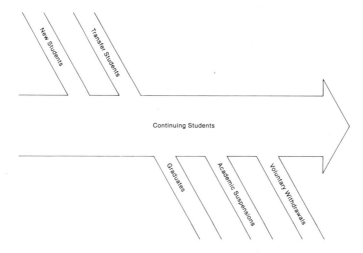

New Students

Transfer Students

Continuing Students

Graduates

Academic Suspensions

Voluntary Withdrawals

Fig. 3. Institutional Enrollment Flow.

former students returning to school? Is the institution gaining or losing ground in terms of its ability to recruit students?

What types of students is the institution enrolling? Are they the traditional 18- to 21-year-old students that attend a day program? Or is the institution's reliance on part-time and non-traditional students increasing? How have the characteristics of these students changed over the past few years in terms of age, sex, minority composition, entering test scores, family income, or the locale from which they come?

Each question focuses attention on a slightly different aspect of the inflow of students. For example, a recent decrease in the number of applications received by an institution could be caused by a number of factors. If an institution's enrollments have varied inversely with economic conditions in the past, decreased applications may simply mirror changing economic conditions. There may be reason for concern but there is also not much that institutional managers can do about the enrollment changes unless they plan to tap into less economically sensitive enrollment markets. But if an institution's enrollments have not been sensitive to economic conditions in the past, decreased applications may reflect shrinkage in the traditional college-aged cohort or declining demand for the types of programs offered. Both causes require careful attention because they have long-term implications for future enrollments.

Alternatively, perhaps the number of students admitted has remained constant over the past few years but the proportion of admitted students registering has decreased. This type of pattern can result from increasing competition for enrollments and indicate a worsening in the competitive position of the institution in relation to other schools. Such data might indicate a need for curriculum revision to make the institution's programs more attractive to potential students, and for better promotion of those educational opportunities.

The essential point of these brief examples is that one can learn much about an institution's position within the educational marketplace by examining data about changes in the inflow of students over time. Moreover, it is important to ask the same questions about the enrollments of individual academic programs within an institution because there are likely to be variations in the inflow patterns across programs. The answers to these questions, directed at the program level, provide much useful information for the program review process discussed in the next section.

The second set of questions concerns what happens to students once they have entered the institution. For example, what proportion of entering students eventually complete a degree? How long does it take the average undergraduate or graduate student to do so? These questions can be answered by conducting a cohort study, which means tracking a group of entering students to determine the pattern of their behavior over time. What you want to determine is when and where attrition within the cohort group occurs.

Are there variations in the completion rates of distinct subpopulations of students? For example, do 18- to 21-year-old full-time male students show greater persistence in completing their courses of study than older part-time male students? Questions then need to be asked about why the observed differences exist. For example, older part-time students are likely to enroll for reasons different from those of the traditional full-time student, such as for personal development or updating technical skills as opposed to earning a degree. As a result, attrition in this subpopulation may not indicate a problem, because these individuals are achieving their individual goals. On the other hand, if you find that the institution is losing a substantial number of students through transfers to other schools, you may wish to determine why and explore whether the loss of these students is due to controllable factors. If such factors can be identified, they become potential opportunities for institutional action.

What variations are there in completion rates across programs? Some programs are likely to do a better job than others in retaining and graduating students. Once program differences are identified, you should ask why the variations exist. For example, are differences in completion rates due to variations in the quality of the educational and support services provided by those programs, in the types of students that the programs attract, or in the difficulty of the programs? Again, identifying controllable versus uncontrollable causes for attrition creates opportunities for institutional action.

If the information gained through this type of self-examination is displayed in the form of a flowchart, as suggested in Figure 3, it allows institutional managers to condense much complex information about enrollments into a digestible format. Careful consideration of the factors affecting inflows, progressions, and outflows of students can help identify points of managerial intervention that can enhance an institution's ability to attract and retain students. By considering the *overall* flow of enrollments rather than the components, an institution may be more able to identify the types of actions that are likely to have the greatest potential impact on enrollments at the lower cost. For example, should an institution put its limited resources into a retention program, an academic assistance program for underprepared students, or increased student services? The answers to these questions should make the utility of different types of activities clear, and the likelihood of using scarce resources to the best advantage is increased. Thus enrollment-flow analyis is an agenda-setting tool (Ewell, 1985) that can help an institution select enrollment management strategies with the greatest likelihood of enhancing enrollments.

Assessment of the Environment

With the information from the review of past and current enrollments in mind, it is useful for institutional managers to think about the future of the enrollment pools from which their institution attracts students. As was noted earlier, much has been written about the decreasing size of the traditional college-aged cohort nationally. But what is likely to happen to the demographics for the particular populations in the areas from which your institution recruits? Do you recruit from age groups that are growing or decreasing in size within your service area? For example, urban institutions that serve primarily older, nontraditional students are less likely to experience decreasing enrollments as compared to schools that focus on educating 18- to 21-year-old students.

Is the ethnicity of the institution's service area changing? Hodgkinson (1983) noted that the decline in birthrates during the 1960s and 1970s was largely a Caucasian phenomenon. As a result, a larger proportion of the smaller traditional college-aged cohort will be composed of minority group members. In many instances, the participation rates in higher education for these groups is lower than for Caucasians. If there is a shift occurring in the minority composition of an institution's service region, has the institution considered the ramifications and made decisions on how to serve these populations' needs?

Some other relevant questions that institutional managers should ask: How reliant are enrollments on uncertain federal and state support? Would decreasing support detrimentally affect an institution's ability to attract students? Are changes likely in the demand for labor in the institution's service area? How would such changes affect students' interests in the programs offered by the institution?

Similar questions should be asked about institutional revenues. For example, what effect would a cut in federal student aid have on institutional revenues? How would changes in the tax laws or in economic conditions affect charitable contributions to the institution? Are any major contracts or grants nearing completion? Can they be renewed or replaced? How would changes in state appropriations for higher education affect institutional revenues? The intent of these and other questions is to sensitize institutional managers to some of the uncontrollable factors that could have an impact on future enrollments and revenues.

While institutional managers can speculate about trends and events, they can't *know* what will happen with any certainty. Much of the value of environmental assessment is psychological because foresight makes the unthinkable thinkable (Turner, 1976; Zammuto, 1985). Thinking about the unthinkable *now* can decrease the level of stress experienced by institutional managers with the onset of decline by reducing the perception of threat, which—as is shown in a later section—is a major cause of dysfunctional organizational dynamics during a period of decline. Thus thinking about possibly unpleasant future realities can emotionally inoculate institutional managers to potential enrollment and revenue problems (Billings et al., 1980).

Program Review

The program review process enables an institution to assess the fit between academic programs and the institution's mission and to set priorities for resource allocation (Dube and Brown, 1983; Mortimer and Tierney, 1979). Mortimer and McConnell (1978, pp. 275–280) suggested that any consultative process, such as program review, should include at least the following steps:

1. The review process and the attendant criteria need to be the subject of early consultation among members of the institution so that alternatives can be fully explored.
2. Procedures and criteria should be formulated jointly by faculty and administrators.
3. Information from the review should be freely available to all interested parties.
4. Adequate feedback should be given to all relevant parties upon completion of the review process.
5. Decisions made on the basis of the review should be communicated widely.

The first set of criteria is concerned with program quality as reflected by the program's staff and students and by the adequacy of facilities and support services. Some of the questions raised by these criteria are: How good are the faculty and students involved in the program? With regard to students, information from the enrollment analysis can be used to determine the level of entering test scores of new students and grade-point averages of transfer students for different programs, and how the entering qualifications have changed over the past few years. Are the available facilities and academic support services adequate to support each program? Differences in retention rates among programs may indicate that the adequacy of these factors needs to be studied. And do the programs generate desired outcomes?

TABLE 2. Program Review Criteria

Type of criterion	Shirley and Volkwein (1978)	Dube and Brown (1983)	Heydinger (1983)
Quality	Quality of faculty Quality of students Quality of library holdings ' Quality of facilities and equipment	Quality of faculty/staff Quality of students Adequacy of academic support services Creativity and flexibility of the program Effectiveness and worth of the processes used by the program, and their outcomes	Program quality
Need	Centrality to mission Present student demand Projected student demand Demand for graduates Locational advantage Comparative advantage	Goodness of fit between institutional mission and program objectives, services, and priorities Program demand by students and society	Mission fit (integration) Uniqueness Demand Connectedness (to other programs in the institution)
Cost	Cost-revenue Other costs and benefits	Program productivity Adequacy of resources used or required by the program	Cost-effectiveness

The second set of criteria is related to the need for a program. Questions are: How central is the program to the institution's mission? Are its content and delivery consistent with the institution's mission as stated in operational terms? What level of demand is there for the program by current students, and what is the potential future demand? Information from the enrollment analysis will provide insight into how demand has changed over the past few years, and information from an environmental assessment should help in determining how demand could change in the future. What is the demand for program graduates? If the institution offers a placement service, it should be possible to determine the ease with which graduates from different programs obtain employment. Does the program have a comparative or locational advantage over competing programs? How unique is the program in its provision of educational services? Both of these questions relate to the position of the program in the competitive environment and ask whether each program has a well-defined niche within the educational system. Does the program play an essential role in the institution through the educational services that it provides other programs?

The third set of criteria is related to cost–benefit considerations. These criteria raise questions concerning the effective use of an institution's resources. Depending on the institution, some of the questions suggested by these criteria are: Is there a gap between the desired quality of a program and the resources committed to it? How productive is the program in generating resources for the institution through student credit hours and research funding? Are there other noneconomic qualitative costs that should be considered, such as social, legal, or political costs associated with offering or not offering a particular program?

The information acquired through the process of asking these types of questions needs to be synthesized and interpreted. It then should provide the basis for recommendations. Shirley and Volkwein (1978), Belanger and Tremblay (1982), and Dube and Brown (1983) have suggested a number of ways to accomplish this task. Then the remaining three steps suggested by Mortimer and McConnell (1978) should be completed. Information should be made available to all interested parties, feedback should be given to the participants, and decisions based on the review information should be communicated widely.

The program review process also has a number of benefits beyond setting program priorities. For example, Belanger and Tremblay (1982) noted that the review process at the University of Montreal has the effect of "creating a situation whereby units are beginning to questions their own modes of operation, their use of faculty resources, and their instructional activities" (p. 34). Heydinger also noted that the outcomes of the review process at the University of Minnesota enabled faculty members to make "longer-range career choices with much fuller knowledge of where their department stood in the overall priority of the college" (p. 8).

In summary, program review is a useful exercise because it forces an institution to make decisions about program priorities. By actively examining current program quality and cost, projected needs, and mission fit, an institution can remove the "dead hand from the tiller" and actively decide the course it will pursue in the future. If participation by faculty and administrators is widespread, the review process will create a sense of ownership on the part of the participants about future directions, making it much easier to accomplish desired changes.

Contingency Planning

Mingle and Norris (1981) found that institutions having contingency plans for dealing with declining enrollments and revenues were more likely to respond successfully than institutions without such plans. But it also appears that relatively few institutions engage in this process. Bowen and Glenny (1981) found in their case studies of ten California institutions that "all administrators and many faculty attributed lack of plans for stress to the dangers of a self-fulfilling prophecy, concern that however bad conditions might become that immediate impact of widespread alarm at the campus would be worse (p. 144). But Bowen and Glenny (1981) also pointed out why contingency plans are necessary, providing at the same time a plausible rationale for the Mingle and Norris finding:

> Without contingency plans crises will be unavoidable, the crisis paranoia will generally prohibit rational response. Moreover, the longer contingency planning is delayed, the fewer the options—even irrational ones—that will be available. [p. 145]

There are different types of contingency planning. The two that are of concern here are contingency plans that specify how a retrenchment process will operate and those that actually specify the content of retrenchment activities. As Morgan (1982) noted, either contingency planning approach has advantages and disadvantages:

> If the assumed conditions of decline fail to materialize or occur to a substantially lesser degree than anticipated, as is often the case, programmatic areas designed for reduced status have often lost their better faculty and students and find recruitment and placement difficult . . .
>
> On the other hand, one advantage of such plans is that they serve to shock the academic community into recognition of a fundamental crisis and to initiate a learning process at the institutional level. Whether or not such an exercise is a learning as opposed to destructive process depends in large part upon the size of the contraction, the degree of trust and confidence educational administrators enjoy, and the perceived fairness of procedures used in the process.
>
> If the extent of decline appears to be marginal and if there is some reasonable time in which to develop plans, it may be more prudent to concentrate on developing strategic contingency planning policies and procedures rather than a plan specifying programmatic areas. [pp. 562–563]

Based on Morgan's observations, it appears that the type of contingency planning selected depends in part on the extent to which institutional managers believe decline will occur, ranging from not very likely to imminent.

If institutional managers believe that declining enrollments or revenues are not very likely in the near future, they should focus on developing a contingency plan specifying the retrenchment procedures to be used if decline occurs. Such plans should focus on two things: Who will make the decisions, and the criteria on which those decisions will be made. There are a number of reasons that institutions need to create contingency plans of this nature. For example, the atmosphere within an institution will be much less politically charged before a period of declining enrollments and revenues than after their onset.

Moreover, because the largest component of an institution's expenditures is personnel costs, layoffs and terminations are often required to manage declining enrollments and revenues. Legal and contractual requirements specify that notice must be given to faculty, administrators, and staff prior to termination. As a result, notice usually has to be given based on *projections* of declining enrollments and revenues rather than on their occurrence in order for terminations to bring revenues and expenditures into line as revenues decrease

(Alm et al., 1977; Mortimer, 1981).[6] In essence, contingency plans that specify policies and procedures need to be developed before the onset of declining revenues and enrollments so that an institution can move quickly when it becomes apparent that declining enrollments and revenues are imminent.

If institutional managers believe that decreasing enrollments and revenues are likely in the near future, they need to take the contingency-planning process one further step, which is to specify what cuts will be made and where resources will be reallocated. Ishler's description (1981) of the planning process at Emporia State University provides one example. The planning process at Emporia State was developed in response to an enrollment shortfall. The president mandated that each academic unit develop a five-year plan. Each plan was to include two enrollment projections, one based on the recent downward trends in the production of credit hours and an alternate plan based on more optimistic enrollment projections. Included in each school's plan was a statement of goals and objectives in relation to the institution's mission statement, a review of departmental programs, an assessment of academic program priorities, and an analysis of staffing needs. A common set of previously agreed-upon assumptions was used to guide the planning process, which was then carried out at the departmental level by the faculty.

Heydinger (1983) described a similar process at the University of Minnesota, which was implemented in response to a recision in the state budget. Deans of the academic units and directors of the support units were asked to identify areas of high and low priority within their units. For the academic units, a guiding principle of the process was that faculty would play a major role in developing program priorities and plans. (Unlike the situation at Emporia State, the University of Minnesota had implemented an institutionwide planning process two years earlier, and much of the groundwork for identifying priorities had already been laid.) The central administration decided on the level of cuts that was to be absorbed by the broad functional areas of the institution and by academic programs. The academic units were then required to determine how they would accommodate these cuts based on the program priorities identified earlier.

There are three important characteristics common to the planning processes at Emporia State University and the University of Minnesota: faculty participation, consensually agreed-upon criteria, and budget decisions based on program priorities. As both Ishler and Heydinger noted, faculty participation in the process created a sense of ownership in the recommendations, and the whole university community stood behind them. Agreement over criteria resulted in a perception that the criteria and the process were fair, which increased support for the recommendations. Finally, using the identified program priorities to guide budgeting allowed the institutions to cope with their immediate problems while strengthening their position for the future.

Five Critical Questions

The general intent of these activities for positioning an institution to meet the future can be summarized in the form of five questions:

1. Can you state the mission of your institution in specific terms?
2. What has happened to the inflow, progression, and outflow of students through your institution over the past few years?
3. What trends or events might have a significant positive or negative impact on your institution's enrollments and revenues in the foreseeable future?
4. Does the institution have a set of priorities that will enable it to choose among programs and services if resources become increasingly scarce?
5. Is the institution prepared to act quickly if declining enrollments or revenues become a reality?

If you find that you cannot answer any of these questions, it's time to get those answers. As will be shown in the following section, which describes the dynamics of decline, the better an institution is prepared to meet a period of decline, the more likely it is to steer a successful course through an uncertain future.

THE ANATOMY OF A DECLINING ORGANIZATION

This section examines the impact of decline on individuals and organizations. The information is drawn from the literature on business and public-sector organizations as well as on colleges and universities. Although this literature focuses on a variety of different types of organizations, the theories and empirical findings that have emerged are remarkably consistent. As will be seen in the following pages, the planning and assessment activities described in the preceding sections are difficult to accomplish after the onset of decline. The internal dynamics associated with decline severely reduce an organization's ability to look forward and plan and make it more difficult to adapt to changing conditions.

The following scenario is not uncommon. Imagine a college that grew at a fair pace through the 1960s and 1970s and then experienced an unexpected 5% decrease in FTE enrollments during the fall of one academic year in the early 1980s. Institutional managers initially expressed disbelief that decline was occurring, believing rather that the decrease was an aberration. Then a sense of threat pervaded the institution with the realization that decreasing enrollments would result in about a 3% decrease in institutional revenues, and that there was a real possibility that enrollments would continue to decline. As is true of most schools, the institution had small reserves that could be used to fund operating expenses, but the reserves would be rapidly depleted if used in this fashion. Quick action was required to bring projected revenues and expenditures into line and to forestall future decreases in enrollment. Unforeseen, the situation caught the institution with no ready plans for dealing with it. A crisis was born.

Hermann (1963) defined a crisis as having three primary characteristics: "A crisis (1) threatens high priority values of the organization, (2) presents a restricted amount of time in which a response can be made, and (3) is unexpected or unanticipated by the organization" (p. 64). The immediate effect of the onset of an institutional crisis is to increase the level of stress experienced by institutional decision-makers. And it is the effects of stress on individuals that lead to the dynamics of decline. As many authors have noted (e.g., Smart and Vertinsky, 1977; Holsti, 1978, Staw et al., 1981), the surprise, threat, and short decision time associated with a crisis affect the ability of managers to make effective decisions. For example, stress increases the selective filtering of information, reliance on past experience as a guide to future action, and the importance of short-term values in formulating organizational responses. It also decreases decision makers' tolerance of ambiguity, sensitivity to others' perceptions, resistance of the pull to closure in decision making, and the ability to recognize important information when presented. In turn, decision makers exhibit a decreased span of attention, increased cognitive rigidity, and a decreased time perspective, all of which affect the formulation of organizational responses to a crisis.

Structural Effects of Decline

A common first response is the centralization of decision making within an organization (Hermann, 1963; Hall and Mansfield, 1971; Rubin, 1977; Khandwalla, 1978; Bowen and Glenny, 1980; Ford, 1980a; Billings et al., 1980). Centralization occurs because the short response time available and the increased stress create a high need for control on the part of decision makers. Moreover, a decentralized decision structure can create institutional paralysis by immobilizing a system's ability to act under crisis conditions (Yarmolinsky, 1975; Rubin, 1979). Ironically, it is the long tradition of participative decision-making through faculty governance that sets colleges and universities apart from most other types of organizations. But as Mortimer and Tierney (1979) noted, traditional governance procedures are likely to prove futile in a decline situation as conflict increases between and among administration and faculty, and the process breaks down into one of political infighting (Hardy, 1983a).

Centralization may increase the speed with which responses can be formulated, but the quality of those responses often suffers in the process. One reason is that centralization decreases the number of communication channels carrying information to decision makers. At the same time, the information load on the remaining channels increases, creating a large potential for information distortion (Hermann, 1963; Staw et al., 1981). Coupled with the effects of stress on decision makers, there tends to be a reduction in the search for information about the options open to the organization, decreased analysis and evaluation of alternatives and their consequences, and fewer choices made among alternatives (Smart and Vertinsky, 1977; Holsti, 1978; Staw et al., 1981).

These dynamics increase the potential for managers to make bad decisions, which creates a serious problem for the organization because errors become more costly under conditions of decline. As Boulding (1975), Scott (1976), Levine (1978), and Zammuto (1985) have noted, strategic miscalculations that may be painful during periods of resource abundance can be fatal during periods of decline. Consider the case of a college adding a new program. If the program fails to attract sufficient enrollments to become self-supporting while enrollments in other programs are increasing, it may simply slow overall institutional growth. But if overall institutional enrollments are decreasing, the failure of the new program to attract students worsens the overall position of the institution and can be fatal. In essence, centralization is a double-edged sword. It increases the speed with which an institution can respond to decline but simultaneously reduces the likelihood that these responses will correct the problem.

Increased control is also manifested in other ways. For example, Smart and Vertinsky (1977) and Khandwalla (1978) reported an increase in the use of standardized procedures in business organizations during periods of decline. Bozeman and Slusher (1979) also suggested that increased formalization in procedures is a common response to decline by public sector organizations. Schendel et al. (1976) found that business organizations responded to decline by making the profit responsibilities of individual units more explicit. Similarly, Rubin (1977), in her study of retrenchment in universities, found that resource allocation decisions became more systematized through the use of explicit criteria for allocation. The overall effect of these types of actions tends to be an increase in the structural rigidity of an organization.

The combined effect of increased centralization and structural rigidity is a reduction in the ability of an organization to innovate (Whetten, 1981). This problem is particularly acute for colleges and universities because the primary source of programmatic innovations is the faculty, who are excluded from the decision process by increased centralization. Innovation also decreases because of a fear of failure and the associated costs mentioned above (Smart and Vertinsky, 1977; Bozeman and Slusher, 1979). Moreover, the common emphasis on increased efficiency during a period of decline and the lack of slack resources available to fund new initiatives decrease the likelihood that innovative responses can be successfully implemented (Walker and Chaiken, 1982).

In short, the structural dynamics associated with decline are increased centralization accompanied by increased formalization and standardization of procedures. The resulting increase in structural rigidity makes it difficult for an organization to formulate innovative responses to the problems caused by decline. Moreover, the lack of slack resources makes the implementation of innovative responses difficult. As a result, organizations that are not prepared in advance to manage a period of decline find themselves with few response options.

Behavioral Effects of Decline

The organization is also affected by decline's impact on interpersonal dynamics. As Iannacone (1979) noted, latent conflicts in an organization are worsened by decreased resources. With fewer resources available to satisfy the conflicting interests of various institutional units and participants (Levine, 1978), conflict becomes more frequent and intense (Cyert, 1978; Whetten, 1980a,b). Resource allocation decisions then have a tendency to be settled relative to the power of the participants in the decision process (Pfeffer and Salancik, 1974; Salancik and Pfeffer, 1974).

The climate of the institution also suffers. As Levine (1979) noted, "Simply put, it just is not as much fun working and managing in a contracting organization as it is in an expanding one" (p. 180). Moreover, Starbuck et al. (1978) noted that the declining climate of an organization can lead to increased distrust and cynicism.

The dynamics of decline also result in reduced organizational cohesion. Member commitment to an organization under conditions of decline can decrease as a result of increased stress and conflict. Hall and Mansfield (1971) found that the result was decreased organizational cohesion, which was contrary to prevailing theory that an external threat will increase it (Coser, 1956). Hamblin (1958a) conducted an experiment that explains these findings and offers information of practical import. He found that decreased cohesion is likely under crisis conditions when a likely solution to the crisis appears to be unavailable, or when the likely solution creates competition among members or units in the organization. In contrast, he found that cohesion is likely to increase if a cooperative solution is present. In Hall and Mansfield's study, little participation in the formulation of a retrenchment strategy was evident in the organization that they studied, a finding leading them to conclude that increased participation by organization members could increase commitment and cohesion. These findings suggest that the tendency toward centralized decision-making discussed in the above section can be dysfunctional in that it may decrease member commitment and organizational cohesion at a time when they are most needed.

Decline also has a significant impact on leadership in an institution. For example, Hamblin (1958b) found that leader influence increased during the early stages of a crisis. But if leaders were not perceived as having a solution to the crisis, they were replaced. The length of time during which institutional leaders have a window of opportunity to act may be limited. As the literature points out, there are many reasons that replacing leaders during a period of decline can be functional. Many of these reasons have to do with the changes in the myth, ideology, or model of reality describing the organization's situation that usually accompany a turnover in leadership. For example, Jonsson and Lundin (1977) reported that the firms they studied were unable to resolve a crisis until new beliefs about the nature of essential organizational action emerged with the replacement of top management. Similarly, Starbuck et al. (1978) suggested that top managers should focus on creating a new ideology in a crisis-ridden organization, which encourages "people to break with past precedents and root out implicit assumptions" (p. 134). Smart and Vertinsky (1977) also noted that a new model of the situation, with an appropriate repertoire of responses, has to be developed before an organization can reverse a decline situation. A new management team can often accomplish these changes since they are not wedded to the policies of their predecessors (Hamermesh, 1977).

The literature also shows that during periods of decline, the replacement of top management is fairly common in both the private and the public sectors. For example, Schendel et al. (1976) found that the replacement of top management was associated with the successful turnaround of fifty-six firms. Similarly, in a study of 36 matched pairs of declining firms, Schendel and Patton (1976) reported that the firms that had recovered in each pair were more likely to have changed management than were those firms that had not recovered. In higher education, Chaffee (1982) reported that each of the 12 institutions she studied had replaced its president during a period of declining revenues. Similarly, Finkelstein et al. (1984) found that the replacement of the president by a "mover and shaker" was a fairly common response by colleges to a period of decline.

Turnover also becomes a major problem for a declining organization. While the institution may have to terminate some faculty and staff, it also has to find ways to retain the personnel it wants to keep. It is common for the most qualified members of an organization to leave during a period of decline, because they have the most employment options elsewhere (Hirschman, 1970; Levine, 1979). Unless faculty and staff have a high degree of loyalty to the institution, lack employment alternatives elsewhere, or derive some psychic satisfaction from assisting the institution, they will explore alternative employment situations (Kolarska and Aldrich, 1980). Moreover, it is these individuals who are most needed to assist the institution in formulating and implementing a strategy for recovering from decline. And as Whetten (1981) noted, organizations that lose their most able members during the early stages of decline are at a serious competitive disadvantage. As a result, colleges and universities with decreasing enrollments and revenues are in serious jeopardy of experiencing a decline in educational quality unless they can find ways to retain their most qualified faculty and staff.

Further problems are created by the effects of decline on the individuals who remain. The faculty and staff remaining often exhibit psychological withdrawal as a result of the stress created by decline. Morale suffers (Bowen and Glenny, 1980), the need for security becomes more important (Hall and Mansfield,

1971), commitment to the organization decreases (Hermann, 1963), and an individual's self-esteem often declines (Jick and Murray, 1982). Thus the overall picture for the declining organization is one of the most able leaving and those who remain becoming dispirited.

Once these dynamics are exhibited, an institution can enter into "a self-reenforcing downward spiral of declining resources and capabilities" (Behn, 1980, p. 617). An initial decrease in enrollments and revenues forces a first round of cuts. These cuts, in turn, discourage the institution's most talented and productive members, who, being the most mobile, leave. Their departure hurts the institution's quality and productivity and make it more difficult to attract students and financial resources. The subsequent decrease in students and revenues forces a second round of cuts. And so the downward spiral continues. Unless institutional managers can break out of the spiral of decline, institutional demise becomes a real possibility (Cyert, 1978; Bozeman and Slusher, 1979; Mingle, 1982).

The following section examines how organizations should respond once they have encountered declining enrollments and revenues. The purpose of this section is to provide guidance on how to successfully formulate and implement a recovery plan, and how to break out of the spiral of decline.

MANAGING DECLINE

Managing a declining organization is not easy, but neither is it impossible. Part of the difficulty is that few managers have experience in managing declining organizations (Boulding, 1975); even fewer managers have been trained to do so (Easton, 1976; Zammuto, 1982b). Managing decline requires a different mind-set from managing growth. Part of this mind-set is an understanding of the dynamics of decline, which were described in the preceding section. Another part is understanding how to formulate and implement effective strategies for recovering from a period of decline. Developing and implementing appropriate responses is not a cut-and-dried process. Institutional managers must have a thorough appreciation both of the factors causing declining enrollments and revenues and of the constraints under which their institution operates. This section outlines some of the strategic considerations that have to be taken into account. The final section then presents guidelines for cutback management, which is essential for creating the resources necessary to implement an institution's retrenchment strategy.

Strategic Considerations
The first issue that institutional managers must address is the question of what factors are causing declining enrollments and revenues. The types of responses that will assist an institution depend on the cause of decline. In some instances,

making this determination is easy. For example, decreasing revenue at a public college because of a cutback in state funding during a recession is easily identified. But in other instances, pinpointing the cause can be more difficult. For example, declining enrollmentss can be due to a variety of factors, including demographic trends, increased competition for enrollments, changing student interests, and deteriorating physical plant.

Zammuto and Cameron (1985) presented a model that is useful for thinking about the causes of decline. The model focuses on environmental changes that can lead to decline for organizational populations and for the individual organizations within them. These authors argued that different types of environmental change create different decline situations. Moreover, various types of decline situations require different types of organizational responses for successful adaptation.

Zammuto and Cameron's model focuses on two dimensions of change that have the effect of reducing the resources available to organizations. One type of change is a reduction in the *level of activity* that the environment will support. Examples of such environmental changes are shrinkage in the traditional college-aged cohort and reduced state or federal support for higher education. The other is a change in the *type of activity* that the environment will support. An example of this type of environmental change is shifting student interests in fields of study. The first type of change is quantitative in that it affects the number of goods and services that organizations within a population can produce. The second type is qualitative in that such changes are related to the kinds of products and services that organizations can produce. When the level of activity that the environment will support decreases, organizations need to become more efficient at what they have done in the past. When the types of activities that the environment will support change, organizations often need to modify what they are doing to fit the new performance requirements of the environment.

The specific type of decline encountered by an institution and the nature of effective responses to those conditions are a function of the interaction between environmental conditions and the position of the organization in that environment. This statement is important in that it indicates that there are many alternative paths to institutional survival and prosperity. The particular strategy that will work best for a specific institution depends on the factors causing decline and the institution's strengths and weaknesses.

Different types of institutions are more susceptible to some causes of decline than to others. Zammuto et al. (1982), for example, suggested that institutions with specialized programs (e.g., liberal arts, teacher preparatory, and divinity) are more susceptible to decline caused by changing students' interests in fields of study than are institutions offering a broad range of academic and professional programs (e.g., major doctoral and comprehensive institutions). Schools with a broad range of programs often can cope with shifting student interests by reallocating resources among existing programs, whereas specialized schools usually do not have that option. As a result, schools with a broad range of academic programs are more likely to experience decline caused by a decrease in the level of activity that the environment will support.[7]

Moreover, institutions experiencing the same type of decline have a variety of strategic alternatives that they can pursue. For example, during the late 1960s and early 1970s many liberal arts colleges experienced declining enrollments because students' interests shifted from the liberal arts to the professions. As a result of these changes in the environment and the institutional responses to them, the proportion of institutions offering liberal arts programs in American higher education decreased. For example, Birnbaum (1983) showed that the number of liberal arts colleges as a proportion of all colleges and universities in eight states declined between 1960 and 1980. Teacher preparatory schools disappeared in these states altogether. Similarly, Zammuto (1984) found that the absolute number of institutions with specialized liberal arts programs decreased nationwide by about 40% between 1972 and 1981. Both studies indicated that the decrease was a result not simply of attrition but of the interplay of the creation of new liberal arts schools, the closing of others, and the migration of many schools away from an emphasis on specialized liberal arts programs.

A study by Pfnister et al. (1982) of program changes in liberal arts schools during the 1970s illustrates the complexity of the adaptation process. Their sample consisted of 84 institutions that had been classified by the Carnegie Council as Liberal Arts I or II institutions in 1969, and the analysis focused on identifying patterns of programmatic change. The results indicated five different patterns that varied along two dimensions: (1) the extent of a school's emphasis on providing vocational preparation and (2) the extent of a school's emphasis on serving nontraditional students. One group, labeled "elite nonprofessional and nonvocational," consisted of institutions that retained a traditional liberal arts curriculum for full-time, traditional students. At the opposite extreme were "multipurpose institutions," which changed their programs to have a relatively high emphasis on vocational and professional education and to serve significant numbers of part-time, nontraditional students. In between were "professionally oriented traditions," "limited multipurpose I," and "limited multipurpose II" institutions, which differed in the extent to which they offered terminal vocational programs and baccalaureate-level professional programs and in the degree to which they focused on educating traditional versus nontraditional students. Pfnister et al. (1982) noted that all of the institutions appeared to be financially solvent at the time of the study, a fact suggesting that many different patterns of adaptation can be successful.

Given the direction of changes in student interests in fields of study, the addition of professional and vocational programs to a liberal arts curriculum is not surprising. Indeed, adding such programs has been the common remedy for declining enrollments. But what about those schools that increased their commitment to the liberal arts? Zammuto (1984) suggested that this strategy was successful precisely because other institutions diversified their programs into professional and applied-science areas. The exit of some institutions from the liberal arts arena had the effect of reducing the competition for students interested in attending a traditional liberal arts school. In turn, this reduced competition may have made it possible for other schools with a specialized liberal arts program to prosper, even with fewer students interested in a liberal education.

While many types of strategies can be successful in responding to declining enrollments and revenues, how do you choose the one most likely to help your institution? First, consider the likely duration of declining enrollments and revenues. If they are being caused by events or trends that have a projected impact of short-term duration, the best strategy may be to do as little as possible, which is to say, "Conserve resources and ride out the storm." Moreover, such short-term downturns can provide institutional managers with an opportunity to do a little fine-tuning. The discretionary power that institutional managers acquire with the initial onset of declining revenues or enrollment provides leeway to reallocate resources in a manner that is not possible at most other times. But if the projected duration of decline is longer term, institutional managers need to develop strategies to realign the institution to new realities.

The best place to begin in this latter situation is with the institution's mission. Research has shown that institutions that do not deviate dramatically from their traditional missions often have more successful recoveries than those that do (Chaffee, 1982, 1984; Finkelstein et al., 1984). A likely reason is that by staying close to their traditional missions, institutions can capitalize on existing strengths while minimizing the risks of failure. Information from the program review process should be used to identify areas of strength and weakness in an institution's academic program offerings. Institutional managers then need to examine this information carefully and to determine whether there are areas within the existing competencies of the institution that can be more fully utilized.

For example, can programs in which the institution has demonstrated excellence be expanded to new student populations? Or can those programs be expanded in such a way as to serve the need of a different market? An institution with strong programs in the language, history, and culture of a particular region of the world might be able to offer an international studies program that would serve the growing need of industry for internationally oriented managers. Such curricular innovations can allow institutions to capitalize on their existing competencies without deviating substantially from their traditional mission.

Second, institutional managers need to carefully assess the school's position in the educational marketplace and to determine the likelihood that it will be able to carve out a segment of the market. For example, deciding to diversify a liberal arts school's program by adding a business major may be successful, depending on the extent to which other institutions already provide business education. If there is an unfilled demand for business education, adding a major may assist the institution in reversing declining enrollments and revenues. But if the school is in a locale that is saturated with business programs, adding one is unlikely to increase enrollments and is likely to worsen the school's situation.

Third, institutional managers have to carefully assess the strengths and weaknesses of the school's personnel, facilities, and finances before embarking on new initiatives. If an institution does not have an adequate resource base, the development of new initiatives that look sound on paper will fail in their implementation. For example, if existing personnel are not qualified to staff a new program and a reasonable chance of attracting qualified individuals does not exist, the addition of a new program is not likely to be successful (Ferris et al., 1984). The sum effect of attempts to innovate without adequate resources is to worsen the condition of the institution.

Fourth, and often overlooked, is the quality of institutional leadership. An institution will not be able to formulate a coherent strategy without strong leadership. Institutional leaders have to have the ability to pull all of the diverse interests of institutional members and constituencies together in order to move in one direction. Thus the institution's leaders must have a high degree of credibility (Kerchner and Schuster, 1982). Without credibility, institutional leaders will have difficulty in convincing institutional members that a problem exists, in reaching a common definition of the problem, and in setting priorities and developing a consensus of how the institution should respond to the problem. In effect, institutional leaders play a very important role in interpreting the situation for members of the institution, as well as a role in formulating and implementing substantive strategic responses to decline. In fact, Chaffee (1984) showed that institutions whose leaders did not attend to the symbolic and interpretive aspects of leadership were not as likely to recover from a period of decline as those that did, even though they employed the same types of substantive strategic responses as the recovering institutions.

In short, institutional managers need first to identify the factors causing decline and to estimate their projected duration. Then strategies need to be formulated to address the underlying causes of decline. A reduction in available resources calls for strategies that increase institutional efficiency. A change in the types of performance that the environment will support may require rethinking the institution's mission and developing new educational services. Ideally, information from an enrollment analysis and a program review will be available to assist in identifying potential strategic options. Alternative courses of action that are congruent with the institution's mission and that extend an institution's dominant competencies should be considered first because they build on existing strengths. Then alternatives that move an institution away from its traditional mission should be examined carefully with respect to potential demand and resource requirements. If the demand is not sufficient or if the resources required to implement an initiative are inadequate, it should not be undertaken.

Finally, institutional leaders need to attend to the symbolic and interpretive aspects of developing and implementing strategic responses to decline. Leaders need to ensure that there will be a common perception of the problem and of the efficacy of proposed solutions. The next section focuses on the issue of implementing strategic responses to decline through the process of cutback management.

Cutback Management

Institutions usually have to implement retrenchment strategies with available resources. Making resources available for implementation requires cutting back existing operations. The following material does not provide a step-by-step digest of what cuts to make. Conditions vary too much across institutions. Rather, the material focuses on the general pattern of actions for effective cutback management. The theme is one of remaining in *control* of the cutback process, that is, the exercise of managerial choice.

Exercising managerial control means the conscious selection among the options available to the institutional managers. It can be visualized as a dimension ranging from no control to total control. No control implies a lack of choice among the options or the absence of options; control indicates the presence of options, from which the managers select. Control is important in that losing it or not exercising it can lead to the "spiral of decline" described earlier. Once institutional managers lose control of the cutback processes, the likelihood that a period of decline will damage the institution or result in its closure is substantially heightened.

Actions that lead to a loss of managerial control are across-the-board cuts, personnel reductions through attrition, and hiring and salary freezes. Such actions have a great deal of appeal to managers for a number of reasons. First, little time is required to implement them. Second, they do not require that managers make potentially painful choices among individuals or units within the institution (Jick and Murray, 1982). Third, they promote an aura of equality. In the case of across-the-board cuts and salary freezes, everyone is perceived as sharing equally in the problems of the institution (Levine, 1978; Whetten, 1981). Equally sharing the burden helps to prevent the political infighting and conflict associated with the reallocation of scarce resources. Fourth, needed reductions in personnel accomplished through attrition are seen as a humane response to the problem (Mortimer and Taylor, 1984). Institutional managers do not choose those who will leave the organization; individuals make that decision themselves.

Moreover, if an institution is unprepared for a period of decline, it usually has few options available and little time to develop any. As a result, using across-the-board cuts, attrition, and freezes become expedient. They require little thought and no exercise of managerial discretion. Thus these techniques appear to offer a ready answer to the problem of declining enrollments and revenues, particularly if institutional managers believe that decline is a temporary phenomenon. If the period of decline is short, these types of actions may bring revenues and expenditures into balance without damaging the institution. Unfortunately, it seems that most managers believe that most downturns are aberrations and not indicative of a longer term problem. In the public sector, Levine (1979) has called this behavior the "tooth fairy syndrome"; managers believe "that the decline is temporary and the cuts will be restored soon by someone—in some cases as remote as the tooth fairy" (p. 181). For this reason alone, environmental assessment and contingency planning are important. If managers believe that decline is possible, they are more likely to recognize it if it does occur (Zammuto, 1985).

If declining enrollments and revenues are not transitory, actions of this sort worsen the problem rather than resolving it. For example, across-the-board cuts penalize the organization's most efficient units, a phenomenon that Levine (1979) labeled the "efficiency paradox." Efficient units have fewer slack resources with which to absorb budgetary cuts then do less efficient units. As a result, across-the-board cuts have two serious unintended consequences. First, administrators have no incentive to operate efficiently because inefficiencies built into the base budget can be used to absorb cuts, a behavior that becomes self-defeating during a period of decline. Second, the production level of an organization can decrease disproportionately to the extent to which cuts were made. To paraphrase Behn (1980), cutting back any unit beyond the point where slack resources can be used to absorb cuts without reducing output will reduce production by more than the percentage of the cut. Thus, across-the-board cuts have the potential for reducing the output more in efficient than in inefficient units (Bowen and Glenny, 1980). And used over the long run, across-the-board cuts can cause irreparable damage to academic quality and vitality (Mortimer and Tierney, 1979; Milson et al., 1983).

The notions of cutting back through attrition and hiring freezes are much like across-the-board cuts. Attrition appears equitable since it reduces the need for an organization to make decisions about which personnel to terminate. Hiring freezes are seen as relatively painless because they do not represent a targeted reduction in personnel, and no one currently at the institution is hurt. But as Hardy (1983a) pointed out, there are a number of inherent problems.

The process of attrition is slow, and where significant cuts are required, it is often inadequate. Moreover, the organization has little control over who leaves. As a result, if a hiring freeze is strictly enforced, it can result in "gaps" in the organization's personnel.

When a hiring freeze is used in conjunction with a salary freeze, institutional managers almost ensure that the institutional will lose valued personnel and will be unable to replace them. As Carter and Blanton (1983) observed, freezing salaries is a "short-term convenience which could have a devastating long-term impact on an institution. That is one action which could encourage good faculty and other employees to seek other employment, and they will have a good opportunity of getting it in other institutions." (pp. 148–149). Those most likely to leave are the best qualified and, therefore, the most mobile members of an institution. Freezing salaries increases the likelihood that they will leave the institution, a likelihood that is already high during a period of decline.

Overall, across-the-board cuts, personnel reductions through attrition, salary freezes, and hiring freezes results in an abdication of managerial choice and a loss of control. As was indicated earlier, the onset of decline restricts managerial freedom in a number of ways. Using such actions further reduces the degree of freedom left to institutional managers in formulating responses to decline. If declining enrollments and revenues turn out to be a long-term problem, managers using these techniques have simply delayed the need to make decisions. Moreover, they will find themselves in a worsening situation because the resources available for formulating and implementing successful retrenchment strategies have been depleted.

The pertinent question, then, is, How do institutional managers retain control of the cutback process? The answer is through selective cuts and a reallocation of resources that implements the institution's overall retrenchment strategy. Making selective cuts and reallocating resources are predicated on having priorities and a strategic plan that reflects these priorities. If institutional managers have not articulated institutional priorities through a mission and program review, they need to do so with dispatch. Institutional managers may protest that these processes can not be completed quickly. But in their study of cutback management at a number of universities, Mortimer and Taylor (1984) reported that

> while institutions often despair of making judgments about program priorities, or suggest that such judgments can be reached only after years of study, the experience of these universities suggests otherwise. Doubtless all whish they had had more time to do their work, but these institutions very quickly selected criteria to be used to establish program priorities, and then assessed adherence to the criteria. Establishing program priorities may well be the sort of task that fills whatever time is allotted to it. [pp. 19–20]

Moreover, the participation of faculty in developing priorities to be used in developing a retrenchment strategy and for identifying the targets of cuts and reallocations is essential to building acceptance of and commitment to the institution's retrenchment strategy (Hyatt et al., 1984). Widespread participation enhances the legitimacy of the retrenchment process (Mortimer and Taylor, 1984), and it increases the ability of institutional leaders to pull the members of the institution together to move in a common direction.

In short, it is necessary to set priorities that will drive decisions about where to cut and where to reallocate resources. Cuts and reallocation make it possible to implement the institution's retrenchment strategy by freeing the necessary resources. If an institution has already conducted or started mission and program review before the onset of declining enrollments and revenues, the institutional managers will be in a good position to initiate the cutback process quickly. If the institution has not developed explicit priorities, they must be developed quickly to ensure that the institutional managers will remain in control of the cutback process.

It is useful to follow the same general steps described in the earlier section on program review. Generally, the faculty should be involved in setting criteria for identifying program priorities. But as Mortimer and Taylor (1984) noted, faculty should not be asked to identify the targets of cuts. Faculty members are likely to employ a less-than-institutionwide perspective in attempting to identify the areas to be cut. As a result, the process can break down into political infighting as faculty members attempt to protect their own turf. Identified priorities should then be communicated widely throughout the academic community.

Institutional managers should set budget targets for functional and academic units that reflect these priorities. In the priority-setting stage, some programs or functional areas will be identified as likely candidates for cuts or termination, and others will be identified as needing additional resources. The fact that resources will be shifted from one area to another to strengthen and redirect the institution can help the central administration to gain acceptance of the retrenchment plan. For example, Volkwein (1984) reported that at SUNY-Albany

> the reallocation of . . . freed resources was . . . crucial to the acceptance of the program discontinuities on the campus because it created more "winners" than "losers." The resources from each retrenched program could be shifted to four or five continuing ones; for every department that was shattered or hurt by the decisions, there were four or five who saw themselves as able to advance. [p. 398]

Therefore, faculty participation in setting the criteria on which priorities are based, a reallocation of resources that is perceived as strengthening the institution, and strong institutional leadership to guide the process should allow an institution to marshal considerable internal support in implementing its retrenchment strategy.

Once the areas that are to be cut have been targeted, institutional managers should let the individual units make the decisions about how those cuts will be accomplished within the context of the priorities set during the mission and program review. Of course, the central administration should retain control of final approval of the suggested cuts to ensure that they will be consistent with the overall institutional retrenchment strategy. Different units will have different needs and preferences concerning what should be cut to maximize efficiency and to minimize the cuts' effects on unit performance. Decentralizing cutback decisions takes different needs and preferences into account by having the specific cutback decisions made at the level of the institution where these differences are most apparent. In essence, the process of deciding what to cut should follow the same general pattern as that discussed in the section on contingency planning.

McKinley et al. (in press), for example, studied the perceived criticality of two different types of personnel to academic departments in a university: support staff (secretaries, technicians, research assistants, and teaching assistants) and faculty. They found that faculty members in research-oriented departments preferred that faculty positions be reduced and that support staff be left reasonably intact. In contrast, faculty members in departments that were not research-oriented preferred cutbacks in support staff as opposed to faculty positions. McKinley et al. explained these findings as reflecting different departmental needs. In research-oriented departments, faculty saw the support staff as essential to the accomplishment of the research function. In nonresearch-oriented departments, faculty members appeared to be more interested in preserving their own positions (Dallam and Hoyt, 1983; McKinley et al., in press). Moreover, the lack of support staff was seen as having less of an effect on the major activity of these departments, teaching.

These results should be interpreted not literally, but as indicative of the different needs of various functional and academic units. Sometimes these needs are apparent; at other times, they are not. Decentralizing the identification of actual cuts can minimize this problem. One of the interesting implications of these findings is that common "targets of opportunity," such as telephone expenses, photocopying, and travel funds, may be treated on more of a unit-by-unit basis. Institutionwide cuts of these various types of expenditures are likely to have a more detrimental impact on some units than on others.

There are a number of checks and balances that have to be incorporated into any effort to decentralize the cutback process. For example, some units may choose to pay lip service to the retrenchment plan while engaging in active or passive opposition. One mechanism that seems fairly common is recommending cuts that will be deemed unacceptable. The intent is usually one of pleading that resources cannot be reduced since there is no other place to cut. As a result, the central administration has to exercise control over the process by retaining the authority to judge the acceptability of the cuts suggested by the units.

Moreover, some of the potential mechanisms available to units, such as an early retirement plan, have to be developed on an institutionwide basis. Similarly, other options to increase an institution's cash flow (e.g., debt refinancing, reducing health insurance costs, tuition pricing, and financial aid) and changing the asset mix of the institution (e.g., the sale or lease of surplus facilities and ownership versus leasing of portions of the physical plant) require action by the central administration (O'Neill and Grier, 1984). In short, institutional managers should, whenever appropriate, decentralize the cutback process to the areas being affected. The central administration's role should be one of developing and identifying options that the units might consider, as well as that of final approval of the recommended cuts. Areas that do not fall within a specific unit's responsibility should be addressed by the central administration. Finally, institutional self-study and contingency planning should continue after the first round of cuts to ensure that the institution will be prepared to manage further reductions in enrollments and revenues if they occur.

These general guidelines for cutback management can be used to prevent many of the dysfunctional dynamics of decline. Decentralization and participation in setting criteria, identifying priorities, and targeting cuts can effectively broaden the narrowed focus of decision making that accompanies decline. Moreover, if institutional members feel that they are participating in the revitalization of their institution, then commitment, morale, and institutional cohesion are likely to increase rather than decrease. In essence, if institutional managers remain in control of the retrenchment process, there is a good chance that their institution will emerge from a period of decline in a stronger position than when the episode began.

CONCLUSION

A period of declining enrollments and revenues need not be a crisis for an institution. It can provide an opportunity for institutional managers to strengthen programs, personnel, and services. The keys to making a period of decline work for the institution are being prepared and understanding how to avoid the dysfunctional dynamics associated with organizational crises. If managers can retain control of the retrenchment process, they will very likely preside over the institution's revitalization rather than its disintegration. As Starbuck et al. (1978) noted, "The Chinese symbol for crisis combines two simpler symbols, the symbol for danger and the one for opportunity" (p. 135). A period of declining enrollments and revenues can be a time of danger for colleges and universities, but it also can be a time of opportunity. Determining which it is lies within the control of institutional managers.

Acknowledgments. I would like to express my appreciation to Paul Brinkman, Peter Ewell, Shelia Hood, and William Tierney for their comments on an earlier draft of this chapter.

NOTES

1. Unlike other projections, Dresch's included only degree-credit enrollments and not nondegree-credit enrollments. This partly explains why his projected decline was so much more severe than others.
2. Most of the differences in projections are a function of differing assumptions. See Dresch (1975), Leslie and Miller (1974), Leslie (1980), and Frances (1980) for discussions.
3. The enrollment data for the 1973-1976 and 1976-1979 periods were originally published by Zammuto (1982a).
4. For ease of presentation, the term *declining enrollments and revenues* has been used to signify the concept of "declining enrollments and/or revenues" throughout the rest of the chapter.
5. Much of the material in this subsection is based on conversations with Dr. Peter Ewell, Director of the Kellog Student Outcomes Project at NCHEMS. Readers interested in learning more about the specific techniques associated with enrollment management should refer to Beal and Noel (1980), Ewell (1984), Hossler (1984), and Kemerer et al. (1982). Ewell (1984) contains an extensive bibliography on the subject.
6. Articles by Furniss (1974), Alm et al. (1977), Strohm (1981), Gray (1981), Mortimer (1981), and Saunders (1984) discuss the institutional and legal ramifications of these issues in much greater detail. They also provide histories of the experiences of individual institutions during the process of terminating faculty and staff, as well as discussions of relevant court decisions.
7. On the other side of the coin, Zammuto (1983) showed that institutions with specialized programs are also more likely to grow rapidly than are institutions with more comprehensive program offerings. While a variety of programs may buffer an institution from the effects of declining student interests in a particular field of study, it also tends to reduce the rate at which an institution grows. As a result, specialized institutions grow more rapidly than institutions with comprehensive programs when the environment favors the specialized institution's area of program emphasis.
8. It's useful to note that Dallam and Hoyt did not find the same type of distinction between departments as did McKinley et al. The findings of these two studies probably reflect differences in the types of institutions studied. Dallam and Hoyt's institution emphasized the teaching function, while it appears that there was a fair amount of variation in departmental emphases between teaching and research in McKinley et al.'s institution.

REFERENCES

Alm, K.G., Ehrle, E. B., and Webster, B. R. (1977). Managing faculty reductions. *Journal of Higher Education 48:* 153-163.
Baldridge, J. V., Kemerer, F. R., and Green, K. C. (1982). *The Enrollment Crisis: Factors, actors, and impacts.* Washington, DC: American Association for Higher Education.
Beal, P., and Noel, L. (1979). *What works in student retention.* Iowa City: American College Testing Program and the National Center for Higher Education Management Systems.

Behn, R. D. (1980). Leadership for cutback management: the use of corporate strategy. *Public Administration Review 40:* 613–620.

Belanger, C. H., and Tremblay, L. (1982). A methodological approach to selective cutbacks. *Canadian Journal of Higher Education 12* (3): 25–35.

Billing, R. S., Milburn, T. W., and Schaalman, M. L. (1980). A model of crisis perception: A theoretical and empirical analysis. *Administrative Science Quarterly 25:* 300–316.

Birnbaum, R. (1983). *Maintaining Diversity in Higher Education.* San Francisco: Jossey-Bass.

Boulding, K. E. (1975). The management of decline. *Change,* June: 8–9, 64.

Boulding, K. E. (1982). Irreducible uncertainties. *Society 20;* 11–17.

Bowen, F. M., and Glenny, L. A. (1980). *Uncertainty in public higher education: responses to stress at ten California colleges and universities.* Sacramento: California Postsecondary Education Commission.

Bowen, F. M., and Glenny, L. A. (1981). Institutional responses to financial stress: the California study. In L. L. Leslie and J. Hyatt (eds.), *Higher education financing policies: states/institutions and their interactions,* pp. 141-150. Tucson: Center for the Study of Higher Education.

Bowen, H. R. (1984). What's ahead for higher education? *Change,* April: 8–13.

Bozeman, B., and Slusher, E. A. (1979). Scarcity and environmental stress in public organizations: a conjectural essay. *Administration and Society 11:* 335–355.

Brantley, P. S., Miller, C. S., and McAlpine, T. (1979). To be or not to be—survival profiles of emerging institutions. *New Directions for Institutional Research 24:* 11–26.

Carnegie Council on Policy Studies in Higher Education. (1980). *Three thousand futures: the next twenty years for higher education.* San Francisco: Jossey-Bass.

Carter, E. A., and Blanton, J. C. (1983). Institutional management flexibility: a strategy for dealing with funding reductions. In R. A. Wilson (ed.), *Survival in the 1980s: quality, mission, and financing,* pp. 146-155. Tucson: Center for the Study of Higher Education.

Cartter, A. (1965). A new look at the supply of college teachers. *Educational Record 46:* 267–277.

Chaffee, E. E. (1982). *Case studies in college strategy.* Boulder, CO: National Center for Higher Education Management Systems.

Chaffee, E. E. (1984). Successful strategic management in small private colleges. *Journal of Higher Education 55:* 212–241.

Combs, C. D. (1982). Beyond cutback management: alternative responses to resource scarcity. Paper presented at the annual meeting of the Urban Affairs Association, Philadelphia.

Coser, L. (1956). *The functions of social conflict.* New York: Free Press.

Crossland, F. E. (1980). Learning to cope with a downward slope. *Change 12:* 18, 20–25.

Cyert, R. M. (1978). The management of universities of constant or decreasing size. *Public Administration Review 38:* 344–349.

Dallam, S., and Hoyt, D. P. (1983). Faculty and department head preferences for dealing with retrenchment demands. *Research in Higher Education 19:* 407–421.

Dresch, S. P. (1975). Educational saturation: a demographic-economic model. *AAUP Bulletin 61:* 239–247.

Dresch, S. P. (1977). Dynamics of growth and decline. *New Directions for Higher Education 19:* 17–31.

Dube, C. S., and Brown, A. W. (1983). Strategic assessment—a rational response to university cutbacks. *Long Range Planning 16:* 105–113.

Easton, A. (1976). *Managing for negative growth: a handbook for practitioners.* Reston, VA: Reston.

Ewell, P. T. (1984). *Conducting student retention studies.* Boulder, CO: National Center for Higher Education Management Systems.

Ewell, P. T. (1985). Recruitment, retention, and student flow: a comprehensive approach to enrollment management research. Paper presented at the annual meeting of the Association for Institutional Research, Portland, OR.

Ferris, G. R., Schellenberg, D. A., and Zammuto, R. F. (1984). Human resource management strategies in declining industries. *Human Resource Management 23:* 381–394.

Finkelstein, M., Farrar, D., and Pfnister, A. O. (1984). The adaptation of liberal arts colleges to the 1970s: an analysis of critical events. *Journal of Higher Education 55:* 242–268.

Ford, J. D. (1980). The occurrence of structural hystersis in declining organizations. *Academy of Management Review 5:* 589–598.

Frances, C. (1980). Apocalyptic vs. strategic planning. *Change* July/August: 19, 39–44.

Furniss, W. T. (1974). Retrenchment, layoff, and termination. *Educational Record 55* (3): 159–170.

Gray, J. A. (1981). Legal restraints on faculty cutbacks. In J. R. Mingle (ed.), *Challenges of retrenchment,* pp. 171–193. San Francisco: Jossey-Bass.

Hall, D. T., and Mansfield, R. (1971). Organizational and individual responses to external stress. *Administrative Science Quarterly 16:* 533–546.

Halstead, D. K. (1980). Higher education prices and price indexes: 1980 update. *Business Officer 14* (Oct.): 17–20.

Hamblin, R. L. (1958a). Group integration during crisis. *Human Relations 11:* 67–76.

Hamblin, R. L. (1958b). Leadership and crisis. *Sociometry 21:* 322–335.

Hamermesh, R. G. (1977). Responding to divisional profit crises. *Harvard Business Review* (March–Apr.): 124–130.

Hardy, C. (1983a). Is strategy-making a political process? The example of retrenchment. Unpublished manuscript, McGill University, Montreal.

Hardy, C. (1983b). Managing retrenchment: the human resource element. In M. C. Baetz (ed.), *Proceedings of the Annual Conference of the Administrative Science Association of Canada 4* (6): 45–58.

Hermann, C. F. (1963). Some consequences of crisis which limit the viability of organizations. *Administrative Science Quarterly 8:* 61–82.

Heydinger, R. B. (1983). *Using program priorities to make retrenchment decisions: the case of the University of Minnesota.* Atlanta: Southern Regional Education Board.

Hirschman, A. O. (1970). *Exit, voice and loyalty.* Cambridge: Harvard University Press.

Hodgkinson, H. L. (1983). *Guess who's coming to college: your students in 1990.* Washington, DC: National Institute of Independent Colleges and Universities.

Holsti, O. R. (1978). Limitations of cognitive abilities in the face of crisis. In C. F. Smart and W. T. Stanbury (eds.), *Studies of crisis management,* pp. 39–55. Toronto: Butterworth.

Hossler, D. (1984). *Enrollment management: an integrated approach.* New York: College Entrance Examination Board.

Hyatt, J. A., Shulman, C. H., and Santiago, A. A. (1984). *Reallocation: strategies for effective resource management.* Washington, DC: National Association of College and University Business Officers.

Iannacone, L. (1979). The management of decline: implications of our knowledge in the politics of education. *Education and Urban Society 11:* 418–430.

Ishler, R. E. (1981). Academic planning model for a declining enrollment: a model for institutions of higher education. *Capstone Journal of Education 2* (1): 51–57.

Jick, T. D., and Murray, V. V. (1982). The management of hard times: budget cutbacks in public sector organizations. *Organization Studies 3:* 141–169.

Jonsen, R. W. (1984). Small colleges cope with the eighties: sharp eye on the horizon, strong hand on the tiller. *Journal of Higher Education 55:* 171–183.

Jonsson, S. A., and Lundin, R. A. (1977). Myths and wishful thinking as management tools. P. C. Nystrom and W. H. Starbuck (eds.), *Prescriptive models of organizations,* pp. 157–170. New York: North Holland.

Kerchner, C. T., and Schuster, J. H. (1982). The uses of crisis: taking the tide at the flood. *Review of Higher Education 5* (3): 121–141.

Khandwalla, P. N. (1978). Crisis responses of competing versus noncompeting organizations. In C. F. Smart and W. T. Vertinsky (eds.), *Studies on crisis management,* pp. 151–178. Toronto: Butterworth.

Kolarska, L., and Aldrich, H. (1980). Exit, voice, and silence: consumers' and managers' responses to organizational decline. *Organization Studies 1:* 41–58.

Krakower, J. Y., and Zammuto, R. F. (1983). *A report on the retrenchment activities of colleges and universities.* Boulder, CO: National Center for Higher Education Systems.

Krakower, J. Y. and Zammuto, R. F. (in press). Enrollment projections: The case against generalizations. *Review of Higher Education.*

Leslie, L. L. (1984). Changing patterns in student financing of higher education. *Journal of Higher Education 55:* 313–346.

Leslie, L. L., and Miller, H. F. (1974). *Higher education and the steady state.* Washington, DC: American Association for Higher Education.

Levine, C. H. (1978). Organizational decline and cutback management. *Public Administration Review 38:* 316–325.

Levine, C. H. (1979). More on cutback management: hard questions for hard times. *Public Administration Review 39:* 179–183.

McKinley, W., Cheng, J., and Schick, A. (in press). Perceptions of resource criticality in times of resource scarcity: the case of university departments. *Academy of Management Journal.*

Milson, A., O'Rourke, A. R., Richardson, G. A., and Rose, H. F. A. (1983). Strategies for managing resources in a declining resource situation. *Higher Education 12:* 133–144.

Mingle, J. R. (1982). *Redirecting higher education in a time of budget reduction* (Issues in Higher Education Report No. 18). Atlanta: Southern Regional Education Board.

Mingle, J. R., and Norris, D. M. (1981). Institutional strategies for responding to decline. In J. R. Mingle, (ed.), *Challenges of retrenchment,* pp. 47–68. San Francisco: Jossey-Bass.

Morgan, A. W. (1982). College and university planning in an era of contraction. *Higher Education 11:* 553–566.

Mortimer, K. P. (1981). Procedures and criteria for faculty retrenchment. In J. R. Mingle (ed.), *Challenges of retrenchment,* pp. 153–170. San Francisco: Jossey-Bass.

Mortimer, K. P., and McConnell, T. R. (1978). *Sharing authority effectively.* San Francisco: Jossey-Bass.

Mortimer, K. P., and Taylor, B. E. (1984). Budgeting strategies under conditions of decline. Unpublished manuscript, Pennsylvania State University.

Mortimer, K. P., and Tierney, M. L. (1979). *The three "R's" of the eighties: reduction, reallocation, and retrenchment.* Washington, DC: American Association for Higher Education.

O'Neill, J. P., and Grier, P. M. (1984). *Financing in a period of retrenchment: A primer for small colleges.* Washington, DC: National Association of College and University Attorneys.

Peck, R. D. (1984). Entrepreneurship as a significant factor in successful adaptation. *Journal of Higher Education 55:* 269–285.

Pfeffer, J., and Salancik, G. R. (1974). Organizational decision making as a political process. *Administrative Science Quarterly 19:* 135–151.

Pfnister, A. O., Finkelstein, M., Gordon, W., and Farrar, D. (1982). Change and continuity in the undergraduate college: adaptation and its consequences. Paper presented at the annual meeting of the Association for the Study of Higher Education, Washington, DC.

Rubin, I. (1977). Universities in stress: decision making under conditions of reduced resources. *Social Science Quarterly 58:* 242–254.

Rubin, I. (1979). Retrenchment, loose structure and adaptability in the university. *Sociology of Education 52:* 211–222.

Rusk, J. J., Leslie, L. L., and Brinkman, P. T. (1982). The increasing impact of economic conditions upon higher education enrollments. *Economics of Education Review 2:* 25–48.

Salancik, G. R., and Pfeffer, J. (1974). The bases and use of power in organizational decision making: the case of a university. *Administrative Science Quarterly 19:* 453–473.

Saunders, M. K. (1984). Legal issues in terminating tenured faculty members because of financial exigency. *Educational Record 65:* 12–17.

Schendel, D. E., and Patton, G. R. (1976). Corporate stagnation and turnaround. *Journal of Economics and Business 28:* 236–241.

Scott, W. A. (1976). The management of decline. *Conference Board Record 13:* 56–59.

Shirley, R. C., and Volkwein, J. F. (1978). Establishing academic program priorities. *Journal of Higher Education 49:* 472–488.

Smart, C. F., and Vertinsky, I. (1977). Designs for crisis decision units. *Administrative Science Quarterly 22:* 640–657.

Starbuck, W. H., Greve, A., and Hedberg, B. L. T. (1978). Responding to crisis. *Journal of Business Administration 9:* 111–137.

Staw, B. M., Sandelands, L. E., and Dutton, J. E. (1981). Threat-rigidity effects in organizational behavior: a multilevel analysis. *Administrative Science Quarterly 26:* 501–524.

Strohm, P. (1981). Faculty responsibilities and rights during retrenchment. In J. R. Mingle (ed.), *Challenges of retrenchment,* pp. 134–152. San Francisco: Jossey-Bass.

Turner, B. A. (1976). The organization and interorganizational development of disasters. *Administrative Science Quarterly 21:* 378–397.

Volkwein, J. F. (1984). Responding to financial retrenchment: lessons from the Albany experience. *Journal of Higher Education 55:* 398–401.

Walker, W. E., and Chaiken, J. M. (1982). The effects of fiscal contraction on innovation in the public sector. *Policy Sciences 15:* 141–165.

Whetten, D. A. (1980a). Organizational decline: a neglected topic in organizational science. *Academy of Management Review 5:* 577–588.

Whetten, D. A. (1980b). Sources, responses, and effects of organizational decline. In J. Kimberly and R. Miles (eds.), *The organizational life cycle,* pp. 342–374. San Francisco: Jossey-Bass.

Whetten, D. A. (1981). Organizational responses to scarcity: exploring the obstacles to innovative approaches to retrenchment in education. *Educational Administration Quarterly 17* (Summer): 80–97.

Yarmolinsky, A. (1975). Institutional paralysis. *Daedalus* (Winter): 61–67.

Zammuto, R. F. (1982a). Growth, stability, and decline in American college and university enrollments. *Educational Administration Quarterly 19* (1): 83–99.

Zammuto, R. F. (1982b). Organizational decline and management education. *EXCHANGE: The Organizational Behavior Teaching Journal 7* (3): 5–12.

Zammuto, R. F. (1983). Three propositions on growth and decline in organizational populations. *Proceedings of the 43rd Annual Meeting of the Academy of Management,* pp. 271–275.

Zammuto, R. F. (1984). Are the liberal arts an endangered species? *Journal of Higher Education 55:* 184–211.

Zammuto, R. F. (1985). Managing decline: lessons from the U.S. auto industry. *Administration and Society 17:* 71–95.

Zammuto, R. F., and Cameron, K. S. (1985). Environmental decline and organizational response. *Research in Organizational Behavior 7:* 223–262.

Zammuto, R. F., Whetten, D. A., and Cameron, K. S. (1983). Environmental change, enrollment decline and institutional response. *Peabody Journal of Education 60* (2): 93–107.

Zemsky, R., and Oedel, P. (1983). *The structure of college choice.* New York: College Entrance Examination Board.

THE IMPORTANCE OF BEING GENERAL:
Philosophy, Politics, and Institutional Mission Statements

Gordon K. Davies
State Council of Higher Education for Virginia

The generative thesis of this essay is that college and university mission statements are usually shaped by a kind of garden-variety philosophical idealism. Institutions appear to argue that their mission is to become as much like some general idea, or ideal form, as they possibly can (Hodgkinson, 1971). For some, this ideal form is the comprehensive community college; for others, the regional state university or comprehensive research university. For some, it is Harvard. For almost all, the logic of the argument proceeds from an identification of the characteristics of the ideal form (for instance, the regional state university) to an identification of the disparities between that form and the institution itself ("A regional state university offers an MBA, and we do not") to a programmatic or financial justification of some sort ("Therefore, we should be permitted to offer an MBA").

This is the generative thesis, and I still think it is valid. But as I looked through the master plans of several states, I realized that most of them do not define institutional missions precisely, and that the garden-variety idealism that I had come to suspect is the basis of most mission statements certainly is not articulated in any detail. Even the small body of higher education literature that talks about mission does not, with few exceptions, recognize the actual imprecision of mission statements and the unexamined presuppositions upon which they are grounded.

Veysey (1965) wrote about the failure of the leaders of American higher education at the turn of the century to articulate the "most fundamental assumptions" upon which they acted. He concluded that the shape of the modern university was determined by men who "almost always evaded . . . deliberate debate" about key issues and choices. Perhaps they sensed that it was easier to get forgiveness than to get permission and so never said what they were about. The result is a pair of disjunctions: between the literature and actual practice, and between mission statements and activities.

So the operative thesis of this essay is different from the generative. It is that there are very good reasons not to define institutional missions, especially within state-supported systems of higher education. It is safer to talk about missions than to define them, politically more astute to avoid the confrontations that would be inevitable if mission statements were to be made more precise than they usually are.

The higher education literature about institutional mission often recognizes the dangers implicit in trying to be "everything to everybody" but does not offer much practical help in setting precise mission statements. Lenning and Micek (1976) worked with a standard hierarchy of mission, goals, and objectives, defining an institution's mission as a "statement of its enduring purpose or aspiration." They recognize that such mission statements are couched in "broad, vague, 'high sounding' and often intentionally inconsistent terms" but nonetheless maintain a standard conception of their place as general statements from which concrete objectives are deduced.

Schwerin (1980) argued that an institutional mission should not be changed by retrenchment or financial exigency, although "the approaches to its accomplishment must." Carruthers and Lott (1981) treated the subject more extensively, starting with the assertion that the "assumption that an organization understands its mission is embedded in . . . systems approaches to planning and management." They recognized an important distinction between the *current* and the *desired* missions of an institution, stating that the current mission statement describes what an "institution does (or can reasonably expect to do)."

American higher education has experienced several decades of rapid growth, most of it unplanned and certainly uncoordinated among institutions within each of the states. There has been an enormous commitment to increasing the capacities of colleges and universities, and to extending access to all who want to participate in postsecondary education. The GI Bill was a critical component of the social programs that enabled this country to return to a peacetime economy after World War II. It channeled veterans into colleges and universities, providing them education as an alternative to work while the economy shifted gears. The role of higher education as a major agent of social change became firmly established.

Education, including higher education, is not only an effective agent of social change, but also a relatively inexpensive benefit to provide. Drawing an analogy with the right to vote, the federal government and the states expanded the concept of accessibility beyond the GI Bill to include a universal educational franchise. The dramatic increases in higher education enrollment that occurred between 1960 and 1980 are the result of this commitment.

There has been a price to pay, of course. Open access means less selectivity within higher education as a whole, and wide variations in the standards of admission, performance, and graduation. On balance, it has probably been worth the price, but higher education could have been better prepared for the reaction that now has set in. The pressures for school reform have reached higher education, and those who speak for higher education are now being asked to account for the quality of the student learning that occurs in their institutions (for instance, *Involvement in Learning,* 1984, and *Integrity in the Curriculum,* 1985).

Higher education's leaders could have been better prepared for the reaction, but it was probably inevitable they would not be. Habits have been developed over the years, and patterns of relationships have been established between the resources to acquired build and operate institutions and constantly increasing enrollment. Little attention has been paid either to cost control or to quality control. A hiring mistake could be absorbed as the next cohort of students brought with it new faculty positions. Rather than constructing the buildings and then accepting the students, leaders learned that if they accepted the students, the buildings would follow. Resources chased enrollment, up to a point.

George Eliot observed in *Middlemarch* (1901) that "all of us, grave or light, get our thoughts entangled in our metaphors, and act fatally on the strength of them." So it is in higher education, whose leaders are trapped in the *building* metaphor while the demands placed upon them are changing quickly. Other metaphors, implying adaptive failure, have been applied to higher education with good reason (for instance, the dinosaur and, more optimistically, the railroads). With some few exceptions, there have been no clear statements of intent to govern the growth that has occurred in higher education during the last 25 years. There are several reasons for this.

First, it is easy to say "yes" and hard to say "no." As institutions grew, various interest groups presented their requests for inclusion: law schools, veterinary schools, football teams, teaching hospitals, dormitories, and occupational programs of various sorts. Every request that is rejected diminishes the pool of support—the support of the president by the faculty, of the institution by the community, or of the entire system by those who assign priorities to statewide operations. It is not only easier to say "yes," it may be unwise to say "no."

Second, to be something is not to be something else. The more precisely an institution's plans for growth are specified, the less latitude it has to respond to unanticipated opportunities. In addition, precise definition requires those who lead institutions to say "no" far more often than they would like.

Finally, only a very few colleges and universities can aspire to national or international recognition. In fact, relatively few can aspire to regional or even statewide standing. The primary function of most institutions is to provide adequate higher education to average people. As the preamble to a master plan for growth, recognition of this harsh reality will not do. The president who comes to his or her board with a proposal that the college or university is what it does will more than likely be sent off on the next train.

While there have been few clear statements of intent to govern the recent growth of American higher education, most states have attempted to control duplication of programs and services within their systems of state-supported colleges and universities. To some degree, they have typed and stratified their institutions: major research universities, other doctorate-granting universities, regional state universities, community colleges, and so on. They have been careful to say that quality is a function of mission and that all missions are equally important, thereby avoiding the unpleasant consequences of formally acknowledging a hierarchy of value or of quality. "The phrase 'differing roles' does not imply better or worse, or more important or less important roles" (*Complete Issue Papers of the Governor's Commission on Higher Education in Michigan,* 1984). But like the animals in Orwell's barnyard, some institutions are more equal than others. The stratification of institutions is held in place by differential funding in the state budget. It is affirmed by inaction rather than by action.

In this way, a curious kind of oblique planning technique has developed at the state level. It is highly political, indirect, and situational. It aims at doing what is possible at any given time and does not attempt to provide a complete set of goals or strategies for public debate. It uses whatever tools are available to move the institution or system toward an objective, but it often does not acknowledge the objective itself.

The dishonesty of this oblique planning is a result of its not being confrontational. Institutional leaders are allowed to say whatever they want, to claim whatever mission or manifest destiny appeals to their various constituencies, without challenge. But not having disagreed is different from having agreed, and state leaders provide money for the missions they want, disregarding the institutional rhetoric.

The tradition of institutional autonomy, whether honored in deed or merely in word, and the political power of institutional constituencies (alumni, regional and commercial interests, students, and faculty) make the price of precision about mission very high for governors, legislators, state governing or coordinating boards, and sometimes even for institutional leaders.

The scholarly literature about mission is dissociated from practice primarily because, except for the theorists, it is to no one's interest that missions be defined clearly. Institutions do not appear to engage in rigorous definition of their missions because the prevailing incentives are to do otherwise. The recruiting slogan of the U.S. Army, "Be all that you can be," is parodied in higher education as "Get all that you can get." Do not get boxed in; remain flexible and alert to every opportunity.

This is not bad management. In some ways, indeed, it is rather good management, given the incentives that condition behavior in higher education. Bowen (1980) wrote a set of "laws" about the costs of higher education:

1. The dominant goals of institutions are educational excellence, prestige, and influence.
2. In quest of excellence, prestige, and influence, there is virtually no limit to the amount of money an institution could spend for seemingly fruitful educational ends.
3. Each institution raises all the money it can.
4. Each institution spends all it raises.
5. The cumulative effect of the preceding four laws is toward ever-increasing expenditure.

To these rules can be added one more about mission: No statement of institutional mission should ever limit access to resources.

All of this gives rise to generic mission statements that are, like generic canned goods, bland and of uncertain reliability. A women's college that had originally been a normal school and offered most of its degrees in education became a coeducational college of arts and sciences with heavy business administration enrollments—but claimed that its mission had not changed. Indeed, because its mission was so generally stated ("to provide the best possible educational opportunities and services to the people of the Commonwealth" and so on), the college's representatives were quite right. It is difficult to imagine a change of programs or clientele that could not have been included under the generic mission statement of the institution. But it is today a remarkably different place, and not just because its lavatories have urinals.

Another institution was one among several on both coasts that competed vigorously to become the unofficial naval academy of another nation. Under the terms of the contract, between 500 and 1,000 foreign nationals would have enrolled in engineering curricula at the university, would have lived together in facilities constructed by the foreign government, and would have received ancillary military training while enrolled. Fortunately, the contract was never awarded because the foreign government fell from power. But the university bidding for it claimed that its mission would not change—even if it became the naval academy of another nation! Chait's trenchant observations (1979) about the generic mission statement are right on target:

> The more one seeks specificity, the more various constituencies resist. In the end, vague and vapid goals able to attract consensus are preferable to precise aims that force choices and provoke serious disagreements. Who cannot rally around "the pursuit of excellence" or "the discovery and transmission of knowledge?" Hence, the look-alike statements.

Not only is practice dissociated from theory, but institutional practice is dissociated from state policy. The planning that goes on in colleges and universities is often neither acknowledged nor endorsed by those responsible for the system of state-supported higher education. Carruthers and Lott (1981) suggested that insecure state coordinating or governing boards tend to avoid the confrontations that are almost inevitable if the state board responds to institutional mission claims. But the conditions that lead to avoidance of confrontation are more systemic and are not confined to states whose boards are uncertain of their strength and political support.

While cautioning that an institution should "try to describe itself rather than mirror some abstract model," Carruthers and Lott (1981) defined mission in terms of the past and the future: "A statement of mission should report what the institution has been (its past), what it shall become (its destiny), and what it does not believe itself to be." Their use of the word *destiny* is not casual. It introduces an element of value that the neutral word *future* would not convey, giving the discussion of mission a greater emotional charge.

Organizational theorists tend to argue that clearly defined missions are essential to the well-being of institutions: "Only a clear definition of the mission and purpose of the business makes possible clear and realistic business objectives" (Drucker, 1973). Without firm goals, wrote Perrow (1970), "organizations are subject to vagrant pressures from within and without, even as they may grow and prosper. . . . While this gives the institution flexibility, it also provides few resources for unusual effort of a concerted kind."

There are, nonetheless, good reasons that institutional leaders choose not to be clear about the mission of colleges and universities. Conrad (1974) pointed out that "in most universities, goals are often implicit, residing in an extended body of collective understandings rather than explicit statements." Such explicit statements as may be contained in recruiting, fund-raising, or other promotional materials may bear little resemblance to what an institution actually does and, therefore, is.

Richardson and Doucette (1984) proposed an empirical approach to mission development. They started from the assertion that the abstractions in which missions are normally couched cannot be translated into concrete terms (p. 1). In terms of the standard hierarchy, they saw no good way to derive highly specific objectives from the standard kind of missions. "Missions," they wrote, "are the expectations that external constituencies have for colleges and universities . . . thus missions exist at the interface between an institution and its environment." Goals, the next step in the hierarchy, "are the aspirations that a college or university has for itself."

Richardson and Doucette concluded that there is no reliable link between general statements of purpose and future and "precise, behaviorably measurable" objectives. They proposed, therefore, that mission definition start with analysis of institutional activities and clientele. A community college, they suggested, can use a survey of its service area population to set operational priorities and funding levels for its various activities. This approach will yield a statement of mission that will differ markedly from those generally proposed in the literature about community colleges.

Whether or not Richardson and Doucette were correct in their judgment that the concrete cannot be derived from the abstract, their proposal avoids the "generic mission" trap. The strength of the empirical mission is that it describes the activities of a college: what it does, where, and for whom. The potential weakness of their approach, if it is applied slavishly, is that the governing body of the college would set a mission based solely on a survey of what its service population wants to support.

Mission statements are used differently by college and university leaders and by state planners and policymakers. The uses all are legitimate, given the incentives that shape higher education, but they are not necessarily compatible.

A university president uses the mission statement to inspire and motivate the constituencies that are vital to the institution. She or he uses it to direct effort toward whatever objectives can be achieved at the moment, and to engender feelings of potential within the academic community and beyond it. It is a sales and public relations tool.

It also is a bludgeon to be used within the institution, by it, or, occasionally, on it. If an institution says that a major part of its mission is to develop programs that support technologically sophisticated industries, for instance, the mission can be used by the board and the administration to justify favorable resource allocations to the engineering and scientific departments at the expense of the arts and sciences. The mission can also be used to pummel state leaders who may be reluctant to allocate as much money as the institution wants.

Conversely, state planners and policymakers can use the same mission as a reason not to permit academic program developments outside engineering and science. They can measure enrollment, degrees conferred, research volume, and space use to ensure that the university does what it claims to do. They can adjust funding based on performance measured against mission.

State governing or coordinating boards sometimes publish institutional statements of mission without endorsement. The preface to Alabama's *Institutional Profiles* (1985) states that the "sections on mission were written by the institutions and were left largely as submitted." Virginia's state plan for higher education, which is revised every two years, includes statements of institutional *aspiration* without endorsement, clearly differentiating them from *mission:*

> The state-supported mission description (of each institution) is followed by a brief statement of institutional aspiration. The Council does not necessarily endorse the aspirations described, but includes them . . . to indicate how an institution hopes to develop in the future. [*The Virginia Plan for Higher Education,* 1983]

The second law of thermodynamics, the law of entropy, applies to colleges and universities when they are left entirely to themselves: They will gradually become more and more alike and so, of course, will their mission statements. This is true in part because, within their respective groups, all aspire to replicate the same ideal form. It is also true because they are being compared with one another—and are comparing themselves with one another—constantly. Whatever one gets, all want, and the generic mission statement allows ample latitude for the degradation of all into sameness.

Hodgkinson (1971) found that insofar as institutions have changed since 1940, they have become more alike:

> Taken as a whole, the amount of institutional diversity in American higher education is decreasing. This is due partially to the existence of a single status system in higher education based on the prestigious university offering many graduate programs and preoccupied with research. There are few alternative models to this system now functioning.

In its report on the baccalaureate degree, *Integrity in the Curriculum* (1985), the Association of American Colleges charges that "the graduate school model, with its single-minded focus on the preparation for research, serves as the standard by which colleges and universities everywhere judge themselves."

In his commentary on Hodgkinson's study, Heywood described the situation more picturesquely. The "model of the great universities permeates many of the thousands of other institutions, and it is no idle statement to say that there is a pecking order based on this model where the compacts strive to be family cars, the family cars to be deluxe models, and the deluxe to be Cadillacs" (Hodgkinson, 1971).

Birnbaum (1983) warned against state controls that reduce diversity among institutions, citing line-item budgeting, program approval procedures, and master planning as particularly offensive. But Birnbaum's thought is entangled in the metaphor of evolutionary natural selection, and he argues for survival in the marketplace as the best way to ensure diversity. What works very well in biology to explain the adaptive behavior of organisms does not apply to the future of colleges and universities. Using the evolution metaphor to explain the development of social institutions is no more valid than using the intestines of birds to predict the fall of cities.

While calling for "mandated limits upon enrollment" and "limitations upon program offerings, or some other management device" to "prevent the stronger from driving out the weaker," Birnbaum did not acknowledge that state governing or coordinating agencies take precisely these actions in order to prevent institutions from copying one another or some common ideal of a "university."

State system boards and those responsible for the state budget apparatus have a critical responsibility to impede the progress of this natural law as it applies to colleges and universities. This is not easy and, for reasons already discussed, is usually done indirectly. Differentiation among institutions is maintained primarily by setting enrollment caps, preferably by course level and by discipline; by resisting attempts to duplicate programs; by providing facilities based on the curriculum; by setting tuition and fee collections based on the distribution of students between in-state and out-of-state, and between undergraduate and graduate levels; and by using budget guidelines that produce different funding per full-time equivalent student at each institution.

Enrollment caps need not be rigid in order to be effective. They can be set only for the budget-planning period of one or two years and can then be revised as the next planning period begins. It is important, however, to disaggregate the enrollment and to approve its component parts: by residence, by discipline and course level, and by part-time or full-time status. In this way, shifts toward the fad of the year and toward greater uniformity can be impeded.

Program duplication is the most visible sign that the law of entropy is at work, and the most intimidating to governors and legislators. The ideology of access has led institutions and their patrons to expect that virtually every academic program should be offered within commuting distance in each region of the state. Against the pressures that result from this expectation, state boards often can only stall, delaying the inevitable on the chance that something—a state budget crisis, for instance—will cause the pressure to subside. Elected officials may be intimidated by unnecessary duplication and the waste it causes, but they are successful because they say "yes" far more often than they say "no." They need the maneuvering room that imprecision about institutional mission provides, and few can afford to say "never" on any particular issue. So the drift toward curricular sameness is inexorable, a process that can be controlled to some extent but not halted.

Ironically, academic degree program approval is an effort to control curricular development at too high a level of aggregation. A degree program consists of courses in several disciplines, and the costs of instruction are incurred by offering the courses. Except in the professional programs, courses in these disciplines will probably be offered in the curriculum even if the degree program is not approved. Few state boards exercise central approval of the courses, and therefore the allocation of instructional costs is not usually controlled by program decisions. If the degree program in Tasmanian archaeology is not approved, but most of the courses that would constitute the program are taught anyway as cognate or support courses in other programs, cost allocation is unaffected and duplication creeps on.

The alternatives to degree program approval are not likely to be acceptable to institutional leaders. They include approval to offer instruction by discipline and approval to employ faculty by areas of specialization. Both are dangerous for obvious reasons having to do with freedom of speech and inquiry, not to mention the endless debates that would occur over what is part of a curricular core and therefore necessarily duplicated at every college or university.

Another approach is to profile the curricular mix of an institution, by discipline and level of instruction, and to approve or disapprove proposals to make significant changes in the profile. The definition of *significant* is, of course, the key here. But definitions, perhaps varying by type of institution or by discipline, could be negotiated. Such negotiation is far more neutral politically than either course or faculty member approval, far less dangerous to constitutional rights, and potentially far more useful than program approval.

Finally, differentiation among institutions is best maintained by affecting the funds to which each has access. Institutions cannot do what they cannot pay for. Without a direct confrontation of the issues, funding decisions are used to control institutional mission.

Different mixes of graduate and undergraduate students, and of in-state and out-of-state residents, usually characterize different kinds of institutions. These mixes can be used to produce different tuition and fee revenues among institutions, either by the setting of specific rates or by the establishment of an aggregate amount of revenue that each institution is expected to produce from tuition and fees.

Different collection-maintenance guidelines for research libraries and staffing guidelines for sponsored research volumes and for instruction at different levels and in different disciplines will combine to produce a unique profile for each institution. Faculty salary averages that are based on comparisons with other institutions across the nation that are quantitatively and qualitatively similar to each college or university in a system will produce further differentiation. Even if every one of these factors is negotiated and compromised to some extent, they will impede the process of entropy.

Institutions respond to all of these impediments in different ways, depending on the political tools at their disposal. They usually display a herd individualism, however, each claiming for the same reasons that it is unique among the others. But *unique* tends to mean that the institution badly wants or needs more money, programs, space, or whatever. Again, perceptions will differ depending on what is happening to or for whom. A major research university, the system flagship, to use a distasteful phrase, sees other institutions acquiring more of a limited pool of resources and decries "homogenization" within the system. A regional state university argues that its growth and acquisition of more resources is equitable recognition of its region's needs and contributions to the state's economy. It decries as favoritism and elitism any rejection of its proposals for growth or development. Both are right to some degree. The trick is to keep anyone from being entirely right or entirely wrong.

The late-medieval philosopher William of Ockham is credited, probably apocryphally, with stating the principle of economy that philosophers since have known as *Ockham's razor*: plurality ought not to be postulated without necessity. State officials apply Ockham's razor whenever and wherever they can. But carefully, because razors are sharp.

The incentives to which college and university managers respond often do not encourage behavior that inhibits entropy and increases institutional effectiveness. Budget guidelines that are tied entirely to enrollment size and that favor awarding graduate degrees encourage institutions to mindless pursuit of growth and escalation to graduate degree-granting status. Accounting procedures that require reversion of year-end balances to the general fund encourage wasteful use of funds. If funds are reverted, the expenditure base for the next budget is diminished, so purchases that may not have high priority are made. It is not possible to accumulate funds over several years for a major equipment acquisition, so equipment needs increase even as all the money is being spent.

Systems that discourage risk and provide no rewards for successful innovation may produce strident rhetoric but probably will not produce risk taking and innovation. It simply is safer for each institution to be like all the others, although every one claims that it is unique. We encourage herd behavior even as we decry it and seek to preserve differentiation among colleges and universities.

Institutional mission statements tend to focus on aspirations: on what institutional leaders want the college or university to become, as opposed to what it is now. This generalization is probably less true of flagship universities than of other institutions. But if every other institution justifies its funding by its aspirations, the flagships are forced to do the same.

In actual operation, institutional aspirations derive from several possible sources. They may reflect a desire to make a university more like the ones that faculty came from as graduate students or young teachers. They may reflect a desire to be more like the other institutions in the system or more like the flagship. They may reflect a desire to become whatever is possible under the circumstances. In the best situations, of course, aspirations derive from a careful assessment of social, educational, and institutional needs, and of the resources that might be available to meet them. They are precise statements of objectives that can be achieved, given certain levels of financial and other support.

In reflecting on what causes events to happen, Aristotle and other philosophers have used the concept of teleology: All things progress toward an end, a fulfillment of their essence. The *cause* of an acorn's becoming an oak tree seems fundamentally different from the *cause* of a billiard ball's rolling across a table. The one appears to be drawn toward a natural end, while the other is struck and pushed into motion. Philosophers who do metaphysics in the tradition of Aristotle (or Plato) hold that there are several different kinds of causality, one of the most subtle being final, or teleological, causality: "to become an oak tree" is the cause of an acorn's growth.

Whether the notion of final causes is attractive because it satisfies our need to feel that we are going somewhere, that we have a purpose, or because it seems to fit organic growth so well, it has found its way into popular thought in a casual, garden-variety form. When it is applied to social institutions, problems arise.

The organic metaphor of natural growth implies that if I cut down an oak sapling, I have interrupted a natural process. Applied to an institution like a university, the metaphor implies the same thing: to impede its development is to violate some kind of natural law. What might otherwise be reasonably sane public-policy debates about how human effort is to be organized and social resources are to be expended take on peculiar, highly charged moral overtones.

Second, the organic metaphor takes on some of the baggage of "manifest destiny" when it is applied to institutions, especially to institutions that enjoy a fair amount of political support. Disagreements over institutional mission then become even more emotionally charged, because development is a matter of high purpose rather than simply a matter of growth. (Recall how Curruthers and Lott, 1981, used the word *destiny* rather than *future* in their definition of mission). Only the strongest oak trees survive, and those that do have a right to their place in the sun.

Missions that describe aspirations, that are statements of what institutions will become, are not useful in resource allocation. They are, however, powerful weapons in arguing for more money. The high ground belongs to those who plead that their institutions be funded for what they are becoming rather than for what they are. They are looking to the future, are optimists and progressives, while the proponents of funding what is are at best reactionaries and at worst blocks, stones, and worse than senseless things.

Disputes over college and university aspirations are inevitable, and they are not particularly rational because they rarely connect with reality. They are often decided by political strength, which is as good a way as any other to decide sandbox arguments that have no basis in fact. Fenske (1980) concluded that "all attempts to mediate effectiveness goals and efficiency objectives have ended up relying upon an interface that is essentially a political process."

Aspirations are not verifiable, even in principle. That is to say, nothing counts toward their being true or false. If I say, "It is raining," you can determine whether I have told the truth by putting your hand out the window. If I say "It is raining in China," you cannot verify my assertion in fact (assuming you are not in China), but you know that in principle my assertion can be verified. Therefore it is a sensible thing to say, even though it may be wrong.

But there is no way to verify a statement of aspiration such as "This university will be one of the top 50 research universities in the nation." Nothing in the present counts for or against it. If the university does not show progress toward becoming a major research institution, it is because the state did not provide it with the resources it requested. The only kind of verification that is possible will come at some future date when the aspirations have or have not been achieved. But if they have not, they are not invalidated. The argument simply shifts gears and goes on.

Flew (1955) tells a parable about two explorers who come upon a neat, patterned clearing in a dense forest. One explorer concludes that the clearing is a remarkable accident, a chance occurrence with no intervention. But the other concludes that the clearing is under the care of a mysterious gardener who comes through the forest to tend it. They wait, but no gardener appears. The one takes this fact as proof that there is no gardener, but the other suggests that the gardener comes only at night and drops into the clearing from the trees overhead. So they cover the clearing with netting and keep watch day and night. Still no gardener appears.

The first explorer takes this fact as proof positive that the clearing is a natural phenomenon, but the other maintains that there must be a gardener. He suggests that the gardener is invisible and incorporeal. No evidence will count against his belief that the clearing is tended.

So it is with statements of institutional aspiration: nothing counts against them. They can be judged realistic or unrealistic, but not true or false, because they are not statements of fact.

This is not to say that they are nonsense statements. Much, probably most, of what we say cannot be verified by an act as simple as sticking a hand out the window. But because such statements are not factual or based on fact, arguments about them are highly charged, politically and personally. They require clarification of values that is extremely dangerous in a political setting. It is little wonder that institutional mission statements based on aspiration are not used in higher education systems' planning and administration.

The Virginia Council of Higher Education has had an unusual experience in dealing with mission change within the state-supported system of higher education. A major legislative study of higher education governance in 1974 concluded that the principle of institutional autonomy should be prescribed, and that each senior college and university should have its own governing board. The system of community colleges, on the other hand, would continue to be governed by a single sector board. The coordinating agency was assigned additional responsibilities and authority.

Because the missions of Virginia's colleges and universities had been set by the legislature and by traditions dating back to the seventeenth century, the Council was assigned responsibility to establish missions only for institutions created after 1974. It was, however, assigned responsibility to approve changes in the mission of any college or university in the state-supported system.

Several years passed during which the statutory provision regarding mission change was hardly noticed. (The incidents of the women's college becoming coeducational and the university's bidding to become a foreign nation's naval academy had occurred just before the new provisions were adopted.) The system grew rapidly, with increased enrollment at several institutions, many new academic programs approved, and almost as many discontinued. One university was authorized to offer doctoral degrees, and one college to offer master's degrees. The Council of Higher Education conducted its business using several broad guidelines to determine which institutions should be permitted to expand their offerings and in what fields expansion should be permitted. It yielded ground slowly to expansion, mindful of the possibility that the system of higher education would be overbuilt once the enrollment wave of the 1960s and 1970s had passed. On occasion, the Council disapproved major expansions in professional programs, particularly law, engineering, and veterinary medicine. It was overruled by the legislature on the establishment of a third state-supported law school and withdrew its objections to a college of veterinary medicine when Maryland agreed to join with Virginia in operating a single school. It continues to be nibbled at in engineering.

Then, during a review of the Council's statutory responsibilities, a member asked how we knew when an institution's mission changed. This question set off a string of discussions that resulted in an empirical conception of mission.

Without a point of reference, we cannot tell when change occurs. This is true of natural phenomena such as the movement of the stars and planets, and it is also true of our sensations: sound, taste, sight, and so on. In the same way, we cannot know that a mission has changed unless we know what the mission of the institution was in the first place. We need a point of reference.

We also need some verifiable criteria by which change is measured, or there will be continual disagreement about our judgments. I can measure the movement of a ship on the horizon by reference to the points of a compass, or the growth of a child by pencil marks on the wall, and there will be no significant quarrels with the results. But if someone says, "Things were better when we were young," there is no way to verify her assertion. I can agree or not, or I can understand the assertion as an expression of the speaker's disposition toward the world rather than as a statement about the world itself. Then I call to mind the old man who once observed that "Things aren't the way they used to be—and they never were."

The point of reference for an institutional mission is an explication of that mission at any given point in time. If we know what Harvard was in 1956, we can begin to judge whether and how Harvard has changed over the past 30 years. But we cannot measure mission change against statements about the future of an institution, unless those statements are forecasts grounded in the institution's present activity. Statements of aspiration are not subject to verification and therefore are not useful in discussions of mission.

The Virginia Council's statement (1981) about missions stresses their descriptive character:

> There are three parts to an institutional statement of mission: a general narrative which includes a statement of purpose, a profile of present activities and characteristics, and a projection of selected activities and characteristics into the future . . . .

The general narrative section of the . . . mission statements includes a summary of the institution's history; a statement of institutional purpose; a description of the relative commitments to instruction, research, and public service; and an indication of the ways in which the institution proposes to develop over the next decade.

Through the data profile section of each mission statement, which graphically demonstrates an institution's present activities and characteristics, aspects of the institution's mission are described more precisely. By projecting changes in selected activities and characteristics, the present and future profiles of an institution indicate, insofar as possible, what services it offers, to whom and by whom they are offered, and when and where they are offered. Among the data components which are included in the institutional profiles are the following:

1. enrollments,
2. academic degree programs,
3. physical facilities,
4. degree-granting levels,
5. institutional organization,
6. institutional operating and capital outlay appropriations and expenditures, and
7. sponsored research.

When the Council approves significant changes in any of the data components, it also may be approving changes in institutional mission. The Council also recommends changes in mission when it reviews some institutional activities as part of the biennial budget submission (for example, the review of public service and sponsored research, two activities which are critical parts of the missions of some institutions) or as part of the approval of institututional . . . curricular plans.

The Council recognizes that neither the general narrative nor the present and future profiles can entirely capture the essence of a rich and complex institution such as a college or university. The combination of all of the elements into a single statement of institutional mission, however, describes each Virginia college and university more precisely than earlier planning documents did. Moreover, the descriptions show more clearly and specifically the diversity of Virginia's state-supported system of higher education. [*The Virginia Plan for Higher Education, 1981*]

The Virginia Council acknowledged that its descriptive missions were incomplete. They lack student characteristic data, for instance, that are important in defining the persons for whom services are provided. But institutions have access to more data than state higher education agencies do and could produce more complete descriptive missions if they were so inclined.

"Mission explication" involves describing what an institution does; whom it serves; and where, when, and how it provides these services. It also involves explaining the implications of the institution's description. For instance, because a university is located in a city and serves many students who are older and attend part-time, it uses its faculty lines and its physical plant in certain distinctive ways. We describe a mission using verifiable criteria. Then we try to say what that description means, because a fact is like a sack: it doesn't stand up until you put something into it.

If an institution is what it does, as opposed to what it wants to do, and what it is, as opposed to what it hopes to become, mission change becomes definable and verifiable rather than a mystery. When what an institution does, or when and where and for whom it does it, changes, then the mission has changed. We are no longer peeling away layer after layer of institutional characteristics, searching for the mission. This is like removing layer after layer of an onion, searching for what makes it an onion.

Again, the more common conception is grounded in philosophical idealism, according to which an entity is composed of a set of attributes and an essence, the attributes being accidental and the essence being necessary and eternal. There are white horses and brown, large and small, plough and show, but they all share the essence of "horse-ness." Remove the accidental attributes, one by one, to find the necessary and eternal essence of being a horse.

By extension, the metaphor is applied to colleges and universities as social institutions. There are accidental attributes—size, location, clientele, and so on—that adhere to the essence of "university" or "college." The mission of a college or university is something that lies beneath the accidental details of "who, what, when, where, and why."

An empirical approach demystifies mission and makes it the sum of the characteristics of a college or university. The Virginia Council's mandate to approve changes in institutional mission becomes redundant. Every time the Council approves a new enrollment forecast, new academic programs, new campuses or off-campus sites, it has approved a change in mission. When an institution becomes more selective in its admissions policies, or when it changes the mix of in-state and out-of-state students, it has changed its mission.

The focus on the present and the immediate future that can be forecast from trends demands that institutional plans be revised continuously and frequently to ensure both that they will reflect accurately what the institutions are, and that the forecasts will be relatively short-term. Virginia, Florida, and other states, for example, revise their state higher education plans every two years. This policy leaves everyone—institutional boards and administrators, legislators, the governor, and the state higher education board—some flexibility while staying close to a description of current institutional characteristics.

Instead of a philosophical conundrum, then, we are left with a practical problem: how to distinguish between those changes that are important enough to warrant attention and those that are not. This is, in part, a matter of statutory authority vested in the governing and coordinating bodies in any particular state and, in part, a matter of good judgment. Overly zealous application of an empirical approach will stifle institutional vitality and produce a glut of petty actions for state-level review and approval. Probably it will also produce a revolution.

But if the characteristics of institutions are profiled, the definitions of *significant change* can be negotiated within the system of higher education. Change will occur, and it should. But it should be examined rather than unexamined, and coordinated rather than random.

The basis for the approach to mission that I have suggested in this chapter is derived in some measure from the tenets of logical positivism, particularly as expressed by Ayer in *Language, Truth and Logic* (n.d.). Ayer's approach to distinguishing sense from nonsense in what we say was a great tonic in its day: it helped to clarify some ancient philosophical muddles, and to sweep cobwebs out of many brains. As an explanation of how we use language, it was wrong but useful.

The notion that the elements of institutional missions must be subject, at least in principle, to empirical verification may also be wrong but can be useful. It permits discussion of mission without the confrontations that must occur if missions are equated with aspirations. It is reasonably clear and simple to explain that a college or university is what it does. Determining what it *ought* to do is the responsibility of whatever governance machinery happens to exist in a particular state, and this is a responsibility that seems on the whole to have been discharged fairly well over the past quarter century. While expansion of higher education has far exceeded the expectations of 1960, state governance systems have been effective in containing institutional aspirations and in maintaining diversity.

Insistence on the principle of verifiability leaves any complex human endeavor vulnerable in that there are some characteristics that cannot be measured. We must remain aware of what Hortense Calisher (1974) called the "currents of the intangible" that flow continuously in any place of learning. The principle of verifiability is not a reality test, so we must not assume that if something cannot be verified, it does not exist.

As a base, however, institutional statements of mission that are susceptible to verification in the present are a good starting point for higher education planning and budgeting. They lead logically to a concern for the measurement of institutional performance: the learning achievements of students, and the quality of sponsored research and public service. Assessment of quality will be a major higher education issue in the coming decade, and an empirical approach to mission is a good starting point for the effort.

REFERENCES

Alabama Commission on Higher Education. (1985). *Institutional Profiles: public four-year institutions.* Birmingham, AL.

Ayer, Alfred J. (n.d.). *Language, truth and logic.* New York: Dover.

Birnbaum, Robert. (1983) *Maintaining diversity.* San Francisco: Jossey-Bass.

Bowen, Howard R. (1980). *The costs of higher education.* San Francisco: Jossey-Bass.

Calisher, Hortense. (1974). *Herself.* New York: Dell.

Carruthers, J. Kent, and Lott, Gary B. (1981). *Mission review: foundation for strategic planning.* Boulder, CO: National Center for Higher Education Management Systems.

Chait, Richard. (1979). Mission madness strikes our colleges. *Chronicle of Higher Education* 18 (36): 36.

Complete Issue Papers of the Governor's Commission on Higher Education in Michigan. (1984). Lansing.

Conrad, Clifton (1974). University goals: an operative approach. *Journal of Higher Education* 45 (7): 505–515.

Drucker, Peter (1973). *Management: tasks, responsibilities, practices.* New York: Harper & Row.

Eliot, George (1901). *Middlemarch.* New York: Doubleday, Page. (Originally published, 1871–1872).

Fenske, R. H. (1980). Setting institutional goals and objectives. In *Improving academic management: a handbook of planning and institutional research.* San Francisco: Jossey-Bass.

Flew, Antony, and MacIntryre, Alasdair. (1955). *New essays in philosophical theology.* London: SCM Press.

Hodgkinson, Harold L. (1971). *Institutions in transition,* with a commentary by Stanley J. Heywood. New York: McGraw-Hill.

Integrity in the curriculum. (1985). Washington, DC: Association of American Colleges.

Involvement in learning. (1984). Washington, DC: National Institute of Education.

Lenning, Oscar T., and Micek, Sidney S. (1976). Defining and communicating institutional mission/role/scope and priorities: the needs of different types of postsecondary institutions. Paper presented at the annual meeting of the American Education Research Assocation, San Francisco.

Perrow, C. (1970). *Organizational analysis: a sociological view.* Belmont, CA: Wadsworth.

Richardson, Richard C., and Doucette, Donald S. (1984). An empirical model for formulating operational missions of community colleges. Paper presented at the American Educational Research Association, New Orleans.

Schwerin, Ursula. (1980). Institutional mission in an era of retrenchment. Paper presented at the annual meeting of the Association of American Colleges, Phoenix.

State Council of Higher Education for Virginia. (1981). *The Virginia Plan for Higher Education.* Richmond.

State Council of Higher Education for Virginia. (1983). *The Virginia Plan for Higher Education.* Richmond.

Veysey, Laurence R. (1965). *The emergence of the American university.* Chicago: University of Chicago Press.

POSTSCRIPT TO "THE IMPORTANCE OF BEING GENERAL," BY GORDON K. DAVIES
The Campus as Chameleon: Rethinking Organizational Behavior and Public Policy

John R. Thelin
College of William and Mary

At one time the symbol of the university was the gryphon—the legendary creature, half eagle and half lion, that protected the light of insight and whose solar rays were the enemy of *chaos* (darkness). Now, however, there is a new addition to the American academic menagerie as the traditional gryphon is joined by the chameleon. According to Gordon Davies's analysis, today many academic institutions do not stand for clarity of purpose; rather they shun clarity in favor of vague and shifting mission statements. The campus, like the chameleon, conveniently alters its identity to blend with the context of a changing environment. The cumulative consequence is that the higher education landscape is increasingly bland and lacking in distinction.

Davies's bold contention complicates the study of organizational behavior in higher education. Certainly, his hypothesis does not stand for a universal truth; at the very least, it does shatter the illusion of consensus for a central strand of conventional wisdom about academic strategy and institutional mission. Namely, much of the professional lore and literature advises that a key to success in both internal and external campus relations is to possess a distinctive mission—and to project it as a clear, forceful image (Keller, 1983; College Entrance Examination Board, 1980). In the parlance of admissions planning, the strategy is to "position" one's college or university in the academic marketplace. This pragmatic advice follows from Clark's study (1970) of the organizational saga, in which he concluded that an integral part of a sustained, successful college operation is the ability to acquire and cultivate a sense of heritage as a distinctive institution—to "stand for something special"—and to transmit this heritage to students, faculty, staff, alumni, and outside publics. Conversely, a number of studies in the 1960s and 1970s expressed concern about the plight of "invisible colleges" (Astin and Lee, 1972) and the low morale of imageless backwater "colleges of the forgotten Americans" (Dunham, 1973).

The Carnegie Foundation for the Advancement of Teaching's 1977 report on the missions of the college curriculum elevated this to orthodoxy by providing campus leaders with guidelines for composing a "good" mission statement. Such statements were to be clear and concise—and were to include focus on "whatever natural, permanent features of the institution may make unique educational activities possible." Instead of having each institution write a tedious, lengthy philosophy of education, the Carnegie study cited the need for a "concise series of statements," characterized by a tone of "realism and humility," which would do the following things:

1. Guide the academic leadership of a college in determining what educational programs are appropriate for accommodation in the institution's curriculum.
2. Provide students with the information about the institution's intentions so that they can compare them with their own interests and needs.
3. Provide the college's governing board, accrediting agencies, and others who might have a legitimate reason to evaluate the performance of the college, the criteria by which the institution chooses, at least in curricular matters, to be governed. [pp. 160–163]

Were colleges and universities practicing what the Carnegie Foundation advocated? Davies's data suggest that such guidelines were usually either ignored or countered by many colleges and universities, especially in the public sector. His description and analysis help the research literature to catch up with the reality of how institutions often behave—rather than how they "ought" to behave—in formulating and projecting mission statements. In so doing, Davies makes some sorely needed contributions to research in higher education.

First, he incorporates *systematic* philosophical analysis into the study of colleges and universities (as distinguished from amorphous "armchair" musings that are erroneously called "philosophical" tracts); certainly, this is a disciplinary perspective that has been grossly underrepresented in the study of higher education during the past decade.

Second, Davies brings to organizational theory a focus on the true *corporate* behavior of institutions—rather than the more familiar emphasis on aggregate attitudes of individuals within colleges and universities.

Third, he includes the state agency and the state capitol view of the campus; this contrasts markedly with the egocentrism of the campus, in which each individual college assumes itself to be the center of the funding cosmos (e.g., Carnegie Foundation for the Advancement of Teaching, 1982); this is a necessary antidote if academic organizational behavior is ever to become an enduring part of public policy analysis.

Finally, the Davies essay helps to rescue organizational behavior from over-reliance on the biological metaphor. Instead of neo-Darwinian assumptions, campus mission statements are depicted as part of the drama of *social* relations among colleges, legislatures, and state agencies. The net contribution is to bring the study of campus governance and public policy close to the realm of ritual that Wildavsky (1964) attributed to the budget negotiations of large-scale federal social programs and the complex sense of play that March (1982) described for decision making within the American campus.

However, as with all good research, Davies raises more questions than he answers. The following commentary suggests an unfinished and altered research agenda:

Amending the Situation. If, in fact, it is neither healthy policy nor healthy practice for institutions to generate vague, shifting statements about what they are and what they will be, what is the root cause? Institutions are at worst co-conspirators in the act of avoiding clear notions of mission and performance. Davies readily admits that because of a combination of political vacuum (legislators and state officers preferring to say "yes," squirming to avoid having to say "no" . . .) and procedural guidelines (institutional compliance with state funding formulae) that promote the ritual of avoidance and vacillation, state colleges are reacting to, rather than creating, the rules of the funding game. Why single out the colleges without equal attention to the inaction (and, possibly, the irresponsibility) of, for example, the legislature in seeking forceful mission statements?

The "culprit" may well be overreliance on enrollment-formula funding—the instrument that prompts public institutions to "play the game" of vagueness, which, in turn, allows a campus to chase enrollments and resources at the expense of clear, enduring academic purpose. If this is so, then one attractive correction would be to replace "enrollment-driven-formula funding" with the "program-funding" notion advanced by the Kentucky Council on Higher Education (Prichard Committee, 1981, p. 114). Unfortunately, such thoughtful reform measures will face political problems—as the Kentucky legislature opposed adoption of the "program-funding" proposal. Nonetheless, the shift to "program funding" could be an attractive option elsewhere in the late 1980s.

One must also bear in mind that the characteristic of vagueness that Davies criticizes in the institutional statements was found to be endemic to the statements of statewide master plans—to the extent that the Education Commission of the States backed down from its original penchant for grandiose thirty-year documents (e.g., the California Master Plans of the 1950s and 1960s) in favor of modest five-year strategic plans (Education Commission of the States, 1980). Campus presidents and deans are most likely to follow the example of the state coordinating councils.

Microanalysis. The most fundamental question is "Who writes a college's mission statement?" Before jumping into the realm of public policy and campus relations with the state coordinating council, one must confront the sad fact that there is little certainty about the authorship of and the responsibility for mission statements at the campus level. In some cases, authorship is a group exercise of a faculty and staff committee—possibly part of the ten-year institutional self-study prepared for regional accreditation. But this need not be the case; in other instances, a president or a provost may compose and forward the statement to the state council. The whim and variance in such a central and elemental document may be the most significant testimony to the drift and complexity of the modern college or university.

Information, Please! Some colleges, especially those in the independent sector, attribute the phenomenon of bland, undistinguished mission statements to the kinds of data collected by federal and state agencies. The logic is that if external agencies collect static and unimaginative data from colleges—and such data are not analyzed in a sophisticated, interesting manner—the result will be perfunctory, characterless institutional behavior. For example, Odell (1976) suggested that state agencies would do well to pay increased attention to institutional results and to *price*-of-instruction data (as differentiated from *cost*-of-instruction data). More recently, Weathersby (1980) called for state councils to use a strategy of "incentives" that would prompt both the public and the independent institutions within a state to perform in distinctive, desirable ways. Familiar categories of HEGIS data probably would not suffice for such analyses and evaluations.

Macroanalysis. Davies's descriptions and analyses are compelling—and probably correct. They are not necessarily complete. In short, the problem of institutional drift toward vagueness and sameness, the tendency to attempt to "be all things to all groups," predates the particular circumstances of state-agency–campus relations on which Davies focuses. As early as 1909, Slosson noted the appearance of the "Standard American University"—a peculiar product that emerged after a period of heroic and unregulated institution founding and building (Slosson, 1909, p. 328). Especially puzzling is the historical fact that the great university builders showed little interest in cooperation or compatibility across institutions—yet they could still see signs that their respective institutions were starting to congeal into the same model.

We still have no thorough explanation of why this happened. Veysey (1965) used the advantage of hindsight to follow up on Slosson's observations and concluded that the syndrome of institutional imitation and accommodation was the "price of structure." The interpretation is that university presidents by 1910 may have pursued a path of least resistance: that is, it was easier to accommodate disparate activities under a university umbrella than it was to make hard choices about what was proper and what was not. Flexner (1930) used this theme of loss of central purpose to organize his classic comparison of the American university with its German and British counterparts. And immediately after World War II, the indefatigable commentator Robert Maynard Hutchins (1948) criticized the 1947 Report of the President's Council on Higher Education for promoting an "omnibus" model for the American campus in which institutions were free to embrace virtually any and all purposes.

Nor was this syndrome confined to the large universities. Townsend's study (1983) of mission and images of community colleges indicates that leaders and planners of the two-year public institutions have long made good use of the vague image as a convenient institutional strategy. Note, for example, that the generic American community college has at one time or another since 1950 shifted its emphasis from the "academic transfer" role to that of "terminal vocational education" and then to the mission of "community service center." Flexibility and diversity of purpose, in fact, are intertwined as rhetoric to constitute an American educational tradition that cuts widely across time, space, and sector.

The Dangers of Reductionism. Davies himself notes that translating mission statements into empirically testable propositions may be useful but wrong. Worth emphasizing is the warning that such a stance at the state agency level runs the risk of reductionism. And such a "corrective" measure may merely engender more of the very blandness and lack of distinction in higher education that Davies laments. One interesting omission in the discussion of research strategies is the possible use of the rich, varied data that institutions compile and present for regional and professional accreditation reports. Might not such data and reports be placed in the public domain, so as to be open for analysis and discussion beyond the particular campus?

Finally, the most interesting puzzle with which researchers are left to work is this: to explain why not all colleges and universities have succumbed to publishing vague, characterless mission statements. Distinction and clarity are potent academic strategies in some cases—but can we isolate and identify these? The public-private dichotomy is an obvious explanation; however, on close inspection, one finds too many textures and variations within those categories to be satisfactory. Davies's philosophical analysis and this subsequent historical commentary ought to be supplemented with the sociological notion of the "organizational charter" advanced by Kamens (1971) more than a decade ago; that is, subsequent research must digest the social and historical fact that faculty, staff, students, alumni, parents, and publics do carry around (albeit implicitly) a notion of what is right and proper for some institutions to do and to be; and to violate this "organizational charter" will have serious consequences for the health and stature of the institution. Thus the study of organizational behavior as a part of public policy in higher education is left to acknowledge Mark Twain's dictum, "It is all right to break laws so long as we obey customs."

108   THELIN

Acknowledgment. Preparation of this manuscript was made possible in part by a summer faculty research grant from the College of William and Mary.

REFERENCES

Astin, Alexander, and Lee, Calvin B. T. (1972). *The invisible colleges: a profile of small, private colleges with limited resources.* New York: McGraw-Hill.

Birnbaum, Robert. (1983) *Maintaining diversity in higher education.* San Francisco: Jossey-Bass.

Carnegie Foundation for the Advancement of Teaching. (1977). *Missions of the college curriculum: a contemporary review with suggestions.* San Francisco: Jossey-Bass.

Carnegie Foundation for the Advancement of Teaching. (1982). *The control of the campus: a report on the governance of higher education.* Washington, DC: Carnegie Foundation for the Advancement of Teaching.

Clark, Burton R. (1970). *The distinctive college: Antioch, Reed, and Swarthmore.* Chicago: Aldine.

College Entrance Examination Board. (1980). *Marketing in college admissions: a broadening of perspectives.* New York: CEEB.

Dunham, E. Allen. (1973). *Colleges of the forgotten Americans: a profile of state colleges and regional universities.* New York: McGraw-Hill.

Education Commission of the States. (1980). *Challenge: coordination and governance in the '80s.* Denver, CO (Report No. 134).

Halstead, D. Kent. (1974). *Statewide planning in higher education.* Washington, DC: U.S. Department of Health, Education, and Welfare.

Hodgkinson, Harold L. (1971). *Institutions in transition: a profile of change in higher education.* New York: McGraw-Hill.

Hutchins, Robert M. (1948). Report of the President's Council on Higher Education. *Educational Record* 29 (April): 107–122.

Kamens, David H. (1971). The college "charter" and college size: effects on occupational choice and college attrition. *Sociology of Education,* 270–296.

Keller, George. (1983). *Academic strategy: the management revolution in American higher education.* Baltimore: Johns Hopkins University Press.

March, James. (1982). Emerging developments in the study of organizations. *Review of Higher Education* 6 (1): 1–16.

Odell, Morgan S. (1976). Information and analysis in the context of state support of private higher education. Proceedings of the 1976 NCHEMS Conference, pp. 107–118.

Prichard Committee. (1981). *In pursuit of excellence.* Frankfort: Kentucky Council on Higher Education.

Slosson, Edwin E. (1909). *Great American universities.* New York: Macmillan.

Townsend, Barbara K. (1983). *Faculty's relation to the identity problem of the community college: a study of faculty support for specific institutional directions for the community college.* Williamsburg, VA: College of William and Mary, doctoral dissertation.

Veysey, Laurence M. (1965). *The emergence of the American university.* Chicago: University of Chicago Press.

Weathersby, George. (1980). Countervailing forces affecting coordination. *Change (Oct.):* 19, 50–52.

Wildavsky, Aaron. (1964). *The Politics of the budgetary process.* Boston: Little, Brown.

Wildavsky, Aaron. (1982). On the uses of adversity in higher education. *Review of Higher Education* 6 (1): 19–29.

AFFIRMATIVE-ACTION EMPLOYMENT DISCRIMINATION:
The Higher Education Fragment

Monique Weston Clague, *University of Maryland*

What, one wonders, do all the readers and users of position advertisements in the *Chronicle of Higher Education* think all the references to "equal employment opportunity" mean? Is an "EEO employer" the same as an "affirmative action, equal opportunity employer" or an "equal access, equal opportunity employer," or a "nondiscriminatory, affirmative action employer" in the minds of all the search committee members and administrators, the "street-level bureaucrats" of academic hiring? Who, among them, believes that they are either legally permitted or legally required to engage in affirmative action discrimination; that is, to accord preferential treatment by gender or race in the name of affirmative action?

For academic institutions that are also federal government contractors, some reference to equal employment opportunity and/or affirmative action has been an obligatory feature of employment advertising since 1972, when the Office for Civil Rights (now in the Department of Education, then in the Department of Health, Education, and Welfare—HEW) issued the Higher Education Guidelines. They interpret for academic contractors the more general employment prohibitions and affirmative obligations that President Johnson's 1965 Executive Order 11246 (as amended in 1967) imposes on all government contractors. Although the guidelines did not specifically require that academic contractors advertise position vacancies, they did require that an explicit commitment to equal employment opportunity be made in all "recruiting announcements and advertisements" (p. 6).

The language of the guidelines is individualistic. No individual is to be denied employment or the related benefits on grounds of race, color, religion, sex, or national origin (p. 3). This is the anti-discrimination prohibition. Positive—affirmative—action requirements were conceived of as a means of ensuring meritocratic nondiscrimination against any individual. Goals are required, but fixed allocation quotas are expressly prohibited (p. 4). There is no reference to any legal or moral imperative of giving preferences on the basis of race, gender, or ethnicity in order to compensate for historic exclusion or injustice, or to increase diversity in the academic workplace. Nevertheless critics (among them a high percentage of eminent Jewish academicians) have been skeptical in the extreme (Van Dyne, 1973, p. 4). Like the building trades, institutions of higher education are required to develop written affirmative-action plans (hereinafter AAP) that set hiring "goals" for minorities and women, based on an analysis of the institution's workplace, the availability of "qualified" women and minorities, and expected turnover in the work force. A goal, it was charged, was a euphemism for "an informal quota system," for reverse discrimination, for preferences (Van Dyne, 1973, p. 4). J. Stanley Pottinger, head of the Office for Civil Rights, responded with a campaign to convince the critics that goals (projected levels of achievement) are not quotas (numerical levels that must be met), and that the objective of affirmative action is to ensure "honest competition" (Fields, 1972, p. 4). President Nixon issued a statement affirming that federal agencies must not use quotas (Fields, 1972, p. 4).

The obligatory statements of commitment to affirmative action or equal employment opportunity remain. They are an inexpensive way of avoiding unnecessary legal trouble if an institution is sued, for their absence might lend support to an inference of discrimination. But in the 21 years since the Executive Order, vast changes have occurred in the law governing employment discrimination. It has grown enormously complicated and confusing. Law has been added to law; extant laws have been applied to new situations; regulations have been added to regulations. Court decisions have multiplied—explaining, revising, reinforcing, and contradicting each other—resulting in an unsettled and highly contextual jurisprudence. The Executive Order is now only one strand in a tangled skein.[1]

The purpose of this chapter is to unravel a part of this tangled skein, that is, to explore the unsettled law of affirmative action discrimination in higher education, primarily in the hiring of minorities and women to the detriment of white males, and, when racial preferences are at issue, to white women and men. Typically, challenges to preferential treatment are formulated as charges of "reverse discrimination," a term not used in the title of this chapter for two reasons. First, not all manifestations of preferential treatment are defended, or can be defended, in the name of affirmative action. Secondly, *reverse discrimination* is a loaded term. It suggests that special treatment favoring minorities is merely the "mirror image" (*Detroit Police Officers Ass'n v. Young*, 1979 p. 697) of invidious discrimination against minorities, a position that ignores or discounts the difference between discrimination inflicted by a dominant racial or social group for the purpose of segregating and oppressing a minority group, and discrimination by the dominant group for the purpose of integrating and improving the social and economic condition of the historically victimized group.

The first part of this chapter provides a brief overview of the national controversy surrounding the evolution of employment discrimination law, from its initial emphasis on individual rights to the present limited acceptance of groups rights' perspectives. In order to place reverse discrimination cases in broader perspective the second part of the chapter presents an overview of case law involving single plaintiff claims of discrimination in academic hiring and promotion. This litigation is "conventional" because of its frequency and because it sets the norm that makes court-approved affirmative-action discrimination the exception. In "conventional" cases the issue posed and debated is whether or not the challenged employment decision was, in fact, discriminatory, not, as in affirmative-action discrimination litigation, whether or not the admittedly preferential employment decision was legally justified. The third part of the chapter turns to an analysis of voluntary affirmative-action discrimination in both the private and the public sectors. When challenged in a reverse discrimination case, the defendant attempts to justify an exception to the principle of nondiscrimination. The fourth part of the chapter, finally, examines judicially mandated exceptions to the principle of nondiscrimination.

The analysis of this chapter (which assesses legal developments through mid-1985) is necessarily exploratory, and to some extent speculative. Not only are there relatively few higher education employment cases in which reverse discrimination has been alleged, but the U.S. Supreme Court has not provided clear and definitive guidelines for permissible race, gender, or ethnic preferences in public or private employment. In June 1984, in *Firefighter's Local Union No. 1784* v. *Stotts*, the Supreme Court ruled that under Title VII of the Civil Rights Act of 1964 (the nation's premier employment discrimination statute), a federal court exceeded its statutory power when it ordered an affirmative-action layoff plan to protect the jobs of newly hired blacks, in contravention of a lawful seniority system. The *Stotts* decision was widely lauded and condemned as delivering a mortal blow to preferential treatment in the name of affirmative action. In September, dissenting Justice Harry Blackman was quoted as saying that as a result of the *Stotts* decision, affirmative action was "pretty well interred" (*Houston Chronicle*, 1984, p. 2). But a close reading of the case suggests that such a sweeping conclusion was premature. Its focus was on the coercive power of the courts under the authority of a particular (albeit important) statute. It did not reverse an earlier decision (*United Steelworkers* v. *Weber*, 1979) upholding, within limits, voluntary racial quotas in the private sector. And it did not address the lawfulness of voluntary affirmative-action plans in the public sector. The Supreme Court's April, 1985 decision to review *Wygant* v. *Jackson Board of Education* suggested that the Court is finally ready to address the constitutionality of voluntary, public sector minority preferences, although the extent to which it will do so is uncertain, for the affirmative action plan challenged in *Wygant* is atypical: it does not set employment goals, or gear its layoff provision to the racial composition of the relevant labor market or applicant pool, the criteria endorsed in most affirmative-action cases. Rather, the plan seeks to create and to maintain a teacher corps whose racial composition reflects the racial composition of the school district's student body. The Court could, therefore, deal with *Wygant* in one of several ways: It could use the case to provide general guidelines within which affirmative action discrimination may be initiated in public employment. Alternatively, it could use *Wygant* to invalidate all preferential affirmative action in the public sector. Or, finally, the Court could limit its decision, likely in the first half of 1986, to one or more specific features of the Jackson School Board's affirmative-action plan (see Clague, 1985).

INDIVIDUAL RIGHTS AND GROUP RIGHTS

In June 1965, four months before Executive Order 11246 went into effect, President Johnson delivered a commencement address at Howard University in which he developed the rationale for his Great Society programs ("To Fulfill These Rights," reprinted in Franklin and Starr, 1967, pp. 225–251). His concern for distributive justice focused on the plight of poor black and Mexican Americans. "[F]or years . . . hobbled by chains," they started the race with a competitive disadvantage. For these groups, therefore, "legal equity" and "equal opportunity" were "essential but not enough." The president depicted the goal of the "next and more profound stage of the battle for civil rights as equality as a fact and as a result."

President Johnson's sensitivity to the economic and educational "roots of injustice" foreshadowed a primary argument in favor of minority employment preferences. But the language of the Executive Order, issued under authority of the Constitution and statutes, remained within an individualistic, equal-opportunity framework. The purpose of affirmative action was to ensure that applicants and employees would be treated "without regard to their race, color, religion, sex (as of 1967), or national origin" (Section 202; see Eastland and Bennett, 1979, p. 131).

But in the 1970s and the first half of the 1980s, the federal executive, the federal courts, and state and local authorities moved beyond a strictly individual-rights interpretation of the Executive Order, statutes, and Constitution, to embrace group rights approaches to the problems of social justice. When, in 1972, a Republican Department of Labor first demanded that construction contractors in Philadelphia conduct future hiring of minorities in accord with "numerical goals and timetables," it was believed that these requirements of the "Philadelphia Plan" were a necessary, practical means of ensuring that the employment outcomes would approximate the results of a race-blind hiring process (Silberman, 1977). Monitoring every discrete employment decision for racial bias was impossible; discriminatory treatment would be presumed if the employer's work force did not reflect the percentage of projected, qualified minority workers available in an employer's labor market. When coupled with a good-faith compliance standard that permitted waivers if qualified minorities could not be found, goals and timetables were, in theory, thought to be compatible with merit-based competition, taking individuals as they are in the here and now. But for equal-individual-rights advocates, the use of goals and timetables soon presented a means–ends dilemma. Without numerical goals, the prohibitions on discrimination contained in the Executive Order, the statutes, and the Constitution could not be adequately enforced (Jencks, 1983, p. 15). Over time, however, numerical goals were transformed into fixed quotas that could not be rationalized within an individualistic theory of employment opportunity. By 1984, the 20th anniversary year of the Civil Rights Act of 1964, and the year in which the nation honored Dr. Martin Luther King, Jr., as a national hero, there were three ways of addressing the means–ends dilemma of affirmative action.

The first, chosen by the Republican Party, is to insist on an all-encompassing, uncompromising, individual rights interpretation of statutes and Constitution, with a consequent weakening of efforts to enhance the employment status of minorities and women. The Republicans walked down what William Bradford Reynolds, Head of the Civil Rights Division of the Justice Department, has called "the high road of race neutrality" (Barbash and Sawyer, 1984), language indicative of the moral righteousness that the problem of affirmative action evokes. In January 1984, the Republican "reconstituted" U.S. Commission on Civil Rights assailed the city of Detroit's court-approved plan establishing race-based promotion quotas in the police department (Statement of the U.S. Commission on Civil Rights Concerning Detroit Police Department's Racial Promotion quota, 1984; *Bratton* v. *City of Detroit,* 1983). Echoing a position repeatedly voiced in Justice Department briefs, the commission insisted that higher seniority status should be accorded only to black police officers who were proven victims of discrimination (U.S. Commission on Civil Rights, 1984). In June 1984, in response to the Supreme Court's decision in *Stotts,* Reynolds announced that he was advising the Equal Employment Opportunity Commission (EEOC) and the Labor Department's Office of Federal Contract Compliance (OFCCP) that they should no longer negotiate anti-discrimination agreements containing numerical quotas (Barbash and Sawyer, 1984). In August, 1984, the Justice Department entered a *Memorandum in Opposition* to the use of "racial 'objectives' and other selection devices for students . . . faculty and staff," contained in a proposed settlement of the protracted desegregation litigation involving Tennessee State University (Memorandum of the United States, *Geier* v. *Alexander,* August 9,

1984). The same month, the Republican Party platform embraced, without qualification, an "Individual Rights" plank repudiating "quota systems and preferential treatment."

For convention Democrats, the quest for justice was not so simple, and so they chose a second response to the means-end dilemma: equivocation. They attacked the Reagan administration for eroding "the force and meaning of constitutionally mandated and court-sanctioned remedies for long standing patterns of discriminatory conduct" and for using the *Stotts* decision "to assault all affirmative action plans." In the last decade, court-sanctioned remedies have included rigid hiring, promotion, and layoff quotas in a variety of legal contexts and employment settings. But the compromise plank adopted by the Democratic Convention—entitled, significantly, "Affirmative Action," rather than "Individual Rights"—neither endorsed nor rejected quotas. It "reaffirmed" instead, with an artful ambiguity, "the use of affirmative action goals, timetables and other verifiable measurements to overturn historic patterns and the historic burdens of discrimination in hiring, training, promotions, contract procurement, education and the administration of all Federal programs." This Democratic formulation was loose enough to accommodate the adherents of both individual and group rights perspectives: (1) those who firmly support individual rights, but who view numerical goals and timetables as means to nondiscriminatory ends; they deal with the means–ends dilemma of affirmative action by denying the existence of a dilemma; (2) those who believe in individual rights but who fear the regressive signals that the Republicans' emphasis on free-market individualism was sending out to the complacent and actively discriminatory; they would rather be impaled sometimes on the "reverse discrimination" horn of the means–end dilemma than dismantle affirmative-action enforcement efforts; and (3) discouraged advocates of individual rights, whose aspiration for collective ascent challenges the slow and costly pace of individual ascent, the latter protected in theory, but inadequately in practice, as President Johnson emphasized, by formal legal equality; sensitive to the economic, social, and educational burdens that handicap disproportionately groups that have suffered a history of segregation and subjugation, they deal with the means–ends dilemma by embracing temporarily a group-rights legal theory. Quotas and preferences may be used to compensate groups until their members achieve a proportionate share of jobs. The logic of this temporary group-rights theory is summed up in Justice Blackman's opinion in *Regents of the University of California* v. *Bakke* (1978): "In order to get beyond racism, we must first take account of race . . . And in order to treat some persons equally, we must first treat them differently" (p. 407).

There is, finally, a group rights perspective that the Democratic plank neither endorsed nor declared apostate. It is a theory of permanent group rights. Affirmative action goals and quotas are conceived of not as means to competitive, individualistic, color-blind ends, as temporary compensatory preferences on the road to a new, historically unburdened starting point. This group-rights approach reacts to the means–end dilemma by redefining the end: It is not fair competition between legally equal individuals; it is a guaranteed fair sharing for selected groups in American society (see La Noue, 1980).

CONVENTIONAL DISCRIMINATION LITIGATION

"Hands Off" Academe
To make sense of affirmative action discrimination cases requires that they be seen in relationship to the broad framework of conventional employment-discrimination law from which they seek to carve out an exception. They must also be understood in relationship to the corpus of "conventional" employment-discrimination litigation in academe. When Title VII was passed in 1964, Congress exempted educational institutions from its coverage. But when this exemption was removed in 1972 Congress made clear its concern about "[pervasive] discrimination against women and minorities in the field of education" (House Report, 1971). Senators characterized discrimination in the professoriate as "truly appalling," "gross," and "blatant" (cited in *Powell* v. *Syracuse University*, 1978). And yet, in spite of the manifest congressional will to apply the full force of Title VII to academic employment in 1972, in the decade that followed federal courts proceeded to shield higher education from its antidiscrimination mandate.

Conventional litigation comprises what courts, in construing Title VII and the equal protection clause of the Fourteenth Amendment (and the Civil Rights Acts that enforce it), have labeled "disparate treatment," that is, intentional discrimination.[2] In general, Title VII makes it an unlawful employment practice to discriminate against "any individual . . . because of such individual's race, color, religion, sex, or national origin." To discriminate is to subject comparably qualified individuals to unequal—disparate—treatment because of the personal characteristics covered the law.

For example, when the Santa Fe Trail Transportation Company fired a white employee, but not a black employee with whom he collaborated in a scheme to steal customer property, the Supreme Court unanimously held that Title VII "proscribe[s] racial discrimination in private employment against whites on the same terms as racial discrimination against nonwhites" (*McDonald* v. *Santa Fe Trail Transportation Co.,* 1976, p. 279).

Three features of *McDonald*'s equal-individual-rights interpretation deserve mention. First, although the case necessarily addressed race discrimination because of the racial nature of the firing, the Court noted that Congress intended the general prohibition on discrimination in Section (703)(a) of Title VII to apply to gender, religious, and national origin discrimination as well. Second, although the Court affirmed the general principle of color-blind nondiscrimination, it reserved the possibility of, if it did not lay the groundwork for, affirmative action discrimination. In *McDonald,* the unanimous court spoke through the voice of Justice Marshall, whose unequivocal support for minority preferences, created as part of an affirmative action program, was fully articulated two years late in *Regents of the University of California* v. *Bakke.* In fact, Marshall's *McDonald* opinion specifically noted that since the Santa Fe Company did not defend its action as part of an affirmative action plan, the lawfulness of such plans, as an exception to the antidiscrimination principle, was not at issue (p. 280, Note 8). Finally, since the existence of discrimination in the *McDonald* case was overt, it was not typical of the overwhelming majority of conventional disparate-treatment cases. In almost all such cases, the defense does not concede the existence of discrimination. Hence, the central inquiry revolves around the factual question of whether an inference can be drawn that the employment decision was improperly motivated, that is, whether it was "because of [an] individual's race, color, religion, sex, or national origin." This inquiry is shaped by a framework that allocates to the plaintiff and the defendant different evidentiary burdens. To the plaintiff falls the burden of establishing a *prima facie* case of discrimination, a claim supported by sufficient evidence to create an inference of discrimination. If this *prima facie* case is made, the defendant need only "articulate," with supporting evidence, a nondiscriminatory reason for its action (the rebuttal stage) (*Texas Dept. of Community Affairs* v. *Burdine,* 1981). To the plaintiff, finally, falls the task of persuading the court that the employer's claim that it acted for "legitimate and nondiscriminatory reasons" is a pretext—a cloak for covert discrimination.

This framework for addressing claims of disparate treatment is sometimes called the *McDonnell-Douglas-Burdine* paradigm, a reference to two in a series of Supreme Court cases creating it. Neither of them involved a claim of discrimination in academic employment. But *Board of Trustees of Keene State College* v. *Sweeney* (1978), the *only* employment discrimination case involving a faculty member in higher education that the Supreme Court has decided, did. And it was also one in the series of cases that attempted to clarify the framework for disparate treatment litigation.

The American Council on Education (ACE), higher education's most comprehensive advocacy organization, had filed a brief *amicus curiae* ("friend of the court") in support of Keene State College's petition for Supreme Court review. For the ACE, the issue was not whether Keene State College had discriminated against Professor Sweeney. It had "no interest" in the disposition of her claim of sex discrimination. The critical issue was the grave threat that "review by the judiciary of academic peer review judgment" posed to "the independence and integrity of the academic enterprise," indeed, to the very "survival of our political system." The case for Keene State College was the case for academic freedom. That Congress, in amending Title VII in 1972, had specifically abolished Title VII's exemption of the professoriate at nonreligious institutions, the ACE simply ignored.

The Supreme Court, in turn, ignored the issue that the ACE attempted to raise. Was it tacitly suggesting, therefore, that academe is not an enclave immune to the sweep of Title VII? Perhaps. A direct consequence of the Supreme Court's procedural ruling in *Sweeney* was that the lower courts confirmed their earlier findings that the reasons the college had advanced in support of its nondiscrimination defense were pretextual. By court order, Dr. Sweeney's promotion to a full professorship was backdated with an accompanying award of back pay.

The circuit court opinion in *Sweeney* was, however, as the ACE noted, a "maverick decision" at the time it was considered by the Supreme Court. For four years, the circuit courts had endorsed the notion that courts, in Title VII suits, should not substitute their judgment of competence for that of a faculty member's peers. Before Title VII's coverage of academic institutions, the same principle was established in suits alleging violations of the equal protection clause of the Fourteenth Amendment. Indeed, judicial reluctance to apply Title VII to academic jobs became so pronounced in the 1970s and early 1980s that it rated the name of a doctrine. It has been called the "academic abstention doctrine" (Edwards and Nordin, 1979, p. 601; see also Edwards, 1977). The Second Circuit Court of Appeals labeled it the "hands-off" doctrine (*Powell* v. *Syracuse University,* 1978). In case after higher-education case, plaintiffs, mostly female, lost (see Lee, 1985).

As Professor Bartholet detailed (1982), this hands-off judicial posture characterizes the case law of employment discrimination addressing "upper level" employment—professional jobs as opposed to blue-collar jobs—in general, not just those dealing with academic employment. Often, in academic cases, judicial abstention has been justified in terms of deference to superior expertise. But the hands-off doctrine is also allied with the conception of academic freedom promoted by the ACE, which borrowed from Justice Frankfurter's celebrated concurring opinion in *Sweezy* v. *New Hampshire* (1957). Justice Frankfurter, eloquently defending the right of faculty to express unpopular views in the classroom without fear of governmental interference, had borrowed, in turn, from the rhetoric of South African scholars urging recognition of the "four essential freedoms of a university," including the freedom "to determine . . . on academic grounds who may teach" (p. 263). The equation of freedom of inquiry and expression in the classroom with freedom of peer judgments from judicial scrutiny was consummated by the Second Circuit Court in 1980 in a case involving the University of Connecticut (*Lieberman* v. *Gant,* 1980). To be sure, the court did not say that academic freedom must include the freedom to discriminate on grounds of race, color, gender, or national origin. Instead, as Judge Friendly put it, academic freedom "cannot be disregarded in determining the proper role of courts called upon to try allegations of discrimination by universities in teaching appointments" (p. 67). What this meant in practice was that the courts made it extremely difficult to win conventional covert-discrimination suits in higher education. Though there are now some straws in a crosswind (*Ford* v. *Nicks,* 1982; *Greer* v. *University of Arkansas,* 1982, 1983; *Kumar* v. *Trustees of the University of Massachusetts,* 1984), in case after case, brought primarily by women against traditionally white institutions with male-predominant faculties, the plaintiffs lost. (This was not true of cases initiated by whites against traditionally black institutions.) Deference to peer review and "subjective evaluation systems" meant that the courts declined to make comparative evaluations of comparatively qualified faculty, and in many instances, the courts also "denied litigants the discovery that would make such assessments possible" (Bartholet, 1982). Although the courts were reluctant to apply the *McDonnell–Douglas–Burdine* paradigm to academic cases, the litigation nevertheless elicited a great deal of testimony about the deliberations of faculty and administrators involved in the personnel decision (see Lee, 1985). Academic freedom amounted, then, to freedom from judicial judgment, but not to freedom from the considerable pains of the judicial process.

If academic freedom has been invoked to justify a judicial hands-off posture toward peer evaluation in academe, the privacy of a marriage relationship was, until 1984, invoked to justify hands-off, tenurelike, up-or-out promotion decisions from associate to partner in law firms. The Eleventh Circuit's treatment of Elizabeth Hishon's sex-discrimination complaint against a prestigious Atlanta law firm (*Hishon* v. *King & Spaulding,* 1980) has been said to epitomize judicial reluctance to apply Title VII to employment discrimination generally, as Congress intended it should (Bartholet, 1982, p. 960). Refusing to apply Title VII's ban on sex discrimination to the firm's selection of partners, the appeals court likened judicial intervention to "the enforcement of a shotgun wedding" (*Hishon* v. *King & Spaulding,* 1980, p. 1305).

As incongruous as it was to use this marital metaphor to protect all male partnerships from female interlopers, the more general principle of freedom of association would not have served the purpose. As a defense to Title VII discrimination claims involving "lower level" jobs, freedom of association failed to persuade. The essential purpose of Title VII is, after all, to interfere with the freedom to associate only with race-, gender-, and ethnic-alike coworkers. Certainly, the purpose of Title VII is not to interfere with the privacy of marital relationships. But neither is its purpose, as expressly articulated by Congress, to permit professional employers to elope from its prohibitions in the disguise of ill-suited metaphors.

In 1984, the Supreme Court unanimously reversed the lower court opinion in *Hishon.* It held that *if* the law firm had obligated itself, by express or implied contract, to consider Hishon for partnership when it hired her as an associate member, she was entitled to bring a Title VII complaint. Whether this decision signals a willingness by the judiciary to apply Title VII to professional employment, including academic employment, applying the same standards used in litigation involving blue-collar employment, remains to be seen. The condition that the Supreme Court placed on the reach of Title VII—if the opportunity to become a partner had been a condition of Hishon's employment as an associate, then the firm would be obligated to consider her without regard to her sex—would not limit Title VII's coverage of tenure-track faculty. The term *tenure-track* implies mutual expectation of consideration for tenure. But the *Hishon* decision suggests that Title VII might not afford faculty on term contracts the right to challenge discriminatory refusals to consider them for tenure-track positions. What is more, the *Hishon* decision did not address the most critical primary limitation on the application of Title VII to professional employment—the refusal to apply to their subjective evaluation systems the same degree of scrutiny as is applied to the subjective evaluation systems of lower-status, but high-skilled, occupations (Bartholet, 1982, p. 962). Indeed, Justice Powell, in his concurring opinion, made it clear (without so much as a nod to *Keene State College* v. *Sweeney*) that the *Hishon* decision did not call into question the academic abstention doctrine: "The courts of appeal" he said, "generally have acknowledged that respect for academic freedom requires some deference to the judgment of schools and universities as to the qualifications of professors, particularly those considered for tenured positions" (*Hishon* v. *King & Spaulding,* 1984, p. 2237, Note 4).

Invoking the principle of academic freedom, and avowing their incapacity to substitute their subjective assessments for those of professionals, the courts carved out, at least until recently, a higher education exception to the general law of employment discrimination in cases brought by women and minorities against traditionally white postsecondary institutions. Or to put it another way, there was little victim-specific relief because the courts were not willing to try very hard to identify the victims.

Answering a Claim of Reverse Discrimination
with a Nondiscrimination Defense

What, then, of cases brought by white men or white women who allege they have been victims of "reverse discrimination"? Faced with such claims, colleges and universities have a choice of defenses. They can respond within the conventional framework by making a nondiscrimination defense at the rebuttal stage of the *McDonnell-Douglas-Burdine* paradigm, or they can respond with an affirmative action defense of admitted preference.

There are, perhaps, cases of covert preferences for women and minorities—cases in which preferential affirmative action "dare not say its name" (see, e.g., *CUNY-Hostos Community College* v. *SHRAB,* 1983). The lack of clarity regarding the permissible scope of gender or race preferences, in combination with the hands-off doctrine, creates an incentive for academic institutions to choose a conventional defense—that is, to claim that a challenged employment decision was made for legitimate and nondiscriminatory reasons, even though, in reality, race, gender, or ethnic characteristics may have played a significant part. If this is the response, judicial deference to subjective evaluation systems can protect affirmative action discrimination, as well as conventional discrimination, at least at traditionally white institutions. Furthermore, courts are inclined to be sympathetic to academic employers, as they are to other employers faced with a reverse discrimination complaint, because the courts have put all employers, in the metaphors of case law, on "a high tight rope" in strong judicial "crosswinds" (*Steelworkers* v. *Weber,* 1979; *U.S.* v. *City of Alexandria,* 1980).

As will be discussed at greater length in the following section, courts have carved out an uncertain affirmative-action exception to the general antidiscrimination principle affirmed in *McDonald* v. *Santa Fe.* They have interpreted Title VII as creating a "spur" or "catalyst" to voluntary employer efforts to rectify the effects of past employment discrimination, at least in the private sector (*United Steelworkers* v. *Weber,* 1979), an understanding of the statute that embraces resort to race preferences. They have recognized that the use of goals and timetables in accord with Executive Order 11246 and Title VI, even if officially premised on an antidiscrimination theory, creates pressures and incentives to prefer minorities, lest employers be subject to federal contract termination, or at least termination proceedings. Recognizing that employers are called on to perform "the difficult acrobatic task" of remedying the effects of past employment discrimination against minorities and women, without liability-provoking injury to white males, the courts have declared themselves reluctant to engage in "active" *post hoc* judicial review of affirmative action plans when charges of reverse discrimination are raised (*Setzer* v. *Novack,* 1981; *Ende* v. *Board of Regents of Northern Illinois University,* 1985).[3] Even though an employer does not invoke affirmative action considerations in making a nondiscrimination defense to a claim of reverse discrimination, such considerations may nevertheless buttress the judicial disposition to defer to the academic employer's employment decisions.

AFFIRMATIVE ACTION DISCRIMINATION

In conventional disparate-treatment litigation, the judicial inquiry focuses on a factual question: What motivated the defendant, or what inferences can be made about what motivated the defendant? In affirmative-action discrimination litigation, on the other hand, the central issue is not *whether* the employer resorted to race, gender, or national origin preferences to the detriment of the plaintiff, but whether the conceded, purposeful resort to preferences (voluntarily, or pursuant to a court order, or a negotiated settlement, or a consent decree) is statutorily and/or constitutionally permissible. In these cases, the employer substitutes an affirmative action defense for a non-discrimination defense at the rebuttal stage of the *McDonnell–Douglas–Burdine* paradigm. Of course, the affirmative action defense does not attempt to rebut the inference of disparate treatment created by the plaintiff's *prima facie* case; it attempts to justify it.

In 1979, in *United Steelworkers* v. *Weber,* the Supreme Court, for the first time, upheld the lawfulness of minority employment preferences in private industry, as lower federal courts had already done. The Court's acceptance of a group rights interpretation of Title VII was grounded in concern about repairing the terrible damage caused by our history of slavery, segregation, and discrimination against American blacks. But it was an acceptance within limits. By embracing a group rights interpretation, the courts have not discarded individual rights. Thus, it is in working out the limits of affirmative action preferences (based on race, gender, and certain ethnic-group identities) that complexity arises in the unsettled law of affirmative action discrimination.

One way in which complexity has shown up in case law is the importance that the courts have attached to "who" it is that initiates affirmative action preferences. The limits of "what" may or must be done depend in large part on "who" it is that decides. For attempts to ensure greater equality in the distribution of jobs to different groups in American society not only sparks controversy over the meaning of social justice, they also generate, when challenged, questions concerning the proper allocation of political power among the three branches of the federal government, the limits of the equitable remedial power of the courts, and, as in conventional cases, the power balance between the courts and academe. The analysis that follows, therefore, links substantive questions regarding the limits on affirmative action preferences to three categories of initiators.

The first section examines the limits on voluntary preferences initiated by private sector employers. There are indications that within this category, a distinction may develop between traditionally white and traditionally black postsecondary institutions. The second section explores the extent to which the courts have sanctioned preferences voluntarily initiated by public sector employers. This discussion entails consideration of another "who" question, for a distinction has been drawn, although not by an authoritative Supreme Court majority, between public institutions that have a history of employment discrimination and public institutions that do not. Of political as well as legal significance is another distinction, also discussed in the second section, between wholly voluntary and induced voluntary affirmative-action preferences. Although the latter are usually created in response to threatened federal executive-branch enforcement of federal civil-rights statutes, ultimately it is the authority of Congress that encourages judicial acceptance of them. As Chief Justice Burger put it, in his opinion upholding the constitutionality of the minority business enterprise set-aside provision of a 1977 statute:

Congress not only may induce voluntary action to assure compliance with existing federal statutory or constitutional antidiscrimination provisions, but also, where Congress has authority to declare certain conduct unlawful, it may, as here, authorize and induce state action to avoid such conduct. [*Fullilove* v. *Klutznick,* 1980, pp. 483–484]

The third section, finally, considers briefly the rare instances of affirmative action mandates that courts have imposed on higher education employers. It includes consideration of court-approved consent decrees as well as remedies awarded in cases litigated to conclusion. Court-mandated affirmative-action preferences speak, of course, to the limits of what must be done in the name of affirmative action, not to the limits of what an employer may do voluntarily.

Voluntary Preferences in the Private Sector

The distinction between state action and private action creates a major divide in American law. The former is subject to constitutional limitations; the latter is not. Therefore, when Brian Weber, a white steelworker, claimed that the affirmative action plan negotiated between the union and the Kaiser Aluminum Corporation discriminated against him because of his race, he framed a claim under the nondiscrimination provisions of Title VII, not under the equal protection clause of the Fourteenth Amendment. When the Supreme Court rejected Weber's complaint in 1979 and upheld the provision reserving 50% of the craft-training provisions for black employees, it emphasized (repeatedly) that its decision did not address the constitutional validity of voluntary affirmative-action preferences in the public sector.

The decision in *United Steelworkers* v. *Weber* is a monumental landmark in the development of employment discrimination law. For the first time, the Supreme Court endorsed judicial enforcement of a racial quota whose preferences ran toward a historically oppressed minority. Confronted with Weber's claim that the affirmative action quota violated the race-neutral language of sections 703(a) and (d) of Title VII, making it unlawful to discriminate against "any individual because of . . . race" in the hiring and selection of apprentices for training programs, the majority acknowledged that the Kaiser plan could not be squared with a "literal interpretation" of the words of the statute (p. 201). But Kaiser's (ostensibly) voluntary, privately initiated employment-training quota, moved with the spirit of Title VII: "the integration of blacks into the mainstream of American society" (p. 202). Or to put it in terms used earlier, the racial quota could be viewed as an expression of the aspiration for black collective ascent, or as a practical response to the means–end dilemma of affirmative action. Individual black beneficiaries had not proved that they were actual victims of Kaiser's discrimination; the voluntary quota was not victim-specific.

If Kaiser's plan moved with the spirit of Title VII, it could also be reconciled with a literal interpretation of Section 703 (j) of the statute, which provides that

"Nothing . . . shall be interpreted to *require* any employer . . . to grant preferential treatment" (italics added) on account of an imbalance in the employer's
workplace. It could be inferred, the majority concluded, that Congress did not
intend to wholly prohibit a private employer from voluntarily initiating preferential affirmative action "to eliminate manifest racial imbalances in traditionally segregated job categories" (p. 197).

In addition to the substantive merits of the Kaiser plan (discussed below),
two "who" considerations supported the majority's interpretation of Title VII.
The first concerned the allocation of authority between the judiciary and Congress. Since the *Weber* decision was based on statutory interpretation, nothing
was set in constitutional concrete. If the court misread the political will, it was,
as Justice Blackmun emphasized, subject to congressional reversal (p. 216).
(Congress has never done so.) The second concerned the allocation of authority
between the federal government and private business. Kaiser's plan fell, the
majority concluded, within a zone of "management prerogatives, and union
freedoms" (p. 206), which Congress, in passing Title VII, had not intended to
disturb. Thus, the liberal plurality, forming a majority, in consort with conservative Justice Stewart, turned a traditional conservative plea for freedom from
governmental interference with "purely private decision-making," into the
service of a substantive policy—hiring quotas—that today's "conservatives"
and yesterday's "liberals" (see Abram, 1984) reject. Certainly, the principle of
autonomy has a more venerable tradition in higher education, since it is
buttressed by the principle of academic freedom, than it has in the steel
industry. One would suppose that if Justice Frankfurter's *Sweezy* opinion can
be enlisted to protect colleges and universities from full enforcement of the anti-discrimination principle in conventional cases, it would reinforce *Weber* to
protect voluntary preferential hiring (within limits) in private higher education.

What May a Private Sector Employer Do? The importance of *Weber* lies not
only in the court's conclusion that a private "who" may initiate minority hiring
preferences (even in the form of a fixed quota); it also delivered a first
installment on an answer to the question "what" a private "who" may do in
the name of affirmative action. Because a number of lower courts have ignored
Weber's express declarations that it was not deciding what a public "who" may
do and have upheld voluntary public-sector quotas in partial reliance on
Weber, the importance of the case has extended far beyond the Court's
approval of the Kaiser plan.

Groping in legally unchartered territory, on the enormously controversial
issue of group rights, the majority declined to "define in detail the line of
demarcation between permissible and impermissible affirmative action plans"
(p. 208). Nevertheless, it singled out three characteristics of the Kaiser plan that
placed it on the lawful side of the line.

First, the training quota was designed to remedy current black under-repre-
sentation in skilled crafts, from which they have been "traditionally" excluded,

not only by the Kaiser Aluminum Corporation but by the industry (and unions) at large. This purpose was not "remedial" in a "victim-specific" sense, to which William Bradford Reynolds would limit civil rights enforcement. It could not be, for that would require case-by-case adjudication and a coercive judicial award of "make-whole" relief to proven victims of the company's discrimination, and this was a voluntary plan. It was remedial in the much broader sense of group reparations for many decades of employment discrimination in the craft trades. *Weber*'s expansion of the concept of remedy beyond the boundaries of victim-specific relief broadened the scope for lawful voluntary affirmative action. Nevertheless, it also implied limits on minority group preferences. They could be used to eliminate racial imbalances in the employer's *own* craft work force, not in the total national work force. In other words, although voluntary preferences need not be victim-specific, they must be employer-specific.

This first limit that *Weber* placed on a race-conscious affirmative-action plan implied a second: that its preferences must be "a temporary measure" (p. 208). The lawful remedial goal was to eliminate racial imbalances, not to maintain them once this desired end had been met. However problematic in practice the notion of temporariness, it preserves the option for an eventual return to a race-blind (or gender-blind) focus on the legal equality of individuals. It signals that while the Court may endorse group-oriented reparations to attack the unequal distribution of employment opportunities, it has not accepted the notion of an ethnically defined nation (see Glazer, 1983).

There was, finally, a third characteristic of the Kaiser plan that saved it from Brian Weber's claim of unlawful reverse discrimination: it did not "unnecessarily trammel the interests of the white employees" (p. 208). Since the Court announced two bottom-line limitations on the pursuit of equitable job distribution, it appears that it really was concerned with excessive injury to nonminority employees in a normative sense, rather than with unnecessary injury in an instrumental sense. The first limitation was that an affirmative action plan cannot absolutely bar whites (as a group) from job advancement. This, of course, is an inherent characteristic of a quota like that involved in *Weber*, based on the racial composition of the labor force (and a reminder that the price whites pay for black ascent is less than the price blacks have paid for white privilege). What was not clear, however, was how *Weber*'s rejection of a "no-whites-need-apply" affirmative-action plan would transpose to the employment context of higher education, in which job vacancies are limited, specialized, and advertised one at a time. This was a question with which the Eighth Circuit Court of Appeals grappled in *Valentine* v. *Smith* (1981), a case (discussed in more detail below) brought by a disappointed white applicant for a faculty position at Arkansas State University.

The second absolute limitation implied by the Court's approval of the Kaiser plan was that an affirmative action plan cannot require the discharge of white employees and their replacement with new black hirees. Although "innocent" white employees might be asked to "share the burden" of remedying the historical exclusion of blacks from access to the craft trades, they may not be asked to pay the price of being displaced from jobs that they already hold. Using a utilitarian calculus reminiscent of Jeremy Bentham's jurisprudence, the *Weber* Court effected a compromise: the conservative principle of security of vested interests, or the "disappointment preventing principle" (Bowring, 1838, pp. 307–308), was given precedence over the "radical" principle of equality (Halevy, 1955, pp. 46–54). Even in conventional employment-discrimination cases, in which minority plaintiffs have proved that they were victims of unlawful discrimination, judicial remedies have never required that the minority discriminatee bump a nonminority employee.

There is, as yet, no precise higher-education counterpart to *Weber*: there is no reported federal case in which a private "mainstream" (traditionally white) institution of higher education has defended itself against a claim of reverse discrimination by using an affirmative action defense in justification of its conceded use of race (or gender) preferences. A number of explanations come to mind. Many outside applicants may be unaware of the race or gender of the candidate ultimately hired. Many white academics may accept, to some degree, the morality of sharing the burden. And since the courts have proved so reluctant to scrutinize institutional assessments of the "elusive and intangible qualities and talents expected of a scholar and teacher" (*Clark* v. *Whiting*, 1979, p. 640), colleges and universities have enormous latitude for justifying personnel decisions in nondiscriminatory terms.

Whatever the explanation for the absence of affirmative-action discrimination cases involving traditionally white private institutions, *Weber* has been invoked, at the margins of litigation, by traditionally black Howard University. In separate Title VII actions, two white faculty members alleged that they had been discriminated against, one in a decision denying promotion and tenure (*Planells* v. *Howard University*, 1983) and the other in a decision denying reappointment as an assistant professor (*Turgeon* v. *Howard University*, 1983). At both district court trials, which ended in judgments for both plaintiffs, the university had attempted, without success, to rebut the claims of disparate treatment discrimination with a nondiscrimination defense. But before trial in the *Planells* case, and following trial in the *Turgeon* case, Howard cast aside the *McDonnell-Douglas-Burdine* framework. It attempted instead to place its actions under the protection of *Weber*, which, the university argued, "makes it clear that the 1964 Civil Rights Act does not prohibit . . . private affirmative action programs to remedy past racial discrimination or segregation" (Defendants' Memorandum, *Turgeon* v. *Howard University*, 1983, p. 7).

Although Howard's *Weber*-based argument was not tested, there were some obvious problems with it. The racial imbalance in Howard's faculty work force, and in the department in which both Planells and Turgeon worked, unlike Kaiser's craft work force, ran in favor of black faculty—in fact, way above the labor-market availability statistics used by the university. Although the Supreme Court acknowledged in *Weber* that the causes of minority underrepresentation may lie beyond the responsibility of the employer, the voluntary elimination of "conspicuous racial imbalances" in the defendant's *own* work force sets the limits of lawful affirmative-action racial preferences. Furthermore, *Weber* involved whites preferring blacks in order to integrate the company's work force. *Planells* and *Turgeon* involved blacks preferring blacks in order to strengthen the university's black identity. This distinction required, therefore, that Howard advance a "novel" affirmative-action defense that transcended the *Weber* framework. In the words of Professor Kenneth S. Tollett (1982), from which Howard's Memorandum borrowed heavily, black colleges are "instruments of affirmative action." Consequently, a black postsecondary institution must be subject to "a different legal standard" (Memorandum, p. 8) from white institutions under Title VII (as well as in every facet of the integration process). The limits of lawful affirmative action in employment at a black college must be measured, the university argued, not by *Weber*'s standard of achieving racial balance in the employer's own work force, but by whether or not "teaching opportunities for blacks in the total workforce would be diminished" (Memorandum, p. 9). Short of a total exclusion of nonblacks, Howard University claimed, as a dismayed Carl Rowan put it, "a unique legal right to discriminate against anyone who is not black" (May 6, 1983). District Judge Pratt, in a footnote to his opinion upholding Planell's Title VII claim, denounced Howard's theory (which was advanced before, but not during, the trial) as "apostate to the cause of racial equality" (p. 345).

Novel as Howard's affirmative-action theory was in the context of a Title VII suit, arguments linking the cultural, social, economic, educational, and political process of blacks to black colleges were not new and were certainly not news to Judge Pratt. In 1973, Judge Pratt had directed HEW to commence funds cut-off proceedings against ten states that HEW had concluded were operating racially segregated systems of higher education in violation of Title VI's prohibition on race discrimination in federally funded programs or activities (*Adams* v. *Richardson,* 1973a). Officials of black colleges were alarmed at the prospect of institutional extinction through assimilation into a white-dominated higher-education system (see Egerton, 1974-1975). In a friend-of-the-court brief, the National Association for Equal Opportunity in Higher Education (NAFEO), a voluntary association of 110 presidents of predominantly black colleges, public as well as private, opposed Judge Pratt's order: it ignored the supportive role—"the compensatory bridge"—that black institutions of higher education play for black graduates of "a crippling and debilitating elementary and secondary education system" (NAFEO Brief, p. 20, 23). The legal goal, the black educators argued, is not equal educational opportunity, but the "equality of educational attainment" (p. 19), a view that echoed but that made no reference to President Johnson's 1965 Howard University speech. Despite differences in emphasis, NAFEO's view of the racial mission of black colleges, as well as a results-oriented view of equity, anticipated arguments made on behalf of women's colleges in the 1980s. "It's important for women to have a place where they are given *every* opportunity, not just equal opportunity" said President Keohane of Wellesley (Ingalls, 1984, p. 19). Champions of black colleges and women's colleges both challenge the atomizing and sometimes crippling effects of competition under the regime of race- and gender-blind equality of opportunity when the "vestiges" of segregation, discrimination, and socialization are internalized in the minds of young blacks and women (see Flemming, 1984). Both also define diversity in postsecondary education in terms of offering students a choice of institutions with distinctive race and gender identities.

NAFEO's plea did not fall on entirely deaf ears. The Court of Appeals, in modifying Judge Pratt's order, admonished HEW to take "into account the special problems of minority students and of black colleges" (*Adams* v. *Richardson,* 1973b, p. 1165). Subsequently, in 1977, in his Second Supplemental Order in *Adams* v. *Califano,* Judge Pratt declared it "the responsibility of HEW to devise criteria for higher education desegregation plans which will take into account the unique importance of black colleges" (p. 120).

Did this mean that black colleges have a unique legal right to discriminate in employment against nonblacks? The 1973 NAFEO brief did not suggest that only black faculty could serve as "healers for wounded minds and restless souls" (p. 27), even though the mood and rhetoric of "black power" was strong on some black campuses. On the contrary, it noted with pride that "The doors of black institutions without exception have . . . been open to all races, sexes, colors, creeds, and they have always collectively offered employment and other incidental privileges to all who passed through their doors" (p. 27). But Howard University's 1983 Memorandum reflects the change in perspective that the decade had wrought. Drawing on the words of Professor Tollett (1982), it advanced a role model theory—the critical link between the concept of the black college as an instrument of affirmative action and the right of the black colleges to give preferences to black faculty. Women's colleges, too, advance a role model argument. But because the supply of female academics is far greater than the supply of black academics, women's colleges are in a better position to achieve their gender goals through nondiscriminatory affirmative action—through "concerted efforts to expand the applicants . . . to make sure women are included" (Keohane, 1984). For black colleges, however, given the scarcity of blacks with doctorates (ACE, 1984, p. 7; Lee et al., 1985, p. 11) and their uneven distribution by field (Blackwell, 1981, p. 296; 1983, p. 88; National Research Council, 1983, p. 29), efforts to achieve racial goals must necessitate discrimination against whites and preferences for blacks. Howard's Memorandum sought support for such a policy. Although the University's argument was not squarely tested in *Planells,* Judge Pratt clearly prejudiced the answer in his harshly negative dictum rejecting Howard's view of affirmative action as unfaithful to the egalitarian ideal (see also *Dybezak* v. *Tuskeegee Institute,* 1984). And in both the *Turgeon* and *Planells* cases, the court took account of positive student evaluations of the white faculty in their finding that Howard had discriminated against them, perhaps intending an implicit rejection of the university's role-model theory.

As far as public black colleges are concerned, Judge Pratt's decision in *Adams* v. *Califano* led to the OCR's staunchly integrationist *Revised Criteria Specifying the Ingredients of an Acceptable Plan to Desegregate State Systems of Public Higher Education* (1978) (sometimes referred to as the Califano Guidelines and hereinafter referred to as the Revised Criteria). The Revised Criteria's recognition of "the unique importance of [public] black colleges" did not exempt those institutions from the statewide approach to desegregation. The transition to a unitary system of higher education was not to place a "disproportionate burden" on black students and black faculty (Revised Criteria, 1978, p. 6660). But the "goal" (explicitly not an "arbitrary quota," p. 6659) of faculty desegregation was a representation of black faculty at *each* institution in a proportion at least equal to the proportion of blacks with master's and doctoral degrees (for positions requiring each), in appropriate disciplines, in the relevant labor market (pp. 6662–6663). The influence of the faculty component of the Revised Criteria can be seen in some *Adams* states desegregation plans (e.g., Arkansas, Florida, Oklahoma, and Texas).[4] But by 1984, if not earlier, the authority of the Revised Criteria was problematic, for, as discussed the following section, neither the Reagan administration nor the courts now consider them binding. Suffice it to note here that as an obvious practical matter, given the growing shortage of black academics (Mackey-Smith, 1984, p. 37; ACE, Office of Minority Affairs, 1983, 1984; Bowen and Schuster, 1985), the ability, if not the legal right, of private (as well as public) black colleges and universities to hire and retain black faculty aggravates the problem for white institutions that seek to increase the presence of black faculty.

Voluntary and Induced Voluntary Preferences in the Public Sector
Weber did not offer a litmus test for determining the lawfulness of all voluntary private-sector affirmative-action plans. It nevertheless provided guidance for making an affirmative action defense to a claim of reverse discrimination. The Supreme Court has provided very little, however, in the way of guidance specifically for public employers. There is no public-sector counterpart to

Weber—no Supreme Court decision in which a coherent majority opinion has explicitly endorsed voluntary group preferences under limiting conditions. Nor has the Supreme Court provided clear guidelines for induced voluntary affirmative-action preferences; that is, those initiated in response to anticipated or threatened administrative enforcement of Title VI, the Executive Order, or Title IX. In its 1984 decision in *Stotts,* rejecting a court-ordered layoff quota (under the authority of Title VII) in the Memphis fire department, the Court emphasized that it had not reached or decided the question of the constitutionality of voluntary preferences in public employment, although a number of lower courts have upheld them (e.g., *Bratton* v. *City of Detroit,* 1983; *Valentine* v. *Smith, 1981; Bushey* v. *New York State Civil Service Commission,* 1984; *Williams* v. *New Orleans,* 1984; *Palmer* v. *Trustees of Saint Petersburg Junior College,* 1984; *Marsh* v. *Flint Board of Education,* 1985; *Wygant* v. *Jackson Board of Education,* 1984). As noted in the introduction, whether or not *Wygant* becomes the test case of voluntary, public-sector affirmative action remains to be seen.

As of mid-1985, the Supreme Court had considered constitutional challenges to government-initiated affirmative-action preferences, designed to benefit racial minorities, on only two occasions. The first was *Regents of the University of California* v. *Bakke,* decided in 1978. Perhaps the affirmative action case best known by name, *Bakke* may well, as one commentator suggested, have left the man (and woman) in the street "confused as hell." A majority of Justices, though not through a majority opinion, held that the public university's minority admissions quota—a 16-seat set-aside at the Davis medical school—violated Title VI's ban on discrimination in federally funded programs. A second majority, though again not through a majority opinion, agreed that race may be taken into consideration in the admissions process. They also agreed that unlike Title VII, Title VI, like the Constitution, is directed only at intentional discrimination (see also, *Guardian's Association* v. *Civil Service Commission of New York,* 1983).

The second case is *Fullilove* v. *Klutznick,* decided in 1980. A majority of Justices concluded, though once again not through a majority opinion (indeed there was not even a plurality opinion), that a provision of the Public Works Employment Act of 1977, requiring that at least 10% of federal funds granted for local public works be used to purchases services and supplies from minority-owned businesses, did not violate the equal protection component of the Fifth Amendment of the Constitution.

What do the lower courts make of *Bakke* and *Fullilove,* cases without majority opinions, but cases in which a majority of Justices agreed on certain results for conflicting reasons? It is clear that a majority of Justices have concluded that not all race-conscious policies are constitutionally impermissible, but that is all that is clear. In neither *Bakke* nor *Fullilove* did the Supreme

Court hold that a public "who" may initiate affirmative-action *employment* preferences. And yet the lower federal courts, drawing selectively from opinions in *Bakke* and *Fullilove,* in combination with *Weber,* have upheld preferences in cases involving the employment of fire fighters, police officers, public-school teachers, prison guards, and even university faculty. Furthermore, not only have lower courts concluded that *Weber* applies to public employees; they have discounted the importance that *Weber* attached to congressional concern with the economic plight of black Americans in particular, and they have held that Title VII does not prohibit voluntary affirmative-action programs designed to remedy sexual and ethnic imbalance in the public work force (see *United States* v. *City of Miami,* 1981; *La Riviere* v. *EEOC,* 1982; *United States* v. *City of Alexandria,* 1980; *Williams* v. *City of New Orleans,* 1984).

As a result of the Supreme Court's decisions, Allan Bakke, a white medical-school applicant, gained access to medical training, while Brian Weber, a white production worker, was denied access to craft training, and white-owned businesses were denied access to a small portion of government contracting opportunities. What explains the difference in outcomes? Is it that *Bakke* focused on educational opportunity and *Weber* on access to employment opportunity? It is unlikely. The lower courts routinely select from the "sometimes inscrutable trilogy" of the *Bakke* opinions in deciding reverse discrimination cases in public sector employment (e.g., *Detroit Police Officers Ass'n* v. *Young,* 1979; *United States* v. *City of Miami,* 1980; *Valentine* v. *Smith,* 1981; *Bratton* v. *City of Detroit,* 1983). Though technically an employment discrimination complaint, Weber's claim that he was denied access to job training was analogous to Bakke's complaint that he was denied access to medical training. And the special deference that the courts accord to academic institutions did not operate to protect the University of California's "fixed-allocation" minority-quota plan.

The difference in outcomes among these three cases reflects both "who" and "what" considerations, at least for Justice Powell, whose swing opinion, because it formed part of both the quota-no, race-yes majorities in *Bakke,* was billed as the judgment of the Court, and for Chief Justice Burger, whose opinion in *Fullilove* was also presented as the judgment of the Court (in the absence of a majority that congealed around a single opinion).

The University of California had never been found guilty of intentionally discriminating on the basis of race in its medical school. Nor did it admit to a history of discrimination. The vice, then, of the University of California plan was, in Justice Powell's view, a consequence of the university's virtue. It had no authority, under statute or Constitution, to initiate preferential racial classifications as a way of contributing to the redress of race discrimination in American society at large. Had the university simply proclaimed a *mea culpa,* it could not have rescued its plan. Nor could it have satisfied Justice Powell by making findings of its own history of past discrimination. College and university governing boards, Justice Powell emphasized later in *Fullilove,* lack authority to make such findings: they are "entrusted only with educational functions" (p. 498).

In addressing the meaning of the equal protection clause of the Fourteenth Amendment and the nondiscrimination provision of Title VI, Justice Powell struggled to remain within an individual rights framework. Since their guarantees of equality are guarantees to individuals, any race classification becomes, in the terminology of Supreme Court jurisprudence, "suspect" and subject to "the most exacting judicial examination" (*Bakke,* p. 291)—in practice, fatal scrutiny, ever since this test of constitutionality had been articulated. It had been fashioned to deal with state-sanctioned discrimination against America's racial minorities. No "compelling governmental interest," the predicate for justifying racial classifications under the Constitution, had ever been identified when those harmed by the classifications were racial minorities. But the *Bakke* case was the first ever to present the Supreme Court with a racial classification benefiting a racial minority—the one that suffered, as Justice Powell put it, from a "tragic legacy" (*Fullilove,* p. 516). Although Justice Powell's opinion was the swing vote that defeated the university's quota plan (joining the four Justices who, unlike Justice Powell, hewed to an absolute, color-blind, individual-rights interpretation of Title VI), it was an opinion that left the door open for the reparations theory of group rights. Remedying an institution's own past discrimination, Powell agreed, could be a compelling governmental interest. If an institution of public higher education is found, by a body with "authority and capability" (p. 309) to make a determination, to have contributed to discrimination against black Americans, then "precisely tailored" remedial preferences could be created (p. 299). Powell's *Bakke* opinion appeared to endorse a violation-specific rather than a victim-specific theory of remedies under the Constitution and the civil rights statutes. It countenanced race-based preferences to remedy identified employer, union, industry, and even societal discrimination even if individual beneficiaries of the preferences are not proven victims of that discrimination.

Who has authority to make a finding of discrimination justifying remedial minority preferences? "Beyond question," Congress has. "Unlike the Regents of the University of California, Congress properly may—and indeed must—address directly the problems of discrimination in our society," Justice Powell wrote in *Fullilove,* in support of the 10% minority set-aside provision (p. 499). The Chief Justice agreed that Congress has the constitutional authority "to initiate a limited racial and ethnic preference" (p. 468) to remedy the present effects of previous discrimination, without the need to identify the precise perpetrators or victims of that discrimination (p. 484).

What government body besides Congress has the authority to make a finding of discrimination justifying a remedial racial preference? Congress alone, in the view of Justice Powell, may initiate group preferences in response to societal discrimination—"an amorphous concept of injury that may be ageless in its reach into the past" (*Bakke,* 1978, p. 304). But administrative and legislative agencies, as well as courts, may impose employer- or industry-specific preferences on their findings of unlawful employer or industry discrimination. Justice Powell suggested that the Office of Federal Contract Compliance Programs could do so: "Every decision upholding the requirement of preferential hiring under authority of Executive Order 11246," he noted with approval, but without elaboration, "has emphasized the existence of previous discrimination as a predicate for the imposition of a preferential remedy" (*Bakke,* 1978, p. 301, Note 40). Powell also seemed to suggest that the Equal Employment Opportunity Commission or the U.S. Attorney General might agree to minority preferences in the settlement of Title VII suits. Rejection of the University of California admissions plan, he noted, "does not call into question congressionally authorized administrative actions, such as consent decrees under Title VII" (p. 302, Note 41). Lower courts have frequently approved consent decrees containing rigid hiring and promotion quotas and, in postsecondary education, goals that are designed to put pressure on the academic hiring process.

Justice Powell also raised the possibility that if the Office for Civil Rights, the responsible administrative agency for enforcing Title VI, had found that the University of California had engaged in discriminatory admissions practices, then some kind of remedial preferences—though possibly not in the form of a fixed number or percentage of minority places—would have met with constitutional approval (*id.*).

Title VI, Title VII, and the Executive Order (a congressionally approved executive-branch initiative), like the minority business enterprise program upheld in *Fullilove,* exemplify, as Chief Justice Burger put it, congressional initiatives to "induce voluntary action to assure compliance with . . . federal statutory or constitutional antidiscrimination provisions" (pp. 483–484). And, he emphasized, especially when Congress induces "voluntary cooperation with remedial measures . . . by placing conditions on federal expenditures," it may experiment with "the limited use of racial and ethnic criteria" (p. 490).

When courts uphold voluntary minority preferences "induced" by an act of Congress, and by the administrative agencies entrusted with "flesh[ing] out" the "bare bones" of the statutory "skeleton" (p. 468), they are deferring to the "politically responsive branches of Government" (p. 490). By contrast, when courts uphold, on constitutional grounds, purely voluntary preferences, initiated without an administrative finding of discrimination pursuant to an act of, or approval by, Congress, they go beyond and possibly against the will of the elected branch. In sum, the question of "who" may initiate group preferences in the public sector implicates the perennial question regarding the proper allocation of political power between the elected and the appointed branches of government.

The common ground in *Bakke* between Justice Powell, who rejected the racial quota, and the four Justices who approved of it (Brennan, White, Marshall, and Blackmun) was the requirement of some finding of discrimination to justify remedial race preferences. For the Brennan four, it sufficed that Congress had made findings of societal discrimination against disadvantaged minorities, entitling the University of California to initiate voluntarily its preferential admissions plan. For Justice Powell, the university could respond in this way only on the basis of judicial, legislative, or administrative findings of the university's unlawful discrimination. But even in the absence of such a finding, Justice Powell's deciding vote did not foreclose voluntary race-conscious (or gender- or ethnic-conscious) decisions in public colleges and universities. Powell's struggle to accommodate minority concerns while remaining within an individual rights framework resulted in his proposition (celebrated or notorious, depending on one's ethical views regarding group reparations) that an academic institution that has not been found guilty of unlawful discrimination by an authoritative body may, in the interest of creating a diverse student body, make race a factor in its admissions decisions (pp. 313–314): score so many points for an oboe player, so many for a running back, and so many for applicants with an African heritage. That was the idea underlying the undergraduate Harvard admissions plan to which Justice Powell drew approving attention. An applicant's race, gender, or ethnicity is treated as one among a number of personal qualifications; it contributes to the well-being of those institutions that value diversity. In theory, there are in this scheme no explicit goals or quotas; no predesignated number of minority places from which other race applicants are precluded from competing, as Allan Bakke had been blocked from competing for the sixteen minority places at the Davis medical school. When an important goal in a generally meritocratic selection process is diversity (of interests, talents, race, culture, and region), individuals are compared to individuals; no one, therefore, can "complain of unequal treatment under the Fourteenth Amendment" (p. 318). For those who adhere to a reparations theory of group rights—to the view that the Thirteenth and Fourteenth Amendments and their implementing civil-rights statutes countenance special redress to black Americans because of their tragic history—Justice Powell's approach was deemed a misguided, even a "dishonest," subterfuge (Calabresi, 1979, p. 427). It is not that educational diversity is an unworthy goal, but rather that diversity is so much less a morally compelling goal than repairing the contemporary inegalitarian effects of segregation and discrimination.

For others, Powell's approach was an astute way of finessing a showdown between the individual and group rights theories of equality. Moreover, an individualized, case-by-case approach, in which race or ethnic background may be deemed a "plus" (p. 318) promised to insulate the "academic process" from judicial interference (p. 319, Note 53). The diversity theory was anchored to the principle of academic freedom. One of the "four essential freedoms" of the university identified by Justice Frankfurter, Justice Powell observed, is the freedom "to determine who may be admitted to study" (pp. 312–314, quoting *Sweezy* v. *New Hampshire*).

Assuming, as the lower courts do, that the opinions expressed in *Bakke* apply to employment as well as to admissions, what does Justice Powell's diversity theory imply? First, public colleges and universities that have never been found to have engaged in illegal discrimination may consider race, gender, and ethnicity a "plus" if these applicant or candidate characteristics contribute to the diversity of the academic work force, and if the position to be filled is not predesignated exclusively for members of a particular group. Assuming that diversification is defined in terms of increasing the presence of poorly represented groups, it is difficult, if not impossible, to separate diversity concerns from affirmative-action equity concerns. The University of Vermont's Affirmative Action Policy Statement, for example, renders them virtually indistinguishable. The university seeks "to redress the consequences of past denial" to women and minorities, "of full participation in all societal functions" and to create "a diverse and heterogeneous campus community."

There is no clear test case, at any judicial level, in which a public college or university has responded to a charge of reverse discrimination in employment exclusively with a diversity defense. In nonacademic contexts, preferential hiring, promotions, and layoffs are primarily defended in the name of affirmative action to address the effects of prior discrimination (Bartholet, 1982, p. 1014). Because there are relatively few cases involving allegations of reverse discrimination in higher education, it is not possible to identify a trend. As suggested, in the earlier section on answering a claim of reverse discrimination, the defense of choice may be the nondiscrimination defense.

There are, however, three hiring cases in which "mainstream" public colleges and universities have answered reverse discrimination complaints with an affirmative action defense. In the first case, *Cramer* v. *Virginia Commonwealth University* (1977), the district court initially rejected a hiring preference for women, and by implication for blacks. Although it finally ground to an inconclusive halt (because it was declared moot before it could be litigated to conclusion, 1980), it deserves comment because of the importance of the issue raised. The second case, *Valentine* v. *Smith* (involving Arkansas State University), is more authoritative. It upheld affirmative-action hiring preferences for blacks, the moral and legal dimensions of which have been more fully, although incompletely, explored by the Supreme Court than has affirmative-action hiring preferences for women. It was affirmed by a federal court of appeals, left standing by the Supreme Court, and has been cited with approval in cases upholding race- and ethnic-conscious preferences in plans involving public-school teachers (*Wygant* v. *Jackson Board of Education,* 1982, 1984), corrections officers (*Kirkland* v. *N.Y. State Department of Correction Services,* 1983), police (*Bratton* v. *City of Detroit,* 1983; *Williams* v. *Vukovich,* 1983) and fire fighters (*Warsocki* v. *City of Omaha,* 1984). The third case, *Palmer* v. *District Bd. of Trustees of St. Petersburg Community College* (1984), follows and reinforces the authority of *Valentine* v. *Smith.* Taken together, the three higher-education cases illustrate the unsettled state of the law of affirmative action.

In *Cramer* v. *VCU* (1977), the plaintiff claimed that he had been denied an advertised faculty position because of his sex. The university, conceding that it had discriminated against Cramer because he was male, defending its action as an attempt "to fulfill the national and State policy of affirmatively seeking women and minority employees as a device to eliminate the effects of past discrimination against these groups" (p. 679). VCU's reparations theory was not a *post hoc* rationalization of whatever decision process was used (a matter of dispute): the policy preface to VCU's public, detailed affirmative-action plan stated upfront that "Fully qualified minorities and women will be given equal consideration for employment as the best qualified male caucasians" (p. 679, Note 4). At the pre-*Bakke,* pre-*Weber* trial in 1976, the university contended that hiring preferences for women and minorities were justified under Executive Order 11246, and that the Executive Order overrode the nondiscrimination provisions of Title VII, on which Dr. Cramer had partially based his complaint. Assuming a conflict between the university's interpretation of the Executive Order and Title VII, a secondary but weighty question implicated by Cramer's complaint was the allocation of power between the executive branch and Congress. The *Cramer* case was not the first to call into question the allocation of power, though it was the first and only one to do so in the context of academic hiring. A number of decisions had upheld the constitutionality of race-conscious affirmative-action plans under the Executive Order, including the decision of the Third Circuit Court upholding the Philadelphia plan (*Contractors Association of Eastern Pennsylvania* v. *Secretary of Labor,* 1971). And in 1972, when Congress amended Title VII, extending its coverage to education and public employment, it had those cases before it. Did Congress intend to exempt the Executive Order from the nondiscrimination language of Title VII? Some commentators (see *University of Chicago Law Review,* Vol. 39, 1972) argued that it did. The circuit court that considered *Weber* did not. Acknowledging, as the Supreme Court did not, that Kaiser's plan had, in fact, been "induced" by threats from the OFFCP, the appellate court held that if the

Executive Order mandated a racial quota, *"in the absence of any prior hiring or promotion discrimination,* the Executive Order must fall before [the] direct congressional prohibition" of Title VII (1977, p. 227, italics in the original). Because the Supreme Court reversed this holding and upheld the lawfulness of Kaiser's "voluntary" affirmative-action plan, *cum* quotas, under Title VII, the Supreme Court sidestepped the issue of the relationship between the Executive Order and the act of Congress. In the *Weber* context, they were not in conflict.

In the context of Professor Cramer's claim of reverse sex discrimination, however, they were. In 1976, before the Supreme Court had handed down its decision in *Weber*, the district court ruled that the presidential Executive Order could not "supersede" what it considered to be Congress's nondiscrimination mandate in Title VII (1976, p. 680). In 1980, although dismissing the *Cramer* case for mootness, the district court left no doubt that *Weber* would not have rescued "the conclusively sexist nature of VCU's hiring process" (1980, p. 189). It treated *Weber* like a disease that had to be quarantined. Beyond its application to Kaiser's plan, *Weber* would not, the court declared, "otherwise guide the lower courts in determining what is and what is not permissible race or sex discrimination" (1980, p. 190). Nothing was made of the fact, in this post-*Weber* dictum, that the *Cramer* case, unlike the *Weber* case, dealt with a public employer. In 1976, however, the district court appeared to rule out any affirmative-action hiring preferences in the public sector as violations of the equal protection clause of the Constitution (1976, p. 677; see also, *Virginia Law Review,* 1977, p. 1389).

Strictly speaking, *Cramer* v. *VCU* set a mood but not a precedent. The views expressed were the dictum of one district judge in proceedings that were dismissed when these ceased to be "a genuine case or controversy." Yet the case illustrates a widely understood affirmative-action dilemma. The Executive Order, as the regulations of the Office of Federal Contract Compliance Programs states (Revised Order No. 4, 41 CFR 60-2.10), is "result oriented." It encourages federal contractors to ensure that their work forces will be generally representative of the available pool of women and minorities. But if openings in a particular job category, such as faculty positions, are scarce and turnover is slow, and if the academic employer has "underutilized" minorities and women in its professoriate (as the *Cramer* court was willing to assume), then the only way for an affirmative action university to bring its academic work force up to "full utilization . . . where deficiencies exist" is to hire at a rate greater than the availability pool, however defined. And that suggests in general terms, if not in every specific hiring situation, preferential treatment. Several authorities have suggested that "An employer who insures that its workplace is generally representative of the area labor market will be, in a practical sense, largely immune from discrimination suits" (Sullivan, et al., 1980, p. 823). But, they caution, citing the *Cramer* case, employers may be vulnerable if a policy of preferences is "overt."

The *Cramer* suggested a position on affirmative action that is in accord with the position of the U.S. Justice Department under the Reagan administration. *Valentine* v. *Smith* looks in an opposite direction and carries more precedential value within the judiciary. Furthermore, because it is embedded within the sprawling and protracted *Adams* litigation, its import is far greater.

In 1970, black students, citizens, and taxpayers initiated the *Adams* litigation, under the aegis of and represented by the NAACP Legal Defense Fund (hereinafter LDF)[5] to compel the OCR to enforce Title VI against ten state systems of higher education (subsequently expanded to nineteen) and over a hundred elementary- and secondary-school districts. At issue in the higher education component of the litigation, as the LDF put it, were "the rights of some one million three hundred thousand students attending segregated public higher education systems continuing annually to receive massive Federal aid" (Brief for Plaintiff-Appellees, No. 72-1273, 1973). By directing its complaint against the federal agency responsible, under Title VI, for eliminating discrimination against recipients of federal funds, the LDF attempted a "wholesale" attack on segregation in public higher education "in lieu of retail individual suits against segregating recipients of Federal funds" (Petitioners Reply Memorandum, *Adams* v. *Bell,* No. 83-643, 1983, p. 5). Arkansas was one of the original ten "*Adams* states" that HEW had determined to be in violation of Title VI. In the mid-1970s, following Judge Pratt's 1973 order (*Adams* v. *Richardson,* 1973a) directing HEW to commence enforcement proceedings, the Arkansas Department of Higher Education responded to HEW pressure by developing a revised statewide desegregation plan. It was endorsed by Arkansas State University (hereinafter ASU) and, in July 1974, by the OCR. But the monitoring of plan implementation led the OCR to conclude that violation of Title VI had continued into 1975. The threat of OCR enforcement actions produced discussion, and in the fall of 1975, ASU's "Affirmative Action Program Pursuant to Title VI" was promulgated. It committed the university to a goal of a 5% black faculty by 1979, a goal that could be met only if 25% of the faculty hired in the next four years were black.

In 1976, Bonnie Valentine, a white female, applied for a position as an instructor of business education at ASU, a position advertised as an entry-level position requiring a master's degree. With seven years of prior teaching experience at ASU (thus ASU's appellate brief labeled the plaintiff an "old boy," 1981) and a master's degree plus thirty hours of credit toward a doctorate, Valentine was initially ranked at the top of the lists submitted by both the division chairman and the search committee to the dean, who, in turn, recommended her appointment to the vice president. At this point the vice-president and ASU's affirmative-action office informed the dean and the division chair of the "hazards of hiring" a white applicant if a black applicant met the minimum qualifications specified in the position announcement (Brief for Appellant, *Valentine* v. *Smith,* 1981, p. 10). Among the perceived hazards was the risk of disregarding a "court order," an allusion to Judge Pratt's 1973 *Adams* order (which was directed, it should be emphasized, at HEW, not ASU), and the prodding of HEW and OCR. Following intrauniversity discussion, Valentine's name was withdrawn, and the names of two black applicants were forwarded instead. Georgia Mitchell, a black applicant whose qualifications matched those of the position advertisement, was hired. Valentine brought suit, claiming race discrimination in violation of Title VI and the Fourteenth Amendment. Despite testimony that ASU had acted in response to perceived federal pressure, the university did not attempt, at either trial or appellate court level, an affirmative action defense. Instead, ASU contended that because Valentine was overqualified for the entry-level position, as those qualifications were advertised (and because she was initially given an unfair chance because she was part of the "old boy network"; ASU, Brief for Appellees, *Valentine* v. *Smith,* 1981, p. 9), the university would be "buying a lawsuit" if it hired her. By not hiring her, ASU, of course, bought a lawsuit anyway.

After winning the case at the appeals court level on an argument that it did not make, ASU finally developed an affirmative action justification (based on *Bakke, Weber,* and *Fullilove*), supplemented by a diversity argument (based on Justice Powell's *Bakke* opinion), in opposing Valentine's unsuccessful petition for Supreme Court review (Respondents' Brief in Opposition, No. 81-745, 1982, pp. 5–9). According to Valentine's attorney, "there was a substantial debate within the [Reagan] Justice Department as to whether an amicus brief should be filed" in support of her request for *certiorari.* But nothing came of it (Bristow, May 6, 1983).

In 1980, the district court, in a cryptic, unpublished opinion, had resolved the case in the university's favor, although it conceded that Valentine's position was "not . . . entirely without merit." Disregarding ASU's contention that race was not a motivating factor, the court upheld the hiring decision on affirmative action grounds. ASU had attempted to reach the goals of its HEW-approved AAP, which the court held, was constitutionally and statutorily permissible, in light of *Bakke* and *Weber.* In addition to this judicially created affirmative action "defense," which ASU had not dared or wished to make, the court called into play the academic abstention doctrine: "since both Georgia Mitchell and the plaintiff were qualified for the vacancy, it was within the expertise and discretion of the university officials as to which applicant would be employed" (*Valentine* v. *Smith,* 1980). Here, a hands-off posture cut in favor of a race-conscious hiring discrimination where the minority applicant met the minimum advertised qualifications.

When the case was appealed, ASU again refused to concede that Valentine had been denied the position because of her race. Again, however, a court concluded to the contrary. The Eighth Circuit Court not only met head-on—and rejected—Valentine's reverse discrimination claim, it provided a Fourteenth Amendment rationale and partial guidelines for and limits to race preferences at a public university, distilled from various opinions in *Bakke, Fullilove,* and *Weber,* as well as lower court decisions upholding racial quotas in public employment. Because the Supreme Court denied review, *Valentine* v. *Smith* was left standing, to be cited, in turn, in employment settings other than academe, as we have seen, in support of voluntary and induced voluntary affirmative-action preferences. In December 1984, the Eleventh Circuit Court affirmed the trial court's decision to grant St. Petersburg Community College a motion for summary judgment as a matter of law (*Palmer,* 1984, p. 601), a disposition of a case that assumed legal clarity and certainty. The college's defense to the claim that it preferred a black over the white plaintiff was that it was acting pursuant to and in compliance with its AAP, which had been accepted by HEW (p. 596). It was a component of the community college segment of Florida's higher education plan designed to comply with Title VI (p. 576). Since the plaintiff acknowledged the validity of the AAP as a remedial measure for past discrimination in Florida's state system of higher education, the appellate court concluded that it passed the *Valentine* "tests" without question (p. 600 and Note 14).

Thus, the qualified ground rules that *Valentine* v. *Smith* set forth, though still leaving many questions yet unanswered, provide the most explicit guidance that any court has yet offered with regard to voluntary and induced voluntary affirmative action in public higher education:

1. A public university may, without violating the equal protection clause of the Fourteenth Amendment, initiate race-conscious affirmative action in hiring, if it is based on a plan that is aimed at the contemporary effects of past discrimination at the institution. (a) This remedial justification requires that some findings of past discrimination be made by "qualified persons" (p. 508). A number of lower federal courts have concluded that nonacademic public employers are competent to make findings of their own past discrimination, ignoring Justice Powell's insistence in *Bakke* and *Fullilove* that there must be an external judicial, legislative, or administrative finding of constitutional or statutory discrimination to justify preferential affirmative action. In *Valentine,* however, the circuit court held open the question of whether or not a public university is competent to make the requisite findings. Under the most restrictive interpretation of *Bakke,* which takes Justice Powell's view into account, there were sufficient findings by "competent" external authorities—a district court and HEW—to justify the remedial purpose of ASU's AAP. (b) The remedial justification for preferential affirmative action also requires that individuals who develop and implement an affirmative action plan understand "the nature and extent of past discriminatory practices" (p. 508); see also, *Setzer* v. *Novack* (1981) and *Lehman* v. *Yellow Freight Systems, Inc.* (1981). *Post hoc*

rationalizations will not satisfy a court that a preferential hiring decision was intended and understood to implement a legitimate remedial plan. The implicit prudential message of the *Cramer* decision for academic institutions may be to veil a specific unlawful affirmative-action preference, intended to make progress toward the goals of a plan, behind a nondiscrimination defense. The message of the *Valentine* opinion, on the other hand, is to link overtly a justifiable preference to the university's AAP.

2. Having established a remedial justification for a race-conscious affirmative-action hiring plan, the *Valentine* court adopted a standard of review to determine whether the particular plan was constitutionally permissible. The "test" was whether the ASU plan was "substantially related" to remedying past discrimination (p. 510). It comprised four components that selectively combined elements of opinions in *Bakke, Weber,* and *Fullilove:*

a. First, employment goals may "not unreasonably exceed" the faculty racial balance that would have existed without past discrimination. Without suggesting criteria for determining what a discrimination-free hiring process would have produced, the court found ASU's 25% four-year hiring goal reasonable. No reference was made to labor market availability, however determined. Instead the court made a cryptic, unexplained allusion to the racial population (23.6% black) of the geographic area from which ASU attracts its students (p. 511). In dealing with elementary and secondary education, a number of lower courts have expressly endorsed and some have mandated affirmative action plans that seek to match the percentage of minority teachers to the percentage of race- or ethnic-alike minority students in the school system, rather than to the racial or ethnic compositions of a teacher population with special qualifications required for the positions in question. (See Clague, 1984, 1985, and cases discussed therein; compare *Wygant v. Jackson Board of Education,* 1982, 1984; *Hazelwood School District v. United States,* 1977). No court, no statute, no executive order, regulation, guideline, or criteria have ever suggested that the proper comparison for setting faculty racial goals in postsecondary education is the racial composition of the student body. All that can reasonably be concluded is that the Eighth Circuit Court would allow considerable latitude to *Adams* colleges and universities in setting their hiring goals.

b. Second, a remedial AAP must be temporary, enduring only as long as it is "reasonably necessary to achieve its legitimate goals" (p. 510). Certainly, as the court acknowledged, the four-year duration of ASU's challenged AAP was not unreasonably long.

Indeed, given the existing and growing scarcity of black academics (of which the court took no note), ASU would have had to engage in heroic efforts to achieve its 25% goal in four years. Recognizing demand constraints, however—the scarcity of faculty openings—the court validated (although only in dictum), a recruitment and hiring technique that ASU disclaimed it had used, that Valentine alleged ASU had employed (in violation of principles established in *Bakke*), and to which some public universities unquestionably resort. A university must, the court asserted, have authority "to reserve a particular position for a qualified minority applicant" to ensure that it will meet its remedial affirmative action goals (p. 511, Note 17). Justice Powell, forming a majority with four other justices in *Bakke,* rejected the University of California's designation of a fixed number of what, in practice, were exclusively minority seats at the Davis medical school. The *Valentine* court, however, took into consideration the difference between admissions (a centralized process for rationing access to a significant number of slots open for annual competition) and faculty hiring (a decentralized process for filling a few uniquely defined vacancies in any one year and relatively few over the course of five years). Accepting that reality and the problem that it creates for meeting hiring goals, the court unequivocally opted for the "reverse discrimination" horn of the means–ends dilemma.

The circuit court's approval of a hypothetical "exclusively minority position" was taken by Valentine as characterizing the procedure actually followed at ASU, and it shaped the issue she presented in her unsuccessful petition for Supreme Court review: "Whether a state university can absolutely preclude consideration of white applicants for selected faculty positions as a means of fulfilling an affirmative action goal" (Brief for Petitioner, *Valentine* v. *Smith,* No. 81-745, 1981, p. 1).

c. Even assuming, as neither the courts nor ASU did, that this accurately characterized the facts, the circuit would still have concluded that such an affirmative-action technique would not violate *Weber* and *Bakke*'s strictures against a "no-whites-need-apply" policy. Looking at all hiring over the duration of ASU's actual plan, the court also concluded that it satisfied *Weber*'s two limitations on burdening the interests of innocent whites: the 25% goal did not completely bar whites from faculty positions at ASU, and it did not require "firing any employees to make room for minority applicants" (p. 511). Valentine's hopes were disappointed; her vested interests were not.

d. Finally, the court identified a fourth "reasonableness" limitation on remedial affirmative action. It must not "unduly stigmatize either the beneficiaries or the persons disadvantaged by the plan" (p. 511). This stipulation, derived from the Brennan–White–Marshall–Blackmun opinion in *Bakke,* touches on the most difficult ethical and emotional objection that affirmative action preferences present, perhaps most critically in work environments in which, however, haphazardly, merit judgments are constantly being made (see, e.g., Sowell, 1972, 1974, 1976, 1978; Bell, 1979, p. 3; Patterson, 1973, p. 32; Greenawalt, 1983, pp. 65-68). Whites, by virtually absolute judicial assumption, do not, because they are members of the socially dominant group, suffer a social stigma when a minority is preferred pursuant to a remedial AAP (*Bakke,* 1978, pp. 374–75). But beneficiaries of race (or gender) preferences, competing in a context in which "individual merit or achievement" counts, may suffer a negatively stereotyping stigma that insidiously attacks self-esteem and undermines interpersonal candor. Recognizing that affirmative action preferences notoriously can hurt as well as help intended beneficiaries (a problem rather cavalierly treated by the Brennan four in *Bakke*), the Eighth Circuit Court set a final reasonableness limit on remedial preferences. A beneficiary must be "fully qualified for the job" (p. 511). No constitutionally impermissible stigma was placed on Mitchell because she had the requisite advertised master's degree (see also, *Bratton* v. *City of Detroit,* 1983, citing *Valentine*). But as most academics agree, not all degrees are equal. The court noted that Mitchell was more than qualified: her job performance, in the five years of litigation had been "very well" rated (p. 511). She was not a minnow recruited into an academic barracuda pond. That the court pointed to evidence of on-the-job competence suggests, however, consolation for queasy judges, rather than to a constitutional requirement, for the legal dispute focused on the constitutionality of the initial hiring decision, before on-the-job performance.

Voluntary and Induced Voluntary, Public-Sector Affirmative-Action Discrimination: A Summary Analysis. Though obviously neither definitive nor complete, the Eighth Circuit Court's opinion in *Valentine* v. *Smith* provides more guidance on the constitutionality of employment preferences for faculty in public postsecondary education than the Supreme Court has yet offered. It is possible that the Supreme Court will use *Wygant* either to endorse public sector preferences within articulated limits, or to reject any deviation from a race- and gender-blind Constitution. The following analysis is grounded in a pre-*Wygant* understanding of legal developments as of mid-1985.

Public colleges and universities, never found by an authoritative external body to have engaged in past discrimination, nor admitting to a self-documented history of discrimination, or at least to evidence that "minority underrepresentation is substantial and chronic" (*DPOA* v. *Young,* 1979, p. 694), will find scant support in case law for an affirmative action defense to a charge of reverse discrimination. Their actions will lack a remedial justification. Although one court determined, following *Weber,* that the professoriate in general is a traditionally segregated job category (*Cohen* v. *Community College of Philadelphia,* 1980), it found no evidence of minority hiring preferences, and therefore did not have to address the question of their lawfulness.

Institutions that make documented findings of their own past history of race discrimination and probably gender discrimination, too (see *Ende* v. *Regents of Northern Illinois University,* 1983, 1985, a salary equity case), will find considerable support for an affirmative action defense. Courts recognize that employers walk on a tightrope, risking liability to minorities for past discrimination, yet threatened with liability to nonminorities for voluntary efforts to remedy minority underrepresentation. Although the *Valentine* decision treated ASU's plan as an induced voluntary plan, it did not rule out wholly voluntary, remedial preferential hiring. It intimated that even if the federal government had not put pressure on ASU, ASU would still have had constitutional "running room" to do what it did. It noted, but did not adopt, Justice Powell's view that a university is not competent to make requisite findings of its own past discrimination. Rather, it noted the contrary view of the Brennan four in *Bakke,* in support of "voluntary efforts to further the objectives of the law" (*Bakke,* 1978, p. 364) by universities receiving federal funds.

The appeals court in *Valentine* also ventured the recommendation that postsecondary institutions create exclusive, minority recruitment positions. In the academic job market, characterized by few, narrowly specialized openings and a small minority availability pool, this approach may be one of the few effective means of increasing minority representation. Since control over faculty lines is a prerogative of top-level administrators, the creation of minority positions not only centralizes control over minority hiring but signals the commitment of the chief executive officers to minority recruitment, a signal more potent than the entreaties of affirmative action officers, or of postselection review. If departments are allocated an extra faculty line as a reward for a successful minority hire, the technique creates positive incentives from the outset of a search and thus may prevent the frustration created, as illustrated by the facts of the *Valentine* case, when upper-level administrators intervene following the conclusion of a search.

The case of an exclusive minority position, though it runs up against Justice Powell's strictures in *Bakke,* should also reduce the risk of being sued (though perhaps not the risk of losing should a reverse discrimination suit be initiated). In *Cramer* and *Valentine,* the universities invited trouble by using gender- and race-neutral advertising for positions subsequently filled on the basis of a gender and racial preference. Advertising resulted in applications from a white male and a white female, who, once rejected, had standing to sue. Federal law and regulations do not, however, as noted at the outset, require that universities advertise. If a minority line is filled by means of an unadvertised search, there are not likely to be any nonminority applicants, especially if the job description is tailored to a particular qualification of the minority candidate. In contrast to the situation in *Bakke,* in which white applicants could apply for some, but not all, of the medical class seats, there won't be anyone who can claim to have been disadvantaged by intentional affirmative-action discrimination. In legal terms, no one will have standing to sue.

Unadvertised recruitment and advertised nonrecruitment for "wired" positions are well known in American universities. Universities also continue to compete for established senior scholars through word-of-mouth recruitment and bonus salaries. Although not motivated by discriminatory intent, this practice is bound to focus overwhelmingly on the hiring of white men. For this reason, it was challenged, unsuccessfully, in a "disparate impact" Title VII suit brought by a class of present and former female faculty and nonteaching professionals at the State University of New York at Stony Brook (*Coser* v. *Moore,* 1984).

Under a Title VII "disparate-impact" theory of unintentional discrimination (in contrast to the more conventional "disparate-treatment" theory of intentional discrimination), the employer must prove that the neutral criteria used in a selection process are job-related (*Griggs* v. *Duke Power Co.,* 1971), if the criteria disadvantage disproportionately the plaintiff group (see Note 2). In the case of Stony Brook, the circuit court concluded that the university's neutral senior-faculty recruitment policy was justified by the desire to hire "highly desirable candidates" (p. 751). Prominence as a respected, sought-after scholar is a job-related criterion for senior faculty positions. But this method of senior faculty recruitment (which, at Stony Brook, departed from the university's mandatory affirmative-action procedures), indirectly and unintentionally diminishes the hiring and promotion opportunities of the late-comers to research universities—women and minorities. This was the point of the plaintiffs' disparate-impact complaint. The adverse effect on women and minorities is aggravated in a retrenchment period, when not only hiring is limited but so are promotional opportunities, by virtue of *de facto,* if not *de jure,* restrictions. Senior faculty recruitment almost begs for a counterbalancing minority-recruitment pool for institutions committed to increasing minority presence. And indeed, both practices coexist at some universities.

Institutions that make hiring decisions that can be justified as implementing desegregation plans accepted by the OCR, or, if not accepted, that are still within the bounds of the Revised Criteria or OCR-accepted plans (e.g., Maryland), should be in a strong position to make an affirmative action defense. Their decisions would seem to fall within Justice Powell's support for induced voluntary affirmative action and clearly are supported by the Brennan four. Plans accepted by the OCR have run out or are running out, however. As explained below, the Revised Criteria, which guided their development, are probably not legally binding.

The era of induced affirmative-action preferences appears to be over, at least for the next four years, unless Congress expressly instructs the executive branch to pursue them. Federal agencies under the Reagan administration, implementing a color-blind, individualistic, victim-specific approach to civil-rights enforcement, have opposed group-based preferences regardless of the "who" it is that initiates them. Witness the Justice Department's filing reverse discrimination suits charging discrimination against white males in the fire departments of Birmingham (*Washington Post,* Feb. 8, 1985, p. 7) and Washington, DC

(*Washington Post*, March 12, 1985, p. 1). The department's earlier initiative, asking over fifty state and local jurisdictions to delete hiring goals for women and minorities provided for in court orders and consent decrees, constituted a direct challenge to the authority of the courts and met widespread political opposition (*Washington Post,* April 3, 1985, p. 1). Witness the decision of the EEOC to change its antibias enforcement policy. The agency announced in February 1985 that it would forsake class actions that pursue gender- and race-based group remedies and concentrate instead on individual relief for proven victims of discrimination (Williams, 1985, p. 1). Witness the settlement agreement between the Department of Education and North Carolina. It ended the University of North Carolina's suit challenging HEW's Title VI enforcement efforts initiated under the Carter administration (Consent Decree, *North Carolina* v. *Dept. of Education,* 1981; see Califano, 1981, pp. 247–248; Dentler, et al., 1983; Ayers, 1982). The settlement's vague, cursory treatment of faculty and administrative employment (pp. 22–33) simply ignored the faculty integration goals of the Revised Criteria (and much else). Witness the government's argument in 1983, in opposition to Judge Pratt's March 11, 1983, order reimposing time limits on the OCR and OFCCP's Title VI compliance reviews (in elementary and secondary education). It claimed that it lacked the personnel resources to carry out its higher-education enforcement responsibilities under the Executive Order (Brief for Appellants, *Adams* v. *Bell,* 1984, p. 21). Furthermore, the government objected, the expenditure of 5.4% of its resources on higher education contractors (which comprise less than 1% of OFCCP jurisdiction) "was not a productive use of [OFCCP's] resources because employment opportunities in higher education are extremely limited" (Brief, p. 21).

But it was not merely a plea of insufficient and inefficient allocation of resources, or opposition to affirmative action remedies, that drove the government's case against Judge Pratt's time-frame order. Of far greater significance was a fundamental "who" question at the heart of the entire *Adams* litigation. The government defendants, including the Secretary of Education and the director of OFCCP, threw down a challenge to judicial intrusion on the responsibility of the executive branch for the determination of substantive standards of compliance with Title VI and Executive Order 11246 (Title IX and Section 504, too) (Brief for Appellants, *Adams* v. *Bell,* 1984, pp. 47–50). "By imposing on the Departments of Education and Labor its views of how the Civil Rights laws should be effectuated," the government argued, the district court had done nothing less than violate "settled principles of separation of powers" (Brief, p. 47). Thus, as one commentator put it, "the real issue in *Adams* is the scope of permissible judicial authority" (Devins, 1984, p. 88) under statutes that set up mechanisms for their administrative enforcement through the lever of funds termination. It is, the government contended, the responsibility of the executive branch to formulate civil rights policy in the first instance, within the gaping interstices of Title VI (and of other statutes patterned on it), not the district court for the District of Columbia. The executive branch would remain subject to a change in (or more detailed specification of) congressional will, and to challenges in federal courts in the states in which plaintiffs are injured by the action or inaction of the OCR and the OFCCP in violation of "specific legal provisions" (Appellants Reply Brief, *Adams* v. *Bell,* 1984, p. 5). But it would not be held accountable through long-term, broad-ranging supervision by a single federal court located where the federal funding agency is located—the objective of the LDF's "wholesale" strategy of attacking segregation in higher education. In September 1984, the Court of Appeals for the District of Columbia strongly suggested, but did not definitely rule, that the district court had exceeded its authority and that LDF plaintiffs lacked standing to invoke it (*Adams* v. *Bell,* 1984). In 1983, three Supreme Court Justices, two of them "liberal activists," remarked that "Congress expected that most intersticial lawmaking [under Title VI] to be performed by administrative agencies, not the courts" (*Guardian's Ass'n.* v. *Civil Service Commission of N.Y.C.,* 1983, p. 3253, Note 12; see also *Allen* v. *Wright,* 1984).

In 1983, the Court of Appeals for the District of Columbia concluded, in response to the LDF's challenge to the settlement of the North Carolina offshoot of the *Adams* litigation, that Judge Pratt's 1973 decree and 1977 Supplemental Order merely directed HEW to initiate an enforcement process against state systems of higher education and "did not dictate specific compliance criteria, but left the choice among lawful criteria to the discretion of the Department and of the states" (*Adams* v. *Bell,* 1983b, p. 165). The Amended and Revised Criteria, developed as a result of Judge Pratt's 1977 order, were, the circuit court held, "never endorsed nor compelled by the District Court" (*id.*). Thus, the court treated them as nonbinding guidelines from which any administration is free to depart. This is what the Reagan administration did in its settlement with North Carolina.[6]

The Revised Criteria are probably moribund as far as future desegregation planning is concerned. The Reagan administration clearly is not going to use the funds termination lever of Title VI (or Title IX) to induce colleges and universities to engage in preferential affirmative action. In its June 1984 decision in *Grove City* v. *Bell,* the Supreme Court concurred in the view, which the Department of Education had already reached, that Congress intended to limit Title IX coverage (and by implication Title VI and Section 504) to the particular "program or activities" receiving federal funds. This reading of congressional intent not only ends institutionwide coverage under Title IX; *a fortiori,* it calls into question systemwide coverage under Title VI, as the Department of Education informed its regional civil rights directors in July 1984 (Singleton,

July 6, 1984; see Sorenson, 1984). In other words, *Grove City* indirectly struck a blow at the fundamental notion on which *Adams* states' desegregation negotiations and planning had been based, ever since the appeals court's 1973 decision directing HEW to deal with higher education "on a state-wide rather than a school-by-school basis" (*Adams* v. *Richardson,* 1973b, p. 1164). (Although the Revised Criteria looked to a systemwide goal of black faculty at each institution in proportion to availability, no *Adams* state developed centralized, systemwide control over hiring.) Barring action by the Ninety-ninth Congress to overturn *Grove City,* over the objections of the administration, as the Ninety-eighth Congress failed to do (see Cohodas, 1984), even executive branch enforcement of the principle of color-blind, gender-blind nondiscrimination will be limited. Moreover, even if Congress does reassert a broad coverage for the civil rights statutes, there is no reason to expect that the executive branch will take the lead in promoting an affirmative duty to integrate in any of the many facets of such an education and social change endeavor.

There is another potential and specific limit on the legal authority of the OCR to deal with faculty (and administrator) desegregation, whatever other Title VI desegregation policies the executive branch pursues. In *Grove City,* the Supreme Court refused to read into Title IX a broad-based jurisdiction for administrative enforcement agencies that the statute's "plain words" and legislative history did not specify. Presumably, this move toward strict construction of statutes patterned on Title VI (shifting the burden to Congress "to supply legislative judgments," Devins, 1984, p. 88) could include a refusal to read into Title VI a jurisdiction that the plain words specifically prohibit. A subsection of Title VI precludes "action . . . by any department or agency with respect to any employment practice of any employer . . . except where a primary objective of Federal financial assistance is to provide employment" (42 U.S.C. Section 2000d-3). In spite of this language, and in spite of the fact that most faculty and administrative salaries are *not* federally funded, not only the Revised Criteria, but Title VI administrative regulations of general applicability to federally assisted programs cover employment practices (45 C.F.R. Section 80.[3]c[3], 1979). Lower courts are divided over the extent to which Section 2000d-3 limits the Department of Education's authority over faculty in the context of school desegregation (*U.S.* v. *Jefferson Co.,* 1966; *U.S.* v. *El Camino Community College Dist.,* 1979; *Caulfield* v. *Bd. of Educ. of City of New York,* 1980).

In 1982, the Supreme Court held that Title IX covers employment (*North Haven* v. *Bell*) and, in 1984, that Section 504 covers employment (*Consolidated Rail Corp.* v. *Darrone*) irrespective of whether the primary purpose of the federal aid is to promote employment. In so holding, the Court relied, in large measure, on the fact that neither Title IX nor Section 504 contain Title

VI's limiting provision (2000d-3). It seems only a matter of time before elementary, secondary, or postsecondary school boards challenge Department of Education authority to regulate faculty employment under Title VI. The Eighth Circuit Court dismissed Valentine's Title VI claim in part because she failed to show, as required by 2000d-3, that ASU received federal assistance for faculty employment (*Valentine* v. *Smith,* 1981, p. 512; see also, *Ass'n Against Discrimination in Employment* v. *City of Bridgeport,* 1981; *Ward* v. *Mass. Bay Transp. Authority,* 1982). In *Guardians Ass'n.* v. *Civil Rights Service Comm'n of New York* (1983), the only Title VI employment discrimination case that the Supreme Court has decided, black and Hispanic police officers challenged the employment practices of the New York Police Department, which had solicited, received, and expended federal funds to recruit, pay, and train its police officers.

Court-Ordered Affirmative-Action Discrimination
Assuming the courts finally block the LDF in its attempt to secure mandatory nationwide desegregation criteria from the District Court of the District of Columbia; assuming the OCR will not use its funds-termination lever to induce preferential affirmative action; and assuming the U.S. Justice Department will no longer initiate suits under authority of Title VI, Title VII, or the Constitution leading to affirmative action preferences, there remains the "retail" strategy: individual suits against public higher-education institutions that exhibit "vestiges" of former state-imposed segregation. The message of the courts in dealing with the North Carolina settlement was that if the federal government continues funding higher education institutions, plaintiffs should repair to the federal courts of the state in which the institutions are located and bring a Title VI challenge there. A judicial finding of federal funding of segregating institutions would signify Department of Education "abdication of its statutory duty" under Title VI (*Adams* v. *Bell,* 1984, p. 167). Instead of one federal court's formulating higher-education compliance standards for the OCR, many federal courts could monitor the conformity of settlements with Title VI. Presumably, in this scenario, many federal courts could be called on to determine whether or not Title VI enforcement satisfies constitutional standards, since the administrative agencies are not bound by any Title VI guidelines. Even assuming that *Adams* v. *Bell* (1984) and *Grove City* signal reluctance on the part of the federal courts to engage in policy formulation under a statute designed to put the executive branch into the business of enforcing desegregation, the design was to complement, not to erase, the role of the federal courts under the equal protection clause of the Constitution.

The Supreme Court has never involved itself in any aspect of the *Adams* litigation, much less its higher-education component. Indeed, in its role as interpreter of the equal protection clause of the Fourteenth Amendment, it has never definitely gone beyond a theory of equality of access based on freedom of student choice in tuition-based postsecondary education, a policy clearly rejected in 1968 as inadequate for compulsory and free elementary and secondary education (*Green* v. *County School Board of New Kent*). At the level of lower public education, the *Green* concept of an affirmative duty to integrate under the Fourteenth Amendment has, of course, resulted in a variety of court-mandated remedies. They include a variety of race-conscious, faculty-related remedies. The Supreme Court has decreed mandatory racial balance in teacher assignments (*Swann* v. *Charlotte-Mecklenburg Bd. of Education*, 1971, p. 17). Some lower federal courts have mandated race-based hiring and layoff quotas for public-school teachers (*Morgan* v. *O'Bryant*, 1982; *Arthur* v. *Nyquist*, 1983; see Clague, 1984; McCarthy, 1984).

Like the Supreme Court's 1984 decision in *Firefighters* v. *Stotts*, these cases implicate questions about the power of the judicial "who" to order a racial quota based on a theory of group rights. Unlike *Stotts*, however, these cases do not involve a determination of the remedial power of the federal courts under Title VII, an act of Congress. With the exception of voluntary private-sector quotas considered in *Weber*, the Supreme Court has interpreted the statutory script that Congress wrote as fundamentally designed to protect individual, not group, rights (see e.g., *Los Angeles* v. *Manhart*, 1978, p. 708). But interpretations of what Congress intended in enacting Title VII do not control judicial interpretation of judicial equity power in creating remedies for violations of the Fourteenth Amendment.

Rarely have the federal courts decided cases involving faculty desegregation in higher education. With one exception, they have never treated faculty, as they have public-school teachers, like fungible, interchangeable parts. That rare case involved the trade schools and junior colleges of Alabama, a segregated system under the centralized control of the Alabama State Board of Education (*Lee* v. *Macon County Bd. of Education*, 1970). With the assistance of the United States (through the Justice Department), plaintiff-intervenor in this case, the court mandated the assignment of faculty so that the ratio of black to white faculty at each institution would substantially match the ratio of the black to the white population of Alabama (not an impossible ratio since there was a higher percentage of black faculty in the system than in the population). Since faculty assignment quotas speak to where, rather than whether, faculty will teach and affect blacks and whites equally, they are not preferential. And since they do not pit the interests of white and black faculty against each other in a winner-take-all contest, they have never stirred as much controversy as hiring and, above all, layoff quotas in elementary and secondary education. Nevertheless, one supposes that because they do violence to academic norms, and must confront the reality of decentralization, diversity, and fine-tuned specialization in higher education employment, they have rarely been contemplated.

The court in *Lee* v. *Macon* did not stop with assignments. It also mandated that faculty vacancies, created as a result of dismissal or demotion, must first be offered to qualified displaced faculty before the employer could recruit a person of a different race from that of the individual dismissed or demoted (p. 110). Here was an early higher education example of judicial protection for minority employment participation, and it undoubtedly reflected concern about the history of black teachers paying with their jobs for the move toward unitary elementary and secondary schools in the South.

The decree in *Lee* v. *Macon* also illustrates a metamorphosis that had occurred in the equity powers of the courts. So, too, did the consent decree in *Geier* v. *Alexander* (1984), the Tennessee desegregation case. (A consent decree is a legal hybrid, a voluntary settlement between the parties to a suit, which, once accepted by the court, becomes the judgment of the court, enforceable by judicial sanctions. Whatever limits apply to the equitable remedial powers of the courts in cases litigated-to-conclusion, apply also to consent decrees.) Since 1945, the federal courts have transformed their traditional, narrowly limited, essentially proscriptive equity power into the fount of prescriptive social policy making (McDowell, 1982, p. 3; see Chayes, 1976; Horowitz, 1977). Unleashed from the limits (some of which Aristotle had delineated) that made of it an "extraordinary" means of granting relief to individuals from the unjust operation of general laws, the equity power of the courts became the controversial vehicle for judicial activism in addressing social problems affecting large groups of people who are not necessarily parties to the litigation.

In September 1984, a federal district court, in the exercise of its equity power, gave its approval to an agreement worked out between the plaintiffs in the Tennessee case and the state attorney general's office, on behalf of the defendants, with the concurrence of the governor, the state board of regents, and the University of Tennessee Board of Regents, with the approval of the LDF, and over the objections of the Department of Justice. It was designed to end, without further litigation, the Fourteenth Amendment challenge to the "vestiges" of Tennessee's dual system of higher education. This challenge has resulted in a finding of unconstitutional segregation in 1968 (*Sanders* v. *Ellington*) and, in 1977, a court-ordered merger of the predominantly white University of Tennessee at Nashville (UT-N) into predominantly black Tennessee State University (TSU) (*Geier* v. *Blanton*). The merger remedy was based squarely on the view that the Supreme Court's holding in *Green*—that the Constitution mandates an affirmative duty to dismantle the vestiges of state-imposed segregation—applies equally to higher education and to elementary and secondary education. But the merger of UT-N into TSU led to increasing black predominance, among students, faculty, and administrators at TSU, allegedly because of TSU's determination to maintain its black identity (*Geier* v.

Alexander, 1984, p. 1266). In an attempt to counter this "disheartening" trend (*id.*, p. 1267), the federal judge accepted a variety of race-conscious measures, including the use of a black at each predominantly white institution, and of a white at each predominantly black institution, to recruit other race students (p. 1270); a preprofessional (non-Ph.D.) program for selected undergraduate black students, which guaranteed admission to Tennessee's state-supported professional schools on successful completion of undergraduate work and achievement of the minimum admissions standards (p. 1271); a five-year interim objective of at least 50% white faculty and at least 50% white upper-level administrators at TSU (p. 1272); a staff development program to enable black staff members to obtain higher degrees (*id.*); an incentive plan to attract black faculty to white institutions and white faculty to TSU; and a plan to increase the pool of qualified black candidates for employment as faculty and administrators (*id.*).

It was, it may be recalled, two months after the Supreme Court's decision in *Stotts* that William Bradford Reynolds, on behalf of the Department of Justice, entered a *Memorandum in Opposition* to the proposed settlement because of racial "objectives" such as these, and because of its provisions for "preferential treatment of persons solely on account of their race" (pp. 11–12) including, it should be noted, whites at TSU (see Cheers, 1984). But what the assistant attorney general unsuccessfully opposed was not just the affirmative action components of the proposed consent decree, but the use of a remedial decree to engage in social problem-solving in constitutional litigation. In resorting to a group rights approach to employment and educational segregation, the Court would, Reynolds argued, exceed its equity powers under the Constitution. Favoring people who have not personally been the victims of unlawful discrimination, the *Memorandum* argued, offends a "first reader principle of equity jurisprudence" (p. 15), which received a "classic" exposition in Pomeroy's 1941 edition of his treatise on equity and Austin's 1863 treatise on jurisprudence (*id.*). The works of Pomeroy and Austin, steeped in an individualistic view of law, predate the era of prescriptive equity. The controversy over affirmative action preferences then, is only part of a debate over judicial activism, the power that the courts have assumed to formulate public policy since 1945 through the transformation of the concept of equity.

The district court, however, did not heed the Justice Department. On the basis of Justice Powell's opinion in *Bakke* and some of the Supreme Court's elementary- and secondary-school desegregation cases, it held permissible racial classifications that aid members of a victim group where there has been a finding of a constitutional violation (p. 1265). It chose a color-conscious road, with the goal of achieving a color-blind higher education system, still marked by the effects of past color-based discrimination (p. 1267).

SUMMARY AND CONCLUSIONS

Although affirmative action preferences have not incited as militant position-taking as abortion in the last few years, the issue remains charged at the level of incompatible first principles. At the beginning of 1986, the law governing affirmative action discrimination remains an elusive will-o'-the-wisp, yielding the following tentative conclusions:

1. Voluntary preferences in private higher education, at least for black Americans, find support in the Supreme Court's *Weber* decision, within the limits of being temporary, of not displacing incumbent whites with new black hires, of not blocking white access altogether (not really an issue in higher education), and of correcting racial imbalances by moving in an integrative direction. Whether the Supreme Court would support preferences for women and other minorities is uncertain. It has equated the conditions of Mexican-American (and Puerto Rican) "Hispanos" with that of black Americans, holding they are an "identifiable class," protected by the Fourteenth Amendment, in the context of school desegregation (*Hernandez* v. *Texas, 1954; Keyes* v. *School Dist. No. 1, 1973*).

2. Although the era of induced voluntary preferences appears to be over, there remain unexpired state desegregation plans that were created in response to pressure from and accepted by the OCR. Should a reverse discrimination suit arise from one of these states, the courts are likely to support a decision that is defended as a way of meeting the goals of the plan. Between Justice Powell's *Bakke* and *Fullilove* opinions and the opinion of the Brennan group in *Bakke,* at least five Supreme Court justices have voiced support for preferences.

3. Until the Supreme Court decides the issue, the lawfulness of purely voluntary affirmative-action preferences in the public sector is likely to vary according to whether the particular lower federal courts treat the opinions of Justice Powell or the opinion of the Brennan four as controlling. Those that rely on Justice Powell's opinion (see, e.g., *Uzzell* v. *Friday,* 1984) are likely to insist that the decision be designed to remedy past institutional discrimination in academic employment, as identified by a competent external body, such as a court, the OCR, or the OFCCP. For courts that treat the opinion of the Brennan group as controlling, a finding by an institution's governing board that it has been guilty of past discrimination will suffice, although the Brennan four also endorsed preferences as a means of remedying societal discrimination (see, e.g., *Bratton* v. *City of Detroit,* 1983; and *Wygant* v. *Jackson Bd. of Education,* 1984, both Sixth Circuit Court opinions). The use of an unadvertised, race-targeted search and hiring, endorsed in *Valentine* v. *Smith,* reduces the risk of a reverse discrimination suit if no nonminority insiders are eligible for and apply for the position, and if there are no nonminority external

applicants. There will be no directly injured private parties with standing to sue. What is more, the use of exclusive minority lines may well result in hiring on a nonpreferential basis. In the normal course of recruiting, institutions may discover highly qualified minorities and women for whom there is no existing position. Departments can later be rewarded with additional lines by hiring these valued individuals.

4. Although the executive branch cannot dictate to judges, it can influence the judiciary in three ways: it can bring reverse discrimination suits of its own or intervene as *amicus curiae* in support of private reverse discrimination plaintiffs; more important, it can influence the federal courts through new appointments. Although President Carter appointed an unusually large number of incumbent appeals-court judges, including "a record number of women, blacks, and Hispanics" (Wermiel, 1984), it is projected that President Reagan will have appointed the majority of appeals court judges by the end of his term (Wermiel, 1984). And of course, he may well appoint new Supreme Court Justices.

5. Most courts that have accepted preferences have reiterated *Weber*'s requirement that they be temporary, however variable and uncertain the criteria for determining when a lawful duration expires. If, as *Weber* implies, the end to preferences is marked by meeting hiring goals, the duration can vary considerably from one employment setting to another, depending on how and under what assumptions the goals are constructed. (No predominantly white institution in the original ten *Adams* states has met its black hiring goals—Wilson, 1982; ACE, 1984). Colleges and universities generally base their goals on "availability" as measured by the number of women and minorities with the relevant degrees in a relevant discipline. At the doctoral level, this means nationally. But universities do not all use the same data sources to determine availability, and because these sources cover different years in which degrees were awarded, goals can be constructed that are more-or-less difficult to meet. Furthermore, measuring availability by the number of degrees rests on at least three questionable assumptions: an assumption that black academics will not disproportionately prefer a black campus; an assumption of perfect geographic mobility; and an assumption that the same percentage of each race with a relevant degree will seek an academic position. Academics, like other mortals, are motivated by quality of life beyond the job description, and beyond the campus boundaries. One would assume, for racial minorities especially, that the presence of a minority community in the surrounding population would play an important role in choice of employment. (West Virginia University's 1981 Title VI plan notes difficulties in attracting black faculty to overwhelmingly white Morgantown—p. 18). And, of course, academe is not the only employer of master- and doctoral-degree recipients. "Temporary," for many colleges and universities sincerely committed to increasing minority presence, could

be a long duration. The end to temporary preferences in the public sector may, however, also be determined by a decision of the Supreme Court, affirming an individual rights interpretation of the Constitution. In that case, the years during which the Court left standing, without affirming, many lower-court cases premised on a group rights theory could be viewed as a *de facto* parenthesis in American constitutional law—a period during which the individualistic norm was suspended in order to allow an experiment in social change, which an individualistic theory of legal equality would not have supported. Because race-conscious desegregation remedies in education (not necessarily preferential) have been mandated and endorsed for so long by the Supreme Court, it is probable that an individual rights decision, foreclosing group-based preferences in public employment, if and when it comes, will focus on employment outside the field of education. And such a decision may leave the lower courts the time and the intellectual space to treat education as an exceptional case.

As an essay on affirmative action discrimination is academic employment (primarily hiring), this chapter focuses on the role of colleges and universities as "buyers" of faculty. Even if some predominantly white institutions meet their goals, the number of blacks and Hispanics will remain among the lowest in "any industry" (Mackey-Smith, 1984). If 500,000 new academic positions open up in the next 25 years, as Bowen and Schuster have projected (Evangelauf, 1984, p. 1), and if the pool of minority doctorates remains exceedingly low, new hires, and in due course newly tenured faculties, will be overwhelmingly white. The opportunity to achieve substantial faculty integration and diversity will be lost for at least another generation. Determined efforts to hire minority-race faculty can succeed, at best, only in stirring up a shrinking pool. The need for targeted incentives and support for minority college (not to mention precollege) students through graduate school is therefore compelling. Concerned about the "supply side," in 1984 the Ivy League schools developed a plan to recruit and support black students for doctoral work (*id.*). The Title VI desegregation plans, accepted by the OCR, of several *Adams* states provide for special assistance programs designed for minority race students to pursue graduate and professional school study (see, e.g., Oklahoma, 1983, pp. 71–74 ["college teaching as a goal"]; University of Missouri-Columbia, 1981, pp. 41–42; South Carolina, 1981, p. 43; Pennsylvania, 1983, p. 63). Some Title VI desegregation plans accepted by the OCR also provide support for minority race faculty to complete their doctoral programs (see, e.g., Florida, 1978, 1983, pp. 26–27; South Carolina, 1981, p. 307; Texas, 1983, p. 162 [Hispanics and blacks]; Oklahoma, 1983 [Hispanics, blacks, and American Indians]). Even the consent decree, settling the Title VI, Fourteenth Amendment action brought by the United States against the State of Louisiana, which was accepted by the Justice Department in the first year of the Reagan administration, contains a provision to increase the pool of black doctorates and professional degree holders. Although written in more race-neutral language than the OCR-accepted plans (since Grambling and the Southern University System are required to nominate one white lacking a terminal degree), the Board of Regents' Graduate Fellowship Program (Consent Decree, 1981, pp. 12–13) was understood primarily as program to assist blacks. Since its inception, 29 of the 32 participants have been black (Beard, 1985).[7]

But in 1984, in opposing the higher-education desegregation settlement in Tennessee, the Justice Department singled out the "set aside program for black students to enter graduate and professional programs" (*Memorandum in Opposition*, p. 6) as the "most palpably discriminatory provision in the proposed decree" (p. 12). Although the Tennessee plan goes beyond support, to include guaranteed graduate and professional school admission if minimum standards are attained, the Justice Department's opposition was addressed to the notion of a separate program benefiting only the minority race.

Whether minority-race-targeted programs will succeed in increasing significantly the pool of minority academics is an important research question. Whether or not the OCR will fall in line under William Bennett or will be pulled into line by the Justice Department[8] and will ignore such programs in the future is a question of enormous importance to higher education. It will be more threatening to purely voluntary efforts if William Bradford Reynold's "high road to race neutrality" leads to an initiative by the nation's Justice Department to bring a Title VI and/or the Fourteenth Amendment suit in quest of a judicial prohibition of such supply-side affirmative-action programs.

NOTES

1. In addition to the Executive Order, the legal provisions most frequently involved in affirmative action litigation are Title VII of the Civil Rights Act of 1964, the nation's most comprehensive employment discrimination statute; Title VI of the Civil Rights Act of 1964, which proscribes discrimination on grounds of race, color, or national origin under federally programs or activities; and the equal protection clause of the Fourteenth Amendment and the equal protection interpretation of the Fifth Amendment of the U.S. Constitution. Title IX, which proscribes discrimination in educational programs or activities on the basis of gender, and Section 504, which proscribes discrimination against otherwise handicapped individuals, have not been involved in reverse discrimination litigation.
2. Title VII, in contrast to Title VI and the Fourteenth Amendment, has been interpreted as covering "disparate impact"—unintentional discrimination—which requires that employers prove that a neutral policy having an adverse impact on protected groups is job-related and a justified "business necessity" (*Griggs* v. *Duke Power Co.,* 1971). "Disparate impact" cases are rare in higher education.
3. Although the court cases discussed in this chapter do not make reference to the EEOC's 1979 "Guidelines on Affirmative Action Appropriate Under Title VII of the Civil Rights Act of 1964, as Amended" (44 Fed. Reg. 4422), Section 1608 was designed to provide employers with protection from Title VII liability when subject to reverse discrimination challenges to "appropriate" voluntary affirmative action.

4. The State of Maryland, one of the original ten *Adams* states, sued HEW and secured an injunction against further enforcement proceedings on the grounds that HEW had failed to provide guidance for complying with Title VI (*Mandel* v. *HEW,* 1976; *Mayor and City Council of Baltimore* v. *HEW,* 1977, 1978; *Lee* v. *HEW,* 1978). Although Maryland did not reach agreement with the Department of Education until May 1985, the 1980 Recommendations of the State Board for Higher Education's Task Force are basically consistent with the faculty goals of the Revised Criteria, goals that the current federal administration rejects (A Plan to Assure Equal Postsecondary Opportunity, 1980–1985. Task Force Report and Recommendations, pp. 6–7).

5. In January 1985, an appeals court reversed a lower court ruling and held that the NAACP Legal Defense and Education Fund, Inc., may use the NAACP initials, though the NAACP LDF had broken away from the NAACP in 1958.

6. On March 24, 1983, Judge Pratt issued an order directing the OCR to require five states to submit revised desegregation plans that would ensure compliance with Title VI and the Revised Criteria, and to commence enforcement proceedings against three states unless the OCR concluded that they had had submitted desegregation plans that "fully conform to the Criteria and Title VI" (p. 84). The government filed a notice of appeal against this order (see Brief for Appellants, *Adams* v. *Bell,* 743 F. 2d 42 [D.C. Cir. 1984], p. 27, Note 35). However, it was dismissed by stipulation on June 30, 1983, after the Circuit Court for the District of Columbia refused to enjoin the settlement of the North Carolina higher-education desegregation case, declared that the Amended and Revised Criteria were neither court compelled nor court endorsed, and that there were "many ways of implementing Title VI's goal of preventing discrimination in federally aided education" (711 F. 2d at 166).

7. The suits initiated by the United States against Alabama and Mississippi have not yet been concluded. The confidentiality of settlement discussions with Mississippi preclude assessment of the Justice Department's current approach to faculty employment. The basic approach to hiring now taken by the Justice Department is to look at applicant rather than hiring goals and to treat the hiring of a black who is less qualified than a white as a violation of the Constitution. (Telephone interview with Jay P. Heubert, Department of Justice, February 27, 1985.)

8. As a result to the 1980 Executive Order 12250 (45 F.R. 72995), the U.S. Attorney General has been given the authority to coordinate the implementation and enforcement, by executive agencies, of the nondiscrimination provisions of Title VI, Title IX, and Section 504.

REFERENCES

Abram, M. B. (1984). What constitutes a civil right? *New York Times Magazine,* June 10, pp. 1, 54, 58, 60, 62, 64.

American Council on Education, Office of Minority Concerns (1983). *Minorities in higher education.* Washington, DC.

American Council on Education, Office of Minority Concerns (1984). *Minorities in higher education.* Washington, DC.

Ayers, Q. W. (1982). Desegregating or debilitating higher education? *The Public Interest* 69: 100–116.

Barbash, F., & Sawyer, K. (1984). Justice Department declares win over quotas. *Washington Post,* June 14, p. A-1.

Bartholet, E. (1982). Application of Title VII to jobs in high places. *Harvard Law Review* 95: 945–1027.

Beard, S., of the Louisiana State Board of Regents. (1985). telephone interview, Feb. 18.

Blackwell, J. E. (1981). *Mainstreaming outsiders: the production of black professionals.* Bayside: General Hall.

Blackwell, J. E. (1983). *Networking and mentoring: a study of cross-generational experience of blacks in graduate and professional schools.* Atlanta: Southern Education Foundation.

Blackwell, J. E. (1985). Telephone interview, May 24.

Bowen, H., and Schuster, J. (1985). *American professors: a national resource imperiled.* New York: Oxford University Press.

Bowring, J. (1838). *The works of Jeremy Bentham,* Vol. 1. Edinburgh: Tait.

Bristow, B. W. (1983). Letter to the author, May 6.

Calabresi, G. (1979). Bakke as pseudo-tragedy. *Catholic University Law Review* 28: 427–444.

Califano, J. A. (1981). *Governing America.* New York: Simon and Schuster.

Chayes, A. (1976). The role of the judge in public law litigation. *Harvard Law Review* 89: 1281–1316.

Cheers, D. M. (1984). Tennessee State U. students fight white quota system. *Jet,* Sept. 24, pp. 14–18.

Clague, M. W. (1985). Voluntary affirmative action plans in public education: matching faculty race to student race—anticipating a Supreme Court decision. *Journal of Law and Education* 14: 309-348.

Clague, M. W. (1984). Beyond the Title VII framework: racial quotas and teacher employment policies in school desegregation litigation. In T. Jones and D. Semler (eds.), *NOLPE School Law Update, 1983.* Topeka, KA: NOLPE.

Cohodas, N. (1984). "Grove City" bill shelved by Senate. *Congressional Quarterly Weekly Report* 42: 2430-2433.

Comment, The Philadelphia plan: a study in the dynamics of executive power. (1972). *University of Chicago Law Review* 39: 723-757.

Dentler, R. A., Baltzell, D. C., and Sullivan, D. J. (1983). *University on trial: the case of North Carolina.* Cambridge, MA: Abt Books.

Devins, N. (1984). Federal courts are becoming reluctant to take the lead in civil rights reform. *Chronicle of Higher Education,* Nov. 28, p. 88.

Eastland, T., and Bennett, W. J. (1979). *Counting by race.* New York: Basic Books.

Edwards, H. T. (1980). *Higher education and the unholy crusade against government regulation.* Cambridge: Institute for Educational Management: Harvard University.

Edwards, H. T., and Nordin, V. D. (1979). *Higher education law.* Cambridge: Institute for Educational Management, Harvard University.

Egerton, J. (1973-1974). Can separate be equal? *Change,* pp. 29-37.

Evangelauf, J. (1985). Colleges must hire 500,000 professors in the next 25 years, new study finds. Report on study by H. Bowen and J. Schuster. *The Chronicle of Higher Education,* May 8, p. 11.

Fields, C. M. (1972). Civil rights chief defends drive against job bias. *Chronicle of Higher Education,* Sept. 25, p. 4.

Fleming, J. (1984). *Blacks in college: a comparative study of students' success in black and white institutions.* San Francisco: Jossey-Bass.

Fullinwider, R. K. (1980). *The reverse discrimination controversy.* Totowa, NJ: Rowman & Littlefield.

Glazer, N. (1983). The politics of a multiethnic society. In *Ethnic dilemmas,* Cambridge: Harvard University Press.

Greenawalt, K. (1983). *Discrimination and reverse discrimination.* New York: Borzoi Books.

Halévy, E. (1955). *The growth of philosophical radicalism.* Boston: Beacon Press.

Horowitz, D. L. (1977). *The courts and social policy.* Washington, DC: Brookings.

Houston Chronicle. (1984). Brennan raps high court's rights and rulings, Oct. 25, 1984.

Ingalls, Z. (1984). Womens colleges show renewed vigor after long, painful self-examination. *Chronicle of Higher Education,* Sept. 12, pp. 1, 18–19.

Jencks, C. (1983). Special treatment for blacks? *The New York Review of Books,* March 17, p. 12.

Johnson, L. B. (1967). To fulfill these rights, in J. H. Franklin & I. Starr (eds.), *The Negro in 20th century America,* pp. 225–251. New York: Random House.

Keohane, N. O. (1984). Letter to the author, Dec. 28.

La Noue, G. R. (1980). Equal employment opportunity: three conflicting theories. Paper presented at the annual meeting of the American Society for Public Administration, San Francisco.

Lee, B. A. (1985). Federal courts involvement in academic decision-making: impact on peer review. *Journal of Higher Education* 56: 38–54.

Lee, J. B., Rotermund, M. K., and Bertschman, J. A. (1985). *Student aid and minority enrollment in higher education.* Washington, DC: American Association of State Colleges and Universities.

Mackey-Smith, A. (1984). Large shortage of black professors in higher education grows worse. *Wall Street Journal,* June 12, p. 47.

Martin, T. (1984). Why blacks do better at black colleges. *Ebony,* Nov., pp. 125–128.

McCarthy, M. (1984). Racial quotas versus seniority rights. *Education Law Reporter* 20: 1063–1073.

McDowell, G. L. (1982). *Equity and the constitution: the Supreme Court, equitable relief, and public policy.* Chicago: University of Chicago Press.

Morris, A. A. (1984). Seniority, tenure and affirmative action layoffs under Title VII. *Education Law Reporter* 20 (2): 459–467.

National Research Council (1983). Summary report 1982: doctoral recipients from United States universities. Washington, DC.

Patterson, O. (1973–1974). On guilt, relativism and black-white relations. *American Scholar* 43: 129–132.

Rowan, C. T. (1984). Race, justice, and Howard University. *The Washington Post,* May 6.

Silberman, L. H. (1977). The road to racial quotas, *Wall Street Journal,* Aug. 11, p. 14.

Smith, A. R., Craver, C. B., and Blank, L. D. (1982). *Employment discrimination law.* Charlottesville, VA: The Michie Co.

Sorenson, G. (1985). Title IX: current judicial, legislative, and administration activity. In T. Jones and D. Simler (Eds.), *NOLPE School Law Update, 1984.* Topeka, KA: NOLPE.

Sowell, T. (1972). *Black education: myths and tragedies.* New York: David McKay.

Sowell, T. (1974). The plight of black students in the United States. In S. W. Mintz, (ed.), *Slavery, colonialism, and racism.* New York: Norton.

Sowell, T. (1976). "Affirmative action" reconsidered. *The Public Interest* 42 (Winter): 47–65.

Sowell, T. (1978). Are quotas good for blacks? *Commentary* 65 (June): 39–43.

Sowell, T. (1976). A black "conservative" dissents. *New York Times Magazine,* Aug., p. 14.

Sullivan, C. A., Zimmer, M. J., and Richards, R. F. (1980). *Federal statutory law of employment discrimination.* Indianapolis: The Michie Co.

Tollett, K. S. (1982). *Black colleges as instruments of affirmative action.* Washington, DC: Institute for Educational Policy, Howard University.

Twenty-Second Annual Survey of Virginia Law: Constitutional Law. (1977). *Virginia Law Review* 68: 1388–1390.

United States Commision on Civil Rights. (1984). Statement, Jan. 17. *United States Law Week* 52. (Jan. 31): 2417.

Van Dyne, L. (1973). Colleges white men assail 'preference' for minorities. *Chronicle of Higher Education,* Feb. 5, p. 4.

Wermiels, S. (1984). The new judiciary: Reagan picked judges put the federal courts on conservative path. *Wall Street Journal,* Dec. 18, p. 1.

Williams, J. (1985). EEOC shifting its anti-bias policy. *Washington Post,* Feb. 13, pp. 1–8.

Wilson, R. (1982). Preface to *Race and equity in higher education.* Washington, DC: American Council on Education.

Cases

Adams v. *Bell,* No. 70-3095 (D.D.C. June 25, 1981).

Adams v. *Bell,* March 11, 1983 order.

Adams v. *Bell,* March 23, 1983 order.

Adams v. *Bell,* 711 F. 2d 161 (D.C. Cir. 1983)b, *cert. denied,* 52 U.S.L.W. 3610 (1984). 104 S. Ct. 1272 (1984).

Adams v. *Bell,* 743 F. 2d 42 (D.C. Cir. 1984).

Adams v. *Califano,* 430 F. 2d 118 (D.D.C. 1977).

Adams v. *Richardson,* 356 F. Supp. 92 (D.D.C. 1973)a.

Adams v. *Richardson,* 480 F. 2d 1159 (D.C. Cir. 1973)b, *modifying and aff'g,* 356 F. Supp. 92 (D.D.C. 1973).

Allen v. *Wright,* 104 S. Ct. 3315 (1984).

Arthur v. *Nyquist,* 712 F. 2d 816 (2d Cir. 1983), *cert. denied,* 104 S. Ct. 3555, 1984.

Ass'n Against Discrimination in Employment, Inc. v. *City of Bridgeport,* 647 F. 2d 256 (2d Cir. 1981), *cert. denied* 455 U.S. 988 (1982).

Bd. of Trustees of Keene State College v. *Sweeney,* 439 U.S. 24 (1978), *vacating and remanding Sweeney* v. *Board of Trustees of Keene State College,* 569 F. 2d 169 (1st Cir. 1978).

Bratton v. *City of Detroit,* 704 F. 2d 878 (6th Cir. 1983), aff'g. *sub nom. Baker* v. *City of Detroit,* 438 F. Supp. 919 (E.D. Mich. 1979), *cert. denied,* 104 S. Ct. 703 (1984).

Bushey v. *New York State Civil Service Commission,* 733 F. 2d (2d Cir. 1984), *aff'g,* 571 F. Supp. 1562 (N.D.N.Y. 1983), *cert. denied,* 105 S. Ct. (1983).

Carmi v. *Metropolitan St. Louis Sewer Dist.,* 620 F. 2d 672 (8th Cir. 1982), *cert. denied,* 449 U.S. 892 (1982).

Carter v. *Gallagher,* 452 F. 2d 315 (8th Cir. 1971), *cert. denied,* 406 U.S. 950 (1972).

Caulfield v. *Board of Education of City of New York,* 632 F. 2d 999 (2d Cir. 1980), *cert. denied,* 450 U.S. 1030 (1981).

Clark v. *Whiting,* 607 F. Supp. 634 (4th Cir. 1984).

Cohen v. *Community College of Philadelphia,* 484 F. Supp. 441 (E.D. Pa. 1980).

Consolidated Rail Corp. v. *Darrone,* 104 S. Ct. 1248 (1984).

Contractor's Ass'n of Eastern Pennsylvania v. *Secretary of Labor,* 442 F. 2d 159 (3rd Cir., 1971).

Coser v. *Moore,* 739 F. 2d 746 (2nd Cir. 1984), *aff'g* 58 F. Supp. 572 (E.D.N.Y. 1983).

Cramer v. *Virginia Commonwealth University,* 415 F. Supp. 673; *remanded* 586 F. 2d. 297 (4th Cir. 1978); *vacated as moot,* 486 F. Supp. 187 (E.D. Va. 1980).

CUNY-Hostos Community College v. *SHRAB,* 59 N.Y. 2d 69, 449 N.E. 2d 1251 (1983).

Detroit Police Officers Ass'n v. *Young,* 608 F. 2d 671 (6th Cir. 1979), *cert. denied* 452 U.S. 938 (1980).

Dybczak v. *Tuskegee Institute,* 737 F. 2d 1524 (5th Cir. 1984).

Ende v. *Bd. Of Regents of Northern Illinois University,* 565 F. Supp. 501 (N.D. Ill. 1983), *aff'd* 757 F. 2d 176 (7th Cir. 1985).

Firefighters Local Union No. 1784 v. *Stotts,* 104 S. Ct. 2576 (1984).

Ford v. *Nicks,* No. 77-3203 (M.D. Tenn. 1982).

Fullilove v. *Klutznick,* 448 U.S. 448 (1980).

Geier v. *Alexander,* 593 F. Supp. 1263 (M.D. Tenn. 1984).

Geier v. *Blanton,* 427 F. Supp. 644 (M.D. Tenn. 1977).

Geier v. *Univ. of Tennessee,* 597 F. 2d 1056 (6th Cir. 1979), *cert. denied,* 444 U.S. 886 (1979).

General Bldg Contractors Ass'n v. *Pennsylvania,* 458 U.S. 375 (1982).

Green v. *County School Bd. of New Kent County, Virginia,* 391 U.S. 430 (1968).

Greer et al. v. *University of Arkansas Bd. of Trustees,* 719 F. 2d 950 (8th Cir) *aff'g* 544 F. Supp. 1085 (E.D. Ark 1982), *cert. denied,* 52 U.S.L.W. 3791 (April 30, 1984).

Griggs v. *Duke Power Co.,* 401 U.S. 424 (1971).

Grove City v. *Bell,* 104 S. Ct. 1211 (1984).

Guardians Ass'n. v. *Civil Rights Service Comm'n of New York City,* 103 S.Ct. 3221 (1983).

Hazelwood School Dist. v. *United States,* 433 U.S. 299 (1977).

Hernandez v. *Texas,* 347 U.S. 475 (1954).

Hishon v. *King & Spaulding,* 678 F. 2d 1022 (11th Cir. 1983), *aff'g* 24 Fair Emp. Prac. Cas. (BNA) 1303 (N.D. Ga. 1980).

Hishon v. *King & Spaulding,* 104 S. Ct. 2229 (1984).

International Brotherhood of Teamsters v. *United States,* 431 U.S. 324 (1977).

Keyes v. *School Dist. #1, Denver,* 413 U.S. 189 (1973).

Kirkland v. *New York State Dept. of Correctional Services,* 711 F. 2d. 1117 (2d Cir. 1983).

Kumar v. *Bd. of Trustees of Univ. of Massachusetts,* 34, FEP Cases 1231 (1984).

La Riviere v. *EEOC,* 682 F. 2d 1275 (9th Cir. 1982).

Lee v. *Macon County Bd. of Educ.,* 317 F. Supp. 103 (M.D. Ala. 1970).

Lehman v. *Yellow Freight Systems Inc.,* 651 F. 2d 520 (7th Cir. 1981).

Lieberman v. *Gant,* 630 F. 2d 1275 (9th Cir. 1982).

Los Angeles v. *Manhart,* 435 U.S. 702 (1978).

Mandel v. *HEW,* 411 F. Supp. 542 (D.Md. 1976); *aff'd in part Mayor and City Council of Baltimore* v. *Matthews,* 562 F.2d 914 (4th Cir. 1977); *vacated* 571 F. 2d 1273 (4th Cir. 1978); *cert. denied Lee* v. *HEW,* 439 U.S. 862 (1978).

Marsh v. *Board of Education of Flint,* 581 F. Supp. 614 (E.D. Mich. 1984) *aff'd* No. 84-1240 (6th Cir. April 4, 1985).

McDonald v. *Santa Fe Trail Transportation Co.,* 427 U.S. 273 (1976).

McDonnell Douglas Corp. v. *Green,* 411 U.S. 792 (1973).

Meyerson v. *State of Arizona,* 740 F. 2d 684 (9th Cir. 1984).

Morgan v. *O'Bryant,* 671 F. 2d. 23 (1st Cir. 1982), *cert. denied sub nom. Boston Ass'n of School Administrators and Supervisors* v. *Morgan,* 459 U.S. 827 (1982).

North Carolina v. *HEW,* 48 o F. Supp. 929 (E.D.N.C. 1981).

Palmer v. *District Bd. of Trustees of Saint Petersburg Junior College,* 748 F. 2d. 595 (11th Cir. 1984).

Planells v. *Howard University,* 32 FEP Cases 337 (D.D.C. 1983).

Powell v. *Syracuse University,* 580 F. 2d 1150 (2d Cir. 1978).

Regents of University of California v. *Bakke,* 438 U.S. 265 (1978).

Sanders v. *Ellington,* 288 F. Supp. 937 (M.D. Tenn.) 1968).

Setzer v. *Novack Ins. Co.,* 657 F. 2d 962 (8th Cir. 1981); *cert. denied,* 454 U.S. 1064 (1981).

Swann v. *Charlotte-Mecklenberg Bd. of Educ.,* 402 U.S. 1 (1971).

Sweezy v. *New Hampshire,* 354 U.S. 234 (1957).

Systems Federation v. *Wright,* 364 U.S. 642 (1961).

Texas Dept. of Community Affairs v. *Burdine,* 450 U.S. 248 (1981).

Turgeon v. *Howard University,* 571 F. Supp. 679 (D.D.C. 1983).

United States v. *El Camino Community College Dist.,* 600 F. 2d 1258 (9th Cir. 1979), *cert. denied* 444 U.S. 1013 (1980).

United States v. *Jefferson County Bd. of Education,* 372 F. 2d 836, decree corrected, 380 F. 2d 385, *cert. denied, sub nom. Caddo Parish School Board* v. *United States, 389 U.S. 840 (1967).*

United States v. *Louisiana* 527 F. Supp. 509 (D.C. La 1981).

United Steelworkers v. *Weber,* 443 U.S. 193 (1979).

Uzzell v. *Friday,* 592 F. Supp. 1502 (M.D.N.C. 1984).

Valentine v. *Smith,* No. J-76-C-78 (D. Ark. 1980).

Valentine v. *Smith,* 654 F. 2d 503 (8th Cir. 981), *cert. denied* 454 U.S. 1124 (1981).

Ward v. *Mass. Bay Transportation Authority,* 550 F. Supp. 1310 (D.C. Mass 1982).

Warsocki v. *Omaha,* 726 F. 2d 1358 (8th Cir. 1984).

Weber v. *Kaiser Aluminum & Chemical Corp.,* 563 F. 2d 216 (5th Cir. 1977).

Williams v. *City of New Orleans,* 729n F. 2d 1554 (5th Cir. 1984), *aff'g* 543 F. Supp. 662 (E.D. La. 1982).

Williams v. *Vukovich,* 720 F. 2d 909 (6th Cir. 1983).

Wygant v. *Jackson Bd. of Educ.,* 546 F. Supp. 1195, (E.D. Mich. 1982).

Wygant v. *Jackson Bd. of Educ.,* 746 F. 2d 1153 (6th Cir. 1984), *cert. granted* 53 U.S.L.W. 3739 (April 15, 1985).

Briefs, Motions, and Memoranda

Appellants Reply Brief, *Adams* v. *Bell,* 743 F. 2d 42 (D.C. Cir. 1984).

Brief for Appellants, *Adams* v. *Bell,* 743 F. 2d 42 (D.C. Cir. 1984).

Brief for Plaintiffs-Appellees, *Adams* v. *Richardson,* 480 F. 2d 1159 (D.C. Cir. 1973).

Reply Memorandum for Petitioners, *Adams* v. *Bell,* No. 83-643, *cert. denied,*   U.S. (1984).

Motion of the National Association for Equal Opportunity in Higher Education for Leave to File Brief as Amicus Curiae, *Adams* v. *Richardson,* 480 F. 2d 1159 (D.C. 1983).

Memorandum of the United States in Opposition to Entry of Proposed Stipulation of Settlement, *Geier* v. *Alexander,* 593 F. Supp. 1263 (M.D. Tenn. 1984).

Memorandum in Support of Defendant's Motion for Judgment Notwithstanding the Verdict or in the Alternative for A New Trial and Remittitur, *Turgeon* v. *Howard University,* 571 F. Supp. 679 (D.D.C. 1983).

American Council on Education, Brief as Amicus Curiae, *Bd. of Trustees of Keene State College* v. *Sweeney,* 439 U.S. 24 (1978).

Brief for Applicant, *Valentine* v. *Smith,* 654 F. 2d 503 (8th Cir. 1981).

Brief for Appellees, *Valentine* v. *Smith,* 654 F. 2d 503 (8th Cir. 1981).

Brief for Petitioner, *Valentine* v. *Smith,* 454 U.S. 1124 (1981).

Respondents' Brief in Opposition, *Valentine* v. *Smith,* 454 U.S. 1124 (1981).

Documents

Consent Decree, *North Carolina* v. *Dept. of Education,* No. 79-217-Cir-5 (E.D.N.C. 1981).

Commonwealth of Pennsylvania, Plan for Equal Opportunity in the State-Supported Institutions of Higher Education (July 1982).

Florida Revised Plan for Equalizing Education Oppportunity in Public Higher Education in Florida, 1978 and 1983 Addendum.

Maryland State Board for Higher Education, A Plan to Assure Equal Postsecondary Educational Opportunity, 1980–85. Task Force Report and Recommendations (September 1980).

Oklahoma State Regents for Higher Education, Compliance with Title VI of the Civil Rights Act, Extended Revised State Plan (October 1982).

South Carolina Commission on Higher Education, South Carolina Plan for Equity and Equal Opportunity in the Public Colleges and Universities (July 1981).

University of Missouri-Columbia, Plan for Continuing the Achievement of Equal Opportunity for Students and Faculty, Part One. (July 1981).

West Virginia University, Title VI, Compliance Plan (May 1981).

Executive Order 11246, 3 C.F.R. 339 (1965), as amended by Executive Order 11375, 3 C.F.R. 339 (1965).

Executive Order 12250, 45 F.R. 72995 (1982).

Title VII of the Civil Rights Act of 1964, 42 U.S.C. 2000e *et seq.* (1964), as amended, 86 Stat. 103 (1972).

Title VI of the Civil Rights Act of 1964, 42 U.S.C. 2000d *et seq.* (1964).

Amended Criteria Specifying Ingredients of Acceptable Plans to Desegregate State Systems of Public Higher Education, 43 Fed. Reg. 40780 (August 11, 1977).

Revised Criteria Specifying the Ingredients of Acceptable Plans to Desegregate State Systems of Public Higher Education, 43 Fed. Reg. 6658 (February 15, 1978).

Title VI Regulation, 45 C.F.R. {80.3 (C) (3) (1979).

Equal Employment Opportunity Duties of Government Contractors, 41 C.F.R. {60.2.10 (Revised Order No. 4).

Higher Education Guidelines for Executive Order 11246, U.S. Department of HEW, Office for Civil Rights, October 1972.

EEOC Affirmative Action Guidelines, 29 C.F.R. {1608.

EVALUATION RESEARCH AND EDUCATIONAL DECISION-MAKING:
A Review of the Literature

Jonathan Z. Shapiro, *Louisiana State University*

This chapter examines the role that program evaluation occupies in the process of decision making in education. The chapter is divided into four sections, two that concern evaluation research in general and two that pertain to evaluation in higher education in particular. The first section describes the emergence and development of program evaluation from the 1960s to the present. The second section introduces several evaluation taxonomies that have been constructed to represent the field conceptually. The third section recounts various evaluations that have been conducted in higher education to illustrate the applications of evaluation to different decision situations. Finally, the last section considers the conditions under which program evaluation is likely to exert its greatest impact on the process of decision making in higher education.

THE DEVELOPMENT OF PROGRAM EVALUATION
FROM THE 1960s TO THE PRESENT

The perspective on evaluation adopted in this paper is based on an assumption that the enterprise has undergone fairly identifiable changes in a short span of time. Three phases in the development of the field are proposed, corresponding to initial high expectations, followed quickly by the realization that the expectations are not being achieved, leading into a relatively long period of research and development predicated on more realistic (and sobering) perceptions of the problems and potential contributions of evaluation. The developmental stages are labeled the *construction,* the *deconstruction,* and the *reconstruction* of evaluation.

The Construction of Program Evaluation
Although it is difficult to establish the origins of evaluation with precision (for

example, Ingle, (1984) characterized Moses' decision to lead the children of Israel out of Egypt as being based on evaluation data), it is clear that the large-scale, formal practice of evaluation did not—indeed, could not—begin until the early 1960s. In the interests of completeness, most reviews of evaluation cite particular research efforts as early examples of evaluation. Among these are Rice's research (1897) on spelling, Binet's work (1905) on intelligence, Thorndike's research (1927) on generalized intellectual power, and Smith and Tyler's eight-year study (1942) of progressive education and success in college, which introduced the notion of measuring the attainment of objectives.

It is argued here that the inclusion of these citations is more likely because each contains characteristics associated with evaluation than because they contributed to the development of evaluation. An article more directly related to the formal field of evaluation, "Course Improvement Through Evaluation," was authored by Cronbach (1963). Cronbach argued, in discussing curriculum evaluation, that evaluation should be directed to the needs of decision makers, should be conducted while the course is being developed, and should focus on performance characteristics.

Madaus et al. (1983) suggested in their historical overview of evaluation that reviews in which evaluation is regarded as a recent phenomenon are mistaken, and they traced the origins of the field to the early 1800s. Despite Madaus et al., it is argued in this chapter that the field of evaluation dates from approximately 1965. The basis for this assertion is an examination of the conditions under which the need and opportunity for evaluation emerged, as well as the argument that such conditions did not exist before 1960. Consequently, from a functional perspective, it is asserted that the development of evaluation is best accounted for by reference to social conditions that were not in place till the 1960s, and therefore, identification of early research activities that occurred under different environmental conditions are unlikely to explain the current state of the field.

The formal field of evaluation did not begin to develop until the 1960s because it was only in that decade that the two necessary and sufficient conditions for the rise of the field emerged. Mosteller and Moynihan (1972) described these two important conditions. The first was a combination of political, economic, and social events that led to unprecedented national commitments to restructure the society so as to overcome the injustices and instabilities associated with the historic problems of poverty and race. The second was the development of new methodologies in social science research, particularly those associated with advances in computer technology, so that large-scale, complex investigations became possible to a degree that had not previously existed. It was from the synthesis of the favorable political and technological conditions that the field of evaluation research arose. The high expectations for evaluation research in this early period were closely tied to the great expectations that were attached to governmental attempts to ameliorate social problems and the great expectations for advances in social science knowledge and application that were appended to the developments in computer technology. Weiss (1972) described the high expectations of early proponents of evaluation:

> Evaluation research is viewed by its partisans as a way to increase the rationality of policy making. With objective information on the outcomes of programs, wise decisions can be made on budget allocations and program planning. Programs that yield good results will be expanded, those that make poor showings will be abandoned or drastically modified. . . . The production of objective evidence is seen as a way to reduce the politicking, the self-serving maneuvers and the log-rolling that commonly attend decision making at every level from the Congress to the local school. Data will replace favors and other political negotiations. [pp. 2–3]

A large part of the early confidence in the ability of evaluation to contribute to the amelioration of social problems was based on an assumption that rigorous, "scientific" data could effectively inform the policy process. From the policymaking perspective, the introduction of the planning–programming–budgeting system (PPBS), borrowed from General Motors in 1961, reflected a sense that "government should make decisions as systematically as possible—arraying alternative policies, assembling information on the advantages and disadvantages of each, and estimating the costs and benefits of public action" (Rivlin, 1971). The political impetus for evaluation was assisted by the passage of the Elementary and Secondary Education Act in 1965, which mandated the evaluation of the Title I and Title III programs (Ingle, 1984).

The predominant response within the field of evaluation to governmental demands for rigorous, scientific data was to promote the field research designs of Campbell and Stanley (1966), with their primary emphasis on the internal validity of the research inference as the appropriate methodological approach to evaluation research. There are at least three reasons for the almost exclusive reliance on experimental and quasi-experimental research designs in evaluation at that time. The first was the notion that government policymaking should be viewed as a form of "social experimentation (Rivlin, 1971). The view was explicated in a significant article authored by Donald T. Campbell entitled "Reforms as Experiments" (1969). Campbell argued that significant advances in solving social problems would occur only when policymakers advocated policies as experiments. Campbell contended that it is characteristic of policymakers to justify policy promulgation by acting as if policy effects are certain to be positive. He argued that the commitment to policy based on this *a priori* promise of success made it impossible for policymakers to attend to evaluation findings and to adjust policies based on these findings. Campbell suggested that an alternative to this form of policymaking would be a shift from the advocacy of a specific reform to the advocacy of the significance of the problem, and to the advocacy of persistence in alternative reform efforts should the first one fail. Campbell concluded that the shift from advocating specific policies to the advocacy of solving social problems (i.e., reforms as experiments) would permit policymakers to use evaluation findings and to abandon experimental policies that were not working. Campbell then suggested, not surprisingly, that if policies and programs were implemented as experiments, it would be most appropriate to employ experimental and quasi-experimental research designs to evaluate such programs and policies.

A second influence on the early commitment to the experimental approach to evaluation research was an argument that social action programs are structured so that the research setting resembles a laboratory experimental situation. Rossi observed that, "in principle, the evaluation of social action programs appears to be most appropriately undertaken through the use of experimental designs (Caro, 1977, p. 239). Two examples he offered are the control that sponsoring agencies exert over their programs and the general condition that ameliorative programs are not intended for general audiences, suggesting the availability of natural control groups. Stanley (1967) suggested that controlled, comparative experimentation can be of value, particularly in the early stages of program development, because the powerful principle of factorial design can be used to structure the components of a program systematically in order to see which are effective and in what combination.

Finally, the most powerful explation for the prominent position accorded experimentation in the 1960s may also be the simplest. Perhaps because much social legislation, particularly President Lyndon Johnson's War on Poverty, focused on education as a means of alleviating social problems, it appears that many of the evaluators working and writing in the 1960s had backgrounds in education and educational psychology. Consequently, the Campbell and Stanley approach to research may have been the most familiar and comfortable methodology to employ in the conduct of evaluation research.

Thus, the period of high expectations in evaluation research was characterized by a hope that policymakers were ready to use the findings of social science and of evaluation research in particular to inject an element of rationality, based on the production of scientific data, to confront and solve the significant social problems of the day. It was further presumed that such scientific information on the effectiveness of social policies and programs could be generated by applications of experimental and quasi-experimental research designs.

The Deconstruction of Program Evaluation

The period of high expectations was quickly followed, beginning in the late 1960s, by the acknowledgment that evaluation had failed to meet those expectations. Conner et al. (1984) noted that following the first euphoric years, evaluation research began to institutionalize itself: "Both evaluation researchers and those who were the intended users of evaluation research began to look closely at the conduct and outcomes of the many evaluations that had been completed. What they found did not always please them" (p. 15). This subsequent period was characterized by the rejection and redevelopment (by some but not all evaluators) of two broad aspects of evaluation: its conduct and its use.

Many evaluators began to challenge the notion that the experimental and quasi-experimental approach to research based on the work of Campbell and Stanley (1966) was, in fact, the optimal way to carry out evaluation. The experimental approach tended to be criticized along four dimensions: the scope or focus of experiments, the *a priori* specification of goals and outcome variables by the evaluator, the preeminent status accorded internal validity in the Campbell and Stanley scheme, and the exclusive reliance on quantitative data.

In a summary statement of the problems facing evaluation, Guba (1969) suggested that the "clinical signs of evaluation failure" were that evaluation was avoided whenever possible, that it was anxiety-provoking in those exposed to it, that the field was characterized by immobilization rather than responsiveness to evaluation opportunities, and that evaluators misguided their clients and failed to provide useful information. Guba argued that the failure was due to a series of lacks: lack of an adequate definition of evaluation; lack of an adequate evaluation theory; lack of knowledge about decision processes; lack of criteria on which judgments might be based; lack of approaches; lack of mechanisms for organizing, processing, and reporting evaluative information; and lack of trained personnel.

The Reconstruction of the Conduct of Program Evaluation

Among the first significant alternatives to the Campbell and Stanley approach was that advanced by Stake (1967) in an article entitled "The Countenance of Educational Evaluation." The major thesis of Stake's article was that evaluation required more than the analysis of program outcome data. He argued that program theory and evaluation judgments must become part of the educational evaluation process. Stake also indicated that data on antecedent conditions and the program process must be analyzed before data on program outcomes is even interpretable.

A similar criticism of the limited utility of focusing on outcomes exclusively was raised by Stufflebeam (1969) in his context–input–process–product (CIPP) approach to evaluation. Stufflebeam introduced the CIPP model by criticizing the application of experimental designs to evaluation. He noted that the experimental approach does not indicate directions for program improvement, does not translate well from the laboratory to the field, and does not promote the external validity—that is, the generalizability—of evaluation findings.

As implied by its name, the CIPP model advances a more comprehensive approach to understanding and assisting programs than does the outcome-focused experimental design. The CIPP model maintains a system-level approach to educational decision-making, examining the implications of the synthesis of the elements of an educational system. The general orientation is toward helping to maintain and improve the quality of institutional operations, because within the context of ongoing organizational activity, the bottom-line question of the overall impact or worth of program outcomes is mostly irrelevant.

The suggestion that evaluators need to focus on program process and to offer recommendations for program improvement led Scriven (1970) to develop the concepts of summative and formative evaluation. The notion distinguishes the two roles that an evaluator can adopt in the evaluation of programs. In the summative role, evaluation is the systematic and objective determination of the worth or merit of a program or product, which is best rendered by an independent evaluator conducting comparative analyses. In the formative role, evaluation is the collecting and reporting of data and judgments, which assist the development of a program. Scriven contended that summative evaluation was fundamentally more important than formative evaluation, and he criticized the CIPP model for ignoring summative judgments (Stufflebeam, 1983). Stufflebeam's subsequent (1971) development of the CIPP model attempted to enlarge the summative or "evaluation-as-accountability" aspect of CIPP.

Another article by Scriven (1976) focused on the problem of the *a priori* definition of program goals and outcomes. Scriven was concerned that the indication of intended program goals and outcomes by program personnel to the evaluator before the evaluation would bias the research by reducing the scope to a focus on a small set of variables. Scriven suggested an approach that he labeled "goal-free evaluation," in which an evaluator is given no *a priori* indication of program intents. This approach has the effect of preventing over-favorable evaluations and the exclusion of unintended consequences. Goal-free evaluation, which has not achieved widespread success, maintains an implicit criticism of the experimental approach, which requires the specification of dependent variables before data can be collected.

The significance accorded internal validity is a Campbell and Stanley notion that has been challenged by Cronbach (1982) and Shapiro (1982). Campbell and Stanley (1966, p. 5) declared that internal validity, the demonstration that a treatment has made a difference in a specific case, is the *sine qua non* of research, a position echoed by Cook and Campbell (1979, p. 83) in their priority ordering of validity concerns in basic and applied research. Both Cronbach and Shapiro argued that the external validity—that is, the generalizability—of an evaluative inference is most significant. Program decisions are forecasts into a blind future, and the utility of an evaluation finding is a function of its generalizability. Cronbach (1982) pointed out that, based on the Cook and Campbell position, internally valid inferences are correct, historical references, and that the generalizability of such inferences are limited because of the inverse relationship between internal and external validity. Shapiro (1982) advocated "evaluation as theory testing" as a method for increasing the generalizability of evaluation findings.

The most significant break with the experimental approach was that associated with arguments for a qualitative approach to evaluation. The debate among those advocating quantitative and qualitative evaluation methodologies has been intense, persistent, and complex. Part of this issue concerns the level at which the debate should be carried out, and the foci of contention include competing methodologies, competing paradigms, the focus of evaluation questions, and the use of evaluation findings.

Initial criticisms of the use of quantitative data were advanced essentially by implication. When evaluators such as Stake (1967), Provus (1971), and Stufflebeam (1969) advocated the significance of assessing program processes in evaluation, the nature of that assessment generally implied the collection of descriptive information based on interviews, observations, and documentary evidence.

Stake's countenance model (1967), for example, required the collection of data to fill two matrices: a program description matrix and a judgment matrix. Both matrices contain rows labeled *antecedent conditions, transactions,* and *outcomes.* The columns of the description matrix are labeled *intents* and *observations.* The intents column contains the presumed antecedent conditions, the planned program transactions, and the expected program results. The observation column contains data describing the realization of each intent.

The observed-transaction cell of the description matrix contains data on the level of treatment implementation, data that are most likely to be based on observations or interviews. Shapiro's evaluation (1985a) of a work-site program in health science employed Stake's description matrix approach. For each of several worksites, the intended-transaction cell contained lists of work activities that students were to be engaged in, and the observed-transaction cell contained observation data on which work activities the students had actually engaged in.

Provus' discrepancy model (1971) also implied the need for qualitative evaluation data, mainly supplied by expert judgment and participant interviews. The basic components of discrepancy evaluation are S (standards of worth) and P (performance information describing the object being evaluated). Discrepancy is then defined as $S-P$. The use of expert judgment and the reliance of the expert judge on the perceptions of program personnel imply that much of the evaluation information will be qualitative.

In a similar vein, Stufflebeam's process evaluation (1969), as a component of the CIPP model, requires recording and judging procedural events and activities through monitoring, interacting with, and observing program activities. The common thread running through the writing of Stake, Provus, and Stufflebeam is that quantitative evaluation data are at least not adequate—if not, in fact, inappropriate—for the comprehensive evaluation of educational programs. The development from Tyler and Smith's focus on objectives (1942) to an emphasis on program improvement and decision making implied that the experimental approach was no longer sufficient.

Parlett and Hamilton (1976) explicated this implicit argument by observing:

> Characteristically, conventional approaches have followed the experimental and psychometric traditions dominant in educational research. Their aim (unfulfilled) of achieving "objective methods" has led to studies that are artificial and restricted in scope. We argue that such evaluations are inadequate for elucidating the complex problem areas they confront, and, as a result, provide little effective input to the decision making process. [p. 114]

Subsequent support for qualitative evaluation included more direct assaults on quantitative data and methods. Weiss and Rein (1972) argued that, in the main, much of the difficulty inherent in evaluating broad-aim programs stems from the commitment to experimental design. They asserted that, in evaluating broad-aim programs, it is difficult to select satisfactory criteria, the situation is essentially uncontrolled, the treatments are not standardized, and the information is limited. They suggested, somewhat sketchily, an alternative approach, characterized as (1) process-oriented qualitative research; (2) historical research; or (3) case-study or comparative research. Stake (1978) also advocated case studies as the preferred method of evaluation research because they may be in harmony epistemologically with the user's experience and are therefore a natural basis for generalization.

In an introductory chapter to a text on qualitative evaluation research, Willis (1978) argued that

> quantitative evaluation, due to both its inherent limitations and to the aura that now surrounds it, neither asks nor answers many basic educational questions dealing with personal meaning and social significance. Educational evaluation in the United States will not develop into a mature and socially responsible enterprise until it widely accepts artistically developed and skillfully employed techniques of qualitative evaluation that directly confront both the significance of and the quality of personal experience within education [p. 2]

Willis's reference to artistic techniques is based on Eisner's model (1976) of connoisseurship and criticism adapted from the arts. Eisner argued that the view of education and educational development that led to an acceptance of the experimental approach was based on a positivist notion of science. Such an approach, predicated on the notion of prediction through control, was reflected in the desire to make schools more efficient and, presumably, more effective.

Eisner argued that the search for "laws of learning" has significant negative implications for education. First, the pursuit of generalizations necessarily treats unique qualities of individual situations as noise or error, leading ultimately to an "oversimplification of the particular" as expressed in a single quantity or index. Second, the attempt to objectify knowledge is based on positivist assumptions currently challenged in many fields. Finally, if the notion of standardizing is put in place, the standardization of outcomes may follow, and individuality may be placed in jeopardy.

Eisner suggested as alternative principles of evaluation the twin concepts of *connoisseurship* and *criticism*. Because Eisner presumed that teaching in classrooms is ideographic, that is, unlikely to be explained or controlled by behavioral laws, he argued that the major contribution of evaluation is a heightened awareness of the qualities of life so that teachers and students can be more intelligent within it. Just as connoisseurs of art, literature, and music possess heightened levels of apprehension in their areas of expertise, so the educational connoisseur can discriminate among subtle elements and characteristics of teachers, students, and classrooms.

Criticism is, then, the process of articulating and explicating apprehensions to others, what Dewey (1934) termed the reeducation of perception. According to Eisner (1976)

> the task of the critic is to adumbrate, suggest, imply, connote, render, rather than to translate. In this task, metaphor and analogy, suggestion and implication are major tools. The language of criticism, indeed its success as criticism, is measured by the brightness of its illumination. The task of the critic is to help us to see. [p. 340]

The growing sentiment against experimentation was not a consensual position, as many evaluators continued to subscribe to the Campbell and Stanley view of experimentation and the experiment (1966) "as the only means for settling disputes regarding educational practice, as the only way of verifying educational improvements, and as the only way of establishing a cumulative tradition in which improvements can be introduced without the danger of a faddish discard of old wisdom in favor of inferior novelties" (p. 2). Riecken and Boruch (1974) adopted the position that experimental trials of proposed social programs have important advantages over other ways of learning about programs. They argued that experiments allow inferences of superior dependability concerning cause and effect in comparison to simple observational or retrospective studies. Houston (1972) suggested that in the effort to persuade decision makers about evaluation validity, "to the skeptical ears of behavioral scientists, mere human testimony is less persuasive than the mathematical rhetoric of the impact effectiveness model" (that is, experimentation). More recently, Cook and Campbell (1979) promoted the experiment, not only as a method appropriate to the concerns of many philosophers of science with respect to cause and effect, but as being consistent with the way in which modern individuals perceive the world around them.

As a culminating statement illustrating the deeply held convictions on both sides of the quantitative/qualitative debate, consider Guba and Lincoln's introduction (1981) to a volume on naturalistic inquiry:

It is our deepest hope, however, that this book will provide a modicum of legitimization to the many evaluators who have concluded that traditional evaluation methods are inadequate but have not felt powerful enough to throw off the yoke of the orthodoxy that now surrounds the evaluation process. Michael Scriven has suggested that the social science model is doomed, that is, what we have called the scientific model—but that "the establishment will rot away before they give way" in their point of view. If we cannot help to persuade the establishment of the inadequacy of that view, we can at least aspire to contribute to the enhancement of the rate of rot. [p. xii]

Despite the intensity of feeling on both sides, some evaluators have argued that the widening gap is dysfunctional and have attempted to promote a synthesis between the approaches. Such sentiment is usually expressed in a call for "triangulation" (Campbell, 1974; Cook and Reichardt, 1979), the combination of multiple data sources and methods in the analysis of behavior. In analyzing the debate, Cook and Reichardt (1979) suggested that "there is nothing to stop the researcher, except perhaps tradition, from mixing and matching the attributes from the two paradigms (quantitative and qualitative) to achieve the combination which is most appropriate for the research problem and setting at hand" (p. 18).

However, Eisner (1976) and Bednarz (1983) have pointed out that the debate between the advocates of qualitative and quantitative evaluation gets confused between the methodological and paradigmatic levels of argument. Willis (1978) observed that there are two ways to differentiate quantitative and qualitative evaluation in education. While both types of studies begin with observations of phenomena and are empirical in that sense, the logic of inference in quantitative evaluation is one of classification, seriation, and numerical comparison, while in qualitative studies the logic is one of direct comparison of phenomena, resulting in insight and clarification.

The second method of differentiation concerns the ways in which evaluators apprehend the world. Quantitative studies often consider only the most easily observed and empirically verifiable characteristics of the environment. Qualitative studies usually attempt to consider more fully both observed characteristics and special qualities, that is, the perceived context within which the characteristics exist.

The significance of the two types of differentiation is based on the distinction between methods and paradigms. Methodologically, quantitative and qualitative evaluation represent alternative ways to make comparisons. Paradigmatically, however, quantitative and qualitative evaluation represent different definitions of what it means to make comparions. In methodological terms, quantitative and qualitative approaches are alternative; in paradigmatic terms, they are mutually incompatible. Consequently, triangulation or synthesis of methods can occur only if methods and paradigms are uncoupled.

It is the relationship between method and paradigm that is the focus of contention between those who advocate (Cook, 1974; Cook and Reichardt, 1979;

Heilman, 1980) and those who oppose (Eisner, 1976; Rist, 1975; Bednarz, 1983) the notion of synthesis between quantitative and qualitative evaluation. Cook and Reichardt, for example, attempted to demonstrate that paradigms and methods are not directly linked by presenting a set of counterinstances. They concluded that "there seems to be no reason to choose between qualitative and quantitative methods either. Evaluators would be wise to use whatever methods are best suited to their research needs, regardless of the methods' traditional affiliations. If that should call for a combination of qualitative and quantitative methods, then so be it." Similarly, Louis (1982) recommended that "the methodological imperative inherent in the narrow two paradigms should be rejected" (p. 14).

Bednarz (1983) pointed out that the argument for triangulation or synthesis is essentially based on a misunderstanding of the notion of paradigms as developed by Kuhn (1970). Kuhn wrote not of alternative paradigms but of competing paradigms, so that acceptance of one necessarily implies rejection of the other. This is true because paradigms represent not alternative views of the world but the assertion of different types of worlds. The qualitative approach, based on phenomenology and ethnomethodology, and the quantitative approach, based on positivism, represent not different methodological perspectives but fundamental disagreements about whether notions such as causality, validity, reliability, and generalizability have any meaning at all to educational researchers.

From this perspective, calls for synthesis or triangulation represent not genuine reconciliation but the attempt to subsume two methodologies under a dominant paradigmatic perspective. As Bednarz (1983) argued,

> Because of these philosophical differences, definitions of data, validity, reliability and causality differ; and so does each approach's definition of social science mission. I claim the picking and choosing of methods from each approach is not done outside of any given approach. Any synthesis must adopt necessarily the perspective of one over the other, so that any effort to reach a middle ground does so only in terms of a single perspective. [p. 30]

The debate between the proponents of qualitative and quantitative evaluation continues. As further technical refinement goes on within the different approaches, the gap between them increases. The ultimate outcome of this debate—triangulation, the development of two fields of educational evaluation, or perhaps subsets of evaluators subscribing to one outcome or the other—remains to be decided.

Reconstruction of the Utilization of Program Evaluation
The second area of major redevelopment concerns the issue of evaluation use. Simply stated, during this period, the perception developed that evaluation findings were mostly not used by policymakers and program administrators. Throughout this period, observations such as House's (1973) that even under

favorable conditions evaluation data may account for only 20% of a decision; Worthen and Sanders's (1973) that evaluation is widely discussed but little used; Novak's (1977) that the apparent nonuse of evaluation findings is one of the most vexing problems; Kilbourne's and De Gracie's (1979) that most evaluation studies are being used for little more than doorstops, and Guba and Lincoln's (1981) that the failure to use evaluation findings has almost assumed the proportions of a national scandal have culminated in what Thompson and King (1981) labeled "the tragedy of nonuse."

It was the perception of nonuse as the modal response to evaluation findings that truly dashed the high expectations. As Thompson and King (1981) observed, "reading the literature on evaluation utilization can contribute to chronic depression" (p. 3). The great expectation of evaluators, prompted in part by their invitation to participate in the policy process by policymakers, was that evaluation data would exert a clear and powerful impact on the policy process. A somewhat hyperbolic characterization of this expectation is Holley's statement (1979) that "in an ideal world we wouldn't have to worry about utilization. Educators would be eagerly waiting our findings and would promptly rush to put them into practice" (p. 2).

The realization that the expectations for evaluation were not being met led to the development of two lines of research on utilization. One line of inquiry focused on the explication and specification of the concept of utilization, in an attempt to define exactly what the term meant and how its occurrence could be identified. The second line of inquiry concerned stategies that evaluators could employ to promote the use of evaluation findings, that is, factors related to use.

Conner et al. (1984) noted that the realization that the evaluation data was not being used caused a great deal of "soul searching" in the field. They suggested that the definition of use at that early time was restricted to an instrumental view, where immediate and direct details of use were examined, usually those that the evaluator had recommended. If these things did not occur, the judgment was that no use had resulted from the evaluation.

Patton et al.'s empirical study (1977) of the use of health evaluations at the federal level challenged the notion of dramatic use operative during the period of high expectations. Contrary to the idea that policymakers use evaluation by acting in a manner recommended by an evaluator, Patton et al. discovered that the impact of evaluation was most often experienced as a reduction in the uncertainty faced by individual decision-makers as they attempted to deal with the complexity of programming reality. Thus, the effect of an evaluation was unlikely to be manifested in administrative behavior.

Patton's results and his subsequent text *Utilization-Focused Evaluation* (1978) challenged the rationality assumptions on which the utilization literature had been based (DeYoung and Conner, 1982) and indicated the need for research on the conditions under which use is most likely to occur, as well as what form use is likely to take. A growing body of literature on evaluation use has begun to develop.

Others have argued that the situation was even worse during the period of high expectations, that rather than maintaining a narrow definition of use, there was simply no notion of what constituted use during this period. Tittle (1977) argued that "papers concerned with analysis of impact and impact assessment methodology have not always dealt with the problem of how to define impact" (p. 3). Similarly, Weiss (1979) observed that "until we resolve questions about the definition of use, we face a future of non-comparable studies of use and scant hope of cumulative understanding of how evaluation and decision making intersect" (p. 13).

Although some studies, such as Patton et al.'s (1977), have deliberately avoided defining the term *utilization,* there has been an attempt in the literature to refine the concept. Most researchers during the 1970s concluded that dramatic, large-scale changes based on evaluation recommendations was simply an unlikely response on the part of decision makers. In discussing an empirical study of use, Patton (1978) stated:

> The view of evaluation research that emerged in our interviews stands in stark contrast to the image of utilization that is presented as the ideal in the bulk of evaluation literature. The ideal held forth in the literature is one of major impact on concrete decisions. The image that emerged in our interviews is that there are few major, direction changing decisions in most programming, and that evaluation research is used as one piece of information that feeds into a slow evolutionary process of program development . . . utilization of evaluation is there to see, but not if one is looking for impact of great moment. [pp. 32–33]

One strategy for refining the definition of utilization has been to categorize or classify different decision-maker responses to evaluation. Rich (1977) suggested employing the term *use* rather than *utilization* to demonstrate minimal expectations for the impact of evaluation data on decision making. He further distinguished instrumental use and conceptual use. Instrumental use occurs when documentation of the decision maker's response to data is possible. *Conceptual use* refers to influencing a decision maker's thinking about an issue without putting information to any specific purpose.

King et al. (1981) extended this notion to include the category of symbolic use. They observed that

> in cases of instrumental and conceptual use, evaluation results are applied to the political context in immediate or long term ways. In contrast, symbolic use comes from the political context; knowing what they want to do, decision makers turn evaluation results to their own ends, whether appropriate or not. To do this is not necessarily unethical or manipulative. It may be a method for survival. [p. 14]

Weiss (1982), however, argued that use is more appropriately thought of as a continuous rather than a categorical variable. She asserted that while the categories have been useful in making the transition from the original, exclusive preoccupation with instrumental use, such categories are essentially arbitrary and that the use of research and evaluation is actually a continuum.

More recently, Leviton and Boruch (1983) suggested differentiating use from impact. *Use* is defined as serious consideration of evaluation findings that may or may not relate to decisions. *Impact* is defined as actual changes in programs resulting from use. Such impact may be manifest as amendments, regulations, and management changes.

To date, the growing literature on use has not led to a consensual definition of the concept. At best, the current literature has led to a broadening notion of what constitute legitimate decision-maker responses to evaluation data and recommendations. Braskamp and Brown (1980) argued that "although the expanded definition makes utilization less dramatic and more difficult to explicitly measure and demonstrate, it represents a view of evaluation in which the role of human interaction in the communication process is given more credence" (p. viii). However, as others (Weiss, 1982) have contended, without an agreed-upon definition of what constitutes use, there is a serious question about whether it can be determined when use has occurred.

Validation for the position that the lack of an agreed-upon definition of *use* is detrimental to the development of the field can be seen in the fact that while the literature on use grows at an ever-increasing rate, no great arguments or debates are being carried on by those writing in this area. Perhaps because a standard definition is lacking, much of the literature on use seems unconnected. In this area of inquiry, there exist no schools of thought, no controversial assumptions, no passion, unlike the nature of the literature on qualitative versus quantitative evaluation. Thus, conceptual growth and development through the clash of ideas are not characteristic of the literature on evaluation use.

As an agenda for future research that would lead the field toward broad, consensual notions of use, Weiss (1982) suggested that the following questions concerning use must be answered through research: (1) What is used? (2) How direct is the derivation from the study? (3) By whom is it used? (4) By how many people is it used? (5) How immediate is the use? And (6) how much effect is required (to count as use)?

Interestingly, the lack of a clear-cut conceptual or operational definition of use has not seemed to hamper research on strategies for promoting or maximizing use. Perhaps the term has taken on the status of a primitive (Rudner, 1966); that is, the evaluation community simply acts as if a consensual definition exists. The literature on evaluation use has been categorized in different ways by those who attempt to describe systematically the lines of inquiry in this field.

Weiss (1982) suggested that investigators have adopted four approaches to the study of use. One approach is to focus on a single evaluation or research study and to follow the effects of the study on subsequent decisions. The most common methodology used is the case study technique with particular emphasis placed on informant interviews. Examples of this approach include Datta's investigation (1976) of the effects of the Ohio-Westinghouse investigation of Head Start, Boeckmann's analysis (1976) of the New Jersey negative-income-tax experiment, and Rich's dissertation research (1975) on the Continuous National Survey project.

A second approach to the study of use is to begin with people who are prospective users of research and evaluation information. The basic strategy is to interview decision makers about their uses of research: which studies they used, when they used them, how they used them, and the consequences of use. Examples of this type of study include Patton et al.'s study (1977) of federal-level use of health policy research, Duggan's study (1983) of clients of the Office of Evaluation Research of the University of Illinois at Chicago, and Leviton and Boruch's study (1983) of federal-level decision-makers.

A third approach is to start with an issue and to examine the ways in which evaluation and research influence the resolution of the issue. This approach presumes that the effects of research can be separated out from other influences. Weiss (1982, p. 139) pointed to Aaron's research (1978) on poverty, education, and unemployment issues as a prime example of this type of research.

The final approach is to begin with a particular organization and to investigate the impact of research and evaluation on the life history of that organization. It is presumed in these studies that researchers can track the ripple effect of research and evaluation on organizational behavior. Examples include Brown and Jaques's study (1965) of the Glacier Metal Company and Klein's research (1976) on Esso Petroleum. Weiss went on to suggest (pp. 140–142) that the type of study employed by a researcher influences the methodology, the questions best answered, the questions less well answered, and the probable limitations on the research effort.

Duggan (1983) categorized the research on evaluation use into simulation studies, empirical studies, and analytical studies. Three examples of use simulations are Brown et al. (1978, 1980) and Braskamp et al. (1978). Each of these studies examined the relationship between use and variables derived from communication theory.

The Brown et al. (1978) study examined the influence of jargon on clients' perceptions of an evaluation report and of an evaluator. The researchers created evaluation reports that varied by being jargon-free objective, jargon-free subjective, jargon-loaded objective, or jargon-loaded subjective. MANOVA results suggested that jargon-loaded reports were perceived as more difficult to understand than jargon-free reports, but there were no statistically significant differences in the acceptance of the recommendations.

The Braskamp et al. (1978) study examined use as a function of the status of the evaluator, the program component under evaluation, and the client's role in the organization. In part, the results suggested that evaluator status did influence clients' perceptions of the objectivity of the evaluator but did not influence agreement with the recommendations.

The Brown et al. (1980) study focused on three questions: the effect of reading an article concerning the need for evaluation on the perceived usefulness of an evaluation, the effect of reading an article concerning the importance of evaluation on the participants' extent of agreement with recommendations, and the effect of a perceived need for evaluation on the assessment of an evaluation report. Among the findings that were reported were no effect of reading the article on the need for evaluation, a positive effect of reading the article concerning the importance of evaluation on the assessment of the evaluation report, and an influence of perceived need for evaluation on the extent of agreement with recommendations.

Obviously, the findings of these simulations constitute a mixed bag of statistical and theoretical conclusions; no general pattern of the influence of communication-theory-based variables on use emerged. Thompson and King (1981) suggested that both the theoretical rigor and the generalizability of these studies are questionable.

Empirical studies of use tend to employ naturalistic methods, mainly interviews, to accumulate evidence on the influence of evaluation on the influence of evaluation on decision making. Patton et al.'s study (1977) of twenty federal-level health evaluations examined two issues: (1) the nature and extent of use of evaluations and (2) factors that resulted in varying degrees of evaluation use. For each evaluation, the researchers interviewed an evaluator and a decision-maker. Based on the data, Patton et al. concluded that two general factors—political considerations and the personal involvement of the evaluator—significantly influenced evaluation use.

Weiss and Bucuvalas (1977) conducted research on the use of evaluation information by officials of mental health agencies. The basic research design was based on presenting the officials with actual research reports and surveying them on how they would respond to the information contained in the reports. The researchers determined that mental-health decision-makers at the federal, state, and local levels believe that social science research can contribute to policy and that it should be used. Factors positively related to usefulness were relevance, quality, conforming to user expectations, action orientation, and challenge to the *status quo.*

A study by Alkin et al. (1979) examined five educational programs. The data in this study consisted of interviews with program staff, interviews with evaluators, and program document information. The respondents were interviewed several times to that cross-sectional and dynamic corroboration of perceptions could be obtained. Among the significant factors identified in the study were the orientation of the clients, organizational factors, and information content and reporting.

A slightly different approach to assessing use was King and Thompson's survey (1981) of administrators' perceptions of evaluation. They reported that 60% of the local-education-agency users rated the evaluation of programs in their school as useful, but 72% of the respondents felt that the most significant program effects could be measured only indirectly (Duggan, 1983, p. 23).

Duggan (1983) asserted that the bulk of literature on evaluation use is analytical in nature; that is, it consists of reviews of the literature, thought pieces, and experientially based writing. The analytic literature tends to focus on six factors related to use: (1) communication factors (Patton, 1978; Wise, 1978; Raizen and Rossi, 1981), or the exchanges of information between evaluators and decision makers during the evaluation process; (2) the characteristics of the decision maker (Alkin, 1975; Kiresuk, 1980; Haenn and Owens, 1981), or the qualities and needs of those who must make program decisions; (3) the nature of the evaluator (Patton, 1978; Cronbach et al., 1980; Thompson and King, 1981), or the image projected by the evaluator to program personnel and decision makers; (4) the nature of evaluation findings (Weiss, 1972; Nathan, 1979; Shapiro, 1984), or the implications for change contained in evaluation results; (5) the technical quality of the findings (Davis and Salasin, 1975; Nachmias and Henry, 1980; Raizen and Rossi, 1981), or the degree of belief based on the methodological rigor of the study; and (6) the organizational setting (Weiner et al., 1977; Dickey, 1979; Isaac, 1980), or the political influences on decision makers, particularly as the influences constrain the degree to which decision makers can respond to evaluation information.

Shapiro (1984) argued that a consistent bias in the literature on use leads to only partial understanding of the utilization process. The bias is due to a two-cultures perspective of use maintained in the literature. The two-cultures perspective, developed by Snow (1962) and modified to apply to social science research and policymaking by Caplan (1979) as the two-community theory, asserts that social scientists and decision makers reside in two professional communities separated by a communication gap. As Rich (1981) described it:

> Among social scientists, the prevailing belief is that empirically grounded knowledge is seriously underutilized in important policy decisions: Social science still accumulates in libraries and impractical retrieval systems rather than policy and government practices . . . Policy makers, however, feel that they cannot understand the reports they receive, that the reports do not deal with the immediate problems on their agenda, and that the reports are not sensitive to bureaucratic and political pressures [p. 6]

A significant implication of the two-community theory (that nonuse is due to a communication gap) is that use will be optimized by attending to the interpersonal transactions between evaluator and decision maker.

Rich (1981) asserted that the two-community theory is at the core of most studies of utilization, and it is argued here that the research on evaluation use is also dominated by the two-community perspective. Duggan's identification (1983) of communication factors, the nature of the decision maker, the nature of the evaluator, the nature and the technical quality of the results, and organizational factors supports this argument because all but the last factor concern the "knowledge transfer" aspect of the evaluation process, that is, the generation and movement of evaluation information from the evaluator to the decision maker. In effect, the essential determinants of use, based on the current literature, are the characteristics of the data, the characteristics of the evaluator and the decision maker with respect to the communication relationship they share, and the nature of that relationship itself.

Research on the significance of the evaluation data indicates the need for data of high technical quality (Nachmias and Henry, 1980) that is relevant to the particular decision under consideration (Rieker, 1980). It is argued that the design must be flexible in order to cope with unanticipated problems (Braskamp and Brown, 1980), but there is disagreement on whether formative evaluation data (Haenn and Owens, 1981) or a combination of summative and formative evaluation data (King and Thompson, 1981) is more likely to be used.

The literature on the nature of the evaluator, not surprisingly, suggests the utility of a positive, nonthreatening approach (Alkin and Law, 1980), in which the needs of the organization are identified first (Dickey and Hampton, 1981). It is argued (Shapiro, 1985b) that an evaluator must be politically adept, but the primary concern of the evaluator must be the individuals within the organization (Davis and Salasin, 1975). The decision maker must develop a stake in the evaluation (Talmage, 1982), and the evaluator must be aware of the decision maker's perception of the evaluation process (Alkin et al., 1979). Finally, Patton (1978), Cronbach et al. (1980), and Thompson and King (1981) concluded that the single most significant influence on use is the "personal" factor," that is, the personality of the evaluator and that of the decision maker. According to Cronbach, "Nothing makes a larger difference in the use of evaluations than the personal factor—the interest of officials in learning from the evaluation and the interest of the evaluator to get attention for what he knows" (Thompson and King, 1981, p. 35). This statement suggests that the informal communication between the evaluator and the decision maker may be of particular importance in the process of utilization.

Two related problems can be derived from the prominence of the two-community hypothesis in the utilization literature. The first, identified by Rich (1981) and Shapiro (1984), is that reliance on the hypothesis implies that if relevant information is provided in a timely, comprehensible manner by a supportive, nonthreatening evaluator, then the decision maker will use that information. Because the two-community theory attributes nonuse to a communication gap, it implies that closing the gap will necessarily lead to use. This approach ignores the fact that once evaluation information enters an organization, it is routinely processed and interpreted before it is used. Thus, the current literature underestimates the effect of the organizational structure and the decision process on the likelihood of use.

Rich (1981) asserted that levels of use may best be explained through an examination of routine bureaucratic roles and procedures. The set of rules, practices, and traditions may be expressed in terms of formal or informal policy that dictates how officials will produce, process, and apply information. In short, utilization may well be a function of how organizations make decisions, independent of the manner in which an evaluator produced and delivered that information to the organization.

While some research on the influence of the organizational environment on utilization has been conducted (Patton, 1978); Hansen, 1981), the focus has been mainly on the relationship between organizational structure and the evaluator–decision-maker relationship rather than on the utilization process itself. Shapiro (1984) examined the implications for utilization of four models of organizational decision making: rational choice, bureaucratic politics, organizational behavior, and cognitive processing. He argued that the organizational decision process constrains the use of evaluation information by advancing other decision criteria, such as self-interest, political consensus, organizational persistence, and cognitive distortion, as more salient. This view suggests that the two-community theory, with its focus on knowledge transfer, can establish only a necessary but not a sufficient explanation for use, that is, only partial understanding of the process of use.

The related problem associated with the two-community theory is that the emphasis on knowledge transfer results in portraying the evaluator as the central figure or the energizing agent in the process of utilization. Shapiro (1985c) argued that more realistic assessments of the role of evaluation in the policy process will occur when models are used that locate the decision maker as the central figure and the evaluator as one of the elements of the decision-making environment. In this type of specification, evaluation is construed as being one of a series of decision cues to which a decision maker responds.

Shapiro (1985) observed that what is required is a reformulation of the utilization problem statement from "how can an evaluator induce a decision maker to utilize evaluation findings?" to "under what conditions will a decision maker incorporate evaluation findings into the decision process?" (p. 5). He argued that this reformulation will result in a more realistic set of expectations for the role of evaluation data in the policy process.

In sum, the development of program evaluation from the 1960s to the present can be described in terms of two broad issues: the conduct and the use of

evaluation. The initial period of high expectations was one when only simple—in fact, naive—assumptions were maintained about the conduct and the
use of evaluation. It was presumed that the experimental methodology was the
appropriate way to generate evaluation information, and that decision makers
would respond to that information immediately, directly, and wholeheartedly.

The subsequent period, when it was acknowledged that the high expectations
for evaluation were not being met, was characterized by criticism and rejection
of the experimental approach by many evaluators, as well as criticism and
rejection of the dramatic notions of utilization by all evaluators. This period,
extending perhaps from the late 1960s to the late 1970s, also marked the advancement of alternatives to the experimental approach to evaluation, as well
as broadening notions of what constitute realistic expectations for the use of
evaluation information by decision makers.

The current period, beginning around 1980, is one in which the issues of
evaluation conduct and utilization continue to be central questions in the literature. One development pertinent to both conduct and use is the examination of
fields outside evaluation in order to extend the limits of evaluation. With
respect to evaluation conduct, several evaluators have begun to ask what evaluation can learn from law, architecture, geography, and painting (Smith, 1981).
With respect to use, it has been suggested (Shapiro, 1985b) that an understanding of what constitutes use, and of what factors are associated with use
can be improved by an examination of the literature on ethics, social welfare
economics, organizational theory, and political science.

It is clear that the field of evaluation has yet to resolve the issues of what constitutes appropriate conduct and use. It is the progress achieved in generating
useful, appropriate, and consensual conceptual definitions of conduct and use
that reflects the process of development and maturation of the field of program
evaluation.

A REVIEW OF TAXONOMIES: THE CONCEPTUALIZATION OF
PROGRAM EVALUATION

The first section of this chapter discussed the development of evaluation, with a
focus on the problems of evaluation conduct and use. The literature in the first
section concerned the issue of evaluation behavior, that is, how we do evaluation, or what we do to generate results and have them used. In contrast, this
section deals not with how we do evaluation but with "how we think about
evaluation" (House, 1984), that is, conceptualization of the evaluation enterprise. Of necessity, this section is shorter than the first because evaluation, as a
practitioner-oriented field, has always been more concerned with behavior than
with conceptual analysis. Nonetheless, a comprehensive understanding of evaluation is facilitated by an examination from both a microlevel (i.e., behavioral)
and a macrolevel (i.e., conceptual) perspective.

One way in which to examine how people think about anything is to identify the metaphors they use. House (1984) observed that "much of our everyday thinking is metaphorical in nature. That is, we experience one thing in terms of another" (p. 81). The function of metaphor is to structure how we think about the world. Rein and Schon (1977) suggested that metaphors are frames (a metaphor in itself) that enable us to (1) highlight certain features of a situation; (2) ignore or discard certain features as irrelevant; and (3) bind together the salient features of a situation into a pattern that is coherent and graspable. Metaphors, as frames, help us to organize what we will address and what we will neglect.

Rein and Schon (1977) further contended that frames impose structure on ambiguous situations because they contain metaphors that enable us to reason from the unfamiliar to the familiar. Familiar concepts are brought to unfamiliar situations and, in the process, transform unfamiliar situations into familiar and therefore explicable situations. House (1984) explained that this process occurs because metaphors are usually brought from phenomena in which the user is immersed.

Rein and Schon (1977) presented two examples to illustrate the framing function. The first concerns the metaphors employed to describe a family situation where, through death, divorce, separation, or desertion, children live without both parents. Two metaphors that have been used to frame this situation are "broken homes" and "single-parent families." The first metaphor implies that the salient aspects of the situation are those that decay or rot, while the second points toward those functions, most likely supportive, that any parent, living alone or as part of a couple, can perform. The metaphoric function is particularly significant when it is understood that most metaphors operate at an unconscious level of thought. As a second example, Rein and Schon (1977) asked what different frames are generated by the metaphors "backward," "undeveloped," and "developing" in discussions of nations.

In this section, four evaluation taxonomies are used to examine how we think about evaluation. Taxonomies are particularly appropriate objects for metaphoric analysis because taxonomies are frames, they point to what is salient and what is irrelevant, and frames generate metaphors. Because the relationship between taxonomies and metaphors is reasonably direct, they indicate how we think about things. The taxonomies analyzed in this section are those constructed by Gardner (1977), House (1978), Stufflebeam and Webster (1980), and Talmage (1982). Table 1, on p. 189, summarizes the four taxonomies.

Metaphor I: Evaluation as Information Production

Gardner's taxonomy (1977) focuses on evaluation as information production. Gardner identified five approaches to evaluation that yield different types of information. Using the terminology of Rein and Schon (1977) and of House

(1984), Gardner explicated these five approaches by employing the metaphor of evaluation as information production to generate the following frame factors: (1) the principle focus of the approach: (2) examples of the approach in current practice: (3) the basic premises and assumptions of the approach: (4) advance organizers (variables that characterize the approach), including basic values, typical research designs, typical evaluator roles, typical methodologies, and types of communication and feedback; and (5) the nature of the expected outcomes and the modes of interpretation.

Gardner used these frame factors to interpret what he called five frameworks or definitions of evaluation. The first approach is evaluation as measurement, which implies that to evaluate is to "measure results, effects, or performance using some type of formalized instrument which produces data that can be compared to some sort of standardized scale" (p. 575). Examples of this approach include applications such as using scores on the Scholastic Aptitude Test or the Graduate Record Examination to evaluate academic aptitude and using instructional-cost-analysis studies based on data collected from faculty-activity-analysis questionnaires.

A second evaluation approach is evaluation as professional judgment, where a qualified professional is asked to examine an object and to render an expert opinion of its merit or worth. Examples of this definition would include Eisner's connoisseurship model (1976) and Provus's discrepancy model (1971), discussed above.

The third major framework was labeled by Gardner as the assessment of congruence between performance and objectives. He suggested that methodologies that fall into this category "define evaluation as the process of specifying or identifying goals, objectives or standards of performance; identifying or developing tools to measure performance, and comparing the measurement data with the previously identified objectives or standards to determine the degree of discrepancy or congruence that exists" (p. 577). Gardner noted that familiar goal-oriented topics include competency-based teacher education, equal educational opportunity, and career education (pp. 577–578).

Unfortunately, Gardner's own definition makes clear that Provus's discrepancy model (1971) can fit this framework as well as the previous one. Since one of the requirements of a good taxonomy is that the categories must be mutually exclusive, the taxonomy (of definitions) obviously has some problems. Gardner did state that "hybrid types are abundant, but the principal emphasis or focus of a particular effort will almost always be identifiable as belonging to one of these categories" (p. 573). However, Provus's model (1971) is based on an expert assessing discrepancy; thus, the ambiguity does not seem resolvable.

The fourth major approach is labeled *decision orientation evaluation*. Gardner suggested that all models that fit into this category are based on the CIPP model (Stufflebeam, 1969) discussed above. Central to these models is the definition of evaluation as the process of delineating, obtaining, and providing useful information for judging decision alternatives. Gardner asserted that the essence of these models is an institutionalized feedback mechanism for a continuous assessment of decision-information needs and the obtaining and providing of information to meet those needs.

The final approach, labeled *goal-free/responsive evaluation,* actually subsumes two models of evaluation. The goal-free model (Scriven, 1976), discussed above, was designed to avoid certain problems of bias. Responsive evaluation, developed by Stake (1975), is based on an evaluation design driven by the needs of program personnel. Gardner combined the two because neither requires the *a priori* specification of goals and objectives.

By applying the frame factors to these five major approaches, Gardner concluded (pp. 590–591) that the type of decision that must be made should determine the choice of evaluation approach. He suggested that the dimensions (that is, the frame factors) that he used illustrate that the type of information produced in each approach varies with respect to objectivity, time demands, goal orientation, and context specificity. Thus, if one takes into account the decision needs in a particular situation, the most appropriate approach should be revealed.

Metaphor II: Evaluation as Political Philosophy
House's taxonomy (1978) is based on the metaphor of evaluation as political philosophy. House set out to explain or distinguish eight approaches to evaluation: the systems approach, for example, the PPBS system (Rivlin, 1971) discussed above; the behavioral objectives approach originally suggested by Tyler (1950): a decision-making approach, exemplified by Stufflebeam's CIPP model (1969); Scriven's (1975) goal-free approach; Eisner's (1976) art criticism approach; an accreditation approach, such as that employed by the North Central Association; an adversary approach based on legal argumentation and jury procedures (Smith, 1981); and a transaction approach such as that in Stake's responsive model (1975).

House actually used two sets of frame factors to analyze the differences among the approaches. The first set of frames includes proponents, audiences, assumptions, methodology, outcomes, and typical questions. The generative metaphor is evaluation as research activity because the factors connect the clients of research, the conduct of research, and the findings of research.

House's second set of frame factors identifies aspects of the philosophy of democratic liberalism, essentially, the degree to which individual perspectives and values are characteristic of the alternative approaches. The two frame factors are the degree of pluralism, defined dichotomously as elite or mass, and the nature of the criteria for judging worth, defined as either utilitarian, in which all value is defined by a unitary criterion, or intuitionist, in which individual, subjective criteria are employed. The two dichotomous factors yield four philosophic categories in which the approaches are located.

Elite-utilitarian approaches (systems analysis, behavioral objectives, and decisionmaking) involve the participation of a select few and a unitary criterion for judging outcomes. Goal-free evaluation is the sole mass-utilitarian approach because it requires input from many sources, but the evaluator's criterion of worth determines the nature of the evaluation assessment.

Art criticism and accreditation are labeled *elite-intuitionist* because these processes involve a small number of experts, and each expert applies his or her own criterion of worth in judging outcomes. Finally, the adversary and transactional models are mass-intuitionist because many are involved in the process and the subjective assessment of each individual impacts on the final evaluation determination.

Metaphor III: Evaluation as Organizational Strategy

The third taxonomy considered in this section is Stufflebeam and Webster's evaluation as purposive organizational behavior (1980). They analyzed thirteen evaluation approaches with the intent of identifying them as politically oriented (also called *pseudoevaluation*), question-oriented (*quasi evaluation*), or values-oriented (*true evaluation*). Stufflebeam and Webster used the following frame factors to assess the different approaches: definitions, study types, advance organizers (the main cues that evaluators use to set up a study), purpose, source of questions, main questions, and typical methods.

Stufflebeam and Webster differentiated among the approaches by characterizing each in terms of the issue of assessing the worth of objects. They defined political orientation studies (politically controlled studies and public relations studies) as those that promote a positive or negative view of an object irrespective of its true worth. Stufflebeam and Webster suggested that pseudoevaluations are a prominent part of the educational evaluation scene. They emphasized that evaluators must be alert to the fact that administrators often require pseudoevaluations; otherwise, evaluators may become "unwitting accomplices in efforts to mislead through evaluation" (p. 7).

Question-oriented studies are so labeled because they start with a particular research question to be answered, and they use the appropriate methodology for answering the question. These approaches are termed *quasi evaluation* because the questions and methodologies are sometimes appropriate for supporting value claims. Among the quasi-evaluation approaches are objective-based studies, experimental research, testing programs, and management information systems. Stufflebeam and Webster concluded that "quasi-evaluation studies have legitimate uses apart from their relationship to evaluation; hence the main caution is that these types of studies not be equated with evaluation" (p. 8).

True evaluation studies are those that manifest a values orientation; that is, they are studies designed to assess the true worth of an object. Among these study approaches are accreditation, policy analysis, decision orientation, con-

sumer orientation, and the client-centered and connoisseur models. Stufflebeam and Webster asserted that, in many organizational settings, clients (e.g.,
program administrators) want a pseudoevaluation, evaluators are most comfortable conducting quasi evaluations, but program audiences mostly desire
true evaluation. These authors suggested that if evaluators are ignorant of the
likely conflict in purpose, the evaluation effort is probably doomed to failure
from the start. Thus, evaluators must be aware of the differing expectations of
researcher, client, and audience and should attempt to negotiate a consensus
before an evaluation begins.

Metaphor IV: Evaluation as Research Paradigm
The last taxonomy discussed in this section is Talmage's evaluation as research
paradigm (1982). Talmage defined four broad approaches to the conduct of
evaluation: experimental, eclectic, descriptive, and benefit–cost. The frame
factors on which the approaches are analyzed are the philosophic and
disciplinary origin, the methodology, the nature of the variables, the use of
control groups, the participants' role, the evaluator's role, political pressures,
and the focus of the evaluation report.

Talmage described experimentalists as those engaged in "strong" research
designs with a focus on establishing causal links between programs and outcomes. Examples of experimentalists include Cook and Campbell (1979),
Riecken and Boruch (1974), and Rivlin and Timpane (1975). This approach
represents the mainstream thinking in evaluation research during the early
1960s.

Talmage identified Suchman (1967, 1969) as an early link between the experimentalists and the eclectics. The eclectics generally use experimental designs
in combination with methods that describe the process of program implementation, as well as contextual variables affecting the program. Talmage suggested
that in this way an evaluation design can search for multiple causes or generate
plausible explanations that approximate reality. Among the eclectic evaluators
are Bryk (1978), Cronbach et al. (1980), and Weiss and Rein (1972). Eclectics
also concentratrate on multiple program effects and reject the experimentalists'
emphasis on achievement as the most important outcome of educational programs. As expressed by Bryk (1980), the eclectic position is that "we should attempt to draw on the strengths of each approach—the objectivity of quantitative data, the richness of qualitative data—to create an integrative view of program impact" (p. 40).

The epistemological orientation of the describers rejects the utility and
validity of quantitative research in favor of phenomenologically based evaluation information. In contrast with the preselection of variables by experimentalists and eclectics, the describers assert that the critical indices emerge in the
process of describing program structure and activities. As people interact in the

program, a holistic portrait of the program and its context is identified. Examples of describers include Parlett and Hamilton (1976), Patton (1980), and Stake (1975).

The final evaluation approach, benefit–cost analysis, is based on social-welfare economic theory and accounting procedures. The purpose of benefit–cost analysis is to determine the anticipated costs and benefits associated with alternative programs. This approach requires the valuation of program goals in market terms, often stated as dollar equivalents. In circumstances where market valuation is not feasible, cost-effectiveness approaches can be used in which the valuation is expressed in physical, cognitive, and psychological values (Levin, 1975). Examples of the benefit–cost approach are contained in the work of Haller (1974), Levin (1975), and Thompson (1980).

Talmage argued that the origin of each methodological approach lies in alternative disciplines of social science: The experimental approach derives from research principles and practices in psychology. The eclectic approach is based on elements of psychology, sociology, and political science. The descriptive approach stems from the ethnographic and participant-observation techniques of sociology and anthropology. The benefit–cost approach is clearly based on the principles and practice of economics and accounting. Talmage suggested that the contribution of several social-science disciplines to evaluation is significant because the problems and limitations inherent in one approach may be overcome by the application of another in particular situations. Thus, the taxonomy of evaluation as research paradigm promotes understanding of the interdisciplinary nature of evaluation research as it is practiced currently.

The four taxonomies presented in this section (see Table 1) suggest four metaphors for explicating and understanding the evaluation enterprise through the analysis of various evaluation approaches. The contrast between evaluation metaphors is illustrated by a comparison of Gardner's and House's descriptions of the goal free approach to evaluation. Gardner (1977) "sees" goal-free evaluation as an approach in which the real effects of a program are identified, a holistic orientation is employed, and data are interpreted in response to constituent concerns (p. 586). House (1978), on the other hand, "sees" goal-free evaluation as a pluralist approach that yields a utilitarian assessment of the worth of a situation, which means that judgment is based on a unitary criterion of worth.

Similarly, Stufflebeam and Webster (1980) "see" experimental research as an activity designed to address specific questions whose answers may or may not assess an object's worth, and it is therefore a form of quasi evaluation. On the other hand, Talmage (1982) "sees" experimental research as a discipline-based paradigm, reflecting the values of positive social science as developed in psychology.

TABLE 1. Taxonomies as Metaphors for Evaluation

Author	Metaphor	Frame factors	Conclusion
Gardner (1977)	Evaluation as information production	Principal focus Basic assumptions Advance organizers Nature of outcomes	Evaluation approaches yield various qualities of information
House (1978)	Evaluation as political philosophy	Nature of participation Nature of value criteria	Evaluation approaches exhibit various levels of liberalism
Stufflebeam and Webster (1980)	Evaluation as organizational strategy	Organizational intent Definition Advance organizers Purpose Source of questions Main questions Typical methods Pioneers/developers	Evaluation approaches represent different organization interests
Talmage (1982)	Evaluation as research paradigm	Philosophical base Disciplinary base Focus of methodology Variables Control or comparison group Participants' role Evaluator's role Political pressures Focus of report	Evaluation approaches are based on different social-science disciplines

Two implications of taxonomic analysis are suggested by these comparisons. The first is that—as revealed by Gardner's conclusion that goal-free data are interpreted in the aggregate, by House's view that goal-free data are interpreted by individual criteria, by Stufflebeam and Webster's identification of experimental research as a methodological approach, and by Talmage's interpretation of research as a paradigm—the location of models within taxonomic categories is a highly subjective enterprise. Of greater significance, however, is the fact that Gardner's, House's, Stufflebeam and Webster's, and Talmage's taxonomies can be seen as complementary approaches to the perception and understanding of evaluation research. Gardner's implicit argument is that one can understand goal-free evaluation by examining the nature of the information that is produced, while House's implicit argument is that one can understand goal-free evaluation by examining the political philosophy on which the model stands. Stufflebeam and Webster's implicit argument is that experimental research can be understood through an examination of the organizational motives underlying it, while Talmage's implicit argument is that experimentation can be understood through an examination of its epistemological bases. Taken together, the arguments suggest that even greater understanding will result when one considers both the nature of information and the underlying political philosophy of goal-free evaluation and both the organizational purpose and the epistemological basis of experimentation.

The use of metaphors not only advances the conceptual understanding of evaluation but, in fact, also has implications for evaluation practice. As House (1984) pointed out, "underlying metaphors provide some of the basic concepts that instruct us on how to proceed" (p. 101). He concluded that

> In retrospect, perhaps it is not so surprising that metaphoric thinking is important in evaluation. Black (1962) has explored the similarity between scientific models and metaphors and concludes that both models and metaphors play an indispensable role in scientific thinking. In fact, all intellectual pursuits rely upon such "exercises of the imagination. . . . Perhaps every science must start with metaphor and end with algebra; and perhaps without the metaphor there would never have been any algebra (Black, 1962, p. 242). [p. 101]

EVALUATION RESEARCH IN HIGHER EDUCATION

The development of evaluation in higher education is in some ways analogous to, and in other ways quite different from, the development of the general field of evaluation described in the first section of this chapter. The ESEA Title I legislation that promoted the field of evaluation by mandating the assessment of Title I programs was paralleled by the Higher Education Act of 1965, which provided federal funds for continuing-education and community-service programs (Oliver, 1970). Evaluation of Title I programs—for example, in Wisconsin (University of Wisconsin, 1967) and California (Farmer et al., 1972)—focused on the selection, funding, and implementation of programs for adults in urban environments, of cooperative extension programs, and of urban extension programs. A similar evaluation effort (McGuffy, 1967) was conducted to assess the effects of the Higher Education Facilities Act of 1963 with respect to the accommodation of expanding enrollments, increased physical facilities, and improved academic programs in the participating institutions of higher education.

While the origins of evaluation research in higher education can be ascribed partially to federal legislative initiatives analogous to the general field of evaluation, the period cannot be characterized as one of high expectations for the influence of evaluation on higher education policymaking. The higher education literature on evaluation during this period focuses mostly on technical aspects of the evaluation process, such as the development of measurable objectives (Ciampa, 1971), program planning and analysis procedures (Dahnke,

1971), and strategies for program implementation (Bogue, 1971), rather than on the role of evaluation research in social change. The relatively nonpolitical focus of the meta-evaluation literature during this period was likely because, unlike preschool and elementary programs, such as Head Start and Follow Through, higher education was not seen as a primary vehicle for ameliorating social problems.

As a consequence, the 1960s and the early 1970s can be characterized by a view of evaluation as a procedure for assisting internal higher-education decision-making. Despite the origin of higher education evaluation in federal legislation, as well as some evaluation of college- or university-sponsored enrichment programs for disadvantaged secondary students (Dispenzieri, 1968; College Entrance Examination Board, 1972), evaluation was motivated mainly by the assumption that knowledge about a program's strength and weaknesses would lead to an improved program. Evaluation appeared to be based on internal initiatives for knowledge generation, geared to internal decision-making, and directed toward internal audiences. Evaluation questions that were examined during this period concerned university grading systems (University of Wisconsin, 1973), correspondence education (Washington University, 1968), self-directed study programs (Morgan, 1970), and the effects of master's and doctoral programs (Nichols, 1967; Preston, 1970; Keith, 1971).

The expanding enrollments and the relative financial security of institutions of higher education permitted their insulation from public scrutiny and influence. Local evaluation projects focused on overseas study programs (Pfnister, 1969, 1972), year-round academic calendars (Suslow and Riley, 1968), and internship programs (MacDougal, 1972; Goebel, 1972; Finnin, 1971). External reviews of higher education programs—for example, state agency audits—tended to be managerial in nature and not directly related to academic performance (Harcleroad, 1980). Furthermore, most evaluations conducted during this period did not use the Campbell and Stanley experimental approach then prominent in the general field. With the exception of some evaluations that used survey research, most employed only qualitative methods.

Significant changes in the environment in which institutions of higher education operated—and consequently in the nature of evaluation in higher education—occurred in the early 1970s. The economic crisis, coupled with subsequent declining enrollments, led to a period of retrenchment and accountability in which the operations and outcomes of higher-education academic programs came under close public inspection. One result of this new economic reality was the notion of using evaluation data to facilitate the management of scarce resources. Harcleroad (1980) noted that the 1973 task force on coordination, governance, and structure of the Education Commission of the States recommended "that the function of program review and evaluation be expanded to include in its scope recommendations on allocation, reorganization or even discontinuance" of academic programs (p. 13).

The period extending approximately from 1973 to 1980 was one in which the demands for increased evaluation information created a need for improved methods and models of evaluation in higher education. Bowen (1974, p. xi) observed that accountability is the wish of officials, taxpayers, and the public in general that the increasing sums laid out for public services be justified by reliable estimates of the outcomes. Thus, one significant aspect of the accountability movement was that the demands for evaluation were external to institutions of higher education, which meant that the nature of evaluation questions had to change from an internal to an external focus. Bowen (1974) suggested that the questions raised in the interests of accountability have positive implications for the management of higher education, but that the higher education community, on the whole, does not have the capability of answering these questions.

Bowen (1974, p. 1) argued that the significant steps in attaining true accountability are (1) to define the goals and to order the priorities; (2) to identify and measure the outcomes; (3) to compare the goals and the outcomes and then to judge the degree to which the goals are being achieved; and (4) to measure the cost and then to judge the degree to which it approaches a reasonable minimum. This formulation suggests that another result of the accountability movement was the emerging notion of using experimental and quasi-experimental research designs in the conduct of higher education evaluation.

Astin (1974) argued that the most difficult aspect of generating evaluation data to meet the demands of accountability is developing methods to measure the outcomes of higher education. He asserted that most educational evaluation studies focus on means rather than ends because higher education policymakers seem to reward administrator for means (acquiring funds, bright students, and prestigious faculty) rather than ends. He added that this focus occurs because the causal connections between means and ends are not well understood and are difficult to study. Astin then developed a taxonomy of different higher-education outcomes and suggested ways in which each could be measured.

Astin categorized student outcomes into cognitive and affective, and research data into psychological and behavioral (p. 31). Cognitive psychological outcomes include knowledge, general intelligence, critical thinking ability, and basic skills. Affective psychological outcomes include self-concept, values, attitudes, and beliefs. Cognitive behavioral outcomes include educational and occupational attainment, while affective behavioral outcomes include choice of a career or major, avocations, mental health, and interpersonal relations.

Fincher (1973) agreed that the demands of accountability require changes in the conduct of evaluation research. Among the necessary modifications are an increasing emphasis on tests and measurements and an increasing advocacy of problem-solving data and research that is action-oriented, that is, that indicates directions for program improvement.

A review of the higher-education evaluation literature during this period reveals the influence of external demands on the conceptualization and conduct of evaluation research. One example of this influence was a new focus on systemwide and statewide evaluations. Barak (1975) identified a steadily increasing role of statewide coordinating and governing agencies in the process of program review. Heldman (1975) stated that the increased significance of the external program review was due, at least in part, to the inability of funding sources to maintain levels of support to ensure quality in all program operations. The need to select among competing program components led to a consideration of criteria that could be used to make judgments of relative worth (Elmore, 1974; Francis, 1978; Ayers, 1979). One example of an early criterion used as an indicator of program worth was the teaching effectiveness demonstrated by program graduates (California State University, 1975; Johnson, 1979).

In general, the period from 1973 to 1980 was characterized by increasing external demands for the documentation of higher education outcomes and the initial attempt of those involved in the management of higher education to meet those demands. It is argued in this chapter that since 1980, the complex interrelationships among external demands, internal data needs, and alternative strategies for generating evaluation data have begun to be conceptualized in a systematic manner. The requirement has been research on (1) the levels of external demands; (2) internal decisions facilitated by evaluation data; and (3) the organizational units that can generate the required information, in order to meet the organizational needs created by the accountability movement.

Harcleroad (1980) identified four levels of external agencies that demand accountability in the administration of higher-education academic programs. Among the external levels that pass judgment on instructional departments and degree programs are institutions, multicampus-system coordinating boards, statewide boards of higher education, and regional and national accreditation organizations. The primary focus of institutional concerns is on the distinctiveness and compatibility of program objectives within the compass of the institution's mission and, subsequently, on providing resources to enhance quality and effectiveness (Munitz and Wright, 1980).

Craven (1980, p. 106) perceived a trend among institutions toward increasing self-study to determine the best allocation of resources to maximize institutional goals and missions. However, Munitz and Wright (1980) argued that comprehensive institutional evaluation is not feasible, and that it may be better to generate substantive insights into a few facets of academic programs than to generate information of little substance about many facets. They suggested that even if institutional academic-program evaluations do not reveal patterns for maximial resource allocation, they increase one's ability to understand current allocation patterns and can provide information about alternative resource allocation among departments and colleges.

Trends at the system level (Harcleroad, 1980) probably represent the main reason for the increasing activity in academic program review (see, for example, Green, 1981; Wilson, 1980; Rowland, 1978). Program review has traditionally been a function of coordinating commissions and governing boards, and the trend to more centralized control often results in the restriction or elimination of campus programs. Smith (1980) observed that of the nineteen multicampus systems of higher education in the United States in 1975, all maintained the authority to evaluate academic programs offered by the institutions in the system. Among the relevant evaluation issues at the system level are establishing institutional missions, approving new program proposals, creating institutional evaluation policies, monitoring the consequences of these policies, and requiring rejustification of programs not meeting specified criteria.

The most significant development at the statewide level is the newfound importance ascribed to program review activities. Harcleroad (1980, pp. 16–17) pointed out that in 1977, academic program review was considered the tenth most important activity engaged in by state boards, but by 1978, it was ranked fifth, deemed to be more significant than capital-outlay, enrollment, and faculty-salary issues. Bogue (19080) observed that state-level agencies conduct evaluations for the purposes of continuing, ending, or improving existing programs, purposes identical to those at the institutional and system levels. This fact suggests the importance of the interaction and coordination of evaluation activities among the levels of external agencies in higher education. One unique role of the state board is to link institutions or systems with accreditation organizations. Groves (1979) presented a case study identifying the interactions among the Illinois State Board of Education, the governing boards, and the individual institutions in the process of program review.

In order to track the changing nature of academic program approval and review, Barak (1982) surveyed over 1,000 postsecondary institutions and obtained a 68% response rate (p. 4). The sample included both private and public schools with two-year, four-year, and graduate programs. In addition, 53 site visits were conducted, some superficial, others involving interviews with students, faculty, administrators, state agency staff, board members, and legislators. The survey covered both the internal and external aspects of academic program approval and review.

With respect to the internal approval of programs, Barak (1982, p. 9) identified a general trend toward increasing formalization of the process. The stated purposes of the internal approval process include a desire to determine if documented needs justify the program, to determine if resources are sufficient to support a quality program, and to determine if the program is consistent with institutional role and mission.

Typically, on completion of internal approval, the next step in the process is the system- and state-level review. Barak (1982, p. 27) noted that by 1981, all but 7 states had conducted at least some new-program approval for public institutions. By contrast, an earlier study by Barak and Berdahl (1978) found that agencies at that time were still very much in the developmental stage. In that study, 21 states reviewed new program proposals; as of 1985, 47 states exercise that responsibility. Another trend identified by Barak was the broadening scope of programs that come under review. He suggested that the increase in the number of state-level agencies follows a proportionate decrease in institutional credibility in the eyes of many state administrators and legislators. In particular, state agency approval is being used as a means monitoring resource allocation.

Internal program review is the most common form of evaluation in higher education. Barak (1982) noted that one way of distinguishing program approval from program review is by the amount of controversy involved because "when resources must be reallocated, courses cancelled, or programs or faculty terminated, the review process becomes a topic of fervid debate" (p. 33).

Consistent with the chronology established in this section of the chapter, Barak (1982, pp. 33–34) observed that internal program-review processes have a fairly long tradition: 12% of the reporting institutions indicated that their program-review policies had been in place before 1965. What is new, however, is the dramatic increase in program review activities since the early to mid-1970s. Approximately 70% of the institutions surveyed had initiated their present policies after 1970, and more than half of those had begun after 1976.

Additional comparisons over time reveal that reviews are more likely to use multiple indicators, to use more sophisticated data collection and analysis procedures, and to involve external evaluators. Barak (1982) concluded that "Perhaps the most significant impact of recent reviews is their growing role in institutional decision making. The two decisions most commonly linked to evaluation information are the improvement of academic programs and the redistribution of resources" (p. 37).

At the system level, Barak's survey indicated that approximately half of the system-level offices for both four-year and community-college institutions had undertaken some degree of program review. At the state level, all 50 states had some sort of review process, and there was great variation in the nature of specific responsibilities. Among the stated goals of state-level review (Barak, 1982, p. 64) were: (1) to improve resource allocation; (2) to help in making difficult program decisions on a statewide basis; (3) to make the termination of programs less hectic at institutional levels; and (4) to clarify institutional missions. Barak also identified problems associated with program reviews (p. 84): (1) the apparent unnecessary duplication of evaluation efforts; (2) state-institution friction about the way program reviews were carried out; (3) the involvement of private and independent institutions in statewide reviews; and (4) whether or not program reviews did, in fact, save money.

Finally, Harcleroad (1980) observed that current trends in the accreditation process focus on the improvement of the current self-study and visitation approach to evaluation. One emerging issue is the use of voluntary accrediting organizations by federal agencies to determine which institutions should be eligible for federal funds. Accreditation is based on the notion that the best-qualified persons to make judgments about academic programs are peer educators and others who themselves are involved in or devoted to postsecondary education (Young and Chambers, 1980, p. 91). Craven (1980, pp. 106–107) predicted that accrediting agencies will seek to refine the process of accreditation by focusing on educational outcomes and uniform expectations that will standardize the process to a greater degree. Young and Chambers (1980, p. 100) argued that national standards will be developed and will attain significance only when institutions (1) deal with nationally recognized accrediting bodies; (2) follow guidelines for good practice in reporting their accredited status in catalogs and other published materials; (3) centrally coordinate relations with accrediting agencies; and (4) provide leadership for recognizing accrediting agencies.

The external demands for accountability, as well as the declining enrollments and budgets within higher-education academic-program areas, have also served to change the nature of information needs within academic programs. While the evaluations of the 1960s were intended to provide avenues for program improvement, the internal environment of the 1970s and 1980s has required decisions about internal resource allocation and program discontinuation as well as improving program effectiveness. This focus has led to an emphasis on more formal evaluation approaches at the department level. Among the issues of concern in the conduct of evaluation at the department level are the legitimization of programs (House, 1982), the need for adaptive evaluation systems (Petrie, 1982), and the role of values and value judgments in evaluation (Dressel, 1982; Braskamp, 1982). Thus, the current concerns in the evaluation of higher education are those that have previously interested researchers involved in general evaluation.

It has been argued in this section that the insulation of institutions of higher education from public scrutiny and financial dependence led to a focus on evaluation for program improvement during the 1960s. From the early 1970s on, the economic crisis, the accountability movement, and declining enrollments have imposed a set of external information demands on academic program administrators that require an emphasis on demonstrating program outcomes and effectiveness. The nature of the external demands, as well as the internal problems created by the period of scarcity, have required more rigorous and formalized evaluation procedures, as well as different internal information needs, to cope with resource allocation, program termination, and program effectiveness.

EVALUATION IN HIGHER EDUCATION:
CONDITIONS FOR UTILIZATION

The final section of this chapter considers the conditions under which the increasing collection of evaluation data is most likely to impact on the process of decision making in higher education. In a sense, the accountability movement in higher education echoes some of the aspects of the period of great expectations in the general field of evaluation research. The ultimate implication of accountability is the use of evaluation data to produce maximally effective institutions of higher education. This implication is clearly predicated on the notion that the behavior of decision makers will be guided by the evaluation of higher education programs, a perspective on utilization already discarded by those in the general field as discussed in the first section.

Some of the literature on the future of evaluation in higher education suggests a tendency toward rising expectations. Harcleroad (1980, p. 19), predicted—given the likelihood of increasing demands for accountability, particularly in terms of resource allocation—that academic program evaluation, both internal and external, will be instrumental in this ultimate decision-making process. Craven (1980, p. 113) stated that at a time of important issues and significant challenges, institutional research can play a vital role in ensuring a positive future for higher education. Wilson (1982) identified four challenges to evaluators in higher education: better measures of quality, methods for assessing nonacademic units, methods for evaluating cross-program institutional characteristics, and the need for establishing the effect of evaluation on performance. His emphasis on technical problems in evaluation implies a form of the two-community hypothesis underlying his perspective.

It is argued here that expectations for the role of evaluation research in higher-education decision-making can be rendered more realistic by an application of the lessons learned in the development of the general field of evaluation. First, it is important to distinguish between internal and external demands for evaluation information. Accountability is the external demand for the documentation of program outcomes of higher education programs. In terms of the evaluation demand, the call for accountability is similar to the call for evaluation as a means of solving social programs in the 1960s. In light of the period of deconstruction, there is an *a priori* reason to predict that the current call for data may not lead to the use of these data in the decision process.

The problem is that the nature of accountability requires evaluation data on higher education outcomes that are then compared with institutional goals. However, the analysis of models of organizational decision-making and evaluation-use discussed above (Shapiro, 1984) indicates that decision makers usually interpret information in terms of personal goals or relatively simple institutional goals, such as persistence and stability. Furthermore, literature from social welfare economics, political science, and organization theory suggests that decisions are often influenced by political, ethical, and organizational pressures on a decision maker (Shapiro, 1985b). The greater the political implications of the decision (who gets what, when, and how), the greater the influence of these factors and, correspondingly, the less the influence of evaluation data. Given the political milieu of the system and state levels of higher education policymaking, it is suggested that utilization is most likely to occur at the institutional, and particularly at the academic, level of decision making.

The nature of utilization can also be derived from literature on organizational decision-making. Feldman and March (1981) suggested that the primary motivation for the organizational search for information is symbolic. They contended that organizations gather information to take on the appearance of rationality and competence in decision making, but that the nature of organizations is such that the options for behavior are limited. It is therefore the gathering rather than the analysis of information that is valued by organizations.

Despite this motivation, once information search becomes part of the organizational routine, it can become instrumental. Feldman and March argued that organizations use information to scan the presumably hostile environment, searching for indications of threats to the organization. Thus, a primary function of information is surveillance. Feldman and March further contended that since information can be subject to strategic misrepresentation, decision makers learn routinely to discount much information. Since the type of information most susceptible to strategic misrepresentation is interpretive information, the judgments generated by outcome evaluation are least likely to be used by evaluators.

Taken together, these arguments imply that the type of information most likely to be used by decision makers consists of relatively neutral descriptions of the organizational environment. The function of such information is to reduce uncertainty about appropriate organizational behavior within the vague, but presumably hostile, environment. Such information can be provided by offices of institutional research or by departmental management-information systems on a routine basis. On the other hand, the judgments of value or relative worth conventionally afforded by evaluation are less likely to be used because of the need to discount the information to a significant degree.

Braskamp (1982) emphasized the fact that evaluation is more than information product because evaluations requires the making of value judgments. The dilemma suggested by Feldman and March (1981) is that the making of value judgements is inconsistent with what is likely to be useful information from the organizational perspective. The basic operation of evaluation is the assessment of worth or value, yet it is becoming increasingly clear that the type of information valued by organizations is neutral social-indicator data that reduce uncertainty about the nature of the environment within which the organization operates.

Validation of the Feldman and March position can be found in the increasing reliance of organizations on offices of institutional research and management information systems. The most common activities of these units are the systematic, or routinized, collection and provision of descriptive information. Thus, the making of value judgments and the use of information would seem to be mutually exclusive evaluation purposes. While data help clarify the implications of alternative value judgments, the bases for such judgments are political, organizational, and ethical pressures on a decision maker. It is predicted here that evaluation and evaluators will continue to move toward a role of producing maximally useful—that is, relatively neutral—data, and to abandon the original role of generating expert value judgments at all levels of the educational system.

Acknowledgments. I would like to acknowledge the invaluable assistance of Ernie Pascarella, Ed Kelly, and Larry Braskamp through their criticisms and suggestions on earlier drafts of this chapter. Of course, the ultimate responsibility for any errors of commission or omission contained in this chapter, but also for any significant insights, is entirely mine.

REFERENCES

Aaron, H. J. (1978). *Politics and the professors: the great society in perspective.* Washington, DC: Brookings Institution.
Alkin, M. C. (1975). Evaluation: who needs it? who cares? *Studies in Educational Evaluation* 1: 201–212.
Alkin, M. C., Daillak, R., and White, P. (1979). *Using evaluations: does evaluation make a difference?* Beverly Hills: Sage.
Alkin, M. C., and Law, A. (1980). A conversation on evaluation utilization. *Educational Evaluation and Policy Analysis* 2: 73–79.
Astin, A. W. (1974). Measuring the outcomes of higher education. In H. R. Bowen (ed.), *Evaluating institutions for accountability: new directions for institutional research.* San Francisco: Jossey-Bass.
Ayers, J. B. (1979). *Followup studies at Tennessee Technological University: a model teacher evaluation.* Paper presented at the annual meeting of the National Association for Research in Science Teaching, Atlanta.
Barak, R. J. (1979). *State-level higher education program review.* Boulder, CO: State Higher Education Executive Officers/National Center for Education Statistics.
Barak, R. J. (1979). *Program review in higher education.* Boulder, CO: National Center for Higher Education Management Systems.
Barak, R. J., and Berdahl, R. O. (1978). *State-level academic program review.* Denver: Education Commission of the States.
Bednarz, D. (1983). *Quality and quantity in evaluation research: a divergent view.* Paper presented at the annual joint meeting of the Evaluation Network and the Evaluation Research Society, Chicago.
Black, M. (1962). *Models and metaphors.* Ithaca: Cornell University Press.
Boeckmann, M. E. (1976). Policy impacts of the New Jersey income tax experiment. *Policy Sciences* 7: 53–76.
Bogue, E. G. (1971). *Strategies for action: an outline of factors which influence decisions on program plans.* Paper presented at the American Association of Collegiate Registrars and Admissions Officers Convention, St. Louis.

200   SHAPIRO

Bogue, E. G. (1980). State agency approaches to academic program evaluation. In E. C. Craven (ed.), *Academic program evaluation: New directions for institutional research.* San Francisco: Jossey-Bass.

Bowen, H. R. (1974). Editor's notes. In H. R. Bowen (ed.), *Evaluating institutions for accountability: new directions for institutional research.* San Francisco: Jossey-Bass.

Braskamp, L. A. (1982). Evaluation Systems are more than information systems. In R. Wilson (ed.), *Designing academic program reviews: new directions for higher education.* San Francisco: Jossey-Bass.

Braskamp, L. A., and Brown, R. D. (eds.), (1980). *Utilization of evaluative information: new directions for program evaluation.* San Francisco: Jossey-Bass.

Braskamp, L. A., Brown, R. D., and Newman, D. L. (1980). Credibility of a local educational evaluation report: author source and client characteristics. *American Educational Research Journal* 15: 441–450.

Brown, R. D., Braskamp, L. A., and Newman, D. L. (1978). An investigation of the effects of different data presentation formats and order of arguments in a simulated adversary evaluation. *Educational Evaluation and Policy Analysis* 4: 197–204.

Brown, R. D., Newman, D. L., and Rivers, L. S. (1980). Perceived need for evaluation as an influence on evaluation's impact on decision making. *Educational Evaluation and Policy Analysis* 2: 197–204.

Brown, W., and Jaques, E. (1965). *Glacier project papers.* London: Heinemann.

Bryk, A. S. (1978). Evaluating program impact: A time to cast away stories, a time to gather stories together. In S. B. Anderson and C. Coles (eds.), *Exploring purposes and dimensions: new directions for program evaluation.* San Francisco: Jossey-Bass.

California State University and State Colleges. (1975). *The challenge of creative change. The program for innovation and improvement in the instructional process.* Los Angeles: California State University and Colleges, Office of the Chancellor. (ERIC Document Reproduction Service No. ED 119534.)

Campbell, D. T. (1969). Reforms as experiments. *American Psychologist* 24: 409–29.

Campbell, D. T. (1974). Qualitative knowing in action. Paper presented at the annual meeting of the American Psychological Association, New Orleans.

Campbell, D. T., and Stanley, J. C. (1966). *Experimental and quasi-experimental designs for research.* Chicago: Rand McNally.

Caplan, N. S. (1979). The two-community theory and knowledge utilization. *American Behavioral Scientist* 22: 459–470.

Caro, F. (ed.). (1977). *Readings in evaluation research.* New York: Russell Sage.

Ciampa, B. J. (1971). The instructional process in higher education: a perspective. Unpublished manuscript. (ERIC Document Reproduction Service No. ED 065072)

College Entrance Examination Board. (1972) *Project Opportunity reports: Research and evaluation report, number 1972-5; post-secondary enrollment patterns of group III Project Opportunity students, number 1972-6: college choices of outstanding black students in Project Opportunity.* Atlanta: Southern Association of Colleges and Schools.

Conner, R. F., and Associates (eds.). (1984). *Evaluation studies review annual,* Vol. 9. Beverly Hills: Sage.

Cook, T. D., and Campbell, D. T. (1979). *Quasi-experimentation.* Boston: Houghton Mifflin.

Cook, T. D., and Reichardt, C. (1979). *Qualitative and quantitative methods in evaluation research.* Beverly Hills: Sage.

Craven, E. C. (ed.). (1980). *Academic program evaluation: new directions for institutional research.* San Francisco: Jossey-Bass.

Cronbach, L. J. (1963). Course improvement through evaluation. *Teachers College Record* 64: 672–683.

Cronbach, L. J. (1982). *Designing evaluations of educational and social programs*. San Francisco: Jossey-Bass.

Cronbach, L. J., and Associates. (1980). *Toward reform of program evaluation*. San Francisco: Jossey-Bass.

Dahnke, H. L., and Associates. (1971). *Program planning and analysis: The basis for institutional and systemwide facilities planning: higher education facilities planning and management manual six (rev)*. Boulder, CO: Western Interstate Commission for Higher Education.

Datta, L. (1976). The impact of the Westinghouse/Ohio evaluation of the development of Project Head Start: An examination of the immediate and longer-term effects and how they came about. In C. C. Abt (ed.), *The evaluation of social programs*. Beverly Hills: Sage.

Davis, H. R., and Salasin, S. E. (1975). The utilization of evaluation. In E. L. Struening and M. Guttentag (eds.), *Handbook of evaluation research*, Vol. 1, pp. 621–666. Beverly Hills: Sage.

Dewey, J. (1934). *Art as experience*. New York: Minton, Balch.

DeYoung, D. J., and Conner, R. F., (1982). Evaluator preconceptions about organizational decision making. *Evaluation Review* 3: 431–440.

Dickey, B. (1979). Effective problem solving for evaluation utilization. Paper presented at the annual meeting of the Evaluation Research Society, Minneapolis.

Dickey, B., and Hampton, E. (1981). Effective problem solving for evaluation utilization. *Knowledge: creation, diffusion, utilization* 2: 361–374.

Dispenzieri, A., and Associates. (1968). Characteristics of the College Discovery Program students: 1964–1967. Unpublished manuscript. (ERIC Document Reproduction Service No. ED 036815.)

Dressel, P. D. (1982). Values (virtues and vices) in decision making. In R. Wilson (ed.), *Designing academic program reviews: new directions for higher education*. San Francisco: Jossey-Bass.

Duggan, J. G. (1983). Client use of evaluation findings: an examination of salient variables. Paper presented at the annual meeting of the American Educational Research Association, Montreal.

Eisner, E. W. (1976). Educational connoisseurship and criticism: their form and functions in educational evaluation. *Journal of Aesthetic Education* 3–4: 135–150.

Elmore, R. (1974). An analysis of change in a competency based, teacher education program at the University of Georgia. Paper presented at the annual meeting of the American Educational Research Association, Chicago.

Farmer, J. A., Jr., and Others. (1972). *Evaluation of the Title I (HEA, 1965) program in California, 1966–1971: developing community service and continuing education programs in California higher education institutions*. Sacramento: California State Coordinating Council for Higher Education.

Feldman, M. S., and March, J. G. (1981). Information in organizations as symbol and signal. *Administrative Science Quarterly* 26: 171–186.

Fincher, C. (1973). Program evaluation: approaches and procedures. Paper presented at the annual forum of Association for Institutional Research, Vancouver, B.C.

Finnin, W. (1971). *North Carolina Environmental Internship Program 1971*. Raleigh: North Carolina State Board of Higher Education.

Francis, J. B., and Neff, C. B. (1978). *The recognition and reward of teaching excellence: an evaluation*. Washington, DC: Fund for the Improvement of Postsecondary Education.

Gardner, D. E. (1977). Five evaluation frameworks. *Journal of Higher Education* 48: 571–593.

Goebel, C. (1972). *Evaluation of the WICHE Intern program in the State of Oregon.* Portland: Oregon State University, Western Interstate Commission for Higher Education. (ERIC Document Reproduction Service No. ED 071599.)

Green, K. C. (1981). Program review and the state responsibility for higher education. *Journal of Higher Education* 52: 67–80.

Groves, R. T. (1979). Program review in a multi-level state governance system: the case of Illinois. *Planning for Higher Education* 8: 1–9.

Guba, E. G. (1969). The failure of educational evaluation. *Educational Technology* 9: 29–38.

Guba, E. G., and Lincoln, Y. S. (1981). *Effective evaluation.* San Francisco: Jossey-Bass.

Haenn, J. F., and Owens, T. R. (1981). Utilization frameworks for evaluation reporting. Paper presented at the annual meeting of the American Education Research Association, Los Angeles.

Haller, E. J. (1974). Cost analysis for educational program evaluation. In W. J. Popham (ed.), *Evaluation in education.* Berkeley, CA: McCutchan.

Hansen, J. B. (1981). Uses of Title I evaluation data: implications for technical assistance. Paper presented at the annual meeting of the American Education Research Association, Los Angeles.

Harcleroad, F. F. (1980). The context of academic program evaluation. In E. C. Craven (ed.), *Academic program evaluation: new directions for institutional research.* San Francisco: Jossey-Bass.

Heilman, J. (1980). Paradigmatic choices in evaluation methodology. *Evaluation Review* 4: 693–712.

Heldman, D. R. (1975). Academic program review—concerns and justifications. Unpublished manuscript. (ERIC Document Reproduction Service No. ED 122690)

Holley, F. (1979). Catch a falling star: promoting the use of research and evaluation findings. Paper presented at the annual meeting of the American Educational Research Association, San Francisco.

House, E. R. (1973). *School evaluation: the politics and process.* Berkeley, CA: McCutchan.

House, E. R. (1978). Assumptions underlying evaluation models. *Educational Researcher* 7: 4–12.

House, E. R. (1982). Alternative evaluation strategies in higher education. In R. Wilson (ed.), *Designing academic program reviews: new directions for higher education.* San Francisco: Jossey-Bass.

House, E. R. (1984). How we think about evaluation. In R. F. Conner and Associates (eds)., *Evaluation Studies Review Annual,* Vol. 9. Beverly Hills: Sage.

Houston, T. R., Jr. (1972). The behavioral sciences impact-effectiveness model. In P. H. Rossi and W. Williams (eds.), *Evaluating social programs.* New York: Seminar Press.

Ingle, R. B. (1984). Evaluation methodology: Past, present and future. Paper presented at the annual meeting of the American Educational Research Association, New Orleans.

Isaac, S. (1980). Increasing the relevance of national evaluation to schools: a school district's view. Paper presented at the annual meeting of the American Educational Research Association, Boston.

Johnson, R. R. (1979). Innovation and influence among American colleges and universities. Paper presented at the annual meeting of the American Educational Research Association, San Francisco.

Keith, N. R., Jr. (1971). *A study of the Ph.D. graduates at the University of Georgia 1966–1970.* New York: Ford Foundation.

Kilbourne, R., and DeGracie, J. (1979). The use of L.E.A. research at the local level: the picture of a dropout. Paper presented at the annual meeting of the American Educational Research Association, Los Angeles.

King, J. A., and Thompson, B. (1981). A nationwide survey of administrators' perceptions of evaluation. Paper presented at the annual meeting of the American Educational Research Association, Los Angeles.

King, J. A., Thompson, B., and Pechman, E. M. (1981). *Evaluation utilization: a bibliography.* New Orleans: Orleans Parish Public Schools, 1981. (ERIC Document Reproduction Service No. ED 207984.)

Kiresuk, T. J. (1980). Planned change and evaluation. *Knowledge: Creation, Diffusion, Utilization* 1: 405–420.

Klein, L. (1976). *A social scientist in industry.* New York: Wiley.

Kuhn, T. (1970). *The structure of scientific revolutions.* Chicago: University of Chicago Press.

Levin, H. M. (1975). Cost-effectiveness analysis in evaluation research. In M. Guttentag and E. L. Struening (eds.), *Handbook of evaluation research,* Vol. 2. Beverly Hills: Sage.

Leviton, L. C., and Boruch, R. F. (1983). Contributions of evaluation to educational programs and policy. *Evaluation Review* 7: 563–598.

Louis, K. S. (1983). Multisite/multimethod studies. *American Behavioral Scientist* 26: 6–22.

MacDougall, B. (1972). *Oregon's WICHE intern program.* Portland: Oregon State University: Western Interstate Commission for Higher Education. (ERIC Document Reproduction Service No. ED 071600.)

Madaus, G. F., Scriven, M. S., and Stufflebeam, D. L. (1983). *Evaluation models.* Boston: Kluwer-Nijhoff.

McGuffey, C. W. (1967). *An evaluation study of the College Facilities Program. Final report.* Tallahassee: Florida State University. (ERIC Document Reproduction Service No. ED 020627.)

Morgan, G. A. (1970). *Final report to the National Endowment for the Humanities for Hiram College: the Hiram College Freshman Year program.* Washington, DC: National Endowment for the Humanities. (ERIC Document Reproduction Service No. ED 060815.)

Mosteller, F., and Moynihan, D. P. (eds.). (1972). *On equality of educational opportunity.* New York: Random House.

Munitz, B. A., and Wright, D. J. (1980). Institutional approaches to academic program evaluation. In E. C. Craven (ed.), *Academic program evaluation: new directions for institutional research.* San Francisco: Jossey-Bass.

Nachmias, D., and Henry, G. T. (1980). The utilization of evaluation research: problems and prospects. In D. Nachmias (ed.), *The practice of policy evaluation.* New York: St. Martin's Press.

Nathan, R. P. (1979). Federal grants-in-aid: how are they working in 1978? Paper presented at the converence "The City in Stress" sponsored by the Center for Urban Policy Research, New Brunswick, New Jersey.

Nichols, R. F. (1967). A reconsideration of the Ph. D. *The Graduate Journal* 7: 325–335.

Novak, C. D. (1977). An involvement approach to the evaluation of local district programs. Paper presented at the annual meeting of the American Educational Research Association, New York.

Oliver, L. P. (1970). Title I of the Higher Education Act of 1965: its promise and performance. Unpublished dissertation. (ERIC Document Reproduction Service No. ED 042110.)

Parlett, M., and Hamilton, D. (1976). Evaluation as illumination: A new approach to the study of innovatory programs. In G. V. Glass (ed.), *Evaluation studies review annual,* Vol. 1. Beverly Hills: Sage.

Patton, M. Q. (1978). *Utilization-focused evaluation.* Beverly Hills: Sage.

Patton, M. Q. (1980). *Qualitative evaluation methods.* Beverly Hills: Sage.

Patton, M. Q., and Associates (1977). In search of impact: an analysis of the utilization of federal health evaluation research. In C. H. Weiss (ed.), *Using social science research in public policy making.* Lexington, MA: D. C. Heath.

Petrie, H. G. (1982). Program evaluation as an adaptive system. In R. Wilson (ed.), *Designing academic program reviews: new directions for higher education.* San Francisco: Jossey-Bass.

Pfnister, A. O. (1969). Evaluation of undergraduate programs: in what way should evaluation of overseas study programs be included in the accreditation process for colleges and universities? Paper presented at the annual membership conference of the Council on International Educational Exchange, Tarrytown, NY.

Pfnister, A. O. (1972). General evaluation of studies abroad programs under the auspices of American colleges and universities. Paper presented at the meeting of the National Association for Foreign Student Affairs, Atlanta.

Preston, M. A. (1970). *The first three years of appraisal of graduate programs.* Toronto: Ontario Council on Graduate Studies. (ERIC Document Reproduction Service No. ED 071556.)

Provus, M. (1971). *Discrepancy evaluation.* Berkeley, CA: McCutchan.

Raizen, S. A., and Rossi, P. H. (eds.). (1981). *Program evaluation in education: when? how? to what ends?* Washington, DC: National Academy Press.

Rein, M., and Schon, D. A. (1977). Problem setting in policy research. In C. H. Weiss (ed.), *Using social science research in public policy making.* Lexington, MA: D. C. Heath.

Rice, J. M. (1897). The futility of the spelling grind. *The Forum* 23: 163–172.

Rich, R. F. (1975). An investigation of information gathering and handling in seven federal bureaucracies: a case study of the continuous national survey. Unpublished dissertation. Chicago: University of Chicago.

Rich, R. F. (1977). Uses of social science information by Federal bureaucrats: knowledge for understanding versus knowledge for action. In C. H. Weiss (ed.), *Using social science research in public policy making.* Lexington, MA: D. C. Heath.

Rich, R. F. (1981). *Social science information and public policy making.* San Francisco: Jossey-Bass.

Riecken, H. W., and Boruch, R. F. (eds.). (1974). *Social experimentation.* New York: Academic Press.

Rieker, P. R. (1980). Evaluation research: the design-to-use process. *Knowledge: Creation, Diffusion, Utilization* 2: 215–235.

Rist, R. C. (1977). On the relations among educational research paradigms: from disdain to detente. *Anthropology and Education* 8: 42–49.

Rivlin, A. M. (1971). *Systematic thinking for social action.* Washington, DC: Brookings Institution.

Rivlin, A. M., and Timpane, P. M. (eds.). (1975). *Planned variation in education: should we give up or try harder?* Washington, DC: Brookings Institution.

Rowland, H. R. (1978). Participation in a statewide program review. In H. K. Jacobson (ed.), *Evaluating advancement programs: new directions for institutional advancement.* San Francisco: Jossey-Bass.

Rudner, R. (1966). *Philosophy of social science.* Englewood Cliffs, NJ: Prentice-Hall.

Scriven, M. (1970). Critique of the PDK Book, Educational evaluation and decision making. Paper presented at the annual meeting of the American Educational Research Association, New York.

Scriven, M. (1976). Evaluation bias and its control. In G. V. Glass (ed.), *Evaluation studies review annual,* Vol. 1. Beverly Hills: Sage.

Shapiro, J. Z. (1982). Evaluation as theory testing: an example from Head Start. *Educational Evaluation and Policy Analysis* 4: 351–353.

Shapiro, J. Z. (1984). Conceptualizing evaluation use: implications of alternative models of organizational decision making. In R. F. Conner and Associates (eds.), *Evaluation studies review annual,* Vol. 9. Beverly Hills: Sage.

Shapiro, J. Z. (1985a). Evaluation of a worksite program in health science and medicine: an application of Stake's model of contingency and congruence. *Educational Evaluation and Policy Analysis* 7: 47–56.

Shapiro, J. Z. (1985b). A perspective on evaluation: where we are and where we need to go. *Educational Evaluation and Policy Analysis* 7: 245–248.

Shapiro, J. Z. (1985c). Toward a theory of evaluation use: implications of the rational calculus. Paper presented at the annual meeting of the American Educational Research Association, Chicago.

Smith, D. K. (1980). Multi-campus system approaches to academic program evaluation. In E. C. Craven (ed.), *Academic program evaluation: new directions for institutional research.* San Francisco: Jossey-Bass.

Smith, E. R., and Tyler, R. W. (1942). *Appraising and recording student progress.* New York: Harper.

Smith, N. L. (1981). *Metaphors for evaluation.* Beverly Hills: Sage.

Snow, C. P. (1962). *Science and government.* London: Oxford University Press.

Stake, R. E. (1967). The countenance of educational evaluation. *Teachers College Record* 68: 523–540.

Stake, R. E. (1975). Some alternative presumptions. Unpublished manuscript, Urbana, IL, Center for Instructional Research and Curriculum Evaluation.

Stake, R. E. (1978). The case study method in social inquiry. *Educational Researcher* 7: 5–8.

Stanley, J. C. (1967). Elementary experimental design—an expository treatment. *Psychology in the Schools* 4: 195–203.

Stufflebeam, D. L. (1969). Evaluation as enlightenment for decision making. In W. A. Beaty (ed.), *Improving educational assessment and an inventory of measures of affective behavior.* Washington, DC: Assoc. for Supervision and Curriculum Development.

Stufflebeam, D. L. (1971). The relevance of the CIPP evaluation model for educational accountability. *Journal of Research and Development in Education* 5: 19–25.

Stufflebeam, D. L. (1983). The CIPP model for program evaluation. In G. F. Madaus, M. Scriven, and D. L. Stufflebeam (eds.), *Evaluation models.* Boston, Kluwer-Nijhoff.

Stufflebeam, D. L., and Webster, W. J. (1980). An analysis of alternative approaches to evaluation. *Educational Evaluation and Policy Analysis* 2(3): 5–20.

Suchman, E. A. (1967). *Evaluative research: principles and practice in public service and action programs.* New York: Russell Sage.

Suchman, E. A. (1969). Evaluating educational programs. *Urban Review* 3: 15–17.

Suslow, S., and Riley, M. J. (1968). *Year-round operation at Berkeley: background and implementation.* Berkeley: University of California, Office of Institutional Research. (ERIC Document Reproduction Service No. ED 043937).

Talmage, H. (1982). Evaluation of programs. In H. E. Mitzel and Associates (eds.), *Encyclopedia of educational research,* Vol. 2. New York: Free Press.

Thompson, B., and King, J. A. (1981). Evaluation utilization: a literature review and research agenda. Paper presented at the annual meeting of the American Educational Research Association, Los Angeles.

Thompson, M. S. (1980). *Benefit-cost analysis for program evaluation.* Beverly Hills: Sage.

Thorndike, E. L. (1927). *The measurement of intelligence.* New York: Teachers College, Columbia University.

Tittle, C. K. (1977). Evaluation and decision making: developing a method to link program funding decisions and outcome evaluation. Paper presented at the annual meeting of the American Educational Research Association, New York.

University of Washington. (1968). *Correspondence study: faculty evaluation: Phase I of the state-wide correspondence study: faculty evaluation.* Seattle: University of Washington, Office of Institutional Educational Research. (ERIC Document Reproduction Service No. ED 028317.)

University of Wisconsin (1967). *Progress and evaluation report, a summary of activities in Wisconsin under Title I of the Higher Educational Act of 1965, an historical and evaluative report of fiscal year 1966 and fiscal year 1967 programs, July 1, 1965 to September 1, 1967.* Madison: University of Wisconsin, University Extension. (ERIC Document Reproduction Service No. ED 017864.)

University of Wisconsin (1973). *An evaluation of the pass-fail grading policy at UW-Stevens Point.* Stevens Point: University of Wisconsin, Office of Institutional Research. (ERIC Document Reproduction Service No. ED 076098.)

Weiner, S. S., Rubin, D., and Sachse, T. (1977). *Pathology in institutional structures for evaluation and a possible cure.* Stanford, CA: Stanford Evaluation Consortium.

Weiss, C. H. (1972). *Evaluation research.* Englewood Cliffs, NJ: Prentice-Hall.

Weiss, C. H. (1979). Conceptual issues in measuring the utilization of research and evaluation. Paper presented at the annual meeting of the Evaluation Research Society, Minneapolis.

Weiss, C. H. (1982). Measuring the use of evaluation. In E. R. House and Associates (eds.), *Evaluation studies review annual,* Vol. 7. Beverly Hills: Sage.

Weiss, C. H., and Bucuvalas, M. J. (1977). The challenge of social science research to decision making. In C. H. Weiss (ed.), *Using social science research in public policy making.* Lexington, MA: D. C. Heath.

Weiss, R. S., and Rein, M. (1972). The evaluation of braod-aim programs: Difficulties in experimental design and an alternative. In C. H. Weiss (ed.), *Evaluating action programs: readings in social action and education.* Boston: Allyn and Bacon.

Willis, G. (ed.). (1978). *Qualitative evaluation.* Berkeley, CA: McCutchan.

Wilson, R. F. (1980). Institutional participation and reciprocity in state-level program reviews. *Journal of Higher Education* 51: 601–615.

Wise, R. I. (1978). What we know about the decision maker and decision setting. Paper presented at the annual meeting of the American Educational Research Association, Toronto.

Worthen, B. R., and Sanders, J. R. (1973). *Educational evaluation: theory and practice.* Worthington, OH: Charles A. Jones.

Young, K. E., and Chambers, C. M. (1980). Accrediting agency approaches to academic program evaluation. In E. C. Craven (ed.), *Academic program evaluation: new directions for institutional program evaluation.* San Francisco: Jossey-Bass.

RATES OF RETURN TO HIGHER EDUCATION:
An Intensive Examination

Larry L. Leslie, *University of Arizona*
and
Paul T. Brinkman, *National Center for Higher Education Management Systems*

Many years ago in a dissertation proposal-writing seminar, a fellow student, with merciless regularity as each proposal was presented, asked his fellow "proposers" a single question: "Why would anyone want to know that?" This question, in the minds of many in higher education, surely pertains to rate-of-return studies and analyses. We in higher education are supremely skeptical in regard to such studies, and properly so.

To those with even a cursory knowledge of how rate-of-return analyses are conducted, skepticism about the study method is generally extreme. Even more questionable, in the minds of critics, is the entire matter of public-policy criterion appropriateness: How can only the *economic* returns to higher education be considered an adequate test of the value of the higher education enterprise?

It is not the purpose of this chapter to argue the case for the rate-of-return estimate as a public policy criterion. As will soon be apparent, the chapter authors possess adequate skepticism of their own. So, why is this topic the focus of a *Handbook* chapter?

First, studies aimed directly at calculating the economic benefits to schooling and especially at solving the numerous, related analytical problems are probably the most numerous of all empirical studies in higher-education finance research. Although the rates-of-return studies are frequently characterized by questionable assumptions, poor data, and analytical shortcomings, the topic is so important that efforts do not seem to diminish over time.

Second, as befitting a handbook of theory and research, attention is given to questions of research method. Of some 130 rate-of-return papers reviewed, approximately two thirds deal with methodological issues, such as how the dependent variable (the "return") should be specified and what controls or adjustments should be exercised. These and other issues related to rate-of-return research methods will be examined, although the primary focus is on study results.

ORGANIZATION OF THE CHAPTER

This chapter seeks to examine numerous issues related to rates of return to higher education and to provide synthesized estimates of the magnitude of those returns. Above all, what is desired is reader understanding of the limitations and proper use of rate-of-return information: What can be made of these estimates and what cannot? If nothing else, it is the objective of this chapter to instill in the reader the ability to place the results of rate-of-return studies in their proper perspective.

The remainder of the chapter is organized as follows. First is a discussion of the uses to which rate-of-return studies are conventionally put, why economists devote so much energy to these studies, and why policymakers and the public apparently pay so much attention to them. In order to carry out this discussion, a second section considers how returns to education may be measured. This section blends into a brief methodological section.

The core of the chapter is presented next. Here is found the product of an ambitious effort to synthesize the results of the major empirical studies of rates of return to higher education. Although the studies are not strictly comparable, a meta-analytical matrix of the studies along with considerable comparative information is provided, and average results from the twenty-five studies are calculated. Subsections isolate the rates of return for graduate education, by field of study, by college type and quality, over time, and for other countries. The focus of the results section is to present synthesized quantitative estimates and generalizations rather than to discuss individual studies. Indeed, the effort is to draw attention away from isolated results, as is characteristic of meta-analytic approaches.

The last part of the chapter is the most vital. It is here that the true utility of rate-of-return studies is discussed—what they really do and do not show. Included are treatments of what is known about the important nonpecuniary benefits of higher education, what are called *psychic benefits* and *externalities*. The chapter closes with a brief conclusions section.

The desire throughout the chapter is to translate an esoteric body of important knowledge into a form that higher educators, both practitioners and scholars, can understand and use.

WHY ECONOMISTS STUDY THE RETURN TO EDUCATION

Among the several reasons for examining the economic returns to higher education, the foremost is allocative efficiency, the cardinal concern of public finance: Where will society gain the maximum benefit from its investments or, more practically, from the investment of any new money that may become available? The corollary question to the individual is, Where will one's investment yield the highest return? Both questions are in three parts: (1) How do the benefits from higher education compare with those of noneducational alternatives? (2) How do the benefits from higher education compare with those of educational alternatives? And (3) how do the benefits compare by field of study within higher education? If it can be shown that the returns for one alternative are greater than for another, then society's and the individual's choice is clear, and resources can be directed accordingly. At least, so the orthodoxy goes.

HOW ARE THE RETURNS TO BE MEASURED?

Calculation of the "yield" on higher education investment requires a determination of costs and of benefits, each of which must be discounted to reflect the fact that the present value of money is normally greater than the future value: "A dollar isn't worth what it used to be." The returns to education are most commonly stated in terms of income differentials, which reflect benefits only; cost–benefit ratios; net present values (NPV); or internal rates of return (IRR).

Debate in the literature has centered on the latter two alternatives. NPV is simply the worth in dollar terms of the difference between the cost of education and the associated monetary gain, each properly discounted to reflect "present value." IRR is the rate of interest or discount that sets one's stream of lifetime earnings back to its present value and equates this value to one's total educational costs compounded forward to educational termination. Proponents of the NPV approach would seem to have the best of the technical arguments but not the practical ones. As Joy and Bradley (1973) pointed out, IRRs are generally satisfactory when one is facing a simple go or no-go decision; besides, they say, IRRs are more easily understood. For our purposes here, Psacharopoulos and Hinchliffe (1973, p. 19) made the practical choice for us by observing that rates of return are by far the most commonly reported. Detailed discussions of the use of IRR versus NPV are contained in Hirshleifer (1958), Bailey (1959), Cohn (1972), and Joy and Bradley (1973). Calculations of internal rates of return, as used herein, are clearly laid out in Eckaus (1973, p. 71).

Internal rates of return may be assessed in two ways, the choice depending on whether it is the relative efficiency of society's or the individual's educational decision that is at issue. The former involves calculation of a social IRR, the latter of a private IRR. To the educator, the economist's standard specification of costs and benefits for analytical purposes will appear, to say the least, dubious.

Rate-of-return studies, at least under ideal conditions, identify private costs as the student's tuition and fees, books and supplies, net forgone income (earnings forgone while enrolled in college), and other education-related expenditures; private benefits are defined in most cases as after-tax earnings. Social costs are definied most commonly as the educational expenditures of institutions, and social benefits as before-tax earnings of individuals. Many issues surround these definitions (see Becker, 1975, pp. 194–200), and some of the most serious related difficulties are addressed in later sections. Suffice it to say here that these definitions include only the nonconsumption pecuniary benefits.

Finally, in the way of introduction, needed also are interest rate standards with which the (pecuniary) returns to higher education may be compared. That is, what yield can be expected from comparable, alternative investments? Although Taubman and Wales (1975, p. 42) set a relatively high 13%–15% standard for evaluating social IRR, most analysts select a 10% social and private IRR as suitable for the degree of risk represented by investment in education.[1]

METHODOLOGICAL ISSUES

Of some 130 references examined, less than one third were aimed specifically at providing rate-of-return estimates. The remainder addressed, in some fashion or other, related methodological problems. Because our primary focus here is not on research methods, suffice it to say that these methodological issues may be collected into the following: (1) standardizing reporting of IRRs (Are marginal or average rates reported, and what does *marginal* mean in this context?); (2) specifying the dependent variable (Should earnings or income be used, and if the former, which earnings?); (3) adjusting to enhance data compatibility (What adjustments are necessary for differences due to mortality, taxes, secular growth, unemployment, and hours worked?); (4) assessing the advantages of cross-sectional versus time-series databases (Which yields more valid results?); and (5) interpreting the residual (What conclusions may be reached about the sources of unexplained variance?). The implications of these and other issues for the validity and application of study results are discussed in the final section.

Standardizing Reporting.
Rates of return are not always reported consistently. Most studies report marginal rates of return, social or private. As conventionally used, however, the term *marginal* refers to the return not from one additional year of

schooling, but from an additional degree or other such increment, for example, the B.A. versus the high-school diploma (Psacharopoulos, 1973, p. 22). Returns by year of schooling are difficult to interpret for policy purposes. Average returns, on the other hand, conventionally reflect the mean return to higher education versus no education at all—again, for policy, a not very useful figure.

Specifying the Dependent Variable

The next issue concerns the use of earnings versus total income as the dependent variable. Most studies use earnings or wage rates rather than income, at least in part because of the form of the available data. The major argument in favor of using earnings is that income may contain inheritances, gifts, and other such revenues not readily attributable to education. Most of the literature fails to acknowledge that in saving more and in investing more wisely, college graduates realize more "unearned" income than do others. In any case, the rate-of-return literature routinely criticizes studies such as Jencks et al. (1972) massive-inequality work for using annual income as the personal revenue measure.

The subordinate question involves selection from among earnings figures. Most early and many more recent studies have used annual earnings as the dependent variable. The use of annual earnings, however, confounds labor–leisure choices (e.g., opting to work more hours) and the more transitory effects of unemployment; therefore, hourly wages—or perhaps even better, weekly earnings—are preferable (Griliches, 1977). The labor-leisure issue is reflected in the fact that years of schooling are correlated positively with number of hours worked (Mincer, 1975, p. 83). The seriousness of this problem is illustrated clearly in the results of Mennemeyer (1978), who showed that large earnings differentials favoring physicians over dentists and lawyers are essentially eliminated when controls for hours worked are executed. To some extent, the highly educated do trade off leisure for work; however, whether earnings should be controlled for hours worked, seems a debatable matter.

Adjustments for Data Compatability

Almost all rate-of-return studies use cross-sectional data sources to identify relationships among age (or experience), earnings, and education. The assumption is that the various relationships for workers of all age–experience, earnings, and educational levels are represented in the data cross-section and that the lifetime earnings stream of any given worker is thus known. However, adjustments are generally recognized as being necessary to reflect the varying impacts on earnings of factors that differ by educational level. The factors most commonly considered important to control are (differences in) mortality, taxation, unemployment, secular growth,[2] and hours worked. Carnoy and Marenbach (1975) estimated empirically that errors emanating from failure to adjust for mortality, taxes, and unemployment are "not large," and Raymond and Sesnowitz (1975) showed that the combined effects of progressive taxation at national, state, and local levels are about equal by degree held, except at the very high and very low income levels. Danielson's estimates (1969–1970) of the size of potential errors are considerably higher, but he found that the effects of mortality, progressive taxation, and secular growth essentially cancel out. Even though in many cases the combined effects of all factors may balance each other (Psacharopoulos, 1973, p. 39), errors from secular growth and hours worked are known to be large, and errors from the other factors may be substantial; therefore, it is generally believed that each should be accounted for.

Still another set of adjustments involves differences, by degree level, in personal traits such as socioeconomic status (SES), sex, motivation, and ability, with by far the most having been written about the importance of making ability adjustments. One would expect that all else being equal, the college-educated would earn more than high-school graduates because presumably the former are more motivated and more able. Estimates of the upward bias on rate-of-return estimates due to omission of ability and other personal traits range from practically nothing (Griliches, 1977) to perhaps 35% (Cutwright, 1969). Among those who have attempted to measure the ability bias are Taubman and Wales (1975), Griliches and Mason (1972), Hause (1972), and Weisbrod and Karpoff (1968). Others who have discussed the importance of the ability problem include Hause (1972), Wachtel (in Juster, 1975), Ashenfelter and Mooney (1968), Becker (1975, p. 158), Chamberlain and Griliches (1975), Chiswick (1972), Goldberger (1978), Marin and Psacharopoulos (1976), Weisbrod (1972), and Wessel (1971). Gintis (1971), in a creative approach to the problem, suggested that the theory is wrong, that education does not raise cognitive achievement so much as it inculcates changes in personality traits important to personal income growth. Still others argue that the so-called ability issue in rate-of-return estimates is a nonissue, that ability in this regard is ability to earn, and that this is what the dependent variable measures. Limited reviews of works on the ability topic are found in Gintis (1971), Leibowitz (1974), and Raymond and Sesnowitz (1975).

Cross-Sectional Versus Time-Series Studies

A modest controversy has surrounded whether cross-sectional studies yield valid IRR estimates. The central issue is whether a cross section of an entire work force can accurately represent the lifetime earnings streams of individuals. Freiden and Leimer (1981) showed that cross-sectional results may be biased downward, and Danielson (1969–1970), in comparing cross-sectional to time-series results from the same database, concluded that the former yield "clearly wrong" results in describing the earnings profile of a single cohort. In arguing for cross-sectional analyses, Miller (1960) seemed unwittingly to reinforce this view in pointing out that cross-sectional studies are free of variants such as economic depressions. In reflecting conditions at one point in time, an IRR taken at that time will reflect only present, rather than long-term, average circumstances. As will be seen later, this apparently is the major reason that Freeman's IRR estimates (1975b) for the early 1970s were low in comparison to others: Freeman's data reflect, in part, economic recession and, in part, the effects of an atypically large college-aged cohort size.

Interpretation of the Residual

Although the error is rarely straightforward, the IRR literature shows a periodic and troubling tendency to ascribe any earnings not explained by conventional factors to whatever may be the issue at hand. For example, one can find papers concluding that any differences in education-related earnings by sex or race, after normal controls are set, are due to discrimination. As Griliches (1977) observed, "Studies which identify the 'residual' with something particular such as discrimination, are much more dependent on the original equation having accounted for *'everything else'* ". Discussions of this and similar alleged errors are illustrated in Weisbrod (1972), who charged Hause (1972) with assigning too much of the explanation of earnings to ability on the assumption that other correlates of earnings are uncorrelated with ability, schooling level, and background variables, particularly motivation; and in Goldberger (1978), who charged Taubman (1976) with assigning unexplained variance to heredity and environment.

RESULTS OF EMPIRICAL WORK

Besides cost–benefit approaches such as IRR analysis, there are two other ways of viewing the contribution to earnings from education. Each is useful for public policy purposes. One is the contribution of education to growth in the economy, and the other is the share of earnings differences that can be explained by education.

Denison (1962) ascribed 23% of the growth in total real national income to education and another 20% to the advancement of knowledge and "change in lag in the application of knowledge" over the period 1929–1957. Later (1964), he found that education accounted for 15% of national economic growth between 1957 and 1962, and his projection for 1960–1980 was that education would account for 19% of total real-income growth. A related approach is described in Psacharopoulos (1973, Chapter 7), who put the percentage of growth from education at 17.9% (p. 116).

More common in assessing the impact of education on earnings are studies that offer estimates of an "alpha factor," the portion of earnings differences that is explained by education. Almost all such studies have controlled for ability, which is generally considered the largest source of potential bias in earnings differentials by educational level. And most studies have controlled for additional variables, such as parents' education, income, and occupation; marital status; family size; health; religion; and region of the country.

The average alpha value for thirteen studies of the B.A. degree is .79; that is, the portion of the difference in earnings between B.A.-holders and non-B.A.-holders that can be explained by the B.A. is 79%. Values tend to be lower for two-year and technical degrees. Alpha values of .90 are found for the graduate level. In the seventeen studies found, the pattern seems to support the generalization in the literature that the alpha factor increases with educational level. Coefficients for schooling levels below higher education are consistently lower.

THE META-ANALYTICAL MATRIX

Table 1 contains rate-of-return estimates from twenty-five studies. The results are not strictly comparable because of varying data sources, the populations studied, the time periods reflected, the social and private cost specifications, the controls and adjustments made, the dependent variable specifications, the inclusion or exclusion of nonpecuniary or psychic variables, and whether the study was of cross-sectional or time-series data. Primarily because of differences in controls and adjustments (Column 10), the results could not be standardized readily. The most important factors for comparing results are listed in Column 12.

The final rows of the table present average estimates by level of higher education. After carefully reviewing the 25 empirical results and over 100 conceptual and methodological papers dealing with analytical issues, the authors' general sense is that, especially for the B.A. degree, the averages roughly reflect pecuniary rates of return to higher education over the past twenty or so years. The average private and social rates of return are 11.8% and 11.4% for 22 and 14 studies, respectively. The social rate of return is probably upwardly biased by about 1% in relation to the private rate. Both rates compare favorably to conventional benchmark rates for alternative investments, especially if one considers the ups and downs of the equities (stock) market. (See McMahon and Wagner, 1982, p. 161, Figure 2.) The trends by higher education level seem valid, too.

The lower return for less than the B.A. (10.1%) is consistent with generalizations in the literature. Though not tabled here, the returns for elementary and secondary education tend to be higher than those for the postsecondary level. The major reason is that private and social costs increase by level; it is not that benefits decrease.

TABLE 1. Rates of Return

(1) ID No.	(2) Author(s), Year	(3/4) Year of Data/ Population	(5/6) Publication Source/ TS or CS	(7/8) Data Source/ Cost Specification	(9/10) Grade Levels/ Controls Adjustments	(11) Dependent Variable Specification	(12) Special Notes	(13) Includes Psychic?	(14) Results (%) Private / Social	
01	Ashtenfelter and Mooney, 1968	1966 Woodrow Wilson fellows	J CS	Woodrow Wilson fellows FI + ?	All graduate A, not M, Ta	Annual income by graduate level/years	Early income, high ability, prestige colleges, fellowships	No	9.1	
02	Becker, 1975	1939, 1949 Census	B CS	Census .75 FI + DC	High school and college A, M, S, Ta	Earnings	Results after all adjustments	Some-what	10	13
03	Becker and Chiswick, 1966	1959 White males	J CS	Census FI + DC + (?)	0-8, 8-12, > 12 NA	Earnings in South and non-South	Average IRR to all college years	No	8.5	
04	Carnoy and Marenbach, 1975	1939, 1949, 1959, 1969 Whites	J CS and TS	Census Pvt. = 75% of FI; Soc. = "insti-tutional cost" + FI	Elementary, high-school, college graduates Ta (men only), U, not M, S	Annual income and earnings	No DC, whites only	No	14.3	9,3

215

Abbreviations and symbols: J = journal, B = book, S = secondary source; CPS = current population surveys, NBER-TH = National Bureau of Economic Research. Thorndike; CS = cross section, TS = time series; DC = direct costs, FI = foregone income, Pvt. = private cost, Soc. = social cost; E & G = educational and general, T = tuition; A = ability, H = hours worked, M = mortality, S = secular growth, Ta = taxes, U = unemployment; $\propto$ = % of earnings attributed to education, NA = not applicable; IRR = internal rate of return.

TABLE 1. *(continued)*

(1) ID No.	(2) Author(s) Year	(3/4) Year of Data/ Population	(5/6) Publication Source/ TS or CS	(7/8) Data Source/ Cost Specification	(9/10) Grade Levels/ Controls Adjustments	(11) Dependent Variable Specification	(12) Special Notes	(13) Includes Psychic?	(14) Results (%) Private	Social
05	Danielson, 1969–1970	1956–1966 Males	J TS	CPS 1956–1966 Woodrow Wilson fellows FI (perceived) + DC	B.A.–Ph.D. M, S, Ta	Annual income	B.A.IRR for GA	No	16.2	
06	Duncan, 1976	1970–1971, 1973 Working white non-farm males, age 21–65	J CS	Quality of Employment Survey, Panel Study of Income Dynamics None	All A + others	Wage rates	Nonpecuniary and pecuniary items	Yes		
07	Eckaus, 1973	1959 White males, age 14–64	B CS	Census FI + DC	Elementary-college H, Ta, M, U, S	Hourly wage	Excellent adjustments	No	11.5	
08	Freeman, 1975b	1959, 1969, 1972, 1974 Males	J CS	Census and CPS Soc. = E + G ÷ enrollments; Pvt. = T - scholarships	High school vs. 4-year college T	Annual earnings	E and G, no FI, 10% discount rate	No	10.4	9.7
09	Greer, 1976–1977	1960, 1970 Census	J CS	Census FI, T	College vs. high school T, M	Net annual earnings	Low cost estimate	No	16.1	

216

#	Study	Year & Sample	Type	Source/Method	Schooling & Variables	Earnings Measure	Comments		Rate	Rate
10	Hanoch, 1967	1959 Males	J CS	Census Assumes student earnings = DC	K-17 Demographic variables + M, S, Ta, U	Annual earnings	Study highly regarded	No	10	
11	Hansen, 1963	1949 Males	J CS	Census Soc. = institutional + FI + incidentals; Pvt. = same except T for institutional	1-16 M, T	Income		No	10.1	10.2
12	Hunt, 1963	1947 College graduates	J CS	Time magazine, 1947 survey of college graduates "Expense/ pupil," graduate is 2 X undergraduate	College A + others		Very small N, old data; not really Pvt. RR; ignore		6	
13	Johnson and Stafford, 1973	1965 White, male, urban employed	J CS	Survey Research Center "Soc. Cost" .75 FI	12, 16	Hourly earnings		No		8.8
14	Koch, 1972-1973	1968-1969 Graduates	J CS	Illinois State Undergraduate cost at Illinois State	Undergraduate A, Ta, and others	Annual earnings by discipline	Illinois State		7	

TABLE 1. *(continued)*

(1) ID No.	(2) Author(s), Year	(3/4) Year of Data/ Population	(5/6) Publication Source/ TS or CS	(7/8) Data Source/ Cost Specification	(9/10) Grade Levels/ Controls Adjustments	(11) Dependent Variable Specification	(12) Special Notes	(13) Includes Psychic?	(14) Results (%) Private	Social
15	Liberman, 1979	1958–1976	S			Pre-tax income				14
16	Mattila, 1982	1956–1979 Males	J TS	CPS .75 X wages of high-school graduates + net T	High school, some college, continuing college Business cycle	Annual earnings	Mixed earnings-income	No	12	
17	McMahon and Wagner, 1982	1976 B.A. graduates	B CS	ACT College Investment Decision Study FI, books, net of scholarships and institutional expenditures	B.A. A, S+ others, ($\propto$ = .66)	Annual earnings	Pvt.—expected IRR	No	18	13.3
18	Mincer, 1962	1950 Census	J CS	Census FI + DC	College Not A, S, U; a correction factor; part-time employment	Pre-tax income	Downward biased	No	11	13

	Study	Sample	Type	Cost measure	Education levels / quality controls	Income measure	Ability adjustment		
19	Raymond and Sesnowitz, 1975	1969 Census	J CS	Census .75 FI net of taxes, T, books and supplies	College A, S, T, PT workers	Annual income	No	15.7	14.3
20	Solmon, 1975	1969 Male air cadets	J CS	NBER-TH FI	Some college College qual-ity and other	Annual earnings	No	9.7	
21	Taubman and Wales, 1973	1955, 1969 Male air cadets	J CS	NBER-TH Soc.: 71% of EandG +FI plant; Pvt.:T+FI + incidental	High school and college A + others	Deflated, before-tax monthly earnings	Adjust- ment for teach- ers	9	8
22	Wachtel, 1976	1955, 1969 Male air cadets	J TS	NBER-TH School ex- penditures T + (.75) FI	High school, some college, college graduates A + others, α factor	Monthly earnings	No		10

Pvt. = per year RR; Soc. = return to expenditures

TABLE 1. *(continued)*

(1) ID No.	(2) Author(s), Year	(3/4) Year of Data/ Population	(5/6) Publication Source/ TS or CS	(7/8) Data Source/ Cost Specification	(9/10) Grade Levels/ Controls Adjustments	(11) Dependent Variable Specification	(12) Special Notes	(13) Includes Psychic?	(14) Results (%) Private	Social
23	Weiss, 1971	1966 NSF scientific and technical personnel	J CS	National Register of scientific and Technical personnel NSF, 1966 FI and academic expenses	Graduate S + demographic variables	Annual earnings	Registered time	No		
24	Witmer, 1983	1967–1982 Men and women	J TS	Census Pvt.: full cost net of aid; Soc.: full cost	High school and college A, M, Ta, U, and other	Annual earnings	Average per year	No	16	13
25	Witmer, 1980	1961–1972 Men and women	J TS	CPS E and G net of research and public service	Higher education NA	Estimated earnings		No	1 4	

	Two years or some college	B.A. 4 years	Graduate	Master's	Ph.D. or Ph.D./professional
Private IRR	10.1	11.8	8.3	7.6	8.1
Social IRR	NA	11.4	NA	NA	NA

GRADUATE EDUCATION

The private rates of return for graduate education (generally), the M.A., and the Ph.D. at 8.3%, 7.6%, and 8.1, respectively, also support the generalizations in the literature: returns within graduate education tend to increase as one moves upward toward the Ph.D.[3] The variation in results for the graduate school studies is relatively large, ranging from a negative value (Maxwell, 1970) to as high as 20% or more (Curtis and Campbell, 1978). The principal reason for this high variation is that most IRR studies of graduate education are of special groups, as opposed to the broad national samples characteristic of undergraduate IRR studies. Also, costs of graduate education vary more widely. Ashenfelter and Mooney (1968, 1969) obtained quite high results (IRR) by studying the early earnings of Woodrow Wilson fellows who were graduates of prestigious universities. Not only were these former students highly able, but their costs were low because they received stipends, increasing rates of return by roughly a factor of 2 (Siegfried, 1972–1973). At the other extreme, Maxwell (1970) obtained negative results (rates of return), apparently in considerable part because he oversampled education students at a nonprestigious mid-western university (Wessel, 1971). Bailey and Schotta (1972) observed very low returns (.8%) in studying persons who later entered the academic profession and who studied, and thus incurred costs, over longer periods of time. Weiss (1971) showed that returns are greater within every graduate field and level for persons later employed in private industry and management than in academia. Curtis and Campbell (1978) reanalyzed the Bailey and Schotta data and—showing the importance of regional markets for graduates and the proper corrections for risk, for taxes, and for leisure time—reported that graduate IRR could vary between .04% and 20% and more.

BY FIELD

Although space does not permit elaboration here, several studies have compared rates of return by field of study (Eckaus, 1973, Chapter 2; Hanoch, 1967; Koch, 1972; Seeborg, 1975; Thurow, 1968; Taubman and Wales, 1974; Wilkinson, 1966). McMahon (1981) and McMahon and Wagner (1981, 1982) have calculated *expected* rates of return by occupation. Returns tend to be highest in the mature professional fields and lowest in the striving professions, such as education and nursing, and in the humanities and the fine arts. Problems in conducting rate-of-return studies by field are discussed by Eckaus (1973, pp. 17–21). Among the problems cited are selecting the appropriate comparison group (To whom should the IRR of a physician or a history major be compared?), difficulties in separating education from noneducation sources of knowledge and skills, psychic income differences, and worker movement among occupations. Seeborg (1975) pointed out that the various curricula attract persons of quite different abilities, thus again raising comparability questions.

BY COLLEGE TYPE AND QUALITY

One of the more interesting questions addressed in the IRR studies is whether returns vary by type of college and by college quality. The only known extensive study comparing rates of return across institutional types is a carefully controlled effort by McMahon and Wagner (1982, pp. 161–169). The authors showed that community and junior colleges, which offer many technical courses of study, yield high returns, as do private and public research universities and public and private comprehensive colleges. Graduates of liberal arts colleges do not fare as well, except for those who go on to graduate school.

Determining what constitutes institutional quality is itself a complex matter;[4] but regardless of the measure, a positive association with earnings is uniformly found. Using the Project Talent index of freshman attitudes, Reed and Miller (1970) reported a generally linear relationship between college quality and earnings. Based on the quality values of the Gorman Report (1967), Taubman and Wales (1973) concluded that the contribution of college quality to earnings was large, but only for the top-quality one-fifth, whereas Solmon (1975) found differences for only the bottom- and top-quality quartiles. Ribich and Murphy (1975) reported a positive relationship between school quality and later earnings, but primarily because of the additional quantity of education induced by higher quality institutions. On the other hand, Johnson and Stafford's findings (1973) were strong enough to allow them to conclude that institutional quality was more important to earnings than was educational quantity (years of schooling), a conclusion supported by Link and Rutledge (1975). A very thorough discussion of the related issues and research is contained in Solmon (1975).

OVER TIME

One of the most contentious and important issues to arise in higher education finance in recent years is the alleged decline in the value of a college education. Freeman, in a series of publications (1975a,b,c,; 1977, 1979, 1980), and Freeman and Holloman (1975) purported to show that the private rate of return had declined markedly between 1969 and 1974, to a point (about 7.5%) where the investment in higher education was not justified. Witmer (1980), Schwartz and Thornton (1980), McMahon and Wagner (1982, pp. 152, 155), and Smith and Welch (1978a,b) wrote critiques in which, among other things, it was pointed out that Freeman's calculations were only for males in their very early employment years and that Freeman's cost estimates were badly flawed. Freeman's response (1980) made a strong case for the general pattern of his results over time; that is, his results do appear to be biased downward,[5] but since his method is consistent over time, a decline probably did occur. Whether Freeman's IRR was below benchmark levels is another matter.

In retrospect, Freeman's findings were neither unexpected nor alarming. It had been known for some time and has since been verified, both theoretically (Psacharopoulos, 1973, p. 9) and empirically (Miller, 1960; Psacharopoulos, 1973, pp. 95–97; Welch, 1970, 1979; Ashenfelter and Ham, 1979; Bartlett, 1978; Cline, 1982; Mattila, 1982), that cohort size (the so-called vintage effect) and business cycles affect earnings.[6] In the past, the growth of college-educated cohorts had been matched essentially by growth in technical and related labor markets (Welch, 1979).[7] Freeman's data covered a period in which both cohort size and business recession placed a dampening effect on the earnings of new college-educated entrants into the work force. Indeed, Freeman (1975b, 1979) explained his results as reflecting the interaction of recessions and the vintage effect and suggested that the observed effects might only be temporary. One could observe that, at worst, even if the trend had persisted, the value of a college degree had not declined so much as cohort sizes had grown—a temporary phenomenon that would begin to pass by the early 1980s.

Regardless, more recent works have shown either that Freeman's decline did not really occur (Witmer, forthcoming) or that the decline was temporary (Mattila, 1982; Liberman, 1979; Rumberger, 1980), as rates appear now to have returned to near their historic level. Smith and Welch (1978a) were prophetic when they wrote, "If the size of the cohort produces only a temporary decline until the market absorbs the new workers, it remains plausible that this recent 'depression' is only 'market indigestion.'" Cline (1982) argued that what has changed over time is the composition of the college-educated group: those who graduate from college today are quite different kinds of persons (in aptitudes and interests) from those who graduated in decades past, and their earnings reflect this difference.

INTERNATIONAL STUDIES

Rate-of-return studies are by no means unique to the United States, and much can be learned about earnings and education relationships in other countries. Psacharopoulos's 1973 book is by far the most complete work on the subject. He showed, for example, that the returns to education are greater in developing than in developed countries; that primary education yields the highest returns in most countries; that differences in national incomes are more a function of human than of physical capital differences; that education contributes importantly to the rate of growth of output, particularly in developing countries; that the earnings inequalities associated with education are the greatest in the less developed countries; and that labor substitution (using persons of varying educational levels for various jobs) among workers of varying educational levels is great, arguing for education cost-benefit analysis over manpower planning programs as public policy devices. Other and more recent, though more limited, works in this area include those by Belanger and Lavalee (n.d.), Dougherty and Psacharopoulos (1977), Okachi (1983), and Ziderman (1973).

ISSUES AND PROBLEMS: WHAT DO THE IRR STUDIES TELL US?

The rate-of-return studies are held up as a way of judging optimum investments in education. But do they succeed? Very large questions arise on both the cost and the benefit sides.

As noted earlier, rates of return are particularly sensitive to cost variations. When one speaks of rates of return, most persons think of benefits to education and do not contemplate the cost side; yet, differences in rates of return (especially private rates) by educational levels reflect differences primarily in costs, rather than in earnings. Private rates of return to elementary education are very high, sometimes approaching infinity, because the elementary student pays very few of the direct costs, and the forgone earnings (indirect costs) are almost nil (Carnoy and Marenbach, 1975). At the other extreme, the direct and indirect costs of higher education are relatively very high. Social costs vary in the same fashion, although not as drastically. From a utility perspective for public policy purposes, a rate-of-return result generally tells the policymaker more about the relative public subsidies of the students' costs at each educational level than it tells her or him about the benefits of the education. Low private IRR may be increased most easily by a lowering of costs to the student, and the cost reduction need not be very large to impact IRR substantially. Or put another way, subsidies to alternative educational levels may be reduced if rates are found to be high. The point is that private IRRs are artificial in that they do not represent the value of education in some absolute sense; rather, more than anything, they represent the degree of public subsidy obtained, or simply a low cost of educational production. For example, Wachtel (1975, pp. 158–162) estimated that the rate of return on higher education for those receiving the GI Bill after World War II was almost double the rate for nonrecipients. Similarly, Siegfried (1972–1973) showed that graduate economics students on fellowships realized rates of return ranging from 11.4% to 23.6% compared to 13% for those using solely private funds.

Therefore, a vital issue is the accuracy of cost estimates in rate-of-return studies. In regard to social costs, Becker (1975, pp. 192–193) pointed out the arbitrariness and inconsistency in determining what shall be included in college costs. Although authors typically do not specify clearly the social costs that they use, many appear to use, for the large institutional contribution, total Educational and General Expenditures. This category contains all components of the annual operating budget, including organized research and public service, even though the implicit *benefit* measured is earnings from instruction.[8]

Private cost estimates are even more problematic. First, for direct cost, researchers almost exclusively employ national averages of student expenditures. As Eckaus (1973) noted, "The use of such averages introduces strong qualifications in the interpretation of the internal rates of return associated with college especially" (p. 84). He observed, "Although I have no more to apologize for in this respect than other investigators, the procedure is felt to be particularly unsatisfactory" (p. 84). One of the more obvious "qualifications" is that expenditures vary tremendously between the public and the independent sectors, so that, other factors being equal, using an "average" cost significantly understates the IRR to the student enrolled in the public sector. Studies using aggregate data that obscure variations in postschool investment may even understate aggregate rates of return (Knapp and Hansen, 1976).

Based on actual numbers of hours worked by students, Parsons (1974) showed that most studies err seriously in imputing opportunity costs by ignoring or misstating student earnings. Discussing the five ways of estimating forgone earnings used in the literature, he showed (from hours worked by students) that the errors ranged from -28% to $+31\%$ (pp. 262–264). Becker's (1975) and Hanoch's (1967) technique of using three fourths of the earnings of nonstudents to compute forgone income seems to yield the most accurate results. Less accurate estimates fail to reflect the greater sacrifice of leisure for work by students than by nonstudents (Parsons, 1974). The data of Freiden and Leimer (1981), however, seem to suggest that the three-fourths estimate is too high and thus bias the rate-of-return estimates downward. Again, the reason is that students earn a good deal. Freiden and Leimer estimated that 18-to 21-year-old males earn from 53% to 68% of the amount earned by comparable male nonstudents, and females earn from 32% to 46% of what female nonstudent earn. The earnings of 18- to 24-year-olds are even higher. Using the National Longitudinal Study of 1972, Crary and Leslie (1978) controlled for ability and socioeconomic status to equate college-goers and nonattenders in order to assess forgone earnings directly. Only Becker's 1964 estimates were found to approximate actual total average costs, whereas others have overestimated costs (and thus understated IRR) by 16% to 56%. Further, it was found that the annual amounts forgone in four-year schools were several times greater than in two-year and proprietary schools. Crary and Leslie also shed considerable light on variations by ability and SES. Surprisingly, high-ability students have the lowest opportunity costs, often very much lower, suggesting a very high IRR, while the reverse is true for low-ability students.

Finally, and most important from the cost side, by assuming that all costs are paid by the student, analysts have greatly understated private rates of return. From an individual's perspective, the judgment of whether higher education represents a good investment is based, not on some published gross price, as commonly used in rate-of-return studies, but on the student's actual net cost. It has already been seen that IRR calculations are sensitive to cost estimates. Very few IRR studies take student aid into account, and of the many references examined, none acknowledged that parents often pay a large part of higher education costs. If indeed the *student's* net cost is much less than the published price or the total cost paid from whatever sources, then the student essentially realizes a much higher IRR than all studies show. Thus, from a student's perspective, if student aid or family support is substantial, on average, higher education represents an investment almost without equal. It may not be overstating the case to liken this student's situation to striking gold after a few weeks in the goldfields.

Using data that for the first time allow comparisons of comparable student and nonstudent earnings, Crary and Leslie (1978) showed that student indirect costs are actually much less than is generally thought. Further, Leslie (1984) found that the net cost to the student was only some 32% to 40% of total private direct costs in 1980, having declined by about 10 percentage points between 1973 and 1980. Parents and governments directly subsidize the remainder. For most individuals, IRR must be much higher than reported above. Perhaps it is not surprising that higher education participation rates have been maintained at high levels during a period when the IRR has been said to be declining.

There are also factors on the benefits side that bias rate-of-return estimates downward. The major omission is the nonpecuniary benefits of education. As defined above, the measures of neither the social nor the private benefits employed in IRR analysis extend beyond the pecuniary or dollar earnings realized. Indeed, it may have struck the reader as bizarre that social benefits would be defined as *private* earnings, before taxes are paid. This matter did not escape Becker (1975, p. 195), who labeled the before-tax definition as only "a first approximation" to rate-of-return estimation. He recognized the "common criticism" that earnings greatly understate the social productivity of college graduates. McMahon and Wagner (1982) were quite direct on this point, which is often glossed over in the literature:

> This should not imply that the incremental taxes paid by college graduates are a fully adequate measure of the external benefits of education, or of education's overall contribution to equity, but they are the best measures of society's estimate of the value of these social contributions. [p. 152]

Becker (1975, pp. 117–120) estimated that the total return to higher education may be as much as twice the private return obtained from conventional IRR analyses. Additional issues addressed above suggest that even this estimate may be far too low for many students.

The nonpecuniary benefits may be subdivided into consumption benefits and postcollege psychic benefits. Consumption benefits are those benefits that the student enjoys as a part of student life, including, for example, the pleasures of living in college housing, belonging to collegiate organizations, and attending athletic and cultural events, as well as the pleasure component of learning—in short, all activities from which a later "return" will not be realized. Wachtel (1975, p. 160) made the interesting observation that the substantially higher IRR on direct cost investments over the IRR on indirect cost investments (forgone earnings) demonstrates that full-time study, in comparison to part-time study, yields largely a consumption benefit.

POSTSCHOOLING PSYCHIC BENEFITS

There exists a substantial literature regarding the "psychic" or nonpecuniary benefits that follow higher education enrollment. It is known that education, especially that of the wife and mother, is associated with better health; each additional year of schooling appears to extend life by .4 percentage points or almost 3% for a Ph.D. graduate over a high school graduate (Grossman, 1976). The better educated also experience less work disability (Lando, 1975); the children of better-educated women are generally more healthy (Grossman, 1982); and when combined with the mother's "home investment" (reading, writing, and storytelling), her education appears to raise children's IQ considerably (Leibowitz, 1974).

Rosen (in Juster, 1975, p. 23) reported that people often accept lower-paying jobs for the opportunity to advance their education. McMahon (1976, p. 322) found that parents' education contributes to the number of years of college planned by their children.

Education is related positively to savings, investment management, and the willingness to take financial risks (Solmon, 1975). The better educated tend to be wiser spenders, indirectly enhancing their incomes by between 10% and 50% (Michael, 1975), and to have fewer children, especially "unwanted" births (Michael, 1982). Schooling is known to be correlated positively with the selection of a spouse whose earnings potential is relatively high (Michael, 1982). A wife's schooling has been found to raise her husband's earnings (Welch, 1974), but divorce rates are higher for educated women. The work of the better educated is more interesting and challenging and is more likely to lead to advancement (Beaton, 1975). Unemployment is less likely (Erlich, 1975), and depreciation of one's human capital (e.g., formal education), as well as obsolescence of job skills, is slower or less likely (Rosen, in Juster, 1975). The better educated tend to place less importance on "luck" and "connections" in their employment behaviors.

Efforts to quantify these benefits for inclusion in IRR estimates have been creative though modest in number. Dunn (1977) surveyed textile plant workers and asked them to identify the dollar and hours-of-work values that they would trade off for certain fringe benefits, such as sick leave and retirement. Lucas (1977) showed that the omission of psychic job considerations, such as repetitiveness and the physical conditions of the workplace, understates the returns to education. The reader is referrred to McMahon (1982a) for a current and broad summary of all nonpecuniary benefits of education, to Witmer (1970), and to Michael (1982).

EXTERNALITIES

There is also considerable literature on the external benefits of education, that is, the "spillovers" or benefits gained by society from the education of individuals. The direct pecuniary benefits of that education are presumably captured in the social rate-of-return calculations that reflect extra taxes paid by the more highly educated; however, productivity gains realized through a highly educated work force and nonpecuniary gains that spill over from individuals to society must be taken into account. Becker (1975, p. 32) observed that this omission is the main reason that rate-of-return studies have not been well accepted.

Again, McMahon (1982b) wrote a concise review of the externalities of education, as did Weisbrod (1964, 1966), Bowen (1982), and Witmer (1970). Empirical work in this area depends on imputing dollar values and using shadow prices.

Education, especially inequality in education, has been observed to have an effect on the crime rate, the theory being proved when crimes of "profit" are separated from other crimes; that is, the relationship of (lack of) education to crime can be demonstrated for crimes of profit but not for profitless crimes when other factors are controlled. The better educated are also more able to prevent crimes (Erlich, 1975). Education reduces juvenile delinquency (Spiegelman, 1968). The cost of crime that can be associated with the educational deficiencies of adult prison inmates was put at $19.8 billion for 1982 (Webb, 1977).

High welfare and Medicaid costs have been associated with low educational levels (Garfinkel and Haveman, 1977, p. 53). Higher levels of education seem to yield greater liberality on issues such as integration and freedom for youth (Beaton, 1975), and many community agencies enjoy voluntary assistance and leadership that come heavily from more highly educated groups (Weisbrod, 1962).

A reading of this literature leaves one with the distinct impression that traditional rates-of-return estimates almost invariably and rather decisively understate the true social rates of return.

CONCLUSIONS

Where, then, does this leave us in the use of rate-of-return studies? First, the rates presented should not be considered a sufficient basis for higher-education allocative decision-making. These rates understate the true return to education by a substantial margin, probably by a wide margin. Berg (1981, p. 102) was quite right when he observed that rate-of-return studies capture only a few of the elements in educational productivity.

Raymond and Sesnowitz's pertinent statement (1975) that it is better to have imperfect information than none at all is problematic. Suppose that imperfect information leads to a conclusion contrary to that reached with complete knowledge. The experiences of the last ten or so years in American higher education seem clearly to tell us that this is precisely what has happened. Governments have shifted funding priorities away from higher education to areas such as prisons and welfare, and they have done so on grounds that, if complete, would almost certainly have led to contrary conclusions. Similarly, individuals have reduced their propensity to enroll in higher education. It seems clear that the so-called declining value of a college education has been greatly oversold.

Present rate-of-return studies can offer a "go" decision; they cannot yield a "no-go" decision. If pecuniary rates of return, as now constructed, show that the returns are greater than benchmark rates, additional educational investment is supported. If such benchmarks are not exceeded, additional information is probably required.

One could argue that the rate-of-return issue should be viewed solely from a field-of-study perspective. In a sense, the policy question is not whether *higher education* pays off. Clearly and overwhelmingly, it does pay off financially in many fields of study, and it clearly pays off less well in many others. Yet, it is a fact of life that governments, at least, tend to think in terms of support of higher education generically. Society might benefit more by making public allocations on a field-by-field IRR basis, but practically, such an approach would raise other serious issues. Would we allocate less money to fields such as teacher education, nursing, theology, and social work because we know that the rates of return there are relatively small? Clearly not. Perhaps this sort of field-by-field analysis points up most clearly the inadequacy of traditional IRR analyses, which neglect the nonpecuniary benefits to society and to the individual.

NOTES

1. For a discussion see Becker (1975, pp. 192–193) and Joy and Bradley (1973, p. 1255).
2. The rate of productivity growth.
3. Psacharopoulos's summary (1973) from fewer studies sets the master's and Ph.D. private IRR at 7.5% and 9.1%, respectively (p. 71). His private and social RR estimates for the B.A. are 13.6% and 9.7%, which bracket the 11.8% and 11.4% figures reported here.
4. Solmon (1975) treated this issue more thoroughly than anyone.
5. Dresch (1980) discussed the reasons that Freeman's estimates are biased downward.
6. Miller (1960) argued that it is primarily unemployment, not cohort size, that explains IRR differences over time; Smith and Welch (1978a) are more convincing that cohort size is the major factor. Rosen and Taubman (1982) have taken the most recent look at this important question and concluded that cohort size is not as important as previously thought. They included a discussion of other studies on the subject.

7. Carnoy and Marenbach (1975) found stable IRRs for college graduates between
   1939 and 1969, a finding reported earlier by Welch (1970). Bartlett (1978) found
   that the decline for *all* workers reported between 1939 and 1969 was due entirely to
   declines between 1939 and 1949, a period marked by the end of the Great
   Depression, World War II, and the postwar recovery.
8. Witmer (1980, pp. 114–115), for example, charged Freeman (1975b) with this
   error.

REFERENCES

Ashenfelter, O., and Ham, J. (1979). Education, unemployment, and earnings.
Journal of Political Economy 87: S99–116.
Ashenfelter, O., and Mooney, J. (1968). Graduate education, ability, and earnings. *Review of Economics and Statistics* 50: 78–86.
Ashenfelter, O., and Mooney, J. (1969). Some evidence on the private returns to graduate education. *Southern Economic Journal* 35: 247–256.
Bailey, D., and Schotta, C. (1972). Private and social rates of return to education of academicians. *American Economic Review* 62: 19–31.
Bailey, M. J. (1959). Formal criteria for investment decisions. *Journal of Political Economy* 67: 476–488.
Bartlett, S. (1978). Education, experience and wage inequality: 1939–1969. *Journal of Human Resources* 13: 349–365.
Beaton, A. (1975). The influence of education and ability on salary and attitudes. In Juster, F. T. (ed.), *Education, income and human behavior,* pp. 365–404. New York: McGraw-Hill.
Becker, G. S. (1964). *Human capital.* New York: National Bureau of Economic Research.
Becker, G. S. (1975). *Human capital, a theoretical and empirical analysis with special reference to education* (2nd ed.). New York: National Bureau of Economic Research.
Becker, G. S., and Chiswick, B. (1966). The economics of education: Education and the distribution of earnings. *American Economic Review* 56: 358–369.
Belanger, C. H., and Lavalée, L. (n.d.) *Economic returns to schooling decisions.* Montreal: Université de Montreal, Office of Institutional Research.
Berg, I. (1981). The effects of inflation on and in higher education. *Annals of American Academy of Political and Social Sciences* 456: 99–111.
Bowen, H. R. (1982). *The costs of higher education.* San Francisco: Jossey-Bass.
Carnoy, M., and Marenbach, D. (1975). The return to schooling in the United States, 1939 to 1969. *Journal of Human Resources* 10: 312–331.
Chamberlain, A., and Griliches, Z. (1975). Unobservables with a variance components structure: ability, schooling and the economic success of brothers. *International Economics Review* 16: 422–449.
Chiswick, B. (1972). Schooling and earnings of low achievers: comment. *American Economic Review* 62: 752–754.
Cline, H. (1982). The measurement of change in the rate of return to education: 1967–75. *Economics of Education Review* 2: 275–293.
Cohn, E. (1972). Investment criteria and the ranking of educational investments. *Public Finance* 27: 355–360.
Crary, L. J., and Leslie, L. L. (1978). The private costs of postsecondary education. *Journal of Education Finance* 4: 14–28.
Curtis, T. D., and Campbell, J., Jr. (1978). Investment in graduate human capital: an evaluation of rate of return approach. *Review of Business and Economics Research* 14: 74–89.
Cutwright, P. (1969). *Achievement, military service, and earnings.* (Contract No. SSA 67-2031). Washington, DC: Social Security Administration.

Danielson, A. (1969-70). Some evidence on the private returns to graduate education: comment. *Southern Economic Journal* 36: 334–338.

Denison, E. F. (1962). The source of economic growth in the United States and the alternates before us. (Supplementary Paper No. 13). New York: Committee for Economic Development.

Denison, E. F. (1964). Measuring the contribution of education, and the residual, to economic growth. *The residual factor and economic growth.* Paris: Organization for Economic Cooperation and Development.

Dougherty, C., and Psacharopoulos, G. (1977). Measuring the cost of misallocation of investment in education. *Journal of Human Resources* 12: 446–459.

Dresch, S. (1980). *Deflating, discounting and the returns to schooling: clarifying the Schwartz-Thornton vs. Freeman "debate."* New Haven: Yale Institute for Demographic and Economic Studies.

Duncan, G. J. (1976). Earnings function and nonpecuniary benefits. *Journal of Human Resources* 11: 462–483.

Dunn, L. P. (1977). Quantifying nonpecuniary returns. *Journal of Human Resources* 12: 347–359.

Eckaus, R. S. (1973). *Estimating the returns to education: a disaggregated approach.* Berkeley, CA: Carnegie Commission on Higher Education.

Erlich, I. (1975). On the relation between education and crime. In F. T. Juster (ed.), *Education, income and human behavior,* pp. 313–338. New York: McGraw-Hill.

Freeman, R. (1975a). Legal "cobwebs": a recursive model of the market for new lawyers. *Review of Economics and Statistics* 57: 171–179.

Freeman, R. (1975b). Overinvestment in college training. *The Journal of Human Resources* 10: 287–311.

Freeman, R. (1975c). Supply and salary adjustments to the changing science manpower market: physics, 1948–1973. *American Economic Review* 65: 27–39.

Freeman, R. (1977). Decline in economic rewards to college education. *Review of Economics and Statistics* 59: 18–29.

Freeman, R. (1979). The effect of demographic factors on age-earnings profiles. *Journal of Human Resources* 14: 289–317.

Freeman, R. (1980). The facts about the declining economic value of college. *Journal of Human Resources* 15: 124–142.

Freeman, R., and Holloman, J. (1975). The declining value of college going. *Change* 7: 24–31, 62.

Freiden, A., and Leimer, D. (1981). The earnings of college students. *Journal of Human Resources* 16: 152–156.

Garfinkel, I., and Haveman, R. (1977). *Earnings capacity, poverty, and inequality.* Institute for Research on Poverty Monograph. New York: Academic Press.

Gintis, H. (1971). Education, technology and the characteristics of worker productivity. *American Economic Review* 61: 266–279.

Goldberger, A. (1978). Genetic determination of income: comment. *American Economic Review* 68: 960–969.

Gorman, J. (1967). *The Gorman Report.* Phoenix: Continuing Education Institute, Inc.

Greer, C. R. (1976). Returns to investments in undergraduate education by race and sex in 1960 and 1970. *Review of Business and Economic Research* 12: 57–68.

Griliches, Z. (1977). Estimating the returns to schooling: some econometric problems. *Econometrica* 45: 1–22.

Griliches, Z., and Mason, W. (1972). Education, income, and ability. *Journal of Political Economy* 80: S74–103.

Grossman, M. (1976). The correlation between health and schooling. In N. Terleckyj, (ed.), *Household production and consumption,* pp. 147–211. New York: Columbia University Press for NBER.

Grossman, M. (1982). *Determinants of children's health.* (Report PHS 81-3309.) Washington, DC: National Center for Health Services. (NTIS P380-163603.)

Hanoch, G. (1967). An economic analysis of earnings and schooling. *Journal of Human Resources* 2: 310-329.

Hansen, W. L. (1963). Total and private rates of return to investment in schooling. *Journal of Political Economy* 71: 128-140.

Hause, J. (1972). Earnings profile: ability and schooling. *Journal of Political Economy* 80: 108-138.

Hirshleifer, J. (1958). On the theory of optimal investment decision. *Journal of Political Economy* 66: 329-352.

Hunt, S. J. (1963). Income determinants for college graduates and the return to educational investment. *Yale Economic Essays* 3: 305-358.

Jencks, C., et al. (1972). *Inequality: a reassessment of the effects of family and schooling in America.* New York: Basic Books.

Johnson, G. E., and Stafford, F. P. (1973). Social returns to quantity and quality of schooling. *Journal of Human Resources* 8: 139-155.

Joy, O. M., and Bradley, J. O. (1973). A note on sensitivity analysis of rates of return. *Journal of Finance* 28: 1255-1261.

Juster, F. T. (ed.). (1975). *Education, income, and human behavior.* New York: McGraw-Hill.

Knapp, C. B., and Hansen, W. L. (1976). Earnings and individual variations in postschool human investment. *Journal of Political Economy* 84: 351-358.

Koch, J. V. (1972). Student choice of undergraduate major field of study and private internal rates of return. *Industrial and Labor Relations Review* 26: 680-685.

Lando, M. (1975). The interaction between health and education. *Social Security Bulletin* 38: 16-22.

Leibowitz, A. (1974). Home investments in children. *Journal of Political Economy* 82: S111-131.

Leslie, L. L. (1984). Changing patterns in student financing of higher education. *Journal of Higher Education* 55: 313-346.

Liberman, J. (1979). *The rate of return to schooling: 1958-1976.* Faculty Working Paper. Urbana, Ill.: University of Illinois, Department of Finance.

Link, C. R., and Rutledge, E. C. (1975). Social returns to quantity and quality of education: a further statement. *Journal of Human Resources* 10: 78-89.

Lucas, R. E. B. (1977). Hedonic wage equations and psychic wages in the returns to schooling. *American Economic Review* 67: 549-558.

Marin, A., and Psacharopoulos, G. (1976). Schooling and income distribution. *Review of Economics and Statistics* 58: 332-337.

Mattila, J. P. (1982). Determinants of male school enrollments: a time series analysis. *Review of Economics and Statistics* 64: 242-251.

Maxwell, L. (1970). Some evidence on negative returns to graduate education. *Western Economic Journal* 8: 186-189.

McMahon, W. W. (1976). Influence on investment by blacks in higher education. *American Economic Review* 2: 320-324.

McMahon, W. W. (1981). *Expected rates of return to education.* (Faculty Working Paper No. 832.) University of Illinois at Urbana-Champaign.

McMahon, W. W. (1982a). *Consumption benefits of education.* (Faculty Working Paper. No. 856.) University of Illinois at Urbana-Champaign.

McMahon, W. W. (1982b). *Externalities in education.* (Faculty Working Paper No. 877.) University of Illinois at Urbana-Champaign.

McMahon, W. W., and Wagner, A. P. (1981). Expected returns to investment in higher education. *Journal of Human Resources* 16: 274-285.

McMahon, W. W., and Wagner, A. P. (1982). The monetary returns to education as partial social efficiency criteria. In W. W. McMahon and T. G. Geske (eds.), *Financing Education,* pp. 150–185. Urbana: University of Illinois Press.

Mennemeyer, S. (1978). Really great returns to medical education? *The Journal of Human Resources* 13: 75–90.

Michael, R. T. (1975). Education and fertility. In F. T. Juster (ed.), *Education, income and human behavior,* pp. 339–364. New York: McGraw-Hill.

Michael, R. T. (1982). Measuring nonmonetary benefits of education. In W. W. McMahon and T. Geske (eds.), *Financing education: overcoming inefficiency and inequity,* pp. 119–149. Urbana: University of Illinois Press.

Miller, H. P. (1960). Annual and lifetime income in relation to education: 1939–1959. *American Economic Review* 50: 962–986.

Mincer, J. (1962). On-the-job training: Costs, returns, and some implications. *Journal of Political Economy* 70: 50–79.

Mincer, J. (1975). Education, experience, and distribution of earnings and employment: an overview. In F. T. Juster (ed.), *Education, income and human behavior,* pp. 71–93. New York: McGraw-Hill.

Okachi, K. (1983). Analysis of economic returns to Japan's higher education and its application to educational financing. *Journal of Educational Finance* 9: 185–212.

Parsons, D. O. (1974). The cost of school time, foregone earnings, and human capital formation. *Journal of Political Economy* 82: 251–266.

Psacharopoulos, G. (1973). *Returns to education.* San Francisco: Jossey-Bass.

Psacharopoulos, G., and Hinchliffe, K. (1973). *Returns to education: an international comparison.* San Francisco: Jossey-Bass.

Raymond, R., and Sesnowitz, M. (1975). The returns to investments in higher education: some new evidence. *Journal of Human Resources* 10: 139–154.

Reed, R. H., and Miller, H. P. (1970). Some determinants of the variation in earnings for college men. *Journal of Human Resources* 5: 177–190.

Ribich, T. L., and Murphy, J. L. (1975). The economic returns to increased educational spending. *Journal of Human Resources* 10: 56–77.

Rosen, S. (1975). Measuring the obsolescence of knowledge. In F. T. Juster (ed.), *Education, income and human behavior,* pp. 199–234. New York: McGraw-Hill.

Rosen, S., and Taubman, P. (1982). Changes in life cycle earnings: what do social security data show? *Journal of Human Resources* 17: 321–338.

Rumberger, R. W. (1980). The economic decline of college graduates: fact or fallacy? *Journal of Human Resources* 15: 99–112.

Schwartz, E., and Thornton, R. (1980). Overinvestment in college training? *Journal of Human Resources* 15: 121–123.

Seeborg, M. C. (1975). The effect of curricular choice on alumni income. *Journal of Behavioral Economics* 7: 151–172.

Siegfried, J. J. (1972–1973). Rate of return to the Ph.D. in economics. *Industrial and Labor Relations Review* 26: 420–431.

Smith, J. P., and Welch, F. R. (1978a). *The overeducated American? A review article.* Santa Monica: Rand Corporation.

Smith, J. P., and Welch, F. R. (1978b). *Local labor markets and cyclic components in demand for college trained manpower.* Santa Monica: Rand Corporation.

Solmon, L. C. (1975). The definition of college quality and its impact on earnings. *Exploring Economic Research* 2: 537–587.

Spiegleman, R. G. (1968). A benefit/cost model to evaluate educational programs. *Socio-economic Planning Sciences* 1: 443–460.

Taubman, P. (1976). Earnings, education, genetics and environment. *Journal of Human Resources* 11: 447–461.

Taubman, P., and Wales, T. (1973). Higher education, mental ability, and screening. *Journal of Political Economy* 81: 28–55.

Taubman, P., and Wales, T. (1974). *Higher education and earnings.* New York: McGraw-Hill.

Taubman, P., and Wales, T. (1975). Mental ability and higher education attainment in the twentieth century. In F. T. Juster (ed.), *Education, income and human behavior,* pp. 47–70. New York: McGraw-Hill.

Thurow, L. (1968). *The occupational distribution of the returns to education and experience for Whites and Negroes.* Washington, DC: Joint Economic Committee, Federal Programs for the Development of Human Resources (90th Cong., 2nd Sess.) 1: 276–284.

Wachtel, P. (1975). The returns to investment in higher education: another view. In F. T. Juster (ed.), *Education, income and human behavior,* pp. 151–170. New York: McGraw-Hill.

Wachtel, P. (1976). The effect on earnings of school and college investment expenditures. *Review of Economics and Statistics* 58: 326–331.

Webb, L. D. (1977). Savings to society by investing in adult education. In *Economic and social perspectives on adult illiteracy,* pp. 52–73.

Weisbrod, B. A. (1962). Education and investment in human capital. *Journal of Political Economy* 80: 106–123.

Weisbrod, B. A. (1964). *External benefits of public education.* Princeton: Industrial Relations Section.

Weisbrod, B. A. (1966). Investing in human capital. *Journal of Human Resources* 1: 5–21.

Weisbrod, B. A. (1972). Comment on John Hause JPE paper. *Journal of Political Economy* 80: S139–141.

Weisbrod, B. A., and Karpoff, P. (1968). Monetary returns to college education, student ability, and college quality. *Review of Economics and Statistics* 50: 491–497.

Weiss, Y. (1971). Investment in graduate education. *American Economic Review* 61: 833–852.

Welch, F. (1970). Education in production. *Journal of Political Economy* 78: 35–59.

Welch, F. (1974). Comment. In T. W. Schultz (ed.), *Economics of the family,* pp. 390–393. Chicago: University of Chicago Press for NBER.

Welch, F. (1979). Effects of cohort size on earnings: the baby boom babies' financial bust. *Journal of Political Economy* 87: S65–98.

Wessel, R. H. (1971). Ability and the returns on graduate education. *Western Economic Journal* 9: 208–210.

Wilkinson, B. W. (1966). Present values of lifetime earnings for different occupations. *Journal of Political Economy* 74: 556–572.

Witmer, D. R. (1970). Economic benefits of college education. *Review of Educational Research* 40: 511–523.

Witmer, D. R. (1980). Has the golden age of American higher education come to an abrupt end? *Journal of Human Resources* 15: 113–120.

Witmer, D. R. (1983). Let's increase college quality, funding and tuition. La Crosse, Wisconsin: Office of the Vice Chancellor.

Ziderman, A. (1973). Rates of return on investment in education: recent results for Britain. *Journal of Human Resources* 8: 85–97.

RESEARCH ON ACADEMIC PROGRAMS:
An Inquiry into an Emerging Field

Clifton F. Conrad, *University of Arizona*
Anne M. Pratt, *College of William and Mary*

Broadly defined, academic programs or curricula denote those educational experiences that encourage purposeful learning. Academic programs are forms at
the core of higher learning that organize the acquiring, transmitting, and applying of knowledge. Moreover, by housing and defining academic knowledge,
curricula serve as the major arena for academic decision-making and expression of institutional values, the focal point in the professional lives of most students and faculty, and the *raison d'etre* of American colleges and universities.
In short, although a form, the curriculum reflects the very substance of the educational enterprise. Form and substance, in turn, become synonymous, and
any discussion of curricular forms becomes a substantive discourse as well
(Pirsig, 1976).

There is a large and diverse body of scholarship on college and university academic programs. This corpus includes both an applied strain of essay and
opinion and a growing number of studies. Since the mid-1960s especially, the
subject has engaged scholars not only in higher education but also in such disciplines as history, sociology, and political science. Still, the literature on college
and university curriculum is unquestionably amorphous. Aside from a paper
by Toombs (1982), which helped in the preparation of this review, not a single
journal article or book offers a comprehensive review of the research on academic programs.

In light of this lacuna, we undertake to isolate and describe the major threads
of research on academic programs and to acknowledge major and representative studies within each of those threads. Our secondary purpose is to examine
critically each line of research by inquiring into the condition of scholarship
and making suggestions for future research. Therefore, we seek above all to
bring a fresh analytical perspective to extant knowledge about academic programs in colleges and universities. "The arrangement of material is new. . . .

Just as the same thoughts differently arranged form a different discourse, so the same words differently arranged form different thoughts," wrote Pascal (*Pensees,* 1670; Pantheon ed., 1950, p. 358). We hope that the comparisons invoked offer an illuminating and meaningful perspective that will engage scholars in the field.

FRAMEWORK AND METHOD

This review is largely exploratory and is not an "integrative review" in the sense of being aimed at inferring generalizations about substantive issues from studies that address those issues (Jackson, 1980, p. 438). Therefore, the various techniques of integrative reviews, such as meta-analysis (Glass et al., 1981), were inappropriate to our purposes. Nevertheless, a framework and method were needed both to organize and analyze the literature and to flesh out major areas of research on academic programs.

As Toombs (1982) suggested, research on academic programs is analogous to field study in the social sciences. Zelditch (1962) developed a framework for classifying field-study information, a framework that provides a useful point of departure for organizing studies of academic programs. In brief, the Zelditch framework identifies three broad categories of information or data: (1) incidents and histories, (2) distributions and frequencies, and (3) generally known rules and statuses. This typology is limited only to placing data into classes and is not intended as a structure for classifying what can be "inferred" or "explained" from such data. As we noted earlier, however, consideration of the forms of any phenomenon (whether it be the forms of curricula or of research on curricula) likewise includes consideration of the substance of that phenomenon.

Our overall analytical framework derives not only from the Zelditch classification scheme but also from a perspective that views colleges and universities as information-processing organizations (Miller, 1978). In essence, this perspective rests on the proposition that curricular forms are basically a "shared language" used to describe academic programs (Katz and Kahn, 1966). This shared language provides abstract concepts that academe employs as part of the process of "informing" or shaping higher learning. Similarly, it can be said that our review involves organizing a part of the shared information on curricula in order to distinguish the discernible shapes of curriculum research.

In describing some of what we know about these information-processing organizations, we also consider colleges and universities and the curricula lodged in them as evolving social systems (Miller, 1978; Boulding, 1984). Compatible with this view is the supposition that colleges and universities have only two principal categories—information and matter-energy—of those many elements comprising their makeup (Miller, 1978). We further propose that the kind of information transformation that occurs signals the kind of change or learning—individual and organization—that takes place.

Within the context of this analytic framework, we employed the constant comparative method to delineate major threads of research and to identify major and representative studies. While this method, as first developed by Glaser and Strauss (1967), is an inductive approach aimed at discovering theory, it is appropriate to our purposes even though we are not developing theory. In brief, the constant comparative method is a process by which the researcher systematically sorts and analyzes data while moving from the empirical to the conceptual and theoretical level through the identification of underlying patterns in the data. (For a discussion of the constant comparative method, see Conrad, 1982; Glaser and Strauss, 1967.)

Our literature review draws from four sources. First, we used two indices, *Dissertation Abstracts International* and the *Educational Research Information Clearinghouse,* to identify studies of academic programs published between 1974 and 1984. Second, over the same period, we searched for articles on curriculum in seven scholarly journals: *Review of Higher Education, Journal of Higher Education, Research in Higher Education, Review of Educational Research, Teachers College Record, American Educational Research Journal,* and *History of Education Quarterly.* Third, references cited in the above two categories pointed to additional books, articles, and book chapters. Finally, we perused the recent social science and higher education literature to identify the most current publications.

Our review of the literature yielded some 465 publications concerned with academic programs. We reduced this number through two major delimitations. First, we excluded the extensive body of essay and opinion on curriculum. Second, we omitted all other applied strains of scholarship, such as the literature on program evaluation and guidelines for curriculum planning. Applying these limitations, we reduced the total number of relevant books and articles examined to 210 publications.

Consistent with our analytic framework and the guidelines of the constant comparative method, our data collection and analysis focused on the following research question: What are the major lines of inquiry to which researchers continue to adhere in scholarship on academic programs? The systematic review of the 210 publications included in the final pool led to the identification of six major lines of inquiry.

This paper is divided into three major sections derived from Zelditch's tripartite classification scheme. For each of the six lines of inquiry, we identify major and representative studies, critique the literature, and make some suggestions for future research.

INCIDENTS AND HISTORIES

Zelditch (1962) defined the study of "incidents" as the consideration of individual cases at particular times and places. One such type of incident identified in this review is the case study of academic program innovations. A second type of incident, of the same kind but of a more complex configuration, denotes "sequences of incidents" or "histories" of academic programs. Finally, a third kind of incident, a complex configuration based on repeated observations spanning multiple cases, is that of studies of the process of academic change. These three lines of research, all of which fit within Zelditch's scheme (1962) for classifying information, are considered below.

Case Studies of Innovation

Whether as detailed case studies or as unfettered descriptions of innovative academic programs, the scholarship of the last 15 years evinces a fascination with curricular innovation and reform. Despite the attention given to the topic, however, relatively few studies place program innovations in any sort of context: the majority focus more on isolated incidents than on either patterns within eras or evolving histories. In instances where scholars have attempted to isolate contemporary trends—that is, to define trends during the very era in which such (purported) trends have been manifested—the objectivity of the description or analysis is suspect. It is difficult to make clear, useful distinctions between mere incidents and the more important trends when one is standing amid the phenomenon being described. No less telling, because each incident or trend is usually treated as separate from the evolving history of a program, most studies fail to provide the historical context essential for a deeper understanding of the innovation process.

In studying innovation, we must be constantly on the alert for surprises. Innovative programs are, in one view, "happenings" or events that did not have to occur just when they did (Boulding, 1984; March, 1978). The very celebratory tone of the innovation literature provides testimony to the value placed on freshness. Boulding (1984) asserted that information, to be information, must be surprising. Thus, when surprises do occur, an ability to discern and identify such surprises as such lies at the heart of acquiring "know-how" (Simon, 1981) about the system. The fact that so many surprises do appear in the literature lends credence to the notion of indeterminacy or uncertainty as regards curricular innovation. Yet, at the same time, it also suggests that we should inquire into whether the innovative incidents described really are surprises. They may be variations on a durable curricular form. This consideration may be a critical one, for durability does bias our images of what we know and how we know it. Making conceptual distinctions between variation and innovation involves a willingness, first, to evaluate our own methods for making meaning, and next, to determine the extent to which we are able to learn from surprise, and then, to analyze the curricular characteristics that we have invented to organize learning.

How, then, have scholars described innovative incidents? One widespread tendency has been to provide brief descriptive portraits, usually of popular reforms. For example, Brick and McGrath (1969, p. 2) surveyed 882 colleges to develop a "picture of novel and creative practices" in liberal education. They identified numerous curricular innovations, such as interdisciplinary studies and freshman seminars. Drawing on secondary sources, Heiss (1973) published a lengthy listing (including brief descriptions) of popular reforms that still stands as the most comprehensive inventory of curricular innovations in higher education.

In their study of undergraduate education, Levine and Weingart (1973) examined seven areas of experimentation at twenty-six schools. The areas investigated include advising, general education, comprehensive examinations, concentration, and student-centered curricula. Levine and Weingart went beyond mere description in their fieldwork: they also examined the successes and failures of the various innovations as perceived by those involved in the programs.

Bergquist et al. (1981) and Conrad (1978b) have offered vignettes of innovative programs and practices derived from secondary sources. Bergquist and his colleagues gave little indication of their methods, so it is difficult to relate their findings to how they came by the knowledge. Conrad, in contrast, explicated his approach to identifying curricular innovations and delineated his definition of an innovation—a useful clarification for researchers seeking to remain alert to surprises. By the same token, the framework offered by Bergquist et al. may prove useful to researchers. The authors identified six dimensions of curricula and curricular innovation: time, space, resources, organization, procedures, and outcomes.

For some years Levine's *Handbook on Undergraduate Curriculum* has functioned as the curriculum encyclopedia for some in the field. Levine shed some light on historical and comparative perspectives worthy of consideration by those studying the curriculum, and he attempted to distinguish successful innovations from ephemeral ones. As in so many treatments of innovation, however, Levine's handbook offers little more than brief descriptions of innovative practices, such as new forms of general-education distribution requirements and novel calendar arrangements.

Studies by Conrad and Wyer (1980), Fitzgerald (1980), and Gaff (1983) focus on innovations in a limited segment of the curriculum: liberal and general education. While these studies have somewhat better articulated methodologies than the aforementioned works, the representativeness of what is reported remains in question, and not much sense of the richness of contexts and consequences is provided. "Know-what" and "know-how" about the system (Simon, 1981) remain separate, and to make distinctions between information (e.g., a new informing structure) and repetition (e.g., variations on an older, durable structure) in these studies is a trying task.

There also exists a body of more extensive descriptive and analytic portraits of curricular innovations. These treatments are based, for the most part, on ethnographic research and are richer than the studies mentioned thus far. Furthermore, these works emphasize "telic" as well as "popular" reforms (Grant and Riesman, 1978), a distinction that offers a useful point for explanation, analysis, and departure. In differentiating between the two, Grant and Riesman (1978) suggested that

> some of the reforms have a large resonance, representing attempts not only to change the university but to set forth new ideals. We call these telic reforms, reforms pointing toward different conceptions of the ends of undergraduate education, to distinguish them from the more popular reforms of the last decade. [p. 15]

The distinction between popular and telic is reminiscent of the difference some theorists note between information and entropy. According to these theorists, "negentropy," or information, moves in the direction of a less probable course (surprise), while "entropy" moves in the direction of a more probable course. Information has descriptors such as form, regularity, accuracy, pattern, order, and organization (Miller, 1978). Despite these properties, which seemingly denote a high degree of stability, information constantly expands. Consequently, it is important to know what is new and what is not. What is imitative, form- or rule-following? What is not? Grant and Riesman's definition (1978) of telic reform implies information; their definition of popular reform does not. The systematic analysis of this issue may itself comprise a productive research avenue: Where did values, ideals, and norms change, and where did procedures and routines change but not the organizing principle?

Numerous studies have emphasized in-depth analysis of curricular innovations. For example, two largely quantitative treatments, one by Lehmann and Ristuben (1983) and the other by Bush (1979), emphasize popular reforms in consortia. Although neither is a seminal piece, each evidences some useful description and analytic grist essential to the comparative millwork required to refine our notions about academic innovation. In order to carry these two studies further to ascertain what is information and what is not, we would need an initial set of distinctions in two areas: that of the notion of consortia as new and that of the notion of newness as regards the particular incident(s) we are investigating. An analogy to elucidate: The writing of a new poem may provide not new information so much as new meaning (Miller, 1978); likewise, a new curricular arrangement may fall into a category marked less by new information than by new meaning.

We can combine and recombine information to yield new meanings that eventually may turn into new forms. This phenomenon—the evolution from old to new—is not well documented in curriculum research. In turn, it remains difficult to be on the alert for surprise when the background necessary for differentiating the old from the new has not been filled in. To be sure, some of the finer treatments do move in this direction. While based on secondary sources, Bell's case studies (1968) of three telic reforms in general education (at Columbia, Harvard, and the University of Chicago) provide an encompassing perspective. In straining these institutional experiences through the sieve of historical and sociological contextual analysis, Bell came to attribute meaning to reforms in provocative ways. The third chapter of his book, "Tableau of Social Change," reflects a thoroughness of traditional sociological analysis rarely seen in the literature on academic programs. On the one hand, the self-documented processes of Bell's thought as he categorized information might prove useful to those wishing to better understand how we have tended to think about curriculum innovation. On the other hand, the implied developing curricular hierarchies or sociological inevitabilities that surface in Bell's work may well overshadow, by comparison, any surprises on which learning might turn.

From a perspective less provocative than that of Bell, Belknap and Kuhns (1977) reviewed a telic reform in general education at Columbia University. Using a quasi-historical emphasis, Belknap and Kuhns traced the evolution of general education at Columbia and suggested that revitalization has been a prevailing theme. Again, the question arises: Did people (at Columbia, in this instance) try to breathe new meaning, more relevant to a particular age and locality, into old, durable forms that traditional norms and values in the university would accommodate? Or did they attempt to create information (new informing patterns) in suitable, workable ways that altered the traditional norms and values of the university? Or did they try to do both?

The remaining literature reviewed here in brief involves the extensive work spearheaded by four individuals: Riesman, Grant, Gusfield, and Gamson. Much of the "refined grist" heretofore mentioned as necessary to promote thinking about curricula may emerge from ethnographic works of high quality. Riesman et al. (1971) offered first-rate case studies of popular institutions, Oakland and Montieth, that began in the late 1950s. While the authors stated their concerns as being those primarily related to faculty, their work lends valuable insight into incidences of institutional response to social change. Specifically, in interpreting how these two institutions responded to an influx of "new students," the authors not only delved critically into several aspects of information processing in academe but illustrated the dilemma that would-be reformers faced as they struggled with the interfacing of traditional with unfamiliar forms.

Grant and Riesman (1978) stressed the important distinction between popular and telic reforms as they wove rich ethnographic tapestries. Their wonderfully descriptive case studies, both of three telic reforms (St. John's College, Kresge College at Santa Cruz, and the College for Human Services) and of several popular reforms (New College, Santa Cruz and two experimental public colleges in New Jersey) display sustained analytic temper.

Finally, Grant et al. (1979) and Gamson et al. (1984) have presented well-done case studies of popular reforms. Grant and his associates looked at competence-based reforms, Gamson and her colleagues at fourteen innovative programs in diverse institutions. The strength of both of these works lies in their authors' attempts to render contextually grounded analyses. Furthermore, these studies convey a sense of the importance of two considerations that would surely benefit curriculum researchers: (1) the shared language of curricula, which can be applied across institutions with variations in meaning from one place to another and (2) the similarities of curricular design across institutions, with variations in application from one place to another.

Histories

A second matter demanding attention in research on academic programs involves knowledge of how a curriculum has evolved to its current state. Institutional histories and historical descriptions of the underpinnings of an institution's curriculum can provide a meaningful historical context for the present. As Miller (1978) wrote, a college or university "carries its history with it in terms of altered structure and consequently of altered function also" (p. 23). For purposes of research, then, it may be useful to distinguish the structures of a college or university as they exist at any single point in time or space. Yet another useful distinction involves the recognition that information and structure are connected so that one can speak of the structure(s) (or forms) of the curriculum—a conceptual or temporal configuration. For example, the structure of knowledge in a discipline involves patterns of conceptual variables. The department that houses the discipline involves patterns of spatial variables. Indeed, much of the business of higher education involves translating information from one state or place or configuration to another. Moreover, patterning among conceptual or temporal variables can compare with patterning among spatial variables. For instance, transforming a written design for a curriculum into a desired sequence of educational experiences or happenings is, in a very real sense, a translation of conceptual variables to spatial variables and the reverse (Miller, 1978, pp. 22–23). Since this translation process is a difficult one to delineate empirically, the distinction between spatial and temporal dimensions, between physical space and conceptual space, remains an important one for researchers.

For example, an institution's charter represents a blueprint similar to DNA. As DNA provides a chemical blueprint for human growth and development, so does the charter establish a conceptual template by which one can organize the institution and its curriculum in a manner faithful to the legal mandate. Also, like DNA, charters evolve to keep pace with the environment. Often collective perceptions or public mandates (which themselves are evolving) greatly influence what can and will occur on college campuses (Kamens, 1974).

Moreover, the evolutionary nature of colleges and their curricula makes them rather unpredictable beasts, inasmuch as the factors that contribute to their makeup are so many and varied and events border on the random: such evolutionary systems have as a part of their histories events that did not have to occur when or even in the manner in which they did. We can view evolution itself as basically a process in which information and its derivatives provide the "know-how" for the informing structure(s). And if, indeed, "printing is the social equivalent of DNA" (Boulding, 1984, p. 20), then one can see how the process of information replication in academe expands what we know, as we wish to know it, even as the future state of the system becomes increasingly probabilistic.

To be sure, most series of events have identifiable trends, so that we can assume that some events are more likely to occur or recur than are others. Certainly histories can enhance our ability to prognosticate, even though such commentaries suffer from imperfections in the record and limitations of human evaluation. We must be careful as we read them, moreover, about placing a high value on phenomena we recognize and like and placing a low value on phenomena we dislike or find unfamiliar. Nevertheless, beyond these residues or effects of past events, what do we have? The "right stuff" from which fruitful historical research on curricula derives no doubt demands two basic characteristics of the researcher: the patient scholar's well-honed penchant for humble skepticism (Phenix, 1971) and the self-aware lover's awe at subtle surprise. Otherwise, we will not be able to learn from surprise, adapt our perspectives, and eliminate our more unrealistic images of how things are and how they might affect our future (Boulding, 1984).

We begin our review of curricular histories by identifying two distinct approaches to the history of higher education: the so-called traditionalist perspective and the revisionist perspective. While a linear or continuous motif seems to underlie substantial portions of each approach and thus makes them somewhat similar, the interpretations of these two schools provide points of divergence, contrast, and comparison. To begin with, the traditionalists seem to be infinitely more readable than the revisionists because of their use of anecdote and personality to provide the glue to bind their theses; by contrast, revisionist histories often tend to be dry reading, perhaps as a result of quantitative approaches. Nevertheless, each approach suffers from what we could call the objective reality syndrome, an approach that tends to obscure any surprises that might surface, either now or in the past. To be sure, the revisionists (to their credit) have uncovered some unanticipated quantitative data, but they fail to apply their statistics in a nonlinear fashion that illuminates the probabilistic manner in which evolving processes converge to result in a historic event. Our view of information transformation looks upon surprises as improbable convergences, which, in turn, suggests the need for a different kind of historical synthesis from the one that is currently evident.

The traditional histories of higher education are, for the most part, well known. In his history of American colleges and universities, Rudolph's discussion (1962) of curricula interpenetrates his entire volume. Veysey (1965) focused on the period from 1865 to the early twentieth century; in so doing, he offered some organizing concepts that may prove useful to future researchers. Brubacher and Rudy (1976) linked historical data cross-sectionally, lending a clear sense of overriding themes.

Two slim volumes of historical essays, one by Handlin and Handlin (1970) and the other by Thelin (1982), sketch broad perspectives of the evolution of higher education. Each volume occasionally addresses the topic of curriculum, though more thoroughly in Handlin and Handlin's than in Thelin's work. Each work attempts to place academic programs within the context of their respective societies; each also points to the difficulties inherent in relating contemporary themes or issues to past events.

These general histories of higher education share two important features. First, all point to the significant stature of the academic program in the legacy of higher education. Second, all emphasize the vital relation of the curriculum to society. Nevertheless, all share an unfortunate defect: thoroughness of historical synthesis remains a rare occurrence.

This lack of thoroughness, in part, has provided fuel for the revisionist inquiries. Blackburn and Conrad (1985) provided some insight into the traditionalist-revisionist debate. By using such organizing categories as curriculum and instruction, learning, leadership, and exclusiveness, Blackburn and Conrad provided useful tools for the analysis of evolving academic programs and examined the evidence for the revisionists' claims. They suggested that curriculum should be a primary test site for the nascent revisionist perspective.

In defending the antebellum college, the revisionists assume the very reverse of several traditional postures toward higher education's past. They suggest that the curriculum was not hostile to science, that teaching was not uninspired, that the extracurriculum was not impoverished, that students were not cloistered in closely held residences, that enrollments did not fail to remain abreast of population growth, and that college birthrates had not been incontinent and death rates extremely high (Metzger, 1984, p. 420). Still, revisionist research scarcely evidences thoroughness of historical synthesis. It is too early to tell whether revisionist reinterpretations depict historical reality more accurately than do traditional perspectives.

At this juncture, the importance of the revisionists' postures lies in their willingness—indeed, their zest—in rethinking issues of evolutionary academic systems. For example, Potts (1981) examined enrollments to assess the popularity of antebellum colleges. Yet, while Potts persuasively questioned the traditional evidence, he did not provide counterevidence with which to revise the standard posture. Perhaps Burke (1982) stands foremost among those calling for a revised perspective. He described, and gave supporting evidence for, the antebellum colleges as "flexible and dynamic" institutions (p. 6); as anything but adrift in a sectarian or provincial, conservative backwater; and as a collegium responsive to the nation's expanding economy. Moreover, Burke took Tewksbury (1932) to task by refuting the latter's reported birth and death rates for institutions in the first half of the nineteenth century.

A modest number of general histories specifically address the curriculum; two representative ones are by Butts (1939) and by Rudy (1960). In particular, Butts's portrayal of the debates between Hutchins and Dewey in the 1930s and his overall historical development of the college curriculum stand as exemplary traditionalist interpretation. Similarly, Rudolph's (1977) standard history of curriculum from 1636 to 1977 has offered the revisionists a potentially vulnerable target.

In contrast, Oleson and Voss (1979) refined their research aperture to review selectively the organization and development of knowledge in colleges and universities from 1860 to 1920. Oleson and Voss paradoxically pointed to the absence of research on some basic "informing" structures of college and university curriculum that fall under the rubric of the organization and structure of knowledge. Given the contemporary emphasis in several disciplines on the technologies of information and on information organization, one wonders about the comparative void of similar analysis of information "technologies" and organization in college and university curricula. Certainly, scant commentary exists in histories of American higher education. For example, Sloan (1971) discussed current difficulties in higher education and its analytic literature and reconstructed several historical incidents. However, his article stops short of doing more than suggesting a need for better reinterpretation and analysis of some older organizing forms of curricula.

Finally, there are the more specialized histories of general or liberal education. Thomas (1962) traced the development of general education from 1800 to 1930 and then examined more recent practices in general education in eighteen colleges and universities. In addressing the problem of liberal education in the modern university, Wegener (1978) provided a selective history of the evolution of American higher education. In doctoral dissertations, LeBlanc (1980) and Koch (1979) have traced the recent history of general education and have occasionally offered fresh perspectives.

Perhaps most engaging of recent dissertations is Kimball's work (1981), which represents fine scholarship marked with a clarity of analysis seldom seen in conjunction with the topic of liberal or general education. Of particular interest to students of the history of curricular forms (for liberal and general education) is Kimball's delineation of two ideals and two accommodations. These ideals and accommodations—*"artes liberales,"* "liberal-free," *"artes liberales* accommodation," and "liberal-free accommodation"—encourage us to consider the ontological grounding of curricula. If carried further, such treatments of evolving curricular histories might become less suggestive of continuous or consistent processes. We might be able to envision better how events have happened as a result of improbable occurrences. To a large extent, Kimball's thorough discussion accomplishes this very task, even as he carefully separated issues of definition and philosophy of liberal education. Furthermore, and no less important, Kimball's work underscores the need for more inquiry into the historic foundations of the information transformation process in academe.

Academic Change
Contemporary studies of academic change would also benefit from the examination of change as a process of information transformation. Until the late 1960s, there was a paucity of research on the dynamics of change in higher education. To be sure, opinion pieces and case studies of innovation broached the topic, but few scholarly works examined change as a process. The last 15 years, however, have witnessed a sharp upturn. The current scholarly focus on change, which includes studies of the initiation and implementation of curricular innovations and reforms, is one manifestation of the more general focus on processes of organizational change.

Given the "newness," the apparent timeliness, and the volume of research, diversity of scholarship on the topic is hardly surprising. Not only do the various change studies often employ different theoretical frameworks, but some focus on the initiation stage, others on the implementation stage, and still others on both stages. Moreover, while nearly all studies seek to delineate factors associated with change, emphases shift from one study to the next. Some scholars examine agents of change, some the process of change, some the obstacles to change, and some most or all of these dimensions. Despite this diversity, however, students of academic change seldom address the phenomenon as a process of information transformation (except indirectly as a communication phenomenon).

In related research, which one might use as a point of departure in addressing this oversight, Argyris (1976) has equated change with learning and, in so doing, has drawn a distinction between kinds of observable learning behaviors. Argyris's use of the terms *single-loop* and *double-loop learning behaviors* (p. 363) is not unlike some theorists' use of the terms *positive* and *negative feedback* (Miller, 1978). Single-loop learning (or change) behavior appears to be

more imitative, routine, or rule-abiding, characteristics that also mark a negative feedback loop. Double-loop learning behavior looks more like rule- or
policy-changing behavior, which is akin to a positive feedback process. In an
attempt to maintain dynamic equilibrium, negative feedback is adaptive and
adjustment-oriented; positive feedback processes serve to upset dynamic equilibrium. Unchecked positive-feedback processes result in chaos and ultimately
in a system's demise. Although the higher education literature attempts to delineate the positive and negative aspects of change, such evaluations rarely encourage comparisons to positive or negative feedback processes as they relate to
organizational or curricular change.

Extant reviews of the literature on organizational change, both changes in
higher education in general and academic change in particular, abound and
vary in perspective (Conrad, 1980; Dill and Friedman, 1979; Lindquist, 1978,
pp. 1–30; Nordvall, 1982; Parker, 1980). Given the volume and diversity of the
research, we limit ourselves to proposing some initial organizing foci. We begin
by discussing several major, encompassing studies. Next, we examine some representative studies in two major areas of research on change—change in general
education and academic change in community colleges. Finally, in partial summary and as a touchstone both for criticism and for thinking about future research, we consider a review of the research by Dill and Friedman (1979).

Of the comprehensive studies, Hefferlin's study (1969) is a landmark one,
the first comprehensive, theoretically framed study of the modern period.
Hefferlin looked at 110 institutions to examine the sources, processes, correlates, and agents of academic change. In the wake of Hefferlin's work, other
studies soon followed, turning on such generalizations by Hefferlin as follows:

> Students are seen as more influential in having courses added to the curriculum than
> in any other development. Faculty members are most influential in getting a program
> of study added to the curriculum. Administrators are most influential in getting
> requirements changed and in adding new units to the institution and trustees and out-
> side agencies are most influential in altering the entire status of the institution [p. 79]

Future research might fruitfully explore Hefferlin's generalizations about
influential participants in certain aspects of a change process. His suggestions
about who usually attends to certain kinds of information and what the influence of their attention is represent useful points of departure.

In research on academic change based on 11 case studies, Ladd (1970) examined both the reasoning behind the changes and various dimensions of the
change process. Following his presentation of individual cases, Ladd made
comparisons across cases and identified numerous factors that had either
helped or hindered change. He considered the following elements of the change
process: institutional climate, committee makeup and procedures, degree of
involvement, reports, leadership, and institutional size and character (pp.
197–209).

Lindquist (1978) reviewed existing theories of change and knowledge utilization and then tested these theories through case studies of colleges and universities that had attempted to introduce curricular, administrative, or instructional reform. Lindquist's treatment may prove instructive for future research on change as information transformation. As the following excerpt illustrates, he combined several useful organizing concepts:

> Colleges and universities combine deeply rooted norms, values, structures, subgroups and power-relations with great complexity, low formalization and de-centralization of control. Many new ideas penetrate such organizations, but very few can budge the status quo . . . rarely does reform or innovation of much magnitude get implemented. [pp. 29–30]

Lindquist's conclusions broadly correspond to notions of single- and double-loop learning or positive and negative feedback, and they point to the kind and complexity of feedback processes involved.

In a study of the successes and failures of innovation, Levine (1980) focused on the institutionalization, or termination phase, of change. He proffered a theory of change in organizations and then examined his theory in a study of 14 structurally similar innovations in the experimental colleges of the State University of New York at Buffalo. Of significance for future inquiry is Levine's perspective of boundaries in the change process. According to Levine, any innovation abets institutional instability as a result of its encounter with established boundaries. When several such boundaries are confronted at once against a backdrop of scarce resources, conflict emerges. Only boundary expansion, to include the change, or boundary contraction, to exclude the change, can resolve such conflict. Moreover, Levine pointed out two additional dimensions of the change process—compatibility and profitability—which are relevant to any conceptualization of information processing.

One other encompassing study of the change process merits mention here, for its method as much as for its findings. Newcombe and Conrad (1981) used the constant comparative method to study the process of mandated academic change. In studying programmatic changes, they identified conditions that facilitated the effective implementation of Title IX of the Higher Education Amendments of 1972 in eight Virginia colleges and universities. The authors' investigations of feedback cycles and institutional subsystems are an important feature of their research. Newcombe and Conrad suggested stages for a mandated change process, but they stressed the dynamic, situational nature of these stages (pp. 565–572).

Turning to the literature on curricular change in two topical areas—general education and the community college—we cite several representative studies. Studies of change in general education have taken several directions (Conrad, 1978a; Gaff, 1980; Ighodaro, 1980; Manns and March, 1978; Pratt, 1984). The treatments of the topic discussed here reflect varied approaches, both in method and in conceptualization.

Using the constant comparative method, Conrad (1978a) examined changes in general education at four colleges and universities. He identified several processes that link pressures for change to a policy decision for change: conflict and interest-group pressures followed by power exertion, administrative intervention, faculty leadership exercised through interest-group advocacy, and compromises negotiated through administrative leadership.

In examining the initiation and implementation of a diffusion process, Ighodaro (1980) used a case study approach to study change in a core-centered curriculum. He drew from three prevalent models of organization—bureaucratic, collegial, and political—in order to identify organizational variables and then analyzed their impact on the two stages of the change process. Ighodaro found that, taken alone, none of the three traditional organizational models could adequately explain the process of decision making and change. His study also confirmed two widely held beliefs about change: (1) congeniality and effective conflict management facilitate both the initiation and the implementation of the diffusion process and (2) decentralization and low formalization impede the implementation of innovation.

In a study that can best be described as ethnographic, Gaff (1980) consolidated some of the information gleaned from the Project on General Education Models (GEM), a project designed to help facilitate curricular change at 12 diverse institutions. Basing his observations on the work of general education reform committees in the 12 institutions, Gaff addressed the flaws in 43 common strategies for change and suggested alternative strategies. Gaff's proposed strategies for reforming general education provide some useful insights but few surprises—nearly all of his strategies find support in the literature on academic change.

On a different tack, Manns and March (1978) looked at curriculum change in times of adversity. Where many have approached studies of change qualitatively, they employed a quantitative lens as well as a framework that can help to channel thinking about information usage. They found that curricula seem to change more under adverse financial circumstances than in times of favorable economic climate. Moreover, in using a market metaphor to analyze routine curricular changes, Manns and March made some noteworthy departures from the bulk of the change literature. They noted, for example, that the "organized anarchy" of academe results in inconsistent information processes. Such inconsistencies make it difficult to predict how educational ideals and pragmatics will combine to produce the effects we record. In turn, these observations suggest a whole series of possible avenues of research from the viewpoint of the curriculum as a temporal, information-processing structure in colleges and universities. For example, March and Simon's theories (1958) of limited attention, which incorporate their ideas of organizational slack and search, correspond roughly to theories of positive and negative feedback. In turn, research could examine these authors' notions of organizational learning behaviors as they compare to kinds of feedback.

In related qualitative research, Pratt (1984) extended a portion of Manns and March's work in a case study of routine changes over a ten-year period at a single institution. Examining such variables as change in course description, course additions, and change in prerequisite designations, Pratt found that change in one variable—course additions—reflected a concern with enrollment markets. Despite the exploratory nature of Pratt's research and thus the tentative aura surrounding her findings, some useful information-related themes emerged: she discussed notions of positive and negative feedback, of limited or selective attention, and of signs and symbols in curricular organization.

Numerous studies of academic change in community colleges have been conducted in the last several years (Allan, 1979; Chiaro, 1984; Drum, 1979; Roark, 1985; Zoglin, 1981). These studies evince a diversity of focus and analytic framework. For example, Drum (1979) submitted a questionnaire to 188 community colleges to collect data for a trio of reasons: to examine community college services to the elderly, to test the predictive accuracy of claims made by the services-to-the-elderly movement, and to test the power of certain internal and external organizational variables for predicting the introduction of distinctive courses (services) for the elderly. Drum's dissertation research showed that a social movement (represented in this case by services to the elderly) encourages the institutionalization of certain changes.

Yet another study of change in community colleges is also a dissertation, one that merits mention here for its organizing concepts. Allan (1979) viewed planned change as occurring in the manner of a gestalt and used Lewin's well-known model of change (1961) to examine the "unfreezing" phase of the process. In a survey of some ninety respondents, Allan examined whether respondents were "unfrozen" relative to their willingness to participate in a new project. Such a widely respected metaphor as Lewin's may well have paved the way for later studies concerning how limited or selective attention processes influence the ability to change. For example, boundaries "unfreeze" to admit new pieces of information and "refreeze" when new information has found an acceptable fit in the system. Moreover, the system's attention to information is allocated in relation to numerous competing demands on time and energy (March and Simon, 1958). And a system "learns" to select the appropriate information for survival, given all the demands placed on the system. In terms of basic organizing concepts, this approach has the effect of relating our notions of boundary permeability to ideas about positive and negative feedback.

With a narrower focus, Zoglin (1981) primarily examined the agents involved in changing curricular content. She found that "community college decision making is a pluralistic process that permits each segment of the curriculum to respond to a distinct set of determinants of particular relevance to its unique function" (p. 418). Unfortunately, Zoglin's lack of focus on the sources or correlates of change tends to limit her findings. In contrast, Chiaro

(1984) investigated the sources, processes, and agents of curriculum change in a two-year institution. He identified factors and agents associated with change in both a general education program and an occupational educational program.

Lastly, Roark's study (1985) represents one of the more vigorous examples of research in the area. In case studies of three community colleges, Roark examined changes in educational technology. Since technologies can be viewed as discrete areas of information (March and Simon, 1958), Roark's research provides a useful point of departure for future research on information transformation in colleges and universities. Roark identified a range of factors affecting the implementation of new educational technology as a means of better understanding the processes associated with the effective implementation of innovations.

To summarize this treatment of academic change, it is instructive to proceed from a well-known critique of the change literature by Dill and Friedman (1979). These two authors outlined four frameworks for research on academic change that were originally advanced by Gamson (1974): complex organization, conflict, diffusion, and planned change. In regard to the complex organization framework, Dill and Friedman noted that research usually proceeds from an analysis of the rate of organizational change. The variables typically investigated in this mode include age, complexity, formalization, centralization, stratification, system environment, and size; an innovation itself can even serve as a variable of change.

The conflict or political framework emphasizes interest groups as influential forces in the change process. Variables frequently examined in political frameworks include intensity of conflict, job mobility, duration of conflict, level of satisfaction with a change, and effectiveness of change. In addition, this framework tends to focus on the natural history of one particular innovation at a time, emphasizing the formulation of policy over its execution. In short, the conflict framework tends to emphasize the circumstances leading to change more than the implementation of change (Dill and Friedman, 1979, pp. 417–419).

The diffusion framework focuses on the way in which a change "diffuses" throughout a system. Studies using this model have attempted to distinguish between "adoptor" and "nonadoptor" units. Such variables as cosmopolitanism, location in social structure, and past record of innovativeness have been found to be useful in making such discriminations. Dill and Friedman (1979) pointed to a major limitation of this framework: the assumption that innovation is "good" and in need of adoption by all units (pp. 419–420).

The last framework, planned change, focuses on managing change through a change agent. This model assumes self-motivation by participants and emphasizes intervention and implementation. Depending on the kind of change examined, this framework tends to include such variables as level of intervention and attitudinal acceptance. Perceptions of the effectiveness of intervention strategies underlie this thread of research, and Dill and Friedman (1979) cited this as a limitation (pp. 420–425).

Dill and Friedman's analysis of the four frameworks is highly instructive, offering many organizing principles for future research. We also offer it for its representation of prevailing approaches to change research. Relatedly, the authors go from their review to propose forms for causal modeling that, while not necessarily assuming linearly related variables, emphasize monotonic relationships; that is, positive effects are always positive and negative effects negative (Dill and Friedman, 1979, p. 424). In our view, the incomplete information that we have about evolving curricula is not sufficient for us to generalize as yet about effects in such a fashion. Moreover, the subject–object dualism implicit in much of the change research remains a distinguishing characteristic of such causal models. If one's conceptual and analytic processes indeed remain ontologically grounded, as some current theory suggests, attempts at such "objective" research will be, at best, relative (Wolf, 1981). The heavy emphasis on qualitative research in the area of change suggests the nature of the difficulty of dealing quantitatively with the learning or change process. We scarcely suggest that quantitative research on change is unnecessary. Rather, we propose that empirical descriptions of change processes need a wide berth and that March (1978) and several of his colleagues in the study of organizational change seem to know the beast, albeit metaphorically.

DISTRIBUTIONS AND FREQUENCIES: NORMS AND OUTCOMES

Distributions and frequencies provide a foundation for comparative analysis in a field. We have identified two types of distributions and frequencies in our review of the literature on academic programs. One type consists of descriptive studies aimed at creating and maintaining normative data about academic programs across postsecondary education. A second type includes studies that examine the "outcomes" or "effects" of curricula on students.

Distributions and frequencies reported in the literature tend to be in a quantitative analytic mode. Even most qualitative-minded researchers underpin their work with some familiar assumptions that support a quantitative paradigm. From our perspective, the most important of these assumptions is that we can most fruitfully view distributions and frequencies as linear and sequential and thus can depict their directionality and/or sequence in logical mathematical statements.

To be sure, comprehensive mathematical pictures can offer useful points of contrast and departure as we seek to capture both curricular patterns and their effects on students. Yet, at the same time, we need to acknowledge the limitations of solely mathematical representations of reality in regard to evolving systems. As Boulding (1984) put it: "It has been said that if a proposition is not obvious, it is not mathematics, although it may take a considerable amount of intellectual work to show that something is in fact obvious" (p. 20). If something is mathematically "obvious," then the relationship depicted cannot be otherwise.

Herein lies a fundamental turning point for research on information-processing organizations. Wherever humans transfer information, the unpredictable often occurs: relationships are not always the same. In turn, the research on academic programs offers scant evidence of the "obvious" phenomena that are reported in fields such as physics. To complicate things further, contemporary description and explanation continue to suffer the biases of the researcher. In other words, our very notion of how humans transform, combine, or replicate information depends largely on the particular aspect to which we choose to attend, as does any "logical" description of any event. Even when statistics paint a mathematical picture of a curricular incident, the uncertainty absorbed (March and Simon, 1958) as one infers "meaning" from the statistics to elucidate the incident illustrates the burden of determining fixed relationships in evolving systems. In short, accurate measurement and prediction in relation to curricula suffer from the uncertainty and ambiguity inherent in their evolution.

Accordingly, we must view with caution all normative data that emerge in descriptive studies about curricula. The same caveat applies to studies of the outcomes or effects of curricula. Both kinds of studies lend only a snapshot of the remnants, residues, or visible aspects of a process. To extend the metaphor, the learning process for which the curriculum provides a structure remains, at this time, largely unphotographed. Therefore, we may predict the future from chronicled past events or trends with, at best, a considerable amount of uncertainty.

Normative, Descriptive Studies

Researchers and educators can employ the normative data that derive from descriptive studies as partial indicators of "what is" or "what was" about academic programs at particular times and from particular viewpoints, of course. When applied in contexts other than those of the original descriptions or measurements, however, commentaries on past or current curricular patterns do not reveal mathematically "obvious" representations: how people or institutions were operating may be well documented; but whether or how that information pertains to learning in another setting is not "obvious." Whether anyone—students, faculty, or administration—requires the recognition or approval of the people or institutions depicted in descriptive studies in order to encourage desirable learning outcomes in the future is not revealed as "obvious" information either. Nevertheless, we have traditionally used this kind of information to describe "norms" and to compare systems against these norms.

Notwithstanding this caveat, one major tactic of gathering normative evidence has involved the analysis of catalogs over time. Dressel and DeLisle

(1969) and Blackburn et al. (1976) provided a straightforward monitoring of trends in undergraduate requirements. Dressel and DeLisle's study stands as the first of the contemporary catalog studies, while Blackburn and his colleagues began their study shortly after the earlier one left off.

Dressel and DeLisle's investigation was concerned with current practices and with changes over the period from 1957 to 1967. With a sample of 322 institutions, Dressel and DeLisle reviewed the following areas of the undergraduate program: general education, majors, electives, individualizing and integrating experiences, and comprehensive curricular patterns both traditional and unusual. While offering a well-designed, comprehensive empirical study of current and changing requirements, Dressel and DeLisle noted the limitations of catalog analysis:

> There exist ambiguities and contradictions, and there is ever the problem of poor organization and of readability. A specific course in history is required, but it is not made clear whether this is in addition to or a part of the humanities requirement which lists history as an alternative. Inquiry in one such case elicited the response that advisors made their own interpretation! [p. 78]

This limiting statement clarifies the difficulties inherent in dealing with systems that continue to produce "happenings" (i.e., events that do not have to occur when they do).

On a tack similar to Dressel and DeLisle's, Blackburn et al. (1976) reviewed changing requirements from 1967 to 1974. While this study did not examine the very same curricular requirements as the earlier one, the research nevertheless suffered many of its limitations. The first phase of the Blackburn study focused on general education, the major, electives, and overall degree requirements at the undergraduate level. Among other interesting findings, Blackburn et al. found a decline in the proportion of general education courses as part of the total undergraduate program, an increase in the number of electives that students may submit to meet degree requirements, and virtually no change in the number of courses required for individual majors (pp. 33–35).

The Carnegie Catalog studies of 1975 and 1980, although unpublished, have been cited in several texts (Boyer and Levine, 1981; Carnegie Foundation, 1977; Conrad, 1983; Levine, 1978). On occasion, the literature discusses data on the major or on general education that are drawn from these two studies. Such occasions are far too few; these two studies deserve better illumination than from the once-removed perspective of selective citation. More direct interpretation of such data within institutions, for example, offers opportunities for contextually grounded contrast and comparison.

The studies by Dressel and DeLisle (1969) and by Blackburn and his colleagues (1976) endeavored to display the range and frequency of certain curricular events, and the authors' interpretations of these data have added the potential for increased depth of analysis. To seek further such depth, Blackburn and his associates (1976) narrowed somewhat the focus of the second phase of their study. By examining student transcripts from ten institutions (none of them two-year institutions) from 1967 to 1974, they investigated how students partook of curricula. The contribution of this phase of the Blackburn et al. study lies in the progress made toward painting a more detailed picture of events occurring at certain points in time. For example, Blackburn and his colleagues found students increasingly choosing to take electives in areas of specialization or depth rather than in the breadth portion of the curriculum (pp. 29-30). Following the lead of Blackburn, other studies (Beeken, 1982; Grace, 1984; Mapp, 1980) have used transcript analyses to investigate student course-taking behavior.

Qualitative analyses of trends in undergraduate education also appear in the literature (Conrad, 1983; Conrad and Wyer, 1980; Gaff, 1983; Gamson et al., 1984). These studies deserve consideration for their attempts to delve into features lying beneath the visible surface of a curriculum as depicted in a catalog or planning document. Nevertheless, these studies seem to fall short of providing illuminating insights: on the whole, they forego any analysis of the unpredictablity of the trends they delineate. In the process, the discontinuous, uncertain nature of events combining to produce a so-called trend receives short shrift. In these studies, trends often look as if they were built by successive stages, with little evidence of contrasting perspectives of the same phenomena. The absence of alternative perspectives with which a system might be usefully contrasted or compared limits the scope of many of these studies.

Conrad and Wyer (1980) sought to identify trends in liberal education by starting from a historical perspective rooted largely in Greek ideals of a liberal education. After reviewing documents from 100 institutions, they presented seven current trends in liberal education: the movement back to a required, integrated group of courses for students; the renewed interest in relating the outcomes of a liberal education to academic programs; the redefinition of liberal education in terms of process; the expansion of the curriculum beyond an emphasis on intellect to embrace the affective domain; the focus on values or moral education; the development of new relationships between the liberal arts and the professions; and the introduction of new ways to "deliver" the curriculum (pp. 25-35).

Concerning information transformation, a more productive research focus may involve less concern with trends in events *per se* and more analysis of the circumstances underpinning shifting events. This observation holds for the four studies mentioned above: Conrad's study (1983) of general education in community colleges, Gaff's study (1983) of general education, Gamson et al.'s study (1984) of fourteen innovative programs, and Conrad and Wyer's examination (1980) of trends in liberal education. All four studies penetrate, in varying degrees, the surface of the events that they delineate. Still, the embedded processes in individual and organizational learning, though raised occasionally as examples, remain largely beyond the careful treatment usually given to identifying trends. Until researchers adopt an equal consideration of the discontinuous elements that help to forge events—elements that relate to how people and the institutions they create make choices—we stand either to miss or be taken aback by significant events rather than to be pleasantly surprised by them.

Outcomes

This same lack of attention to embedded processes, circumstances, or conditions is particularly evident in the literature on outcomes. The studies of the outcomes or effects of higher education have provided veritable "laundry lists" of characteristics that people think are by-products of the academic enterprise. Indeed, it is vital to know the product of a learning process. Without such knowledge, it is difficult to evaluate the present or to set a future course. At the same time, much of the contemporary research on outcomes or effects may best serve as familiar indicators of some familiar events occurring at certain points, given some equally familiar assumptions. There is an underlying research question that, if appropriately examined, might provide insight into higher learning. This question has barely begun to be asked.

Such a research question is multifaceted. An initial facet involves asking about how students change in college (e.g., What is the impact of college?). Many data have surfaced here. So also have data surfaced antipodally: Does college make a difference (e.g., What is the difference between a college person and a noncollege person?)? Inquiring about a specific condition (attending college or not attending) that could be associated with an effect precipitates still another question: What other conditions contribute to higher learning? Unfortunately, this last question, though addressed repeatedly by researchers, has yielded few "obvious" data on learning, either inside or outside a college setting.

In the reviews of research on the outcomes of college, three major works stand out. Feldman and Newcomb (1969), Bowen (1977), and Pace (1979) have provided virtual compendia on college impact. Again, the studies cited in these volumes encourage linear thinking about college outcomes; they tend to emphasize the outcomes without giving equal treatment to those conditions or variables that may be associated with various outcomes. Feldman and Newcomb (1969), who reviewed 40 years of studies, focused mostly on affective outcomes. Bowen (1977) viewed both affective and cognitive effects, while Pace (1979) concentrated on cognitive ones. Analysis of curricular variables that might be associated with various outcomes is largely missing (except in the Feldman and Newcomb review, which examined the impact of major field of study).

In a major study of the outcomes of college, Astin (1977) confirmed many of Feldman and Newcomb's observations. From several longitudinal studies conducted between 1965 and 1974, Astin reported results on a number of questionnaire items: persistence in college, satisfaction with college, career plans, degree aspirations, extracurricular activities, self-concept, and attitudes and beliefs. Astin also examined whether various outcomes were related to certain characteristics of colleges (e.g., four-year versus two-year). Similarly, Winter et al. (1981) focused on cognitive and affective outcomes and linked various characteristics of liberal arts colleges to certain effects.

How the topic of curriculum fits in the research on college outcomes is difficult to ascertain. There simply has not been much research that examines the relationship between various curricular features and educational outcomes. Perhaps Chickering (1969), over 15 years ago, gave the best approximation of the current state of this genre of research: "At the outset it must be recognized that research documenting relationships between curricular systems and particular aspects of student development is like Vermont dirt roads in spring—muddy and soft" (p. 206).

We should not be put off by the mud, however. The lack of substantive research on the curriculum as a variable associated with learning processes is plainly evident. Even in the less-attended-to area of cognitive outcomes, there have been few attempts to relate curricula to effects. In turn, the overarching need to fill this gap demands more and different kinds of research. Even mud grows firm under proper conditions. It is premature to conclude, as some have, that the curriculum is not an important factor in learning. Research is badly needed that examines the relationship of the curriculum to learning or information transformation or change (which is the larger question being asked in an impact study): What is the learning or change which takes place, and what seems to encourage this kind of learning or change?

To be sure, some studies conducted in a single setting have attempted to differentiate between two curricular types as they may relate to differential outcomes. Usually the study has compared a traditional curriculum or curricular feature to an innovative one. As yet, research in this area has not come to incorporate comparisons of curricular types across a number of settings.

Two examples in this area are the work of Hendel (1977) and of Berson (1979). Hendel investigated transcripts of a group of graduates from an elective liberal-arts degree program and compared them with the transcripts of traditional liberal-arts graduates. He found that elective program graduates had more individualized programs and concentrated less within an academic discipline than did traditional liberal arts graduates. Further, elective program graduates tended to have slightly lower overall GPAs at graduation than did the comparison group (pp. 257–267). Basically, however, Hendel found few differences between students of the two groups when comparing performance on a number of traditional measures of academic success.

Similarly, Berson (1979) investigated the effects of an experimental, value-oriented liberal-arts curriculum on moral development. Contrasting a standard ethics course of study with the experimental one, and using an instrument designed by Kohlberg to measure moral development, Berson examined the curricular history of two groups of freshmen students participating in the comparison programs. Berson found the experimental curriculum to have no significant effect on moral judgment as measured by Kohlberg's instrument. Further, he suggested that the experimental program exhibited a lack of either any legitimate novelty (i.e., a genuinely changed program) or faculty and institutional support for the new, more interdisciplinary approach.

In noting that faculty, curriculum, and institutional ethics require attention when one focuses on the ethical growth of students, Berson raised an important point for all research in the general area of distributions and frequencies. These kinds of studies need to address what a curricular structure brings (or contributes) to the learning process as well as what the faculty (individually and collectively), the student, and the institutional environment bring.

Thus far, whether the outcomes under scrutiny are cognitive or affective, this genre of research has rarely touched on the learning relationships that describe academe. Instead, research has focused on the products that one might expect to realize from a college education. Without incorporating more information about the producers (faculty, students, administration, alumni, and participating "significant others") and the producing (acquiring, transmitting, and applying information in productive ways), such a body of research will remain inchoate. Thus, we remain uncertain about the underlying nature of the information transformation that occurs when both teacher and student learn—that is, when both walk away from an exchange wiser than they were before the exchange.

As if to address this elusive notion, two other approaches to college impact research have emerged. The first involves studies that have examined the paths of individuals developing through their college (undergraduate) years. As two examples, Perry (1968) and Heath (1968) have provided well-known data on student development that have spawned numerous follow-up studies. Perry looked at intellectual and ethical development, Heath at cognitive and affective development. Each of these studies also examined a male population and proceeded on assumptions of development that involve moving from some relatively simple and concretely related growth phases toward more complex and abstractly related ones, the phases being hierarchically arranged.

The strength of these studies lies in their attempts to seek out the substance that might link to some rather visible forms (e.g., traditional notions of curriculum and human development placed in a four-year period). The obvious limitations of these studies by Perry and Heath reside in their narrowness of research focus—on males in traditionally conceived settings (Harvard and Haverford).

Nevertheless, these studies do comprise a modest beginning toward identifying experiences or characteristics that may be associated with a curriculum. Moreover, if the curriculum is a form that faculty and students will use for purposes of organization, researchers need somehow to associate the substance of the learning process with the visible forms. The compelling caveat for assuming such an association is, stated broadly, that the learning process for which understanding is sought may be, in essence, an evolutionary one that is neither linear nor hierarchical, as many of the developmental studies imply.

Research in this area may take a cue from the findings by Pascarella and Terenzini (1976, 1978) on informal student-faculty interaction and the experience of students in their first year of college. The earlier study (Pascarella and Terenzini, 1976) examined freshmen perceptions of academic and nonacademic experiences associated with varying amounts of informal contact with faculty. The later study (Pascarella and Terenzini, 1978) looked at the relationship between student–faculty interactions and three freshman-year educational outcomes. Each study found positive correlations between student–faculty interaction and such factors as student persistence and self-perception of personal growth. Each study also emphasized the correlational nature of the research and advised caution in attributing causality or directionality to informal interaction and student outcomes.

Students who interact frequently with faculty beyond the classroom may do so because they are extracting academic or nonacademic meaning from classroom exchanges and hence are seeking additional association or exchange with those who abet such a process. Another possibility is the reverse: faculty who interact frequently with students beyond the classroom may do so because they are making meaning (in an academic sense) or personally meaningful use (in a nonacademic sense) of a classroom exchange and seek further association or exchange with those who encourage that. According to this view of information transformation, both faculty and students are learners in a complex exchange organized within certain curricular forms.

Along similar lines of reasoning, Pace's research (1980) has proceeded from the assumption that "what a student gets out of college depends, at least to some extent, on what he or she puts into it" (p. 10). In emphasizing that learning requires both time and effort, Pace suggested that time is a frequency dimension and effort a quality dimension. Using a method that employs fourteen scales related to use of college facilities and opportunities (as part of a more comprehensive questionnaire), Pace attempted to measure quality of student effort. The questionnaire, which was sent to thirteen colleges and universities, also requested extensive information about students' background and perceptions of the college environment. In addition, Pace gathered information concerning each student's "estimate of gains" regarding his or her college progress.

Computing all possible correlations among his measures of effort, environment, and outcomes, Pace reached the following conclusion:

> These relationships suggest a basic wholeness about the college experience. Personal and social experiences contribute to intellectual competencies and to general education; academic and intellectual experiences contribute to personal and social development and understanding. . . . [Q]uality of effort is clearly related to degree of attainment—the greater the effort, the greater the gain. Moreover, quality of effort is the most influential single variable in accounting for students' attainment. [p. 16]

Pace expanded on his findings for the National Commission on Excellence in Education (1982) and later in a monograph, *Measuring the Quality of College Student Experiences* (1984). In turn, a number of researchers have examined Pace's measures of quality of effort, sometimes in relation to a value-added concept of learning (Friedlander, 1980, 1981; Shaver, 1979; Lara, 1981; Porter, 1983). Friedlander (1980), for example, found substantial differences among students in quality of effort invested in certain opportunities and found these differences to be related positively to gains that students made toward educational goals. Similarly, Shaver (1979) found that students in different institutions invested their efforts differently.

Finally, the suggestion emerging from this vein of research is one of encouraging researchers to look at, among other things, quality of effort (both student and faculty) and its relation to the curriculum. As noted earlier, curricular forms serve as organizing mechanisms and exist at the center of the academic experience that research seeks to delineate. To be sure, research has produced a number of measures of such things as achievement, quality of effort, and outcomes. Some studies have attempted to link outcomes to particular curricular environments (Baird, 1977; Forest and Steele, 1978). But there is a need to define meaningful associations between the variables of the learning processes to which a particular curriculum provides some shape and even direction (by virtue of the progressive nature of requirements in certain programs). Such associations include comprehensive descriptions of the adaptive behaviors of participants, the exchanges taking place, and the outcomes of the process.

GENERALLY KNOWN RULES AND STATUSES: CONCEPTUAL FRAMEWORKS

One line of scholarship in the higher education literature corresponds roughly to what Zelditch (1962) referred to as "generally known rules and statuses." This scholarship has focused on the development and refinement of concepts and terminology in order to capture key features of academic programs. To be sure, the literature in this vein is, by definition, nonempirical and often includes a prescriptive dimension. Yet, at the same time, this literature represents an important thread in the research on academic programs, not least because it enables us to examine the extent to which the field has begun to develop conceptual building blocks on which a volume of research can firmly rest. Further, such conceptualization processes offer opportunities for associating problem-solving elements with fitting metaphors and perhaps, at some point, with appropriate theories (Saccaro-Battisti, 1983; Morgan, 1980).

Conceptual Frameworks

In an attempt to provide some closure, this concluding section seeks to pencil in portions of the literature where the communicative thrust has been one of outlining, designing, modeling, or sketching with broad strokes on a conceptual canvas. Mere sketching can in itself prove a useful tool to aid in organizing thought and action. Blau (1960) and Crane (1972), among others, have suggested that the development of a cognitive structure and a system of social interaction are two dimensions of any maturing field of study; indeed, the kind of collective sketching that occurs when a social system supports a field of study can at once help to define the field even as the field continues to evolve beyond successive temporal definitions. The importance of such sketching concerning information transformation in academic organizations lies in the creation of a design and in the taking of risks by so doing, in concert with others likewise willing to brave an exchange of such mental road maps. In essence, the higher learning resides in such exchanges.

So what do people suggest that the exchange of higher education is all about? The first block of literature treated here deals with models drawn mainly from work done in the area of general or liberal education. These specifically focused models tend to emphasize curriculum planning in a normative sense; we present them to lend a sense of special focus in modeling. For example, Vars (1982) outlined five curriculum designs in general education: (1) distribution requirements, (2) required courses, (3) correlated courses, (4) combined courses, and (5) integrative seminars. Through a discussion of the strengths and limitations of the five designs, Vars purported to illuminate alternative approaches to curriculum integration.

In comparison, Hursh et al. (1983) offered a single interdisciplinary model as a means of achieving the aims of general education. Noting that little agreement exists over the methods of such achievement, the authors addressed the integration of curriculum design and learning theory. Hursh et al. suggested, moreover, that

> the discipline-based recipe for general education could be improved upon and that one key for doing so [is] the introduction of multiple perspectives upon specific issues in order to exercise, among other things, skills of comparison, contrast, analysis, and above all, synthesis. [p. 44]

The authors juxtaposed the multiple perspectives of the disciplines with the "metaperspectives" characterizing each discipline. These metaperspectives include major disciplinary assumptions, major units of analysis, preferred forms of experimentation, preferred methods of data collection, preferred methods of data analysis, rules of evidence for asserting fact, relevance to specific problem, and definition of relevant concepts (p. 48). They also emphasized the perpetual aspect of learning in a world of competing goals, rapidly growing information bases, and shifting perspectives.

In a piece that deals with community college curricula, Myers (1979) offered yet another approach to design. He developed and evaluated a model for "curriculum engineering" that tends to address normative system maintenance. Myers's emphasis on the normative is not unusual in the literature. Such approaches can, if conducted in wholesale fashion, encourage a narrowness of perspective that tends to undercut the benefits of designing.

Where information is concerned, an important design perspective continues to be the broad philosophical underpinnings of a modeling process. Few models address personal or educational philosophy explicitly but evince a tendency only to imply that philosophical frameworks undergird the practical, necessary comparative renderings of curricular types (see Bucci, 1981). Since philosophies represent mental blueprints, we wonder at the wisdom of continued implicit allusion to these templates. Should not those drafting curriculum models employ the tools of the philosopher? If such tools were more explicitly evident, the users of the models would at least have more discrete ideas about the modeler's self-conscious distinctions of design. Further, normative models would show some connection with a value system, where philosophy remained outlined alongside values and norms.

One scholar has attempted such philosophical outlining. In a piece that is extremely helpful in explaining the notion of curriculum design, Toombs (1977–1978) arranged five philosophies of curriculum amid his ten design considerations. In his analysis of general education in eight colleges and universities, Toombs described the "problems and paradoxes" inherent in dealing with the curriculum as a field of study or as a structure at the center of the higher learning. Many of these problems, Toombs argued, may well have resulted from individual and collective acceptances of some rather arbitrarily chosen formal orders. Formal orders include such phenomena as the structure of knowledge in a field or modes of practice in a profession (some of which one sees posited as norms). Toombs wisely noted, however, that errors in dealing appropriately with curricula to date lie "not with the formal order but with the attempt to conceive of a curriculum from a limited frame of reference" (p. 20). Moreover, Toombs suggested that design represents an appropriate level of abstraction for dealing with curricula at this point. If it is necessary, as a part of problem setting and solving, to formulate an array of symbols, signs, numbers, and words to represent an event (Simon, 1969), then designing encourages the formation of such sets. In turn, the distant future may hold distinct possibilities for an eventual juxtaposition of carefully crafted curriculum designs with the constructs of another blueprint, such as evolving information transformation in concrete systems.

Moreover, it is useful, as a prelude to such a juxtaposition, to investigate existing approaches to design. Toombs' design considerations (1977–1978) fall under the general rubrics of content, context, and form (p. 24), components that he drew from various literatures. By way of comparison, Conrad and Wyer (1980) took an anecdotal approach to grouping models of liberal education, defending the appropriateness of this tack in light of the fledgling state of curricular definition and conceptualization. Conrad and Wyer outlined three models of general or liberal education based on actual usage. Their discussion of distributive, integrative, and competence-based models uses content, process, and outcomes as bases of analysis and comparison (pp. 43–49). These authors also made useful distinctions regarding the differences in several well-known attempts at generic—rather than content-specific—curricular modeling.

In a similar but more encompassing vein, a discussion of a number of influential generic curriculum models follows. Such a discussion can help to accomplish several tasks necessary to future comprehensive design efforts by, first, sketching an outline of the evolution of curricular modeling in higher education; second, underscoring the terminology common to modeling; and third, acknowledging any other apparent strengths and weaknesses of contemporary design efforts.

As an approach to curriculum description, planning, and analysis, Axelrod (1968) suggested thinking about academic programs in terms of systemic curricular dimensions or elements. Axelrod's three structural dimensions are content, schedule, and certification; his three implemental elements are group-person interaction, student experience, and freedom and control.

To provide guidance in constructing programs for undergraduates, Dressel (1971) presented a "structure for curriculum analysis." His modest model could function as a planning tool as well as an analytic framework, given his attempt at broad conceptualization. Moreover, the relationship between broad, cogent conceptualization and practical application remains a compelling impetus for ongoing modeling attempts at several levels of academic organization (e.g., department, school, institution, and system). Where information transformation or exchange takes place, such conceptual attempts remain an essential part of information organization.

In his model for curriculum analysis, Dressel (1971) first outlined four continua: individual student and disciplines; problems, policies, actions and abstractions, ideas, and theories; flexibility, autonomy or rigidity, and conformity; integration, coherence, and unity in and from learning experiences and compartmentalization, inconsistency, and discord in learning experiences. Next, he proposed five essential elements of curricula: liberal and vocational education, breadth and depth, continuity and sequence, conception of learning and teaching, and continuing planning and evaluation (pp. 21–29). Dressel's is one of the early efforts to address systematically such elements as breadth and depth in higher-education curricular models.

Mayhew and Ford (1971) also sought to describe "prevailing curriculum analysis" for a new decade by describing existing programs and critiquing the ideas of such figures as Tyler (1950) and Phenix (1964). They suggested that "with improved techniques of social research, and with improved information systems, it seems possible to obtain a great deal of information as to how the curriculum is working" (Mayhew and Ford, 1971, p. 91). Further, Mayhew and Ford thought that the building blocks of curriculum theory would eventually derive from gathering and disseminating routine evidence from faculty, administration, students, and alumni about what each was doing as it related to the curriculum. Comprehensive institutional research, held Mayhew and Ford, would approximate for faculty the insights that had previously been the province of the philosophers (p. 92).

Unfortunately, more and different kinds of information do not necessarily result in insight, philosophy, or theory. In the extreme, such abundance can result in an information overload that can encourage a retreat from philosophical or theoretical organization, so complex does the task appear, so uncertain do the results seem, so dense is the atmosphere surrounding insight. As noted earlier, people have limitations on their time, energy, and attention and thus will attend only selectively to incoming information (March and Simon, 1958). How would anyone be encouraged merely by the presence of more data to select more or different items to which to pay attention? Indeed, people "learn" what to take in and what to ignore, given a situation. Without some impetus for refocusing on more or different information, people are not likely to change their attention patterns. Mayhew and Ford (1971), while contributing to the discussion on curriculum modeling as it may lead to theory, did little to enhance conceptual organization to this end. They presented a number of helpful kinds of evidence (basically more normative information) for designers to employ but offered few substantive recommendations about conceptual organization. However, Mayhew and Ford did illuminate a number of curricular issues. The following issues have gradually come to be accommodated in more recent curriculum designs: cultural versus utilitarian emphases, general versus specific orientations, elective versus prescribed, elite versus egalitarian, student-oriented versus subject-matter-oriented, discipline-centered versus problem-centered, and scientific versus humanistic (pp. 2–5).

One of those later designs belongs to Bergquist (1977), who combined Mayhew and Ford's issues (1971) with Dressel's continua (1971) and added three curricular approaches that he had identified, all to produce eight categories of nontraditional curricula. Bergquist named his categories or models as follows:

heritage-based, thematic-based, competency-based, career-based, experience-based, student-based, values-based, and future-based. Bergquist (1977) acknowledged that his eight categories represent a "mixed bag of curricular dimensions. Several categories specifically refer to the content of the curriculum, while others refer to the way in which decisions are made about the curriculum or ways in which students are likely to learn" (p. 85). Bergquist then suggested five other dimensions worthy of design consideration: curricular breadth, locus of control, instructional process, curricular structure, and curricular outcomes.

Concerned with curriculum planning and analysis, Conrad (1978b)—like Bergquist—considered innovations in the development of his schema. Conrad's framework provides for traditional and nontraditional curricula by using four continua reminiscent of Dressel (1971) and five organizing principles that compare to those of Bergquist (1977). Conrad (1978b) proposed groupings "not primarily distinguished from one another at a broad philosophical level. . . . The crucial distinctions . . . lie in the way knowledge is organized and communicated" (pp. 13-14). Conrad differentiated five alternative principles for organizing the undergraduate curriculum: academic disciplines, student development, great books and ideas, social problems, and selected competencies.

The use of continua and typologies as means of approaching program planning surfaces frequently in the literature. In a later book, for example, Dressel (1980) expanded on his earlier continua. More recently, Bergquist et al. (1981) presented a typology of six curricular types, types that reflect a hierarchy of six curricular dimensions. These dimensions, which can serve as a generative system for curriculum categorization, include time, space, resources, organization, procedures, and outcomes (pp. 6-7).

Bergquist and his colleagues (1981) suggested that their dimensions are hierarchical "with reference to the profundity of change required when a decision is made to alter existing curricular structures within one or another dimension" (p. 6). For example, time and space changes are viewed as lower-order dimensions (and thus easier to change) than are procedures and outcomes. One should note, however, that this observation holds for change according more to prevailing Western than to Eastern conceptions of time and space. If, as many of these designers have noted, the curriculum needs to respond to multiple cultures, then such dimensions as these may function differently. Curricular structures will necessarily shift to accommodate multiple perspectives of time, space, organization, resources, procedures, and outcomes. Some of these shifts (relating to other perspectives) may not include the same linear progressions or hierarchical arrangements of curricula that we have traditionally depicted.

In an attempt to address a shift in perspectives, Conrad and Pratt (1983) incorporated many of the characteristics of the earlier-mentioned models and added the decision maker to the schematics. This approach has the effect of associating individual learning and organizational learning. Their suggestion that deciding and thus designing is an "everything-at-once" phenomenon introduced metaphor as an important design tool. In effect, by noting the holographic nature of human decision-making, these authors pointed to a contemporary means of dealing with the complexities of comprehensive curriculum design. That is, the linear thrust of current design efforts (to include Conrad and Pratt's model) might be alleviated by a holographic approach to design. To be sure, curricular conceptualization seems a long way from holographic presentation. For example, it remains difficult to draw full-dimensional pictures representing philosophy, epistemology, learning theory, or politics in a way that benefits current notions of design. In the meantime, however, our designs can begin to delineate the hand-in-glove layers of a fuller picture of these many aspects of a learning process.

In a modest way, the Toombs, Dressels, and Bergquists have begun this layering process. More recently and in reconceptualized summary, Conrad and Pratt (1983) have underscored internal and external curricular considerations, to include administration, faculty, students, alumni, and other important groups (business, the community, and the professions). Conrad and Pratt also noted the simultaneity of processes—political, social, educational, curricular, and professional—in an organized system for learning, outlined curriculum variables that relate to form and content, and wedded many of the continua and essential elements of other models to represent the interface of instructional practices, curriculum organization, and human resources. Such formative interfaces include considerations of content coverage, time dimension, locus of learning, instructional strategies, faculty expertise, and student development. These two authors also presented the delivery systems of a curriculum as options occurring along continua dealing with flexibility of program, design of program sequence, evaluation procedures, calendar, and credit options (pp. 27–28). Finally, Conrad and Pratt asserted that feedback is an important design consideration as it affects one and many parts of a system. In their model, outcomes begin to look as much like a means of feedback as they do like ends of a learning process.

Largely absent from the curriculum literature and thus from design efforts to date are "high context" (Hall, 1976) representations of a complex exchange process (Boulding, 1970) between people and groups. Transformation of information in academic institutions seems to be a process of exchange that is realized at once internally, individually, distinctively and externally, collectively, and differentially. Each person transforms information in his or her own unique way; yet, at the same time, the process occurs in relation to groups (at various levels of organization) that also are transforming information in ways unique to the group. Individual learning probably influences group learning, and group learning processes probably influence individual learning. Research needs to come to scholarly terms with such a paradoxical notion.

The size of the system can give some valuable clues about realistic approaches to designing for regenerative learning. Generalizations about individual learning, for example, do not seem appropriate to predictions regarding organizational learning, because open systems and closed systems have different properties. The smaller, individual system has the greater potential to function in a relatively open fashion. An individual functions in an environment that is relatively stable from her or his vantage point. The larger a system is, however, the more it may tend to function in a relatively closed fashion. Larger systems have larger social, political, economic, biological, and physical structures to consider. The more closed a large system, the more it is its own environment. And the more difficult it becomes to form accurate images of the system, much less to evaluate the images. Not only do we lack familiar references for how the large system works, but it is also difficult to acknowledge in an orderly fashion all of the evolving processes that we recognize that might contribute to an event. It is important, then, to remain aware that systems of different size apprehend information differently (Boulding, 1984; Miller, 1978). The critical interface that curriculum design can address, nevertheless, is that of the decision maker (faculty member, student, administrator, or graduate) in an institutional setting. Design, by definition, represents an attempt to depict the properties of a system and simultaneously to convey some knowledge to those who wish to choose among system options. In this view, those involved in conceptualizing curricular organization and functioning need to focus more on the adaptive behaviors of the institution, to monitor institutional and curricular history, and to continue to consider creative options (March, 1984, p. 2).

Finally, the conceptual effort must be decisively tentative. While this may sound like a contradiction in terms, the central suggestion here is not: Simply, the designer must ensure that curricula are open to change. Indeed, the evidence over the last 15 years suggests that curricula are changing—as demographics, public perceptions, and societal demands are changing: "The view that what has been always will be is not borne out by the record of evolution, as the disappearance of the dinosaurs certainly indicates" (Boulding, 1984, p. 20). Moreover, trends will end; regenerative designs need only to take note of the trendy or the trend setters. Models need to allow for surprise. And modelers need to risk sharing with each other any good fortune that comes their way in the form of insight about uncertain pathways. In this regard, today's researchers of higher education curricula, having come a long way, have much solid work to monitor, many possible futures to consider directly, and numerous energetic colleagues with whom to embrace the immediate inquiry.

Acknowledgment. We would like to express our appreciation to John Birk, a doctoral student in higher education at the University of Arizona, for his many valuable comments and suggestions.

REFERENCES

Allan, B. B. (1979). An empirical investigation related to the forces impinging upon planned change implementation. Unpublished doctoral dissertation, University of Virginia.

Argyris, C. (1976). Single-loop and double-loop models in research on decision-making. *Administrative Science Quarterly* 21: 363–375.

Astin, A. (1977). *Four critical years: effects of college on beliefs, attitudes, and knowledge.* San Francisco: Jossey-Bass.

Axelrod, J. (1968). Curricular change: a model for analysis. *The Research Reporter* 3: 1–3.

Baird, L. L. (1977). Structuring the environment to improve outcomes. *New Directions in Higher Education* 16: 1–23.

Beeken, L. (1982). A study of the general education component at three Virginia community colleges. Unpublished doctoral dissertation, Virginia Polytechnic and State University.

Belknap, R. L., and Kuhns, R. (1977). *Tradition and innovation: general education and the reintegration of the university.* New York: Columbia University.

Bell, D. (1968). *The reforming of general education: the Columbia College experience in its national setting.* New York: Anchor.

Bergquist, W. H. (1977). Eight curricular models. In A. W. Chickering, D. Halliburton, W. H. Bergquist, and J. Lindquist (eds.), *Developing the college curriculum: a handbook for faculty and administrators.* Washington, DC: Council for the Advancement of Small Colleges.

Bergquist, W. H., Gould, R. A., and Greenberg, E. M. (1981). *Designing undergraduate education: a systematic guide.* San Francisco: Jossey-Bass.

Berson, R. J. (1979). Ethics and education in the freshman year: impact and implications of an experimental value oriented curriculum. Unpublished doctoral dissertation, Teachers College, Columbia University.

Blackburn, R. T., and Conrad, C. F. (1985). The new revisionists and the history of higher education. Manuscript submitted for publication.

Blackburn, R., Armstrong, E., Conrad, C., Didham, J., and McKune, T. (1976). *Changing practices in undergraduate education.* Berkeley, CA: Carnegie Council on Policy Studies in Higher Education.

Blau, P. M. (1960). Structural effects. *American Sociological Review* 25: 178–193.

Boulding, K. N. (1970). *A primer on social dynamics.* New York: Free Press.

Boulding, K. N. (1984). The fallacy of trends: on living with unpredictability. *National Forum* 54: 19–20.

Bowen, H. R. (1977). *Investment in learning: the individual and social value of American higher education.* San Francisco: Jossey-Bass.

Boyer, E. L., and Levine, A. (1981). *A quest for common learning.* Washington, DC: Carnegie Foundation for the Advancement of Teaching.

Brick, M., and McGrath, E. J. (1960). *Innovation in liberal arts colleges.* New York: Teachers College, Columbia University.

Brubacher, J. S., and Rudy, W. (1976). *Higher education in transition* (3rd ed.). New York: Harper & Row.

Bucci, P. T. (1981). The importance of integration for general education reform: a conceptual analysis and case study. Unpublished doctoral dissertation, State University of New York.

Burke, C. B. (1982). *American collegiate populations: a test of the traditional view.* New York: Columbia University.

Bush, M. A. (1979). Institutionalization and utilization of a cross registration program in a higher education consortium. Unpublished doctoral dissertation, State University of New York at Albany.

Butts, R. F. (1939). *The college charts its course: historical conceptions and current proposals.* New York: McGraw-Hill.

Carnegie Foundation for the Advancement of Teaching. (1975). Carnegie catalogue study, 1975. Unpublished data and report, Carnegie Foundation.

Carnegie Foundation for the Advancement of Teaching. (1977). *Missions of the college curriculum: a contemporary review with suggestions.* San Francisco: Jossey-Bass.

Carnegie Foundation for the Advancement of Teaching. (1980). Carnegie catalogue study, 1980. Unpublished data and report, Carnegie Foundation.

Chiaro, K. R. (1984). Academic change in the community college: an institutional case study. Unpublished doctoral dissertation, University of Arizona.

Chickering, A. W. (1969). *Education and identity.* San Francisco: Jossey-Bass.

Chickering, A. W., Halliburton, D., Bergquist, W. H., and Lindquist, J. (1977). *Developing the college curriculum: a handbook for faculty and administrators.* Washington, DC: Council for the Advancement of Small Colleges.

Conrad, C. F. (1978a). A grounded theory of academic change. *Sociology of Education* 51: 101–112.

Conrad, C. F. (1978b). *The undergraduate curriculum: a guide to innovation and reform.* Boulder, CO: Westview.

Conrad, C. F. (1980). Initiating and implementing change. In J. G. Gaff (ed.), *General education: issues and resources.* Washington, DC: Association of American Colleges.

Conrad, C. F. (1982). Grounded theory: an alternative approach to research in higher education. *The Review of Higher Education* 5: 239–249.

Conrad, C. F. (1983). *At the crossroads: general education in community colleges.* Washington, DC: Council of Universities and Colleges, American Association of Community and Junior Colleges; Los Angeles: ERIC Clearinghouse on Higher Education.

Conrad, C. F., and Pratt, A. M. (1983). Making decisions about the curriculum: from metaphor to model. *The Journal of Higher Education* 54: 16–30.

Conrad, C. F., and Wyer, J. C. (1980). *Liberal education in transition.* (AAHE-ERIC/ Higher Education Research Report No. 3.) Washington, DC: American Association for Higher Education.

Crane, D. (1972). *Invisible colleges: diffusion of knowledge in scientific communities.* Chicago: University of Chicago Press.

Dill, D. D., and Friedman, C. P. (1979). An analysis of frameworks for research on innovation and change in higher education. *Review of Educational Research* 49: 411–435.

Dressel, P. L. (1971). *College and university curriculum.* Berkeley, CA: McCutchan.

Dressel, P. L. (1980). *Improving degree programs.* San Francisco: Jossey-Bass.

Dressel, P. L., and DeLisle, F. H. (1969). *Undergraduate curriculum trends.* Washington, DC: American Council on Education.

Drum, R. A. (1979). Selected factors related to adoption and implementation of an innovation in community colleges. Unpublished doctoral dissertation, University of Texas.

Feldman, K. A., and Newcomb, T. M. (1969). *The impact of college on students: An analysis of four decades of research,* Vol. 1. San Francisco: Jossey-Bass.

Fitzgerald, M. L. (1980). Interdisciplinary studies in letters and science: the idea, the program, the method of teaching. Unpublished doctoral dissertation, University of California, Berkeley.

Forest, A. F., and Steele, J. M. (1978). *College outcomes measures project.* Iowa City: American College Testing Program.

Friedlander, J. (1980). The importance of quality of effort in predicting college student attainment. Unpublished doctoral dissertation, University of California at Los Angeles. (Shorter version presented as a paper at the annual meeting of the Association for the Study of Higher Education, Washington, DC, March, 1980).

Friedlander, J. (1981). Influences of length of time in college versus quality of time on college student development. Paper presented at the annual meeting of the American Educational Research Association, Los Angeles.

Gaff, J. G. (1980). Avoiding the potholes: strategies for reforming general education. *Educational Record* 61: 50–59.

Gaff, J. G. (1983). *General education today: a critical analysis of controversial practices and reforms.* San Francisco: Jossey-Bass.

Gamson, Z. F. (1974). Course outline: G804, sociological approaches to collegiate innovation. Unpublished course syllabus, University of Michigan, Center for the Study of Higher Education.

Gamson, Z. F. and Associates. (1984). *Liberating education.* San Francisco: Jossey-Bass.

Glaser, B. G., and Strauss, A. C. (1967). *The discovery of grounded theory.* Chicago: Aldine.

Glass, G. V., McGaw, B., and Smith, M. L. (1981). *Meta-analysis in social research.* Beverly Hills: Sage.

Grace, J. D. (1984). Higher education as a profession: a curriculum analysis. Unpublished doctoral dissertation, University of Arizona.

Grant, G., and Associates. (1979). *On competence: a critical analysis of competence-based reforms in higher education.* San Francisco: Jossey-Bass.

Grant, G., and Riesman, D. (1978). *The perpetual dream: reform and experiment in the American college.* Chicago: University of Chicago.

Hall, E. T. (1976). *Beyond culture.* New York: Anchor/Doubleday.

Handlin, O., and Handlin, M. T. (1970). *The American college and the American culture: socialization as a function of higher education.* New York: McGraw-Hill.

Heath, D. (1968). *Growing up in college.* San Francisco: Jossey-Bass.

Hefferlin, J. L. (1969). *The dynamics of academic reform.* San Francisco: Jossey-Bass.

Heiss, A. (1973). *An inventory of academic innovation and reform.* Berkeley, CA: Carnegie Commission on Higher Education.

Hendel, D. D. (1977). Curricular choices and academic success of students enrolled in an elective studies degree program. *Research in Higher Education* 7: 257–267.

Hursh, B., Haas, P., and Moore, M. (1983). An interdisciplinary model to implement general education. *Journal of Higher Education* 54: 42–59.

Ighodaro, A. A. (1980). Beyond a new graduation requirement: the diffusion of curriculum innovation in an academic organization. Unpublished doctoral dissertation, University of Southern California.

Jackson, G. B. (1980). Methods for integrative reviews. *Review of Educational Research* 50: 438–460.

Kamens, D. (1974). Colleges and elite formation: the case of the prestigious American colleges. *Sociology of Education* 47: 357–379.

Katz, D., and Kahn, R. L. (1966). *The social psychology of organizations.* New York: Wiley.

Kimball, B. A. (1981). A historical and typological analysis of ideas of liberal education in America. Unpublished doctoral dissertation, Harvard University.

Koch, G. A. (1979). The general education movement in American higher education: an account and appraisal of its principles and practices and their relation to democratic thought in modern American society. Unpublished doctoral dissertation, University of Minnesota.

Ladd, D. R. (1970). *Change in educational policy: self-studies in selected colleges and universities.* New York: McGraw-Hill.

Lara, J. (1981). Differences in quality of academic effort between successful and unsuccessful community college transfer students. Paper presented at the annual meeting of the American Educational Research Association, Los Angeles.

LeBlanc, M. E. (1980). The concept of general education in colleges and universities, 1945-1979. Unpublished doctoral dissertation, Rutgers University.

Lehmann, T., and Ristuben, P. J. (1983). Colleges in partnership: four ventures in successful program collaboration. *Journal of Higher Education* 54: 381-398.

Levine, A. (1978). *Handbook on undergraduate curriculum.* San Francisco: Jossey-Bass.

Levine, A. (1980). *Why innovation fails.* Albany: State University of New York.

Levine, A., and Weingart, J. (1973). *Reform of undergraduate education.* San Francisco: Jossey-Bass.

Lewin, K. (1961). Quasi-stationary social equilibria and the problem of permanent change. In W. Bennis, K. Benne, and R. Chin (eds.), *The planning of change.* New York: Holt.

Lindquist, J. (1978). *Strategies for change.* Berkeley: Pacific Soundings.

Manns, C. L., and March, J. G. (1978). Financial adversity, internal competition, and curriculum change in a university. *Administrative Science Quarterly* 23: 541-552.

Mapp, R. (1980). A comparison of purpose statements and representative course requirements for general education in public two-year college occupational programs. Unpublished doctoral dissertation, Virginia Polytechnic and State University.

March, J. G. (1978). Bounded rationality, ambiguity, and the engineering of choice. *Bell Journal of Economics* 9: 587-608.

March, J. G. (1984). Shaping the future of American higher education. *The Pen,* American Educational Research Association, Division J-Postsecondary Education.

March, J. G., and Simon, H. A. (1958). *Organizations.* New York: Wiley.

Mayhew, L. B., and Ford, P. J. (1971). *Changing the curriculum.* San Francisco: Jossey-Bass.

Metzger, W. P. (1984). Review of *American collegiate populations: a test of the traditional view* by C. Burke. *Journal of Higher Education* 55: 419-422.

Miller, J. G. (1978). *Living systems.* New York: McGraw-Hill.

Morgan, G. (1980). Paradigms, metaphors, and puzzle-solving in organizational theory. *Administrative Science Quarterly* 25: 605-622.

Myers, J. R. (1979). A model for curriculum engineering for use in multi-college/campus community and junior colleges. Unpublished doctoral dissertation, Florida State University.

Newcombe, J. P., and Conrad, C. F. (1981). A theory of mandated academic change. *Journal of Higher Education* 52: 555-577.

Nordvall, R. C. (1982). *The process of change in higher education institutions.* (AAHE-ERIC/Higher Education Research Report No. 7.) Washington, DC: American Association for Higher Education.

Oleson, A., and Voss, J. (1979). *The organization of knowledge in modern America, 1860-1920.* Baltimore: Johns Hopkins University.

Pace, C. R. (1979). *Measuring outcomes of college: fifty years of findings and recommendations for the future.* San Francisco: Jossey-Bass.

Pace, C. R. (1980). Measuring the quality of student effort. In *Current issues in higher education*. Washington, DC: American Association for Higher Education.

Pace, C. R. (May 1982). Achievement and the quality of student effort. Paper presented to the National Commission on Excellence in Education, Washington, DC.

Pace, C. R. (1984). *Measuring the quality of college student experiences*. Los Angeles: Higher Education Research Institute, Graduate School of Education, University of California at Los Angeles.

Parker, C. A. (1980). The literature on planned organizational change: A review and analysis. *Higher Education* 9: 429–442.

Pascarella, E. T., and Terenzini, P. T. (1976). Informal interactions with faculty and freshman ratings of the academic and nonacademic experience of college. *Journal of Educational Research* 70: 35–41.

Pascarella, E. T., and Terenzini, P. T. (1978). Student-faculty informal relationships and freshman years educational outcomes. *Journal of Educational Research* 71: 183–189.

Perry, W. F. (1968). *Forms of intellectual and ethical development in the college years*. New York: Holt, Rinehart & Winston.

Phenix, P. H. (1964). *Realms of meaning: a philosophy of the curriculum for general education*. New York: McGraw-Hill.

Phenix, P. H. (1971). Transcendence and the curriculum. *Teachers College Record* 73: 271–283.

Pirsig, R. M. (1976). *Zen and the art of motorcycle maintenance*. New York: Bantam.

Porter, O. (1983). The role of quality of student effort in defining institutional environments: an attempt to understand college uniqueness. Unpublished doctoral dissertation, University of California at Los Angeles.

Potts, D. B. (1981). Curriculum and enrollments: some thoughts on assessing the popularity of ante-bellum colleges. *History of Higher Education* 1: 89–104.

Pratt, A. M. (1984). Making routine curriculum changes at the College of William and Mary in Virginia: are faculty influenced by trends in students' pursuits? Unpublished doctoral dissertation, College of William and Mary.

Riesman, D., Gusfield, J., and Gamson, Z. (1971). *Academic values and mass education*. New York: Doubleday/Anchor.

Roark, D. D. (1985). Factors affecting the implementation of new educational technology in higher education. Unpublished doctoral dissertation, University of Arizona.

Rudolph, F. (1962). *The American college and university: a history*. New York: Vintage Books.

Rudolph, F. (1977). *Curriculum: a history of the American undergraduate course study since 1636*. San Francisco: Jossey-Bass.

Rudy, W. (1960). *The evolving liberal arts curriculum: a historical review of basic themes*. New York: Bureau of Publications, Teachers College, Columbia University.

Saccaro-Battisti, G. (1983). Changing metaphors of political structures. *Journal of the History of Ideas* 44: 31–54.

Shaver, J. (1979). An examination of the quality of effort that college and university students invest in their own learning and development. Unpublished doctoral dissertation, University of California at Los Angeles.

Simon, H. A. (1969). *The sciences of the artificial*. Cambridge: Massachusetts Institute of Technology.

Simon, J. (1981). *The ultimate resource*. Princeton: Princeton University.

Sloan, D. (1971). Harmony, chaos, and consensus: the American college curriculum. *Teachers College Record* 73: 221–251.

Tewksbury, D. G. (1932). *The founding of American colleges and universities before the Civil War*. New York: Teachers College, Columbia University.
Thelin, J. R. (1982). *Higher education and its useful past*. Cambridge, MA: Schenkman.
Thomas, R. (1962). *The search for a common learning: general education, 1800–1960*. New York: McGraw-Hill.
Toombs, W. (1977–78). The application of design-based curriculum analysis to general education. *Higher Education Review* 1: 18–29.
Toombs, W. (1982). Finding exemplars of research on academic programs. Paper presented at the annual meeting of the American Educational Research Association, New York.
Tyler, R. W. (1950). *Basic principles of curriculum and instruction*. Chicago: University of Chicago.
Vars, G. F. (1982). Designs for general education: alternative approaches to curriculum integration. *Journal of Higher Education* 53: 216–226.
Veysey, L. R. (1965). *The emergence of the American university*. Chicago: University of Chicago.
Wegener, C. (1978). *Liberal education and the modern university*. Chicago: University of Chicago.
Winter, D. G., McClelland, D. C., and Stewart, A. J. (1981). *A new case for the liberal arts*. San Francisco: Jossey-Bass.
Wolf, F. A. (1981). *Taking the quantum leap*. New York: Harper & Row.
Zelditch, M., Jr. (1962). Some methodological problems of field study. *American Journal of Sociology* 67: 566–576.
Zoglin, M. L. (1981). Community college responsiveness: myth or reality? *Journal of Higher Education* 52: 415–426.

TRENDS AND ISSUES IN CURRICULAR DEVELOPMENT

Cameron Fincher, *University of Georgia*

The National Institute of Education (NIE), the National Endowment for the Humanities (NEH), and the Association of American Colleges (AAC) have issued reports on the status of undergraduate education in American institutions of higher learning. Each report addresses the decline in liberal or general education and calls for national efforts to strengthen undergraduate programs in community colleges, senior colleges, and universities. The dominant theme of all three reports can be expressed as a belief that the quality of undergraduate education has declined over the past two decades and that quality can be restored by concerted attention to liberal and/or general education. The particular thrusts of the three reports can be identified as:

1. The inducement of more active involvement in learning on the part of students (NIE);
2. The restoration of the humanities to their central position in college curricula (NEH); and
3. A redefinition of the meaning and purposes of baccalaureate degrees (AAC)

The strength of the NIE report lies in its recommendation that students must become more actively involved in their own education. The recommendation stems from theories of learning in which active participation by learners has always been a crucial variable. To that effect, research is cited as showing that learning is directly related to the quantity and quality of learning efforts.

The NIE recommendations are based on the premise that colleges and universities must produce demonstrable improvements in knowledge, capacities, skills, and attitudes between time of entrance and time of graduation. To produce these demonstrable improvements, colleges and universities must establish clearly expressed and publicly announced standards of performance for awarding degrees.

The NIE report testifies that if excellence is to be achieved in undergraduate education, the expectations of both teaching faculty and students must be raised. Faculties and chief academic officers should agree on and disseminate a statement of the knowledge, capacities, and skills that students must develop before graduation. All four-year college degrees would require at least two full years of liberal education. Should this requirement make necessary the extension of undergraduate programs beyond the usual four years, colleges should not hesitate to impose such a requirement. In expanding the requirements of liberal education for baccalaureate degrees, the report states that curriculum content should be addressed not only to subject matter but to the development of analytic problem-solving and communication skills. In addition, students and faculty should work together to integrate knowledge from the various academic disciplines.

The NEH report, written by William J. Bennett before he was appointed U.S. Secretary of Education, makes a special case for the humanities in undergraduate education. The report, as well as the deliberations of the study group appointed by Bennett, is predicated on the observation that the humanities have lost their central place in baccalaureate programs. A substantial majority of students now graduate from college without exposure to Western civilization, American literature and history, and the civilization of classical Greece and Rome. The dominant recommendation in the report thus states that:

> The nation's colleges and universities must reshape their undergraduate curricula based on a clear vision of what constitutes an educated person, regardless of major, and on the study of history, philosophy, languages, and literature [p. 2].

Closely related to this recommendation are encouragements to college and university presidents to take responsibility and to reward excellent teaching—and to college faculties in escaping the confines of narrow departmentalism and in helping establish a core of common studies. The report is particularly appealing in its encouragement of academic programs that would permit "all students to know a common culture rooted in civilization's lasting vision, its highest shared ideals and aspirations, and its heritage" (p. 4).

In many respects, the report is an eloquent plea for cultural literacy. Much needed is a better balance between breadth and depth; more frequent use of original literary, philosophical, and historical texts; better continuity in humanistic studies; improved teaching or greater faculty competence and expertise; and a conviction that the humanities are not merely an educational luxury. The report is quite explicit in its preferences for the particular books and authors that undergraduate students should read, discuss, and assimilate.

The core of the recommendations in the AAC report is some kind of "study in depth" before individuals complete degree requirements. This study in depth evidently would meld together most of the requirements for synthesizing student learning and demonstrating student performance.

The requirement of such a study evidently would ensure that learners comprehend some complex structure of knowledge, gain some degree of understanding and control, and (by implication) overcome the disadvantages of the narrow specialization that major fields now encourage. In-depth study would presumably present a central core of method and theory that introduces learners to the explanatory power of academic disciplines, provides a basis for subsequent study, and "forces" the student to experience the range of disciplinary topics and the variety of disciplinary tools. Studies in depth are presumably as relevant to professional and applied fields as they are to the traditional disciplines in arts and sciences.

In discussing "the methods and processes, modes of access to understanding and judgment, that should inform all study," the AAC report recalls many traditional objectives and expected outcomes of undergraduate education. In addition to studies in depth, the report calls for an unusual mixture of knowledge, information, skills, competencies, attitudes, beliefs, and values. Included in its list of "methods and processes" are

1. Inquiry, abstract logical thinking, and critical analysis;
2. Literacy: writing, reading, speaking, and listening;
3. Historical consciousness;
4. Science; values; art; and
5. Multicultural experiences.

The NIE, NEH, and AAC reports have much in common—and provide good insight into the difficulties of undergraduate education and the many good intentions that have gone astray over the past twenty years. All are on target in pointing to a national need to strengthen baccalaureate degree programs and to declare in more affirmative, constructive terms the objectives and expected outcomes of a college education. And to a noticeable degree, all are correct in their inferences that if undergraduate education is to be strengthened and if it is to give better evidence of quality or excellence, the challenge must be accepted by college and university faculties, and a concerted effort must be directed to the academic programs by which college students earn college degrees.

The glaring weakness of the NIE, NEH, and AAC reports is in the direction and guidance they give for the strengthening of undergraduate curricula. More specifically, the NIE, the NEH, and the AAC failed to address the substance and content of college curricula in ways that make sense to the majority of college faculty. The three reports ignore the judgment of the Carnegie Foundation (1977) in its description of major fields of study as "a success story," and they make only passing reference to many indications that American colleges and universities teach well what they are best prepared to teach: those areas of specialization that merit and sustain the research and teaching interests of the faculty. To a similar degree, the reports do not take sufficient notice of the conflict that we now have between the learning needs and interests of students *and* the teaching interests of faculty. But most of all, the three reports may perpetuate the confusion of the liberal arts, liberal learning, general education, and the humanities.

The purpose of this chapter is to identify the dominant trends and issues of college curricula and to discuss their relevance to curricular reform in the remaining years of the twentieth century. A value premise on which the chapter is based is the obvious need for improvement in learning and teaching at the college and university level of education. In other words, the need for reform is taken for granted, and a national need for curricular reform is addressed for the practical reason that academic programs and courses, with all their resistance to reform, will still be easier to change than college faculties and students.

Another critical assumption rests on the belief that college curricula are always changing. What students learn in college and what faculty members teach are always in a state of flux. To invoke the classical Greeks, college courses and programs are Heraclitean rivers into which no students step twice; they are devoid of the Parmenidean unities that would appeal to classicists and others who would hold to traditional and/or elitist notions of a college education. To soften such a view, it is well to concede that academic programs and courses may, indeed, have many similarities. At the same time, there are pronounced differences that will often be more important. In most colleges and universities, there is an unbelievable array of teaching styles and learning strategies that serve both teachers and faculty well. It is banal to believe that all teaching styles and/or learning strategies are equally effective. It is not banal to state that there is no proven one-best-way to learn, and that there surely is no demonstrated one-best-way to teach (Fincher, 1985).

In much the same manner, the ensuing discussion assumes that to understand the problems, issues, and concerns of college curricula, serious and concurrent thought must be given to secondary-school curricula and the quality of instruction at that level. Whatever the problems and issues of learning and teaching at the college level, they are not independent of problems and issues that begin early in public schooling and become quite pronounced in the closing years of high school. "The crucial years" in education must surely be identified as the last three years of high school and the first two years of college. These are the years in which the American people have invested their fondest hopes, and these are the years in which there is the greatest disappointment.

A fourth premise that should be mentioned is the fact that curricular debates and controversy are not strangers to college and university faculties. It is distinctly possible that there is absolutely nothing in the viewpoints of the 1980s that has not been expressed frequently in the past. Indeed, there are ample reasons to believe that curricular reform is a perennial issue in higher education and that serious efforts to trace the ebb and flood of curricular debate would be an insightful undertaking. To some extent, much of what follows is such an effort for the years following World War II and leading up to the mid-1980s.

TRENDS IN CURRICULAR DEVELOPMENT

The demand for curricular reform in the 1980s is the result of growth and expansion over a twenty-five-year period, followed by a period of financial difficulty, uncertain enrollments, and changing demands and expectations on the part of students and the general public. Some curricular issues are the function of institutional success in meeting the challenge of increased demand, while others are caused by increased competition for students, funds, and other public resources. More than a few curricular issues are a function of mistakes or ill-advised concessions to the problems of the 1960s and the early 1970s. Reactions to student protests, faculty restiveness, financial difficulties, and the "new student" in higher education have left many residues that affect college curricula in various and subtle ways.

Four obvious trends affecting undergraduate curricula are: (1) the continuing convergence of secondary and graduate curricula on the course content and substance of four-year degree programs; (2) the diversification of undergraduate course work as the result of teaching interests and learning needs; (3) the increasing specialization of academic disciplines and fields of study; and (4) the increased professionalization of education to satisfy the career objectives of students and the requirements of accrediting agencies and professional societies. The effect of each of these trends suggests that college curricula are indeed dynamic, ongoing, and continuously changing.

Convergence and diversification as continuing trends are most clearly seen in the influence of secondary-school and graduate curricula on undergraduate college programs and courses. As early as 1959, Jacques Barzun and other critics pointed out that four-year college-programs were being eroded by the downward gravitation of course content to the high school and by the imposition of entrance requirements from above by graduate and professional schools. Over the years, high schools have adopted many characteristics of the four-year college and have borrowed appreciable substance and content from courses once taught only at the college level. In a similar manner, many college courses have borrowed much from graduate and professional education, as admission to higher or advanced levels of education has become more selective.

During the 1950s and 1960s, the purpose and content of high-school curricula were severely criticized. Rapid social change, technological developments, the changing occupational structure of the nation, and differences in standards of living produced a strong reform movement. In 1957, the launching of the Russian sputnik represented a turning point in educational thought and discussion as it became a major impetus to federal support for secondary and postsecondary education. James B. Conant (1959) and John Gardner (1961) became frequently cited authorities on the need for educational reform. Other accounts of the nation's schools and the need for curriculum reform were given by Martin Mayer (1961), Admiral Hyman Rickover (1959), Arthur Bestor (1955), Paul Goodman (1965), and Edgar Friedenberg (1953).

In 1959, a group of well-known scholars, scientists, and educators met at Woods Hole, Massachusetts, to discuss how science should be taught. The views and opinions of this distinguished group were summarized by Jerome Bruner (1963), who quickly earned national respect as an authority on curriculum and instruction. Obviously influenced by the conference at Woods Hole were a series of energetic commissioners of education, an incredibly large number of professional associations, numerous business corporations, and the nation's representatives in Congress. With wide acceptance that the subject matter of science could be made intellectually respectable when taught to students of any age, there was even stronger agreement with certain assumptions that the way in which science had previously been taught was educationally unsound.

From 1963 to 1968, a total of 28 major legislative acts were passed by the U.S. Congress in an effort to re-create an educational system for the nation. Recalling the establishment of the National Science Foundation and the enactment of the National Defense Act, the Congress moved to redirect and support education through such legislation as the Manpower Development and Training Act, the Vocational Education Act, the Economic Opportunity Act, the Elementary and Secondary Education Act, and the Higher Education Act of 1965. Each of these acts, with their subsequent amendments, gave unusual force and direction to the improvement of education in schools and colleges.

Not unrelated to these legislative acts was the advent of an educational technology that was strongly supported by corporate industry. The outcome was an amazing set of strategies for curriculum changes, including (1) the funding an establishment of regional educational laboratories; (2) an increasing concern with planning and development models; and (3) the development of high-school courses that emulated in many ways the structure and content of college courses in science, mathematics, and foreign languages. The development of new strategies for curriculum change was predicated on a number of emerging concepts and principles, including: (1) global concepts of school and college curricula as programs of study; (2) an intense concern with outputs, objectives, and cost-effectiveness; (3) a new focus on students and their changing expectations for education; (4) the extension of education on both ends of the traditional years of schooling; and (5) continuing education and in-service training for virtually all participants in the educational process. Closely related to these changes were psychological and sociological factors related to adolescence as a stage of growth and development. Physiological factors resulted in an increasingly early entry into adolescence, and sociocultural factors resulted in an increasingly later departure.

The most influential critic, of course, was James B. Conant in his study of the American high school (1959). Conant presented a view of the high school as providing a general education for all, through specialized elective programs for those who would use their acquired skills on graduation and through satisfactory preparation for those who would continue their education in a college or a university. Conant found English, social studies, and foreign languages to be less than satisfactory and an insufficient challenge to superior students. He believed that the high school should eliminate extracurricular activities that curtailed more serious study. Algebra and foreign languages should begin in the lower schools; science courses should be modernized; history courses should be improved and at least one theme a week should be required in English. From his study, Conant concluded that the small high school that could not provide a comprehensive program should be eliminated; a core curriculum should be provided for all students, and better academic counseling and guidance should be given bright students, especially capable girls. Many of Conant's findings and recommendations were supported by *Project Talent* (Flannagan et al, 1964). Most of the nation's high schools were still located in small towns or rural areas and could not provide the kind of curricula that contemporary students needed. Pronounced differences were obvious among the nation's high schools, and there was little that could be interpreted as either uniform or rigorous.

For those interested in curriculum building, the decade of the 1960s was an energetic and highly productive period. The subject matter and course content of numerous high-school programs were altered or modified to meet new educational challenges and national needs. Whatever the high schools had been teaching in the past, they were challenged in the 1960s to teach something different and to teach it better. Outside agencies and associations took an active role in reorganizing course content, devising instructional materials, and providing in-service training for teachers. Funding for curriculum projects were generously provided by private foundations and the federal government. Curriculum design became a package deal that included experimental or provisional textbooks that would undergo numerous revisions before acquiring the bound authority of a hardback book. Laboratory guides, teachers' manuals, films, tapes, and other supplementary materials were part and parcel of the deal.

Nothing less than total redesign was intended in many cases. The major thrust of the curriculum designers was to present their particular subject in terms of its inherent structional features. The purpose of education was to teach students that knowledge is never finite and seldom stable. Only by grasping the structure of an academic discipline could students prepare themselves for continued learning in the field. The student was to explore and to discover knowledge in the same manner that proven scholars in academic disciplines did. Students were to discover for themselves that the pursuit of knowledge was an active, ongoing, ceaseless activity, with immense intellectual pleasure as the only reward worthy of the name.

But perhaps equally important, the new curricula for high schools were to be packaged in such a manner that they would be teacher-proof. This meant not only an extensive and ambitious program of in-service training for teachers, but an alteration of the teacher's central role in the classroom. The teacher was no longer to be the source or transmitter of knowledge but a curriculum manager. The teacher's expertise was directed to modes of inquiry and channels of information, and the teacher's role was to function as a facilitating agent for the student's own learning efforts. At best, the teachers might serve as knowledge brokers; at worst, they became completely subservient to the curriculum and served only to pass out the materials and supplies that the students would need in educating themselves.

For specific fields of study, the changes in course objectives and content were quite extensive. Some of the predominant changes made in specific fields can be identified as follows.

Physics, biology, and chemistry. The curriculum designed by the Physical Science Study Committee (PSSC), the Biological Sciences Curriculum Study (BSCS), the Chemical Education Materials Study (CHEM), and the Chemical Bond Approach Project (CPA) are the better-known projects of the era and more-or-less set the style and tone for other curricular projects. Together, these projects made the general science course obsolete. They shifted, with pronounced effect, the emphasis from the accumulation of knowledge to methods of inquiry; from technological application to theoretical structures; from facts and figures to competencies in inductive inquiry. Whatever science was, it was a set of problem-solving skills that were to be taught for their own sake and not for the factual knowledge that they had produced in the past.

Mathematics. As in the physical and biological sciences, curricular reform in mathematics began in the 1950s and set the stage for curricular change in other fields. The major emphasis can be identified as the complete formalization of mathematics and its propagation as a field of inquiry in its own right. This emphasis means less concern with computation as such and less attention to the practical applications of mathematics in business, science, and technology.

English. The new English became an active concern with language, literature, and composition as inductive, ongoing processes instead of standardized forms or products. Curriculum movements were influenced by developments in the field of linguistics and represented an effort to reestablish the teaching of English as a viable, meaningful effort.

Foreign languages. Curricular change in the foreign languages represents radical reform in objectives, methods, and instructional materials. The emphasis was shifted from reading foreign languages to audiolingual approaches that were predicated on the belief that languages begin with listening and speaking. Curricular change in this area may demonstrate more cogently than any other the impact of technological innovation.

Social sciences. Curricular change in the social sciences was less successful than that observed in other curricula. Efforts were made to imitate the breaking out of separate disciplines in the physical and biological sciences, but there is still confusion about what constitutes the social sciences. Bruner's views (1960) on instruction were influential in the social sciences, but the controversy surrounding MACOS (Man: A Course of Study) was indicative of the difficulties of reform in secondary schools (Goodlad, 1966).

Critics of the new curricula of the 1960s were quick to point out that the methods of inquiry employed by the mature and experienced scholar might not be the best model for immature and inexperienced students. Morris Kline (1973) was one critic of the new mathematics who believed that it quickly degenerated into a set of hollow formalisms unrelated to what students knew or wanted to learn. Other critics suspected that the new curricula had succeeded in slaying certain dogmas but were unsuccessful in demonstrating their effectiveness in developing skills of inquiry and attitudes of open-mindedness. Equally cogent is the suspicion that curricular reform in the 1960s was insufficiently tuned to the broadening base of public education, did not recognize the changes in minority group access, and placed too high a premium on the education of the upper half of high-school classes.

Whatever the successes of curricular reform, they were not sufficient to head off another cycle of vehement criticism aimed at the public schools in the early 1970s. A host of new critics arose in opposition to much that the public schools presumably stood for and wrote with consummate scorn of their weaknesses and failures. Although concerned primarily with the elementary schools, the reactions of George Dennison (1969), James Herndon (1968), John Holt (1970), Jonathan Kozol (1963), and Ivan Illich (1971) had stinging implications for what was being taught in high schools.

The most intelligent, and the most fair-minded, of the new critics was Charles Silberman (1970). His thesis was that schools are grim, joyless places where there is a mindlessness about the purposes and consequences of education. By mindlessness, Silberman meant the failure or refusal to think seriously about educational purpose and the reluctance to question established practice. If mindlessness was indeed the central problem, the solution should be found in serious thought about purpose and the ways in which techniques, content, and organization can fulfill purpose.

Criticisms of the new curricula came from within the educational profession as well as from without. Daniel Tanner (1971) likened secondary curricular reform to urban renewal and city planning. Both, he wrote, are predicated on the expectation that the individual will be transformed to improve the efficiency of the system. Curricular reform was thus viewed as disjointed innovation. Schoolteachers were utilized more efficiently through modular scheduling, team teaching, independent study, technological devices, and the alteration of physical facilities, but these have little or nothing to do with curricular improvement.

Curricular Change in the College

Given the turbulence of the 1960s and the frantic efforts of colleges and universities to cope with social, economic, political, and cultural change, it is difficult to specify the effective or lasting changes that might have taken place in traditional college programs. Laurence Veysey (1973) wrote that in qualitative ways that really matter, universities seem to change, but that their formal curricula structures have a way of remaining somewhat unaffected. The course remains the most durable element in American higher education. Only slightly less tenacious is the letter grade as the logical way of reporting student achievement, and almost equally durable are the ideas of unit credit for courses completed and the division of the school year into semesters or quarters.

As a historian, Veysey contended that the decades between 1870 and 1910 witnessed the only genuine academic revolution experienced on American college campuses. These were the years in which the American university and the undergraduate colleges were created. These were the years in which higher education became fully utilitarian, incorporated science and empirical research, and embraced liberal or general education. Veysey believes that undergraduate curricular needs must be placed in the context of a broad pattern of academic development and suggested that the paperback revolution of the 1950s may have done more to improve academic quality than any curricular innovation of the last seventy years. Economic constraints rather than intellectual ones loom larger in explaining why undergraduate classes remain large in size and why lectures still predominate. Course proliferation is well known in every academic discipline, but the major means of introducing experimentation in course content may be through interdisciplinary courses.

One effort to answer critics such as Jacques Barzun was seen in Daniel Bell's committee-of-one report, which was prepared for Columbia University and published as *The Reforming of General Education* (1966). Bell believed the university to be a striking example of endurance among social institutions and made an appealing effort, if not an effective one, to restore general education to its proper place in the four-year curriculum.

Viewing the secondary schools, Bell rightly pointed out that curriculum change was necessarily limited. The reforms initiated in mathematics and the physical sciences could not carry over to the humanities and social studies because of inherent differences within the various disciplines. The acquisition of knowledge in the physical and biological sciences is largely sequential, while the achievement of understanding in the humanities is largely concentric. Still, Bell could see an orderly division of labor between high schools and colleges. College curricula should be reorganized, therefore, with these distinctions clearly in mind. The liberal arts program should retain its vital functions; it does have a "hidden and instinctive wisdom" and it should permit an "unforced intellectual maturing."

Bell was in agreement with other curriculum designers in rejecting a quota of eternal verities or a set of invariant truths that must be taught to all students. He thought that the purposes of a liberal education are (1) to overcome intellectual provincialism; (2) to appreciate the centrality of method; (3) to gain an awareness of history; (4) to show how ideas relate to social structures; (5) to understand how values infuse all inquiry; and (6) to demonstrate the civilizing role of the humanities.

Bell's effort, of course, was to propose a new intellectual structure for general education. The problems in doing so were a matter of organizational and intellectual flexibility. Other limitations on doing so were the limited amount of talent and the increasingly political role of the university. Another might be the disjunction between culture and social structure. Bell quickly spotted the building tension between technocratic and apocalyptic modes of thought as those distinctions were then discussed within the university.

Other efforts to study curricular change in the college should be mentioned. A study of undergraduate curricular patterns by specialists in the U.S. Office of Education (Haswell and Lindquist, 1965) did not reveal striking differences between the course requirements for B.A. and B.S. curricula in the six undergraduate areas of the humanities, the social sciences, the physical sciences, the biological sciences, engineering, and agriculture. Uniformity and similarity were more characteristic of distributional requirements than the rhetoric of specialization and program diversity would suggest.

One of the few places where comparative data can be found for the assessment of curricular change is in Dressel and DeLisle's study of 322 colleges and universities chosen in a national sample for the years 1957 and 1967. Their data reveal a number of changes that occurred during the 1960s, many of which are in keeping with changes in the high school. Some of the conclusions drawn by Dressel and DeLisle may be stated as follows:

1. Formal requirements for English composition, literature, and speech had decreased, but foreign language requirements had increased.
2. Philosophy and religion were more likely to be an option than a requirement, while mathematics was increasingly a requirement or an option.
3. A slight tendency to reduce physical education requirements and to eliminate grades or credit was observed.

An important conclusion drawn from Dressel and DeLisle's survey is the balance that undergraduate colleges sought between liberal and professional course work. In brief, few colleges were attempting to be exclusively liberal arts and were quite sensitive to the professional or career interests of students and to the admissions requirements of professional or graduate schools. Colleges were still trying to provide breadth, however, by distributional requirements among the humanities, the natural sciences, and the social sciences. The pattern that could still be detected in most undergraduate curricula, nonetheless, was the provision of general education (or breadth) before specialization (or depth). In the first years of academic programs, general education was emphasized through interdisciplinary courses and, in the later years, through the coordination or integration of separate courses.

Dressel and DeLisle did not regard the curricular trends detected in their study as revolutionary. Much more impressive were the relative stability of course requirements in the curriculum and the corresponding efforts to loosen or individualize such courses through arrangements such as study abroad, work–study programs, community service, honors programs, independent study, and comprehensive examinations. These arrangements also included a host of quasi-formal learning situations such as study abroad, tutorials, senior theses or projects, and fieldwork experience.

Richardson (1971), in a study for the National Laboratory for Higher Education, concluded that most curricular reform might be regarded as academic window-dressing. His review and analysis of the literature led to the conclusion that most curricular improvements had been made at the clerical-distributive level and did not represent sophisticated or comprehensive reform. He believed, however, that considerable pressure for curricular improvement was mounting in the early 1970s because of the broader social order in which institutions of higher education had to function, the influence of external agencies and organizations, the knowledge explosion, and forces peculiar to the colleges and universities.

The dynamics of curricular reform in the college were described by Hefferlin (1969) in terms that should permit a better understanding of why reform is not always successful. Hefferlin estimated that, through the addition of new courses and the deletion of obsolete ones, the curriculum changes, on the average, every 22 years. Lewis Mayhew (1967–1972), in a series of monographs for the Southern Regional Education Board, described the numerous eddies at work in the mainstream of higher education. For the most part, these concern organizational displacements only and may be regarded without undue scorn as tinkering with the curriculum for the sake of looking busy with the solution of momentous problems. It is evident from Mayhew's wide-ranging views that innumerable efforts were made to cope with the demands for change. The gamut of alterations and modifications is incredible, but the permanency and genuine effect of such tinkering must be assessed with better data than those available.

The Carnegie Commission on Higher Education was established in 1967 and was initially funded for a five-year period at an annual rate of approximately $1 million. Its mission was initially conceived of as an effort to study the financial difficulties of colleges and universities, but it was quickly expanded to include the structure, function, and governance of higher education; the necessity of innovation and reform; demand and expenditures; and the availability and uses of public resources. The activities of the commission included research studies by experienced investigators in the social and behavioral sciences; a series of descriptive profiles of various segments of the higher education community; a series of reflective essays dealing with critical issues and trends; the review and analysis of selected policies; new developments and alternative processes; and the preparation of special reports and recommendations. Before its work was concluded, the Carnegie Commission had issued over 100 volumes appraising higher education and providing guidance for its continued development.

The joint problems and issues of secondary and higher education were addressed in several of the Carnegie Commission reports. Remedial work for college students was discussed in *A Chance to Learn* (1970). The duplication of effort and the waste of student time between high school and college was considered in two reports: *Less Time, More Options* (1970) and *Reform on Campus* (1972). The creation of new places for entering high-school graduates was recommended in the volume *New Students and New Places* (1971). A report focusing specifically on the relationships of schools and colleges, however, was entitled *Continuity and Discontinuity: Higher Education and the Schools* (1973). The general theme was that while some discontinuities are harmful and disruptive, there is a need for some discontinuity between high school and post-secondary education.

The Carnegie Commission stressed the reciprocal influence of school and college curricula, as well as the desirability of new structural patterns for academic progression through high school and college. The complex interactions between schools and colleges meant that the traditional college preparatory course had little meaning in an era of universal access, since students find a place in college regardless of their high-school preparation.

The commission was of the opinion that schools and colleges are still worlds apart; that there are broad moats separating schoolteachers and college professors; and that the two groups artificially and harmfully impede the learning experiences of students. The commission believed that the schools should relieve colleges of remedial work. In return, the colleges should not force conformity on the schools and should not impede curricular experimentation. Both could cause less trouble for students if they provided better counseling and if the admissions process was less of a rat race. The commission stated emphatically that unnecessary duplication is contemptuous of the students' time and sensibilities.

A report from the Hazen Foundation entitled *The Student in Higher Education* (1968) called for major qualitative changes in the role of students in colleges and universities. Such changes should begin with a reorganization of instruction and a restructuring of faculty relations that would break the power of academic guilds over undergraduate instruction. Written at the height of student protest, this report was especially sensitive to the boredom, frustration, and alienation of students. The theme of alienation was later revisited by Levine (1980) in ways that suggested that colleges and universities still have much to learn about their own students.

ISSUES IN CURRICULAR REFORM

Despite the rapid turn of curricular events since World War II, most problems and issues of curricular development persist. No decrees from either Mount Sinai or Mount Olympus have yet resolved the issues of (1) who is to decide the curricular content of schools and colleges in a democratic society; (2) to what extent students *should* be involved in curricular planning and development, and to what extent they can be involved; (3) what are the relative rights and responsibilities of teachers within the schools and of societal interests outside the school; (4) how the curriculum itself is to be organized, and whether courses of instruction should be given traditional, functional, or solicitous titles; (5) to what extent the curriculum can reflect instructor interests and student needs without contradiction; (6) how curricular content is to be related to the world of work; and (7) how instruction within the classroom and experience outside the classroom can be tied together for educational relevance.

Other problems and issues that are recurrent in education pertain to (1) the sectioning or grouping of students for purposes of instruction (for examples, advanced placement, course exemption, or credit by examination), (2) the timing or sequencing of instructional content (when and where specific topics, units, or subjects will be taught); and (3) the methods of instruction that will be employed (how the teacher will engage the student in the curriculum). Underlying these issues are age-old questions concerning (1) the extent to which the curriculum is to be general or specialized; (2) the development of some acceptable procedure whereby courses can be deleted from the curriculum as well as added to it; (3) the compromise that must be found between course and curricular content that is final or terminal and that which is instrumental or preparatory; and (4) the extent to which education at any level, time, or place is to be concerned with attitudes, values, or feelings as opposed to knowledge, competencies, and skills.

Following a period in which numerous efforts have been made to establish new curricula in the nation's colleges and universities, it is not inappropriate to ask:

1. How does curricular change take place?
2. In what ways are rapid, innovative changes possible?
3. To what extent are those changes enduring or substantive?
4. Are there well-tested procedures that will enable us to plan and develop more effective curricula for colleges and universities?

How Change Takes Place

Curricular changes at the secondary and postsecondary levels of education have been both extensive and frequent in the past 30 years. Curricula in both high school and college have changed in efforts to accommodate societal and cultural changes that could not be ignored—and curricular change has, in turn, affected social, economic, and political events that have reacted by calling for additional curricular change. For example, some observers are satisfied that grade inflation and test-score decline are reflections of curricular change in the secondary schools—and of little else. Public reaction to grade inflation and test-score decline, however, has usually taken the form of further changes in the curriculum. Alternative schools would give secondary students different subjects to study and different ways of studying them; a "back-to-the-basics" movement would ostensibly insist that all students study some of the same subjects and master them in ways about which there would be no doubt; and efforts at the college level would reestablish core curricula that ensure common funds of knowledge or basic academic competencies.

Concurrent with efforts to revise college curricula are continuing efforts to develop new programs that will serve the educational needs of new student clienteles. A new majority of "part-time students," an increasing proportion of older, adult students in college student bodies, and the increasing numbers of educationally disadvantaged students are indicative of a changing composition of student groups that require curricular adjustments or alterations (Commission on Non-Traditional Study, 1973). The challenge in curriculum development, therefore, is to reestablish the central or basic features of academic programs while fashioning new or different programs that will serve other purposes.

In the second edition of his book *College and University Curriculum,* Paul Dressel (1971) wrote:

> The curriculum may be likened to sundry and assorted bricks, blocks, and stones. An uncoordinated professoriate and confused students pile these bricks, blocks, and stones in assorted patterns to construct the walls of an edifice that no one envisions clearly. No unified structure ever becomes apparent because between lack of order . . . and lack of coordination . . . what is reared one year falls or is torn down the next. It is a tribute to the intellect and resilience of youth that, in some fashion, they still acquire the rudiments of an education. [p. iii]

A few sentences later, Dressel added:

> The curriculum is a result of gradual cumulative actions, and it involves so many and uncorrelated, if not conflicting interests, that it is not easily replaced. When there is a readiness to confront the higher education curriculum tasks *de nova,* there is very little available in the way of principles of structures to provide guidance. [pp. iii–iv.]

Although Dressel was writing during years of widespread concern with college curricula, the intensity of that concern has increased during the following decade. Since 1971, there has been a returning concern with general education or core curricula, continuing efforts to design new curricula, and an accelerated advocacy of curricular reform. Various models for curricular design and development have been applied with varying effectiveness. If higher education has not undergone a period of active experimentation, it has at least displayed an active concern with accommodations for adjustment believed to be necessary for undergraduate curricula in the nation's colleges.

Change as Innovation

The development of any college curriculum would seem to be a process that is poorly understood by both participants and observers. When genuine innovation is possible, there seems to be a period of initial success, followed by a period of disillusionment, and eventually by attitudes that border on bitter rejection. Institutional histories are rife with curricular innovations that did not outlive their innovators. Where innovation does succeed, it often becomes a pale shadow of what was envisioned at the start. Usage and daily routine grind down the finer features of innovation, and it is a rare baton that is passed without being dropped.

Gerald Grant and David Riesman (1978) studied at close hand the innovations and reforms of the 1960s. They discussed in appreciable detail the reforms attempted at St. John's College, Kresge College, and the College for Human Services. They also discussed New College at Sarasota, the cluster-college effort of the University of California at Santa Cruz, and the experimental public colleges of New Jersey—Stockton and Ramapo. The gist of Grant and Riesman's work may well be that experiment and reform have been tried; have been found quite interesting and sometimes exciting; and have failed. There is no doubt that many colleges in recent years have tried to change the basic purposes of collegiate education and have tried in creative ways. Grant and Riesman classified such "telic reforms" as neoclassical revivals, communal-expressives, and activist-radical impulses. St. John's College provides a case study of the first; Kresge College is a case study of the second; and the College for Human Services is a telling example of the third.

It was Grant and Riesman's conclusion that universities—our modern secular cathedrals—remain strong and retain their hegemony over other institutions. Experimenters and reformers have won relatively few adherents and have met with "only mixed success." Where they have succeeded, it has been through a partial incorporation of their aims, goals, and purposes within the modern university itself. The university can add new functions with relative ease because it is a pluralistic institution where "different sects may worship at the side altars" (p. 335). Of all the books written on curricular change, innovation, or reform in the past thirty years, Grant and Riesman's may be the one that could be read by college administrators and faculty with the most benefit. Grant (1979) gave further credence to the conclusion that innovation is the most difficult form of change.

Change as a Developmental Process

Although curricular reform is the most challenging issue in higher education, there is no theory of curriculum development that adequately explains how curricula change, develop and mature. There are no consistent notions about the phenomena of decay, dissolution, or death in curricula—and no funeral directors to handle last rites in a humane manner. Yet no one should doubt that curricula are bred and born, occasionally blooming and flourishing, sometimes growing too rapidly and too large, and occasionally reaching maturity, and just as surely, some enter an age of senescence, and a few live long beyond an obvious usefulness.

As much as we write about curriculum design and development, teach courses in curriculum and instruction, or graduate curriculum specialists for public schools and two-year colleges, there is a lingering suspicion that curricula develop at their own pace with or without the assistance of those who presumably understand the process. Even authors of influential reports may despair of planned and directed change in curricular matters:

> American legal education, like most is a mindless growth. It has evolved by accretion, sometimes spurred by a faith in the divinity of all education, sometimes diverted by professional vanity, sometimes retarded by the excessive admiration of students, but always the product of what teachers have learned from their students. This is the way that such institutions should grow; not from a single arrogant concept, but as a flourishing of many individual wisdoms. [Carrington, 1972, p. 95]

Despite the availability of curriculum development handbooks (Chickering et al., 1977) and excellent advice on the evaluation of academic programs (Dressel, 1976; Anderson and Ball, 1978), there is little reason to believe that curricular deficiencies are easily remedied or that new, creative, radically different curricula are easily designed, planned, and implemented. There are, indeed, marketplaces that courses, programs, and degrees must eventually be tested in, and the provisional variations made by curriculum innovators must be seen as just that—provisional. Success or failure is a judgment that must be suspended until students graduate, assume societal roles and responsibilities, and register their pleasure or displeasure with their preparation. If society is inclined to select graduates well-adapted for survival, there is little reason to doubt the similar selection of courses, programs, and degrees.

Observation of curricular change over a period of many years must surely suggest that curricula develop through a process of accretion, gradual adjustment, mutual accommodation, and frequent compromise. Most curricular innovations must be understood in terms of what preceded the efforts to bring about curricular change and the specific faults, defects, or inconveniences with which those concerned with curricular change were trying to cope.

Most curricular changes that are in any way enduring would seem to resolve some issue or conflict in a manner that is generally accepted as being better than whatever they replaced. Herbert Simon's concept (1957) of satisficing would seem especially appropriate to curricular development. Curricular problems are seldom amenable to solutions that are optimal, ideal, or comprehensive, and most participants in the process evidently reach some arrangement that is sufficiently satisfactory and then turn their attention to other matters.

Curricular development may be explained best as a form of sociocultural evolution with something similar to natural selection as the mechanism that eventually decides what survives and what doesn't. There is a marketplace that courses, programs, and degrees must be tested in, and many curricular innovations may be damned by premature judgments of their success. Changes in education frequently benefit from a "novelty effect" that suggests students will welcome almost any kind of break in routine. Substitute teachers are almost always welcome in public schools, and most college students are unlikely to complain when professors cut classes. New degree programs are frequently welcome because they promise relief from painful requirements in older or better established programs. Indeed, it is not ridiculous to hypothesize that any kind of tinkering with course, program, or degree requirements will meet with the initial approval of students. A corollary might be that dissatisfaction sets in when students realize what the personal costs and inconveniences are.

Campbell's theory (1975) of blind-variation-and-natural-selection would explain many curricular changes if the term *provisional* were substituted for *blind*. Many developmental efforts are predicated on systematic or experimental change, while others opt for a conscious selection based on experience, thinking perhaps that natural selection is a mechanistic or determinate process unsuited for enterprises as rational as education. Yet it is not unseemly to remember that competition based on merit was regarded as essential in the science development efforts of the National Science Foundation, and that competitive decision-making has been consistently favored over central planning in most efforts to develop institutions and curricula.

A model of provisional-variation-and-selective-retention in curriculum development thus has appreciable explanatory value. Yet it obviously lacks the degree of prediction and control that advocates of curricular reform seek. There are many who would reform and not know why they have failed. If a program of study in an academic community cannot be rationally designed, developed, and disseminated, there may be reason to question the rationality of higher education itself. The exercise of rational, analytical methods is obviously due in planning and organizing curricular variations. The selective retention of such variations, however, is a function of forces and influences that may not be rational or orderly. A nation infatuated with automobiles should not have a lack of competent automotive mechanics.

Thus, there are reasons, quite sound, to believe that college curricula are always in a stage of becoming. Whatever the college curriculum is, it is never finished and it is never complete. If a metaphor of a living, breathing creature may be stretched a bit, the college curriculum would indeed appear to expand and contract; converge and diverge; open and close—and to show many other characteristics of a distinct pulsation within cycles and phases that we poorly understand.

The gist might be that curricular change can be advantageously regarded as a developmental process in which trial-and-error, cut-and-try, or provisional efforts play a dominant role. Comprehensive design and grand strategy are not as characteristic of curricular change as piecemeal, incremental efforts are. The outcomes of curricular reform thus are seldom seen in retrospect as earth-shaking, radical, or innovative as they were in the beginning by advocates or adherents. Any curricular change that is dependent upon faculty committees for approval must surely be sensitive to the deliberative process that many faculty members believe to be the college's or university's own brand of rationality.

THE CHANGING STRUCTURE OF COLLEGE CURRICULA

Academic disciplines are believed to have a structure of relative endurance. Mastery of the structure is regarded as essential to the socialization of newcomers to the discipline, and a significant feature of most professional or graduate programs is what observers could call *structural courses*. The belief that students can learn the methods of inquiry by which scientists and scholars investigate and "structure" their respective disciplines has, as indicated earlier, shaped many of the curricular reforms attempted.

The undergraduate curriculum in most colleges can be described as a loose collection of courses. The major groupings of such courses are usually identified as electives, major field, general education, and "other"—a field that usually includes supplementary courses such as physical education and ROTC. The courses that make up the general education requirements of undergraduate degrees usually include English, mathematics, science, and various combinations of the humanities. As a rule, these courses are offered in the freshman and sophomore years and are often referred to as a *lower-division course work*. A basic assumption underlying such courses is that they constitute background knowledge or basic academic competencies that will be needed for specialization or concentration at the upper-division level.

The major field, or area of specialization, usually represents the subjects in which students are most interested and for which they have ostensibly attended college. We often assume that a higher degree of mastery will be exhibited in such courses because of student interest and faculty proficiencies. The group of courses identified as electives may contain courses similar to those in the general education requirement, or they may include fields related to the student's major. To some extent, they also reflect student interest but also serve to grant academic credit for courses that are not applicable to the student's basic curriculum as defined.

The distribution of courses among the groupings of electives, major fields, and general education varies according to the degree earned, but not dramatically. As Haswell and Lindquist (1965) showed, there is little difference between a bachelor of arts degree and a bachelor of science degree if one looks at the distribution of course work. In the biological sciences, for example, the major field constitutes approximately one fourth of the student's undergraduate course work. Electives may range from 21% for the B.S. degree to 25% for the B.A. degree, while the humanities constitute approximately one fifth of the student's course work. The major difference in distributional requirements may be that students working for a B.S. degree take a larger proportion of their courses in other sciences.

For students majoring in the humanities, the primary distinction may be the relatively few courses they take in sciences and mathematics. According to Haswell and Lindquist, well over one fourth of the course work is in the major field, while almost 30% of the courses are designated as electives. An additional one fifth of the course work is apparently taken in "other humanities."

Students majoring in the physical sciences apparently show a smaller proportion of electives but do show approximately one fourth of their course work in the humanities. Students majoring in social sciences show a much larger proportion of their course work in electives and a relatively small proportion of their course work in their major field. Sciences and mathematics for social science majors constitute only 10% for the B.A. degree and 12% for the B.S. degree.

Dressel and DeLisle (1969) found that changes in college curricula vary greatly in scope, depth, and rationale. Some changes in curricula could be attributed to changes in institutional mission. For example, as teacher colleges and two-year institutions were upgraded to state colleges or universities, corresponding changes in curricula were made. More important, Dressel and DeLisle found basic or general educational requirements to constitute approximately 37% of degree requirements. Of the degree requirements, 17% were in the humanities while 10% each were in the social sciences and the natural sciences. The departmental major remained the most common pattern, but there was evidence of an increase in divisional or interdepartmental approaches. Major requirements were supplemented by courses in related fields in 60% of the responding institutions, but some decrease in the specification of such requirements was indicated. Although there was still variation in the degree of concentration for a major, the modal practice remained as 24 to 32 credits.

In a later study Blackburn et al. (1976) found that students increasingly used electives to pursue interests within their field of concentration. Students continued to take approximately a third of their course work in their major field but decreased the proportion of total course work taken in general education. The percentage of course work devoted to electives increased from 24% in 1967 to 34% in 1974 and reflected, for the most part, additional courses in the student's area of specialization. The Carnegie Foundation (1977) attributed the increase in electives to a loosening of curricular requirements in efforts to satisfy student demands for relevance. The council concluded, however, that it is doubtful if further electives in the curriculum could be justified.

CHANGING PURPOSES AND FUNCTIONS

The resistance to change that is evident in the structure or basic organization of undergraduate curricula is not true of the functions served by college degree programs. The purpose, functions, and meaning of college curricula have changed in significant ways during the years of rapid growth and expansion, stress and reaction, financial difficulties, and uncertain missions and roles. The outcome of such changes is a continuing debate about: (1) the meaning of the liberal arts in undergraduate programs; (2) the purpose and functions of general education; (3) the specific benefits and advantages that accrue to college graduates on the completion of program and degree requirements; and (4) the particular significance and meaning that can be attached to a college education in an era of mass or universal education. To many critics and observers, the traditional liberal arts program of four-year colleges no longer has the purpose and value it should have. Many four-year colleges are seen as preprofessional colleges in which the value of the programs is attested to by the number of graduates entering graduate or professional school. The content and substance of their undergraduate courses is seen as more in tune with professional entrance requirements than with the traditional values of a liberal education. Similar arguments are heard concerning general education and the significance or value of undergraduate degrees that do not result in career placement.

It is not inaccurate to say that the baccalaureate is now viewed by many students as a means to other ends. The intrinsic value or quality of the degree is "an unknown quantity" and the outcomes of undergraduate education are measured by criteria that are not inherent in traditional notions of a college education. In the words of econometricians, the college degree is judged in terms of its "externalities." Because a college degree no longer accounts for a sufficient portion of the variance in occupational status, starting salary, and lifetime earnings, policymakers are warned of "overeducated Americans" and parents are advised to invest their money not in tuition but in the money market. Because the attainment of a college education has not had the expected distributive effect on socioeconomic status, sociologists have recommended alternative forms of education and other societal arrangements for what used to be called *upward mobility* (Fincher, 1979).

A Historical Perspective
There is irony in the fact that the Carnegie Commission on Higher Education, despite issuing over 100 volumes, devoted only a volume edited by Carl Kaysen (1973) to college curricula. In a critical look at the commission's work, Donald

McDonald, executive editor of *The Center Magazine* (1973), severely criticized commission members for ignoring teaching and the curriculum in its $6-million effort. McDonald cited Clark Kerr's opinion that the commission could not be helpful in matters of curriculum and instruction because these were responsibilities of college faculties. Implied in Kerr's opinion was the low probability that commission findings and recommendations would be influential with the teaching faculties of American colleges.

Where the Carnegie Commission on Higher Education was negligent, its successor—the Carnegie Council on Policy Studies in Higher Education—was most successful. The Carnegie Council commissioned a respected historian to write a historical survey of undergraduate curricula, issued through the Carnegie Foundation for the Advancement of Teaching a remarkable volume entitled *Missions of the College Curriculum* (1977), and issued under its own label a 662-page handbook on undergraduate curriculum (Levine, 1978). In doing so, the Carnegie Council obviously extended the work of the Carnegie Commission and rendered invaluable service in its critical look at the problems and issues of curriculum development.

Frederick Rudolph (1977) discussed in detail the development of higher education from its beginnings at Harvard and gave an unusually helpful perspective to the difficulties of developing undergraduate programs in American colleges and universities. In particular, his chapter on "The Last Fifty Years" gave curriculum planners cause to believe that the twentieth century had seen such a diversity of "purpose, style, and institutional form that the word curriculum becomes a concept of convenience rather than precision" (p. 244). Rudolph believed that the liberal arts, as "a set of values and expectations, let alone subject matter," had lost much of their meaning. The B.A. degree had become, in his estimation, an umbrella degree with titles that were "intentionally job descriptive." The excessive "concentration" of bachelors' degrees had created a need for testing, counseling, and guidance as a means of coping with increased specialization and "vocationalism" in curricula. He drew close attention to the failure of undergraduate curricula to define or support general education and was almost scornful of scientists who had no interest in the general education of nonscientists.

Among Rudolph's many cogent observations is the following judgment of student protests:

> As unsettling as it was to the serenity of college and university campuses, the student movement of the 1960s wrought no great transformation either in the curriculum or in the lecture system. The movement, whatever its source, was not an attack on the curriculum or instruction, as such. [p. 270]

In concluding his historical survey, Rudolph was of the opinion that the conditions currently prevailing (1977) in higher education were not disadvantageous:

The time may be at hand when a reevaluation of academic purpose and philosophy will encourage the curricular developments that will focus on the lives we lead, their quality, the enjoyment they give us, and the wisdom with which we lead them. If such a development does take place, human beings, as distinct from trained technicians, will not be at a disadvantage in the job market. And perhaps, once more, the ideal of an educated person will have become a useful idea. [p. 289]

Missions of the College Curriculum is the most relevant statement issued on college curricula since *General Education in a Free Society* (Report of the Harvard Committee, 1945). As a commentary, the volume was issued in a context of "considerable change" in college curricula; "changes of substantial significance" in the composition and capacities of students; and a perspective of "no growth" for higher education but fundamental social changes for society. The commentary was cognizant that curricular review is never easy and that most colleges have few effective mechanisms for examining and revising curricula. In particular, the Carnegie Foundation was appreciative that in curricular matters:

> There are eternal points of tension; scholarship versus training; attention more to the past or to the present or to the future; integration versus fragmentation; socialization into the culture versus alienation from the culture; student choice versus institutional requirements; breadth versus depth; skills versus understanding versus personal interest; theory versus practice; ethical commitments versus ethical neutrality; among others. These conflicts are temporarily adjusted now one way and now another; but they never cease. There are no easy or permanent solutions. [pp. 1–2]

Other observations made in the Carnegie Foundation commentary are equally relevant to the changing purposes and functions of undergraduate curricula. The basic components of the curriculum are identified as (1) advanced learning skills; (2) general education; (3) breadth; (4) major field; and (5) electives. Advanced learning skills should be learned in high school but must also be taught in college. The general understanding components of general education should include what is common to undergraduate learning experience, while the breadth components should expose students to the broader grouping of subject matter, such as social sciences, humanities, and the physical or natural sciences. Although the Carnegie Foundation regarded general education as "an idea in distress," there was an expression of confidence that intellectual trends were now in the direction of integration. Biochemistry, the behavioral sciences, and systems and operations analysis gave promise of restoring some of the coherence that had been lost in fields of human knowledge. A particularly appealing statement in the commentary, however, was to the effect that:

> The curriculum is the major statement any institution makes about itself, about what it can contribute to the intellectual development of students, about what it thinks is important in its teaching service to society. It deserves more attention and merits less neglect than has been accorded it by most institutions of higher education in recent years. [p. 18]

Levine's handbook on undergraduate curriculum is a helpful companion to the first two volumes. Part One is a topical outline of such matters as general education, majors or fields of concentration, tests and grades, and methods of instruction; each treatment is relevant to the needs of curricular planning and reorganization. Part Two is an effort to provide historical and comparative perspectives. Chapters 11 and 12 give curriculum "highlights" from 1900 to the present, and Chapter 14, perhaps the weakest in the entire book, gives an overview of strategies for curricular change.

Liberal Learning

The fact that the purpose and meaning of a liberal education is again debatable is, by its own evidence, an indictment of higher education in the 1980s. Yet, a prestigious commission examining the status of the humanities in 1980 found little evidence that the humanities are greatly valued in contemporary society. The commission believed that the value of the humanities should be reaffirmed, and it recommended that the highest priority be assigned the improved quality of elementary and secondary education. Research in the humanities should be supported, and cultural institutions should receive sufficient funds to conserve and propagate humanistic values. Such recommendations came at a time when, as pointed out by Theodore Hesburgh (1981) in *Change* magazine, accounting was the most popular course on college campuses.

Although the Commission on Humanities (1980) was much better at explaining the humanities than it was in recommending public action, its report implies that there is in contemporary society no deep, pervasive, abiding concern with philosophical, literary, and historical insights into the nature of the human condition. The humanities must struggle to maintain a respectable position in undergraduate curricula, and their potential value to many students is quickly nullified by charges of elitism or by the demands they make on what the Carnegie Foundation (1977) called advanced learning skills.

The extension of educational opportunity has challenged all notions of a "common culture" and a "unified curriculum." As a result, the humanities were "especially vulnerable to the wave of the vocationalism that swept undergraduate learning in the 1970s" and few colleges have been able to "maintain a firm commitment to a liberal education." The commission was not equivocal when it asked for the knowledge and mental capacities for:

(a) effective command of written and spoken English;
(b) enjoyment and informed judgment of the arts;
(c) understanding of other cultures;
(d) analysis and assessment of ethical problems, issues of public policy, and the questions of value underlying science and technology. [p. 69]

The commission was also mindful that no single curriculum is appropriate for all colleges, but it recommended "general strategies" such as instruction in writing that spreads across the course of study; courses with integrating themes and subjects; clear sequences of courses in each of the disciplines; and the development of new materials for teaching the humanities.

The status and the dubious value of the humanities in the 1980s are not unrelated to the changing economic conditions identified by the National Enquiry into Scholarly Communication (1979) as affecting libraries, university presses, and the distribution of scholarly books and journals. The crisis in scholarly communication is defined by that group as "not dramatic enough to kill the patient, but able, if left unattended, to produce a lingering, wasting disease" (p. 3).

The goals and objectives of the Commission for the Humanities were given a new impetus with the NEH report written by Bennett (1984), then director of the National Endowment for the Humanities. It was Bennett's contention that while the humanities are taught well in many colleges, they are taught poorly in too many other institutions. His case for restoration of the humanities was not for more students who would specialize in or major in the humanities, but for broader, better in-depth coverage of the humanities in the undergraduate education of all college students.

Further support for liberal learning was given by Zelda Gamson and associates (1984). This volume gives particular emphasis to expressing more clearly what the goals of a liberal education are; how students can be educated for critical awareness, use more effectively what they learn, and make the many choices that living requires. Although some excellent advice is given to college faculty and others responsible for the personal development of students, it is not easy to determine who the audience of the book might be. There is much in Gamson's views that will strike long-term critics and observers as being unrealistically suited for education in the 1990s.

General Education
The national need for core curricula and/or the reestablishment of general education has been strongly advocated by Ernest Boyer, a former Commissioner of Education and then president of The Carnegie Foundation. Writing first with Martin Kaplan (1977) and later with Arthur Levine (1981), Boyer argued persuasively that the college curriculum has a common core of verities and values to which colleges are returning. Although academic programs have long lost the unity they once had, there is again a need to emphasize the common foundations of academic disciplines and intellectual inquiry. With Kaplan, Boyer gave an informative summary of the continuing tensions between general or common educational purposes and the pressures toward specialization. With Levine, he discussed the subject matter that he believed to be the "proper concern of general education."

The theme of his "modest proposal" is that we share a common heritage and confront a common set of challenges in contemporary society. As we understand the past and deal with the present, we are building a future that necessarily involves ethical choices. To do this in any kind of rational or intelligent manner, we must understand how it has been done in the past and what the specific challenges of the present might be. A core curriculum is the forum in which we can deal with our common past, present, and future.

General education should be the means by which we concentrate on our common experiences in a community that we may be losing. What we have in common, obviously, is (1) a shared use of symbols; (2) membership in groups and institutions; (3) a concern with producing and consuming; (4) an interlocking relationship with nature; (5) a shared sense of time; and (6) shared beliefs and values. Boyer and Levine rightly viewed their broad, sweeping themes not as a single set of courses but as program objectives to be achieved formally or informally, on campus or off, and with credit or without, but as they acknowledged, "faculty and classrooms are still the heart of the enterprise."

Other publicized efforts to deal with the issues of core curricula and general education may be seen in Harvard's development of a core curriculum (O'Connell, 1978; Schiefelbein, 1978; Wilson, 1978). Extensive revisions were approved by the Harvard faculty after lengthy consideration and signified that institution's efforts to reemphasize "basic literacy in major forms of intellectual discourse." Begun in 1982, the core curriculum required Harvard undergraduates to devote almost one fourth of their studies to literature, the arts, social and philosophical analysis, and other courses designed to ensure strength in academic competencies and areas. Less publicized but equally interesting was a continuing effort by Columbia University to "reintegrate" the university through general education (Belknap and Kuhns, 1977). The Columbia effort defined general education as the opposite of training and proceeded on the principle that doctors, lawyers, historians, and physicists could be trained but that human beings should be educated. Academic disciplines were seen by the Columbia faculty as highly fragmented, resulting in a contradiction that exalted training over education. The means of coping with this contradiction were the organizing and conducting of general education seminars for the faculty and courses that were self-consciously planned to introduce students to Western culture.

Gaff (1983) gave an overview of general education that is particularly relevant to its role and function in undergraduate degree programs. He was encouraged by the returning concern with general education and with its continuing importance for the liberal traditions of American higher education. Greatly needed, however, was "a new philosophy" in which general education could be viewed as a necessary complement to both specialization and professional education. Some forms of knowledge should be seen as more important than other forms, but "certain subjects" should be required of all students.

Some degree of coherence and more emphasis on common learning should be evident in all degree programs, and undergraduate education should be strengthened without undue concern that such a strengthening will weaken the base for research and/or graduate training. General education is, in Gaff's estimation, everyone's business and should incorporate advances that have only recently been made in scholarship.

Adult Development

The implications of adult development for higher education have been persuasively presented by Weathersby and Tarule (1980). Its importance in adult, continuing, and professional education has been discussed in appreciable detail by Knox (1977). Its bearing on faculty development and administrative development has been pointed out by Hodgkinson (1974). And its relevance to undergraduate teaching and learning is the subject of an impressive volume published by Jossey-Bass (Chickering, 1981).

If accepted with full implications, adult development would give the nation's colleges and universities an entirely new thrust or mission. The movement, of course, is influenced by the baby-boom generation as that generation has affected education at other levels. In 1990, the largest age group in the national population will be the baby-boomers, who will then be between twenty-five and thirty-four years old. Just as the generation imposed different demands and expectations on elementary and secondary education, so will they pose new challenges for higher education as they move out of the traditional college-age group of eighteen to twenty-four years and become older adults. Clearly implied by the adult development movement is the obligation of higher education to see the baby-boomers through their midlife crises and the remainder of their life cycle.

Adult development has profound implications for higher education—*if* several basic premises are granted. Stages of development have been described with good fidelity at preschool, school, and adolescent ages; and developmental psychology has been quite serviceable in its applications to elementary and secondary education. There should be serious reservation, however, about immediate and direct applications of developmental theory to education beyond the high school. Nevitt Sanford's classic *The American College* (1962) suggests, however, that the applicability of developmental themes and research findings to institutions of higher education may be limited by misapprehensions of curricular purposes, contents, and methods. Successful implementation of developmental psychology in higher education may require too much redirection of institutional missions and roles for adoption by faculty and administrators, and the applications of social science theory and research may be more relevant to extracurricular activities than to formal classroom instruction and what students study and learn as degree requirements.

It is doubtful that adults will attend college on the scale envisioned by some observers of adult learning; it is particularly doubtful that colleges and universities can or should redirect their central mission or thrust to assist adults in their passages through the life cycle. Institutional resources and capabilities are still needed for the transitions involved in becoming an adult, and it will be impossible for institutions of higher education to accept responsibility for the entire sequence of stages and transitions depicted in the life cycle. Bowen's commendable volume on *Investment in Learning* (1977) gives good reasons to believe that colleges are successful in helping students to learn, develop, and mature. That *is,* in the opinion of many observers, precisely their function. To ask that they continue their service to adults through midlife and senior citizenship is to ask once again that they "be all things to all men." Advocates of adult development have not heard Clark Kerr (1981) in his assessment of the work of the Carnegie Commission on Higher Education and the Carnegie Council on Policy Studies. In retrospect, Kerr stated that both the commission and the council underestimated the willingness of institutions to "entertain and undertake reform"; the strength of "certain forces" in American society, such as the intensity of competition among institutions; and the inability of the council to make "adequate contact with faculty opinion." As Kerr expressed it:

> The overall mistakes of judgment were to be too optimistic about the future, too charitable about the attitudes and performances of some groups of individuals, and too convinced that all problems have reasonable and possible solutions. [p. 60]

Competency-Based Education

The most prominent influence on college curricula since the 1960s has been the push for measured or assessed outcomes that would ensure the competency, proficiency, and/or achievement of college graduates. A concern about minimal competency has been expressed in the enactment of laws requiring minimal competency tests before high school graduation; in the requirement of system-wide reading and writing tests for college sophomores; and in the increased use of comprehensive examinations for graduating seniors. The basic skills of reading, writing, and computation have become a pervasive concern for education at virtually all levels, and there have been innumerable attempts to define the skills, competencies, and abilities that schools and colleges should develop in all students receiving diplomas, degrees, or other forms certifying or attesting to what they have studied and presumably learned.

In 1983, at least nine national reports addressed the curricular needs of the nation's secondary schools and left no doubt that the quality of education had become a matter of public policy and debate. Without exception, the national reports of 1983 were explicit in calling for (1) more explicit requirements for high-school graduation; (2) better specification by colleges and universities of preferred or required precollege curricula; (3) more explicit college admission standards that are educationally relevant; (4) national educational policies that address the problems and issues of education in a culturally pluralistic society; and (5) academic programs and services that are guided by sound educational policies.

At the heart of each report was an active concern with academic competence and its apparent erosion over a twenty-year period. Leading the national chorus of critics was the National Commission on Excellence (1983) that had been appointed by Secretary of Education Terrell H. Bell. The National Commission's report was unusually effective in calling attention to the difficulties of public education at the secondary level. Among the many recommendations made was a call for "the new basics" of public education. The commission took a strong stand for a command of English, mathematics, science, social studies, and computer science that would equip high-school graduates for useful employment and education beyond the high school. The commission also advocated a curriculum in the eight years preceding high school that would provide the basis for the continued development of academic competencies.

The Education Commission of the States' Task Force on Education for Economic Growth (1983) was even more explicit in placing the plight of public schools within the context of international competition. The ECS Task Force also called for more emphasis on reading, writing, speaking, and listening competencies along with the scientific, mathematical, and reasoning competencies that were needed for employment and economic competition. Boyer's report (1983) for the Carnegie Foundation for the Advancement of Teaching was again a strong plea for a core of common learning and for the restoration of a basic curriculum. Among the noteworthy recommendations of this report were reduced teaching loads for teachers and concerted efforts to attract brighter students to teaching as a career. Reports from the National Science Foundation, the 20th Century Fund, the National Society for the Study of Education, and the National Association of Secondary School Principals followed suit in calling attention to the failures of secondary schools and in recommending immediate, concerted public action. Without doubt, the most interesting of the reports issued in 1983 was the *Paideia Proposal* written by Mortimer Adler. The *Paideia Proposal* is a truly radical call for reform in the nation's high schools and is quite explicit in suggesting ways by which that reform could be achieved.

In all of the reports issued in 1983, there is a sense of urgency. All urge schools and colleges to cooperate on matters of mutual and national importance. The transition of students from high schools to colleges must be less disruptive, and both schools and colleges must declare and hold to academic standards that will attest to the integrity of education.

The College Board, in its Educational EQuality Project, took commendable care to specify the basic academic competencies that all college students should demonstrate at the time they enter college. The Tennessee Higher Education Commission (Branscomb et al., 1977) defined the minimal competencies that all college graduates should master by the time they complete degree and program requirements. Other state commissions, national task forces, and innumerable faculty committees have considered the indispensable skills and basic understandings that would enable high-school and college graduates to meet their respective responsibilities as citizens, employees, parents, and consumers. Implied in all these deliberations is the belief that school and college curricula can be modified or revised to develop the skills, competencies, and abilities desired by state and society.

Thus, in the mid-1980s, there is once again a concern with the distinction that must periodically be made between education that is instrumental and education that is consummatory or terminal. One form of education is valued for the learning that it permits at later stages of personal and intellectual development; the other form is valued for the benefits and advantages that accrue to students on completion of their formal education and/or career preparation. In many respects, the back-to-basics movement is predicated on the belief that basic skills of literacy have a special meaning in a democratic society. Those who would participate fully in modern or contemporary life must master the skills and competencies that give them access to informed opinion and public dialogue.

Colleges and universities have a specific challenge to define or refurbish a meaningful concept of functional literacy that will serve a pluralistic society; to develop realistic and useful standards of academic competence; and to refine and promote criteria by which societal and institutional objectives can be realized.

CONCLUSIONS AND IMPLICATIONS

When college curricula are systematically studied, changes in purpose, structure, and function can be detected. Given the intensity of concern with curricular innovation and reform over the past 30 years, however, the extent or magnitude of many changes is less than dramatic. Despite intensive efforts by the federal government and other external agencies to bring about substantive, enduring changes in curricula, the academic programs of colleges and schools display a remarkable indifference. Educational institutions are apparently happy to accept the funds of foundations and federal agencies, and they are apparently willing to do such tuning, tinkering, or touching up as the funds might permit. But highly significant, profound, impressive change has not taken place in most college and school curricula as the result of planned, directed, and externally funded change. The changes that have taken place may be accurately described as gradual, cumulative, and provisional. It is quite possible that many changes can be described as temporary and inconsequential.

The systematic studies of curricular change reviewed here indicate that the basic structure of college curricula has not been altered in a truly appreciable manner. There is little doubt that course content has changed as knowledge has expanded, but college students continue to earn their baccalaureates in much the same manner that their parents did: they earn academic credit by taking so many courses from specified divisions or areas of instruction; when they have accumulated enough credits with proper distribution and acceptable perform- ance, they are awarded degrees.

Although college curricula are characterized by scope, sequence, depth, con- tinuity, and coherence, the quality of these characteristics is difficult to detect in studies of curricular change. The structure of most college curricula is more readily seen in efforts to balance general and specialized course work. Undergraduate curricula are still presented as a two-layer cake in which the lower division and the upper division are neatly ordered. General education is still presented as a function of lower-division instruction, while advanced or specialized study is seen as an inherent feature of upper-division instruction. Rational divisions of academic disciplines still constitute the subject matter of most college courses, and subjects instead of skills or competencies are still the content of most courses.

Degree requirements continue to be specified in terms of distributional re- quirements, and course enrollments continue to be dictated by prerequisites that imply continuity in subject matter. Yet sequence and continuity are diffi- cult to demonstate, and coherence is difficult to judge. Only in depth or in area and extent of specialization do most college curricula show genuine, substantive strength. It is understandable why the Carnegie Foundation for the Advance- ment of Teaching has called the college major a "success story" and general ed- ucation "an idea in distress." There is no little irony in the observation that college curricula try so hard to ensure breadth and succeed primarily in achieving depth.

The concern about college and high-school curricula is unlikely to diminish in the foreseeable future. Efforts to cope with declining, or uncertain, enrollments may well result in curricular changes that could not be imple- mented under more favorable circumstances. And if there is an increasing con- cern with the integrity of academic programs and degrees, curricula at all levels of education must be studied more intensively and more systematically. The problems and issues of curricular change in the 1990s may be much what they were in previous decades. As Hollis Caswell, President Emeritus of Teachers College, Columbia University, has written:

> Three curriculum problems . . . seemed very important to my generation, namely: (1) the problem of dealing with "the basics" in the curriculum in a way which recognizes both social needs and individual potentialities; (2) the problem of developing tested procedures that improve the curriculum; (3) the problem of developing a viable general education curriculum. We did not develop adequate solutions to them. From a sidelines view, I doubt that this generation is solving them either. [1978, p. 110]

REFERENCES

Academic preparation for college: what students need to know and be able to do.
(1983). New York: College Board.

Action for excellence: a comprehensive plan to improve our schools (1983). Denver:
Education Commission of the States (ECS).

Adler, M. (1983). *The Paideia proposal.* New York: Macmillan.

Anderson, S. B., and Ball, S. (1978). *The profession and practice of program evaluation.* San Francisco: Jossey-Bass.

Barzun, J. (1959). *The house of intellect.* New York: Harper & Row.

Belknap, R. L., and Kuhns, R. (1977). *Tradition and innovation: general education and
the reintegration of the university.* A Columbia Report. New York: Columbia
University Press.

Bell, D. (1966). *The reforming of general education.* New York: Columbia University
Press.

Bennett, W. J. (1984). *To reclaim a legacy: a report on the humanities in higher education.* Washington, DC: National Endowment for the Humanities.

Bestor, A. (1955). *The restoration of learning.* New York: Knopf.

Blackburn, R., Armstrong, E., Conrad, C., Didham, J., and McKune, T. (1976). *Changing practices in undergraduate education.* Berkeley, CA: Carnegie Council on Policy
Studies in Higher Education.

Bowen, H. R. (1977). *Investment in learning.* San Francisco: Jossey-Bass.

Boyer, E. L. (1983). *High school: a report on secondary education in America.* New
York: Harper & Row.

Boyer, E. L., and Kaplan, M. (1977). *Educating for survival.* New Rochelle, NY:
Change Magazine Press.

Boyer, E. L., and Levine, A. (1981). *A quest for common learning: the aims of general
education.* Washington, DC: Carnegie Foundation for the Advancement of Teaching.

Branscomb, H., Milton, O., Richardson, J., and Spivey, H. (1977). *The competent college student: an essay on the objectives and quality of higher education.* Nashville:
Tennessee Higher Education Commission.

Bruner, J. S. (1960). *The process of education.* Cambridge: Harvard University Press.

Campbell, D. T. (1975). On the conflicts between biological and social evolution and
between psychology and moral tradition. *American Psychologist,* 1103–1126.

Carnegie Commission on Higher Education. (1970a). *A chance to learn.* New York:
McGraw-Hill.

Carnegie Commission on Higher Education. (1970b). *Less time, more options.* New
York: McGraw-Hill.

Carnegie Commission on Higher Education. (1971). *New students and new places.*
New York: McGraw-Hill.

Carnegie Commission on Higher Education. (1972). *Reform on campus.* New York:
McGraw-Hill.

Carnegie Commission on Higher Education. (1973). *Continuity and discontinuity.* New
York: McGraw-Hill.

Carnegie Foundation for the Advancement of Teaching. (1977). *Missions of the college
curriculum: contemporary review with suggestions.* San Francisco: Jossey-Bass.

Carrington, P. D. (1972). Training for the public professions of the law. Reprinted as
Appendix A in H. L. Parker, T. Ehrlich, and S. Pepper (eds)., *New directions for legal education.* New York: McGraw-Hill.

Caswell, H. L. (1978). Persistent curriculum problems. *The Educational Forum* 43:
99–110.

Chickering, A. W., ed. (1981). *The modern American college: responding to new realities of diverse students and a changing society.* San Francisco: Jossey-Bass.

Chickering, A., Halliburton, D., Bergquist, W. H., and Lindquist, J. (1977). *Developing the college curriculum: a handbook for faculty and administrators.* Washington, DC: Council for the Advancement of Small Colleges.

Commission on Non-Traditional Study. (1973). *Design for diversity.* San Francisco: Jossey-Bass.

Commission on the Humanities. (1980). *The humanities in American life.* Berkeley: University of California Press.

Committee on the Student in Higher Education. (1968). *The student in higher education.* New Haven, CT: The Hazen Foundation.

Conant, J. B. (1959). *The American high school today.* New York: McGraw-Hill.

Dennison, G. (1969). *The lives of children.* New York: Random House.

Dressel, P. L. (1971). *College and university curriculum* (2nd ed.). Berkeley, CA: McCutchann.

Dressel, P. L. (1976) *Handbook of academic evaluation.* San Francisco: Jossey-Bass.

Dressel, P. L., and DeLisle, F. H. (1969). *Undergraduate curriculum trends.* Washington, DC: American Council on Education.

Educating Americans for the 21st Century: a plan of action for improving mathematics, science, and technology education for all American elementary and secondary students. (1983). Washington, DC: National Science Foundation.

Fincher, C. (1979). Economic and sociological studies of educational effects. *Educational Forum, 43*, 139–151.

Fincher, C. (1985). Learning theory and research. In John C. Smart (ed.), *Higher education: Handbook of theory and research, Vol. 1,* pp. New York: Agathon Press.

Flanagan, J. C. et al. (1962). *Studies of the American high school.* Pittsburgh: Project Talent.

Friedenburg, E. Z. (1963). *Coming of age in America.* New York: Random House.

Gaff, J. G. (1983). *General education today: a critical analysis of controversies.* San Francisco: Jossey-Bass.

Gamson, Z. F., and Associates. (1983). *Liberating education.* San Francisco: Jossey-Bass.

Gardner, J. W. (1961). *Excellence: can we be equal and excellent too?* New York: Harper & Row.

Goodlad, J. I. (1966). *The changing school curriculum.* New York: Fund for the Advancement of Education.

Goodlad, J. I. (1983). *A place called school: prospects for the future.* New York: McGraw-Hill.

Goodman, P. (1965). *Growing up absurd.* New York: Vintage.

Grant, G., and Riesman, D. (1978). *The perpetual dream: reform and experiment in the American college.* Chicago: University of Chicago Press.

Grant, G., et al. (1979). *On competence: a critical analysis of competence based reforms in higher education.* San Francisco: Jossey-Bass.

Haswell, H. A., and Lindquist, C. B. (eds.). (1965). *Undergraduate curriculum patterns: a survey of baccalaureate programs in selected fields, 1962–63.* Washington, DC: U.S. Government Printing Office.

Hefferlin, J. B. (1969). *Dynamics of academic reform.* San Francisco: Jossey-Bass.

Herndon, J. (1968). *The way it spozed to be.* New York: Simon & Schuster.

Hesburgh, T. M. (1981). The future of liberal education. *Change* 13: 36–40.

Holt, J. (1970). *What do I do on Monday?* New York: Dutton.

Illich, I. (1971). *Deschooling society.* New York: Harper & Row.

Integrity in the college curriculum: a report to the academic community. (1985). The findings and recommendations of the project on redefining the meaning and purpose of baccalaureate degrees. Washington, DC: Association of American Colleges.

Kerr, C. (1981). Clark Kerr looks back. *AGB Reports* 54–64.

Kline M. (1971). *Why Johnny can't add.* New York: St. Martins.

Knox, A. B. (1977). *Adult development and learning.* San Francisco: Jossey-Bass.

Kozol, J. (1968). *Death at an early age.* Boston: Houghton Mifflin.

Levine, A. (1978). *Handbook on undergraduate curriculum.* San Francisco: Jossey-Bass.

Levine, A. (1980). *When dreams and heroes died: a portrait of today's college students.* San Francisco: Jossey-Bass.

Making the grade: Report of the TCF task force on federal elementary and secondary education policy (1983). (Background paper by Paul E. Peterson included). New York: The Twentieth Century Fund.

Mayer, M. (1961). *The schools.* New York: Harper & Brothers.

Mayhew, L. B. (1967a). *The collegiate curriculum: an approach to analysis.* Atlanta: Southern Regional Education Board.

Mayhew, L. B. (1967b). *Innovation in college instruction, strategies for change.* Atlanta: Southern Regional Education Board.

McClure, R. M. (ed.). (1971). *The curriculum: retrospect and prospect.* Chicago: National Society for the Study of Education.

McDonald, D. (1973). A six million dollar misunderstanding. *The Center Magazine,* Sept.–Oct., pp. 32–52.

National Commission on Excellence in Education. (1983). *A nation at risk: the imperative for reform.* Washington, DC: U.S. Government Printing Office.

O'Connell, B. (1978). Where does Harvard lead us? *Change,* Sept., pp. 35–40.

Report of the Harvard Committee. (1945). *General education in a free society.* Cambridge: Harvard University Press.

Richardson, L. P. (1971). *Undergraduate curriculum improvement—a conceptual and bibliographic study.* Durham, NC: National Laboratory for Higher Education.

Rickover, H. (1959). *Education and freedom.* New York: Dutton.

Rudolph, F. (1977). *Curriculum: a history of the American undergraduate course of study since 1636.* San Francisco: Jossey-Bass.

Schiefelbein, S. (1978). Confusion at Harvard: What makes an educated man? *SR* 4: 12–20.

Scholarly communication: the report of the National Inquiry. (1979). Baltimore: Johns Hopkins Press.

Silberman, C. E. (1970). *Crisis in the classroom.* New York: Random House.

Simon, H. A. (1957). *Models of man.* New York: Wiley.

Sizer, T. R. (1984). *Horace's compromise: the dilemma of the American high school.* Boston: Houghton Mifflin.

Tanner, D. (1971). *Secondary curriculum.* New York: Macmillan.

Veysey, L. (1973). Stability and experiment in the American undergraduate curriculum. In Carl Kaysen (ed.), *Content and context: essays on college education.* New York: McGraw-Hill.

Weathersby, R. P., and Tarule, J. M. (1980). *Adult development: implications for higher education.* Washington, DC: American Association for Higher Education.

Wilson, J. Q. (1978). Harvard's core curriculum: a view from the inside. *Change,* Nov., pp. 41–43.

THE NORMATIVE STRUCTURE OF SCIENCE:
Social Control in the Academic Profession

John M. Braxton, *Loyola University of Chicago*

The mastery and control of a basic body of abstract knowledge and the ideal of service—the client's welfare above that of the professional—are the core generating traits of professionalism (Goode, 1969). The claim to professional autonomy by an occupational group is derived from these core characteristics. The larger society is willing to grant autonomy to professions that control the work of members in the interests of their clients (Goode, 1969). Social control of professional behavior is also of importance at the level of the profession, as the individual has autonomy over the performance of professional tasks without external controls (Clark, 1963; Scott, 1966; Moore, 1970).

Social control is exercised through the community of the profession (Goode, 1957). Formal and informal codes of conduct serve to exercise such control as they provide guides for professional behavior (Goode, 1957; Greenwood, 1966; Strauss and Bucher, 1961). Such control mechanisms define appropriate professional behavior with respect to the larger community, colleagues, and clients (Goode, 1957). Thus, the content of various formal and informal control mechanisms and the extent to which such mechanisms induce conformity in practice are fundamental topics in the study of professions.

These topics are also of significance to the study of the academic profession. Like other professions, claim to professional autonomy is also made by college and university faculty (Clark, 1963; Kadish, 1970). This claim is uniquely embodied in the notion of academic freedom (Hofstader and Metzger, 1955; Kadish, 1970).

Social control, however, is particularly problematic in the academic profession, as it is differentiated from other professions along three dimensions: mode of interaction with the knowledge base, the ideal of service, and the socialization process. Such professions as law and medicine interact with their

309

body of knowledge through the application of knowledge to concrete problems. In contrast, the advancement of knowledge is one of the core activities of the academic profession. Thus, the body of knowledge is in a tentative state, as extensions, revisions, and new directions are made. The unformalized forces of creativity, and problem solving underlying such a mode of interaction results in loose social control by the community of the academic profession. In contrast, the routine and formalized applications of knowledge to professional tasks makes social control less problematic in other professions.

In addition to the tentative condition of the knowledge base, two other factors attenuate social control. First, the research process requires the highest level of professional autonomy (Clark, 1963). Second, the high level of specialized knowledge and skill or expertise centered in disciplinary subspecialties makes self-regulation difficult for all but those academics with the same expertise (Clark, 1963).

The larger society exchanges autonomy for professional self-regulation in the interests of clients (Goode, 1969). In the case of the academic profession, the identification of the clients served is ambiguous (Goode, 1969; Schein, 1972). Goode contended that the term *client* is not in the vocabulary of academics, as the cause of learning, not individuals, is served. Thus, the cause of learning or the knowledge base itself may be the client. As in research, the client served in the role of teaching is unclear. Although the student may be the client, groups of students, not individuals, are usually served (Schein, 1972). As much teaching is predicated on the development of well-educated and responsible citizens, society may also be the client (Schein, 1972). Schein also suggested that the discipline professed may also be the client. Such ambiguity in the notion of the client results in loose social control, because the focus of professional practice, in terms of the client served, is difficult to ascertain. In contrast, the clients of other professions are more easily identified.

Although the doctoral socialization process in the academic profession is functional to the activity of research and scholarship, this process fails to provide the needed link between training and the teaching function of the academic profession. Unlike in other professions, where training and practice are closely related, training for college teaching is neglected. More specifically, the thrust of the doctoral socialization process is on the development of the attitudes, values and skills of research (Hagstrom, 1965; Rosen and Bates, 1967; Cole and Cole, 1973). However, training in the skills of teaching is neglected during doctoral study (Jencks and Reismen, 1968). Thus, the absence of a common base for practice in teaching renders social control difficult to achieve.

Like research, skill and expertise in the teaching of disciplinary subspecialties also poses a problem for professional self-regulation of teaching.

In sum, social control by the community of the academic profession is, at best, loose. Despite such an assessment, a normative structure of science, which is binding on the scientist, has been described (Merton, 1942). As norms are prescribed, preferential, permissive, or proscribed patterns of behavior (Merton, 1942, 1968b), the norms of science are of special importance as mechanisms of informal social control, given the problematic condition of self-regulation in the academic profession. As mechanisms of control, these norms prescribe appropriate behavior with respect to the advancement of knowledge and toward colleagues.

Thus, the primary purposes of this chapter are (1) to review the literature concerned with the conceptual underpinnings of the normative structure of science and (2) to review the literature and research concerned with the extent to which the norms of science are adhered to in practice. Such a review will serve not only to increase our understanding of the mechanisms of social control in the academic profession, but also to provide additional clarity and meaning to practice. Moreover, directions for further research on the normative structure of science will also be outlined.

Before we turn to the endeavor at hand, it should be noted that the norms of science are directed toward the advancement of knowledge (Merton, 1942). Although teaching and research form an integrated core of activities for the academic profession (Parsons and Platt, 1968, 1973), attention to informal social control of research activity is consistent with the thrust of the doctoral socialization process, with its emphasis on the attitudes, values, and skills of research, as well as with the value pattern of cognitive rationality (Parsons and Platt, 1968; 1973), both of which are defining characteristics of the academic profession.

Moreover, the literature and research to be reviewed are also almost exclusively concerned with scientists in research universities in the natural and physical sciences or in the social sciences. Consequently, no claims are made for generalizability to other types of colleges and universities and other academic disciplines. With these delimitations in place, it should also be noted that the terms *academic profession* and *science* are used interchangeably throughout this chapter.

In addition to these provisos, there are two other delimitations regarding the literature base of this chapter. First, the literature reviewed is derived almost exclusively from the sociology of science, in particular, and from sociology, in general, in order to keep the topics theoretically and conceptually *in situ*. Thus, other disciplines that may have addressed some of the topics covered in this chapter are not reviewed. Second, scholarly books and articles published in refereed academic journals are the sole source of the literature for this chapter. The literature reviewed was confined to these sources in order to represent a minimal level of scholarly quality, a quality assured by the peer review process.

This chapter begins with a review of the literature concerned with the conceptual underpinnings of the normative structure of science.

The Normative Structure of Science

The formulations of the normative structure of science were developed by Robert Merton (1942). Merton advanced the norms of science as constituting an ethos of science or an affectively toned complex of values and norms. The norms of science are expressed as prescriptions, proscriptions, preferences, and permissions. Such norms are legitimized by the values of science and are transmitted by precept and example and reinforced by sanctions. Moreover, the norms of science are internalized in varying degrees by the scientist. The four norms that comprise the ethos of science are universalism, communism (communality), disinterestedness, and organized skepticism. These norms are defined as follows.

1. Universalism holds that truth claims, or the findings of research, must be assessed on the basis of preestablished impersonal criteria, as opposed to an assessment based on such particularistic criteria as race, nationality, class, and personal qualities. The norm of universalism also generates the expectation that scientific careers will be predicated on talent rather than particularistic criteria.

2. The norm of communism (communality) prescribes that the findings of research be made public, as such findings are owned by the community of scientists. However, this norm does allow for recognition and esteem as the sole property rights of a scientist for his or her contribution. However, this norm calls for the full and open communication of findings, and thus, secrecy is prohibited. Because of its negative connotation with *communism,* Barber (1952) urged the use of the substitute term *communality. Communality* will be used in this chapter.

3. The preference for the advancement of knowledge as opposed to the individual motives of the scientist is the content of the norm of disinterestedness.

4. Organized skepticism is the fourth norm of science identified by Merton. The thrust of this norm is that no knowledge claims or research findings should be accepted without an assessment based on the technical norms of science: empirical and logical criteria. Put differently, a critical stand toward the results of research is prescribed.

According to Merton (1942), the norms of science are more than moral imperatives, as they are derived from the goals and the methods of science. Thus, the norms of science enhance the institutional goal of science: the advancement of certified knowledge claims.

Merton (1957) also linked the norms of science to the reward system of science, as he posited that the institution of science allocates rewards to those individual scientists who adhere to the norms of science. The reward system of science also entails the allocation of rewards for the performance of roles or for those individuals who produce research characterized as original.

CRITIQUES OF THE NORMS OF SCIENCE

Merton's formulations of the norms of science have not gone without criticism. Among those offering critiques have been Mulkay (1969), Barnes and Dolby (1970), Mulkay (1976), Rothman (1972), and Mitroff (1974). As Rothman (1972) and Mitroff (1974) were concerned with the extent to which norms guide the behavior of scientists, their critiques are not to be discussed here. However, later in this chapter, the review of empirical studies will address the extent to which behavior reflects the norms of scientists.

Mulkay (1969) took the stance that scientific theories and methodological rules are the sources of normative control in science. Put differently, he posited that technical, not social, norms guide the behavior of scientists. Mulkay also suggested that the influence of technical norms hinders the development and acceptance of new theories. Using the case of the scientific community's reaction to Velikovsky's controversial *Worlds in Collision* as a case in point, Mulkay contended that the negative reaction to Velikovsky was a consequence of socialization involving the technical aspects of science. Velikovsky's claims produced cognitive dissonance in scientists, which was reduced by the position that accepted knowledge about the natural world was not consonant with Velikovsky's claims.

In a later critique, Mulkay (1976) contended that the norms of science are social realities, but that they can best be regarded as an ideology rather than as a normative structure. Put differently, he posited that the normative structure of science is better conceived of as a set of vocabularies of justification that are employed to evaluate, justify and describe the professional behavior of scientists. However, such vocabularies are not institutionalized within the scientific community so as to induce conformity. Such vocabularies are also used, according to Mulkay, by the leaders of science to portray science in a way that gives justification to the lay public for special political status. Moreover, such vocabularies of justification, which support collective interests, are tantamount to an occupational ideology.

Barnes and Dolby (1970) offered a perspective similar to Mulkay's earlier criticisms (1969). They also took the stance that technical, not social, norms are adequate for social control in science. Moreover, Barnes and Dolby contended that organized skepticism, for example, is not unique to science, as such a norm is present in society, and thus, this norm is not unique to science and cannot be a norm of science.

However, Gaston (1978) retorted to this contention of Barnes and Dolby by positing that the formulations of Merton do not state that the norms of science cannot also exist in society. According to Gaston's interpretation of Merton, the norms of science as a set, however, are peculiar to science.

Although the contentions of Schmaus (1983) pertain to the norm of disinterestedness, his perspective is similar to those of Mulkay (1969) and Barnes and Dolby (1970). He adduced that fraud is not a violation of a special norm proscribing the self-interested behavior of scientists but is, rather, a violation of a more general rule of honesty in the performance of role-related responsibilities. Thus, the norm of disinterestedness is not unique to science but is a moral rule applicable to the larger society. This stance is supportive of that of Barnes and Dolby. Schmaus also concurred with Mulkay's contention that methodological or technical considerations guide the behavior of scientists, as criticism and replication of one another's work provide an adequate warranty of honest work.

A provisional assessment of the current status of Merton's normative structure of science was offered by Stehr (1978). After reviewing various criticisms concerning the propositions advanced by Merton, Stehr concluded that the original theoretical perspective can best account for both social norms of science and for the cognitive or technical norms of science. Stehr's position is derived from the distinction or bifurcation between cognitive and social norms found in the positions of those individuals who are critical of Merton's ideas.

HAGSTROM'S THEORY OF SOCIAL CONTROL

Collins and Restivo (1983) identified Hagstrom's (1965) theory of social control in science as the first general sociological theory of the scientific community. Hagstrom postulated that social control in science is realized through an exchange system in which gifts of information are exchanged for recognition from colleagues. As a consequence of their desire for social recognition, scientists adhere to the goals and norms of the scientific community. To elaborate, the contribution of a scientist's discoveries, in the form of publications, is an act of giftgiving. Publication, in turn, establishes the individual's status as a scientist and assures prestige within the community of scientists.

Although Hagstrom did not specifically delineate the norms of science putatively adhered to in exchange for recognition, his emphasis upon the act of publication seems indicative of the norm of communality delineated by Merton (1942). Moreover, the exchange of recognition and esteem for contributions is also prescribed by this norm. Thus, it would seem that Hagstrom's theory of social control applies to a particular norm rather than to a range of norms of science. However, Hagstrom does appear to have provided an elaboration upon Merton's contention (1957) that rewards are allocated to those individuals who conform to the norms of science.

Conformity to the Norms of Science

Having reviewed the conceptual underpinnings of the normative structure of science, I now address the question of the extent to which scientists conform to the norms of science. The literature to be reviewed is organized around the four norms of science described by Merton (1942).

NORM OF COMMUNALITY

Priority of discovery, originality, and competition are the key concepts in the assessment of the extent to which scientists conform to the norm of communality. Each of these concepts is reviewed here.

Through a review of the history of science, Merton (1957) observed that disputes over priority of discovery have occurred with great frequency. Conflicts over priority of discovery occur when the same discovery is made simultaneously by different scientists. Merton also stated that the alleged or actual anticipation of an idea occasions disputes over priority.

In the assessment of the possible explanations for disputes over priority of discovery, Merton ruled out such possibilities as the egotism of individual scientists or the irascible nature of scientists. He did, however, posit the norms of science as the root cause of such disputes. The institutionalized role of the advancement of knowledge and the recognition of originality in discovery are dimensions operative here. Thus, the prescriptions of the norm of communality are manifested in conflicts over the priority of discovery. Put differently, this norm prescribes the publication of original discoveries as well as the recognition of the individual scientist for his or her contribution. Moreover, Merton also pointed to the moral indignation expressed by scientists when priority over discovery is either denied or challenged. Such indignation is an indication that a norm of science has been violated.

Recognition for an original discovery can take many forms. According to Merton, the highest form of recognition is eponymy, or the practice of naming a discovery after the discovering scientist. Examples are the Copernican system, Halley's comet, and Hookes's law. Crediting the formation of a new science, or a branch of science, is another application of eponymy cited by Merton. The application of eponymy to laws, theories, hypotheses, and instruments is another level of recognition. The Nobel Prize is also mentioned by Merton as a preeminent type of recognition.

The value of originality in discovery and the concern about recognition for this originality can also lead to various forms of deviancy. The most deviant response suggested by Merton is fraud. However, he indicated that existing evidence suggests that fraud occurs very infrequently. Fraud can also be taken as a violation of the norm of disinterestedness. Such a stance, which was outlined by Zuckerman (1977) and Weinstein (1979), is discussed under the subheading of the norm of disinterestedness. Merton specified plagiaries, slanderous charges, and charges of plagiary as more likely forms of deviant behavior in response to the high value placed on originality in discovery. However, he offered the assessment that plagiary is not a frequent event in science.

Fraud, plagiary, and slander are all active forms of deviant behavior. However, Merton also identified retreatism or role attrition (Zuckerman and Merton, 1972) as a passive form of response to the pressures for originality in contribution. Retreatism or role attrition is the withdrawal from research as an activity by either leaving the academic profession or by taking the role of teaching or administration.

VALUE OF ORIGINALITY

Like Merton, Hagstrom (1965, 1974) and Gaston (1971) emphasized the value of originality in science. Gaston (1971) stated that originality is valued because some important aspect of the natural world is identified and demonstrated for the first time. Thus, only original research is a contribution.

Hagstrom (1965) also emphasized first presentation. Like Merton (1957), he suggested that originality in discovery is the basis for recognition, although he did state that some recognition may be given for replications and rediscoveries.

The value placed on originality and the desire to receive recognition for an original discovery lead to competition among scientists. Competition is an important concept in the consideration of whether the norm of communality is manifested in the behavior of the academic profession. Competition is important because one of its consequences is secretiveness about research (Hagstrom, 1965, 1974; Gaston, 1971), which is a violation of this norm (Merton, 1942). Before a review of research on secretiveness, the extent of competition in science is reviewed.

EXTENT OF COMPETITION IN SCIENCE

Merton (1957) stated that competition has almost become a basic dimension of social relations between scientists. However, the empirical work of Hagstrom (1965, 1974) and Sullivan (1975) provides more than an impressionistic indication of the extent of competition in several scientific fields.

Hagstrom (1965) defined competition as the situation in which two or more scientists or a group of scientists are working on the same problem and only one individual or group will obtain priority of discovery and subsequent recognition. Competition, Hagstrom posited, is the experience of being anticipated in the presentation of research results. He applied this definition in interviews conducted with scientists in five universities, four of which ranked among the top 25 in the United States. Represented in this nonrandom sample were 33 individuals from departments of mathematics, philosophy, and statistics (formal scientists); 27 physical scientists, including physicists and physical chemists; and molecular biologists. Hagstrom noted that this group of scientists contains a disproportionate number of leading scholars.

Through his interviews, Hagstrom found that anticipation is a frequent experience of scientists, as 61% of his interviewees had been anticipated in their research at least once in their careers. Severity of competition was measured as concern about the possibility of being anticipated. Hagstrom noted that 50% of his sample did indicate concern about the possibility of being anticipated. He also detected an association between having experienced anticipation and concern about being anticipated in the future. The possibility of being anticipated was also of greater concern to younger scientists than to older scientists.

The experience of anticipation, as well as concern about anticipation, was also analyzed for differences between scientific fields by Hagstrom (1965). The experience of being anticipated was observed to be the greatest in the physical sciences, followed by molecular biology and then by the formal sciences. However, the greatest concern about the possibility of being anticipated was evidenced in the formal sciences, followed by molecular biology. The least amount of concern was indicated by physical scientists.

Recognizing the limitations of the generalizability of the research described above, Hagstrom (1974) examined the extent and severity of competition through the administration of a survey instrument to a random sample of mathematicians and statisticians, physicists, chemists, and biologists in U.S. graduate universities offering advanced degrees in these fields. He limited his consideration of competition and its severity to those respondents who were currently involved in research.

The experience of having been anticipated at least once in a career appears to have occurred quite frequently in science, as over 60% of the scientists who responded to Hagstrom's survey indicated having been anticipated at least once during their careers. This observed incidence of competition compares very favorably to the extent of competition observed by Hagstrom (1965) in his more restricted sample of scientists. Contrary to the findings in his previous work (Hagstrom, 1965), Hagstrom (1974) observed no disciplinary differences either in the incidence of competition or in concern about the possibility of being anticipated.

Hagstrom's definition (1975) of competition in science was also employed by Sullivan (1975) in his study concerned with the extent of competition in biomedical science. From interviews conducted with biomedical scientists from two biomedical research institutions, both having research and teaching functions, Sullivan learned that 54% of these biomedical scientists had experienced anticipation of their research. Once again, the majority of scientists had experienced anticipation, although a smaller percentage than Hagstrom observed (1965, 1974).

Sullivan also examined the extent to which biomedical scientists are concerned about the possibility of being anticipated. The majority of biomedical scientists reported being at least slightly concerned about the possibility of being anticipated. This finding is consistent with those of Hagstrom (1965, 1974).

These studies suggest that the majority of scientists not only have experienced the anticipation of their research (Hagstrom, 1965, 1974; Sullivan, 1975) but also have some concern about the possibility of being anticipated (Hagstrom, 1965, 1974; Sullivan, 1975). Such levels of competition and severity of competition in the academic profession raise a question concerning the extent to which secretiveness about research findings occurs in science. Put differently, the question raised is to what extent the norm of communality is violated. Research concerned with secretiveness is reviewed next.

SECRETIVENESS IN SCIENCE

Those scholars who have considered competition in science have likewise addressed secrecy in science (Hagstrom, 1965, 1974; Sullivan, 1975). Through his interviews with leading scientists, Hagstrom (1965) observed the tendency to be secretive among those scientists who were worried about the possibility of being anticipated through the theft of their ideas. Few individuals, however, admitted engagement in secretiveness. Hagstrom attributed this reticence to admit to secrecy to the norm of communality. Thus, it is difficult to estimate the amount of such behavior. However, Hagstrom's more extensive survey of scientists (1974) provides a firmer indication of the effect of secrecy in science. This was measured by asking respondents to indicate whether they felt safe in discussing their current research with other persons doing similar research in other institutions. Most of the respondents felt safe in discussing their current research with most or all other scientists (93%). However, such openness decreased with an increase in concern about the possibility of being anticipated.

Through a path analysis, Hagstrom portrayed some of the direct and indirect effects on secretive behavior. Concern about being anticipated exerted a positive influence, while the average number of collaborators had a negative direct effect on secrecy. The later effect suggests that scientists working in research groups are less likely to engage in secrecy. The path analysis also indicated that the average number of years since Ph.D was earned had a negative indirect effect upon secrecy, an effect that was indicated by concern about being anticipated. The frequency of being anticipated also had an indirect positive effect upon secretiveness that was mediated by concern about being anticipated in research.

From his interviews with biomedical scientists, Sullivan (1975) provided results consistent with those found by Hagstrom (1974). Sullivan asked his respondents the same question used by Hagstrom to measure secrecy (1974) and observed that 14% of his biomedical scientists felt safe in discussing their work with only a trusted few, thus, exhibiting a relatively low level of secrecy. Moreover, Sullivan also learned that concern about the possibility of being anticipated increased the likelihood of secretiveness in discussing research.

In passing, it should be noted that in his critique of the Mertonian norms of science, Rothman (1972) drew attention to the practices of invisible colleges as potential violators of the norm of communality. He pointed out that invisible colleges are selective and closed groups of scientists in specific research areas. Members of such groups exchange reports, preprints, and reprints on a selective basis.

With the extent of secrecy as a consideration, the research reviewed suggests that the norm of communality is adhered to by U.S. scientists. However, conformity to the norm of communality appears to be conditional, as working in isolation and concern about being anticipated increase the level of nonconformance to this norm. Put differently, working alone and severity of competition lead to violations.

THE COMMUNICATION PROCESS IN SCIENCE

In addition to secrecy in research, the extent to which the visibility and awareness of research results is conditional on a scientist's location in the prestige hierarchy of science is an index of conformity to the norm of communality. The component of this norm that specifies the full and open communication of findings is germane. Selected dimensions of the communication process in science were the foci of research by Cole and Cole (1968) and by Cole (1978). Although visibility and awareness of research were the selected dimensions of the communication process in science, only awareness is pertinent to the norm of communality.

In their research, Cole and Cole (1968) defined awareness as the degree to which the social characteristics of an individual scientist, or the prestige of her or his department, influences the extent to which the work of other scientists is known. The more efficient the communication system, the less the various social variables would affect awareness. Obversely, an inefficient system would be influenced by social factors.

The analyses conducted on awareness were based on the responses to a survey administered to a sample drawn from the population of U.S. graduate departments in physics. Awareness was measured as the number of names on a list of 24 physicists with which the responding physicists were familiar. The 24 names were drawn from various universities, institutes, and specialities within physics. The results of these counts indicated that the majority of the survey respondents were familiar with the research of about one half of the 24 listed physicists. Cole and Cole took this as an indication that the communication system in physics is somewhat efficient.

The various variables selected to ascertain the extent to which various social characteristics influence awareness were professional rank, age, prestige of highest award, number of awards, and rank of current department and quality of work (number of citations). Awareness was regressed on each of these six variables in a multiple-regression analysis. Professional age, prestige of highest award, prestige of current department, and quality of work were all moderately associated with awareness. Cole and Cole concluded that there were differences in awareness across different social characteristics, but that these differences were not great. Thus, the research of Cole and Cole (1968) implies that there is a fairly full and open communication of research in physics and that this dimension of the norm of communality is conformed to by physicists. However, this adherence is somewhat variable according to the various social characteristics of individual physicists.

Although Cole (1978) was primarily concerned with the reward structure of five scientific fields, this research is also pertinent to the question of the influence of various social characteristics on awareness in four fields in addition to physics. In this study, Cole (1978) found that a social characteristic such as prestige of doctoral department exerted little or no influence on awareness in each of the five fields included: biochemistry, chemistry, psychology, sociology, and physics. Although the same measure of awareness was used as in the research by Cole and Cole (1968), such social characteristics as professional age and prestige of current department were not used. As in Cole and Cole (1968), quality of research exerted a positive independent effect on awareness across the five fields. The pattern of findings of this study also suggests a full and open system of communication across the five fields of varying degrees of paradigmatic development.

THE NORM OF DISINTERESTEDNESS

Two different interpretations of the meaning of the norm of disinterestedness exist in the literature. One view holds that this norm prohibits the desire for professional recognition as an explicit goal, as well as doing research in order to garner prestige or financial gain in the lay community (Rothman, 1975; Stehr, 1978). Put more succinctly, this reading of the norm of disinterestedness proscribes research and discovery as ends in themselves.

Wunderlich (1974), however, interpreted surveillance by fellow scientists as a prescription of this norm. Surveillance or policing protects the goal of the extension of certified knowledge by preventing faulty or fraudulent research from entering the stockpile of certified knowledge. Wunderlich added that science may be said to be conforming to the norm of disinterestedness as long as surveillance or policing occurs. Thus, this norm prescribes behavior at the institutional, rather than the individual, level of science.

Both interpretations are evident in discussions of the extent to which this norm is adhered to in practice. In his critique of the Mertonian norms of science, Rothman (1978) questioned whether discovery and research or individual recognition is the principal motivation of scientists. In comparison, Zuckerman (1977a) and Weinstein (1979) discussed fraud in science and surveillance or policing. Although the perspectives advanced by Rothman, Weinstein, and Zuckerman are heuristic, the question of conformity to the norm of disinterestedness begs for empirical investigation.

Rothman (1972) took the stance that this norm is violated because the ethic of success is prevalent in science. He cited the race for the priority of discovery, as well as the reporting of experiments before they are conducted. Reports to the popular press are also made to obviate the lag time in the publication of articles in scientific journals. Rothman also pointed out that James Watson, who was a codiscoverer of the structure of DNA, reported his use of science as a vehicle for his own success and prestige. Rothman believed that Watson may be typical of the new scientist.

Opposing viewpoints on surveillance or policing in science were taken by Zuckerman (1977a) and Weinstein (1979). Although there is no institutionalized surveillance function in science to differentiate between error and fraud, Zuckerman contended that the requirement that research contributions be reproducible serves such a function through deterrence and detection. Potential deviants who fear being caught faking evidence are deterred by the requirement of reproducibility. This requirement also provides for the detection of fraud both when it occurs and in the future through efforts to replicate research findings.

In contrast, Weinstein (1979) was leery of the efficacy of the requirement of reproducibility. She stated that replications are not as highly rewarded as original contributions and thus occur too infrequently for effective policing. Zuckerman, however, recognized the limits of replications or reproducibility for policing in science. She stated that scientific fields differ not only in their potential for replication, but also in the extent of replication. Replication occurs more frequently in such fields as physics, biochemistry, and genetics, while infrequently occurring in psychology. Moreover, Zuckerman also advanced the intriguing notion that the more significant or consequential the research finding, the more likely replication is to occur. Concomitantly, error or deception is more likely to be detected.

In addition to questioning the incidence of replication, Weinstein contended that specialization in science has led to ineffective policing in science. She maintained that specialization has made it necessary for scientists to trust or accept the results of their colleagues, as the prestige of the scientist and the shared assumption of a paradigm have displaced the critical examination of research findings. Zuckerman, however, suggested that specialization provides a deterrence to fraud, as scientists are aware that others working in their own specialty or related areas are all potential detectives, as replication and utilization in further research by colleagues can result in detection of errors or deception.

A final point of difference concerns the application of appropriate sanctions when fraud has been detected. Zuckerman stated that expulsion from the community of scientists can and does occur, whereas Weinstein contended that loss of career does not occur when fraud has been identified.

NORM OF ORGANIZED SKEPTICISM

As in the case of the consideration of conformity to the norm of disinterestedness, essays also address adherence to the norm of organized skepticism. Rothman (1972) posited that the application of empirical and logical criteria is necessary for the careful scrutiny of research and the suspension of judgment before acceptance can occur. With acceptance contingent on scientific criteria in place, Rothman stated, evidence that deviates from conventional thinking or that has been generated by unknown scientists frequently serves as the basis for the rejection of some "truth claims." Although skepticism is operative, it is not rooted in the application of empirical and logical criteria. Thus, Rothman was dubious about the extent to which organized skepticism is adhered to in practice in science.

Although Weinstein (1979) was primarily concerned about an explanation for the lack of policing in science, some of her contentions also apply to the norm of organized skepticism. She pointed to the role of shared paradigms in the limitation of organized skepticism. More specifically, the research of colleagues working within the framework of a shared paradigm are less likely to be seriously questioned. An additional inhibitor of adherence to organized skepticism is the tendency of scientists to trust the work of colleagues with whom they have social ties.

The ideas advanced by Rothman (1972) and Weinstein (1979) are provocative. However, empirical research on conformity to the norm of organized skepticism is needed.

NORM OF UNIVERSALISM

The norm of universalism prescribes preferential behavior not only for the evaluation and acceptance of research findings, but also for the careers of scientists. The preferred behavior is that universalistic, rather than particularistic, criteria be applied to both the evaluation and the acceptance of knowledge claims and the career process of scientists. Universalistic criteria are impersonal cognitive standards, whereas personal or social characteristics are particularistic criteria. Of the four norms of science identified by Merton, the norm of universalism has spawned the most literature. This literature is grouped into two major categories: evaluation and acceptance of knowledge claims and the career and reward system. These two threads of literature correspond to the two forms of behavior governed by the norm of universalism. Each of these two strands is reviewed.

Evaluation and Acceptance of Knowledge Claims

The literature reviewed under this heading can be grouped into two categories: the functioning of scholarly journals and the reception and use of research. The characteristics of contributors, the role of particularistic criteria in publication decisions, selections of editors or referees, and journal policies and procedures are topics addressed in the literature.

Studies that examine the characteristics of contributors are primarily concerned with the prestige of their institutional affiliation (Goodrich, 1945; Zuckerman and Merton, 1971; Miller, 1980). Goodrich (1945) classified the manuscripts received by the *American Sociological Review* from May 15, 1944 to September 1, 1945. The authors' institutional affiliation was classified either as a major institution—public or private—or as "other institutions," based on the prominence of the department of sociology. Percentage distributions indicated that 37.4% of the article submissions were from the less prominent universities, while 25% were received from authors at the more prominent universities. In contrast, the manuscripts from the major institutions were accepted at a 4-to-1 ratio over those submitted by authors from the less prominent sociology departments. Goodrich stated that the editors of the *American Sociological Review* made no attempt to accept manuscripts on the basis of institutional affiliation. Goodrich suggested that the marginality of the subject matter to sociology may have accounted for the ratio of acceptances observed. Thus, the role of such particularistic criteria as prestige of institutional affiliation was judged not be operative.

From an examination of manuscripts submitted to the *Physical Review* from 1948 to 1956, Zuckerman and Merton (1971) noted that manuscript submissions from the top 16 physics departments averaged 2.62 contrasted with 2.49 from all other physics departments. However, 91% of the articles from the physicists at the top departments were published, while 72% of the manuscripts from other departments found their way into print.

Given that manuscripts submitted to the *Physical Review* are not subjected to blind review, Zuckerman and Merton offered two possible interpretations of the observed differential acceptance rate. One interpretation was that the status of both the referee and the author influenced the judgement process. Put differently, particularistic criteria based on status, rather than merit, were used. In contrast, the other interpretation holds that differences in paper quality were involved in the higher-quality papers' being produced by physicists from the top departments, while lesser-quality manuscripts were submitted by authors from the other physics departments. This interpretation suggests the application of universalistic criteria.

In an analysis of articles submitted to the *Journal of Marriage and the Family* during a two-year period, Miller (1980) found that an author from a high-prestige university was slightly more favored in the acceptance process than were authors from universities of less prestige. The difference in acceptance rates, however, was less than six percentage points. Miller suggested that this difference may have been due to more competitive environments, more research funds, and more graduate students at the more prestigious universities than at the less prestigious institutions. The specialty of marriage and the family is a low paradigmatic interdisciplinary area of inquiry.

Studies that classify articles on the basis of institutional affiliation raise questions concerning conformity to the norm of universalism. However, several studies (Crane, 1967; Zuckerman and Merton, 1971; Pfeffer et al., 1977; Miller, 1980) have addressed whether particularistic criteria are manifested in the manuscript acceptance process.

In an exemplary study, Crane (1967) compared the characteristics of authors whose articles were anonymously evaluated with those of individuals whose articles were not anonymously reviewed. The two scholarly journals selected for these comparisons were the *American Sociological Review* (ASR), which follows anonymous review procedures, and the *American Economic Review* (AER), which does not follow anonymous review procedures. Articles submitted between 1956 and 1965 were included in the comparisons. Comparisons of the institutional affiliations of the authors whose manuscripts were selected for publication indicated that authors from minor universities fared better under anonymous review procedures than under nonanonymous review. This finding suggests that nonanonymous review may involve the application of particularistic criteria.

As previously indicated, a higher rate of acceptance of manuscripts from physicists in top-ranked departments than from those in lower-ranked departments was observed by Zuckerman and Merton (1971). They also examined the acceptance patterns of referees of differing status in the prestige hierarchy and found that referees of differing status accepted the same proportion of manuscripts across all prestige levels of author. Zuckerman and Merton inferred the application of a similar standard to manuscripts submitted, regardless of the authors' institutional affiliation. Further support for their contention was provided, according to Zuckerman and Merton, by the observation that referees of minor universities did not display a greater tendency to accept manuscripts from authors from minor universities than did referees holding appointments in higher-ranked departments. This pattern of findings suggests conformity to the norm of universalism, as the relative institutional status of both the referee and the author did not appear to be an influential factor in the acceptance of a manuscript for publication.

The acceptance of manuscripts by authors from the same institution as a journal editor or an editorial board member is another form of particularistic behavior. Pfeffer et al. (1977) addressed this topic and hypothesized that low paradigmatic fields are more likely to exhibit such particularistic behavior than are high paradigmatic fields, above and beyond the effects of institutional quality. The research procedures of this study involved the examination of several leading journals of chemistry, sociology, and political science for a ten-year period (1963–1972). As the institution was the unit of analysis, editors, editorial board members, and authors were classified by name of institution. The quality of each institution was also measured by the use of the 1969 Roose and Anderson rankings of graduate programs.

As the authors reasoned that any possible observed relationship between author and editorial-board institutional affiliation may be specious because both are related to institutional quality, two analyses were done using different measures of institutional quality. One set of analyses used articles published in the previous years as such an index, whereas another set of analyses employed the Roose–Anderson graduate-department ratings as the other measure of institutional quality.

Regardless of which indicator of institutional quality was used, the same pattern of results was obtained. The editorial board members in political science and sociology were more likely to accept manuscripts from their own institution than were editorial board members in chemistry. As political science and sociology are low paradigmatic fields and chemistry is a high paradigmatic field, it can be inferred that particularistic criteria are more likely to be employed in low paradigmatic fields than in high paradigmatic fields. Moreover, the authors noted no evidence of particularism in the manuscript acceptance patterns of chemists.

Although Miller (1980) did not control for institutional quality for submitting authors, her results support the work of Pfefer et al. (1977). Her analysis of manuscripts submitted to the *Journal of Marriage and the Family* suggests the influence of the paradigmatic development of a field on particularism in the manuscript acceptance process. She found that when the author of a submitted manuscript knew the journal editor, the rate of acceptance of such manuscripts was 40.2% as contrasted to a 14.8% rate of acceptance for other authors. Although this suggests particularism, slightly more than 10% of the authors knew the editor.

The editorial appointments of the editors-in-chief of academic journals have also been the focus of studies concerned with conformity to the norm of universalism in the functioning of scholarly journals (Yoels, 1971, 1974). Yoels (1971) addressed the relationship between the doctoral origins of editors-in-chief and their appointments of individuals as assistant editors or associate editors for the *American Sociological Review* from October 1948 to December 1968. The idea was to examine the doctoral origins of those individuals concerned with the review and referral of manuscripts submitted to the ASR. For this twenty-year time period, Yoels observed that the highest percentage of editorial positions on the ASR were held by holders of doctorates from

Chicago, Harvard, and Columbia. The data for these three schools were collapsed into one category labeled CCH, so that the representation of these three institutions could be compared with the representation of all other institutions. These comparisons indicated that when the doctoral origin of the editor-in-chief was CCH, the percentage of editorial appointments from CCH was the highest. Conversely, the percentage of appointments with CCH doctoral origins were lowest under editors-in-chief with doctorates from other institutions. Yoels noted that as the professional standing of the appointees was unknown, it is difficult to infer the application of particularistic criteria when universalistic criteria may have been applied to these editorial appointments.

In a later study, Yoels (1974) extended to seven academic disciplines the examination of the relationship between the doctoral origins of both editors-in-chief and editorial appointees. The seven disciplines were physics, chemistry, biology, economics, psychology, political science, and sociology. The four social sciences were classified as being low paradigmatic, while the three physical and natural sciences were classified as being high paradigmatic. Yoels postulated that social science editors-in-chief are more likely to use particularistic criteria in their editorial appointments, whereas natural and physical science editors-in-chief are more likely to be universalistic in their editorial appointments.

Particularism was defined as the degree to which editors-in-chief with doctorates from Harvard or Columbia were likely to offer editorial appointments to holders of doctorates from either of these two institutions. In comparison, universalism was defined as operative when editors-in-chief with doctorates from Harvard or Columbia were just as likely to select individuals with doctorates from other institutions as they were holders of doctorates from either Harvard or Columbia.

A twenty-year period was also selected in this study by Yoels to test his formulations. The official journals of all the fields except biology were selected for the analyses. The results of the tabulations made suggest that there was no statistically significant relationship between the doctorates of editors-in-chief and the doctoral origin of editorial appointees for the physical sciences. In contrast, a statistically significant association between doctoral origins of editors-in-chief and their editorial appointees was found for the social sciences. This pattern of findings suggests that fields with a low consensus on basic paradigms are more likely to be particularistic in journal editorial appointments, whereas fields with a high degree on consensus on paradigms are more likely to be universalistic in such matters. The use of the notion of paradigmatic development as a conceptual framework for viewing editorial appointments made by editors-in-chief tends to strengthen the inference that conformity to the norm of universalism in editorial appointments is conditional upon the paradigmatic development of a given field.

In addition to doctoral origin, the importance attached to various criteria by editors in their selection of editorial board members has also been the topic of research. Beyer (1978) focused upon the relationship between paradigmatic development and the importance of universalistic and particularistic criteria in the selection of editorial board members. She surveyed the editors of 36 leading journals in the fields of chemistry, physics, political science, and sociology and asked them to rank the importance of various criteria for the selection of both the editorial board members and the editor for their journal. Three particularistic and three universalistic criteria were provided for both rankings. As performance was emphasized, previous publication in the journal, prestige in the discipline, and prestige in a disciplinary subspecialty were classified as universalistic criteria. In contrast, such criteria as institutional affiliation, personal knowledge of an individual, and position within the professional association were classified as particularistic.

Beyer hypothesized that editors of journals in fields with lower paradigmatic development would endorse particularistic criteria to a greater extent than editors in higher paradigmatic fields. The results of the analyses of variance conducted indicated that previous publications in the journal, a universalistic criterion, was ranked higher in chemistry that in any other field as a basis for editorial board appointments. In contrast, institutional affiliation, a particularistic factor, was significantly different across fields, with the highest ranking given by sociologists. Beyer concluded that the results suggested mild support for the hypothesis advanced, as only chance differences were observed for the other criteria listed. Although this inquiry was conceptually well grounded in the notion of paradigmatic development, mean rank differences were observed as different after significant analyses of variance were calculated without the use of appropriate *post hoc* group mean comparisons. *Post hoc* group mean comparisons are requisite for ascertaining the validity of the findings of this inquiry.

While particularism is evident to some degree in the criteria used to select editorial board members to a greater extent in low paradigmatic than in high paradigmatic fields, editorial board members in such low paradigmatic fields as agriculture (Lacy and Busch, 1982) and psychology, sociology, and social work (Lindsey and Lindsey, 1978) are more likely to apply universalistic criteria than particularistic criteria in assessing manuscripts submitted for publication. Both Lindsey and Lindsey (1978) and Lacy and Busch (1982) used the same list of criteria for manuscript review and found that journal editorial-board members rated such universalistic criteria as the value of the author's findings to the advancement of the field and the creativity of ideas in the article as having a much higher level of importance than the background and reputation of the author, a criterion indexing particularism. This highly particularistic criterion was ranked the lowest in importance among the 12 criteria in the fields of psychology, sociology, and social work combined (Lindsey and Lindsey, 1978) and was ranked next to the bottom of this list of criteria in the agricultural sciences (Lacy and Busch, 1982).

The influence of the characteristics of editorial board members on editorial concurrence in manuscript recommendations made by such board members has also been the focus of research. Lindsey (1978) tabulated the percentage of suggestions for publication that were followed by social work journals from the results of a survey administered to editorial board members. Through a path analysis, Lindsey observed that editorial-board-member publication productivity had the strongest independent effect on editorial concurrence, while being an university administrator exerted a negative direct effect on concurrence. This pattern of findings evinces universalism in the process of journal concurrence with recommendations made for manuscripts by editorial board members in the low paradigmatic field of social work. However, citations of the published work of editorial board members exert a modest negative effect on concurrence. If citations are viewed as an index of author's repute, then further evidence of universalism is suggested. If citations are viewed as an index of the quality of scholarly work, then some particularism may be indicated, as quantity rather than quality of publications is more influential. Nevertheless, on balance, a greater degree of universalism than particularism is indicated.

From the literature reviewed, two inferences seem reasonable. In the selection of editorial board members, adherence to the norm of universalism is contingent on the paradigmatic development of the field in question. Where paradigmatic development is high, universalism appears to be followed. Conversely, particularism appears to be operative in low paradigmatic fields. However, a mixed pattern of results suggests that the manuscript review process is more universalistic than particularistic in low paradigmatic fields. In fact, the use of anonymous manuscript review procedures seems to vitiate the effects of paradigmatic development (Crane, 1967).

Reception of Research Findings. In addition to the assessment of research on the basis of merit, the norm of universalism also prescribes that knowledge claims should also be accepted or received on the basis of merit rather than on the basis of the personal characteristics of the author. The conceptual foundation for viewing conformity to this component of the norm of universalism is provided by the formulations of the Matthew effect (Merton, 1968a). Merton advanced the proposition that "a scientific contribution will have greater visibility in the community of scientists when it is introduced by a scientist of high rank than when it is introduced by one who has not yet made his mark" (p. 59). This proposition was derived from interviews with Nobel laureates (Zuckerman, 1977b) and from data in letters, notebooks, scientific papers, diaries, and biographics of other scientists. Merton stated that the Matthew effect is generally operative either in collaboration between scientists or in independent multiple discoveries made by scientists of differing status. This effect has both functional and dysfunctional effects. According to Merton, the Matthew effect is functional in the communication of scientific findings, as the results offered are more likely to be quickly disseminated if produced by a scientist of high professional standing. As the careers of relatively unknown scientists are affected, the Matthew effect is dysfunctional in the reward system of science. Perhaps most important is the occasion of the transformation of the Matthew effect into an idol of authority. At this point, Merton contended, the norm of universalism is violated and the advancement of knowledge is impeded.

Although Merton was concerned with vast differentials in rank or status, empirical tests of the influence of status on the reception of research have defined rank or status in terms of scientific reputation (Cole, 1970; Blau, 1976; Bayer, 1982; Stewart, 1983; Oromaner, 1983), the prestige of the department of academic employment (Cole, 1970; Blau, 1976; Oromaner, 1983; Stewart, 1983), the prestige of doctoral origin (Bayer and Folger, 1966; Stewart, 1983), chronological age (Cole, 1970), and professional age (Blau, 1976; Oromaner, 1977; Stewart, 1983; Oromaner, 1983).

Citations of previous work was the measure of scientific reputation used by Cole (1970), Bayer (1982), Stewart (1983), and Oromaner (1983). In contrast, editing and refereeing papers were used as such a measure by Blau (1976).

Cole (1970) was concerned with the effects of the author's reputation on the early reception of high-impact articles published in the *Physical Review*. High impact was assumed when a paper that was first published in 1963 had six or more citations in the 1966 edition of the Scientific Citation Index (SCI). Cole reasoned that the effect of the author's scientific reputation, as well as other factors, on early recognition could be assessed if the number of 1966 citations (the quality of the paper) was held constant. The number of citations of other papers was employed as the measure of scientific reputation or repute. With the effects of 1966 citations, or the current quality of papers, controlled for, partial coefficients between early recognition (or 1964 citations) and scientific repute, rank of department of academic employment, membership status in the American Physical Society (APS), number of honorific rewards, prestige of highest award, and chronological age in 1963 were computed. Scientific repute had a mild independent effect on early recognition, but other measures of the scientists' stature—such as being a fellow of the APS, the number of honorific awards, and the prestige of the highest award in 1963—all exerted little or no influence on early recognition. These findings suggest that the Matthew effect was operating to a modest degree as, all other things being equal, a scientist's repute, as measured by citations in other works, had a mild effect on early recognition of research.

Like Cole, Oromaner (1983) also used citation counts as the unit of analysis. However, he was concerned with all citations of articles published in four economic journals rather than with high-impact papers, as was Cole. All citations

of 124 articles published in the 1968 editions of the four core economic journals were tabulated by means of the Social Science Citations Index (SSCI) for
1969–1977. Early recognition was defined as the number of citations observed
in the 1969–1971 SSCI, while scientific repute was measured as the total number of citations received in 1966–1968. Oromaner found that the higher the repute of the economist, the more likely was early recognition to occur. More
specifically, the economists of the highest repute (25 or more citations) averaged 7.6 citations of their articles published in 1968 during 1969–1971, while
economists of medium repute (6 to 24 citations) received an average of 3.1
citations, and economists of low repute (0 to 5 citations) had an average of 1.1
citations. The Matthew effect also appears to have been operating in the early
recognition of work in the field of economics.

Evidence concerning the Matthew effect in an interdisciplinary social-science
field was also provided by Bayer (1982). Citations of all refereed articles in all
issues of the *Journal of Marriage and the Family* from 1970–1973 were the
data source for this study. With the effects of three other variables controlled,
the scientific reputation of the author was positively associated with the reception of research in the area of marriage and the family.

Although Stewart (1983) was concerned with the assessment of both author
and article characteristics on citations of articles in geophysics over a six-year
period, the effects of author characteristics assisted in the assessment of the
Matthew effect. Stewart tabulated the citations of 139 articles on geochemical,
geological, or geophysical topics that appeared in selected journals. The years
1969–1974 were used. These citations were regressed on five author characteristics: 1965–1969 citations of works, authors' institution of current employment as well as authors' doctoral department, authors' professional age, authors' professional rank, and the quality of authors' previous work or research
of scientific repute. This last variable, of interest here, was defined as the number of citations of pre-1967 articles (divided by the number of articles published
in 1967–1968) cited in the 1965–1969 SCI. Of these five variables, scientists'
repute once again had the largest effect upon citations or the reception of
research in geophysical science.

Different measures of both reception and recognition of research and scientific reputations were employed by Blau (1976). This research focused upon
theoretical high-energy physicists employed at universities in North America. In
order to construct the measure of reception or recognition of scientific contributions, these theoretical physicists were asked to name no more than three individuals who were doing the most important work in their area of research.
Thus, this measure was defined as the total number of times a physicist was so
mentioned. Editing and refereeing papers can also be used as an indicator of
scientific reputation. This measure of repute was introduced into a multiple-regression equation along with nine other variables. Of these nine variables, departmental quality and professional age were germane to a consideration of the

Matthew effect. With the effects of the other nine variables held constant, editing or refereeing had little or no effect on recognition.

The prestige or quality of either a scientist's doctoral institution or current departmental affiliation are also particularistic indicators of rank or status. In his study of early recognition of high-impact contributions published in the *Physical Review,* rank or quality was one of the variables controlled by Cole (1970). The partial coefficient observed for rank or quality of current academic employment was .18. This finding suggests that physicists employed in more prestigious departments are more likely to receive early recognition than physicists employed in lower-ranking departments. In his study of recognition for contributions in economics previously discussed, Oromaner (1983) found a similar result. Economists employed in one of the nineteen most highly rated graduate departments were more favored in early reception of their work ($x =$ 5.0 citations) than were economists employed in lower-ranking graduate departments ($x = 2.8$ citations).

In contrast, Stewart (1983) and Blau (1976) did not find any evidence of the effect of the quality of the department employing a scientist on the reception or recognition of his or her work. Stewart also observed that quality of doctoral origin of geophysicists had little or no effect on the reception of their research contributions. For biochemists, however, a moderate relationship between graduate department quality and citations of published research was observed by Bayer and Folger (1966).

Before we turn to a review of those studies that have addressed the effect of age (professional or chronological) on the reception of scientific discoveries, the Zuckerman–Merton (1972) hypothesis will be outlined, as it provides a conceptual framework for viewing the studies to be reviewed.

Zuckerman and Merton (1972) advanced the notion that the effects of the age of the contributing scientist upon the reception of research varies by the degree of codification that exists in a given field of inquiry. Briefly, codification is the integration of extant empirical knowledge into theoretical formulations that are succinct and interdependent. Thus, new ideas or research findings are less clearly identified as important in the less codified, or largely descriptive, fields. In contrast, the theoretical importance of new findings is more easily discerned in the more codified fields. These formulations suggest that the contributions of younger scientists are less likely to be accorded recognition than those of older scientitists, while age has little or no effect upon the reception of findings in the more codified fields. This hypothesis suggests that the Matthew effect, with age as an indicator of status, may vary as a function of the codification (paradigmatic development) of a field.

The findings of the research to be reviewed can be considered within the framework of the Zuckerman–Merton hypothesis. Physics represents the case of a highly codified field. Several studies were concerned with the effect of age on the reception of research in the field of physics. Cole (1970) found little or no relationship between chronological age and early reception of scientific work. A similar finding was also obtained by Blau (1976) in her study of high-energy theoretical physicists.

However, Allison and Stewart (1974) found that inequalities in the number of citations received in 1966 increased with professional age for physicists. Thus, their findings did not support the Zuckerman–Merton hypothesis. Their research involved a random sample of U.S. scientists in graduate departments awarding advanced degrees in biology, mathematics, chemistry, and physics. As the measure of inequality in this study, Allison and Stewart used the Gini Index, which has a value of zero when all scientists are equally productive and near unity when productivity is the result of the individual productivity of one. Allison and Stewart also found that inequalities in citations increased with professional age in chemistry, another highly codified field.

The tendency for older chemists, chemical engineers, and physicists to receive greater attention for their contributions was also noted by Bayer and Dutton (1977) in their study of doctorate-holding natural and social scientists having teaching-faculty status in a nationally representative sample of universities, and four-year and two-year colleges. While Bayer and Dutton found little or no relationship between professional age and citations of published work for earth scientists, Stewart (1983) found that younger geophysicists were more likely to receive recognition for their contributions than were older geophysicists.

These findings suggest a mixed pattern of support for the Zuckerman–Merton hypothesis as it predicts the effects of age on the reception of research in the highly codified fields. However, biology, sociology, and economics are examples of less codified fields. Allison and Stewart (1974) found that professional age had little or no effect on increasing inequalities in citations in biology. Such a finding fails to support the Zuckerman–Merton hypothesis of a positive relationship between age and the reception of research contributions in less codified fields.

Moreover, Oromaner (1977) found no apparent relationship between professional age and reception of sociological articles either during the first ten years after their publications or within the first two years after publication (early recognition). In contrast, a positive relationship between professional age and citations of published work was observed for sociologists by Bayer and Dutton (1977). Perhaps, differences in the method of tabulating citations accounts for the difference in findings between these two studies. Oromaner tabulated citations of articles published in three core sociological journals that were made in ten sociological journals. In contrast, Bayer and Dutton used all citations recorded in the Social Science Citation Index. Thus, the more comprehensive method of tabulating citations used by Bayer and Dutton may have resulted in greater variability in citations, thereby resulting in a statistically significant relationship.

However, support for the Zuckerman–Merton hypothesis in the less codified fields of economics and experimental psychology has been provided, as increasing professional age is related to reception of research contributions (Bayer and Dutton, 1977; Oromaner, 1983).

Cole (1979) and Allison et al. (1982) have also focused on the relationship between age and citations of published work. These two studies employed longitudinal analyses of cohorts of scientists. Allison et al. were concerned with testing the hypothesis of cumulative advantage for differential publication productivity, while Cole (1979) addressed the question of whether age affects research productivity. These studies are not reviewed here, as both address questions different from the Zuckerman–Morton hypothesis. Moreover, and more important, a cross-sectional, not a longitudinal, analysis is the appropriate methodology for addressing the question of whether the age of a scientist affects the reception of her or his contributions to knowledge.

In addition to the various author characteristics reviewed, an assessment of the effect of article characteristics on the reception of research is also pertinent to the Matthew effect. Stewart (1983) contended that if various author characteristics, which have been listed above, remained statistically significant after the inclusion of article characteristics in a multiple-regression analysis, then particularism would still be evident in the reception of research findings. However, a high degree of universalism would be indicated if the importance of author characteristics evidenced reduction. In the regression analyses conducted, Stewart observed that the length of the article, the relevance of article to theory in geophysics (plate tectonics), research based on laboratory or field studies, and the number of references had a positive influence upon citations, above and beyond the effects of such author characteristics as scientific reputation and quality of departmental affiliation. However, publication delays for articles on geophysical topics have a negative effect on the reception of a contribution. Almost 70% of the variance in reception to research was accounted for by author and article characteristics. With article characteristic entered first, 67% of the variance was explained. The addition of author characteristics yielded an additional 8% explained variance. Thus, Stewart concluded that universalism appears to be more important in the reception of scientific discoveries; however, the Matthew effect was still somewhat evident in the case of geoscience. Such article characteristics as references to theorists in the area of marriage and the family and references to other articles published in the *Journal of Marriage and the Family* were also related to citations of published work (Bayer, 1982).

The findings of the studies reviewed suggest that the Matthew effect does operate to some extent in the reception of research. The scientific reputation of the author appears to be the most consistently influential factor in the reception of scientific findings. This probability was particularly well tested by Cole

(1970), as he focused only upon those contributions that were of a similar level of quality or impact, while Stewart (1983), Bayer (1982), and Oromaner (1983) included all articles in their analysis.

Unlike in the functioning of scholarly journals, paradigmatic development does not seem to be an obviating factor in the Matthew effect. High paradigmatic fields (physics and geophysics) and low paradigmatic fields (economics, marriage and the family, and sociology) alike exhibit the Matthew effect. However, the effects of article characteristics found by Bayer (1982) and Stewart (1983) provide some indication of universalism in the reception of scientific discoveries. Future research concerned with the Matthew effect should include article characteristics in order to show the influence of universalism. This suggestion is discussed in more detail later in this chapter.

Careers and Recognition

The norm of universalism also prescribes that faculty careers and recognition or rewards be predicated upon achievement or merit rather than the personal characteristics of academic professionals. The extent to which the faculty appointment process as a reward system in science conforms to the norm of universalism is reviewed below.

Faculty Appointment Process. In the faculty appointment process, publication productivity is one indicator of achievement or merit, while the prestige of a candidate's doctoral department is representative of particularistic criteria (Crane, 1970; Long, 1978; Long et al., 1979). These two criteria are employed in most of the studies to be reviewed. Moreover, these studies can be classified into two groups. One group is concerned with the appointment process in general (Caplow and McGee, 1958; Crane, 1965; Cole and Cole, 1973; Stehr, 1974; Crane, 1970). A differentiation between first and subsequent academic position characterizes the second group of studies (Hargens and Hagstrom, 1967; Shichor, 1975; Long, 1978; Long et al., 1979; Reskin, 1979).

General Process of Appointment. Through their interviews conducted with department chairpersons and department faculty members where faculty vacancies had occurred at ten major universities, Caplow and McGee (1958) learned that departments select candidates based almost entirely on their anticipated contributions to the prestige of the department. Instead of an emphasis on the candidates' written work, who recommends them and their doctoral origin are given attention in the selection process. Particularistic criteria appear to be used in the faculty selection process at these ten major universities.

Crane (1965) also found some evidence of particularism, as she observed that graduates of major universities are more likely to be placed at a major university than are graduates of a minor university. This relationship holds regardless of the prestige of the faculty member's sponsor. Crane adduced that particularistic elements affect the careers of talented faculty who are not graduates of the top graduate schools. These findings were derived from interviews conducted with faculty at three universities: a major university, a high minor university, and a low minor university. The disciplines of biology, political science, and psychology were represented among the faculty interviewed. Both the quality of the doctorate-granting institution and the quality of the institution of current employment were classified according to categories described by Berelson (1960). Although prestige of sponsor and quality of doctoral department, which are both particularistic criteria, were controlled for, faculty members' publication productivity, which is a measure of achievement or merit, was not used. Thus, a universalistic factor was left possibly undetected in Crane's analysis.

In a later study, Crane (1970) focused on the characteristics of faculty hired by the top twenty departments in four categories of disciplines during the 1963-1964, 1964-1965, and 1965-1966 academic years. The four disciplinary categories were the natural sciences (chemistry and physics), the biological sciences (psychology), the social sciences (economics), and the humanities (English and philosophy). The top twenty departments in these four disciplines were identified by means of rankings by the American Council on Education (Carter, 1966).

Rank of doctoral origin, number of honors, number of citations of published works, and number of publications were the data collected by Crane on the faculty hired during the three-year period by the top twenty departments. Using these data, Crane found that twice as many graduates of the top five graduate departments were hired by the top twenty departments as were hired from those ranked sixth to tenth (38% contrasted with 20%); also, only 12% of the faculty hired by these top twenty departments were graduates of departments ranking below the top twenty. Moreover, Crane computed correlations between the rank of the hiring department and such universalistic or achievement-based criteria as number of publications ($r = -.051$) and the number of citations ($r = -.001$). Consequently, Crane stated that prestige of doctoral origin appears to be the best predictor of securing an appointment in one of the top twenty departments in the four discipline groupings. As doctoral prestige has more influence than scholarly performance in the attainment of faculty appointments at the leading institutions, Crane adduced that despite the normative commitment to universalistic criteria in the academic profession, such criteria are not used in practice.

Stehr (1970) was concerned with the relationship between the quality of doctoral origin of sociologists and the prestige of their academic appointment at two points in time for those sociologists who changed positions between 1959 and 1970. Although publications were not included, such career contingencies as professional experience, type of graduate degree, and age were introduced as controls in the assessment of the influence of prestige of doctoral origin on the prestige of academic appointment in 1959 and in 1970.

The membership directory of the American Sociological Association (ASA) for 1959 and 1970 was used to compile the data for this study. Using the 1970 ASA directory, Stehr drew a sample of sociologists. From a name-by-name comparison of the entries in the 1970 and 1959 directories, individuals appearing in both directories were identified. Sociologists who had changed institutions at least once were used in the analyses performed.

With the effects of the five control variables held constant, the prestige of doctoral origin had a moderate association with prestige of the academic appointment in 1959. However, Stehr found that this effect decreased to one of little or no relationship when prestige of doctoral origin was regressed on prestige of academic appointment in 1970. However, the prestige of previous academic position had a mild association with the prestige of current academic affiliation in 1970.

Although such universalistic criteria as publications were notably absent, this pattern of findings suggests that particularistic criteria such as prestige of doctoral origin and prestige of previous institutional affiliation play a role in the careers of sociologists over time, but that attenuation in such criteria does occur. Perhaps then, as Stehr posited, achievement-based criteria may assert themselves to a greater degree in the careers of sociologists with passage of time.

Although Cole and Cole (1973) conceptualized appointment to a major academic department as a form of positional recognition, their findings are pertinent to a consideration of conformity to the norm of universalism in the faculty appointment process. In their sample of university physicists, Cole and Cole noted that quality of research (citations) had a larger net effect than quantity of publications on the rank of a scientist's academic department when both measures were controlled. When quality of work was controlled, the prestige of the doctoral department had a moderate effect on the prestige of the current academic appointment, while citations also had a moderate influence. These findings suggest that both achievement-based and particularistic factors are involved. The research of Cole (1978) in five scientific fields also supports this contention.

A somewhat similar pattern was found by Hargens and Hagstrom (1967) in their study of biological and physical scientists employed in graduate universities, as publication productivity and the prestige of the doctorate-granting institution had equal effects on the prestige of the current academic appointment.

Further analyses made a differentiation among the prestige rankings of the current institution: highest, top two categories, and above the lowest category.

Hargens and Hagstrom noted that both the prestige of the doctoral institution and productivity had almost equal effects upon the attainment of a position in the top or one of the top two prestige categories. However, publications, not prestige of doctoral origin, were most influential in the avoidance of placement in bottom-tier graduate universities. This finding suggests the possibility that lower-ranking institutions conform more to the norm of universalism than do higher-ranking graduate institutions.

First and Subsequent Appointments. The studies reviewed in this segment of the chapter are concerned either with factors associated with the attainment of the first academic appointment or with the first and subsequent appointments in a longitudinal design. Such distinctions provide clearer indications of the role of achievement or personal characteristics in the faculty appointment process, as selected variables are measured longitudinally, rather than cross-sectionally.

Hargens and Hagstrom (1967) found a moderately strong relationship between prestige of doctoral origin and prestige of first academic appointment for newly minted Ph.D.'s. However, the strength of the association between the prestige of the current institutional affiliation and publication productivity was not reported. Thus, firm inferences about adherence to the norm of universalism are problematic. This result suggests particularism.

The influence of publication productivity was also neglected in a study of recent Ph.D. sociologists by Shichor (1970). However, the demonstrated relationship between the prestige of the doctoral department in sociology and the prestige of the hiring department suggested particularism. Using the Cartter (1966) rating categories of distinguished, strong, good, and adequate plus, Shichor found that the "better" departments hired the vast majority of their new faculty from the "better" departments (86.5%). These findings were derived from data contained in the 1967 ASA directory that were collected for those sociologists who received their Ph.D.'s during 1964–1966 from an American university.

With the work of Long (1978), Long et al. (1979), and Reskin (1979), the analyses become crisper and the conclusions clearer. These three studies are exemplary in their methodological rigor and their inclusion of relevant variables to address the question of adherence to the norm of universalism in the faculty appointment process.

Using data collected on the male biochemists who received their doctorates in 1957, 1958, 1962, and 1963, Long examined the relative effects of educational experience and scholarly productivity immediately before the first academic appointment. He reasoned that to assess the strength of the effect of productivity on the appointment to a prestigious post, productivity must be measured at the time the position is secured, not several years later. To assess the influence of the prestige of doctoral origin and scholarly performance upon the prestige of the first appointment, Long regressed the prestige of the first position upon the prestige of doctoral origin, the mentor's eminence, the selectivity of undergraduate institution, publications prior to appointment, and citations of work published prior to appointment. The net effects of each of these five variables upon the prestige of the departmental appointment are discernible through the multiple regression conducted. The regression analysis indicated that both publications and citations had little or no effect (statistically nonsignificant) upon the prestige of the appointment. In contrast, the prestige of doctoral origin had a strong, positive, statistically significant influence upon the prestige of the first academic position obtained by biochemists. These results are sharply contrasted with the findings of Cole and Cole (1973) and Hargens and Hagstrom (1967) but are consistent with those of Crane (1970).

Long also examined the influence of various variables upon the prestige of subsequent academic appointment for biochemists who changed institutions after remaining at their first job for at least three years. Both publication productivity and citations were measured at the time of change in institutions. In this multiple-regression analysis, the net effects of the prestige of the initial appointment and productivity prior to the move could be assessed to determine if particularism had abated later in the career process. Long regressed the prestige of the subsequent institutional appointment on the prestige of the initial institution, the prestige of doctoral origin, the eminence of the sponsor, the selectivity of the undergraduate institution, publication, and citations prior to the move.

Because of the lack of statistical power ($n = 47$), none of these variables had a statistically significant effect upon the prestige of the subsequent institution. From both sets of analyses, Long adduced that there was no evidence for the importance of publication productivity in the faculty career attainment process. However, the prestige of the doctoral department appeared to play a major role in the career attainment process, as did the eminence of the mentor as measured by citations of the mentor's work. These findings suggest the influence of particularism in the faculty career process, at least in the case of biochemistry.

In consideration of the processes by which departments select new faculty members, Long et al. (1979) posited that adherence to the norm of universalism would require the use of publications as a basis for selection among candidates. However, they noted that new doctorates may not have had ample time to demonstrate their merit through publications. Furthermore, many predoctoral publications are coauthored with mentors. Thus, these authors contended that a universalistic department might base its selection upon the potential for future productivity. If such were the case, then prestige of doctoral origin might be a good index of future productivity.

To test these formulations, Long et al. addressed the question of the influence of prestige of doctoral origin on future productivity. They used the same data set used by Long (1978) and found that the future level of productivity was most greatly influenced by predoctoral publications, while prestige of doctoral origin was not statistically related to future productivity. Future publication was defined as the number of publications for the three-year period ending in the sixth year of the first position. However, prestige of doctoral origin was a moderately strong predictor of future quality of work (future citations). These findings were derived from a multiple-regression equation with the effects of not only prestige of doctoral origin and predoctoral publication but also five other variables held constant. Although prestige of doctoral origin did have an influence on future citations, Long et al. pointed to predoctoral publications as the best single predictor of future productivity. Consequently, they suggested that their results supported Caplow and McGee's observation (1958) concerning attention to doctoral origin rather than to the written work of the candidate. From these findings, the influence of the prestige of doctoral origin appears to reflect a particularistic faculty appointment process.

In considering the findings by Long et al. (1979) that predoctoral publications, not prestige of doctoral origins, is the best single predictor of postemployment productivity, Thompson and Zumeta (1985) contended that their findings might be an artifact of bias in the estimation of the obtained coefficients. They indicated that one approach to the estimation of the effect of prestige of doctoral origin upon postemployment productivity is to test this effect in those institutions most likely to be supportive of research. Thompson and Zumeta postulated that if prestige of doctoral origin is overly emphasized in the hiring process, then high-prestige doctorate-holders should be less productive than individuals who obtained their degrees from less prestigious institutions.

To test this idea, Thompson and Zumeta regressed postemployment publication productivity on prestige of doctoral origin. The results indicated that prestige of doctoral origin had little or no effect on publication activity. This finding supports the contention of Long et al. (1979) that doctoral origin is given too much emphasis, while too little emphasis is given to factors that are better predictors of postemployment productivity. The data source used by Thompson and Zumeta was more encompassing than that used by Long et al., as their sample was comprised of 3,098 faculty in the disciplines of biology, chemistry, and physics holding academic appointments at the major U.S. research universities.

Sponsors can also exert both universalistic and particularistic influences on the career attainment process of faculty (Reskin, 1979). Reskin contended that some of the variation in scientists' careers that is unexplained by prestige of doctoral origin may be explained by the characteristics of sponsors. In her study, which is composed of a random sample of chemists who received their doctorates from U.S. universities between 1955 and 1961, Reskin focused upon the effects of sponsors' scientific performance (a universalistic factor) and sponsors' eminence (a particularistic factor) on the attainment of the first academic appointment. Sponsors' eminence was measured as the number of honorary degrees and the numbers of science advisory committees, while sponsors' scientific performance was defined as the number of publications during the four-year period prior to their students' receipt of the Ph.D.

With the first job defined as either a university tenure-track position or "all other jobs," the first job was regressed on the prestige of doctoral origin, sponsors' characteristics, predoctoral publications, prestige of postdoctoral fellowship, and three other variables. Of these variables, only prestige of doctoral fellowship and number of advisory committee memberships held by the individual's sponsor had statistically reliable positive effects upon the attainment of a tenure-track university post. Noteworthy are the nonsignificant influences of prestige of doctoral origin and predoctoral publications. Reskin contended that both the sponsor's influence and the prestige of the postdoctoral fellowship are evidences of particularism in the attainment of the first academic post of a chemist.

As Reskin's data were longitudinal, the effects of sponsor's characteristics on chemists who changed positions—to tenure-track university posts or other jobs—were tested. In this regression analysis, predoctoral publication was regressed upon the faculty-member publication productivity during the 3- to 5-year period after the attainment of the first position. Only early citing of the individual's published works and having secured the initial appointment at a university had positive, statistically significant effects on later positional attainment.

Of the 11 studies reviewed, only two indicate the operation of a combination of universalism (publication) and particularism (prestige of doctoral origin) in the faculty appointment process. The remaining nine studies, which are of varying degrees of methodological rigor, specify the operation of particularistic, not universalistic, factors in the appointment of faculty members. Because of their longitudinal design, their simultaneous statistical control of relevant variables, and their measurement of pertinent variables in a casually ordered sequence, the findings of Long (1978), Long et al. (1979), and Reskin (1979) offer particularly sound evidence of particularism in the faculty hiring process, for the first job in particular. Thus, the norm of universalism appears to be violated in the case of the faculty appointment process in the academic profession.

Reward System in Science

Rewards are allocated to those academic professionals who adhere to the norms of science (Merton, 1957). More specifically, academic professionals contribute their scientific discoveries in order to obtain social recognition from their colleagues (Hagstrom, 1965). Such recognition or rewards, however, should be allocated on the basis of merit or achievement rather than on the personal or social attributes of the scientist. This section of the chapter reviews those empirical studies that address conformity to the norm of universalism in the allocation of rewards and recognition in science.

Although promotions in rank and the granting of tenure are forms of rewards and recognition at the level of the employing institution, sociologists of science have attended almost exclusively to the allocation of rewards and recognition at the level of science as a social institution. As this chapter draws almost exclusively from the literature of the sociology of science, only the allocation of rewards and recognition external to the employing institution is reviewed.

Election to associational offices, postdoctoral fellowships, advisory panel memberships, and, of course, the Nobel Prize are examples of the forms of recognition allocated in science. As many of the forms of recognition are either a nominal category of some of the variables constructed or are parts of composite scales, the studies reviewed are arranged in more-or-less chronological order.

Two categories of recognition were used by Crane (1965) in her study of scientists at three universities of varying prestige. The higher category of recognition included the Nobel Prize, the presidency of a disciplinary association, honorary degrees, and membership in such an honorary society as the National Academy of Science. Such forms of recognition as postdoctoral fellowships, prizes for outstanding service, service on governmental advisory boards, and membership on journal editorial boards were classified as lower forms of recognition. Through contingency table analysis, recognition was related to such particularistic variables as the prestige of the current academic affiliation, the prestige of the graduate school, and the prestige of the graduate school sponsor. Publication productivity, an indicator of universalism, was also related to recognition with various combinations of the particularistic measures used as controls.

With prestige of graduate school controlled for, the prestige of the current academic affiliation was related to the type of recognition received. Regardless of the prestige of doctoral origin, faculty at a major university were more likely to receive higher forms of recognition that were faculty employed at less prestigious universities. Despite the finding that highly productive scientists were more likely to receive recognition, highly productive faculty at major universities were more likely to receive recognition than were their highly productive counterparts at minor universities.

Moreover, scientists with low productivy, but whose sponsors had high prestige, were more likely to receive recognition than were highly productive scientists whose sponsors had low prestige. Crane's analyses were conducted with the data aggregated across the disciplines of biology, psychology, and political science. Violation of the norm of universalism in the allocation of recognition appears to be indicated by this pattern of findings.

Three forms of recognition were used by Cole and Cole (1967) in their study of 120 physicists in U.S. graduate departments. These forms of recognition were honorific awards and memberships in honorific societies, which were measured as numerical counts and as the prestige of the highest award, an appointment in a top-ranked graduate department, and the extent of firsthand familiarity that a sample of physicists had with the work of the 120 physicists. Correlation analyses indicated that both the quantity of publications and the quality of publications, measured as citations of published works, were associated with all these forms of recognition. However, quality of work was more highly associated with each of the forms of recognition. Cole and Cole contended that these correlations indicate that the reward system in physics allocates recognition on the basis of the quality of work accomplished. This contention seems to be indicative of universalism; however, these analyses failed to control for the effects of particularism.

In a subsequent reanalysis of their data, Cole and Cole (1973) assessed the effects of such particularistic factors as the prestige of the doctoral department and the rank of the current academic affiliation, as well as the effects of the quality and quantity of research. In the case of the number of honorific awards, the standardized partial regression coefficient was .10 for the prestige of the doctoral department, with the quality of research controlled. Cole and Cole concluded that such recognition is not influenced by a scientist's doctoral origins. However, prestige of doctoral origin did have an equal and independent effect, with quality of work, on appointment at a top-ranked graduate department in physics. Thus, universalistic and particularistic criteria seem to be equally applicable in this particular form of recognition.

Recognition in the form of firsthand familiarity with a scientist's work had a stronger association with both quality of work and quantity of research than with prestige of doctoral department. These relationships suggest that universalism plays a larger role in the allocation of this form of recognition than does particularism. If prestige of current affiliation is used as an indicator of particularism, a different assessment emerges. When familiarity is regressed upon quality of research and prestige of current academic appointment, both indices have equal and independent effects upon the allocation of this form of recognition. Taken as a whole, Cole and Cole (1973) concluded that the reward system in science is not entirely universalistic, but that it is more universalistic than stratification systems in other major social institutions (p. 122).

Both universalism and particularism appear to be operative in the process of recognition in the discipline of sociology (Lightfield, 1971). Two forms of recognition were used in Lightfield's study of U.S. sociologists holding academic appointments in graduate departments of sociology. Like Cole and Cole (1967, 1973), Lightfield defined the prestige of the current academic appointment as one type of recognition, while peer recognition, which is much like the measure of familiarity used by the Coles, was the other form of recognition used. To yield this measure of peer recognition, a group of judges were asked to specify whether they were familiar with "most" or "some" of the work of each of the sociologists in the sample, or if they had only heard or never heard of each individual. With quality and quantity of publications used as indices of universalism, and with prestige of doctoral department of sociology used as the index of particularism, the strength of the effects of these indices differed for the type of recognition received. Both quality of research and quantity of publications had stronger independent influences on peer recognition than did the prestige of the doctoral department. In comparison, the prestige of the doctoral department had a stronger independent effect on recognition in the form of the prestige of the current academic appointment than did the quality of publications. Quality of publications, however, had little or no effect on this form of recognition.

In a limited group of biological scientists doing summer research at the Woods Hole Biological Laboratory (MBL), O'Rand (1977) found evidence of both universalism and particularism in the allocation of recognition. Two forms of recognition were used: professional standing and peer consultation status. The frequency of appointment to advisory boards, editorial boards of journals, and professional association offices, as well as top honorific awards, comprised the measures of professional standing. Peer consultation status was defined as the number of times an individual was contacted for consultation on research matters at the MBL.

Both particularism and universalism were evident in the allocation of the two types of recognition used. A multiple-regression analysis indicated that professional age (a particularistic criterion), quantity of publications, and quality of publications (citation counts) had independent effects on professional standing, while both prestige of current appointment and prestige of doctoral department exerted little or no influence. Professional age had the largest independent effect, as 38.4% of the variance in professional standing was explained by this particularistic factor. Quantity of publications explained 8.3% and quality of publications 3.9%. This pattern suggests that particularism plays a stronger role in professional standing than does universalism.

For peer consultation status, however, a multiple-regression analysis indicated that quality of publication ($R^2 = .11$) had the strongest independent influence, as contrasted with the effects of age ($R^2 = .034$) and prestige of current academic affiliation ($R^2 = .045$). Thus, universalism appears to play a larger role than particularism in this form of recognition. These findings were derived from interviews conducted with biological scientists during summer research at the MBL.

Comparison among three disciplines were made by Gaston (1978). Biology, chemistry, and physics, which are arranged in ascending order of paradigmatic development, were the three disciplines selected for comparison. Gaston used two forms of recognition to determine adherence to the norm of universalism: citations of published works and the number of awards received. Pertinent variables were classified as being either performance (universalistic) or ascriptive (particularistic) by Gaston. He classified predoctoral publications, postdoctoral publications, and citations of predoctoral publications as universalistic factors. Gender, professional age, prestige of current academic appointment, prestige of doctoral origin, and prestige of undergraduate institution were classified as particularistic factors.

To make the comparisons, a universalism statistic was developed. This statistic involved the subtraction of the percentage of variance explained by universalistic factors when entered first, subtracted from the percentage of explained variance by particularistic factors when entered first, and divided by the total explained variance for both sets of variables. The values of this ratio range from -1.00 to 1.00, with minus values indicative of strong particularism and positive values indexing a strong degree of universalism.

In the allocation of recognition through awards received, physics was the most universalistic, followed by biology and then by chemistry. Physics was also the most universalistic in recognition through citations of published work. Chemistry and biology were both universalistic, but chemistry was slightly more so than biology.

Using measures similar to those of Cole and Cole (1973), Cole (1978) studied the reward system in five scientific fields of varying levels of paradigmatic development. Arrayed in descending order of paradigmatic development, these fields were physics, chemistry, biochemistry, psychology, and sociology. Although awareness of research was used in this study as a measure of recognition the correlates of this form of recognition are not discussed here, as attention has been given them elsewhere in this chapter.

Like Cole and Cole (1973), Cole (1978) used prestige of current academic department as a measure of recognition. Both universalistic and particularistic criteria seemed to be operative, as both rank of doctoral department (an index of particularism) and quality of published work had positive and independent effects upon this form of recognition across the five scientific fields. However, the effects (path coefficients) of prestige of doctoral origin upon the allocation of this form of recognition was slightly larger than was the quality of published work. Number of publications had no effect on this form of recognition. This pattern of findings provides support for the findings of Cole and Cole (1973). Moreover, Cole (1978) concluded that the same process of allocation of recognition occurs in the five scientific fields studied. This conclusion suggests that paradigmatic development has little effect upon conformity to the norm of universalism in the reward system of science.

In a final study, Shin and Putnam (1982) focused on the role of age, a particularistic criteria, in the allocation of recognition. Winning the Nobel Prize and election to an associational presidency were the forms of recognition used applicable to this chapter. Shin and Putnam's findings indicate that the mean age at selection for these two forms of recognition is older than the median age of other scientists. However, Nobel Prize winners are younger at time of selection than are professional or scholarly association presidents. Moreover, Nobel Prize winners in scientific fields—physics, chemistry, and medicine—are younger than those in literature. Thus, a paradigmatic effect is suggested. Less consistent results, however, were obtained for selection as an associational president.

If we summarize the findings of the studies reviewed, the conclusion most consistent with these findings is that both universalism and particularism play a role in the process of the allocation of recognition in science. This conclusion suggests the inference that the norm of universalism is neither totally violated nor totally adhered to in the allocation of recognition in the academic profession.

COUNTERNORMS

The research and literature reviewed have been exclusively concerned with whether or not each of the four norms of science described by Merton (1942) are followed in the academic profession. An alternative perspective on conformity to these four norms is the possibility of counternorms to each of these norms that induce ambivalence in scientists concerning conformity.

Four such counternorms were advanced by Mitroff (1974). Most of these counternorms emerged during interviews with forty-two Apollo moon scientists. For the norm of universalism, Mitroff proposed particularism as a counternorm. The essence of this counternorm is that the social and psychological character of the scientist are important criteria in the assessment of research contributions. Moreover, the priority of discovery should be given to some scientists over others.

For communism (communality), Mitroff offered the counternorm of solitariness. The norm prescribes that secretiveness about discoveries is necessary, as property rights should include protective control over the dissemination of discoveries.

Interestedness was advanced as a counternorm to disinterestedness. Interestedness prescribes that scientists achieve self-interested work satisfaction and prestige through serving their special communities of interest.

Finally, Mitroff adduced organized dogmatism as a counternorm to organized skepticism. Two dimensions are present in this norm. First, organized dogmatism prescribes that each scientist clearly identify the authors of previous work used so that any deficiencies in the previous work are credited to others, while any possible credit goes to oneself. The other dimension of the counternorm of organized dogmatism holds that each scientist must believe in her or his own findings with great conviction, while doubting the findings of others also with great conviction.

Although Mitroff contended that such counternorms exist, he stated the norms and counternorms are not necessarily equally prevalent in every situation. More specifically, norms dominant in one situation may be subordinate in a different situation. Dominance of norms is dependent on various factors such as the paradigmatic development of a field. Mitroff suggested that future research focus on understanding the conditions that promote the dominancy of one set of norms over another. Perhaps, these counternorms, as well as some yet to be identified, account for some of the findings regarding conformity to the Mertonian norms of science reviewed in this section of the chapter.

Directions for Further Research

The studies reviewed and the summaries provided by no means close the door on further research on the normative structure of science. Such needed further research is outlined in this section. The directions for further research on the normative structure of the academic professions to be outlined fall into three categories: (1) general directions pertinent to the Mertonian norms of science; (2) suggested directions for further research on each of the four norms of science; and (3) extension of the notion of professional self-regulation or social control through norms to non-scientific disciplines and to the faculty role of teaching.

GENERAL RESEARCH DIRECTIONS

The mechanisms by which the norms of science are communicated, rewards for compliance and sanctions for deviance, and counternorms are general topical areas for future research on the normative structure of science. Merton (1942) posited that the norms of science are transmitted by precept and example. He also contended that the scientist internalizes them to varying degrees so as to develop a scientific conscience or superego. These formulations raise the basic question of the mechanisms by which the norms of science are transmitted by precept and example; a question that has been the focus of little or no empirical research. The doctoral socialization process is one such mechanism. Future research should focus on various dimensions of the socialization process through which the various prescriptions for behavior may be communicated. Some of the more obvious dimensions of the socialization process through which norms could be transmitted are faculty–student interactions, in general, and research collaboration by students with faculty, in particular. Counternorms, to the extent to which they exist, may also be communicated through these same and other mechanisms.

In addition to the doctoral socialization process, professional disciplinary associations and the academic department of employment may also be settings for the transmission of norms. Reports, presidential addresses, and committees formed at the level of the disciplinary association may have normative content. Letters written in disciplinary association newsletters may also, on occasion, express norms. Memoranda, topics discussed in meetings, and informal conversations with colleagues are possible mechanisms at the level of the academic department. Additional quetions are: Do these mechanisms vary by paradigmatic development of academic disciplines? Do these mechanisms vary by institutional and departmental quality? The identification of such mechanisms presents a difficult challenge for research and will require a range of methodologies and sources of data. Both quantitative and qualitative methodologies seem appropriate to this task.

Reward for normative compliance and sanctions or punishments for deviancy from norms are dimensions of social control exercised by the community of the profession (Goode, 1957). Merton (1957) contended that rewards are allocated to those scientists who adhere to the norms of science. The norms of science are also reinforced by sanctions (Merton, 1942). Although these important dimensions of social control are hypothesized to be in place, little is known about the application of rewards and sanctions in the academic profession. Although some of the research reviewed in this chapter focuses on adherence to the norm of universalism in the allocation of rewards or recognition, the question of whether conformity to the norms of science leads to rewards and recognition is a neglected topic.

Several research questions emerge: (1) To what extent are rewards and sanctions applied? (2) What are the rewards and sanctions applied? (3) Who are the professional agents responsible for the application of rewards and sanctions? And (4) do the rewards and sanctions, as well as the responsible agents, differ by the paradigmatic development of academic fields? The role of the institution should also be the topic of research. If the discipline or academic department fails to apply sanctions in deviant cases, what role does the institution play? In such cases, does the institution form review committees composed of peers, or do such individuals as the dean or the provost review such cases? If institutional review does take place and norm deviancy is determined, what sanctions are applied? Not unlike the research directions suggested for the identification of the mechanism for the transmission of the norms of science, these five research questions also require a range of methodologies and sources of data. Quantitative and qualitative approaches are also appropriate to the addressing of these research topics.

The counternorms identified by Mitroff (1974) provide an important research lead for understanding conformity to the Mertonian norms of science. Mitroff's sample, however, was limited, as the four counternorms identified were obtained through interviews with an eminent group of scientists. Thus, the identification of counternorms across various academic disciplines, as well as various types of institutions, should be the focus of future research. The mechanisms by which counternorms are transmitted, as well as the application of rewards and sanctions, should also be addressed. Moreover, as Mitroff suggested, research directed toward an understanding of the conditions under which the Mertonian norms or counternorms are predominate should also be conducted.

FURTHER RESEARCH ON SPECIFIC NORMS

Future directions for research on each of the four norms of science are outlined in this section.

Norm of Communality

The extent of secrecy has been examined in the academic fields of biomedical science (Sullivan, 1975), high-energy physics (Gaston, 1971), and the physical sciences, the formal sciences, and molecular biology (Hagstrom, 1965, 1974). Thus, academic fields with high or medium paradigmatic development have been included in these studies.

The extent of secrecy in research also needs to be examined in the social sciences, or those disciplines lower in paradigmatic development. Secrecy may be greater in low paradigmatic fields, as research has indicated that collaboration is less frequent in low than in high paradigmatic fields (Biglan, 1973). As will be recalled, working in isolation is more likely to lead to secrecy than working in collaboration with other scientists. Hagstrom's method (1974) for ascertaining secretiveness should be used. Moreover, future research on secretiveness in research should also address whether scientists employed in institutions other than research universities exhibit a greater or lesser tendency toward secrecy.

A fuller picture of conformity to the norm of communism would be gained by attention to these two suggested topics for further research.

Norm of Disinterestedness

As there are two interpretations of the prescriptions of this norm, two research directions are suggested. As previously noted, no empirical research has been conducted on conformity to either interpretation of this norm.

One reading of this norm asserts that conducting research for personal recognition, prestige, or financial reward is eschewed. As values shape and motivate behavior (Rokeach, 1973), conformity to this norm could be assessed by having respondents choose between a series of paired statements. Such statements would reflect various motivations, attitudes, and values concerning engagement in the process of research. The basic idea of this technique would be to identify tendencies toward the pursuit of research either for the advancement of knowledge or for personal prestige or financial gain. The scaling of these paired statements should be designed so as to produce ipsative measures.

Research using such scales should be conducted using both high and low paradigmatic disciplines, as well as a variety of institutional settings. Such inquiries would provide a first step in ascertaining conformity to this interpretation of the norm of disinterestedness.

A research challenge is also provided by determining conformity to the other reading of this norm. This interpretation holds that policing or surveillance by fellow scientists is prescribed. One research approach would be to ask respondents whether they or their disciplinary colleagues would report incidences of faulty or fraudulent research. Statements of varying degrees of severity about poor research or fraud could be developed. Such scaling would help determine the possible point at which policing might occur in a discipline. Another approach is to provide such statements and to ask respondents to indicate the extent to which policing occurs in their disciplines, as well as the extent to which it should occur. Strains toward normative conformity could be identified through computed discrepancy scores. A third approach would be to determine the extent to which academics write letters or make telephone calls to authors of poor published research. Each of these three approaches should be applied to disciplines of varying levels of paradigmatic development, as well as in colleges and universities of various types.

Although the suggested research approaches advanced for both interpretations of the norm of disinterestedness would provide indices of predispositions toward conformity, conformity in behavioral terms would not be tested. Nevertheless, the suggested research directions are needed first steps in empirical research on conformity to the norm of disinterestedness.

Norm of Organized Skepticism. It will be recalled that this norm prescribes that research findings not be accepted without an assessment based on empirical or logical criteria. Although studies of the social character of scientific practice (Knorr-Cetina and Mulkay, 1983) have focused on the assessment of knowledge claims, this program of research has not directly addressed conformity to the norm of organized skepticism. Thus, the research to be outlined comprises first steps toward addressing this topic.

A discrepancy approach is again suggested. Various empirical and logical criteria for the assessment of research could be identified. Respondents could be asked to indicate the extent to which knowledge claims are assessed by means of such criteria, as well as the extent to which such criteria should be applied. Research using such an approach should also cover academic disciplines of varying degrees of paradigmatic development, as well as various types of colleges and universities.

Moreover, the various studies concerned with the social character of scientific practice (Knorr-Cetina and Mulkay, 1983) might also be viewed with conformity to the norm of organized skepticism as an analytical framework.

Norm of Universalism

Further research directions are suggested for the assessment of universalism in the functioning of academic journals, the acceptance of research findings, the faculty appointment process, and the allocation of rewards and recognition.

The influence of the relative statuses of authors and reviewers on manuscript acceptance has been assessed (Zuckerman and Merton, 1971). Moreover, the acceptance of manuscripts by authors from the same institution as a journal editor or editorial board member has also been studied (Pfeffer et al., 1971). Although the manuscript review process, which is the crux of the assessment of research, has been addressed in empirical research, the work of Lindsey (1978) on the process of journal concurrence with editorial board members should be extended.

This suggested extension involves the case of disagreement between reviewers over the acceptibility of a submitted manuscript. In such a case, the decision of the journal editor is the focus. If editors tend to decide to accept manuscripts from authors affiliated with high-prestige institutions or from authors of high scholarly repute (the Matthew effect) but reject those from authors either of unknown repute or from low-prestige institutions, then particularism would be indicated. In contrast, the lack of a systematic relationship between social or personal characteristics and the editorial decision would suggest universalism. Such research should be conducted from the records of disciplines of varying levels of paradigmatic development.

The research reviewed indicates that the Matthew effect does exert an influence on the acceptance of knowledge claims, as scientific reputation affects such acceptance. In tests of the Matthew effect, the logic of the design employed by Cole (1970) is exemplary and should be replicated in fields other than physics. Cole assessed the effect of scientific reputation on the reception of articles of relatively equal quality. Control for the quality of articles provides a rigorous test of the Matthew effect, as scientific repute may be expected to exert an influence when articles are of varying degrees of quality. If scientific repute exerts an influence upon the reception of articles of equal quality, then stronger support for the Matthew effect is provided. Thus, future research on the Matthew effect should hold the quality of the articles constant.

The results of mathematical modeling of the distribution of citations among researchers of a field by Hargens and Felmlee (1984) suggest that further research on the Matthew effect should also consider such variables as the growth rate of a field and the degree to which recent, rather than older, contributions are cited. The modeling procedures indicate that older scientists are cited at a higher rate in rapidly growing fields than are younger scientists. However, younger scientists are cited more often than are older scientists in those fields that cite more recent contributions than older contributions.

A promising research lead on the Matthew effect was also suggested by Bayer (1982) and Stewart (1983). Bayer and Stewart assessed the effects of both author and article characteristics upon the reception of research findings. As article characteristics accounted for the most explained variance in Stewart's research, the characteristics of articles should be incorporated into the assessment of the Matthew effect in fields other than geoscience, especially fields of varying levels of paradigmatic development.

Improvements upon the design used by Bayer and Stewart could be made by using articles of equal quality as suggested above, as well as by testing for conditional or interactive effects between author and article characteristics.

Compensatory and accentuating factors that account for the reception of knowledge claims might be revealed by tests for interactions. A possible compensatory factor would be that certain article characteristics interact with low scientific repute to produce a higher level of acceptance. In comparison, an accentuating factor would be that certain article characteristics interact with high repute to produce a high level of acceptance. Such tests would further our understanding of the Matthew effect and its concomitant particularistic influence on the acceptance of knowledge claims.

Further research directions on the faculty appointment process are indicated by the exemplary research of Long (1978) and Reskin (1979). These studies not only are longitudinal in design but also measure productivity variables at a point in time before the appointment process. Thus, more accurate estimates can be made of the independent effects of such variables as prestige of doctoral origin and preappointment publications and citations on the prestige of first academic appointment.

However, these studies are limited only to biochemists and chemists. Further research using longitudinal designs and productivity measures taken before the appointment process should be conducted in disciplines of varying degrees of paradigmatic development.

Moreover, such studies should also be conducted on institutions other than ranked graduate departments. The full range of the Carnegie Classification of Institutions (1976) should be used. By the use of this range of institutions our knowledge of the extent to which the norm of universalism is adhered to in the faculty appointment process would be enhanced. Separate regression equations, however, should be developed for each institutional type, as the graduates of prestigious graduate departments have "trickled down" to less prestigious colleges and universities (Muffo and Robinson, 1981). Separate equations would obviate the possible specious attenuation of the effects of prestige of doctoral origin on the faculty appointment process.

Moreover, tests for interactions between various particularistic and universalistic criteria should also be made in future research on the faculty appointment process. Compensatory and accentuating factors may also be operative. A possible compensatory factor might be that lower prestige of doctoral origin interacts with high levels of preemployment publication to make possible the attainment of a post at a highly ranked institution. An accentuating factor might be that an interaction between low prestige of doctoral origin and low preemployment publication results in the attainment of a faculty post at a less prestigious institution. Thus, the case is made for possible conditional relationships in the faculty appointment process.

The last research direction suggested entails an assessment of the influence of universalistic and particularistic factors on faculty posts attained after the first job. Such research should be longitudinal and should use prior measurement of pertinent variables. This needed research would extend our understanding of conformity to the norm of universalism in the faculty appointment process.

The final direction for further research concerns the allocation of recognition. Gaston's study (1978) is exemplary and should be replicated on academics from social science disciplines. Of particular significance in this study is the development of the universalism statistic, which provides a composite measure of the degree of universalism or particularism in the process of the allocation of recognition. Future studies should also include this statistic. An additional suggestion entails the population of inference. As Gaston sampled an eminent group of scientists, future research might include academics from institutions of various types and levels of quality. Such a broader sampling frame not only would increase the generalizability of the findings, but would also provide a fuller test of conformity to the norm of universalism in the allocation of recognition external to the employing institution.

EXTENSION OF THE CONSTRUCT OF NORMS

The research directions to be outlined here call for the extension of the construct of norms as a mechanism of social control not only to nonscientific disciplines, but also to other activities of the academic profession.

As previously stated, empirical studies focusing on conformity to the Mertonian norms have included the biological, physical, or social sciences. Moreover, the four norms of science are binding on the scientist (Merton, 1942). Thus, the norms or ethos of science does not prescribe professional behavior for the nonscientific disciplines, such as the humanities and the fine arts.

For a greater understanding of self-regulation or social control in the various fields of study of the academic profession, the construct of norms needs to be extended to the nonscientific disciplines. The suggested research task is to identify possible norms that prescribe appropriate behavior in the scholarship of these disciplines.

The norms of science may be operative in the focal disciplines, but research techniques should be designed to identify or describe either different norms or different meanings of the Mertonian norms. Both quantitative and qualitative methodologies may be appropriate to such a research task.

As noted at the outset of this chapter, the norms of science are directed toward the advancement of knowledge. However, teaching is also one of the core activities of the academic profession (Parsons and Platt, 1968, 1973). As students are clients in the eyes of the lay public, a knowledge of self-regulation or social control of teaching is needed. Consequently, research on the identification of norms that prescribe for both undergraduate and graduate teaching is needed. The natural sciences, the biological sciences, the social sciences, the humanities, and the fine arts should be the focus of such research.

By analogy or transference, the norms of science may guide such behavior. However, research designs should be flexible enough to identify norms unique to undergraduate and graduate teaching. The literature on needed reforms in undergraduate and graduate instruction and ethics in teaching is also a rich source for the development of possible prescriptions for behavior. A list of possible norms derived from this literature and analogies to the norms of science could be included in a survey instrument. Respondents could be asked to indicate the extent to which each possible norm is an expectation of their colleagues. An alternative approach would be to identify norms through a more qualitative approach. Norms identified by qualitative methodology would be expressed in the words of the respondents rather than in *a priori* definitions of possible norms. As teaching is the primary orientation (Fulton and Trow, 1974) and activity of most academic professionals (Baldridge et al., 1978), research on the normative structure of teaching cannot be postponed. Such research would increase our knowledge and understanding of self-regulation or social control of this core activity of the academic profession.

Concluding Thoughts

The research directions outlined indicate that definitive conclusions regarding social control in the academic profession cannot be advanced. These directions also point to significant gaps in our knowledge. The research reviewed, however, does suggest that social control in the academic profession is a complex and variable phenomenon, as conformity varies from one dimension of a given norm to another (communality and universalism).

Such complexity may be explained by the pressure of counternorms, which produce ambivalence in academics. Perhaps, some norms are ideologies, as Mulkay contended (1976), while others are, in reality, norms. Sanctions and rewards may also be differentially applied from one situation to another. Moreover, the effects or lack of effects of doctoral or organizational socialization may also account for the complexity and variability of social control suggested. These possible explanations reinforce the need for research in those directions for further inquiry presented above.

In addition to the research on such informal social control mechanisms as norms, conformity to formal codes of conduct such as the AAUP statement on professional ethics in general and that of the American Sociological Association in particular (1968) should also be the focus of research on social control in the academic profession. In addition to conformity to the tenets of such formal control mechanisms, such additional topics as mechanisms for the internalization of such formal codes in academic professionals and rewards for compliance and sanctions for deviance should also be pursued as research topics.

This chapter lays down a foundation for a topic that is worthy of attention by scholars of the academic profession. Addressing the gaps in knowledge outlined will not only further our understanding of self-regulation in the academic profession, but may also help to preserve the autonomy granted by the lay public to the academic profession, an autonomy struggled for and well cherished.

354   BRAXTON

REFERENCES

American Sociological Association (1968). Toward a code of ethics for sociologists. *The American Sociologist* 3: 316–318.
Allison, P. D., Long, J. S., and Krauze, T. K. (1982). Cumulative advantage and inequality in science. *American Sociological Review* 47: 615–625.
Allison, P. D., and Stewart, J. A. (1974). Productivity differences among scientists: evidence for accumulative advantage. *American Sociological Review* 39: 596–606.
Baldridge, J. V., Curtis, D. V., Ecker, G., and Riley, G. L. (1978). *Policy making and effective leadership.* San Francisco: Jossey-Bass.
Barber, B. (1952). *Science and the social order* New York: Free Press.
Barnes, S. B., and Dolby, R. G. A. (1970). The scientific ethos: a deviant viewpoint. *European Journal of Sociology* 11: 3–25.
Bayer, A. E. (1982). A bibliometric analysis of marriage and family literature. *Journal of Marriage and the Family* 44: 527–538.
Bayer, A. E., and Dutton, J. E. (1977). Career-age and research-professional activities of academic scientists: tests of alternative nonlinear models and some implications for higher education faculty policies. *Journal of Higher Education,* 48: 259–282.
Bayer, A. E., and Folger, J. (1966). Some correlates of a citation measure of productivity in science. *Sociology of Education* 39: 381–390.
Beyer, J. M. (1978). Editorial policies and practices among leading journals in four scientific fields. *Sociological Quarterly* 19: 68–88.
Biglan, A. (1973). Relationships between subject matter characteristics and the structure and output of university departments. *Journal of Applied Psychology* 57: 204–213.
Blau, J. R. (1976). Scientific recognition: academic context and professional role. *Social Studies of Science* 6: 533–545.
Caplow, T., and McGee, R. J. (1958). *The academic marketplace.* New York: Basic Books.
Carnegie Council on Policy Studies in Higher Education (1976). *A classification of institutions of higher education.* Berkeley: Carnegie Council.
Cartter, A. M. (1966). *An assessment of quality in graduate education.* Washington, DC: American Council on Education.
Clark, B. R. (1963). Faculty organization and authority. In T. F. Lunsford (ed.), *The study of academic administration,* pp. 37–51. Boulder, CO: Western Interstate Commision for Higher Education.
Cole, J. R., and Cole, S. (1973). *Social stratification in science.* Chicago: University of Chicago Press.
Cole, S. (1970). Professional standing and the reception of scientific discoveries. *American Journal of Sociology* 76: 286–306.
Cole, S. (1978). Scientific reward systems: a comparative analysis. In R. A. Jones (ed.), *Research in sociology of knowledge, science and art: an annual compilation of research,* pp. 167–190. Greenwich: JAI Press.
Cole, S. (1979). Age and scientific performance *American Journal of Sociology* 84: 958–977.
Cole, S., and Cole, J. R. (1967). Scientific output and recognition: a study in the operation of the reward system in science. *American Sociological Review* 32: 377–390.
Cole, S., and Cole, J. R. (1968). Visibility and the structural bases of awareness of scientific research. *American Sociological Review* 33: 397–413.
Collins, R., and Restivo, S. (1983). Development, diversity and conflict in the sociology of science. *The Sociological Quarterly* 24: 185–200.

Crane, D. (1965). Scientists at major and minor universities: a study of productivity and recognition. *American Sociological Review* 30: 699–714.

Crane, D. (1967). The gatekeepers of science: the selection of articles for scientific journals. *American Sociologist* 2: 195–201.

Crane, D. (1970). The academic marketplace revisited: a study of faculty mobility using the Cartter ratings. *American Journal of Sociology* 75: 953–964.

Fulton, O., and Trow, M. (1974). Research activity in American higher education. *Sociology of Education* 47: 29–73.

Gaston, J. (1971) Secretiveness and competition for priority of discovery in physics. *Minerva* 9: 472–492.

Gaston, J. (1978). *The reward system in British and American science.* New York: Wiley-Interscience.

Goode, W. J. (1957). Community within a community: the professions. *American Sociological Review* 22: 194–200.

Goode, W. J. (1969). The theoretical limits of professionalization. In A. Etzioni (ed.), *The semi-professions and their organization,* pp. 266–313. New York: The Free Press.

Goodrich, D. W. (1945). An analysis of manuscripts received by the editors of the *American Sociological Review* from May 1, 1944 to September 1, 1945" *American Sociological Review* 10: 716–725.

Greenwood, E. (1957). Attributes of a profession. *Social Work* 2: 44–55.

Hagstrom, W. O. (1965). *The scientific community.* New York: Basic Books.

Hagstrom, W. O. (1974). Competition in science. *American Sociological Review* 39: 1–18.

Hargens, L. L., and Felmlee, D. H. (1984). Structural determinants of stratification in science. *American Sociological Review* 49: 685–697.

Hargens, L. L., and Hagstrom, W. O. (1967). Sponsored and contest mobility of American academic scientists. *Sociology of Education* 40: 24–38.

Hofstadter, R., and Metzger, W. P. (1955). *The development of academic freedom in the United States.* New York: Columbia University Press.

Jencks, C., and Riesman, D. (1968). *The academic revolution.* Garden City, NY: Doubleday.

Kadish, S. H. (1972). The theory of the profession and its predicament. *AAUP Bulletin* 58: 120–125.

Knorr-Cetina, K. D., and Mulkay, M. (eds.). (1983). *Science observed: perspectives on the social study of science.* London: Sage Publications.

Lacy, W. B., and Busch, L. (1982). Guardians of science: journals and journal editors in the agricultural sciences. *Rural Sociology* 47: 429–448.

Lightfield, E. T. (1971). Output and recognition of sociologists. *American Sociologists* 6: 128–133.

Lindsey, D. (1978). The operation of professional journals in social work. *Journal of Sociology and Social Welfare* 5: 273–298.

Lindsey, D., and Lindsey, T. (1978). The outlook of journal editors and referees on the normative criteria of scientific craftsmanship. *Quality and Quantity* 12: 45–62.

Long, J. S. (1978). Productivity and academic poosition in the scientific career. *American Sociological Review* 43: 889–909.

Long, J. S., Allison, P. D., and McGinnis, R. (1979). Entrance into the academic career. *American Sociological Review* 44: 816–830.

Merton, R. K. (1942). Science, technology in a democratic order. *Journal of Legal and Political Sociology* 1: 115–126.

Merton, R. K. (1957). Priorities in scientific discovery. *American Sociological Review* 2: 635–659.

Merton, R. K. (1968a). The Matthew effect in science. *Science* 159: 56–63.

Merton, R. K. (1968b). *Social theory and social structure.* New York: Free Press.

Miller, S. E. (1980). Journal of marriage and the family. (Review.) *Journal of Marriage and the Family* 42: 1032–1034.

Mitroff, I. I. (1974). Norms and counter-norms in a select group of the Apollo moon scientists: a case study of the ambivalence of scientists. *American Sociological Review* 39: 579–595.

Moore, W. E. (1970). *The professions: roles and rules.* New York: Russell Sage.

Muffo, J. A., and Robinson, J. R. (1981). Early science career patterns of recent graduates from leading research universities. *The Review of Higher Education* 5: 1–13.

Mulkay, M. (1969). Some aspects of cultural growth in the natural sciences. *Social Research* 36: 22–52.

Mulkay, M. (1976). Norms and ideology in science. *Social Science Information* 15: 637–656.

O'Rand, A. M. (1977). Professional standing and peer consultation status among biological scientists at a summer research laboratory. *Social Forces* 55: 921–937.

Oromaner, M. (1977). Professional age and the reception of sociological publications: a test of the Zuckerman–Merton hypothesis. *Social Studies of Science* 7: 381–388.

Oromaner, M. (1983). Professional standing and the reception of contributions to economics. *Research in Higher Education* 19: 351–362.

Parsons, T., and Platt, G. M. (1968). *The American academic profession: a pilot study.* National Science Foundation. (Mimeographed.)

Parsons, T., and Platt, G. M. (1973). *The American university.* Cambridge: Harvard University Press.

Pfeffer, J., Leong, A., and Strehl, K. (1977). Paradigm development and particularism: journal publication in three scientific disciplines. *Social Forces,* 55: 938–51.

Reskin, B. F. (1979). Academic sponsorship and scientists' careers. *Sociology of Education* 52: 129–146.

Rokeach, M. (1973). *The nature of human values.* New York: Free Press.

Rosen, B. C., and Bates, A. P. (1967). The structure of socialization in the graduate school. *Sociological Inquiry* 37: 71–84.

Rothman, R. A. (1972). A dissenting view on the scientific ethos. *British Journal of Sociology* 23: 102–108.

Schein, E. H. (1972). *Professional education: some new directions.* New York: McGraw-Hill.

Schmaus, W. (1983). Fraud and the norms of science. *Science, Technology and Human Values* 8: 12–22.

Scott, W. R. (1966). Professionals in bureaucracies—areas of conflict. In H. M. Vollmer and D. L. Milles (eds.), *Professionalization,* pp. 265–275. Englewood Cliffs, NJ: Prentice-Hall.

Shichor, D. (1970). Prestige of sociology departments and the placing of new Ph.D.'s. *American Sociologist* 5: 157–160.

Shin, K. E., and Putnam, R. H. (1982). Age and academic-professional honors. *Journal of Gerontology* 37: 220–229.

Stehr, N. (1974). Ascriptive career contingencies of sociologists: a longitudinal analysis. *American Sociologist* 9: 206–211.

Stehr, N. (1978). The ethos of science revisited: social and cognitive norm. In J. Gaston (ed.), *The sociology of science,* pp. 172–196. San Francisco: Jossey-Bass.

Stewart, J. A. (1983). Achievement and ascriptive processes in the recognition of scientific articles. *Social Forces* 62: 166–189.

Strauss, A. L., and Bucher, R. (1961). Professions in process. *American Journal of Sociology* 66: 325–334.

Sullivan, D. (1975). Competition in bio-medical science: extent, structure, and consequences. *Sociology of Education* 48: 223-241.

Thompson, F., and Zumeta, W. (1985). Hiring decisions in organized anarchies: more evidence on entrance into the academic career. *The Review of Higher Education* 8: 123-138.

Weinstein, D. (1979). Fraud in science. *Social Science Quarterly* 59: 639-652.

Wunderlich, R. (1974). The scientific ethos: a clarification. *British Journal of Sociology* 25: 373-377.

Yoels, W. C. (1971). Destiny or dynasty: doctoral origins and appointment patterns of editors of the *American Sociological Review, 1948-1968. American Sociologist* 6: 134-139.

Yoels, W. C. (1974). The structure of scientific fields and the allocation of editorships on scientific journals: some observations on the politics of knowledge. *Sociological Quarterly* 15: 264-276.

Zuckerman, H. (1977a). Deviant behavior and social control in science. In E. Sagarin (ed.), *Deviance and social change,* pp. 87-138. Beverly Hills: Sage.

Zuckerman, H. (1977b). *Scientific elite: Nobel laureates in the United States.* New York: Free Press.

Zuckerman, H., and Merton, R. K. (1971). Patterns of evaluation in science: institutionalization, structure and functions of the referee system. *Minerva* 1: 66-100.

Zuckerman, H., and Merton, R. K. (1972). Age, aging and age structure in science. In M. W. Rilesy, M. Johnson, and A. Foner (eds.), *A sociology of age stratification,* Vol. 3 of *Aging a society.* New York: Russell Sage Foundation.

THEORIES OF STUDENT DEPARTURE REVISITED

Vincent Tinto, *Syracuse University*

The past decade has witnessed a marked increase in studies of student retention in higher education. Fueled in large measure by the onset of declining numbers of college entrants, there has been renewed interest in the study of the forces that shape student departure from institutions of higher education. Understandably, there has also been increased interest in the construction of models, and sometimes theories, of student departure to explain both the patterning and the longitudinal occurrence of student departure from varying institutions of higher education.[1]

With this explosion in attention has come some confusion. While we have learned much about the character of student departure, the construction of different theories has led to some disagreement, if not confusion, about the appropriate explanation of student departure in higher education. That this should be the case is understandable, indeed desirable. The advance of our understanding of social phenomena is always the result of our first opening up new ways of thinking about explaining the phenomena we observe. The inevitable conflict that arises between different views is a necessary part of the process through which new insights into social phenomena are gained. New questions are almost always the sources of new answers. But at some point in our debate, we must stand back to reassess where we have been and where we seek to go in the future. At some stage of our work, we need to develop a more synthetic view of departure that integrates the diverse findings of the past and points our way to new questions for future inquiry.

It is to that long-term goal, that of eventually producing a more synthetic theory of student departure, that this chapter is directed. Specifically, it is concerned with the first step in the process of synthesis, namely, the critical assessment.[2] In the pages that follow, we first direct our attention to a critical review

This chapter is drawn in part from a more extended discussion of student departure in higher education by the author entitled *Leaving College: Rethinking the Causes and Cures of Student Attrition.* Chicago: The University of Chicago Press (in press).

of the existing models that have been espoused as providing an explanation for the process of student departure from higher education. That review is followed by an extended discussion of some of the changes that would have to be included in a new theoretical synthesis of student departure. To that end, the outline of a possible synthetic model of student departure is proposed, one that highlights the interactive, longitudinal character of student experience in institutions of higher education. The chapter concludes with an agenda for future research that identifies the critical questions that need be resolved if we are to make further advances in our understanding of the process of student departure from higher education.

THE STATE OF CURRENT THEORY ON STUDENT DEPARTURE

One way of distinguishing theories of student departure from one another is by the emphasis they give to different individual and environmental forces in the shaping of student behavior. Roughly speaking, it is possible to categorize past theories as falling into one of five types of theory, each with its own particular focus and level of analysis. These can be described by the terms *psychological, societal, economic, organizational,* and *interactional.*[3]

The first, psychological, is the category of theory that, as the name implies, emphasizes the role of individual psychological attributes in the departure process. The second, third, and fourth are theories that emphasize in different ways the impact of environmental forces on student behavior. Organizational theories stress the influence of immediate organizational characteristics on student behavior, whereas societal and economic theories look toward broader social and economic attributes and the impact that external social and economic forces have on the process of student departure. The last category, interactional, is the form of theory that sees student behavior as being influenced both by individual attributes and by environmental forces, especially those within the immediate setting of the institution in which students find themselves.

Psychological Theories of Student Departure
Psychological models of student departure, those that dominated our thinking about retention in the decades immediately following World War II, argue that student behavior is primarily the reflection of student attributes, specifically those that describe the individual's psychological characteristics. Models such as those by Summerskill (1962) and Marks (1967) point to the importance of intellectual attributes as shaping the individual's ability to meet the academic challenges of college life, while those by Heilbrun (1965), Rose and Elton (1966), Hanson and Taylor (1970), Rossmann and Kirk (1970), Hannah (1971), and Waterman and Waterman (1972) stress the role that personality, motivational, and dispositional characteristics play in influencing the student's ability and/or willingness to meet those challenges.

Typically, research of the psychological type has sought to distinguish stayers and leavers in terms of attributes of personality that help account for their differing response to supposedly similar educational circumstances. Heilbrun (1965), for example, in comparing stayers and leavers, argued that dropouts were likely to be less mature, more likely to rebel against authority, and more likely to be less serious in their endeavors and less dependable than persisters. More to the point, Rose and Elton (1966) argued that student leaving is an immediate reflection of maladjustment and directed hostility. Students with high hostility who are unable to adjust to the college tend to direct their hostility for their problems toward the institution and either leave higher education altogether or transfer to another institution.

However framed, all these views of departure share a common theme, namely, that retention and departure are primarily the reflection of individual actions and therefore are largely due to the ability or willingness of the individual to complete successfully the tasks associated with college attendance. More important, such models invariably see student departure as reflecting some shortcoming and/or weakness in the individual. Leaving is, in this view, assumed to be reflective of a personal failure of the individual to measure up to the demands of college life. Though external forces may matter, the individual alone bears the primary responsibility for persistence.

There is, of course, some merit to this view of student departure. There can be little doubt that individual actions matter and that differences in intellectual and personality attributes influence student persistence. But at the same time, there is no substantial body of evidence to suggest, as do these theories, that leavers are consistently different in personality from stayers or that such a thing as a "dropout" personality exists. Rather, one is led to the conclusion that observed differences in personality attributes of stayers and leavers are situationally determined.

The work of Sharp and Chason (1978) is, in this respect, most revealing. Though their first study of departure showed differences between stayers and leavers in personality scores on the Minnesota Multiphasic Personality Inventory, their attempt to replicate the results on a subsequent sample of students in the same institution proved negative. As a result, they and others (e.g., Cope and Hannah, 1975) concluded that the significant relationships shown in prior research between broad personality traits and persistence were situational and sample-specific.

The difficulty, then, with the psychological view of student leaving is that it is not truly explanatory. Because it has largely ignored the impact situations may have on student behaviors, the psychological perspective does not provide a suitable model of departure for either institutional research or institutional policy. Though it does point up the necessary role of personality in individual responses to educational situations, this perspective has not yet been able to tell us why it is that some personality attributes appear to describe differences among stayers and leavers in some situations but not in others. As a result, it does not yet provide a suitable guide either for researchers who seek to better explain the departure of different types of students from different types of institutional settings or for institutional officials who seek to enhance student retention by altering institutional actions.

Societal Theories of Student Departure

At the other end of the spectrum from psychological theories are environmental theories of student departure which emphasize the impact of wider social and economic forces on the behavior of students in institutions of higher education. One variant of the environmental perspective, societal theories of student departure, sees educational attainment as only one part of the broader process of social attainment and the success or failure of students in higher education as being molded by the same forces that shape social success generally. Rather than focusing on individual dispositions, societal theories have concerned themselves with those attributes of individuals, institutions, and society, such as social status, race, institutional prestige, and opportunity structures, that describe the person's and the institution's place in the broader social hierarchy of society.

But the manner in which they have done so has varied considerably. Societal theories of departure, like the social theories from which they derive, have differed because their view of the underlying causes of social success has also differed. Take, for example, the work of Karabel (1972) and Pincus (1980). Like most conflict theorists, these authors have argued that social institutions generally and higher education in particular are structured to serve the interests of the prevailing social and educational elites. In their view, student departure must be understood not as an isolated individual event but as part of a larger process of social stratification, which operates to preserve existing patterns of educational and social inequality. Student departure must be seen in light of how its patterned occurrence among different persons and institutions serves to reinforce social inequality generally. Thus, it is argued that individual social status, race, and sex are particularly important predictors of student success and that high rates of departure in two-year colleges reflect the intentional desire of educational organizations to restrict educational and social opportunity to particular groups in society (Clark, 1960; Pincus, 1980).

Other theorists, who share in the structural-functional view of society, see the outcome of schooling as reflecting the largely meritocratic contest among individuals for social attainment (Duncan et al., 1972; Sewell and Hauser, 1973; Featherman and Hauser, 1978). In their view, differences in educational attainment—and therefore, patterns of student departure—tend to mirror differences in individual skills and abilities rather than social status *per se*.

Though social origins as defined by social status and race matter, they tend to be less important than those attributes of individuals and organizations that impact directly on their ability to compete in the academic marketplace.

Whether a derivative of conflict theory or structural-functional theory, societal theories of departure stress the role of external forces in the process of student persistence, often at the expense of institutional forces. Consequently, such theories are frequently insensitive to the institution-specific character of student retention and to important variations in staying and leaving. Though useful in the aggregate, that is in describing broad trends in retention in society generally, these theories are much less useful in explaining the institution-specific forces that shape varying forms of student institutional departure.

Economic Theories of Student Departure

This is not as true for those environmental theories of schooling which stress the importance of economic forces in student decisions to stay or leave. Derived from economic theories of educational attainment, the work of researchers such as Manski and Wise (1984), Iwai and Churchill (1982), Jensen (1981), and Voorhees (1984) share the view that individual decisions about persistence are not different in substance from any other economic decision that weighs the costs and benefits of alternative ways of investing one's scarce economic resources. Thus, retention and departure mirror economic forces, especially those that influence both the economic benefits accruing to a college education and the financial resources that individuals can bring to bear on their investment in continued college attendance.

Understandably, all such theories emphasize the importance of individual finances and financial aid in student retention (e.g., Iwai and Churchill, 1982). More importantly, economic theories, unlike societal theories generally, take account of institution-specific forces by arguing that individual weighing of costs and benefits necessarily reflects individual experiences within a given institutional setting. Nevertheless, economic theories do so only as measured by economic factors. They are generally insensitive to the social or nonpecuniary forces inside and outside institutions that color individual decisions regarding persistence. Though such theories are useful for the study of certain problems, for instance the analysis of the effect of financial aid and tuition upon retention, their ability to explain departure in its various forms has thus far been quite limited.

In any case, there is little evidence to support the contention that financial forces are paramount to individual retention decisions. Though there is little doubt that financial considerations are important to the continued persistence of some students, most notably those from working-class and disadvantaged backgrounds, they tend to be of secondary importance to the decisions of most students. The reasons are twofold: First, the effect of finances upon persistence is most often taken up in decisions regarding college entry, that is, whether to attend and where to attend (Manski and Wise, 1984). Second, though students frequently cite finances as reasons for withdrawing, those reasons normally reflect other forces unassociated with finances, such as dissatisfaction with the institution. When students are satisfied with their institutional experience, they frequently accept a great economic burden in order to continue.[4]

This is not to say, however, that short-term fluctuations in financial resources do not lead to departure among some students, especially those from disadvantaged backgrounds. But such events are most often short-term in character and cannot explain the continuing long-term patterns of student departure that we observe in higher education. A general theory of student departure, if it is to be fully explanatory, must be able to account for the latter as well as the former mode of student departure.

Organizational Theories of Student Departure

Organizational theories of student departure, like environmental theories generally, are also concerned with the impact of environmental forces on student behavior. But rather than focus on broad social or economic forces, they center on the effect of the organization of higher educational institutions. Like studies of role socialization and worker productivity and turnover, from which they are derived, organizational theories of departure, such as those of Kamens (1971) and Bean (1983), see the occurrence of student departure as reflecting the impact that the organization has on the socialization and satisfaction of students. Their central tenet has been that departure is as much, if not more, a reflection of institutional behavior as it is of the individuals within it.

Typically, researchers have looked at the effect of organizational dimensions such as bureaucratic structure, size, faculty–student ratios, and institutional resources and goals on the aggregate rates of student institutional departure. Though individual attributes are sometimes included, they are not of primary theoretical interest. Kamens's multi-institutional study (1971), for instance, focused on the impact of organizational size and complexity on student role socialization and retention. He argued that larger institutions with distinct college "charters" would have lower rates of attrition because of their superior capacity to allocate students to the more prestigious positions in society. Such "charters" are a reflection not only of institutional resources but also of the links that larger institutions maintain with different occupational and economic groups (Kamens, 1971, pp. 271–272). Bean's study (1983) takes a somewhat different view of departure. An offshoot of an industrial model of work turnover (Price, 1977; Price and Mueller, 1981), this study looked at the impact of organizational attributes (e.g., routinization, participation, and communication) and rewards (e.g., grades, practical value, and development) on retention through their impact on student satisfaction. As in work organizations, it is argued that institutional rates of retention—that is, student turnover—would be heightened by institutional policies that increase students' participation and enhance the rewards they obtain for their "work" in the institution.

The strength of the organizational view of student departure lies in its reminding us that the organization of educational institutions—their formal structures, resources, and patterns of association—do impact on student retention. As in formal organizations generally, organizational decisions within higher education necessarily impact on the satisfaction of all members within the organization, students as well as faculty and staff. In this respect, organizational models are especially appealing to institutional planners concerned with the restructuring of organizations to achieve greater institutional effectiveness, for they focus on organizational attributes that are directly alterable by administrative action. These models should also be appealing to researchers interested in the comparative analysis of institutional retention.

As a theory of student departure, however, organizational theories such as Bean's (1983) and to a lesser extent Kamens's (1971) lack in explanatory power in that they do not enable us to understand how organizational attributes eventually impact on student decisions to stay or leave. That is the case, in part, because these theories normally do not point out the intervening factors, such as student subcultures and patterns of student–faculty interaction, that serve to transmit the effect of the organization to student behaviors.[5] Nor do they enable us to understand why it is that different types of students may take on different types of leaving behaviors within the institution. In this regard, these theories implicitly assume that all leavings arise from the same sources—an assumption we know not to be correct.

Though organizational models may be especially suited to comparative studies of rates of retention in different types of higher education organizational settings—for which they have unfortunately been rarely used—they are much less useful in the study of intraorganizational variations in student behaviors. They are not well suited to the task of explaining the patterns of student departure that arise among different types of students within the institution. For this purpose, one has to look elsewhere, specifically to interactional theories of student departure.

Interactional Theories of Student Departure
Interactional theories of student departure, those that have now come to dominate current views of student leaving, take student behavior as reflecting both individual and organizational attributes. But rather than being a simple compilation of psychological and organizational theories, they represent a dynamic, interactive view of student experience, one that has its origins in social anthropological and ethnomethodological studies of human behavior. From the former, interactional theories of student departure have taken the view that student leaving reflects individuals' experience in the total culture of the institution

as manifested in both the formal and the informal organization of the institution. Rather than focusing on formal organization alone, they stress the role of informal social organizations (e.g., student peer groups) and subcultures in student departure. From the latter, they have come to argue that student departure necessarily reflects the interpretation and meaning that individuals attach to their experiences within the institution. Though individual attributes matter, their impact cannot be understood without reference to how they relate to the understandings that different students have of events within the institution.

In this fashion, interactional theories see student leaving as reflecting the dynamic reciprocal interaction between environments and individuals. The two cannot be separated and are intimately intertwined in the manner in which each comes to shape the interpretations that differing individuals give to their experiences. In the final analysis, what matters is the individual's understanding of the situation—an interpretation of events that is necessarily a dynamic outcome of how the individual interacts with other persons and with the broader setting of which he or she is a part.

There are several variants of the interactional view of student departure. The least complex are those that use the notion of role socialization and "person–role fit" to describe student departure (Pervin and Rubin, 1967; Rootman, 1972). For them, socialization into the student role is central to the retention process. As a consequence, the more closely aligned the individual sees himself or herself as being with that role, the more likely is he or she is to stay rather than to leave. Conversely, the greater the perceived discrepancy between the individual's perception of the self and the student role, the greater the likelihood of departure.

Though evidence seems to bear out this view, it does so only for some types of leaving, primarily from relatively homogeneous institutional settings where the notion of *student role* may be more clearly articulated and representative of the wider college culture. In heterogeneous settings or in those with no dominant student subculture (e.g., non-residential colleges), the same notion may provide a less suitable account of student departure. In any event, like other views of departure, the "person–role fit" model tends to asssume that all leavings are the same in character and in source—an assumption that we know to be incorrect. Only some forms of leaving appear to fall within the notion of *person–role fit*. Many others appear to arise from different sources.[6]

A more complex form of the interactional view of departure, and perhaps the most widely cited, is that of Tinto (1975). A derivative of Spady's earlier work (1970), it draws its theoretical origins from the work of the French sociologist Emile Durkheim, in particular his study of social communities and individual suicide. As applied to the question of student leaving, Tinto's model argues that colleges are very much like other human communities, and that the process of persistence—and by extension, that of departure—is very much like those processes within communities that influence the establishing of community membership. In the multifaceted world of the college, student decisions to leave are seen as directly and indirectly influenced by the individual's social (personal) and intellectual (normative) experiences in the various communities that make up the world of the college. Specifically, they reflect the impact that those experiences have on individual goals and commitments both to the goal of degree completion and to the institution. Thus, decisions to leave reflect the individual's interpretation of those experiences and therefore those personal attributes that are associated with how individuals interact with and come to attach meaning to the world around them.

Though quite complex, interactional models provide a more inclusive view of the departure process, one that integrates both the organizational and the psychological view of departure, while enabling researchers to sort out the various forms of leaving that are typically subsumed under the label *dropout* (Tinto, 1982, 1985b). More importantly, they also highlight the various mechanisms through which organization and personality impact upon departure (Pascarella and Terenzini, 1979). By so doing, they move from a largely descriptive view of departure to an explanatory theory that is amenable to the development of testable hypotheses. That is, they go beyond the description of differences between stayers and leavers to an explanation of how those differences arise within the context of a specific institution.

The interactional model is, as Peterson (1985, p. 8) noted, the only theory of student departure to have generated a systematic testing of its ability to explain student departure from institutions of higher education (e.g., Pascarella and Terenzini, 1979; Munro, 1981; Pascarella and Chapman, 1983; Pascarella and Terenzini, 1983; Donovan, 1984; Pascarella and Wolfle, 1985; Pascarella et al., 1985; Fox, 1985; Hall et al., 1985; Cash and Bissell, 1985; Weidman, 1985). For that reason, interactional theories of departure, particularly Tinto's, appear to offer the firmest and most complete foundation on which future developments in theories of student departure can occur.

Nevertheless, the interactional theory of departure is also subject to some important limitations (Tinto, 1982). Not the least of these pertain to its failure to take explicit account of either the formal organizational or external forces (e.g., external communities) which impact upon student participation in college.[7] For that reason, current forms of interactional theory are neither particularly well suited to the study of non-residential institutions and/or of departure among commuting students, nor easily adapted to the practical needs of administrative planners. Tinto's (1975) theory of departure, for instance, is more clearly a social science theory of departure than an administrative one designed for the formulation of policy. More importantly, as is true for virtually all models of student departure, the interactional view of student leaving is not truly longitudinal. Though it is longitudinal in nature, it does not provide substantive details of the manner in which the departure process may vary over time. It assumes, in effect, that the process of leaving is largely uniform over time.

If we wish to produce a truly synthetic theory of departure, we must extend current theory to meet these needs. Specifically we need to address three major areas of concern, namely the need for a more complete longitudinal model of departure over time, for a model which takes account of the effect of external forces upon departure, and for one which allows us to map out the impact of the formal organization of the institution upon student departure.

DIRECTIONS FOR FUTURE THEORY ON STUDENT DEPARTURE

The Longitudinal Nature of Student Withdrawal:
The Stages of Institutional Departure

To address the issue of the longitudinal nature of student departure, we turn to the field of social anthropology and studies of the temporal process of establishing membership in traditional societies. Specifically, we can turn to the work of the Dutch anthropologist Arnold Van Gennep and his study of the rites of membership in tribal societies.[8] Of his numerous concerns, the one most directly related to the process of student departure is his focus on the movement of individuals from membership in one group to membership in another, especially as it occurs in the ascendancy of individuals from youth to adult status in society. In his classic study entitled *The Rites of Passage,* Van Gennep (1960) argued that the process of the transmission of relationships between succeeding groups is marked by three distinct phases or stages, each with its own specialized ceremonies and rituals: separation, transition, and incorporation. Each serves to move individuals from youthful participation to full membership in adult society. They provide, through the use of ceremony and ritual, for the orderly transmission of the beliefs and norms of the society to the next generation of adults and/or new members. In that fashion, such rites serve to ensure the stability of society over time, while also enabling younger generations to assume responsibility from older ones.

According to Van Gennep, each stage in the rites of passage to adulthood consists of a change in patterns of interaction between the individual and other members of society. The first, separation, is characterized by a marked decline in interactions with members of the group from which the person has come. Frequently involving ceremonies whose purpose it is to mark as outmoded the views and norms that characterize that group, separation requires the individual to remove herself or himself, in both physical and normative terms, from past forms of association and patterns of behavior.

The second stage, transition, is a period during which the person begins to interact in new ways with members of the new group in which membership is sought. Isolation, training, and sometimes ordeals are employed as mechanisms to ensure the separation of the individual from past associations and the adoption of behaviors and norms appropriate to membership in the new group. It is during this transitional stage that individuals acquire the knowledge and skills required for the performance of their specific role in the new group. Having given up past forms of association, individuals now prepare themselves for full membership in the new communities of the future.

The third and last phase, incorporation, involves taking on new patterns of interaction with members of the new group and establishing competent membership in that group as a participant. Full membership in or incorporation into the new group is marked by special ceremonies that announce and certify not only the rewards of membership but also the responsibilities associated with it. Though the person may begin to interact once again with past associations, he or she now does so as a member of the new group. He or she has completed the movement from the past and is now fully integrated into the culture of the new group.

Van Gennep believed that the notions of rites of passage could be applied to a variety of situations, especially those involving the movement of a person or group from one place to another.[9] In that movement, the individual or group leaves an old territory or community (separation); in some fashion crosses a border, whether it be physical or ceremonial, to a new setting (transition); and takes up residence in the new location or community (incorporation). For the individual, such movements necessarily entail moving from a position as a known member in one group to that of a stranger in the new setting. The result is often feelings of weakness and isolation not very different from those Durkheim described as being "anomic." Having given up the norms and beliefs of past associations and not yet having adopted those appropriate to membership in a new community, the individual is left in a state of at least temporary normlessness. A consequence of normlessness—that is, of the absence of guiding norms and beliefs—is the likelihood of departure from the community before incorporation.

The work of Van Gennep provides us with a way of thinking about the longitudinal process of student persistence in college and, by extension, about the time-dependent process of student departure.[10] College students are, after all, moving from one community or set of communities to another. Like other persons in the wider society, they too must separate themselves, to some degree, from past associations in order to make the transition to eventual incorporation into the life of the college. In attempting to make such transitions, they too are likely to encounter difficulties that are as much a reflection of the problems inherent in shifts of community membership as they are either of the personality of individuals or of the institution in which membership is sought.

The longitudinal process of institutional persistence can therefore be envisioned as consisting of three major stages or passages through which students must typically pass in order to complete their degree programs. These are, as in the work of Van Gennep, the stages of separation, transition and incorporation. By extension, the process of institutional departure can be seen as being differentially shaped by the difficulties that students encounter in attempting to navigate successfully those stages and to become incorporated into the life of the college.

Separation from the Past. The first stage of the college career, separation, requires students to disassociate themselves, in varying degrees, from membership in past communities, most typically those associated with the local high school and place of residence. Depending in part on the character of those communities, especially their views regarding the worth of college attendance, separation may be quite difficult or merely an accepted part of the process of movement that most persons are expected to make in the course of their lives. Nevertheless, all separations, however small, entail some form of parting from past habits and patterns of affiliation. The adoption of the behaviors and norms appropriate to the college almost always requires some degree of transformation and perhaps rejection of those of the past communities. However close, the life of families and high schools and the demands that they impose on their members are qualitatively different from those that characterize most colleges.

For virtually all students, the process of separation from the past is at least somewhat stressful. For some, it may be so severe as to constrain persistence in college. This may be especially true for individuals who, for the first time, move away from their local high-school communities and families to live away at a distant college, and/or whose colleges are markedly different in social and intellectual orientation from that of the family and the local community. In order to become fully integrated into the communities of the college, these individuals have to disassociate physically as well as socially from the communities of the past. In a very real sense, their persistence depends on their ability to depart from the norms of their former communities.

This may not apply to persons who stay at home while attending college. They need not disassociate themselves from local communities in order to establish membership in the new communities of the college. By the same token, they may be unable to take full advantage of those communities for integration into the social and intellectual life of the college. Though such persons may find movement into the world of the college less stressful, they may also find it less rewarding. They may not be able to reap the full social and intellectual rewards that social membership in college communities brings. Thus, the irony is that though they may find the task of persistence initially easier, it may be measurably more difficult over the long run.[11]

Transition to College. The second stage of the college career, transition, is a period of passage between the old and the new, between the associations of the past and the hoped-for associations with communities of the present. Having begun the process of separating themselves from the past, new students have yet to acquire the norms and patterns of behavior appropriate to integration into the new communities of the college. They have not yet established the personal bonds that underlie community membership. As a result, they are neither bound as strongly to the past, nor firmly tied to the future.

The stress and sense of loss and bewilderment, if not desolation, that sometimes accompany the transition to college can pose serious problems for the individual attempting to persist in college. Though most students are able to cope with the problems of adjusting to the social and intellectual life of the college, many find it measurably more difficult. As a result, many withdraw from college very early in the academic year. They do less from an inability to become integrated into the social and academic communities of the college than from an inability to withstand and cope with the stresses that such transitions commonly induce.

Besides the obvious role of personality, differences in individual coping skills and in educational goals and commitments have much to do with individual responses to the stresses of separation and transition. Quite simply, some students are unable to cope with such situations. They have not learned how to direct their energies to solving the problems they face. Without institutional assistance, they often flounder and withdraw without having made a serious attempt to adjust to the life of the college. But some students stick it out even under the most severe conditions, while others withdraw even under minimal stress. The unavoidable fact is that some students are unwilling to put up with the stresses of transition because they are not sufficiently committed either to the goals of education and/or to the institution into which entry is first made. Others, however, are so committed to those goals that they will do virtually anything to persist.

The point here is simply that the problems associated with both separation and transition are problems that, though stressful, need not in themselves lead to departure. It is the individual's responses to these problems that finally determine staying or leaving. By extension, institutions can do much to assist new students in dealing with conditions that are inherent in the first two stages of the college career.

It should be noted that the scope of the transition stage—that is, the degree of change that it entails—depends on a number of factors, not the least of which is the degree of difference between the norms and patterns of behavior of the past and those required for integration into the life of the college. For example, persons from families, communities, and/or schools that are very different in behavior and norms from those of the college are faced with especially difficult problems in seeking to achieve membership in the communities of the college. Their past experiences are unlikely to have prepared them for the new life of the college in the same way as have the experiences of those persons who come from families that are themselves college-educated. In the "typical" institution, one would therefore expect persons from minority backgrounds and/or from very poor families, older adults, and persons from very small rural communities to be more likely to experience such problems than would other students.

The same may also apply to persons who reside at home during college. In seeking to avoid the pains of separation, they may fail to perceive the need to adjust to the new demands of the college and to become involved in its ongoing intellectual and social life. As a consequence, they may limit the amount of the time they spend on campus. The resulting restriction on their interaction with other members of the college communities may severely constrain the learning of the norms and patterns of behavior required for full incorporation into the life of the college. In the particular case of nonresidential two-year colleges, such transitions are rarely required. Nor is full integration into the life of the institution. Again, what one gains in the way of easier persistence early in the college career, one may pay for in difficulty in persistence later on.

Incorporation into College. After passing through the stages of separation and transition, the individual is faced with the task of becoming integrated, or to use Van Gennep's term, *incorporated* into the community of the college. Having moved away from the norms and behavioral patterns of past associations, the person now faces the problem of finding and adopting norms appropriate to the new college setting and of establishing competent membership in the social and intellectual communities of college life. As social interactions are the primary vehicle through which such integrative associations arise, individuals have to establish contact with other members of the institution, student and faculty alike. Failure to do so may lead to the absence of integration and to its associated sense of isolation. These, in turn, may lead to departure from the institution.

But unlike incorporation into traditional societies, individuals in college are not always provided with formal rituals and ceremonies whereby such contacts are ensured. Nor are they always clearly informed either of the character of the local communities or of the behaviors and norms appropriate to membership in them. Of course, most institutions, especially residential ones, do provide a variety of formal and informal mechanisms for that purpose. Fraternities, sororities, student dormitory associations, student unions, frequent faculty and visiting-scholar series, extracurricular programs, and intramural athletics, for example, may all serve to provide individuals with opportunities to establish repetitive contact with other members of the institution in circumstances that lead to the possibility of integration.

Not all individuals, especially those recently removed from the long-known confines of the family and local high-school communities, are able to make such contacts on their own. As a result, they do not all come to be incorporated into the life of the college and do not establish competent membership in its intellectual and social communities. Many eventually leave because of the ensuing isolation that they experience.

But some students may leave because they choose not to become incorporated into the communities of the college. Having established contact with other members of the institution, some new students may find that the social and intellectual communities of the college are not to their liking. Rather than adopting values and behavioral styles that they see as discordant with their own, they may decide to voluntarily withdraw in order to seek membership in other settings. Their leaving is more a reflection of a perceived lack of fit between themselves and the life of the college than it is of personal isolation. Though isolation may occur, it is the result of their prior decision not to become integrated.

Reflections on the Stages of Institutional Departure and Current Theories of Student Departure. Several observations should be made before we proceed to other areas of theory. The first concerns the relationship between this view of institutional departure and the interactional theories of departure, in particular that of the author. The view described here can be seen as complementary to that theory. Rather than offering a conflicting view of departure, it adds a time dimension to the theory by describing the longitudinal stages of the process of integration, in particular the early phases of separation and transition that precede incorporation into the life of the college. This view is, in effect, a description of the longitudinal character of the student career as it proceeds toward incorporation into the communities of the college, that is, persistence.

The inclusion of the notion of stages or passages also highlights the sorts of difficulties that students typically face in each of those stages. It argues that all students, regardless of personality and prior experience, will encounter difficulties, in some form, that are characteristic of the college career. Consequently, it also argues that institutions must carefully frame and time their actions on behalf of student retention to meet the changing needs of students as they arise at different points during the college career.

It should also be observed that college communities are both academic and social. Persistence in college may arise in either the academic or the social system of the institution and may reflect both the personal and the intellectual integration or incorporation of the individual into the communities of the college. By extension, the longitudinal process of student institutional departure can be seen as being marked by the difficulties that individuals experience in making the social and/or the intellectual adjustment to the formal and informal academic and social life of the new communities of the college. The general notion of stages of passage may be seen, therefore, as applying to the separate passages that new students must make to become incorporated into both the social and the intellectual life of the college.[12]

Finally, it must be recognized that the stages of passage that we have described are abstractions that necessarily simplify, for purposes of analysis, the more complex phenomena that we understand as student departure. In using the stages of separation, transition, and incorporation in our analysis of student departure, we do not mean to oversimplify what is a very complex and quite fluid situation. Though these stages may apply to the process of departure in an abstract form, they need not apply without modification to each and every case. Some students may hardly be aware of the transition required in becoming integrated into the life of the college. Others may not experience the separate stages at the same time or in the same way. For still other students, any or all of the stages may significantly overlap and may occur simultaneously.

Even so, the tasks and problems associated with each stage must be encountered and overcome for all students to become fully incorporated—that is, integrated—into the life of the communities of the college. Most students are eventually faced with very much the same sorts of problems and experience similar types of difficulties in attempting to establish competent membership within the communities of the college that they enter. These are as much a reflection of the process of persistence in college as they are of either the attributes of the persons experiencing them or the institution in which they occur. By extension, the longitudinal process of departure from institutions of higher education is similarly marked in time by difficulties associated with the individual's inability to attend to the problems that arise in those stages. Though the process of departure necessarily reflects the absence of integration into the life of the college, it may arise at differing points of time from different problems. In short, lack of integration, which has been posited elsewhere as a primary cause of student departure, is not necessarily a reflection of an absence of incorporation alone. It may also result from the inability of students to separate themselves from past associations and/or to make the transition to new ones.

External Forces and the Concept of Competing Communities
All this is not to say, however, that individual decisions regarding staying in college are unaffected by events external to college. We know this not to be the case. Though interactional and organizational models of student departure emphasize the role of intrainstitutional experiences, they do not exclude the possibility that external forces may also sway individual decisions regarding departure.

One can think of the problem of external forces in terms of internal and external communities. External communities (e.g., families, neighborhoods, peer groups, and work settings), like those internal to the college, have their own social and normative structure and patterns of interaction, leading to community membership. For any individual, participation in external communities may serve to counter, rather than to support, participation in college communities.

This is so not only because the demands of the former may take away time from participation in the latter but also because the requirements of membership in one may work counter to those of membership in the other.

The normative requirements of membership in one's local peer group external to the college, for instance, may be such as to downplay the appropriateness of membership in the intellectual communities of the college. Membership in the latter may be seen as being a deviant form of activity within the former. Individuals in such situations may be forced to choose between membership in possibly long-standing external communities and membership in the relatively new, still tenuous communities of the college. When these latter communities are either weak—as they may be in nonresidential, commuting institutions—or when one's experiences in them are unsatisfactory, the effect of external communities on decisions to persist may be quite substantial. The direction of their impact may spell the difference between staying and leaving. For persons who are only weakly affiliated with any college community and/or whose local community may be marginal to the life of the institution, the effect of such external forces may be sufficiently great to alter their goals and commitments so as to induce them to leave the college for other pursuits.

External events may also influence departure by altering the mix of competing opportunities for the investment of individual resources. As pointed out by economic models of departure, individual judgments about continued participation in college may be viewed as a weighing of the costs and benefits of college persistence relative to alternative investments of one's time, energies, and scarce resources. Significant alteration in the external mix of opportunities and/or in their relative benefits may change decisions in favor of noncollege activities. Increases in the demand for non-college-graduates or heightened unemployment among college graduates may, for instance, induce some persons to leave college for potentially greener pastures. Similarly, the removal of restrictions that limit the range of external options, such as occurred with the cessation of the draft and the opening up of white colleges to black students, may lead others to do the same.

In this regard, the research of Chacon et al. (1982) on dropouts among Latina women in colleges in the Southwest reminds us of the way in which excessive external demands—in this case, of one's local and extended family—can effectively prevent persistence within college. The demands of the former are so great as to prevent the transition to the world of the college. Though contact within the college may help, for some it may be insufficient to counter the deeply rooted demands of families and family roles on students' time and energies.

This last notion, that of roles, suggests, perhaps, another fruitful area of exploration: role theory and role conflict. Though it is not our intent here to develop this possibility, it should be pointed out that one can envision the conflict between external and internal forces as being comparable to the conflict between competing roles. Persistence requires the individual to successfully play the role of student, whereas family life requires the person to play different roles. When the two are in conflict, that is, when each requires of the person different forms of behavior and allocation of time and energies, the person is placed in a potentially quite stressful situation. Unless individuals are able to cope with that stress, departure from college (or from the family) may be the only viable way of resolving a potentially damaging situation.

Having made this point, we must also observe that student departure most frequently arises because of a change in the person's evaluation of the relative benefits of college activities. This may result not only from a change in the external benefits accruing to college graduates but also from an alteration in the intrinsic rewards arising from college attendance. As argued in Tinto's model of departure, these intrinsic rewards are largely the consequence of one's social and intellectual integration into the communities of the college. The absence of such integration may alter the person's judgment of the relative costs and benefits of continued persistence, regardless of changes in the world external to the college.

The point here is quite simple. Though external events may be important for some students, especially those from less affluent backgrounds, for most students they are of secondary importance relative to experience within the college. While external forces may influence decisions to go to college and may greatly constrain the choice of which college to attend, their impact on departure following entry is generally quite minor.[13] Recent research on retention in a two-year commuting college tends to support this view (Neumann, 1985). Even in that setting, where on-campus contact with faculty is so limited, social and intellectual contact with persons within the institution matters. Students who might not otherwise be expected to finish their degree program apparently do so because of the relationships they establish with other persons on campus.

Bringing in the Organization:
The Mediating Effect of Social and Intellectual Communities
To the same degree that organizational theories of student departure have largely ignored the subtle effects of the informal world of the college, so, too, have interactional models of departure tended to overlook the effect of the formal organization of the institution on student behavior. This need not be the case. As noted earlier, the latter models can very easily be modified to include the effect of organizational attributes on student behavior.

A number of different perspectives on organizations can serve this purpose. In addition to the model of worker turnover used by Bean (1983), one can make reference to Hirschman's analysis (1970) of the effect of participation on worker loyalty, Barker and Gump's study (1964) of the effect of school size on student participation and satisfaction, or Stroup's extended essay (1966) on bureaucracy in higher education. Any of these models of organizations can provide us with a framework for understanding the many ways in which organizational attributes eventually reach down and impact on the lives of students.

But here an important caveat is called for. The application of theories of work organizations, for instance, to the study of student departure must be carried out with care. The primary difficulty with such applications is that they make the implicit assumption that higher education organizations are essentially the same as those in the world of work and, therefore, that one can think of students in those organizations as one would of workers in factories or offices. While the analogy may be stretched to fit faculty and staff, it is doubtful that students would see themselves in the same light as would workers generally. Though the analogy of worker productivity to that of student performance is especially appealing, as it can provide us with a way of addressing both the issue of retention and the issue of student learning, we must be careful not to push such analogies too far. Perhaps we should consider looking to other models of organizations, such as those of the professional or socializing type, as possible guides to our study of the effect of organizations on student departure.

Whatever our referent, it is important that the adoption of organizational models enable us to trace more accurately the direct and indirect effects of organizations on student behavior. Available evidence leads us to believe, for instance, that one of the primary effects of the organization on student departure is indirect, through its influence on the character of the social and intellectual communities within the college. For example, formal academic policies, such as requiring faculty to take attendance, may alter not only the nature of classroom interactions but also the character of the academic communities of the college. By so doing, such policies may have wider, though often unintended, impacts on student retention that extend beyond initial policy goals. In this example, they may undermine rather than aid student learning by affecting how students and faculty view their mutual responsibility in the learning process.

By allowing us to map out the multiple effects of the organization on students, the inclusion of organizational variables in current interactional theories of departures can also lead to a more complete guide for administrative policy formation. They may do so by pointing out the various and often unintended ways in which formal administrative actions impact directly and indirectly on student departure. Currently, interactional theories of departure are, in this regard, particularly weak.

Combined interaction and organizational theories may also serve as an effective tool for the comparative study of student departure in different institutional settings. They may enable us, for instance, to analyze more carefully the ways in which different organizational structures impact upon institutional rates of student departure. Though some very informative attempts have been made to use existing interactional models for this purpose (e.g., Pascarella and Chapman, 1983; Pascarella and Wolfle, 1985), we have only begun to scratch the surface of the multi-layered effects of different institutional settings on student departure.

CONCLUDING COMMENTS: COMMONALITIES IN THE DEVELOPMENT OF A GENERAL THEORY OF STUDENT DEPARTURE

The above discussion leads us finally to consider some of the major elements of a general theory of student departure and some of the research we would have to pursue to develop that theory. Here it would seem to be the case that recent research provides a reasonable guide to what we can expect in the future, namely, that a general theory of student departure will result from an extension and elaboration of the interactional view of departure. That view, especially as elaborated by Tinto (1975), Pascarella and Terenzini (1979), Pascarella et al. (1983), and Tinto (in press), seems to provide the most inclusive theoretical base on which future developments in a theory of student departure can be built. This is the case because it already contains many of the elements that are essential to a general theory of student departure.

First, this view enables researchers to sort out the various forms of leaving that are typically subsumed under the label *dropout*. For instance, it allows one to distinguish voluntary withdrawal from forced dismissal and, within the former, to separate the various roots of voluntary withdrawal. Here, current research is still lacking. Though we have distinguished between forced and voluntary leaving, we have not yet adequately isolated the events that lead persons to leave because of lack of fit from those that give rise to leaving because of social and/or intellectual isolation. Until we do so, it should not be surprising that our models of departure will continue to explain relatively small percentages of variance in leaving behaviors.

Second, this view offers an inclusive model of departure that integrates, in a dynamic and interactive fashion, the full range of environmental and individual influences that impinge on the withdrawal process. It includes both social and academic forces and the formal and informal impact of both personal and intellectual experiences on individual decisions to stay in college. Furthermore, it can, with some of the revisions suggested above, also capture the various direct and indirect effects of the formal organization of the institution on student behavior. In this fashion, it provides us with a way of tracing out the direct and indirect effects that formal organizational structures have on student retention and of isolating how informal structures (e.g., peer subcultures) serve to mediate and sometimes to alter the intended impact of formal administrative decisions.

The mapping out of those effects requires, however, that we carry out many more multi-institutional comparative studies of student departure. Only through carefully drawn comparisons between institutions or settings of different organizational attributes can we come to understand the multidimensional impacts that settings have on student retention. For example, we need to look not only at the experiences of similar types of students in different institutional settings but also at the differences in the experiences of different types of students (e.g., black and white, male and female) in those varying settings. Though the recent work of Pascarella and Wolfle (1985) is a move in the right direction, it is only a first step. Rather than relying on large databases drawn from many institutions—in the case of Pascarella and Wolfle's study, 10,326 students attending 487 colleges and universities—we need to carefully select a few institutions from which we sample a much larger number of students. Only in that way can we expect to tease out the complex patterns of interactions that are likely to describe the experiences of different students in different institutional settings.

Third, this view is a longitudinal explanatory model of retention that can be extended to provide explanatory detail of the time-variable dimension of the process of student departure.[14] A relatively simple extension of the model to include the concept of passages is, as described above, only one possible way to achieve that end. Here is where the need for additional research is clearest. We need to carry out research that explores the character of departure at differing points in the student career. For instance, we must look at departure during the first several months of college separately from departure that occurs at the end of the first year, and we must study departure that arises early in the student career separately from departure in the last years of college. And we must do so for different types of students as they enter and progress through varying types of institutions.

However constructed, future theory must also lead to or be derived from the perceptions that the actors themselves have of the situation. It must be based on the meanings that students place on their experiences. In other words, future theory must be grounded in the everyday reality of the lives of students and must make sense of their experiences in the various realms of college life. Future theory must, in this sense, be understandable to the actors themselves. It must distinguish situations of personal failure from those that represent successful individual adaptation to changing educational circumstances. For the most part, our current theories of departure, with several notable exceptions, continue to treat all leaving as dropout and therefore as reflective of some form of personal failure.

It is for this reason that an agenda for future research must also include more careful qualitative studies of student departure. Though there is much merit in present efforts to provide quantitative tests of existing theory, we should not overlook the important contributions that grounded qualitative research can make to the development of theory. Regrettably, serious qualitative studies of student departure, such as that by Neumann (1985), are infrequent and far between. The development of complete, grounded theory of student departure requires that we carry out similar qualitative studies that explore the experiences of different students (e.g., adult, minority, and part-time) in varying institutional settings (e.g., two-year and nonresidential). We must more frequently combine the strengths of comparative longitudinal studies of departure with those of detailed qualitative studies of the character of those departures.

Finally, in looking at the experiences of students, future theory must be able to make sense of research that indicates the importance of "quality of student effort" and student "involvement in learning" to both retention and the quality of student learning (e.g., Pace, 1984). In pursuing their educational mission, institutions of higher education must act to enhance the quality of student effort and to involve students in the learning enterprise in ways that lead not only to retention but to further education (see Endo and Harpel, 1982). To that end, our theories of student retention and departure must also be theories of student involvement and learning—theories that point up how institutional experiences serve to heighten or hinder student involvement and to enhance or reduce the quality of effort that they are willing to expend on behalf of their own education. In the final analysis, our theories of student departure must also be translatable into theories of student education. Otherwise, they will always be only marginally relevant to the important needs of both students and institutions of higher education.

NOTES

1. The distinction between models and theories is not a trivial one. Not all so-called theories of student departure are theories in the social science sense of the word. Only infrequently have we had theories of student departure that provide for a systematic set of relationships or underlying principles which could be said to explain the observed phenomena of student leaving and that lead to the specification of hypotheses which could be tested and verified by research. Most so-called theories are, in fact, models of departure which focus on some, but by no means all, of the factors and relationships that would account for students' leaving. Though they may be inspired by a theory of behavior, they are more limited in scope than the theories from which they derive. Nevertheless, in the discussion that follows, we will refer to current models of departure as if they were theories of student departure. We will do so because it is our intent to highlight not only the theoretical orientations from which they derive, but also the essential differences in theoretical assumptions that describe their varying approaches to the question of explanation.
2. In many respects, the current discussion parallels that by the author over ten years ago (Tinto, 1975). As in that article, the current chapter reflects an attempt to provide a theoretical assessment of our current state of knowledge about the process of student departure. But now we have the benefit of the considerable body of research and theory development that has taken place over the past decade. Though there are still major gaps in our knowledge of student departure, we are much better informed today of the roots of leaving than we were a decade ago.
3. There are a number of other ways of categorizing theory. We could also distinguish theories by the theoretical orientations from which they spring (e.g., con-

flict versus structural) or by the levels of analyses they use to study departure (e.g., individual, group, or societal). In this case, the distinction between psychological, societal, economic, organizational, and interactional serves to highlight the essential differences between theories in the assumptions they make about the primary causes of student attrition. Of equal importance, this distinction enables us to consider ways in which these disparate perspectives may someday be fused by highlighting the different levels of analysis (individual, organizational, and societal) that can be applied to the study of student leaving.

4. A study by Collins, Turner and Maguire (1979) at Boston College is one of a number of institutional studies which reinforce this contention, namely that student response to economic hardships is dependent upon their level of satisfaction with their educational experience.

5. Bean and Kuh (1984) has recently modified his original model to include both the attributes of and individual forms of participation in the social and intellectual communities of the institution. In this sense, then, his more recent work appears to be an attempt to integrate his organizational model with the interactional models of retention which now have such wide currency.

6. Studies which have supported the notion of student-role fit have been of relatively small and/or quite homogenous institutions such as military academies (Rootman, 1972) and church-related colleges (Cash, 1985). In much larger, heterogeneous institutions, even potentially deviant students sometimes manage to find a niche and stay until degree completion (Simpson, Baker and Mellinger, 1980).

7. It should be noted that most current interactional theories of student departure assume a largely functionalist view of behavior. In arguing that integration is central to persistence, they have made the implicit assumption that retention is functional for both the individual and the institution. But that assumption is not the only one which can be used to frame a theory of student retention. The conflict tradition, already noted, makes the assumption that social structure will reflect the interests of the prevailing social elites. As a result, it is possible that retention may sometimes further the interests of the institution at the expense of the individual. The phenomenological tradition, however, would argue that theorists should suspend judgment until they made reference to the understanding various actors have of retention. Rather than invest in research which seeks to validate preexisting theories, phenomenologists would have theory evolve from the grounded discovery of the meaning different individuals give to student leaving.

8. A year after having completed the first draft of this paper, the author learned of the work of John Gardiner of the University of South Carolina on the same theme. Having worked independent of one another, we had arrived at the same point, namely the application of the notion of Rites of Passage to the study of student persistence. For that reason the reader is urged to look at Gardiner and Jewler (1985) as an example of another application of the same concept to the problems of educational continuance.

9. Solon Kimball, in his introduction to the English translation of Van Gennep's classic *Rites of Passage,* argues that Van Gennep's "scheme du les rites de passage" might be more appropriately translated as "dynamics of the rites of transition", with the term dynamics implying both a sense of process and structure (Van Gennep, 1960, pp. v-xxii). In his view Van Gennep was as much concerned with the process of transitions as with the structure of the ceremonies which marked those transitions.

10. For a more complete discussion of the application of Van Gennep's work to the study of student departure the reader is urged to see Tinto (1985a).
11. It should also be pointed out that by staying at home, students expose themselves to a number of potential risks, not the least of which is the exposure to external forces which pull the person away from incorporation into the communities of the college. If the orientation of the family or local peer group does not support, indeed opposes, participation in higher education, early separation and transition may be measurably more difficult. It may require the person to reject the values of the family or the local peers in order to adopt those appropriate to the college.
12. These varying passages and the differing forms of adjustment that they entail are inextricably linked. In the interactive life of colleges, experiences in adjusting in one domain of the college necessarily impacts on those in other domains of the college. Difficulties that new students encounter in adjusting to the social life of the college, for instance, may affect their ability to adapt to the academic demands of the college. Similarly, problems that new students experience in adjusting to the informal intellectual style of academic life may impact on their ability to make the transition to the formal demands of academic life.
13. Not all institutions would agree with this view. For those institutions, such as the urban two-year colleges, that serve large proportions of part-time and/or less well-to-do students the importance of external events cannot be underestimated. In a similar fashion, technical-vocational institutions that provide direct access to work opportunities are more likely to feel the effects of alterations in job markets than are other institutions.
14. Of course the same can be said of other models of departure. The organizational model, for instance, can also be extended for this purpose. Here, the notion of worker–role socialization may be useful in helping researchers to think about the longitudinal process by which new workers come to adopt behaviors appropriate to their new setting.

REFERENCES

Barker, R. G., and Gump, P. V., (1964). *Big school, small school.* Stanford, CA: Stanford University Press.

Bean, J. P. (1983). The application of a model of turnover in work organizations to the student attrition process. *The Review of Higher Education* 6: 129–148.

Bean, J. P., and Kuh, G. (1984) The reciprocity between student-faculty informal contact and academic performance of university undergraduate students. *Research in Higher Education* 21: 461–477.

Cash, R. W., and Bissell, H. (1985). Testing Tinto's model of attrition on the church-related campus. A paper presented at the annual meeting of the Association for Institutional Research, Portland, OR.

Chacon, M., Cohen, E. G., Camarena, M., Gonzalez, J., and Stover, S. (1982). *Chicanas in postsecondary education.* Stanford, CA: Center for Research on Women, Stanford University.

Clark, B. (1960). The "cooling-out" function in higher education. *American Journal of Sociology* 64: 569–576.

Collins, J. S., Turner, R. M., and Maguire, J. G. (1979). Unmet Need: How the gap is filled. *Journal of Student Financial Aid* 9: 4–15.

Cope, R., and Hannah, W. (1975). *Revolving college doors: the causes and consequences of dropping out, stopping out, and transferring.* New York: Wiley.

Donovan, R. (1984). Path analysis of a theoretical model of persistence in higher education among low-income black youth. *Research in Higher Education* 21: 243–259.

Duncan, O. D., Featherman, D. L., and Duncan, B. (1972). *Socioeconomic background and achievement.* New York: Seminar Press.

Endo, J., and Harpel, R. L. (1982). The effect of student-faculty interaction on students' educational outcomes. *Research in Higher Education* 16: 115–135.

Featherman, R. L., and Hauser, R. M. (1978). *Opportunity and change.* New York: Academic Press.

Fox, R. N. (1985). Application of a conceptual model of college withdrawal to disadvantaged students. A paper presented to the annual meeting of the American Educational Research Association, Chicago.

Gardner, J. N., and Jewler, A. J. (1985). *College is only the beginning.* Belmont, CA: Wadsworth.

Hall, E. R., Mickelson, D., and Pollard, D. (1985). Academic and social integration and student persistence at a commuter university. A paper presented at the annual meeting of the American Education Research Association, Chicago.

Hannah, W. (1971). Personality differentials between lower division dropouts and stay-ins. *Journal of College Student Personnel* 12: 16–19.

Hanson, G. R., and Taylor, R. G. (1970). Interaction of ability and personality: another look at the drop-out problem in an Institute of Technology. *Journal of Counseling Psychology* 17: 540–545.

Heilbrun, A. B. (1965). Personality factors in college dropouts. *Journal of Applied Psychology* 49: 1–7.

Hirschman, A. (1970). *Exit, voice and loyalty.* Cambridge: Harvard University Press.

Iwai, S. I., and Churchill, W. D. (1982). College attrition and the financial support systems of students. *Research in Higher Education* 17: 105–113.

Jensen, E. L. (1981). Student financial aid and persistence in college. *Journal of Higher Education* 52: 280–294.

Kamens, D. (1971). The college "charter" and college size: effects on occupational choice and college attrition. *Sociology of Education* 44: 270–296.

Karabel, J. (1972). Community colleges and social stratification. *Harvard Educational Review* 42: 521–562.

Manski, C. F., and Wise, D. A. (1983). *College choice in America.* Cambridge: Harvard University Press.

Marks, E. (1967). Student perceptions of college persistence and their intellective, personality and performance correlates. *Journal of Educational Psychology* 58: 210–211.

Munro, B. (1981). Dropouts from higher education: path analysis of a national sample. *American Education Research Journal* 18: 133–141.

Neumann, W. (1985). Persistence in the community college: the student perspective. An unpublished Ph.D. dissertation, Syracuse University.

Pace, R. (1984). *Measuring the quality of college student experiences.* Los Angeles: Higher Education Research Institute, University of California, Los Angeles.

Pascarella, E., and Chapman, D. (1983). A multi-institutional, path analytic validation of Tinto's model of college withdrawal. *American Educational Research Journal* 20: 87–102.

Pascarella, E., Smart, J., and Ethington, C. (1985). Tracing the long-term persistence/withdrawal behavior of two-year college students: test of a causal model. A paper presented to the annual meeting of the American Educational Research Association, Chicago.

Pascarella, E., and Terenzini, P. (1979). Interaction effects in Spady's and Tinto's conceptual models of college dropout. *Sociology of Education* 52: 197–210.

Pascarella, E., and Terenzini, P. (1983). Predicting voluntary freshman year persistence/ withdrawal behavior in a residential university: a path analytic validation of Tinto's model. *Journal of Educational Psychology* 75: 215–226.

Pascarella, E., and Wolfle, L. (1985). Persistence in higher education: a nine-year test of a theoretical model. A paper presented to the annual meeting of the American Educational Research Association, Chicago.

Pervin, L., and Rubin, D. (1967). Student dissatisfaction with college and the college dropout: a transactional approach. *The Journal of Social Psychology* 72: 285–295.

Peterson, M. W. (1985). Emerging developments in postsecondary organization theory and research: fragmentation or integration. *Educational Researcher* 14: 5–12.

Pincus, F. (1980). The false promise of community colleges: Class conflict and vocational education. *Harvard Educational Review* 50: 332–361.

Price, J. L. (1977). *The study of turnover.* Ames: Iowa State University Press.

Price, J. L., and Mueller, C. W. (1981). A causal model of turnover for nurses. *Academy of Management Journal* 24: 543–565.

Rootman, I. (1972). Voluntary withdrawal from a total adult socialization organization: a model. *Sociology of Education* 45: 258–270.

Rose, R. A., and Elton, C. F. (1966). Another look at the college dropout. *Journal of Counseling Psychology* 13: 242–245.

Rossmann, J. E., and Kirk, B. A. (1970). Factors related to persistence and withdrawal among university students. *Journal of Counseling Psychology* 17: 56–62.

Sewell, W., and Hauser, R. (1975). *Education, occupation and earnings.* New York: Academic Press.

Sharp, L. F., and Chason, L. R. (1974). Use of moderator variables in predicting college student attrition. *Journal of College Student Personnel* 19: 388–393.

Spady, W. (1970). Dropouts from higher education: an interdisciplinary review and synthesis. *Interchange* 1: 64–85.

Stroup, H. (1966). *Bureaucracy in higher education.* New York: Free Press.

Summerskill, J. (1962). Dropouts from college. In N. Sanford (ed.), *The American college.* New York: Wiley.

Tinto, V. (1975). Dropout from higher education: a theoretical synthesis of recent research. *Review of Educational Resarch* 45: 89–125.

Tinto, V. (1982). Limits of theory and practice in student attrition. *Journal of Higher Education* 53: 687–700.

Tinto, V. (1985a). Rites of passage and the stages of institutional departure. A paper presented at the annual meeting of the American Educational Research Association, Chicago.

Tinto, V. (1985b). Dropping out and other forms of withdrawal from college. In L. Noel (ed.) *Improving student retention.* San Francisco: Jossey-Bass.

Tinto, V. (in press). *Leaving college: Rethinking the causes and cures of student attrition.* Chicago: University of Chicago Press.

Van Gennep, A. (1960). *The rites of passage,* trans. by M. Viedon and G. Caffee. Chicago: University of Chicago Press.

Voorhees, R. A. (1984). Financial aid and new freshman persistence: an exploratory model. A paper presented at the annual meeting of the Association for Institutional Research, Fort Worth.

Waterman, A. S., and Waterman, C. K. (1972). Relationship between freshman ego identity status and subsequent academic behavior: a test of the predictive validity of Marcia's categorization system for identity status. *Developmental Psychology* 6: 179.

Weidman, J. (1985). Retention of non-traditional students in postsecondary education. A paper presented at the annual meeting of the American Educational Research Association, Chicago.

EMERGING PERSPECTIVES ON CONTINUING PROFESSIONAL EDUCATION

Wayne D. Smutz, Mary Beth Crowe,
and Carl A. Lindsay
The Pennsylvania State University

Continuing education is an integral part of a professional career. Broadly defined, continuing professional education (CPE) includes formal and informal learning activities that professionals undertake in order to maintain and enhance their ability to practice. That professionals must update their knowledge and skills throughout their careers is not new. Rather, continuing learning always has been an obligatory part of the professional's role. In the past, this obligation was undertaken primarily on an informal basis through activities such as reading journals, consulting with colleagues, and attending conferences. However, it has become apparent in the last twenty years that an informal approach is no longer sufficient to meet the learning needs of professionals because of the rapid expansion of knowledge, the increased use of technology, and a more critical public, which has become increasingly willing to challenge the professional's competency (Houle, 1980). Also, as the nation has evolved from an industrial to a service and information society, education—and particularly higher levels of education—has become increasingly important to its productive capacity (Cross, 1981). Thus, not only have the traditional professions been faced with an unprecedented learning challenge, but the scope of the total work force in need of constant updating and development has expanded enormously.

For higher education institutions, CPE is both a new idea and an old one. In some fields, such as teacher education (Harrington, 1977a), and at some institutions, continuing professional education has long received attention. However, it was only in the early 1970s that CPE began its rapid expansion

(Harrington, 1977b). In fact, CPE has been the most rapidly growing area of continuing education in terms of dollars and enrollments (Nowlen and Stern, 1981). In response, higher education institutions have made some adjustments by expanding specific CPE offerings to some extent and by making access to their regular degree programs easier in some cases. In general, however, the response has appeared to be uneven, and few institutions have made a substantial commitment to the field (Donnelly, no date). Knox (1982), for example, found in a comparative study of similar higher education institutions that there is extreme variability in the commitment, the range of programs, and the general effort being focused on CPE. Indeed, the development of CPE programs may not be of interest to or it may not be an appropriate activity for all higher education institutions.

The current and potential future role of CPE within higher education institutions is not well understood at this time. Continuing professional education as an area of higher learning has not received much systematic study, although a few major works on CPE have appeared in the past five years. Cyril Houle's *Continuing Learning in the Professions* (1980) was the first major work on the topic and provides an introduction to the foundations of CPE. *Power and Conflict in Continuing Professional Education,* edited by Milton Stern (1983), addresses issues related to the marketplace of CPE. In the health professions, *Mobius* and *The Journal of Continuing Education in Nursing* are devoted exclusively to CPE, and *Continuing Education for the Health Professions* (Green et al., 1984) offers a model and criteria for quality programming. However, the literature regarding CPE is limited in the sense that it has seldom been empirical and is more often based on the perspectives and experiences of individuals actively involved in CPE. Also, much of the literature is profession-specific; medicine, followed by the other health professions, has been the most prolific contributor. There have been few attempts to integrate work across fields or to assume an institutional perspective. Some studies have not distinguished between CPE and continuing education in general and therefore have not addressed the special problems of CPE.

Given the emerging nature of CPE as an endeavor for higher education institutions, as well as the current state of the literature, the purpose of this chapter is to identify issues contained in the available literature and to propose an agenda for research based on them. While the chapter is limited to issues and questions pertaining to the involvement of higher education institutions in CPE, these issues include many aspects of CPE in general, as well as concerns unique to higher education.

The chapter contains four major sections. A brief review of the general area of CPE is presented to provide a perspective for consideration of the interface between higher education and continuing professional education; issues related to CPE within higher education are identified and analyzed; comprehensive

CPE research and development projects located at higher education institutions are described to provide examples of CPE activity and research; and finally, directions for future CPE research are proposed.

CONTINUING PROFESSIONAL EDUCATION: FROM THE EYES OF THE BEHOLDER

CPE is elusive by nature, raising many questions regarding its practice. By definition, CPE refers to learning activities undertaken by individuals subsequent to preparatory occupational training. There is, however, much room for interpretation regarding what constitutes CPE. Suter et al. (1981) offered the following comprehensive definition of CPE for health professionals, which highlights the areas of ambiguity:

> Continuing education of health care professionals is defined as processes aimed at the improvement of health care outcomes through learning either by individual efforts or as part of continuing education provider unit developed activities, products, and services. Learning may result in the maintenance or enhancement of professional competence and performance or in health care organizational effectiveness and efficiency. [p. 691]

The first question raised by this definition concerns the identification of professionals. In this age of increasing knowledge specialization and technological sophistication, more and more occupational groups claim professional status, however informally. The sociological literature offers some guidance regarding the identification of professional status (e.g., Goode, 1960; Vollmer and Mills, 1966), but from the educator's perspective, these criteria may prove unnecessarily exclusive. Characteristics of occupational groups, such as the criteria commonly associated with professional status, may not be related to differences in educational needs. The above definition also indicates several different goals for CPE: improvement of health care outcomes, enhancement of practitioner competence and performance, and improvement of organizational effectiveness. These multiple goals suggest that the identification of realistic expectations for the impact of CPE may be another issue in need of resolution. Whether CPE is limited to organized activities or includes individual efforts by practitioners is another point of debate; individual learning efforts and provider-developed offerings are both included in the definition. Finally, the definition suggests at least two clienteles for CPE: individual practitioners and organizations. Clarification of the market for CPE is another area in need of study.

Perspectives on the questions raised by Suter et al.'s definition of CPE, and on other questions concerning the practice of CPE, vary across the parties involved. There are many stakeholder groups in CPE; chief among them are the public, the professions, the CPE participants, and the providers. Each emphasizes a slightly different interest, and each exerts its influence on the practice of CPE. A brief review of the perspective of each of these groups identifies the major issues currently confronting CPE and provides a basis on which to consider relationships between higher education and continuing professional education.

The Public

The public interest in continuing professional education, represented by state licensing bodies, focuses on the quality of professional services. Mandatory continuing education, a requirement for CPE tied to the renewal of a professional license, has been viewed as a response to concerns raised by consumer groups and governmental bodies regarding the continuing competence of professionals (Edwards and Green, 1983; Frandson, 1980a). Arguments supporting mandatory continuing education maintain that it will (1) protect the public from those professionals uninterested in maintaining their skills; (2) remove from registration those persons no longer practicing and keeping current; (3) increase professional interchange; (4) help maintain and improve public confidence in a profession; (5) pose less threat to practitioners than relicensure examinations; and (6) result in better-informed practitioners (Lowenthal, 1981). Each of these arguments, however, has been debated.

Mandatory continuing education requirements generally involve a specific number of hours of educational activity. Significantly, the choice of activity is usually at the discretion of the individual practitioner. All states require continuing education in at least one licensed occupation. Accountants, nursing-home administrators, and optometrists must meet such requirements in a majority of states (Phillips, 1983). However, the mandatory CPE movement has slowed because of the number of states having passed such legislation already, the impact of sunset laws, and criticism of the effectiveness of such requirements (Phillips, 1983).

Mandatory continuing education has focused attention on the relationship of CPE and professional performance. The rise of mandatory continuing education requirements throughout the past decade reinforces the notion that the ultimate goal of CPE has been to assure the quality of professional services. However, there now appears to be widespread recognition, based on a distinction between competence and performance, that quality assurance itself does not result directly from CPE, even though CPE may be a contributing factor (Cooper, 1981; Gonnella and Zeleznik, 1983; Lowenthal, 1981; Sanazarro, 1982; Caplan, 1983). Educational programs can help to prepare competent individuals who possess the knowledge, skills, and attitudes that comprise the ability to perform (Sanazarro, 1982). However, the performance, as well as the outcome, of professional services is subject to the influence of a variety of contextual factors, including organizational characteristics, the clients themselves, and the competence of the professional (Suter et al., 1981; Gonnella and Zeleznik, 1983; LaDuca, 1980). Therefore, the goals of CPE regarding the individual practitioner must be limited, in the words of Gonnella and Zeleznik

(1983), to "the development of proficiencies that can be translated into professional performance" (p. 61). More accurately, then, education is directly connected not with performance, but with proficiency. Thus, CPE alone may not meet the public interest concerning professional competence, because it is only one component of continuing competence.

The Professions

Houle (1980) listed fourteen characteristics of professions that form the basis of their interest in CPE. These characteristics, derived from the concept of professionalization, which indicates that a profession must evolve continuously in order to survive, include (1) the conceptual characteristic, which calls for the members of a profession to be actively involved in clarifying the profession's defining function; (2) performance characteristics, which include the mastery of a profession's knowledge base, the capacity to solve problems, the use of practical knowledge, and practitioner self-enhancement; and (3) collective identity characteristics, which differentiate a profession from other fields of endeavor, and which include credentialing, the creation of a professional subculture, legal reinforcement, public acceptance, relations with other vocations, relations with users of services, formal training, penalties, and ethical practice. These characteristics suggest a two-sided interest in CPE by the professions. Professions have an altruistic motive to maintain the competence of their practitioners based on their service orientation; however, they also have a need to limit external regulation in order to ensure the most favorable conditions for their members to practice.

A profession's interest in CPE is inherent, and it also occurs in response to the environment. Lauffer (1977) observed that professions, as embodied by their associations, have been under pressure both internally and externally to expand their continuing education function. Members clamor for continuing education to develop new knowledge and skills. External pressures have come from the public and from third-party payers. Response to these pressures, as well as a prior interest by a profession in CPE, is manifested in several ways. Professional associations have assumed the roles of provider and regulator of CPE for their members. As providers, professional associations can maintain control over the content of CPE as well as recognize any revenue to be gained from delivery. Professional associations can regulate CPE at two levels: through monitoring the quality of CPE offered to their members through program approval mechanisms, and through imposing their own CPE requirements, making certification, specialization, or membership dependent on CPE. This latter approach, called "conditional continuing education" by Berlin (1983), can be interpreted as a profession's attempt to preempt legislated mandatory continuing education requirements in order to limit external regulation of the profession.

Providers

Continuing professional education has been frequently characterized with phrases such as "a disorderly market" (Stern, 1983) or "a booming, buzzing confusion" (Caplan, 1983). Contributing to the disorder are fragmented course offerings, lack of standards, and a variety of providers in any one field. Among the different types of providers are educational institutions, professional associations, employers, and private entrepreneurs. The National Center for Education Statistics (NCES) for the year ending in 1981 reported that for courses taken by participants in adult education for trade or professional objectives, approximately 19% were provided by four-year colleges or universities, 14% by business or industry, 5% by labor or professional associations, 8% by government agencies, and 7% by other providers (Kay, 1982).[1] Characteristics formerly differentiating providers have become blurred; for example, higher education institutions are marketing their programs more competitively, and employers are hiring more academic personnel to provide in-house training (Berlin, 1983). In some professions, there are clearly established providers. In public accounting, where mandatory continuing education requirements are common, the American Institute of Certified Public Accountants, in conjunction with state and local accounting organizations, has a well-established system of CPE for its members. Cruse (1983) reported that in 1978, professional associations provided 35% of the CPE participated in by California licensees, a figure well above that reported by the NCES for professional associations. However, in many professions, such as engineering, competition among providers is wide open (Griffith, 1983).

Provider costs in the delivery of CPE are high. They include development, marketing, and delivery expenses, which are balanced against program fees that the market will bear. Hansen (1983) indicated 20%–30% of a total program budget as a normal allocation for marketing for university-provided continuing medical education (an even higher percentage is allocated in some situations) and reported a dollar figure of $70.81 as the marketing cost per enrollment over a five-year period for home study courses for physicians. Anderson (1982) identified classroom costs as most often the largest category of costs in adult education, accounting for 30%–72% of total costs, the remaining costs consisting of administration and overhead. Different types of providers have different perspectives on costs. For example, Weinstein (1982) found that not all professional associations feel that their continuing education programs must generate revenues; some feel that low course fees leading to deficits encourage greater member participation. For continuing education provided by business and industry, participant time away from the job represents a significant category of cost.

It has been frequently observed that CPE activity has grown tremendously in recent years, but some observers have speculated that the market is becoming saturated (Ruhe, 1982). As the market stabilizes, attention must increasingly focus on program issues concerning the nature of the product offered. Recent publications concerning the quality of continuing education are those by Green, et al. (1984) and the Council on the Continuing Education Unit (1984). Some continuing professional educators believe that an important responsibility of providers is to teach professionals to learn in an independent fashion, a skill not usually encouraged in preprofessional training (Suter et al., 1981; Houle, 1980), because it is this mode of learning that is best suited to the professional's needs. This belief creates a kind of provider's paradox: Those engaged in the delivery of formal continuing professional education must encourage an attitude and skill among their clientele that may make them less dependent on these services.

Participants
Specific individual continuing professional education needs are diverse and are largely idiosyncratic to a professional's practice situation and experience. This fact renders a match between CPE programs and individual needs difficult (Gonnella and Zeleznik, 1983) and uniform CPE requirements for individuals irrelevant (Cooper, 1981). Individuals participate in CPE for many reasons, including some that are not performance-related. Groteluschen et al. (1979) found that collegial learning and interaction, personal benefit and job security, professional improvement and development, and professional service were reasons that professionals in general participate in CPE. Cervero (1981) found similar reasons for physician participation: to maintain and improve professional competence, to understand oneself as a professional, to interact with colleagues, and to enhance personal and professional position. Caplan (1983) stressed the potential importance of personal as well as explicit client-care reasons for participation, citing the desirability of intellectual renewal in itself as an outcome of CPE. Thus, the individual's perspective on CPE may be quite different from that of the public or the professional association.

   In considering the participant perspective, it is important to distinguish, as Houle (1980) did, between continuing education and continuing learning. Whereas the term CPE implies participation in a formalized activity, continuing professional learning can occur in independent, informal, or even spontaneous contexts, such as consulting with colleagues or reading a journal article. Surveys of physician preferences for "educational" formats and studies of the introduction of changes into medical practice have repeatedly shown that print materials, particularly professional journals, are the primary means used to acquire new information, and that contacts with colleagues are also frequently used (Green et al., 1984; Caplan, 1983; Geertsma et al., 1982; Lockyer et al., 1985). Griffith (1983) reported that only about 5% of the total time invested in continuing professional development by engineers is spent in formally organized programs; practitioners rely instead on job-rotation, on-the-job training, and self-study. Many continuing professional learning needs result directly from specific on-the-job problems and are most efficiently addressed through individual effort. Informal or individual activities also offer a significant advantage regarding convenience to the practitioner. Although more easily documented, formal activities are likely to take practitioners away from their practice situations, possibly causing them to lose income.

Formal continuing professional education activities are not without their benefits, however. In a recent review of 238 evaluation studies on continuing medical education, Davis et al. (1984) concluded that continuing medical education does have a positive effect on physician competence and performance, but that there is less consistent evidence for an effect on patient outcomes. Caplan (1983) argued against the meaningfulness of statistically significant evidence of impact, stressing instead the importance of changing individuals rather than group means. In addition to specified learning outcomes, formal activities offer individuals opportunities for collegial exchange, which may satisfy practitioner reasons for participation. Thus, individuals are faced with choosing that combination of formal and informal activities best suited to their own needs.

Current Issues in Continuing Professional Education
Several aspects of continuing professional education surface across the perspectives described above, thereby suggesting issues that are currently important in the field. The impact of CPE continues to be a concern for all interested parties. Although in one sense expectations for CPE have become more limited, that is, focusing on proximate rather than ultimate goals, the demands on CPE have also become greater as attention is increasingly focused on practitioner competence and performance rather than on knowledge alone. The impact of CPE is a value question as well as an empirical one. Appropriate outcomes— attitudes versus knowledge and skills, organizational versus individual change— will continue to be debated. The value of informal versus formal CPE activities must also be considered.

The disorder of the continuing professional education market must be addressed. Issues include the means by which providers can work with professions to provide a more meaningful service, the need for overcoming the episodic nature of continuing professional education, and the role of regulation regarding the quality of CPE. Of special importance to the delivery of continuing professional education are questions regarding the financial bases of the activity—not only questions of cost effectiveness, but examination of who will bear the costs, however small or large.

Overriding all of these issues are the implications of the individualized nature of continuing-professional-education needs. As Day and Baskett (1982) noted, "a uniformity of solutions" is being offered to "a multiplicity of problems," an approach far too simplistic to address client demands. Articulation of a comprehensive system of continuing professional education for practitioners within a profession poses a difficult challenge for the field.

CONTINUING PROFESSIONAL EDUCATION AND HIGHER EDUCATION

Higher education institutions must continuously evaluate the scope of their missions, the range of their services, and their relationship to society. The importance or urgency of such evaluation is not constant, however. Periods of societal, political, and economic stability demand less of the process, and minor adjustments in direction are usually sufficient. At other times, changing societal conditions produce developments that demand fundamental organizational reevaluation. Such instances may or may not lead to significant organizational change, but only if the reevaluation is undertaken seriously will organizational direction be set by conscious, institutional choice.

Continuing professional education is one emerging issue within the higher education arena that may force institutions to reevaluate the scope of their activities. Although it is unclear how soon serious consideration must be given to this issue, colleges and universities may be approaching a crossroads that will require them to make a substantial commitment to CPE or to relinquish major responsibility for this dimension of higher learning to other types of organizations.

The fundamental issue confronting higher education institutions with regard to CPE is the extent of their involvement. Currently, many institutions are delivering CPE programs, but few have made a major commitment to integrating CPE into the mainstream of their activities. If higher education institutions were alone on the continuing professional education frontier, such variability of effort would not be an issue. However, higher education institutions find themselves in an extremely competitive struggle for this relatively new education market.

The Case for Active Involvement in CPE

Higher education institutions' ambivalence toward continuing professional education rests in part on conflicting views over the value and/or the need of undertaking such a commitment. Arguments supporting higher education institutions' extensive involvement in CPE can be divided into three categories: (1) those based on the obligations of the university; (2) instrumental motivations related to institutional benefits; and (3) arguments derived from the unique capabilities of the university.

The Obligation Argument. The notion that higher education is obligated to deliver CPE on a broad scale contains three dimensions. One is rooted in the idea that the uniqueness of the American higher-education system rests on its orientation to serving the needs of society, a tradition firmly grounded in the

American scheme of higher education dating back at least to the land-grant movement and epitomized by the "Wisconsin Idea" (Brubacher, 1977). Anderson (1976) argued that the service concept embedded in the land-grant notion had been so well accepted that it was no longer unique to land-grant institutions but had been adopted by most of higher education. And given Kerr's characterization (1963) of the modern American university as a multiversity containing many communities serving a wide range of constituencies in a multitude of ways, it appears that extensive involvement in CPE, with its need for higher-order learning, is an appropriate function of higher education institutions.

However, for some of those who stress the service orientation, the need for acceptance of CPE as a legitimate service function rests on severe economic and demographic problems rather than simply on its appropriateness (Carnevale, 1983). Not only is the total number of professionals growing and the increasing knowledge orientation of the labor market requiring more professionals who need constant updating (Harrington, 1977b; Leslie, 1976; Peterson, 1983), but the shifting age structure of the population means that business and industry will no longer be able to fill their needs for new types of personnel by hiring fresh entrants into the labor market. Instead, they will have to be concerned with retraining the current work force for new tasks through human resource management (Carnevale, 1983; Lynton, 1981). According to this argument, the task is so monumental that higher education's failure to become intimately involved could have serious consequences for the economic status of the country.

A second dimension of the obligation argument pertains to the nature of the education required by practicing professionals. Although professionals must always assume ultimate responsibility for their continuing learning, the explosion of knowledge and the expanded use of technology make it increasingly difficult and, indeed, inefficient for individual professionals to try to keep up-to-date on their own. As Lynton (1983) stated, "The changing insights and skills are of such a nature as to make it increasingly necessary to acquire them through some form of organized instruction rather than individual effort" (p. 18). Given this need, it is the responsibility of higher education institutions to become actively involved in CPE because they are in the business of higher learning (Bowen, 1980). To leave the field completely to other types of organizations deprives CPE of the content and the instructional expertise available in colleges and universities.

The final obligation-related argument centers on the idea that higher education institutions have a responsibility to maintain the competence of those they originally trained for professional roles (Stern, 1975). The perspective taken here is one of social obligation to protect the public. That is, higher education institutions are uniquely qualified to provide CPE because their sole concern is educational. To relinquish such a responsibility to other organizations, such as professional associations, would place the primary responsibility for enhancing competence on organizations that may have conflicting interests—enhancing competence versus responding to the desires of their members—that may or may not have to do with enhanced competence.

Instrumental Motivations. The second category of arguments in support of higher education's involvement in CPE can be labeled *instrumental reasons.* They pertain to the benefits that higher education institutions may accrue from involvement. Probably the most often cited reason here is related to the declining number of 18- to 22-year olds who make up the traditional youth market for higher education. From this perspective, the rising demand for CPE at the very time that the traditional market is shrinking represents an opportunity to ease financial pressures that may be on the horizon (Harrington, 1977b). It is not surprising, of course, that this argument has been challenged on the basis that educational, and not financial, reasons ought to guide the policy decisions of colleges and universities (Queeney, 1984). However, the declining traditional student population argument has been used positively to support the idea that higher education ought to become more involved in the education of adults generally (Bowen, 1980). The basis of this argument is unused capacity; that is, it makes little sense to dismantle major portions of the higher education sector as long as there are underserved segments of the population that can benefit from the level of education appropriately delivered by colleges and universities.

The need for additional students and the appropriate use of unused capacity are not the only instrumental reasons for involvement in CPE. CPE activities can also benefit faculty members and traditional programs. Faculty who provide preservice education for budding professionals should be in constant contact with practitioners to ensure that their understanding of professional practice—and therefore, what they teach preprofessionals—will have a strong relationship to the real world (Harrington, 1977b; Patton, 1975; Wasch, 1980). In addition, Vicere (1981) found that faculty members who participated in CPE programs believed that these experiences enhanced their instructional capabilities and overall teaching effectiveness. Finally, contact with practitioners may provide an opportunity for faculty members to identify research topics that are immediately applicable to practice (Toombs, 1982), although Vicere's study (1981) suggests that faculty members involved in CPE programs do not use the experience for this purpose.

Higher Education Institutions' Unique Capabilities. The third argument in support of higher education institutions' involvement in CPE is related to the unique capabilities of colleges and universities. The key issues here are that universities' research orientation makes them a primary source of new knowledge and that effective communication of that new knowledge to practicing professionals is critical to improved practice (Bowen, 1980; Frandson, 1975a,b;

Queeney, 1984). Beyond these issues, however, it has been noted that the problems that professionals confront in their daily practice are often interdisciplinary. As a consequence, effective CPE requires that professionals have access to a wide spectrum of educational opportunities. Unlike other organizations, universities house experts in the variety of disciplines necessary to professional practice and have the capability, in theory, of making them available to address the broad range of professionals' learning needs (Frandson 1975b, 1980b).

The Case Against Involvement

Explicitly stated arguments against the involvement of higher education institutions in CPE are harder to uncover in the literature. This is somewhat surprising, given the limited progress that CPE has made in the higher education environment. However, because CPE is an emerging development, and because those writing about it are generally already involved, perhaps it is not so surprising. In any case, three reasons are used to dissuade higher education from becoming a major provider of CPE: (1) value differences between higher education and professions; (2) lack of practice-related educational resources; and (3) inadequate financial resources.

Value Differences. Some argue that higher education institutions are ill suited to provide CPE because there are fundamental value differences between the world of professional practice and the world of university. From this perspective, higher education is viewed as a social institution oriented toward reflective thinking and the intrinsic value of knowledge, while professional practice focuses on the applicability and the utility of knowledge (Berlin, 1983; Sneed, 1972). Consequently, there is little convergence between what practitioners need in terms of CPE and what colleges and universities can offer.

Lack of Practice-Oriented Resources. Sneed (1972) noted that an explicit connection must be made between knowledge and practice through illustrative cases if CPE is to be useful and efficient. Higher education institutions, however, generally do not have clients and do not offer services that faculty members can use to link knowledge and application in CPE programs. Without clients, the potential contribution of higher education institutions to CPE is inherently limited. There are a few exceptions; for example, medical schools maintain hospitals, and colleges of education operate laboratory schools.

Inadequate Financial Resources. There has been some concern that effective involvement in CPE will require a substantial investment in resources (Sneed, 1972). In the absence of a clear source of funds, traditional preservice programs may become the source, with a subsequent decrease in the quality of these programs. Whether involvement in CPE is worth that price is questionable from this perspective.

A Receding Opportunity?

As outlined above, arguments have been mounted supporting and opposing higher education's extensive involvement in CPE. Two points of clarification regarding the controversy are in order here. First, higher education institutions clearly should not and cannot be the only providers. There are simply too many different kinds of learning needs (Frandson, 1975a). The real issue is the appropriate role for different providers and higher education institutions' particular role in the overall scheme of CPE. Second, higher education institutions' involvement in CPE in some form is not in question. The issue is whether CPE will remain a tangential concern or whether it will be integrated into the central missions of higher education institutions.

Why should any effort be expended to clarify higher education's role in and commitment to CPE? The answer provided by CPE advocates is that a decision will be made for higher education institutions if they do not make a conscious choice, and the consequence will be that their involvement will be extremely limited because competition in the CPE market is so widespread that other providers will take over. Indeed, some have suggested that higher education institutions' lack of action has already resulted in their losing whatever share of the market they might have had (Berlin, 1983; Stern, 1980).

Two developments can be cited as evidence that higher education institutions' opportunity for involvement in CPE is diminishing. One is the blurring of responsibility for higher learning between business and industry and higher education institutions (Cross, 1981). In recent years, business and industry have been rapidly developing their capacity to offer higher-level learning opportunities to their employees (Cross, 1981; Eurich, 1985). This has happened not only in the CPE field but also in the area of accredited degrees. As Cross (1981) noted, the development occurred not because business and industry wanted to diversify into the educational arena, but often because attempts at cooperation with higher education institutions failed.

A second indication that higher education institutions may be losing ground in CPE relates to faculty involvement in CPE programs offered by external organizations. Two major concerns have been voiced about this development. First, the more faculty members participate in CPE programs offered by others, the less time they have to deliver them for their own institutions. Although extensive data on this matter are not available, one study at the University of Washington Medical School found that faculty members offered twice as many programs for outside providers as for their own institutions (Lein et al., 1981). The second concern about this development is that higher education institutions' primary resource, the faculty, is being used by other groups for profit. The problem, the critics have indicated, is that higher education institutions provide the resources that allow faculty members to develop their expertise (e.g., libraries, laboratories, graduate students, and offices), and yet they receive no reimbursement when that expertise is used outside institutional channels (Lynton, 1981; Stern, 1980).

Those who want higher education to have a major role in CPE have been critical of faculty involvement in externally sponsored programs. As a result, they have suggested that colleges and universities need to work cooperatively with other organizations and/or to develop policies that will enable them to recapture the CPE efforts of the faculty members (Nowlen and Stern, 1981). The key point is not whether faculty CPE activities for other organizations are right or wrong, but whether they ought to continue without higher education institutions' seriously considering their consequences and establishing clear policy guidelines with regard to them.

Perhaps the most important question, however, is why higher education institutions generally have not developed comprehensive policies to commit themselves to CPE, given its growing importance as an educational frontier. One answer has been that the central administrations of higher education institutions simply are not interested in the area (Stern, 1980). However, a more complex answer can be provided by examining the context in which CPE is viewed within higher education institutions.

The Status of Continuing Professional Education

To date, CPE has been categorized as part of the overall continuing education function of higher education institutions. As such, it has been viewed primarily as part of the service mission, requiring no separate set of policies. As noted earlier, the service mission has a long tradition in American higher education. Nevertheless, it is beset with problems when applied to faculty members. One such problem is that the service mission is so broad in scope—including such diverse activities as serving on institutional committees, teaching in continuing education programs, holding office in professional associations, and assisting governmental agencies—that it has no clear meaning when compared to the other primary missions of higher education: teaching and research (Crosson, 1983). Another problem, perhaps a product of the first, is that service runs a distant third behind the other two missions in terms of the value and reward structures of higher education institutions (Crosson, 1983).

But what are the roots of higher education institutions' disaffection with the service concept? While it is not necessary to provide an answer for the concept as a whole, Burton Clark's classic analysis of adult education (1958a,b) does provide clues to why continuing education—and by implication, continuing professional education—has not been accepted into the mainstream of higher education.

The Marginality of Continuing Education. The central theme of Clark's work is that adult education and continuing education operations are marginal to their parent organizations. As Clark saw it, marginality has three main features. First, continuing education operations are located within and dependent on organizations (e.g., universities) whose primary clientele and orientation are different from continuing education. In the university setting, the traditional focus is on youth who are committed to education on a full-time basis. In contrast, continuing education serves adults who attend part time, who routinely enter and exit, and who have multiple obligations besides education.

The second feature of marginality is what Clark called "goal diffusion." That is, continuing education operations rarely have specific educational objectives; rather, they are interested in serving adults' learning needs in general. The problem with this orientation is that a well-defined educational purpose is difficult to specify, and thus, there is no basis for administrative decision making. That is, if response to clientele is the goal, then educational purposes cannot be used as a basis for offering one continuing education program instead of another.

This point leads to the third feature of marginality: the enrollment economy. Continuing education operations are generally required to support themselves financially and even, at times, to produce a profit. When this financial pressure is combined with goal diffusion, the product is a utilitarian orientation whereby continuing education operations are forced to make programmatic decisions based on the size of the demand rather than on educational objectives.

Clark's analysis was completed in the late 1950s and in some respects is dated. Certainly, higher education institutions have made strides, even if grudgingly, in terms of adapting their regular offerings to the growing numbers of adult students. In addition, Devlin (1980) argued that Clark's work provided a solid foundation for understanding the status of continuing education in higher education institutions, but erred in treating marginality in nonelastic terms. As Devlin noted, there are probably degrees of marginality. Research is needed to illuminate the conditions and the characteristics that make continuing education less marginal in some institutions than in others.

Still, portions of Clark's work remain applicable to continuing education. Primary among them is his insight into the conflict between responding to the undifferentiated learning needs of adults and espousing clear educational purposes. The issue is not whether such service is legitimate in a general social sense; rather, the issue is whether such a mission can ever be wholly accepted as appropriate in higher education institutions whose primary foundations are faculty members' expertise and the development and dissemination of sophisticated knowledge. In this regard, Clark's insights regarding the service concept still seem valid. As Blaney and Devlin (1985) recently noted about the current condition of continuing education,

It is commonplace to observe that few extension divisions have statements of operational goals by which specific programs can be judged appropriate or, more importantly, inappropriate as university offerings . . . In most (extension) divisions, all

manner of subject matter coexist in a classless academic state. The principle of curriculum relativity applies: every subject is deemed to be as important as any other. This
practice is justified by an appeal to market forces or as a democratization of higher
education yet it is clearly at variance with the historical character of universities as organizations . . . Universities believe themselves to be exclusive rather than inclusive
organizations. [pp. 9–10]

Illustrative of the long-standing conflict between the service concept and the
exclusive character of universities noted by Blaney and Devlin is a study by
Penfield (1975) of attempts to introduce extension education into the University of California in the early 1900s. Penfield argued that efforts to develop
programs responsive to the learning needs of adults were constantly met with
counterproposals that effectively kept extension education closely linked to the
traditional curriculum. Based on her analysis, Penfield suggested that service
qua service was never considered seriously as a potential legitimate university
function because it conflicted with faculty members' growing desire to establish
their identity as experts. Instead, steps taken to incorporate extension activities
were employed simply as a means of system maintenance; that is, they were intended to placate the public in order to enhance support for the institution or to
prevent the establishment of new institutions that might compete for state
funds. Penfield's conclusion about the potential role of continuing education in
higher education institutions was more than a little pessimistic. As she put it,
"It may be that rather than cling to the university as a base of operation, adult
educators must break away from its hegemony and develop alternative,
possibly autonomous, operating bases" (p. 122).

Alternative Bases of Legitimacy for Continuing Professional Education. To
date, continuing professional education has been associated with continuing
education and the service function in higher education institutions. As just
noted, however, it is unlikely that colleges and universities will make a major
commitment to continuing professional education as long as it is perceived as
being no different from continuing education. Thus a separate base of legitimacy divorced from the service concept must be found. Such a base must be
tied to the traditional missions of teaching and research, to the level of knowledge appropriately addressed by higher education (i.e., sophisticated knowledge), and to specific educational purposes rather than consumer demand. But
is there any evidence that continuing professional education and continuing
education are different? Analysis of this issue has been limited. That which has
been done can be classified into two types: (1) an identification of differences
between CPE and the traditional missions of higher education institutions and
(2) a reconceptualization of higher learning, integrating it with the workplace.

The first type of analysis attempts to distinguish carefully the basic characteristics of continuing professional education and their relationship to higher education institutions' traditional missions. In a general way, Bowen (1980)
addressed this issue by arguing that the legitimacy of higher education institu-

tions' involvement in particular educational endeavors hinges on two matters: (1) the level of the knowledge to be imparted and (2) who is to benefit from the education. From his perspective, education that does not deal with higher-order knowledge or that provides only personal as opposed to social benefits is probably not appropriately delivered by universities.

In a similar vein, Toombs (1982) analyzed the differences between professional education and continuing education and compared continuing professional education to them. Using the frameworks of educational purpose and educational design as the basis for comparison, he concluded that continuing professional education has similarities with both but is not exactly like either. For example, with regard to the purpose of continuing professional education, Toombs argued that there must be some response to the expressed needs of professionals, as in continuing education, because they must be able to apply in practice what they learn. Nevertheless, faculty members' expertise is so critical to advancing professional practice that they, too, must have substantial input into the nature of continuing professional education programs.

The second type of analysis of the nature of continuing professional education is more radical and has been developed to some extent by Ernest Lynton. Rather than carefully delineating the differences between continuing education, continuing professional education, and professional education, Lynton argued that the distinctions are artificial and outmoded. Instead of trying to fit continuing professional education into the traditional scheme of higher education, he proposed that the whole sphere of higher learning be transformed by integration of the world of learning with the world of professional practice. This would involve creating an articulated system of learning and practice, beginning with preservice education. As Lynton (1983) stated,

> responsibility for maintaining professional effectiveness should remain closely linked to the responsibility for its initial development. The two should be seen as components of a single coherent process. The assurance of regular periods of recurrent education should be taken into consideration in designing the initial preparatory phase . . . Every indication suggests that young people as well as older adults will increasingly divide their time between work and learning and . . . will expect both theory and practice from their education. The current lack of this mix is one of the principal criticisms leveled at higher education today. [p. 20]

How such a complex, articulated system could be developed is unclear, but the concept does seem worthy of further exploration by content and instructional design specialists.

Toombs and Lindsay (1985) noted, "Universities today are faced continuously with suggestions, even demands, that they take on additional activities, adapt new visions, or shift to a different set of priorities," and that "among the decisions and choices universities will be well advised to explore are those which promise to fulfil in some way the traditions and strengths of the institution" (pp. 8–9). Extensive involvement in continuing professional education is one choice that may fit well within the higher education environment. Not only is it related to the two primary missions of higher education institutions—teaching and research—but it uses faculty expertise and focuses on a level of knowledge appropriately addressed by higher education institutions. Nevertheless, colleges and universities appear reluctant to commit themselves seriously to the field, partly because CPE is associated with the service function and therefore implies a loss of control over the content and purposes of education. This suggests the need for additional analyses to clarify the conceptual foundations of continuing professional education. While a decision to choose continuing professional education as a major university priority cannot be made immediately, neither can it be postponed indefinitely. For higher education, perhaps the important point is that it must make a clear choice to enter the field or leave it to others. At this time, additional examinations of the nature of continuing professional education are necessary to clarify the implications and consequences of either choice.

INSTITUTIONAL ISSUES: THE ORGANIZATIONAL CHALLENGE OF CONTINUING PROFESSIONAL EDUCATION

The most critical issue facing higher education institutions with regard to continuing professional education is the level of their commitment and contribution to the field. There are many related issues, however, that warrant attention as institutions consider an appropriate posture toward continuing professional education. These include the organization and administration of continuing professional education, faculty attitudes and involvement, and collaborative arrangements with other organizations to develop and deliver programs. Research on these issues is limited, but the available work delineates the range of institutional matters that deserve more attention.

Organizational Placement of Continuing Professional Education

One of the major institutional issues is how to organize for CPE. The key area of debate here is over centralization or decentralization of the function, that is, whether responsibility for it should be given to continuing education divisions or parceled out to professional schools and departments. The issue is not a new one. Continuing education has wrestled with it for some time and has reached no final resolution. As a result, there is great variability, and some institutions have adopted a centralized structure for continuing education, some a decentralized one, and others a mixture of the two (Harringon, 1977b; Houle, 1980; Knowles, 1969; Stern, 1975). Partly because of its association with continuing education, CPE has also confronted the issue with the same result: variability in organizational structure (Knox, 1982).

Arguments have been mounted to illustrate why one form of organization is better than another. In terms of volume, the greatest number support a centralized arrangement, perhaps because most of the writing has been done by continuing education practitioners and administrators. In any case, several arguments have been made in favor of centralization. One relates to the experience of continuing education divisions in working with programs for adults. Over time, continuing educators have developed expertise in delivery systems particularly well suited to adult students and thus are more likely to develop successful programs (Frandson, 1975a; Harrington, 1977a). At the same time, continuing education divisions have developed sound arrangements for handling administrative functions such as registration procedures and promotional techniques. Turning these activities over to separate professional schools can result in a loss of economies of scale (Nowlen and Stern, 1981).

A second argument relates to the content of continuing professional education. Because much of professional practice is interdisciplinary, quality continuing professional education requires that program content be drawn from the range of expertise available in universities rather than from professional schools alone. Since continuing education divisions routinely work across the university, they are in a better position to provide the necessary diversity (Frandson, 1975a).

The third argument is philosophical. Essentially, it is that continuing education divisions' commitment to service means that they are concerned about meeting the diverse learning needs of professionals, whatever they may be. In contrast, professional schools, which may not have a similar commitment, may be more likely to limit their offerings to those that promise the greatest financial return (Knox, 1975). In addition, the commitment to service has implications for the range of programs that an institution can offer for different professions. If CPE is placed in professional schools, each school's offerings will be required to survive financially on their own. But not all professions have an equal ability to pay. As a result, program quality may vary from profession to profession based on the ability to pay. Through centralization, however, resources can be redistributed (Gordon, 1974; Harrington, 1977a). In this fashion, all professions will receive adequate treatment in the long run.

There are arguments against centralization as well. Perhaps the most prominent one is that placement of CPE within individual professional schools will enable faculty members to develop a sense of ownership of the programs (Gordon, 1974). In contrast, when the CPE responsibility resides in continuing education divisions, faculty members see participation as an addition to their regular responsibilities. Whether ownership can be developed in this way is unclear because no research has addressed this particular issue. However, in a study of faculty attitudes toward CPE at one institution, Toombs et al. (1984) found that the faculty preferred placement of the CPE responsibility at the departmental level. Interestingly, the faculty members also indicated that they would support CPE activities in only a limited way. Thus, whether ownership can be affected by structural arrangements remains in question.

Although much of the discussion about organizational structure is tied to the centralization–decentralization debate, it may be that other arrangements are more appropriate. Stern (1975), for example, argued that trying to organize continuing education into one organizational pattern may be a mistake because of its broad range of functions. Thus, he suggested alternative structural arrangements for different functions. For example, responsibility for traditional academic courses offered through continuing education might be given solely to the academic departments because their only unique quality is the time when they are offered. Continuing education programs based on community learning needs and thus strictly service-oriented might be handled best by continuing education divisions alone. Finally, responsibility for CPE might be shared by departments and continuing education divisions because it must draw its educational integrity from the departments but must make use of continuing education divisions' delivery systems (Stern, 1975). If this latter suggestion were adopted, the establishment of a separate satellite operation, such as a CPE institute or center, might be useful in facilitating and coordinating interaction between the two groups and thereby might prevent turning CPE into a political battlefield.

Houle (1980) suggested that the centralization–decentralization conflict will probably continue without a final resolution. That may be the case, but the debate could be placed on firmer ground if research were undertaken to address one issue: What difference does organizational structure make in terms of program quality and output? To date, most arguments seem to reflect the biases of their authors. Illustrative of what might be done is Fox's comparative study (1981) of the effect of organizational structure on the CPE program-planning process in six southern land-grant institutions. Among his findings was that professional practitioners were involved in the planning process of centralized operations substantially more than in decentralized ones. Certainly Fox's study does not settle the centralization–decentralization debate, but it indicates the type of research that can lead to more informed conclusions about the appropriate form of organization.

The Leadership Factor
Although disagreement reigns over organizational structure, there is a consensus that the viability of CPE efforts depends heavily on the quality of leadership provided. For example, in his comparative study of CPE across several professions and institutions, Knox (1982) identified leadership as one of the key elements that enhanced the vitality of CPE operations. Similarly, in a study of external degree programs within the University of California system, Patton (1975) found that the level of faculty involvement depended on the support of

the deans. He also suggested that support from upper-level administration was crucial to the success of nontraditional efforts. As he pointed out, when the vice-president responsible for initiating the external degree effort left the institution, the level of commitment decreased substantially.

Leadership, of course, is crucial to all educational endeavors. However, it may be more critical to CPE efforts in particular and to continuing education efforts in general than to other aspects of higher educational institutions because of CPE's marginal status and low priority within colleges and universities. This status appears to be reinforced by limited positive policy direction for CPE from the central administration at most institutions (Berlin, 1983; Peterson, 1983). In the absence of such policy direction, the onus for generating support for CPE rests solely on its leaders. This puts a tremendous burden on such individuals and means that even more than in other areas of the university, CPE leaders must constantly develop and maintain political networks to ensure support for their operations.

Even though leadership is so crucial to CPE, we know little about its dimensions. For example, there has been little research that identifies key characteristics of CPE leaders, even in those studies that cite leadership as a critical factor in successful operations. Some work has been done with regard to chief administrators and the leadership function within continuing education divisions in general. Moore (1980) and Prisk (1984) conducted surveys that provide basic demographic data about continuing education administrators, such as titles, salary levels, academic ranks, and reporting channels. Hiett and Pankowski (1983) examined job satisfaction among chief continuing education administrators and found that the variables contributing to high satisfaction included high organizational placement of their operations, prestigious titles, substantial salaries, and most important, substantial support from their institutions' central administration. Perhaps most interesting is the work of Schneider (1981), who examined the competencies associated with continuing education leaders who have been particularly successful in getting new programs adopted by their institutions. Among the competencies identified were a strong self-concept, the ability to relate programs to the specific mission of their institution, the skillful use of influence networks both inside and outside their institution, and an entrepreneurial rather than a managerial spirit. Schneider also noted, however, that different competencies may be needed in the areas of marketing, administrative efficiency, and financial management, and therefore, institutions should begin to consider the potential value of relying on teams of leaders rather than on specific individuals. However, the question of whether the leadership requirements in the CPE field are the same as those for continuing education in general has not been addressed. Certainly, the research on continuing education administration provides a base, but much work is needed if we are to better understand the conditions that lead to effective CPE operations.

Faculty Involvement in Continuing Professional Education
Although clear and decisive policy statements from the central administration
of higher educational institutions would seem to be a necessary step in generating commitment to CPE, such action alone may not be sufficient to generate
substantial interest and action, partly because of the widespread distribution of
authority in higher education institutions. Faculty members have considerable
collective power and authority; although they may not be able to take positive
action, faculty members can resist efforts to move them into new endeavors.
Because continuing professional education advocates depend on the faculty in
order to offer effective programs (Gordon, 1974), overcoming such resistance
is critical.

To date, faculty have been reluctant to be extensively involved in CPE
activities. In his comparative study of continuing professional education activities at several institutions, Knox (1982) found that more than half of the CPE
programs offered by any given institution were conducted by institutional faculty, and that one third to one half of the faculty usually made some
contribution to the CPE effort. He also discovered that most of the continuing
professional education work was done by a more limited group of faculty
members.

Two other types of indirect evidence also suggest low levels of faculty involvement in their institution's continuing professional education program. One is
the complaint, noted earlier, that institutions are seeing their faculty more involved in the CPE activities of other organizations than in their own, with the
subsequent demand that efforts be undertaken to recapture the loyalty of these
faculty members (Lein et al., 1981; Nowlen and Stern, 1981; Peterson, 1983).
The other type of evidence is the apparent heavy reliance by higher education
institutions on part-time instructors for their CPE programs (Stern, 1975).
There is nothing inherently wrong with using part-time faculty; indeed, there
are sound educational reasons for using practitioners—and thus part-time
faculty—in CPE programming efforts because of their familiarity with practice
situations. The problem for higher education institutions, however, is the
extent to which they rely on such people. A key strength of universities in CPE
is the expertise of the faculties. If higher education institutions cannot make effective use of that resource in their offerings, then they may become only a
CPE broker with little to distinguish them from other providers.

Faculty Attitudes and Incentives. Why is it that faculty members generally
have not become actively involved in their institution's CPE offerings? Are
they opposed to continuing professional education? Houle (1980) suggested
this may be the case. Reasons for such resistance have been uncovered in research on faculty attitudes toward continuing education generally and toward
continuing professional education in particular. One is that involvement in such
activities tends to upset traditional routines. That is, it often requires teaching

off-campus and during evenings and weekends (Bell, 1979; Patton, 1975). A second is that the faculty role may simply be overburdened with responsibilities, and that the addition of one more seems unreasonable.

Others argue that the lack of faculty involvement reflects a lack of enthusiasm rather than opposition (Patton, 1975; Sneed, 1972). From this perspective, the issue is how to identify the incentives that will result in faculty participation. Indeed, if faculty are opposed to continuing professional education, why is it that substantial numbers are willing to participate in other organizations' CPE activities? In addition, there is some evidence that faculty participation in continuing professional education activities leads to a more positive appreciation of them (Lein et al., 1981; Toombs, 1984). Thus, if incentives can be increased sufficiently to generate initial involvement, then long-term participation may be ensured. Study of faculty attitudes and incentives toward CPE has followed three paths: the effects of extra benefits, linkage with the research function, and examination of the faculty role.

Compensation appears to be one of the barriers to faculty participation. One problem regarding compensation is the amount that higher education institutions pay their faculty for CPE activities. For example, in a study of faculty attitudes toward CPE at one institution, Lein et al. (1981) found that faculty members believed that they should be paid more. A second problem with compensation relates to the restrictions that some institutions place on the amount of extra compensation faculty can receive for participating in CE or CPE activities sponsored by their institution. A consequence of both conditions is that faculty members will often teach for other providers because they are paid more (Nowlen, 1977).

Creative uses of extra compensation may facilitate faculty involvement. Hanna (1981), for example, reported steps taken at the University of Illinois to pay faculty members extra money based on how far they traveled to teach, and to provide extra graduate assistants and other support. He indicated that these steps were associated with a substantial increase in continuing education activities by faculty members. Indeed, Hanna (1981) and Knox (1982) argued that it is critical to rely on multiple incentives if faculty involvement is to be increased.

Whether extra compensation, regardless of how large, is sufficient to attract substantial numbers of faculty to continuing professional education activities has been questioned by some. As Pollicita and Hanna (1983) noted, building a separate reward structure for continuing education or continuing professional education runs the risk of institutionalizing it as a peripheral activity. For those who take this position, the key to faculty involvement is acceptance of continuing professional education as part of the traditional reward structure. There is ample evidence that it is not part of that structure now. Studies of promotion and tenure criteria in higher education have consistently shown that these criteria are hierarchically structured, with research productivity usually being viewed as most important, followed by teaching, and then service, which includes CPE activities (Bess, 1982; Braxton and Toombs, 1982; Pollicita and Hanna, 1983). Importantly, service appears to be a *distant* third in the reward structure. For example, McCarthy (1980) noted that a study by Selden revealed that liberal arts deans considered service of little value in promotion decisions. She also noted that Centra came to the conclusion that public service was not recognized in promotion and tenure decisions at all. In her own study of 169 institutions, McCarthy (1980) was led to a similar conclusion, noting that service received only very limited attention in the reward process, when it was considered at all. Certainly, faculty are not unaware of this differential valuing of activities. As Lein et al. (1981) and Sayre (1980) observed, one of the prime reasons that faculty members say they do not participate in continuing professional education is that it does nothing to advance their careers. Indeed, as McCarthy (1980) argued, not only is service in continuing education not positively rewarded, but it is viewed as a detriment because it takes time away from research.

Given these circumstances, integration of CPE into the traditional reward structure will be difficult. Those who have studied the reward structure in relation to CPE argue that if CPE is to be accepted, steps must be taken to link it clearly to the research function (Pollicita and Hanna, 1983; Toombs et al., 1984). Such a link seems possible because much of what professionals need is the new knowledge that faculty develop through their research. In addition to work that relates theory to practice, studies of practitioner competence also offer areas of research within each professional field that can link the faculty research role to continuing professional education. Such efforts involve not only the identification of competency criteria, but also work on technical problems concerning performance assessment. Matters of instructional design and delivery in CPE may also be of interest to educational researchers. Thus, there are many CPE concerns that can be incorporated into the traditional faculty research role.

Pollicita and Hanna (1983) described efforts at the University of Illinois to provide guidelines and assistance to help faculty clearly delineate the nature of their continuing education activities and their relationship to scholarly productivity when preparing review materials for promotion and tenure committees. The underlying assumption of this effort is that the connection between continuing education and scholarly work has simply not been made well enough in the past to enable such committees to consider it seriously. Unfortunately, whether such assistance and guidelines have had a positive effect, either at the University of Illinois or at any other institution, is not known.

A third pathway that may have some promise for helping to determine how continuing professional education may be incorporated into faculty activities involves a total reexamination of the faculty role. The basic premise of those who have begun work on this issue is that universities are suffering because there is no functional division of labor (Bess, 1982). That is, as universities assume more responsibilities, additional activities are simply added to the faculty role. As a result, it is almost impossible for any given faculty member to do well all the things required. To illustrate, Bess (1982) identified 320 tasks, 69 subroles, and 10 macroroles required of faculty members. Braxton and Toombs (1982) identified 71 separate scholarly activities of faculty members and argued that only part of faculty members' scholarly productivity involves publication. However, given that the reward structure of universities focuses on research, and primarily on publication, many of the other activities are not rewarded. More important perhaps, activities other than those that lead directly to publication tend to receive less attention, and higher education institutions may suffer accordingly.

Bess (1982) believes that the faculty collectively can carry out the multitude of responsibilities, but that individual faculty members are not able to do so. He therefore suggested a matrix organization whereby individual faculty members could contract to perform a limited number of activities with a limited sector of higher education's clientele. This arrangement would permit faculty members to focus on their strengths and to be rewarded according to the extent that chosen obligations are fulfilled. It is unlikely, of course, that wholesale reorganization of higher education institutions into a matrix pattern is on the horizon. Nevertheless, the basic problem of faculty role overload is a real one. Unless efforts are undertaken to restructure the faculty role as well as the reward system, it would seem unlikely that CPE can become an integral part of the mission of higher education institutions.

The Unique Contribution of Higher Education Institutions
If faculty commitment to CPE can be generated, what activities comprise the most beneficial contribution by higher education faculty to CPE? Houle (1984) described three modes of learning that characterize CPE: inquiry, reinforcement, and instruction. In an earlier work, he noted that institutions of higher education can contribute most to organized instruction because they are experienced in this regard and because theory and knowledge developed within universities are well suited to dissemination through the instructional mode. Indeed, to the extent that these institutions have been involved in CPE to date, they have been engaged in instruction.

Institutions of higher education have the potential to expand their contribution beyond the delivery of instruction to address difficult questions regarding curriculum in CPE (Sayre, 1980; Lynton, 1983; Queeney, 1984). Currently available CPE programs tend to be of short duration (i.e., one or two days) and therefore do not provide sufficient time for substantial learning to occur (Harrington, 1977b). Furthermore, the available offerings do not appear to have any curricular coherence and therefore give professionals little chance to build knowledge and understanding from program to program. Exceptions to this state of affairs are the continuing medical education curriculum developed by the medical faculty at UCLA (Sayre, 1980) and a curriculum plan for CPE in accounting developed by the Texas Society of Certified Public Accountants (1981). The extent to which these efforts have been successful is not known; however, they indicate that curriculum development in CPE is possible. Higher education institutions, continuously involved in developing curricula for their degree programs and housing instructional design specialists, are especially qualified to work on curriculum issues in CPE, and thereby to make a major contribution to the area.

Adapting to a New Clientele

If higher education institutions are to become significantly involved in CPE, more will be required than commitment and identification of a unique contribution. Substantial changes in the orientation and operation of colleges and universities must be instituted. For example, a consistent criticism in the literature has been that faculty members treat professionals just like traditional students (Edelfelt, 1977; Lynton, 1981). But unlike traditional students, professionals enter continuing professional education programs with a substantial base of knowledge and with experience in the application of that knowledge. Thus, in addition to being dispensers of knowledge, faculty members must become conveners of educational forums in which professionals are introduced to new theories and concepts and are also allowed to wrestle with the application of theory to practice (Fordham, 1983). This requirement suggests a need for faculty development programs that concern teaching adults effectively (Edelfelt, 1977; Knowles, 1969).

Administrative procedures comprise a second area that reflects a bias against professional learners that is inherent in higher education institutions. Professionals, as a university clientele, differ substantially from the traditional youth clientele. In most cases, professionals are not interested in degrees, and education is not the primary activity in their lives. Serving professionals requires flexibility within higher education institutions, including (1) developing less rigid admission, registration, and residency requirements (Bowen, 1980; Lynton, 1981); (2) making programs available at times and locations more suitable to adults, perhaps through an increased use of instructional technology (Bowen, 1980); and, perhaps most important, (3) streamlining the lengthy program development and approval process (Lynton, 1981). These suggestions are not intended simply as utilitarian efforts to capture a portion of the CPE market. Rather, higher education institutions must carefully consider the criteria necessary to ensure the integrity of their offerings for professionals in addittition to those necessary for traditional clientele. If the conditions and purposes of education for the two groups are different, a determination of the procedures appropriate for each group seems in order.

Control of Program Content: The Need for Cooperation

A most difficult problem facing higher educational institutions in the CPE arena concerns control of program content. Several commentators have noted that higher education institutions must learn to relinquish exclusive control over the CPE program-planning process and to establish a dialogue with various adult clienteles (Cross, 1981; Fordham, 1983; Knowles, 1969; Lynton, 1983). Cross (1981) argued that the failure to do this is in part responsible for the rise of educational systems within business, industry, and professional associations.

Control over content varies with the goals and purposes of an educational program. Historically, postsecondary institutions have had the responsibility (1) of defining the meaning of undergraduate and graduate degrees and (2) of building curricula that enabled youth to become educated in their chosen field. An underlying premise of this system is that traditional college students do not have the wisdom, experience, or vision to perform such tasks, but that the faculty does. In contrast, professionals have a better understanding of their educational needs and wants. As a result, efforts by higher education institutions to define the scope and content of CPE without their cooperation will be rebuffed. This is not to say that higher education institutions—and specifically, faculty members—must give up control completely, but that more than perfunctory attention must be given to the perspectives of the CPE clientele.

Cooperation will not occur easily. There are deep-seated value differences between higher education and business, industry, and professional groups that will be difficult to overcome (Darkenwald, 1983; Lynton, 1981). Those outside education tend to view CPE as a way to enhance the cost effectiveness of their operations, while those within higher education are concerned with the overall growth and development of individuals as professionals (Lynton, 1981). Often, this conflict surfaces as a debate over the differences between education and training. There are, however, reasons for the two groups to join together in CPE. From the professionals' viewpoint, these reasons include access to faculty expertise, use of specialized facilities, and decreased educational costs (Darkenwald, 1983; Lynton, 1981). From the higher education perspective, the reasons for involvement in CPE, as noted above, include the responsibility to disseminate new knowledge, access to new student markets, and meeting of the learning needs of a legitimate university-level clientele.

Many arrangements are possible to bring higher education institutions and professional and business and industry groups together. Cross (1981) argued that cooperation could take several forms, including advisory boards or more tightly constrained collaborative arrangements. Similarly, Cervero (1984) noted that links can range in intensity from the simple exchange of information to long-term legal contracts to cooperate.

There is a substantial need, however, for research that carefully explores the nature, the costs and benefits, and the procedural arrangements associated with cooperative efforts related to CPE, although these issues have received limited attention. Lindsay et al. (1981), for example, outlined a theoretical basis for collaboration between professional associations and universities by drawing on the resource-dependence framework developed in the field of interorganizational relationships. Smutz and Toombs (1985) used a political framework to examine the process by which collaborative partnerships are formed between academic departments and professional associations. They found that the participating organizations selected their representatives strategically. Organizations with a high need for resources and an interest in expanding their CPE efforts selected individuals in high-level positions, who wielded influence in their parent organizations. In contrast, organizations with low resource needs and less interest in expanding their CPE efforts selected individuals in lower-level positions, who wielded less influence. Cervero (1984) examined various links established by a continuing professional education operation at a large midwestern university. Using the resource-dependence framework, he delineated the extensive relationships maintained by the operation and their criticalness to its ongoing program-development function.

Fingeret (1984) conducted an intensive case study of an attempt at collaboration between a power company and a higher education institution to develop a learning package for nuclear-power-plant operators. The prospects for collaboration are not good if her analysis is generalizable. Fingeret found that collaboration foundered on two key issues: (1) who was to control the content of the program and (2) the university's failure to accept participation in the development and delivery of the program as a legitimate faculty activity. She concluded that extensive effort must be put into helping business and higher education institutions to establish relationships across a broad range of activities in order to enhance familiarity before intensive collaborative efforts are undertaken.

Collaboration between higher education institutions and professional groups may be facilitated through organizational units that serve a catalytic rather than a program development or delivery function. Manning et al. (1979) reported the successful development of such a boundary-spanning unit at the University of Southern California Medical School. This unit, made up of educational specialists, works with community hospitals to identify learning needs of physicians and faculty in order to design appropriate educational programs, permitting both internal and external constituencies to contribute to the program development process without either's losing control. In a study of collaborative relationships between academic departments and professional associations,

Smutz (1985) identified a need for a separate facilitator or catalyst. He concluded that faculty members were either unwilling or unable to function effectively as boundary spanners in order to enhance the formation of collaborative relationships. In the absence of effective performance in this area by faculty members, universities must call on others to facilitate the process of partnership formation.

EXAMPLES OF COMPREHENSIVE CPE PROJECTS

The number of comprehensive research-and-development projects that contribute to understanding many of the issues outlined above has grown in recent years. Before this development, CPE practitioners and researchers writing about the field had little contact with each other or with organizations external to the university. This compartmentalized and insular approach to problems in the field is changing now with the advent of these projects, which address selected CPE issues systematically and comprehensively. The projects are distinctive in the following ways:

- Higher education institutions play a leading role in the conduct of the comprehensive projects, either as the primary sponsor or through their contribution of principal investigators. The direct involvement and leadership of higher education institutions through these projects can enhance and accelerate the growth of CPE as a field of practice and as an emerging area of study.
- They are long- rather than short-term efforts, ranging from 4–5 years to 10–12 years. Some are still under way, and others are continuing beyond their original time frame.
- Each features a cooperative team approach in the conduct of the project, involving multiple organizations and interprofessional or interdisciplinary project team.
- These projects have as their broadest goal the enhancement of the quality of professional services, and they attempt, through their operational goals, to advance both the conceptualization and the practice of continuing professional education. In other words, they identify, define, and address issues in continuing professional education through research and programming efforts.

Each of the illustrative projects is summarized below.

The Continuing Professional Education Development Project
This project brings together higher education and the professions to work toward the fundamental goal of Houle's concept (1980) of professionalization, that of enhancing the competence of professionals (Smutz et al., 1982). Begun in 1980, it was a five-year research-and-development effort funded by the W.

K. Kellogg Foundation, The Pennsylvania State University, and fourteen participating professional associations. The project had three major goals: (1) to establish collaborative relationships between the professions and the university in order to strengthen the development and implementation of CPE programs; (2) to develop and implement practice-oriented CPE programs for five professions through the application of a seven-phase needs-assessment-program-development process, the Practice Audit Model (Smutz et al., 1981); and (3) to develop models of university–profession collaboration for CPE that can lead to its institutionalization within the university.

Collaboration, a key concept and goal (Lindsay et al., 1981) was operationalized through a multiparty group, the profession team, for each of the five selected professional groups (accounting, architecture, clinical dietetics, clinical psychology, and gerontological nursing) participating in the project. Each team included representatives from national and state professional associations and from regulatory agencies, Penn State University faculty members from appropriate academic departments, and project staff members. The profession teams carried out the work of the project at twice-yearly meetings, by correspondence, and by telephone calls between meetings. The team efforts were guided by the Practice Audit Model, which focuses attention on what practitioners do rather than on what they know. The first four phases of the model define an empirical approach to needs assessment, while the last three address program design, development, and delivery based on identified learning needs. Each of the five profession teams completed one iteration of the Practice Audit Model, resulting in the delivery and evaluation of a CPE program for their professional group.

Issues associated with the development and implementation of practice-oriented CPE programs have been identified (Smutz, 1984), and an examination of institutionalizing CPE in the academic setting (Lindsay and Smutz, 1984; Toombs et al., 1985) and of selecting professions for collaboration (Queeney and Melander, 1984) was undertaken. Additional information is available through the *Project News,* a twice-yearly publication that reports on project progress and activities.

The Continuing Education Systems Project (CESP)

This project was a well-articulated example of a comprehensive approach to advancing conceptualization and practice dealing with quality assurance in continuing professional education. Its context was a mandate from the project's two cooperating agencies, the Association of American Medical Colleges (AAMC) and the Veterans Administration (VA) to define quality in continuing education for the health professions and to translate the definition into guidelines for the everyday practice of continuing education. Funding for the project, which ran from 1978 to 1983, was provided by a grant from the VA, supplemented by contributions from the AAMC.

The stated goals of the CESP were to improve the quality of CPE for health professionals by defining and describing quality CPE and by assisting CPE providers and accrediting organizations to ensure quality CPE. To reach this goal, the project identified the following objectives: (1) to develop a conceptual model of CPE and a list of quality elements or criteria for applying the model to CPE practice based on a review of the theoretical and experiential foundations of CPE; (2) to develop specifications for an information management and reporting system in support of quality CPE; (3) to produce materials and learning packages that would assist CPE providers in applying the model's concepts to CPE practice; and (4) to pilot-test the criteria, the management system, and the learning materials in various CPE settings.

To date, these objectives have been realized through the publication of a project summary report (Green et al., 1983) and a book (Green et al., 1984). Each publication contains the project's comprehensive conceptual model for CPE and a list of 141 CPE quality elements organized into five categories: (1) "Setting Direction for the CE Provider Unit"; (2) "Organizing the CE Provider Unit"; (3) "Providing CE Activities and Materials"; (4) "Providing Educational Assistance and Services"; and (5) "Administering the CE Provider Unit." A number of organizations, including the American Association of Dental Schools, the American Red Cross, and the Veterans Administration, have been applying the quality elements to the development and provision of CPE in their settings. A recent report describes how Temple University's Office of Continuing Medical Education and 18 affiliated hospitals have attempted to implement the CESP's model of quality for continuing education (Lanzilotti and Finestone, 1985). Directors of Continuing Medical Education (CME) at the 18 hospitals responded to a survey on the current or potential use of the CESP's quality elements in their institutions. Based on the results, the authors proposed that the CME unit be accepted and supported not merely as an adjunct educational service for physicians, but as an agent of the hospital's organizational development.

Commission on Interprofessional Education and Practice

The basic premise of this ongoing project is that an interprofessional perspective can enhance the competence of preservice and practicing professionals. The project began in 1974–1975 when the Ohio Board of Regents gave its forerunner at the Ohio State University a small grant for an experimental program on interprofessional education. It assumed its current goals and structure in 1981, when the W. K. Kellogg Foundation awarded a multiyear grant to the Commission on Interprofessional Education and Practice, the project's governing board.

The project's structure is perhaps as interesting as its goals and activities, providing an example of how working directly with professions can become institutionalized in a higher education institution. The Commission on Interprofessional Education and Practice, a board of project representatives from colleges and state professional associations, brings together six professional colleges and schools of the Ohio State University, the Columbus Cluster of Theological Schools, and seven state professional associations to sponsor and support programs dealing with interprofessional education for both preprofessionals and professionals in education, law, medicine, the allied health professions, nursing, social work, and theology. Another part of the organizational structure is a committee of deans from the respective colleges, chaired by the university provost. While the commission or board sets policy and provides program direction, the committee of deans oversees the fiscal and curriculum matters associated with the project. The funding for project activities comes from the provost's office; the participating colleges, seminaries, and professional associations; the Merchon Center of the Ohio State University; the Columbus Foundation; and a major grant from the W. K. Kellogg Foundation.

The project has four major goals:

1. To develop interprofessional practice in clinical settings that will provide students with opportunities to work in interprofessional teams under faculty supervision in the direct delivery of service.
2. To develop continuing education for professional practitioners that will give them access to interprofessional courses and institutes as well as the present conferences.
3. To develop a program of dissemination of the concept of interprofessional education.
4. To conduct a prospective policy analysis of issues that have cross-professional implications in their impact on society.

Project activities include the development and teaching of preprofessional courses at the Ohio State University, the development and implementation of interprofessional seminars open to both preprofessionals and professionals, and twice-yearly conferences on a broad topic with interprofessional implications. Further information can be found in a newsletter, the *Interprofessional Commentary,* published four times each year, and other publications (Cunningham et al., 1982; Cunningham, 1984).

The University of Georgia Project
The underlying goal of this comprehensive project is to bring theory and practice together in innovative ways to better serve adult learners. Begun in 1984, with a large grant from the W. K. Kellogg Foundation and matching funds from the Georgia legislature, project plans outline a universitywide, multicom-

ponent six-year endeavor to achieve its goal. While its focus is broader than continuing professional education, the project has the potential to have a major impact on theory and practice in this area as well as on the overall field of adult and continuing education.

Directly involved in the University of Georgia Project are the Georgia Center for Continuing Education, the Department of Adult Education, the Cooperative Extension Service, and other faculty and administrators from the university. Central to the project are the development and implementation of a National Center for Leadership Development in Adult and Continuing Education and Lifelong Learning. The goal of this center is to merge practice and theory at the cutting edge of continuing education and lifelong learning in order to benefit practitioners, researchers, teachers, graduate students, and adult learners. The components of the leadership development thrust include plans for a program to stimulate faculty research, teaching, and service through interdisciplinary faculty task forces organized around seven issue areas: (1) the economy; (2) physical resources; (3) governance; (4) the learning society; (5) health and well-being; (6) social institutions and processes; and (7) behavioral norms and social controls. In addition, the Department of Adult Education will expand its faculty and develop a Ph.D. program, a certificate program for practitioners, and other new activities.

The Georgia Center for Continuing Education plans to develop new and to expand current programs, including a learning-support center for adult self-directed learning projects and a certifiable curriculum for adults. Of direct interest to the field of continuing professional education are project plans to establish a council for the improvement of continuing education for the professions. Its goal will be to promote cross-professional sharing and cooperation among providers of continuing professional education. The target groups include lawyers, veterinarians, pharmacists, nurses, physicians, engineers, teachers, dentists, psychologists/counselors, and certified public accountants.

Since the project is very recent, most of the effort has been given to organization and planning. However, the project has begun publishing a newsletter, *Lifelong Learning Forum,* which reports on project progress and theory–practice links.

Development and Demonstration Center in Continuing Education for Health Professionals

Conducted at the University of Southern California, the Development and Demonstration Center in Continuing Education for Health Professionals began in 1980, with funding by the W. K. Kellogg Foundation and the parent university. The project's major goals are to initiate and test innovative and diverse approaches to help integrate the various activities of continuing education, to offer consultive assistance to persons and organizations involved in continuing education, and to coordinate pertinent data in the field for dissemination to educators, professional societies, and legislators (Manning, 1981). A distinguishing feature of the center is the creation of a stable environment where an interdisciplinary team can develop and test long-range plans to improve continuing education.

Examples of the center's work include research on the impact of CME on physicians' prescription-writing behavior (Manning et al., 1979) and on the need for new methods for providing CME to physicians (Manning, 1982).

The Continuing Higher Education Leadership Project (CHEL)
This recent effort brings together a number of parties, including professional associations, higher education, the business community, and federal and state government agencies, to examine issues associated with the broad area of leadership in continuing higher education and to propose and to provide models and opportunities for enhancing this leadership. The CHEL project, begun in 1984, is managed by the National University Continuing Education Association (NUCEA) with funding provided by a five-year grant from the W. K. Kellogg Foundation.

Project activities to date include a planning conference held in December 1984 (Project on Continuing Higher Education Leadership, 1984) and the publication of a quarterly newsletter, *Continuing Higher Education Leadership.* A context for the project's work was given by Munger (1985), and the entire spring 1985 issue of the NUCEA journal, *Continuum,* was devoted to issues that the project addresses.

These exemplary projects, which represent a marriage of private (foundation, professional associations) and public (land-grant universities, federal and state government agencies) funds, systematically address many important issues in CPE. Taken collectively, they represent a force that can accelerate and enhance the development of the field of CPE and provide a forum for the emergence of new issues.

A RESEARCH AGENDA FOR CONTINUING PROFESSIONAL EDUCATION

The available research on continuing professional education reflects not only the relative newness of the area, as distinct from adult education or continuing higher education in general, but also the immediacy of the problems created by the rapid growth in demand and delivery of continuing professional education. Research in this area has not been more orderly than the marketplace itself. However, several issues related to continuing professional education content, design, and delivery surface consistently and call for systematic study. There is also a need for basic data regarding participation, as well as both conceptual analyses and empirical study regarding relationships between CPE and higher education institutions.

Content-Related Issues

This set of issues concerns not specific program content *per se* but the broader topic of professional competence and includes both substantive and methodological questions. Shimberg (1982) provided a thoughtful overview of competency and described methods for its assessment. Watts (1981) referred to these competency issues as "what takes place at the physician/patient care interface"; Caplan (1983) described them as "matching educational needs to patient care needs"; and Diers (1977), as nursing-practice research. The emphasis is on the identification of components of professional competence and determinants of performance. As the goals of continuing education are more clearly related to maintaining competence, empirically determined criteria for competence and performance become an essential ingredient in program design.

Models of professional competence have recently been offered, such as the Professional Performance Situation Model (PPSM) (LaDuca, et al., 1978) regarding the structure of competence in health professions; a model of executive competence by Klemp (1984); and a general competence model by Love (1984). The PPSM, which emphasizes the importance of the practice context in defining competence, has been applied to the field of clinical dietetics in the development of a training program (Engel et al., 1980) and indicates the importance of skills and processes, in addition to knowledge, in both preprofessional and continuing professional education. Other evidence in this regard includes the increasingly numerous role-delineation studies conducted on behalf of professional groups to provide a foundation for training and licensure. Examples include the work of D'Costa and Schreck (1983) in dietetics, Rosenfeld et al. (1983) in psychology, and the National Council of Architectural Registration Boards (1981) in architecture. These studies were undertaken to describe the components of professional practice, including what the practitioner must do, as well as the knowledge and skills necessary to perform the functions described.

Beyond describing professional practice, there is a significant need for empirical work that validates competency criteria or role delineation studies in terms of actual performance and client outcomes. Related to this issue is the need to develop adequate means of measuring professional performance. Scofield and Yoxtheimer (1983) reviewed the recent literature on counselor and therapy competencies and made recommendations for improving the reliability and validity of clinical performance appraisal. Reliability and validity problems in making clinical ratings were noted by McGuire (1983), and problems in setting performance standards were discussed by Meskaukas and Norcini (1980). Recent efforts to ameliorate the former have included patient management problems (McGuire, 1983) and simulations in client treatment planning (Butcher, Scofield, and Baker, 1984). The latter would benefit from empirical work that few have the time, the resources, or the inclination to perform.

These content and methodological issues related to the analysis of professional competence and performance provide a necessary foundation for the substance of continuing professional education, whether or not such research efforts are undertaken in the name of continuing education. Work of this type has occurred primarily in medical and health professions schools or, in other professions, has been initiated by professional organizations and contracted out to private research organizations. Research in this regard represents a potential contribution by higher education faculty to any profession.

Instructional Design and Delivery Issues
The design and delivery of continuing professional education suggest many research questions. Caplan (1983) identified the following topics as being in need of further study: (1) maximizing individualization; (2) helping learners to become more sophisticated; (3) employing "inquiry" methods; (4) using the multiple motivations of learners; (5) characterizing the effective participant; and (6) developing computer literacy.

Professional self-assessment systems, undertaken by the individual practitioner, have been developed in many fields and represent one way in which continuing education systems have been individualized. These systems identify individual needs and serve as learning experiences in themselves because they provide feedback to the individual (Kalman, 1984). Another means of individualizing continuing learning is a mentoring system through which practitioners have access to university faculty. Also related to maximizing individualization is Caplan's suggestion regarding helping learners to become more sophisticated by facilitating the use of learning aids. The use of computers has great potential for impact on practice, as an information-processing tool as well as an instructional device (Piemme, 1984). Thus, research regarding the individualization of continuing professional learning can involve content, instructional technology, and delivery.

Houle (1980) stressed the importance of inquiry methods in continuing professional education. This term refers to learning that arises directly from the practice situation, including the identification of problems to be studied or solved and the identification of solutions. Facilitating learning in the practice setting is another topic for research in continuing professional education. Related to increasing the practice orientation are questions concerning what professions can learn from each other, such as those addressed by the Ohio State Commission on Interprofessional Education.

Perhaps the most frequently raised question regarding continuing professional education has concerned program impact. Recent reviews of the continuing professional education evaluation literature in the area of medicine have indicated that continuing medical education can have a positive effect on competence and performance (Davis et al., 1984; Abrahamson, 1984; Illinois

Council on Continuing Medical Education, 1980). These reviews have also documented the increasing sophistication in the design of evaluation research, ranging from studies of learner satisfaction to examination of practitioner performance and client outcome. Further research on the broad question of the effectiveness of continuing professional education is probably not warranted, because of the individual and situational concerns previously discussed. However, models of the impact of continuing professional education—such as that offered by Cervero and Rottett (1984), which asks the question "Under what conditions and for which types of individuals are which characteristics of continuing education most likely to improve professionals' performance" (p. 136)—show promise in identifying useful information about the influence of continuing professional education on practice.

Institutional Issues
The relationship of higher education institutions to continuing professional education is ambiguous at this time. However, researchers can examine issues in this area for purposes of clarification as well as to provide direction for institutional policymakers who will be increasingly challenged to define an appropriate posture for their institutions vis-à-vis CPE. To this end, three types of research activity would offer some useful dividends.

The first area deserving attention is the establishment of a CPE database within institutions and across them (Stern, 1970; 1984). One real problem in attempting to understand the parameters of CPE is the limited amount of basic data on the level and scope of activity. Several kinds of data are needed. One is enrollment information: How many individuals, with what characteristics, and from which professions are enrolling in what kinds of programs, and how often? Institutional data would also be helpful: What kinds of institutions and how many (inside and outside of the formal postsecondary educational system) are offering what types of CPE programs, to whom, and where? With regard to this latter issue, it has been suggested that CPE is a national market rather than a local or even a regional one (Stern, 1980), so that institutions in one part of the country may be offering their programs in other parts. This possibility has potential implications for the quality of CPE offerings as well as for territorial conflict. Finally, data on faculty participation in CPE activities are needed: How many faculty, in which fields, are spending how much time, providing CPE for what kinds of organizations? Although considerable anguish has been expressed over faculty participation in CPE efforts of outside providers, the extent to which this is happening in unclear.

A second area of needed research involves conceptual analyses of continuing professional education and higher education institutions' relationship to it. At least two issues deserve attention here. One has to do with the fundamental nature and even the definition of CPE: What is CPE, how does it differ from other forms of higher learning, and how does it fit into the educational systems that currently exist? Some work has addressed this issue, such as Toomb's effort (1982) to understand CPE as a unique educational endeavor based on its purpose and design, but considerable clarification is needed. A second issue that could benefit from extensive conceptual analysis is the notion of a CPE curriculum: What are the components of such a curriculum, how would it vary for different professions, how would it relate to the preservice curriculum, and how could it be integrated into various career stages and tracks of professionals?

Third, there is a need for empirical studies that explicate and thus enhance discussions of the relationship between higher education institutions and CPE, especially concerning administrative and organizational matters. A key area for research is the centralization versus decentralization issue. For example, what difference does organizational structure make in terms of an institution's CPE effort? Does one type lead to better, more, or different programs that the other? Do different structures mean that different assumptions underlie the decision-making process regarding what programs to offer? Indeed, how are decisions made in the different structures—who has an input and at what stage of the process? This last question raises the issue of leadership. If leadership is so essential in the CPE field, what are the characteristics specific to effective CPE leaders, how did they reach their current positions, and what are their modes of operation?

Research on the functioning and status of CPE operations within higher education institutions must be guided by some conceptual framework. To date, Clark's marginality framework has dominated our understanding of continuing education in general. Devlin (1980) noted, though, that Clark's framework has been accepted without any attempt to investigate the elasticity of marginality's key features, or whether degrees of marginality and institutional characteristics are associated with such variability. In addition, there may be other theoretical frameworks that might help us to better understand institutions' involvement in CPE as distinct from continuing education. For example, application of the recently developed organization-environment interaction models may tell us more about higher education's relationship to CPE than marginality. Organizational culture may be another important factor affecting involvement. Finally, a political framework might be applied to clarify different levels of institutional receptivity to CPE. Penfield's historical analysis (1975) of one institution's experience with continuing education at the turn of the century indicates that political considerations were paramount in that institution's ambivalent approach to continuing education. Are similar conditions involved in current discussions over the appropriateness of CPE in the higher education context?

An effective relationship between CPE and higher education institutions will require the support not only of institutional faculty and administrators, but also of individuals and organizations outside higher education. Research regarding the attitudes and concerns of each group could provide direction for future CPE efforts. Although some work has addressed faculty perspectives, it has been far from comprehensive. Research on administrators' attitudes toward CPE and the place of CPE in the strategic planning process is nonexistent. Questions concerning relationships with external organizations include how higher education institutions and other organizations can work together, how they might get together in the first place, whether some institutions are better equipped for collaborative relationships than others, and how collaborative relationships can be maintained.

The significant involvement of educational institutions in CPE, if it occurs, will require organizational change. The abundance of literature on organizational change may be used to clarify the problem of incorporating CPE within higher education. There are a few instances of efforts to organize the change literature conceptually to illustrate its applicability to continuing education and/or CPE (Votruba, 1981; Lindsay and Smutz, 1984). With the exception of the work of Pollicita and Hanna (1983), however, there has been less effort to apply what is known about organizational change to the problem of integrating CPE into the higher education context.

The emergence of continuing professional education represents an opportunity for higher education services to expand the educational services they provide while building on long-established traditions of mission and purpose. At the same time, it offers an opportunity for researchers interested in higher education to explore in a new context many educational and organizational issues that have received attention in the past, such as the impact of instruction on learning and the relationship of organizational structure to educational effectiveness. Importantly, the need for such research comes at the very time when its potential contribution to policy considerations related to CPE within higher educational institutions is highest. Perhaps this opportunity will provide the necessary challenge to interest more researchers in the field of continuing professional education.

Acknowledgment. The authors acknowledge the contribution of Dr. C. O. Houle to the early version of this chapter.

NOTE

1. Percentages do not sum to 100 because not all available categories are indicated. For example, elementary schools were omitted because it is unlikely that they would provide continuing professional education.

REFERENCES

Abrahamson, S. (1984). Evaluation of continuing education in the health professions: the state of the art. *Evaluation and the Health Professions* 7: 3–24.
Anderson, G. L. (1976). *Land-grant universities and their continuing challenge.* Lansing: Michigan State University Press.
Anderson, R. E. (1982). Overview and implications. In R. E. Anderson and E. S. Kasl (eds.), *The costs and financing of adult education and training.* Lexington, MA: Lexington Books.
Bell, J. (1979). The role of library schools in providing continuing education for the profession. *Journal of Education for Librarianship* 19(3): 248–259.
Berlin, L. S. (1983). The university and continuing professional education: a contrary view. In M. R. Stern, (ed.), *Power and conflict in continuing professional education.* Belmont, CA: Wadsworth.
Bess, J. (1982). *University organization: A matrix analysis of the academic professions.* New York: Human Sciences Press.
Blaney, J. P., and Devlin, L. E. (1985). Managing organizational renewal in university extension. *The Journal of Continuing Higher Education* 33(2): 8–10.
Bowen, H. (1980). *Adult learning, higher education, and the economics of capacity.* New York: College Entrance Examination Board.
Braxton, J. M., and Toombs, W. (1982). Faculty uses of doctoral training: consideration of a technique for the differentiation of scholarly effort from research activity. *Research in Education* 16(3): 265–282.
Brubacher, J. (1977). *On the philosophy of higher education.* San Francisco: Jossey-Bass.
Butcher, E., Scofield, M. E., and Baker, B. (1984). Validation of a standardized simulation for the assessment of competence in mental health counseling. *The American Mental Health Counselors Association Journal* 6(4): 162–172.
Caplan, R. M. (1983). Continuing education and professional accountability. In C. McGuire, R. P. Foley, A. Gorr, R. W. Richards, et al. (eds.), *Handbook of health professions education* pp. 319–350. San Francisco: Jossey-Bass.
Carnevale, A. P. (1983). Higher education's role in the American economy. *Educational Record* Fall: 6–17.
Cervero, R. M. (1981). A factor analytic study of physicians' reasons for participating in continuing education. *Journal of Medical Education* 56: 29–34.
Cervero, R. M. (1984). Collaboration in university continuing professional education. In H. Beder (ed.), *New Directions for Continuing Education: Realizing the Potential of Interorganizational Cooperation* 23: 23–38.
Cervero, R. M., and Rottet, S. (1984). Analyzing the effectiveness of continuing professional education: an exploratory study. *Adult Education Quarterly* 34: 135–146.
Clark, B. R. (1958a). *The marginality of adult education.* Boston: Center for the Study of Liberal Education for Adults, Boston University.
Clark, B. R. (1958b). *Adult education in transition: a study of institutional insecurity.* Berkeley: University of California Press.
Cooper, S. S. (1981). Myths about continuing education. *Mobius* 1: 69–75.
Council on the Continuing Education Unit. (1984). *Principles of good practice in continuing education.* Silver Spring, MD: Author.
Cross, K. P. (1981). New frontiers for higher education: business and professions. *Current Issues in Higher Education: Partnerships with Business and the Professions,* Vol. 3, pp. 1–7. Washington, DC: American Association for Higher Education.

Crosson, P. H. (1983). *Public service in higher education: practices and priorities.* (ASHE-ERIC Higher Education Research Report No. 7). Washington, DC: Association for the Study of Higher Education.

Cruse, R. B. (1983). The accounting profession. In M. R. Stern (ed.), *Power and conflict in continuing professional education.* Belmont, CA: Wadsworth.

Cunningham, L. L. (1984). Interprofessional collaboration in continuing education for the professional: 10 years of experience and practice. Paper presented at the meeting of the National University Continuing Education Association, Atlanta.

Cunningham, L. L., Spencer, M., and Battison, S. (1982). Expanding professional awareness: the commission on interprofessional education and practice. *Merchon Center Quarterly Report* 7(4): 1-7.

Darkenwald, G. G. (1983). Perspectives of business and industry on cooperative programming with educational institutions. *Adult Education Quarterly* 33(4): 230-243.

Davis, D., Haynes, R. B., Chambers, L., Neufield, V. R., McKibbon, A., and Tugwell, P. (1984). The impact of CME: a methodological review of the continuing medical education literature. *Evaluation and the Health Professions* 7: 251-284.

Day, C., and Baskett, H. K. (1982). Discrepancies between intentions and practice: reexamining some basic assumptions about adult and continuing professional education. *International Journal of Lifelong Education* 1: 143-155.

D'Costa, A., and Schreck, A. L. (1983). *The role of the dietary manager.* Hillside, IL: The Hospital, Institution, and Educational Food Service Society.

Devlin, L. E. (1980). Marginality: some conceptual approaches for university extension. *Canadian Journal of University Continuing Education* 8: 4-9.

Diers, D. (1977). The role of continuing education in promoting research in practice. *The Journal of Continuing Education in Nursing* 8: 54-62.

Donnelly, R. S. (no date). *Continuing professional education: an appraisal.* Amherst: Division of Continuing Education, University of Massachusetts.

Edelfelt, R. A. (1977). The school of education and inservice education. *Journal of Teacher Education* 28(2): 10-14.

Edwards, R. L., and Green, R. K. (1983). Mandatory continuing education: time for reevaluation. *Social Work* 28: 43-48.

Engel, J. O., Sayers, S., LaDuca, J., and Risley, M. E. (1980). *Competence in clinical dietetics.* Chicago: Center for Educational Development, University of Illinois at the Medical Center.

Eurich, M. P. (1985). *Corporate classrooms: the learning business.* Princeton, NJ: The Carnegie Foundation for the Advancement of Teaching.

Fingeret, A. (1984). Who's in control? A case study of university-industry collaboration. *New Directions for Continuing Education: Realizing the Potential of Interorganizational Cooperation* 23: 39-63.

Fordham, P. (1983). A view from the wall: commitment and purposes in university adult education. *International Journal of Lifelong Education* 2(4): 341-354.

Fox, R. D. (1981). Formal organizational structure and participation in planning continuing professional education. *Adult Education* 51(4): 209-226.

Frandson, P. E. (1975a). Continuing education of the professions: issues, ethics, and conflicts. *NUEA Spectator* 38: 5-10.

Frandson, P. E. (1975b). Greater role urged for universities. *Los Angeles Times,* September 28, Part VI, p. 1, 4.

Frandson, P. E. (1980a). Continuing education for the professions. In E. J. Boone, R. W. Shearon, E. E. White, et al. (eds.), *Serving personal and community needs through adult education,* pp. 61-81. San Francisco: Jossey-Bass.

Frandson, P. E. (1980b). Continuing education in architecture: the process, the issues, the challenge. *Continuum* 45(1): 25–36.

Geertsma, R. H., Parker, R. C., and Whitbourne, S. K. (1982). How physicians view the process of change in their practice behavior. *Journal of Medical Education* 57: 753–761.

Gonnella, J. S., and Zeleznik, C. (1983). Strengthening the relationship between professional education and performance. *New Directions for Continuing Education: Strengthening Connections Between Education and Performance* 18: 59–72.

Goode, W. J. (1960). Encroachment, charlatanism, and the emerging profession: psychology, sociology, and medicine. *American Sociological Review* 25: 903–914.

Gordon, M. (1974). The organization of continuing education in colleges and universities. *The NUEA Spectator* 37(17): 20–27.

Green, J. S., Grosswald, S. J., Suter, E., and Walthall, D. B. (1983). *The continuing education systems project.* Washington, DC: Association of American Medical Colleges and the Department of Medicine and Surgery, Veterans Administration.

Green, J. S., Grosswald, S. J., Suter, E., and Walthall, D. B. (1984). *Continuing education for the health professions.* San Francisco: Jossey-Bass.

Griffith, D. E. (1983). Professional continuing education in engineering. In M. R. Stern (ed.), *Power and conflict in continuing professional education.* Belmont, CA: Wadsworth.

Grotelueschen, A. D., Harnisch, D. L., and Kenny, W. R. (1979). *An analysis of the participation reasons scale administered to business professionals* (Occasional paper No. 7). Urbana-Champagne: University of Illinois, College of Education, Office for the Study of Continuing Professional Education.

Hanna, D. E. (1981). Securing faculty involvement in continuing education. *Continuum* 45(4): 51–57.

Hansen, R. H. (1983). Marketing of continuing medical education. *Mobius* 3: 53–59.

Harrington, F. H. (1977a). Continuing professional education: an outside view. *Continuum* 41(4): 4–7.

Harrington, F. H. (1977b). *The future of adult education.* San Francisco: Jossey-Bass.

Hiett, J. H., and Pankowski, M. L. (1983). Job satisfaction: a survey of chief continuing education administrators. *Continuum* 47(3): 39–45.

Houle, C. O. (1980). *Continuing learning in the professions.* San Francisco: Jossey-Bass.

Houle, C. O. (1984). Continuing professional education: An overview. In S. Goodlad (ed.), *Education for the professions.* Guildford, England: SRHE & NFER-Nelson.

Illinois Council on Continuing Medical Education. (1980). *Physicians improve performance through continuing education—Eight research reports.* Chicago: Author.

Kalman, S. H. (1984). *Self assessment.* Proceedings of the National Conference on Continuing Competence Assurance in the Health Professions, pp. 52–55. Bal Harbour, FL: National Commission for Health Certifying Agencies.

Kay, E. R. (1982). *Participation in adult education 1981.* Washington, DC: National Center for Education Statistics.

Kerr, C. (1963). *The uses of the university.* New York: Harper and Row.

Klemp, G. O., Jr. (1984). Conceptions of executive competence. Paper presented at the National Conference on the Development and Assessment of Human Competence, Washington, DC.

Knowles, M. S. (1969). *Higher adult education in the United States.* Washington, DC: The American Council on Education.

Knowles, M. S. (1985). Applications in continuing education for the health professions. *Mobius* 5(2): 80–100.

Knox, A. B. (1975). New realities: the administration of continuing higher education. *The NUEA Spectator* 39(22): 6–9.

Knox, A. B. (1982). Organizational dynamics in university continuing professional education. *Adult Education* 32(3): 117–129.

LaDuca, A. (1980). The structure of competence in health professions. *Evaluation and the Health Professions* 3: 253–288.

LaDuca, A., Engel, J. D., and Risley, M. D. (1978). Progress toward development of a general model for competence definition in health professions. *Journal of Allied Health* 7:149–156.

Lanzilotti, S. S., and Finestone, A. J. (1985). Application of the continuing education systems project. *Mobius* 5(2): 18–27.

Lauffer, A. (1977). *The practice of continuing education in the human services.* New York: McGraw-Hill.

Lein, J. N., Cullen, T., Liston, A., and Lind, P. (1981). The faculty and continuing medical education: an attitude study. *Journal of Medical Education* 56: 737–741.

Leslie, L. L. (1976). Updating education for the professions: the new mission. In G. L. Anderson (ed.), *Land-grant universities and their continuing challenge.* Lansing: Michigan State University Press.

Lindsay, C. A., Queeney, D. S., and Smutz, W. D. (1981). *A model and process for university/professional association collaboration.* University Park, PA: The Pennsylvania State University, Continuing Professional Education Development Project.

Lindsay, C. A., and Smutz, W. D. (1984). Professionals and professors: a change strategy for institutionalizing collaborative continuing professional education program development. In *Mainstreaming continuing professional education: a conceptual approach and an empirical study,* pp. 1–33. University Park: The Pennsylvania State University, Continuing Professional Educational Development Project.

Lockyer, J. M., Parboosingh, J. T., McDougall, G. M., and Chugh, V. (1985). How physicians integrate advances into clinical practices. *Mobius* 5:5–12.

Love, J. M. (1984). Operationalizing conceptions of competence. Paper presented at the National Conference on the Development and Assessment of Human Competence, Washington, DC.

Lowenthal, W. (1981). Continuing education for professionals: voluntary or mandatory? *Journal of Higher Education* 52: 519–538.

Lynton, E. A. (1981). A role for colleges in corporate training and developoment. In *Current Issues in Higher Education: Partnerships with Business and the Professions* 3:8–15. Washington, DC: American Association for Higher Education.

Lynton, E. A. (1983). Higher education's role in fostering employee education. *Educational Record* Fall:18–25.

Manning, P. R. (1981). Development and demonstration center: continuing education for health professionals. *Mobius* 1(1): 54–59.

Manning, P. R. (1982). Continuing education in the health sciences: can we change the paradigm? *Mobius* 2(2): 5–7.

Manning, P. R., Covell, D. G., Mussell, B., Thomas, C. J., Bee, R. S., and Denson, T. A. (1979). Continuing medical education: linking the community hospital and the medical school. *Journal of Medical Education* 54:461–466.

McCarthy, M. B. (1980). Continuing education service as a component of faculty evaluation. *Lifelong Learning: The Adult Years* 3(9): 8–11, 24–25.

McGuire, C. H. (1983). Evaluation of student and practitioner competence. In C. McGuire, R. P. Foley, A. Gorr, R. W. Richards et al., (eds.), *Handbook of health professions education.* San Francisco: Jossey-Bass.

428   SMUTZ, CROWE AND LINDSAY

Meskauskas, J. A., and Norcini, J. J. (1980). Standard-setting in written and interactive (oral) specialty certification examinations: Issues, models, methods, challenges. *Evaluation and the Health Professions* 3:321–360.

Moore, R. L. (1980). NUCEA survey research committee: 1978–1979 survey. *Continuum* 45(1): 11–24.

Munger, P. D. (1985). Future academic leadership: challenges to continuing higher education. *Continuum* 49: 83–87.

National Council of Architectural Registration Boards. (1981). *NCARB examination validation study*. Final report. Washington, DC: Author.

Nowlen, P. M. (1977). Continuing education for the professions. *Continuum* 41(4): 9–11.

Nowlen, P. M., and Stern, M. R. (1981). Partnerships in continuing education for professionals. *In Current issues in higher education: Partnerships with business and the professions,* Vol. 3, pp. 16–23. Washington, DC: American Association for Higher Education.

Patton, C. V. (1975). Extended education in an elite institution. *Journal of Higher Education* 46(4): 427–444.

Penfield, K. R. (1975). Public service vs. academic values: University extension in conflict. *Adult Education* 25(2): 107–124.

Peterson, R. E. (1983, June). Issues in university continuing education in the United States. Paper presented at the OECD Meeting on Adults in Higher Education, Paris, France.

Phillips, L. E. (1983). Trends in state relicensure. In M. R. Stern (ed.), *Power and conflict in continuing professional education*. Belmont, CA: Wadsworth.

Piemme, T. E. (1984). *The impact of technological advances on continuing competence assurance*. Proceedings of the National Conference on Competence Assurance in the Health Professions, pp. 139–143. Bal Harbour, FL: National Commission for Health Certifying Agencies.

Pollicita, J. R., and Hanna, D. E. (1983, April). Research for policy: faculty perceptions and policy modifications to enhance the role of continuing education. Paper presented at the American Educational Research Association annual meeting, Montreal.

Prisk, D. P. (1984). National university continuing education association: Survey of member institutions, 1982–1983. *Continuum* 48(3): 221–227.

Project on Continuing Higher Education Leadership. (1985). *Challenges to higher education*. Washington, DC: National University Continuing Education Association.

Queeney, D. S. (1984). The role of the university in continuing professional education. *Educational Record* 65(3): 13–17.

Queeney, D. S., and Melander, J. J. (1984). *Establishing foundations for university professional association collaboration: the profession selection process*. University Park: The Pennsylvania State University, Continuing Professional Education Development Project.

Rosenfeld, M., Shimberg, B., and Thornton, R. F. (1983). *Job analysis of licensed psychologists in the United States and Canada*. Princeton, NJ: Center for Occupational and Professional Assessment.

Ruhe, C. H. W. (1982). What is the status of continuing education for health professions? *Mobius* 2: 8–13.

Sanazarro, P. (1982). Continuing education, performance assessment, and quality of patient care. *Mobius* 2: 34–37.

Sayre, S. A. (1980). Medical school leadership in CME: a UCLA program. *Journal of Medical Education* 55: 489–492.

Schneider, C. (1981). A selection and development strategy predicting effective leadership. *Continuum* 45(4): 31–39.

Scofield, M. E., and Yoxtheimer, L. L. (1983). Psychometric issues in the assessment of clinical competencies. *Journal of Counseling Psychology* 30(3): 413–420.

Shimberg, B. (1982). What is competence? How can it be assessed? In M. R. Stern (ed.), *Power and conflict in continuing professional education.* Belmont, CA: Wadsworth.

Smutz, W. D. (1984). *Developing and marketing practice oriented continuing professional education: prospects and implications.* Proceedings of the National Conference on Continuing Competence Assurance in the Health Professions, pp. 94–100. Bal Harbour, FL: National Commission for Health Certifying Agencies.

Smutz, W. D. (1985). Differential performance of formal boundary spanners in the formation of university/professional association interorganizational relationships. Paper presented at the annual meeting of the Association for the Study of Higher Education, Chicago.

Smutz, W. D., Davis, D. M., and Lindsay, C. A. (1982). Enhancing professionalization through collaboration for continuing professional education: A role for the university. Paper presented at the Lifelong Learning Research Conference, College Park, MD.

Smutz, W. D., Kalman, S. H., Lindsay, C. A., Pietrusko, R. G., and Seaman, J. J. (1981). *The practice audit model: a process for continuing professional education needs assessment and program development.* University Park, PA: The Pennsylvania State University, Continuing Professional Education Development Project.

Smutz, W. D., and Toombs, W. (1985). Forming university/professional association collaborative relationships: the strategic selection of boundary spanners. Paper presented at the annual meeting of the American Educational Research Association, Chicago.

Sneed, J. T. (1972). Continuing education in the professions. *Journal of Higher Education* 43(3): 223–238.

Stern, M. R. (1970). Continuing education. *Journal of Higher Education* 41(1): 74–77.

Stern, M. R. (1975). The invisible university. *The NUEA Spectator* 39(22): 10–14.

Stern, M. R. (1980). The universities. In P. E. Frandson (ed.), *Power and conflict in continuing education.* Belmont, CA: Wadsworth.

Stern, M. R. (1983). The disorderly market. In M. R. Stern (ed.), *Power and conflict in continuing professional education.* Belmont, CA: Wadsworth.

Stern, M. R. (1984). Research on CME: a prolegomenal comment. *Mobius* 4(4): 121–123.

Suter, E., Green, J. S., Lawrence, K., and Wathall, D. B. (1981). Continuing education of health professionals: Proposal for a definition of quality. *Journal of Medical Education* 56(Suppl.): 687–707.

Texas Society of Certified Public Accountants. (1981). *Continuing professional education curriculum report.* Dallas: Author.

Toombs, W. E. (1982). The institutionalization of continuing professional education. Paper presented at the Faculty Leadership Seminar, Rochester, NY.

Toombs, W. E., and Lindsay, C. A. (1985). Continuing education for professionals: a practice-oriented approach. *The Journal of Continuing Higher Education* 33(1): 8–13.

Toombs, W. E., Lindsay, C. A., and Hettinger, G. A. (1984). Pressure points for change: faculty views of continuing professional education. In *Mainstreaming continuing professional education: a conceptual approach and an empirical study,* pp. 35–75. University Park: The Pennsylvania State University, Continuing Professional Education Development Project.

Toombs, W. E., Lindsay, C. A., and Hettinger, G. A. (1985). Modifying faculty roles to institutionalize continuing professional education. *Research in Higher Education* 22(1): 93–109.

Vicere, A. A. (1981). Faculty development: the other side of continuing professional education. *Continuum* 45(3): 23–28.

Vollmer, H. M., and Mills, D. L. (1966). *Professionalization*. Englewood Cliffs, NJ: Prentice-Hall.

Votruba, J. C. (1981). Strategies for organizational change. In J. C. Votruba (ed.), *New Directions for Continuing Education: Strengthening Internal Support for Continuing Education* 9: 13–28.

Wasch, S. (1980). The role of baccalaureate faculty in continuing education. *Nursing Outlook* 28:(2): 116–120.

Watts, M. S. M. (1981). An anatomy of continuing medical education. *Mobius* 1:5–15.

Weinstein, L. M. (1982). Professional associations. In R. E. Anderson and E. S. Kasl (eds.), *The costs and financing of adult education and training,* pp. 223–242. Lexington, MA: Lexington Books.

AUTHOR INDEX

* Names in parentheses identify the senior author for "et al." references.

SUBJECT INDEX

A

Ability bias, 212-213
Academic abstention doctrine, 117-119
Academic disciplines, 293-294, 300, 305
  common foundations of, 299
  specialization of, 279
  see also Courses
Academic freedom, 116-117, 119, 123, 134, 309
Academic journals, 11, 323-328, 349-350
Academic major, 254, 277, 293-294, 297, 305
Academic profession, *see* Faculty
Academic programs, *see* Curriculum; Program evaluation
Accountability, 191-193, 196-197
Accounting, 95, 298, 390, 410
Accreditation
  program evaluation and, 194, 196
  reports, 107
Achievement, 9-10
Across-the-board cuts, 73-75
Adams litigation, 137-138, 140, 145-148, 153, 154
Administrators
  continuing education and, 405, 423
  curriculum and, 247, 249, 266
  perceptions of evaluation, 179
Admissions
  definition, 141
  discriminatory, 132-133
  opposition to plans benefiting only minorities, 155
  race and, 129
  standards, 34
  see also Bakke case
Adult education, 3, 38-39, 390, 398, 417
  curricular development and, 289, 301-302
  institutional changes and, 32-33
  see also Continuing professional education
Adversary approach, 185-186
Advertisements, 143
Affective psychological outcomes, 192, 256-258
Affirmative action, 109-112
  constitutionally permissible plans, 140-142
  court ordered, 148-151
  debate over judicial activism and, 151
  as a defense, 119-121
    private sector, 122-128
    public sector, 128-134, 134-148, 152-153
  executive/judicial branch conflict concerning, 145-148
  hiring goals and, 110
  individual rights/group rights and, 112-115
  negative stereotyping recipients of, 142
  purpose of, 112
  Stotts decision and, 111, 114
  see also Discrimination
Age
  citation rate and, 350
  professional recognition and, 343-345
  reception of research and, 331-334
Alienation, 287
Alpha factor, 213-214
Alternative schools, 289
American Council on Education (ACE), 116-117
Analytical studies, 117
Antebellum colleges, 244-245
Applications, 54-55
Association of American Colleges (AAC), 275-277
Attrition, 73-75
  student, *see* Students, departure
Autonomy, 22, 88, 97, 123, 353
  professionalism and, 309
  research process and, 310

B

Bachelors degree
  B.A. vs. B.S., 294
  earnings and, 214
  purposes of, 275
  value of, 295-296
Back-to-basics movement, 289, 304
Bakke case, 114, 116, 129-135, 138-143, 151-152
Banking, 4
Benefit-cost analysis, *see* Cost-benefit analysis
Biological Sciences Curriculum Study (BSCS), 282
Black colleges, 125-128
Blacks, *see* Minorities

in professional practice vs. university, 396,
    411
program evaluation and, 198-199
of science, 312
Videodisc technology, 6

Virginia Council of Higher Education, 97-100
Vocational Education Act, 280
Vocational training, 35, 70, 298

W

War on Poverty, 166

Welfare, 228-229
Women, 152
    defense of admitted preference and, 119-121
    discrimination and, 115, 118, 134-136,
        142-143
    hiring goals and, 110
    retrenchment and, 144
    student departure and, 375
Women's colleges, 127
Woods Hole Conference, 280
Work-study programs, 286
Writing, 302-303